SCIENCE, OPTICS AND MUSIC

SCIENCE, OPTICS AND MUSIC IN MEDIEVAL AND EARLY MODERN THOUGHT

A.C. CROMBIE

THE HAMBLEDON PRESS

LONDON AND RONCEVERTE

Published by The Hambledon Press 1990

102 Gloucester Avenue, London NW1 8HX (U.K.)

309 Greenbrier Avenue, Ronceverte WV 24970 (U.S.A.)

ISBN 0 907628 79 6

British Library Cataloguing in Publication Data

Crombie, A.C.
    Science, optics and music in medieval and
    early modern thought.   .
    1. Science – Europe – History
    2. Music – Europe – Theory – 500-1400
    3. Music – Europe – Theory – 15th century
    4. Music – Europe – Theory – 16th century
    I. Title
    509' .4   Q127.E8

Library of Congress Cataloging-in-Publication Data

Crombie, A.C. (Alistair Cameron), 1915-
    Science, optics, and music in medieval and early modern
    thought/ A.C. Crombie.
    Includes bibliographical references.
    1. Science – History.
    2. Science – Europe – History.
    3. Optics – History.
    4. Music – History. I. Title.
    Q125.C686   1990
    509' .02 – dc20   90-30933 CIP

Printed on acid-free paper and bound in Great Britain
by W.B.C. Ltd., Maesteg

CONTENTS

ACKNOWLEDGEMENTS

The articles reprinted here first appeared in the following places and are reprinted by kind permission of the original publishers.

1   *Annali dell'Istituto e Museo di Storia della Scienza di Firenze*, vii. 2 (1982), pp. 29-50.

2   *History of Science*, xiii (1975), pp. 213-30.

3   *Perspectives in Medieval History*, edited by K.F. Drew, and F.S. Lear (Chicago, 1963), pp. 35-57.

4   *Isis*, lii (1961), pp. 143-60.

5   *Avicenna: Scientist and Philosopher, a Millenary Symposium*, edited by G.M. Wickens (London, 1952), pp. 84-107.

6   *Robert Grosseteste, Scholar and Bishop*, edited by D.A. Callus (Oxford, 1955), pp. 98-120.

7   *Critical Problems in the History of Science*, edited by M. Claggett (Madison, Wisconsin, 1959), pp. 66-101.

8   *History of Science*, xviii (1980), pp. 233-46.

9   *Proceedings of the Royal Microscopical Society*, ii (1967), pp. 1-112. Republished as *Historical Aspects of Microscopy*, edited by S. Bradbury and G.L'E. Turner (Cambridge, 1967).

10   *L'Aventure de la Science: Mélanges Alexandre Koyré*, i (Paris, 1964), pp. 135-72.

11   *Saggi su Galileo Galilei*, edited by C. Maccagni (Florence, 1969), pp. 1-23.

12   *Theory and Change, Ancient Axiomatics, and Galileo's Methodology: Proceedings of the 1978 Pisa Conference on the History and Philosophy of Science*, edited by J. Hintikka, D. Gruender and E. Agazzi (Dordrecht, 1981), pp. 271-86; *Physis*, xii (1970), pp. 106-8.

13   *Actes du XIIe Congrès International d'Histoire des Sciences, Paris 1968* (Paris, 1971), pp. 295-310.

14   *Actes du Xe Congrès International d'Histoire des Sciences, Ithaca, N.Y., 1962* (Paris, 1964), pp. 93-114.

15   *Physis*, xvii (1975), pp. 186-204.

16   *Actes du Symposium International des Sciences Physiques et Mathématiques dans la Première Moitié du XVIIe Siècle, Pise-Vinci, 16-18, 1958* (Paris, 1960), pp. 192-201.

17   *British Journal for the History of Science*, iii (1966), pp. 97-108.

18   *History of European Ideas*, vii (1986), pp. 21-31.

     Appendix: History of Science, i (1962), pp. 57-61; *Isis*, lxxv (1984), pp. 25-28.

LIST OF ILLUSTRATIONS

PREFACE

The history of science is the history of argument, an argument deployed in different ways in different periods and contexts to justify and develop a vision of the nature of things able to solve specific problems. It is an argument initiated to the West by ancient Greek philosophers, mathematicians and physicians in their search for principles at once of nature and of argument itself. Of its essence have been its genuine continuity, even after long breaks, based on the study by any generation of texts written by its predecessors; its progress equally in scientific knowledge and in the analysis of scientific argument; and its recurrent critique, varying considerably in different historical contexts, of its presuppositions about nature, about scientific cogency and validity, and about the intellectual, practical and moral justification of the whole enterprise. A subtle question is what continued and what changed through different historical contexts, in the scientific argument and its criteria and in the cultural vision through which experience is mediated, when education and practice could furnish options for a different future. Styles of thinking and making decisions, established with the commitments with which they began, habitually endure as long as these remain. Hence the structural difference between different civilizations and societies and the persistence in each despite change of a specific identity. Hence the need for historical analysis in the scientific movement of both continuity and change. These like most human behaviour begin in the mind, and we its historians who belong at the same time to its history must look in a true intellectual anthropology at once with and into the eye of its beholder.

A comprehensive comparative historical anthropology of science, medicine and technology would address itself to questions at different levels of commitment, some given by nature, some made by man. Thus at the level of nature there is historical ecology: the reconstruction of the physical and biomedical environment and of what people made of it, both from written records and from physical remains as in striking recent work on palaeopathology, palaeodemography, palaeobotany and the history of climate. Reconstruction at the levels of people and their vision requires the exegesis of evidence including in its scope the visual, musical and constructive arts, literature, philosophy, religion, law, politics and so on far beyond simply scientific thought. At all levels historical questions demand in historians exact scientific and linguistic knowledge to enable them to control the view of any present recorded through the eyes and language of those who experienced it. Obviously historians must attempt to place themselves at the viewpoints of the participants at any moment, and equally obviously we find that those participants habitually saw themselves as engaging in a scientific movement with a direction and with facilities and obstacles of which their judgements were an essential part of that movement. It is another subtle question to relate these judgements to those made by successive generations of later historians.

The studies comprising this volume were written originally for a variety of occasions but on a common principle: that the history of science is an integral part of the history of intellectual culture and should be treated as such. Like my books *Augustine to Galileo* (1952, 1959, 1979) and *Robert Grosseteste* (1953, 1971), they are an exploration of the intellectual orientations of the Western scientific movement, of which the historiography of science is itself an integral part. More specifically they are concerned with the development of styles of scientific argument, investigation and explanation within the intellectual culture of medieval and early modern Europe. I have tried to identify certain historical commitments, memories and expectations which have been at once diagnostic signs and determining causes of Western cultural style over a wide range of thought and action, from the mathematical, natural and medical sciences to the constructive arts, ethics, theology and historiography. In this way I have tried to characterize that cultural style, and its changes, in thinking about nature by paying attention not simply to the results achieved but also to the objectives held in view or taken for granted, to the questions admitted and asked or presupposed as well as to the answers found acceptable or unacceptable. A major influence in the orientation of European thinking, through its experience of nature during this long formative period, was the interaction between the objectives of intellectual programmes inherited from antiquity and their success or failure in being realized. This extended historical interaction took place in a diversity of contexts of general beliefs and of scientific and technical competence, and over an ever-widening variety of subject-matters. As commitments and expectations both intellectual and practical changed, and as achievements and failures were identified, different problems came to be seen and different solutions found acceptable. Ancient programmes came to be transformed or replaced by others.

A central historical question addressed in these studies is about the central concern of the scientific movement with man's relations to nature and his fellow beings as perceiver and knower and agent. This has entailed characterizations of both sides of these relations, and views of problems and solutions directed or even imposed by different forms of characterization. My long monograph 'The Mechanistic Hypothesis and the Scientific Study of Vision' (1967) pioneered the historiography of medieval and early modern optics with special attention to this question. With it belong other studies included here of the relations between science and the arts in general and the visual and musical arts in particular.

My other main theme is the relevance of medieval natural philosophy and the technology to the scientific movement. Medieval universities offered a highly structured approach to studying and teaching, both in the *trivium* and mathematical *quadrivium* followed by the three philosophies (natural, metaphysical and ethical) of the arts faculty, and in the three superior faculties of theology, law and medicine. Styles of learning were affected by specialization, for example in mathematics as well as theology at Paris and Oxford, in law at Bologna, and in medicine at Salerno, Padua and Montpellier, and this led to variations in the treatment of scientific disciplines. But studying and teaching were given everywhere a closely similar logical structure by the universal acceptance of Aristotle's conception of true demonstration which provided the theoretical goal of the whole process in demonstrated scientific knowledge. Medieval universities were concerned with methods of acquiring and certifying true knowledge by argument from the true authority both of books and of nature, and with transmitting such methods and knowledge through teaching. Theoretical science then opened the way to the final goal of rational practice, and was in turn itself certified or otherwise by practice. I have explored further the forms of argument analysed in my two earlier books, especially the experimental and quantitative arguments developed in the contexts both of the theoretical sciences and of the practical arts. Here I have stressed the need to study the logic defining where experiment or observation were to be brought into a scientific argument as well as the practices used in the sciences and arts. Both were necessary and neither can be left out of account.

The slightly polemical tone of some of the earlier essays may perhaps be forgiven by remembering that it is only fairly recently that Continental European and American scholarship in these fields started to penetrate a complacent English intellectual insularity which largely excluded from the view of 'ordinary historians' and others not simply the history of science but the history of thought in general and especially of medieval and Continental thought. When I myself began to study the history of medieval science well over forty years ago I found considerable resistance in England (especially in the two ancient universities where I have spent most of my professional life), but not elsewhere, to accepting that there was such a subject. There seemed to be particular resistance to accepting the existence of experimental science in this period, perhaps because this became the most classically characteristic ingredient of the scientific movement. It was a question of invincible ignorance, complacently and sometimes viciously maintained, motivated largely by the peculiar and persisting preoccupation of English historians since the 16th century with establishing and perpetuating a conception of national and theological identity to serve dominant political interests. This phenomenon is of course paralleled elsewhere: for example in the preoccupation of Italian historians with the uniqueness of the Italian Renaissance, and in that of the 19th-century Germans with the medieval origins of their identity. European interest in medieval history, powerfully stimulated by Romanticism, led on the Continent during the 19th century to the methodical study of medieval thought. English historians seeking an historical justification of a conception of identity found it politically in the medieval origins of the English parliament, but otherwise in the Protestant settlement as the source of all they wanted of national value. Medieval philosophy was beyond their focus, and it is only comparatively recently that English medievalists have moved to a more European perspective. But anachronistic English preoccupations and prejudices were slow to fade, and in persisting they imposed on history an intellectual parochialism which could reach a point of hopeless absurdity. This is exemplified by the recent efforts of a small outmoded group, naïvely continuing 16th- and 17th-century disputes, to politicize the historiography of science, notably (if eccentrically) in the treatment by the Neopuritan, Neomarxist persuasion of the early modern scientific movement as an English phenomenon isolated from the historically Catholic Europe in which it had its origin and context. It is a question of the elementary use of the comparative method.

Ordinary historians, who graduate through modern history departments and in this country dominate the study of history as a whole, have another problem. They are essentially political historians (nowadays commonly with social or economic dimensions) and they have habitually presented an intensely narrow view of human experience dominated by these interests. The source of this parochialism is here no doubt the absurdly early and continued specialization imposed by our educational system, which means among other things that philosphy and its history, as well as 'ordinary' history, are studied as a rule without any attention to scientific thought, even though large areas of philosophical thought are scarcely comprehensible if dissociated from the contemporary thought in mathematics and natural science. Continental European and American scholars are usually in this respect better equipped. Ordinary modern English historians in particular have for the most part simply failed to take account of the role of thought, at its highest technical level, in human affairs. They have simply failed to recognize in their conception of history that a specific style of thinking is the central characteristic of any culture, and that the logically structured thought arising from the same search for principles that generated natural science and mathematics is an essential diagnostic characteristic of Western intellectual culture as a whole in comparison with other major cultures. With some notable exceptions they have by and large left it to others, to ancient historians who study ancient philosophy, and indeed to medievalists, to historians of philosophy, science, art, religion and literature, and to anthropologists, to develop a more realistic perception of the main lines of human experience in all its diverse aspects. This after all is the proper object of historical studies, and it should surely be that of 'ordinary' history, and *mutatis mutandis* of ordinary philosophy likewise.

Because these papers were written for separate occasions to which I was invited to contribute on related subjects, some repetition inevitably appears when they are collected together as a whole. (There are precedents in some of the best classical composers.) The main theme will be continued in a second volume of papers entitled *Science, Art and Nature in Medieval and Modern Thought* and more systematically in my forthcoming books, *Styles of Scientific Thinking in the European Tradition* (with extensive bibliography), *Galileo's Arguments and Disputes in Natural Philosophy* (with the collaboration of Adriano Carugo), and *Marin Mersenne: Science, Music and Language*.

The papers included in this volume have been reprinted with continuous pagination, with the footnotes at the bottom of the page when not already there, and with appropriate revision of internal references. Obvious factual errors and some of my earlier interpretations have been corrected. Immediately relevant further bibliography has been added as required at the ends of chapters. The places of original publication are given in the general Bibliography of my writings.

I should like in conclusion to thank all those who provided the occasions for these papers: in Cambridge and Oxford, Paris, Florence, Pisa, Genoa and Erice, Madison Wisc., New York, Cornell N.Y., Princeton and Atlantic City N.J., Houston Texas and Washington DC, the Australian universities, Tokyo and Kyoto, and New Delhi. These agreeable invitations could only reinforce any native disposition to find enlightenment in experience stretching through space as well as time.

15 September 1989

A. C. Crombie
Trinity College
Oxford

BIBLIOGRAPHY OF ALISTAIR CAMERON CROMBIE

(a) Books and Monographs on the History of Science

1952 *Augustine to Galileo: Medieval and Early Modern Science.* London, Falcon Press, 1952; Harvard University Press 1953; 2nd revised and enlarged ed., 2 vols., Harvard University Press and Doubleday Anchor Books, 1959, London, Heinemann Educational Books, 1959; 3rd ed., Heinemann & Penguin Books Ltd., 1971; 4th printing Heinemann & Harvard 1979; French, Polish, Japanese, German, Italian, Spanish, Greek translations.

1953 *Robert Grosseteste and the Origins of Experimental Science 1100-1700.* Oxford Clarendon Press, 1953; 2nd impression, 1962; 3rd impression with revisions, 1971.

1963 *Scientific Change: Historical Studies in the Intellectual, Social and Technical Conditions for Scientific Discovery and Technical Invention from Antiquity to the Present.* Symposium on the History of Science, University of Oxford, 9-15 July 1961, edited with an Introduction and other contributions. London/New York, Heinemann Educational Books/ Basic Books, 1963.

1967 'The Mechanistic Hypothesis and the Scientific Study of Vision', *Proceedings of the Royal Microscopical Society*, 1967, ii, 1-112; volume republished as *Historical Aspects of Microscopy*, ed. S. Bradbury and G. L'E. Turner. Cambridge, W. Heffer, 1967.

1987 *The Rational Arts of Living: Ruth and Clarence Kennedy Conference in the Renaissance 1982*, ed. with N. G. Siraisi. *Smith College Studies in History*, vol. 50, Northampton, Mass., 1987.

1990 *Science, Optics and Music in Medieval and Early Modern Thought.* London, The Hambledon Press.

1991 *Science, Art and Nature in Medieval and Modern Thought.* London, The Hambledon Press.
      Styles of Scientific Thinking in the European Tradition: The History of Argument and Explanation especially in the Mathematical and Biomedical Sciences. London, Gerald Duckworth & Co.
      Galileo's Arguments and Disputes in Natural Philosophy, with A. Carugo, forthcoming.
      Marin Mersenne: Science, Music and Language , forthcoming.

(b) Papers and Chapters on the History of Science

1948 'Some reflections on the history of science and its conception of
       nature', *Annals of Science*, vi, pp. 54-75.
       'Scholastic logic and the experimental method', *Actes du Ve Congrès
       International d'Histoire des Sciences, Lausanne 1947*, Paris, pp. 45-50.
1950 'Die Philosophie der Wissenschaft', in *Jahrbuch der Rheinisch-
       Westfälischen technischen Hochschule, Aachen, 1950*, Essen, pp. 329-48.
       'Galileo's dialogues concerning the two principal systems of the
       world', *Dominican Studies*, iii, 105-6.
1951 'The notion of species in medieval philosophy and science', *Actes du
       VIe Congrès International d'Histoire des Sciences, Amsterdam 1950*, Paris,
       pp. 261-9.
1952 'Cybo d'Hyères: a 14th-century zoological artist', *Endeavour*, xi,
       pp. 183-7.
       'Avicenna's influence on the Western medieval scientific tradition',
       in *Avicenna: Scientist and Philosopher, a Millenary Symposium*, ed. G. M.
       Wickens, London, Luzac & Co., pp. 84-107.
1952/ 'The invention of scientific explanation', *Discovery*, xiii, pp. 346-51;
53   The invention of the experimental method', *ibid*, xiii, pp. 391-7;
       'The 17th-century revolution in mathematical physics', *ibid*, xiv,
       pp. 23-27; 'The idea of organic evolution', *ibid*, xiv, 1953, pp. 92-97.
1953 'Robert Grosseteste on the logic of science', in *Actes du XIème Congrès
       International de Philosophie, Bruxelles, 20-26 Août 1953*, xii: Histoire de
       la philosophie: méthologie, antiquité et moyen âge, Amsterdam/
       Louvain, pp. 171-3.
       'A note on the descriptive conception of motion in the fourteenth
       century', *The British Journal for the Philosophy of Science*, iv, pp. 46-51.
1954 *Oxford's Contribution to the Origins of Modern Science*, A paper read to
       the British Association for the Advancement of Science on 6 Sepem-
       ber 1954, Oxford, Basil Blackwell.
1955 'Grosseteste's position in the history of science', in *Robert Grosseteste,
       Scholar and Bishop*, ed. D. A. Callus, Oxford, Clarendon Press, pp.
       98-120.
       'Galileo's conception of scientific truth', in *Literature and Science:
       Proceedings of the Sixth Triennial Congress of the International Federation
       for Modern Languages and Literature, Oxford 1954*, Oxford, Basil Black-
       well, pp. 132-8.
1956 *Galilée devant les critiques de la posterité*, Les Conférences du Palais de
       la Découverte, Université de Paris, sér. D., no. 45, Paris.
1957 'P. L. Moreau de Maupertuis, F.R.S. (1698-1759), précurseur du
       transformisme', *Revue de Synthèse*, lxxviii, pp. 35-36.
       'Newton's conception of scientific method', *Bulletin of the Institute of
       Physics*, viii, pp. 350-62; reprinted in *A Physics Anthology*, ed. N. Clarke,
       London, Chapman and Hall.

1958 'Galileo: a philosophical symbol', *Actes du VIIIe Congrès International d'Histoire des Sciences, Florence-Milan 1956*, Vinci & Paris, pp. 1089-95.
'Science in medieval England', in *Medieval England*, ed. A. L. Poole, Oxford, Clarendon Press, pp. 571-604.
'Helmholtz', *Scientific American*, cxci, pp. 94-102.

1959 'The significance of medieval discussions of scientific method for the scientific revolution', and 'Commentary on The Scholar and the Craftsman and The Role of Art', in *Critical Problems in the History of Science*, Proceedings of the Institute for the History of Science at the University of Wisconsin, September 1-11, 1957, ed. Marshall Clagett, Madison, University of Wisconsin Press, pp. 66-101.
'Introduction' to *Turning Points in Physics*, A series of lectures given at Oxford University in Trinity Term 1959, Amsterdam, North-Holland Publishing Company.
'Descartes', *Scientific American*, cci, pp. 160-75.

1959/ Reviews of *Histoire générale des sciences*, publiée sous la direction de R.
61   Taton, 1957-59, i-ii and of *A History of Technology*, ed. C. Singer *et al.*, 1956-58, ii-v, in *The English Historical Review*, 1959, lxxiv, pp. 281-4; 1961, lxxvi, pp. 84-7, 330-2.

1960 'Some aspects of Descartes' attitude to hypothesis and experiment', *Actes du Symposium International des Sciences physiques et mathématiques dans la première moitié du xviie siècle, Pise-Vinci, 16-18 Juin 1958*, Collection des Travaux de l'Académie Internationale d'Histoire des Sciences, xi, Paris, pp. 192-201.
'Darwin's scientific method', *Actes du IXe Congrès International d'Histoire des Sciences, Barcelona-Madrid 1959*, Barcelona/Paris, pp. 354-62; reprinted as 'The public and private faces of Charles Darwin', *The Listener*, London, B.B.C., November 1959.
'The scientific revolution of the seventeenth century and its consequences', *Contemporary Physics*, i, pp. 220-29.

1961 'Quantification is medieval physics', in The Conference on the History of Quantification in the Sciences, New York, 20-21 November 1959, *Isis*, lii, pp. 143-60; proceedings republished as *Quantification: A History of the Meaning of Measurement in the Natural and Social Sciences*, ed. Harry Woolf, Indianapolis, The Bobbs-Merrill Company, 1961.

1962 'History and philosophy of science at Oxford', *History of Science*, i, pp. 57-61.
'The history of science as an academic discipline', *International Symposium on Higher Scientific and Technical Education*, Moscow.

1963 'A note on history of science as an academic discipline', in *Scientific Change*, ed. A. C. Crombie, London/New York, pp. 757-64.
'The relevance of the middle ages to the scientific movement', in *Perspectives in Medieval History*, ed. K. F. Drew and F. S. Lear, Chicago, Chicago University Press, pp. 35-57.

1964 'The study of the senses in renaissance science', in Symposium:

Science in the Renaissance, *Actes du Xe Congrès International d'Histoire des Sciences, Ithaca, N.Y. 1962*, Paris, pp. 93-114.

'Kepler: de modo visionis', in *L'Aventure de la science: Mélanges Alexandre Koyré*, i, introduction de I. B. Cohen et R. Taton, Paris, Hermann et Cie., pp. 135-72.

'Early concepts of the senses and the mind', *Scientific American*, ccx, pp. 108-16.

'From living cells to calculating engine', essay review of *Science before Darwin*, ed. H. M. Jones and I. B. Cohen, London, 1963, *The Times Literary Supplement*, 19 March 1964, p. 236.

1966   'Historical commitments of biology', Presidential address to the British Society for the History of Science, Oxford, 1 July 1966, *The British Journal for the History of Science*, iii, pp. 97-108 (revised version of an address to the Fiftieth Annual Meeting of the Federation of American Societies for Experimental Biology, Atlantic City, N.J., 13 April 1966, *Federation Proceedings*, 1966, xxv, pp. 448-54).

1967   'Grosseteste, Robert', 'Mechanism', 'Spallanzani, Lazzaro', 'Swammerdam, Jan', in *Encyclopaedia Britannica*.

'Physics and astronomy', with J. D. North and M. Schramm, in *Atti del Primo Convegno Internazionale di Recognizione delle Fonti per la Storia della Scienza Italiana: i secoli xiv-xvi, Pisa, 14-16 Settembre 1966*, i, Firenze, pp. 3-48.

1968   'Bluttransfusion im 17. Jahrhundert', *Bild der Wissenschaft*, März, 1968, pp. 237-46.

Contribution to *Acta historiae rerum naturalium necnon technicarum*, Special issue 4, Prague, pp. 55-7.

1969   'Historians and the scientific revolution', *Physis*, xi, pp. 167-80.

'The primary properties and secondary qualities in Galileo Galilei's natural philosophy', in *Saggi su Galileo Galilei*, a cura di C. Maccagni, Firenze, G. Barbèra, preprint, pp. 1-23.

'Thomas Harriot (1560-1621)', with J. V. Pepper, D. B. Quinn, J. W. Shirley and R. C. H. Tanner, *The Times Literary Supplement*, 23 October 1969.

1970   'Premio Galileo 1968', *Physis*, xii, pp. 106-8.

'The scientific movement and its influence, 1610-50', with M. A. Hoskin, in *The New Cambridge Modern History*, ed. J. P. Cooper, Cambridge, iv, pp. 132-68.

'The scientific movement and the diffusion of scientific ideas, 1688-1751', with M. A. Hoskin, in *The New Cambridge Modern History*, ed. J. S. Bromley, Cambridge, vi, pp. 37-71.

1970/   'Descartes: philosophy and scientific method', 'Grossetesete, Robert',
74   'Mersenne, Marin' and 'Bacon, Roger' (with J. D. North), in *Dictionary of Scientific Biography*, ed. C. C. Gillispie, New York, Scribner, 1970-74.

1971   'Mathematics, music and medical science', Conférence plénière à la séance de clôture, *Actes du XIIe Congrès International d'Histoire des Sciences, Paris 1968*, Paris, pp. 295-310.

1973 Review of *Dictionary of Scientific Biography*, ed. C. C. Gillispie, in *American Scientist*, lxi, pp. 353-4.

1974 'Du moyen âge au xxe siècle', in *La science et la diversité des cultures*, Colloque international organisé par l'Unesco à Paris en septembre 1971, Paris, Presses Universitaires de France, pp. 61-78.

1975 'Sources of Galileo's early natural philosphy', in *Reason, Experiment and Mysticism in the Scientific Revolution*, ed. M. L. Righini Bonelli and W. R. Shea, New York, pp. 157-75.

'Some attitudes to scientific progress: ancient, medieval and early modern', *History of Science*, xiii, pp. 213-30.

'Marin Mersenne (1588-1648) and the seventeenth-century problem of scientific acceptability', *Physis*, xvii, pp. 186-204.

1976 'Some general effects of mathematics on natural philosophy in the early modern West', *Istoriko-mathematicheskie issledovaniya*, xxi, pp. 22-50 (commemorative volume for A. P. Yushkevich, published in Russian).

1977 'The Western experience of scientific objectivity', in *Proceedings of the 3rd International Humanistic Symposium 1975: The Case of Objectivity*, Athenai, Hellenistic Society for Humanistic Studies, pp. 428-55.

'Mathematics and Platonism in the sixteenth-century Italian universities and in Jesuit educational policy', in *Prismata: naturwissenschaftsgeschichtliche Studien: Festschrift für Willy Hartner*, hrsg. v. Y. Maeyama and W. G. Salzer, Wiesbaden, pp. 63-94.

1980 'Science and the arts in the Renaissance: The search for truth and certainty, old and new', Symposium at the Folger Library, Washington D.C., October 1978, *History of Science*, xviii, pp. 233-46, and in *Science and the Arts in the Renaissance*, ed. J. W. Shirley and F. D. Hoeniger, Washington, D.C., 1985, pp. 15-26.

'Styles of thinking and historiography of science', in *I Congresso de la Sociedad Española de Historia de las Ciencias*, ed. S. Garma, Madrid, pp. 13-25.

1981 'Philosophical presuppositions and shifting interpretations of Galileo', in *Theory Change, Ancient Axiomatics, and Galileo's Methodology: Proceedings of the 1978 Pisa Conference on the History and Philosophy of Science*, ed. J. Hintikka, D. Gruender and E. Agazzi, Dordrecht, Reidel, vol. i, pp. 271-86.

1982 'Pari sur le hasard et choix dans l'incertain', in *Médicine et probabilités: Actes de la journée d'études du 15 décembre 1979, Université de Paris xii*, éd. A. Fagot, Paris, pp. 1-42.

'Historical commitments of European science', *Annali dell'Istituto e Museo di Storia della Scienza di Firenze*, vii.2, pp. 29-51.

1983 'Galileo in Renaissance Europe', in *Firenze e la Toscana dei Medici nell'Europa del Cinquecento: Convegno internazionale de studi 1980*, a cura di P. Galluzzi, Firenze, S. Olschki, vol. ii, pp. 751-62.

'The Jesuits and Galileo's ideas of science and of nature', with A. Carugo, *Annali dell'Isituto e Museo di Storia della Scienza di Firenze*, viii. 2, pp. 1-68.

1984   'Beginnings at Oxford', *Isis*, lxxv, pp. 25-8.

'The European experience of nature', in *The Good Life and its Pursuit*, ed. J. P. Dougherty, New York, Paragon House Publishers, 1984, pp. 239-45.

1985/   'Sorting out the sources', with A. Carugo, *The Times Literary Supple-*
86   *ment*, 22 November 1985, pp. 1319-20, 14 February 1986, p. 165, 29 August 1986, p. 939.

1986   'What is the history of science?', *History of European Ideas*, vii, pp. 21-31; published in part in *The Times Educational Supplement*, 2 March 1984, pp. 14-15.

'Experimental science and the rational artist in early modern Europe', *Daedalus*, cxv, pp. 49-74.

1987   'Introduction' and 'Contingent expectation and uncertain choice: historical contexts of arguments from probabilities', in *The Rational Arts of Living*, ed. A. C. Crombie and N. G. Siraisi, *Smith College Studies in History*, vol. 50, Northampton, Mass, pp. 9-14, 53-101.

'Alexandre Koyré and Great Britain: Galileo and Mersenne', in *The Renaissance of a History: Proceedings of the International Conference Alexandre Koyré*, Paris, Collège de France, 10-14 June 1986, ed. P. Redondi: *History and Technology*, iv, London, pp. 81-92.

'Infinite power and the laws of nature: a medieval speculation', in *L'infinito nella scienza*, a cura di G. Toraldo di Francia, Roma, pp. 223-43.

'*La dioptrique* et Kepler', in *Le Discours et sa méthode*, Colloque publié sous la direction de N. Grimaldi et J.-L. Marion, Paris, pp. 131-44.

'Some historical questions about disease', in *Sida: Epidémies et societies, 20 et 21 juin 1987*, éd. C. Mérieux, Lyon, pp. 115-21.

1988   'Designed in the mind: Western visions of science, nature and humankind', *History of Science*, xxvi, pp. 1-12.

'A propos de *La dioptrique*: l'expérience dans la philosophie naturelle de Descartes', with H. J. Wickes, in *Problématique et réception du Discours de la méthode et des Essais*, textes réunis par H. Méchoulan, Paris, pp. 65-79.

Galileo and the art of rhetoric', with A. Carugo, *Nouvelles de la république des lettres* (1988), ii, pp. 7-31.

1990   'Le arti e le scienze visive e musicali in Galileo', in *Lezioni galileiane*, i: *Atti delle Scuole superiore di storia della scienza della Domus Galileiana*, Rome, Enciclopedia Italiana, pp. 41-64.

'Expectation, modelling and assent in the history of optics, i: Alhazen and the medieval tradition, ii. Kepler and Descartes', *Studies in History and Philosophy of Science*, xxi (1990).

HISTORICAL COMMITMENTS OF EUROPEAN SCIENCE

Plato's Pythagorean friend the mathematician Archytas of Tarentum commented on their immediate predecessors and contemporaries in the 4th century B. C. as follows:

> Mathematicians seem to me to have an excellent discernment and it is in no way strange that they should think correctly concerning the nature of particulars. For since they have passed excellent judgement on the nature of the whole, they were likely to have an excellent view of separate things. They have handed on to us a clear judgement on the speed of the stars and their rising and setting, as well as on geometry

and numbers, and not least on music; for these mathematical studies appear to be related [1]

This comment illustrates both the continuity and the mutations of the Western scientific tradition. It was found with other fragments of Archytas by the 15th-century Italian scholar Giorgio Valla among the Greek manuscripts brought to Italy from Constantinople, published in a Latin translation in Valla's encyclopaedic and influential *De expetendis et fugiendis rebus opus* (1501), and cited in the 16th century to exemplify the foundation of the sciences both of material things and of human perception on mathematical reasoning and quantity [2]. This seems to link us now with Archytas in a continuous living tradition extending from the ancient Greeks to the present. But his words invite us also to ask what he himself meant by "the nature of the whole" in this arcane and somewhat paradoxical context. They invite us to put ourselves at the viewpoint of Archytas's particular vision of existence and of the possibilities of knowledge, at the viewpoint of his interpreters in the 16th century, and in general to treat the history of science (including medicine and technology) as a kind of comparative intellectual anthropology.

Every society has a cultural ecology in which its view of nature and of man is conditioned both by its physical and biological environment and by its mental vision of existence and knowledge and their meaning. I certainly share the belief that one main reason for studying history is to understand ourselves. Today's problems can indeed alert us to formerly unnoticed counterparts in the past. The dramatic irrationalism of our time for example has sensitized us to the irrational in earlier societies and individuals, and likewise our contemporary experience of the relativity of beliefs and values has given emphasis to differences in expectation and action among different societies and cultures, as opposed to an enduring rational similarity of all men. Yet if each generation is pre-

---

[1] H. DIELS - W. KRANZ, *Die Fragmente der Vorsokratiker*, 47 B 1, 6te Aufl. (Berlin, 1951). This fragment was quoted by Porphyry and first printed in Greek in his *In Harmonica Ptolemaei commentarius*, c. 3, ed. in J. WALLIS, *Operum mathematicorum*, III (Oxoniae, 1699) 236-8; cf. PLATO, *Republic*, VII, 530D. This paper is based on the historiographical introduction to my forthcoming book *Styles of Scientific Thinking in the European Tradition*, which contains full documentation with bibliographies.

[2] Published in Venice after Valla's death in 1499 by his son: see dedicatory preface, and lib. VI, c. 4 for his Latin version of the fragment of Archytas quoted by Porphyry; cf. for Valla and his manuscript collection G. CEREDI, *Tre Discorsi sopra il modo d'alzar acque da' luoghi bassi* (Parma, 1567) 11-12; J. L. HEIBERG, *Beiträge zur Geschichte Georg Valla's und seiner Bibliothek* (*Beiträge zum Centralblatt für Bibliothekwesen*, XVI; Leipzig, 1896); R. R. BOLGAR, *The Classical Heritage and its Beneficiaries* (Cambridge, 1954); G. CARDENAL, P. LANDUCCI RUFFO, C. VASOLI, raccolti e presentati da V. BRANCA, *Giorgio Valla tra scienza e sapienza* (Firenze, 1981).

disposed to dismantle the history written by its predecessors in their image, before rewriting it in its own, our critical inheritance itself commits us to distinguishing on evidence between fact and interpretation.

If we are to understand any historical culture now we are not only advised but obliged to investigate the history of its mental commitments which may survive, modified in new contexts, over long periods of time. If we are to understand our own culture with any education, we must try to grasp the moral and intellectual commitments and expectations and achievements of societies that have formed its history remote in time and seemingly remote in character from the present and the immediate past. Societies and situations nearest to us in time and familiarity may indeed be the least enlightening, and for educated awareness of ourselves as we are now yesterday's events may be the least relevant. Can we assume that the intellectual and moral categories expressed in language are sufficiently common to all mankind, and have remained sufficiently stable, from one period and one society to another, for meaningful investigation to be possible? The whole of historical and anthropological scholarship rests on just that assumption.

Of course it is not only through recognition of continuity that history can give us educated understanding. Societies and their mental ecologies may mutate radically or vanish. Cultures may differ radically. It is scarcely necessary to insist that many of the categories in which we in the West understand both man and nature now, the intellectual and moral and material satisfactions that we demand and the methods by which we get them, have never been accepted by all mankind and have become ours only through a long process of orientation and reorientation. In order to understand our contemporary culture we need then to see it in the context both of comparative anthropology and of its own intellectual and social history, which might be seen as comparative anthropology extended into the past. Yet again as we put ourselves into the minds of the individuals or societies we are studying, and try to understand their questions and satisfactions and discontents, we need to control relativity both by objective scientific truth and by the objective continuity of scientific tradition.

The scientific movement has been concerned with man's relations with nature and his fellow beings as perceiver and knower and agent. It can be identified most precisely as an approach to nature effectively competent to solve problems. At the same time it has been as much a moral as an intellectual enterprise, and its moral commitments have been integral and essential to that intellectual competence. We can recognize in the solution of stable problems of nature or of thought an objective continuity which survives the relativity of culture. We can recognize likewise in the acceptance of scientific argument and evidence a moral commitment to truth which survives the relativity of many other varieties of human discourse and behaviour. In looking then for understanding of the history of science in our culture through a relative and comparative history or anthropology of approaches to nature, putting ourselves sympathetically into the minds of our subjects and trying to grasp their questions, we encounter in their answers and in the logic of their arguments a consistency relative not simply to culture but to nature. Antecedent presuppositions and styles of thinking within which problems have been seen and solved have indeed changed through history with period and society; but the universal measures of thinking effectively competent to solve problems in any period or society have been observation and logic. By these objective standards, reflecting the consistency both of nature and of human thinking, science has an objective continuity from its ancient origins to the present. Cogency relative to culture has varied; objective scientific validity has accumulated. Moral validity has also accumulated. Mankind has experienced through its scientific tradition a continuing standard of validity in a field of public knowledge, and hence it has acquired at least one objective measure of what exists, outside the relativities of human motives and desires. In nature man has not been the measure of all things. Engineers who attempted the impossible, wrote Galileo, "as if with their engines they could cheat nature" and her "inviolable law"[3], cheated only themselves and their employers; for "Nature, deaf and inexorable to our entreaties, will not alter or change the course of her effects"[4]. Nature could not be exploited in the spirit of magic or commerce, interrogated in the persuasive style of a legal hearing, or made the subject of mere academic disputation or literary search for philosophical or theological concordance, or of political compromise or propaganda or chicanery or oppression. Galileo's assertion of science as a moral enterprise of freedom for the inquiring mind, of this as a moral norm for all men, points to perhaps the greatest moral contribution of science to mankind. Who doubts, he wrote during his last Copernican campaign, that the novelty "of wanting minds created free by God to become slaves to the will of others is going to give birth to very grave scandals?" But the scandal was not just against human dignity but against objective knowledge, and would be in the end ruinous to political prudence, if propositions condemned from expediency were later "demonstrated by the senses or by necessity"[5].

---

[3] G. GALILEI, *Le mecaniche* (undated), ed. A. FAVARO (*Le opere*, II, nuova ristampa, Firenze, 1968) 155.
[4] G. GALILEI, "Terza Lettera delle Macchie del Sol" (1612; *Le opere* cit., V) 218.
[5] G. GALILEI, notes related to the *Dialogo* (after 1632; *Le opere* cit., VII) 540, 541.

If the goal of historical scholarship is to reconstruct the living past, the only past available for reconstruction is that which we can know in the present. Historiography is then a dialogue between an interrogating present and an interrogated past. The questions may change. The nature of science as an analytical discipline, involved at one and the same time in the uncertainties of discovery and explanation and belief and in the accumulation of objective knowledge, raises some special problems of historical reconstruction. Looking back from the present we can see scientific inquiry as an activity yielding a progressively growing body of universally communicable knowledge, any part of which we, latest heirs of the tradition, can test by stable criteria of logical consistency and comparison with observation, even if all parts of science are not tested in the same way. General statements of regularities or laws can be tested directly by observation, but theories embodying inobservable entities can be tested only indirectly by their consequences. Other statements such as the axioms of Greek logic or mathematics, and likewise general beliefs presupposing the kind of world that exists to be discovered, are challenged not by observation but by rethinking. Here philology can be an indispensable guide to the history of both ideas and actions.

We may see the history of science in the European tradition then as an intellectual enterprise integrated by its explicit historic criteria for choosing among theories and investigations at different levels of the true, the probable, the possible, the fruitful, the sterile, the impossible and the false. By means of these criteria natural scientists have exercised a kind of natural selection of theories and investigations, which has directed scientific thinking as the history at once of solving particular problems and of embodying them in ever more general explanations. The tradition can be characterized truly only by its whole range, not by selecting at one extreme an excessively empirical natural history or technology or at the other the peculiar problems of theoretical physics concerning the knowability of the world. Nor is it much illuminated by a sociological relativism which fails to distinguish the specific history of science from a general history of ideas lacking its specific modes of self-correction and criteria of acceptability. These from antiquity have identified the objective progress of scientific knowledge.

At the same time historical knowledge of the scientific tradition displays the varieties of scientific methods and intellectual manoeuvres on which any properly inductive analysis of scientific thinking must be based, it exposes us to the surprise that effective scientific thinking could be based on assumptions and have aims so various and often so different from our own, and it enables us to distinguish the historically accidental from the logically essential elements in the succession of scientific systems. Thus the reconstructed past throws light both upon its own later consequences and upon historically independent comparable situations. It can reveal constants of scientific thought and social behaviour as well as the circumstances of scientific and social change.

The history of science is defined like every part of history by its sources, and it shares in the general requirement of critical and linguistic techniques to establish valid sources. But like several other parts of history it requires also special knowledge. The sources of special histories distinguish them from general history (still usually conceived in political terms) for the simple reason that to read them requires both special technical capability and particular sensitivity. Anyone to whom a text is a blank unintelligible page can scarcely be an historian of that subject. But if historians of science or music or art, or of law or philosophy or religion and many other aspects of human thinking and experience, by definition need both a sense and a technical mastery of the content of their documentary sources and material artifacts, obviously they need also to include in their sources those for the intellectual and moral commitments, expectations, assumptions, intentions, motives, practical possibilities, social dispositions and opportunities, geography, occasions, accidents and so forth forming its relevant historical context. The nature of the inquiry is an invitation to look beneath the surface of immediate and particular scientific results and theories for the antecedent and concomitant intellectual and social and material conditions and commitments that made them possible and others perhaps impossible, and also for the logical structure that may be common to scientific situations arising in different fields and periods. The history of science so identified within historical scholarship is both an illumination of our historical intellectual culture, and an epistemological laboratory of science. But before all we look in history for people and their vision. The history of ideas is after all the history of people thinking, and when we say that ideas change we mean that people change their ideas, whether by their own thinking or by exposure to that of others in whatever their circumstances may be. If in this way we try to reconstruct events as lived within the mental and technical and social horizons of the persons whose thinking and actions we are analyzing, we get a view of the future lacking the logical appearance of events as seen in reverse. They after all did not know for sure where science was going until they had taken it there. Hence the historical relevance of errors and failures along with successes. For as Francis Bacon put it, "whether or no anything can be known, was to be settled not by arguing, but by trying"; the answers were "a birth of time" as well as "a birth of wit" [6]; and "the

---

6 F. BACON, *Novum organum*, I. 78 (1620).

art of discovery advances with every act of discovery" [7]. The historical questions we put to our sources aim at exegesis of the problems and arguments and expectations prefigured in the questions put in them to nature.

Science has been generated within the characteristically rational Western tradition as an approach to nature effectively competent to solve problems. But before the general direction towards scientific knowledge had been decided, either in ancient or in modern societies, two essential general questions remained open. It was an open question what kind of world men found themselves inhabiting, and so it was also an open question what methods they should use to explore and explain and control it. The characteristically Western tradition of rational science and philosophy may be traced to the ancient Greek commitment to the decision of questions by argument and evidence, as distinct from custom, edict, authority, revelation, rule-of-thumb, or some other principle or practice. They developed thereby the notion of a problem as distinct from a doctrine, and the consequent habit of envisaging thought and action in all fields as the setting and solving of problems. By deciding at the same time that among many possible worlds, the one world that existed was a world of exclusively self-consistent and discoverable rationality, the Greek philosophers and mathematicians and medical men came to commit their scientific successors exclusively to this effective direction of thinking. Thus they rejected the conceptions of nature in the ancient myths of the origin of the world: nature was not a society on the analogy of human societies, events in nature were not the arbitrary actions of divinities great or small, nature they insisted was an unchangeably stable and predictable order. They introduced in this way the fundamental conception of a rational scientific system, separately for each category of thought and of nature and collectively for every category. The exclusive rationality so defined became an essential presupposition both of formal logical systems and of experimental explorations of natural causation, and so of rational control of subject-matter of all kinds from mathematical to material, from ideas to things.

We may then see the primary origins of our science in the grasp and technical development by the Greeks of this conception of an uniquely true scientific system entailing a logic of decision and proof. They introduced decision and proof, a logic of either — or with methods of testing and self-correction, into speculations both about the general nature of the world and about particular questions, about what existed and about what should be done. On this view Greek science was a

---

[7] F. BACON, *Advancement of Learning*, I (1605), ed. J. SPEDDING, R. L. ELLIS and D. D. HEATH (*Works*, III, London, 1857) 392, cf. *Nov. org.*, I. 130.

consequence of a general commitment to habits of intellectual and moral and social behaviour which, while not themselves necessarily producing any immediate scientific results, appear as necessary or at any rate potent antecedent and concomitant conditions for scientific activity. It was also a consequence of a particular rational conception of existence and knowledge embodying a particular logic with a general application. Greek systems of ethics or law, no less than those of mathematics or physics, were envisaged with built-in methods of testing and self-correction. Aristotle meant his ethics to follow as rationally from a theory of human nature as did his physics from a theory of matter and causation. For the heirs of Aristotle, and of Hippocrates and Euclid then, the world that actually existed did so in one discoverable rational way, which excluded others and according to correct reason closed all other directions of speculation. This at least was the dominant commitment of the Greek scientific movement, despite the beliefs in the irrationality of nature and mankind alike which flourished at the same time, despite the growth of general philosophical scepticism about the possibility of human knowledge, and despite the more particular problems brought for example into mathematics by the discovery of 'irrational' numbers and recognized in diverse situations of contingent expectation and uncertain choice.

There seems to be no historical evidence that any other civilization or society committed itself to this logic of systematic science except by cultural diffusion from ultimately Greek sources. The arithmetical skills of the ancient Babylonians and Indians seem to have involved no central conception of mathematical proof, and neither their cosmological speculations nor those of the ancient Egyptians or Chinese seem to have been controlled by any general theory of natural causation embodying a logic of exclusion. They contained for example nothing corresponding to the Greek geometrical model of the universe. By this criterion they all had ingenious technology in an ambience of myth, but not science. The same goes for ancient medicine before the Greek philosophical reform. The first major civilization to absorb the Greek scientific tradition was that of Islam. The Arabic language became a vehicle for Greek scientific logic, modulated by its own native structure. The Western recovery of the Greek scientific tradition after external disaster and internal confusion was a recovery likewise of the Greek logic of rational decision. But not all societies have accepted its potential commitments in the same way. For whatever reason, neither the ancient Greek and Roman nor the medieval Islamic societies exploited their scientific knowledge technologically on a large scale, and in none did natural science come to dominate their intellectual culture. Anthropologists have shown us contemporary societies which use altogether different conceptions of nature and of man's relation to nature, some of which when exposed to Western scientific thinking have either rejected it or held open the question of its relevance or usefulness to them. We can understand such restraints only within the context of the general intellectual and moral and practical commitments and habits of a society. Can we find in that context the antecedent and concomitant conditions for the unique development of modern science in Western Europe, for that persistent search for criteria of dependable knowledge and that waxing appetite of aggressiveness towards nature? Can we by contrast find the contextual conditions for the long failure of Chinese or Indian or Islamic societies to develop anything comparable?

We may see the origins of modern science in the recovery, exegesis and elaboration of the Greek conceptions of rational decision and proof and of a rational system by medieval and early modern Europe. The recovery was made in a series of responses to ancient thought by a new society with some different mental and moral commitments and expectations, with a different view of nature and of man and his place in nature and his destiny, a different theology, a different economy and a different view of technology, but also with a vision of continuity. Much light can be thrown upon the intellectual orientations of European society in making these responses, by attention to its apprehensions of continuity or discontinuity with the past and programmes projected therefrom. When philosophers pictured themselves in the twelfth century as dwarfs standing on the shoulders of giants, or looked in the fifteenth century for guidance from a Hermetic wisdom of supposedly Mosaic antiquity, or insisted in the seventeenth century that they were doing something entirely new, they were all making evaluations of the past which entailed programmes for future action. The same applied to the evaluative use of the historical terms middle ages, renaissance, reformation, scientific revolution, enlightenment and so on. These may tell us more about the periods in which they were invented than about those to which they refer.

To characterize the process by which the science of nature developed its identity within the intellectual culture of medieval and early modern Europe is not easy. We may distinguish three broad stages of intellectual response and orientation brought about by the recovery and exploitation and then transcendence of ancient models. Each acquired a characteristic style of formulating and solving its problems. With the first intellectual impetus given by the recovery of ancient philosophical, scientific and mathematical texts in the twelfth and early thirteenth centuries came a primary intellectual achievement. This was the grasp and critical elaboration by the philosophical community of the medieval schools and universities of the construction of a demonstrative explanatory

system on the models of Euclid's geometry and Aristotle's physics and metaphysics. Together with this came a critical elaboration of logical precision, from methods formalized by Aristotle, for the control of argument
and evidence to decide a variety of questions, including decision by
calculation and observation and experiment. Despite the fundamental
difference in deductive structure between the linear sequence of Euclid's
mathematical argument and Aristotle's argument by syllogism, a source
of much confusion later, their common form of demonstration from
primary principles, to be accepted whether as self-evident or from o-
bservation or revelation or antecedent demonstration, came to establish
an intellectual style and programme over the whole range of intellectual
culture from natural philosophy and the arts to theology and law. Thus
in the twelfth century Domingo Gundisalvo wrote that the "artist is a
natural philosopher who... searches for principles", and the science and
arts of vision or music or engineering were all alike brought under
rational control by finding out and "contriving how one can make all
those things..., of which the measures are expressed and demonstrated
in mathematical theory, agree ... in natural bodies"[8]. An axiomatic
theology was to be deduced likewise from evident articles of faith, as
geometry was from propositions that were self-evident. Aristotelian
syllogistic logic imposed similarly on the science of nature a form of
demonstration relating cause to effect as premise to conclusion.

Starting from the Aristotelian maxim that "the mode of knowledge
must correspond to the matter"[9], philosophical logicians made a classification of logical procedures in rhetorical or persuasive as well as
demonstrative arguments, established rules for the acceptability of evidence and the degrees of available certainty and probability, and defined
the occasions for appeals to the senses, reason, faith, authority, tradition, usage and so on. Their expertise was relevant to a diversity of
scientific questions, whose common forms of argument applied to different matters with a common form. Thus the mathematical techniques
developed for expressing quantitative rates of qualitative change applied
both to moral virtue and to physical kinematics. The logic of diagnosis
applied likewise equally to disease, to witchcraft and magic, to criminals,
to usury, and to heresy. Rules were developed similarly for the exegesis of the scriptural revelation, and for relating it to philosophical reason. These were all pressingly practical questions. The search in all
for grounds for reasoned assent or dissent, and for identifying the kinds

---

[8] D. Gundissalinus, *De divisione philosophiae*, hrg. L. Baur (*Beiträge zur Geschichte der Philosophie des Mittelalters*, IV. 2-3; Münster, 1903) 10, 27, 112, 122.
[9] Th. Aquinas, *Expositio super librum Boethi De Trinitate...* q. 6, art. 1, rec. B.
Decker (Leiden, 1959) 205.

of argument and authority with power to convince, came to be part of the style of the whole intellectual culture. The context of that culture was established above all by the insistence of the theological heirs of Aristotle and Euclid that the truth must be comprehensive and exclusive, over the whole range of principles of thought and action for all that exists. Given the dual source of human knowledge in the divine gifts equally of true reason and of undeniable revelation, the whole enterprise made an urgent issue then of the possibility of error in good faith, of the attitude to be taken to unpersuadable infidels and heretics, and of the commitments and expectations of disagreement as well as agreement. The urgency of this issue, and the evangelical sense of obligation to discover and to spread true knowledge to the whole world towards some better future, have remained enduring characteristics of secular Western scientific culture.

The movement of intellectual orientation generated in Western Europe first then an organized capacity to act with rational intent in the control at once of argument and calculation. It generated at the same time an organized capacity to control a variety of materials and practices. We may distinguish this matching of logical control of argument by a likewise theoretically designed and measured control of matter as the second stage of European response to ancient models. Programmes towards this end already expressed from the twelfth century that urge towards exact analysis and ingenious contrivance for the material mastery of nature, which was to be achieved in action by the practitioners of a variety of arts. Working essentially outside the academic philosophical community but not without academic contacts, this group succeeded by making a rational and where possible quantitative anticipation of material construction or action. The relations between these two groups need further exploration. Contacts were evidently encouraged by changes in both. The superior craftsman improved in education and social position. The *architectus* for example came to be distinguished, in Italy as the designer or *theoricus* of buildings, from the mere *practicus* or artisan working under his direction. When at the end of the fourteenth century one of the architects of Milan Cathedral declared that *ars sine scientia nihil est* [10], he seems to have meant by *scientia* rather aesthetic design than scientific mechanics. Yet by this time the scientific and practical mathematical curricula of the universities had been considerably enlarged, and certainly by the fifteenth century literate craftsmen of many kinds, as likewise merchants, could find an education offering both technical expertise, with an ability to generalize, and

---

[10] J. S. ACKERMAN, "Ars sine scientia nihil est", *Art Bulletin*, XXXI (1949) 84-111.

some philosophy. The well born architect Leon Battista Alberti is not perhaps typical, yet it is relevant that a contemporary asking "in what class of learned men" to put him, should have replied: "Among the natural scientists (*physici*) ... Certainly ... he was born only to investigate the secrets of nature. And what kind of mathematics does he not know? Geometer, arithmetician, astronomer, musician, he wrote marvellously better than anyone for many centuries on perspective... He wrote on painting, he wrote on sculpture... and he not only wrote but also made with his own hands" [11]. Albrecht Dürer similarly presented in his image of a painter, pouring forth figures "from the inner ideas of which Plato writes" [12], the aesthetic theory of at once a craftsman, mathematician and philosopher.

The painters, sculptors, architects, engineers, metalsmiths, assayers, surveyors, navigators, musicians, accountants and so forth comprising this group generated an effective context for seeing and solving the exemplary technical problems shared by the mathematical sciences with the visual, plastic, mechanical, musical, navigational and commercial arts. Training in the arts provided for both theory and practical skill. Their practitioners responding to a diversity of particular demands brought about a general transformation of European intellectual life by their search for precise understanding and control of materials in a variety of circumstances: in the techniques developed for painting in the Netherlands and France as in Italy from the fourteenth century, for navigation and cartography in Portugal from the fifteenth century as in Italy and South Germany, for the construction of clocks and automata, of guns and music, widely across the European world. They demonstrated the consistency of nature and reason alike. They showed how to control vision by applying the postulates of geometrical optics to perspective painting and sculpture, and music by applying the postulates of acoustics to the measured temporal patterns of pitch and interval. They initiated the extension by art of the natural senses with the invention of spectacles in Tuscany at the end of the thirteenth century, of navigation without landmarks with the magnetic compass, of multiple communication with printing. They devised in the mechanical clock both a measure of time in uniform abstract units and an exemplary self-regulating mechanism. Their astronomical and mathematical instruments and computers provided the prototypes for later scientific

---

[11] C. LANDINO, *Commento... sopra la Comedia di Danthe Aligheri* (Firenze, 1491) f. IV[r]; cf. M. BAXANDALL, *Painting and Experience in Fifteenth-Century Italy* (Oxford, 1972) 114 sqq., 159.

[12] Quoted by E. PANOFSKY, *The Life and Art of Albrecht Dürer*, 4th ed. (Princeton, N.J., 1955) 280.

instrumentation. They quantified location and transport in space by techniques of stereographic projection, trigonometric surveying and cartographic coordinates; building and machines whether for lifting or pumping or gunnery by a search for rational mechanics; commerce and administration by systematic bookkeeping and numerical recording in abstract units of value. Was there a transference of practices between the systematic collecting and recording of numerical data required for rational control of commerce and the methods of the observational and experimental sciences and arts developing in the same ambience? That again is a question for further historical research. The goals of the arts whether technological or aesthetic should not be confused with those of philosophy and the sciences, but it does not seem difficult to recognize in them all a common intellectual style in which each reinforced the others. This was a major contribution to European intellectual as to technological history. The common mentality, revealed with varying nuances through changing contexts, as much by the succession of programmes as by the accompanying achievements, together so characteristic of Western Europe from the twelfth century, came to be indicated in Renaissance Italian by the habit of rational *virtù*.

The term *virtù* designated a style of intellectual and consequently practical behaviour. A man of *virtù*, acting rationally in the image of his creator, was a man with active intellectual power (*virtù*) to command any situation, to act as he intended, like an architect producing a building according to his design, not at the mercy of the accidents of fortuitous circumstance or *fortuna*. Whether in mind or matter, in the natural sciences or the constructive arts, in private or public and political life, a man of *virtù* aimed always to be in rational control of himself as a moral being and in relation to his fellow men and to nature, in control of what he did and what he made. He was the rational artist in all things, designing all his actions within the rationally examined limits of the possible. This according to Alberti was to be the felicitous characteristic of all human conduct, whether in family life or in the arts, exemplified by his account of how the painter by the method of perspective "can represent with his hand what he has conceived with his mind" [13]. For the artist, wrote Giorgio Valla later in the fifteenth century, before making something, by reason "fashions and forms it inwardly, and accordingly makes an image for himself of everything that is to be portrayed" [14] and of everything that is to be done. Valla saw both the constructive arts and the experimental science of nature as

---

[13] L. B. ALBERTI, *De pictura* (1435) I. 24, ed. C. GRAYSON in *On Painting and On Sculpture* (London, 1972) 58.
[14] G. VALLA, *De expetendis...* I. 3, 6, 18 (Venetiis, 1501).

products of the imposition of reason upon matter by antecedent analysis, above all, as Archytas had established at the outset of the scientific
movement, through the stable principles exemplified by mathematics.
Hence the unique capability insisted upon by Ficino of man alone a-
mong living things to make progress.   Human art was "a kind of nature handling external matter", just as nature was " art controlling nature
from within", but men alone were equipped to invent arts "of their
own will", so that "human arts construct by themselves whatever nature herself constructs, as if we were not slaves of nature but rivals" [15].
For: "We call arts the sciences using the hands" [16], and through them
man displayed "a genius (so to speak) almost the same as that of the
Creator" [17].

The intellectual style integrating these European movements in the
arts and sciences, from Alberti and from Valla and his contemporaries
Ficino, Leonardo da Vinci and Dürer down to Galileo and beyond, the
style of the rational artist, of the virtuoso whether in action or construction or investigation, entailed both an interpretation of the past
and a programme for the future of the human condition.   Its original
thrust, given especially by the intellectual and moral commitment made
by Plato and Aristotle to the rational consistency of all things and to
reasoned consistency of behaviour in every situation, was directed towards scientific questions in the sixteenth century by further ancient
sources, most revealingly by the Roman architect Vitruvius.   Men he
wrote (*De architectura*, x.1.4) had learnt to devise the machines (*machinae*) and instruments (*organi*) necessary for improving the material
arts by imitating the "devised nature (*natura machinata*)" exemplified
by the celestial revolutions.   The authors of the earliest Italian translation of Vitruvius (1521) developed this, in their philological commentary, into a characterization of scientific inquiry as intellectual contriving
or stratagem.   For "*Machinatio*... may be derived from I cunningly
contrive, ... I deliberate, I think out, ... stratagem, ... whence ... undertaking, thinking, machine and ... mechanic or mechanical operator".
Mechanics was commendable both for "its basic imitative resemblance
to the divine work of the construction of the world" and for its usefulness. It was an illustration of how theoretical philosophers like Archytas,
famous also as a mechanic who had contrived a wooden dove that flew,
must first contrive intellectually what they wanted to "put into practice
through a burning desire to produce in sensible works with their own

---

[15] M. FICINO, *Theologia Platonica*, IV. 1, XIII. 3 (*Opera*, Basileae, 1576) 123, 295-7.
[16] M. FICINO, *In Philebum commentarium*, II. 53 (1576) 1267.
[17] M. FICINO, *Theol. Plat.*, **XIII. 3 (1576) 297.**

hands that which they have thought out with the mind"[18]. In so doing, wrote Daniele Barbaro in another famous Vitruvian commentary, the constructive artist "will imitate nature ... Yet he will not search for impossible things"[19]. On these lines the engineer Giuseppe Ceredi, inspired at once by Greek mathematical thinking and by the example of "nature itself, as if become mechanical in the construction of the world", offered as a method of antecedent analysis of any enterprise the construction of "models, adding, changing and removing many things", as required. Thus he could bring together conveniently the many observations needed to bring about "some new and important effect", recognize errors by experience and correct them by reason, and so direct the whole enterprise "to the stable production of the effect that is expected"[20].

Does all this indicate a mental and social disposition, a dedication as much of will as of intelligence towards material enlightenment and power, that provided an uniquely favourable set of circumstances enabling the West to exploit the intellectual opportunities offered by the recovery of the Greek sciences and arts, with an energy and purpose found in no other society? However this large question of intellectual sociology is to be answered, dedication to exact and quantitative knowledge and control did eventually decide the fundamental identity both of science and of nature.

The self-conscious man of *virtù*, the virtuoso, the rational artist aiming at reasoned and examined control alike of his own thoughts and intentions and actions and of his surroundings, was of the essence of European morality, meaning both habit and ethical valuation, out of which the European scientific movement was generated and engineered. In this context the rational artist and the rational experimental scientist appear as exemplary products of the same intellectual culture. Both were exemplary men of *virtù*, achieving their results by a similar intellectual behaviour. The conception of *virtù* embodied a programme for relating man to the world as perceiver and knower and agent in the context of his integral moral and social and cosmological existence. The programme presupposed the stability of nature and mankind and of their relations, it entailed a commitment to an examined life of reasoned consistency of personal behaviour in intellectual and moral life alike,

---

[18] VITRUVIUS, *De architectura libri dece, traducti de latino in vulgare, affigurati, commentati,* I. 3, X. 1 (Como, 1521) ff. 18^r, 162^r; cf. P. GALLUZZI, "A proposito di un errore dei traduttori di Vitruvio nel '500", *Annali dell'Istituto e Museo di Storia della Scienza di Firenze,* I (1976), fasc. 2, 78-80.

[19] D. BARBARO, *I dieci libri dell'Architettura di M. Vitruvio, tradutti e commentati,* Proemio and 1. 3 (Vinegia, 1556) 9, 26.

[20] G. CEREDI, *Tre discorsi...* I (1567) 5-7.

and it generated a common style in the mastery of nature and mankind alike by the rational anticipation of effects. Thus the moral man could govern his private and public life by the mastery of human nature, and the cultivation of the habit of virtue true to that nature, by practice guided by right reason; the expedient politician could guide his calculations and machinations according to the regularities of experience. "Given that the happiness of man consists in acting according to *virtù* in a perfect life" wrote Alessandro Piccolomini in an essay on education, the essential cause of happiness, as of all effects, was surely not fortune but "what produced the effect according to the intention of that cause, just as an architect produces a house according to his own intention" [21]. This was the style not only of the mathematical sciences and arts but likewise of the right reason of Aristotelian ethics, exemplified by the moral and political philosophy of Thomas More and with perhaps more ambiguous intention of Machiavelli. It was in the same style that the builder and engineer could design by rational mechanics what he would make; that the rational perspective artist could form in his mind a conception of what he would represent by an antecedent analysis of visual clues organized optically by geometrical perspective; that the rational musician could discover the speeds and intervals producing the music heard. The rational experimental scientist proceeded likewise by an antecedent quantitative and conceptual analysis of his subject-matter.

At the same time for the philosophical and scientific community at large the nature and range of the effects that might be anticipated still remained at the beginning of the seventeenth century in varying degrees open questions. There was by no means general agreement on the kind of world men thought themselves to inhabit, how they should investigate it and what kinds of explanation should be accepted as satisfactory, how best to control it and to what ends control was most desirable.

In this context the confident establishment during the 17th century of the rational experimenter and observer as the rational artist of scien-

---

[21] A. PICCOLOMINI, *De la institutione di tutta la vita de l'homo nato nobile e in una città libera...* I. 3 (Venetiis, 1545) f. 16ʳ; 1st ed. 1542; cf. L. OLSCHKI, *Geschichte der neusprachlichen wissenschaftlichen Literatur*, I (Heidelberg, 1919), II (Leipzig, 1922), III (Halle a.S., 1927); E. PANOFSKY, "Artist, scientist, genius: notes on the 'Renaissance-Dämmerung'" in *The Renaissance: Six essays* by W. K. FERGUSON et al. (New York, 1962) 121-82; A. C. CROMBIE, "Science and the arts in the Renaissance: The search for truth and certainty, old and new", *History of Science*, XVIII (1980) 233-46, "Philosophical suppositions and shifting interpretations of Galileo" in *Theory Change, Ancient Axiomatics, and Galileo's Methodology*, ed. J. HINTIKKA, D. GRUENDER and E. AGAZZI, I (Dordrecht, 1981) 271-86, *Mersenne: Science, Music and Language*, CROMBIE and A. CARUGO, *Galileo's Arguments and Disputes in Natural Philosophy* (both forthcoming); S. Y. EDGERTON, "The Renaissance artist as quantifier" in *The Perception of Pictures*, ed. M. A. HAGEN, I (New York, 1980) 179-212.

tific inquiry, designed first in the mind and proceeding by antecedent theoretical analysis before execution with the hands, marked the culmination of European orientation in response to ancient scientific sources in its third stage. The experimental philosopher as the rational artist might make his analysis by means of theory alone, quantified as the subject-matter allowed, or by modelling a theory with an artifact analytically imitating and extending the natural original. Both artist and philosopher could obtain the effect sought only as Galileo put it "according to the necessary constitution of nature... For if it were otherwise, it would be not only absurd but impossible..." [22]. Art then could not cheat nature, but by discovering, obeying and manipulating natural laws, with increasing quantification and measurement, art was seen to deprive nature of its mysteries and to achieve a mastery exemplified by rational prediction, whether in the representation of a scene or the prognosis of a disease or the navigation of a ship. Galileo himself marks the connection and transition between two great European intellectual movements: from the world of the rational constructive artist to that of the rational experimental scientist. It was above all as the designer of an explicit scientific style, providing a philosophical strategy for the sciences of nature, that he illuminates the specific identity of natural science within the contemporary intellectual scene. But sharing a common style, art and science each proceeded to a different end. The artist set out to construct or imitate, the scientist to investigate and explain. A painter used his analysis of visual clues to construct his painting as a perceptual model imitating the natural clues in true perspective. The experimental philosopher conducted his analysis and devised his models as an inquisition aiming to discover an explanation of the natural phenomena. He modelled not clues to imitation but optical physiology.

The leading architects of the classical experimental and mathematical science of the 17th century saw this as the deliberate combination of a theoretical search for common forms of explanation with a practical demand for accurately reproducible results. The former was the commitment of philosophy deployed with logical mastery of argument, the latter of technology as the art of mastering materials. Thus the experimental philosophers of the generations of Gilbert, Galileo, Harvey and Descartes developed, through their characteristic style of rationality in dealing with particular problems, a general theory of discovery and explanation in which their solutions were embodied. Thereby they came to establish a specific identity, largely if not universally accepted,

---

[22] G. GALILEI, *Le meccaniche* (undated; *Le opere* cit., II) 155, 189; cf. above n. 21.

both for nature among the diverse possibilities long entertained, and for natural science as a mode of inquiry and decision in specific distinction from other diverse modes of thinking within contemporary intellectual culture.

The common commitments of the scientific movement offer then an invitation to examine the identity of natural science within any intellectual culture, to relate the styles of scientific thinking in any period to contemporary styles of thinking in the arts, in literature, in philosophy and theology, and in government, law, commerce and other practical affairs. They offer likewise an invitation to analyse the various elements that make up an intellectual style in the study and treatment of nature: conceptions of nature and of science, of scientific inquiry and scientific demonstration and explanation with their diversifications according to subject-matter, the evaluation of natural science within any society, and the intellectual and moral commitments and expectations generating attitudes to innovation and change. These questions again, asked comparatively of different cultures, offer a culturally integrated view of the historical problems of the unique scientific movement generated by the society of Western Europe.

The generations who established the specific rationality of seventeenth-century science gave confidence to its methods of research and criteria of acceptability by defining it as the art of the soluble. The scientific movement brought together in its common restriction to answerable questions a variety of scientific methods diversified by their subject-matters, each of which at the same time united an assembly of cognate subject-matters under a common form of argument. For wrote Alessandro Piccolomini "any discipline should receive its name rather from its way of demonstrating than from its subject-matter" [23]. Thus all the mathematical sciences and dependent arts from optics and music to mechanics and astronomy were united under a common method of postulation. The exploration by experiment and observation of the most diverse subjects from chemistry and biology to the study of human society and language used the same forms of argument by resolution and composition and taxonomy. Hypothetical modelling was likewise an instrument of analysis for society as for physiology and physics. The analysis of probable expectation and choice again took the same forms whether in estimating the outcome of a disease, a legal process, a commercial enterprise, or natural selection, or the reasonableness of assent to a scientific theory. The method of historical derivation was applied first to languages before it was applied to biological evolution.

---

[23] A. Piccolomini, *In Mechanicas quaestiones Aristotelis paraphrasis...* c. 1 (Romae, 1547) f. 6.

The scientific movement brought together also within these objectives an explicit scientific community with commonly acceptable habits of
intellectual behaviour.   The establishment through education and communication of such a community, largely still unorganized in ancient and
medieval societies, was a major achievement of the seventeenth century.
By reaching general even if not universal agreement on the aims, methods and criteria of validity, cogency and relevance in scientific argument, the seventeenth-century natural philosophers established a new
private and public confidence in the ability of men to find generally
acceptable criteria for dependable, self-monitoring and self-correcting
knowledge of the world.   They showed how to reach agreement on
how both to agree and to disagree rationally, and how to give demonstrations from evidence which obliged all rational men to accept their
conclusions.   They brought to conspicuous fulfilment the Western conception of a logically structured philosophical programme tested by its
success or failure in realization.   "Is it not evident in these last hundred years (when the study of philosophy has been the business of all
the virtuosi of Christendom)", John Dryden wrote in 1668, "that almost a new nature has been revealed to us? ... errors ... detected, ...
useful experiments in philosophy ... made ... so true it is that nothing
spreads more fast than science, when rightly and generally cultivated" [24].   They offered a cumulative confirmation of the growing Western
sense of rational purpose and of progress.

Yet for a true historical anthropology of science, a true history of
the experience of nature mediated through the specific vision and commitments of a particular society, we need to remind ourselves again that
successful scientific programmes are only part of the cultural ecology.
Their historical data must be matched from visions of nature that solved
no problems and from theories proved by scientific experience to have
been misguided.   The dominant element in Western culture remained
theology well beyond the seventeenth century, and science shared its
growing but still subsidiary position with many other intellectual activities ranging from philosophy and law to the literary, visual and musical
arts.   These might entail an attitude to nature or, like philosophical
responses to scepticism, an attitude to natural science, but they were
seldom strictly scientific.   Many individuals and sections of society
found their intellectual and moral satisfactions in categories of thought
and explanation not at all concerned with natural science but expressing

---

[24] J. DRYDEN, *Essay of Dramatic Poesy* (1688) in *Essays*, ed. W. P. KER, I (Oxford,
1900) 36-37.

some quite different purpose. The historical problem is to see how these various interests and categories affected and were affected by the sciences of nature found in the same ambience. The specific style of a culture is defined by all of its commitments and expectations and methods of procedure. The style of intellectual and moral behaviour in natural philosophy, in the individual and social processes by which discoveries and inventions have been made and have come to be accepted, may be illuminated as much by that in religion, law, the arts or practical affairs as by natural philosophy itself. The responses made to the challenges of Aristotelian metaphysics in the thirteenth century, of the new Platonism and scepticism and atomism in the fifteenth and sixteenth centuries, and of the new Copernican cosmology in the seventeenth century, all exemplified styles and methods at once of opposition and of accommodation with much in common in both their intellectual and their social dimensions. They marked at the same time subtle changes in both ends and means, in attitudes to innovation and to error, and in the treatment of tensions generated by conflicts of intellectual and moral loyalties both within the minds of individuals and externally in the relation of free inquiry to the habits of society and its institutions. Science and its rational philosophy have generated tensions in Western history at a variety of points in the dominant structure of meaning and power extending from theology or philosophical or political ideology to political or commercial motive and action. These have given a refined discretion to the presentation of arguments for persuasion as also for proof. The debates and practical experience over all these questions promoted in their specialized range a growth of the technical content of the arts and sciences, as likewise of philosophy and theology, law and government, but more generally and more subtly they promoted shifts in their intellectual and moral expectations.

The scientific movement has generated a moral paradox. Modern science has developed its power to solve problems by its selectivity and by its programme of reduction of more and more classes of phenomena to increasingly general theories. From this it has eliminated all values except truth and the aesthetic economy of theories which must also pass the test of truth, and all questions of motive and of the meaning of existence. To all other values and to all such questions its clear logic has made it explicitly neutral. Yet natural science has emerged as the rational norm in the Western search for universally and exclusively dependable principles in all regions of thought and action. This has made it a notable source first of conflicting certitudes and then of disquiet in Western societies, and a notable solvent of the confidence of other cultures to which the West has brought not simply its science and medicine and technology, but also its questioning of the meaning men give to existence as a whole and to human life and decision, in health and disease, within it. The paradoxical culmination of reasoned decision has been an increasing magnification of means with a matching neutralization of ends.

At the present time when, whether in welcome or reluctance, Western science is being appropriated by even the remotest peoples on the globe, and when East and West have met in competition for industrial and political power and in experience of its social consequences, as in more benign knowledge of each other, there are many reasons for looking for mutual understanding through the comparative history of intellectual and moral orientation and reorientation. Of immediate relevance is the comparison of Western with different Eastern and other conceptions of nature and of man's relation to nature as knower and agent, of the potentialities and limitations of different languages for expressing scientific reasoning and theory, and of the intellectual and moral acceptability of Western science to other cultures. How can we relate the mentalities of other historical traditions to the mentality of Western science? Some cultures seem opaque to the presuppositions of scientific argument. The languages of traditional magic and ritual for example and of Western science, lacking fundamental common premises, are mutually untranslatable. Their interpretations of the connections of events cannot be compared or confirmed or falsified in mutually acceptable terms or categories because these do not exist. Closed to each other, any choice must be a total rejection by each side. But the rejection is not symmetrical. The scientific analysis of the physical world common to all mankind yields results that can be applied to the practical problems of engineering or medicine in the expectation that they will work, and that if they do not, the reasons can be discovered by further analysis of the same kind. The occasions when traditional magical or similar means might seem also to produce desired physical effects, by the administration of ethnic drugs for example, can likewise be reduced to scientific explanation. The reverse is not true. The self-critical European tradition has generated at the same time a capacity, albeit for long uncertain, to see Western values through alien eyes and all in comparison with each other. It is surely no accident that anthropology and the critical study of intellectual history were developed systematically in the West as in no other culture, despite sophisticated individual exceptions. A conceptual freedom, won only with effort, that makes possible a detached perception of other intellectual and moral outlooks comprises also the perception of irreducible and perhaps incomprehensible differences. We may the more easily grasp other mentalities by recalling the scientific origins of our own in the Greek commitment to the analytical discovery of truth, and by attending to the different ends as well as means that relate man to nature. Western medicine itself for example, while based on analytical science, has a different objective. Analytical science as a theoretical inquiry has understanding as its end. Having taken its subject-matter to pieces and identified its parts and understood how they fit together, it has completed its mission. The objective of medicine, as of practical morality or engineering or artistic composition or politics, is not the analysis of the parts but the effect produced in the whole. The effect aimed at by medicine is health, the bodily and mental well-being of the individual person, unique and irreplaceable by any other individual person. It shares this end rather with the traditional religions, Eastern and Western, than with analytical science. Where it differs is in the means. Hence the complexity of relating the intellectual and moral history, and the philosophical anthropology, of medicine to those of science. It was the original Greek commitment that established the Western analytical style of both. Yet desired effects may be produced in the human person, by traditional Chinese or Indian medical practices for example as by Western psychiatry, with little real understanding of their causes. This has always been understood in medical practice. It raises questions of delicate discretion alike for mutual understanding among mankind and for the philosophical historian.

2

SOME ATTITUDES TO SCIENTIFIC PROGRESS: ANCIENT, MEDIEVAL AND EARLY MODERN

Taken literally, an essay within the length of a brief article on two thousand years of intellectual history, when the concept of progress as now understood was by no means at the forefront of men's minds, may seem to be an exercise in begging the question and in attempting the impossible. The concept of progress expresses an attitude to man's place in time and history, to the relation of his past to his future, that is both descriptive and prescriptive. It involves insights both into the progress of knowledge and its uses and into the possibilities and sources of knowledge, and also into the sources and progress or regress of happiness, power or moral virtue. The concept implies a desirable direction, hence the possibility of deviation, and value judgements about what ought and ought not to have been, and to be, done in man's dealings with nature, with himself and his fellow creatures, or with God. In other words, the concept of progress is at once profane and sacred, at once epistemological, cosmological and religious, in that it implies beliefs about knowledge, about what exists, and about man's origins, expectations and responsibilities within whatever is accepted as the scheme of knowledge and existence.

The idea is found only at the most critical level of literacy and can be found only in societies with historical records and a historical sense. One would not expect to find a concept of progress in the Western sense in societies that either had no recorded history, or that looked for their meaning, their commitments and expectations, not in a historical relation between future and past but in timeless myths. So far as I know, of the great ancient civilizations, only the Greeks and Hebrews in the West and the Chinese in the East developed this sense of history. The Egyptians, Babylonians and Hindus seem to have been primarily mythopoeic. Equally one would not expect to find a concept of rational progress where the accepted source of knowledge was revelation, custom or authority as distinct from critical argument and evidence. In the West at least, the literary evidence, which perforce is all we have for the period in question, records only the interests and concerns of the highly intellectual. We really do not know much of what the ancient and medieval populace themselves thought; we know only what philosophers, theologians, historians, medical men and poets thought about them and about the societies of which they formed the

* Based on a paper given by invitation at the *Convengo sul Concetto di Progresso nella Scienza* organized by the Società Italiana di Logica e Filosofia delle Scienze at Chiavari on 23–26 September 1974.

bulk. But it is obvious as one reads these writers that their view of both the possibility and the desirability of progress, or the reverse, towards some goal, sacred or profane, was very much influenced, then as now, by the immediate experience of their societies.

I propose then to examine briefly in the light of some recent scholarship some of the crucial episodes in this Western search for meaning in history.[1] As a proper, philosophical use of historiography, we might hope that the history of the idea might throw some light also upon ourselves, especially on that belief, so persistent in Western attitudes even in the midst of disbelief, in "the orgastic future that year by year recedes before us". It is hard to go against old habits, even when we want to. Like Gatsby "we beat on, boats against the current, borne back ceaselessly into the past" that holds before us the ever-promised consummation.

Greek appraisals of the origins of civilization and expectations of its future established contrasting attitudes in Western historiography, depending from the beginning on general philosophy and particular experience. Attitudes to the history of civilization depended, for example, on whether it was held that the world was a product of design or of chance; that knowledge of the world was an open-ended process of finding out or could reach certainty; that there was a natural language of humanity in which true names revealed the nature of things or all languages were again open systems of arbitrary signs; that man could with justice aspire to nobility or was merely an overweening animal. The most optimistic view of civilized man and his future appeared in the fifth century B.C. following the visible Greek achievements in the mathematical sciences, medicine and philosophy. This is reflected in the anthropological preface written four centuries later by Diodorus Siculus to

1. For general histories of the idea of progress and further specialized bibliography see J. Delvaille, *Essai sur l'histoire de l'idée de progrès jusqu'à la fin du 18ième siècle* (Paris, 1910); J. B. Bury, *The idea of progress* (London, 1920); R. Hubert, "Essai sur l'histoire de l'idée de progrès", *Revue d'histoire de la philosophie et d'histoire générale de la civilisation*, ii (1934), 289–305; iii (1935), 1–32; F. J. Teggart, *The idea of progress*, revised with introd. by G. H. Hildebrand (Berkeley, California, 1949); P. Rossi, *I filosofi e le macchine, 1400–1700* (Milano, 1962), trans., 1971, into English as *Philosophy, technology, and the arts in the early modern era*, transl. A. Attanasio, ed. B. Nelson (New York, 1970), ch. 2; L. Edelstein, *The idea of progress in Classical Antiquity* (Baltimore, Maryland, 1967); C. Van Doren, *The idea of progress* (New York, 1967); J. A. Passmore, *The perfectibility of man* (London, 1970), ch. 10; E. R. Dodds, review of Edelstein, *op. cit., Journal of the history of ideas*, xxix (1968), 453–7; *idem, The Ancient concept of progress and other essays* (Oxford, 1973), ch. i; references below, especially in refs 2, 27–31, 40, 52 and 73–75; and *cf.* J. W. Johnson, "Chronological writing: its concepts and development", *History and theory*, ii (1962), 124–45. The quotations that follow are of course from the end of Scott Fitzgerald's *The Great Gatsby*.

his universal history:[2]

> Concerning the first generation of the universe this is the account which we have received. But the first men to be born, they say, led an undisciplined and bestial life, setting out one by one to secure their sustenance and taking for their food both the tenderest herbs and the fruits of wild trees. Then, since they were attacked by the wild beasts, they came to each other's aid, being instructed by expediency, and when gathered together in this way by reason of their fear, they gradually came to recognize their mutual characteristics. And though the sounds which they made were at first unintelligible and indistinct, yet gradually they came to give articulation to their speech, and by agreeing with one another upon symbols for each thing which presented itself to them, made known among themselves the significance which was to be attached to each term. But since groups of this kind arose over every part of the inhabited world, not all men had the same language, inasmuch as every group organized the elements of its speech by mere chance. This is the explanation of the present existence of every conceivable kind of language, and, furthermore, out of these first groups to be formed came all the original nations of the world.

Diodorus went on to stress the role of necessity in stimulating men to raise themselves from their first wretched condition, without clothing, dwellings, fire or the cultivation of food, by discovering these useful things and the arts that furthered social life: "Indeed, speaking generally, in all things it was necessity itself that became man's teacher, supplying in appropriate fashion instruction in every matter to a creature which was well endowed by nature and had, as its assistants for every purpose, hands and speech and sagacity of mind". Necessity became a recurrent theme in Western interpretations of the history of civilization, reappearing for example in the fifth century A.D. in

2. Diodorus of Sicily, with an English translation by C. H. Oldfather, (Loeb Classical Library, Cambridge, Mass., and London, 1936), i.8. What follows is based primarily on Dodds's account of ancient conceptions of time and human history. I should also like to thank for his guidance Mr G. E. M. de Ste Croix of New College, Oxford. For further studies see A. O. Lovejoy and G. Boas, *Primitivism and related ideas in Antiquity* (Baltimore, Maryland, 1935); L. E. E. Robin, "Sur la conception Épicurienne de progrès" (1916), 525–52, in *La pensée hellénique des origines à Epicure* (Paris, 1942); B. A. van Groningen, *In the grip of the past: essay on an aspect of Greek thought* (Leiden, 1953); W. K. C. Guthrie, *In the Beginning: some Greek views on the origins of life and the early state of man* (London, 1957); A. Momigliano, "Time in ancient historiography", *History and theory*, Beiheft vi (1966), 1–23; J. de Romilly, "Thucydide et l'idée de progrès", *Annali della Scuola Normale Superiore di Pisa*, ser. 2, xxxv (1966), 143–91; *cf.* below, ref. 14.

Proclus's account of the origin of mathematics[3] and in the twelfth century in Hugh of St Victor's account of the origin of all the arts.[4] In the fifth century B.C. pride of achievement then and for the future was given to *techné*, skill used to advantage, both of mind and hand. This was how the authors of the Hippocratic works *On ancient medicine* and *On the art of medicine* saw things. The same pride in man's self-reliant intelligence, in discovery by research which raised him to mastery of earth and sea, of animals and minerals, of writing, and of such difficult sciences as mathematics, astronomy and medicine, can be glimpsed in a fragment of Xenophanes and more fully in the Prometheus of Aeschylus. By making Prometheus the giver not just of fire but of all the arts for power over nature, Aeschylus created one of the great symbolic figures of European consciousness. But in saying this in his famous essay on this whole subject, E. R. Dodds has drawn attention also to the sense of divine purpose in Aeschylus, and to the sense of the destructiveness of human cleverness, of man's ultimate helplessness, of the irrational and unteachable elements in his nature, and of the play of sheer chance in history, with which other observers, Sophocles and the historians Herodotus and Thucydides, coupled their recognition of the genuine advances they witnessed.[5]

The experience of the Peloponnesian War brought an altogether more pessimistic outlook, and with it revived two ancient myths, both of which have retained a long, if protean, attraction. The myth of the Golden Age, the Lost Paradise with its Noble Savage, was of course used by Plato in the *Laws* (iii, 677–9) for contemporary social criticism, just as, like all future Utopias, he used the *Republic*. He saw the history of civilization as the history of technical progress and moral decline. Dodds has noted that in this period too appeared the 'hippies' of Antiquity, "the Cynics who preached rejection of all social conventions and a return to the simple life in its crudest form".[6]

The later centuries of the Greco-Roman world offer a fascinating model for us of this continuing tension between awareness of scientific and technical progress and at the same time scepticism of its value in a society seen as being in moral retreat. Scientists like Aristotle (also, of course, a philosopher with his own view of the nature of things) and Archimedes retained confidence in the capability of their scientific methods and the desirability of their results. But leading philosophers of all schools, in diagnosing the sick society of the Hellenistic age, and especially with the crisis of civil war and

3. Proclus Diadochi, *In primum Euclidis Elementorum librum commentariorum . . . libri iv*, Latin translation by Francesco Barozzi (Patavii, 1560), ii.4; first Greek edition, by S. Grynaeus, Basel, 1533; see (editor) G. Friedlein (Teubner: Leipzig, 1873), 65 and English translation with historical introduction by G. Morrow (Princeton, 1970).

4. Below, ref. 34.

5. See Dodds, *The Ancient concept of progress*, 4–13.

6. *Ibid.*, 13 seq.; Lovejoy and Boas, *op. cit.* (ref. 2), 117 seq., 287 seq.

corruption which destroyed the Roman Republic, became more gloomy. The Stoics developed the second ancient myth, of the Great Year, into their deterministic theory of time as an endless succession of cyclical returns. Each cycle ended with the dissolution of the world into its elements in a universal conflagration, followed by its regeneration, and so on and on, exactly repeating the same events over and over again, leaving room only for acceptance without initiative or responsibility. The Epicureans likewise left no room for ultimate hope in developing Democritus's atomism into their cosmogony of meaningless chance which generated the human race. It is perhaps surprising that each school should have produced thinkers in the first century B.C., the Stoic Posidonius and the Epicurean Lucretius, who respected scientific and technical advance and revived interest in its origins (coupled by Posidonius with personal observations on the tribes of Gaul and Lusitania). But neither saw an optimistic future. The rise of civilization for Lucretius was man's intelligent response to need in a world where he stood alone, but with civilization man became at the same time more vainly acquisitive and destructive.[7]

Dodds has noted other opinions from this period: that the Greek way of life had corrupted even the neighbouring barbarians, that nature had done more for the Scythians than philosophy for the Greeks, and that Prometheus was rightly punished for introducing man to the arts of civilization. But most paradoxical of all was another Stoic, Seneca, who a century later was something more than a witness of the reign of Nero. Seneca reported Posidonius's opinions, and was to be quoted on these issues by Roger Bacon and many times in the sixteenth century. He thought, like Lucretius and later Diodorus Siculus, that the Earth might be growing old and less fecund and Rome too losing its vigour. At one point in his *Natural questions* he seems to have envisaged that the final Stoic conflagration of the world was immediately at hand.[8] Yet he wrote also in the same work with an expectation at some future date of indefinite intellectual progress: "The time will come when careful research over very long periods will bring to light things which now lie hidden ... when our descendants will be amazed that we did not know things to them so obvious".[9] But knowledge of nature was for Seneca essentially an intellectual delivery for the few. He did not approve its application.[10]

Contemporary writers on science and technology, for example Vitruvius and the elder Pliny, continued to expect advances in those fields, but belief

7. Dodds, 16–20; for Posidonius see Seneca's *Epistolae*, xc, and see Lucretius, *De rerum natura*, v, 1410 seq.; Robin, *op. cit.* (ref. 2).
8. Seneca, *Naturales quaestiones*, iii.27–30; Dodds, *op. cit.* (ref. 1), 20–22.
9. Seneca, *Naturales quaestiones*, vii.25; *cf.* 30, with an English translation by T. H. Corcoran, ii (Loeb Classical Library, Cambridge, Mass., & London, 1972).
10. *Ibid.*, vi.4; Dodds, *op. cit.* (ref. 5), 23; *cf.* Edelstein, *op. cit.* (ref. 1), 169–77.

in general progress was not characteristic of the ancient world.[11] The vision of existence was limited by *moira*, the normative order of the universe keeping everything both physically and morally within the boundaries of its nature. Lucretius seems to have thought that the arts of civilization had reached their perfection.[12] Plato and Aristotle in their different ways both saw the development of knowledge as the fulfilment of a delimited pre-existing model or form.[13] For Aristotle, the subject of many commentaries after the editing of his collected works in the first century B.C., the advances made by the arts and sciences in each civilization were the fulfilment of the potentialities of their natural form beyond which they could not go. This was a structural rather than temporal view of history, on which he imposed the same structural teleological conception of causation as he used in organizing his biology and cosmology.

Yet in late Antiquity a view of material progress did appear from a seemingly unexpected quarter. To a number of Christian writers, notably the Emperor Constantine's theological adviser and historian Eusebius, and indeed Constantine himself, the recent triumph of the Church was evidence both of the *operatio Dei* in human history and of the material benefits for which Christians could look from the same hand. The Christian Empire and Church had realized the *Pax Romana* under the true God. It projected on to providential history the idea of the unity of mankind which had appeared after the Eastern conquests of Alexander the Great.[14] Even before this glorious transformation, Tertullian had given an arrestingly topical picture of mankind in progress:[15]

If you look at the world as a whole, you cannot doubt that it has grown progressively more cultivated and populated. Every territory is now accessible, every territory explored, every territory opened to commerce. The most delightful farmsteads have obliterated areas formerly waste, plough-land has subdued the woods, domestic cattle have put to flight the wild beast, barren sands have become fertile, rocks are reduced to

11. See Plinius, *Naturalis historia*, ii.13.62; Dodds, *op. cit.* (ref. 5), 22–23; *cf.* Guthrie, *op. cit.* (ref. 2), 78 seq.
12. Lucretius, *De rerum natura*, v, 1457.
13. Dodds, *op. cit.* (ref. 5), 14–16; see especially Aristotle, *Politica* i.,1, 1252a24 seq., ii. 8, 1268b35 seq., vii.10, 1329b25 seq.; *cf.* D. M. Balme, "Aristotle: Natural history and zoology", *Dictionary of scientific biography*, i (New York, 1970), 259–61.
14. C. M. Cochrane, *Christianity and classical culture*, revised (New York, 1944; paperback 1957), 183 seq.; Bury, *op. cit.* (ref. 1), 22 seq. *Cf.* for providential views of history especially in Platonic and Stoic thought, W. Theiler, *Zur Geschichte der teleologischen Naturbetrachtung bis auf Aristoteles* (Zürich, 1925); F. Solmsen, *Plato's theology* (Ithaca, New York, 1942); A. J. M. Festugière, *La révélation d'Hermes Trismégiste*: ii. *Le Dieu cosmique* (Paris, 1949).
15. Cochrane, *op. cit.* (ref. 14), 246.

soil, swamps are drained, the number of cities today exceeds the number of isolated huts in former times, islands no longer inspire fear nor crags terror: everywhere people, everywhere organized communities, everywhere human life. Most convincing as evidence of populousness, we men have actually become a burden to the Earth, the fruits of nature hardly suffice to sustain us, there is a general pressure of scarcity giving rise to complaints, since the Earth can no longer support us. Need we be astonished that plague and famine, warfare and earthquake come to be regarded as remedies, serving as it were to trim and prune the superfluity of population?

The Western vision, pagan or Christian, of man's place in time and history was sharply refocused for almost a millennium and a half by St Augustine. When Rome did fall to Alaric's Visigothic army in the summer of 410 A.D. the event signified something already very different from what it might have done to the tired pagan society of Seneca. Rome was no longer the actual capital of the Empire. But it was still the eternal city, the symbolic capital of the last of the four universal monarchies whose fall, according to the prophecies of Daniel and of the Apocalypse of St John, would herald the persecutions of Antichrist and then the fifth monarchy of the saints lasting till the end of the world.[16] Augustine's great work the *City of God* was yet another response with a general philosophy to a particular occasion. He wrote it, in sections over thirteen years, to dispose of some false responses based on false beliefs, and to establish the true place of mankind in the Christian cosmology of unique creation, incarnation and salvation within which history was now seen to be enacted.[17]

Augustine accepted the apocalyptic prophecy but rejected the symbolism of Rome. The only permanent kingdom was the City of God. He attacked both the pagan assertions that Rome's calamities were a consequence of the neglect of the gods, and the Christian expectation of material advantage from the true religion. Most important of all he attacked the Stoic theory of cyclical returns, of an endless succession of periodic catastrophes and regenerations of the world and the human race.[18] He wanted to make a

16. Augustine, *De civitate Dei*, xx.
17. See for the composition of this work, Augustine, *Concerning the City of God against the Pagans*, trans. H. Bettenson with introd. by D. Knowles (Pelican Classics, London, 1972), xv seq., and T. E. Mommsen, "St Augustine and the Christian Idea of progress: the background of the City of God", *Journal of the history of ideas,* xii (1951), 346–74; *cf.* L. Spitzer, "Classical and Christian ideas of world harmony", *Traditio*, ii (1944), 409–64; iii (1945), 307–64; C. A. Patrides, *The phoenix and the ladder: the rise and decline of the Christian view of history* (Berkeley and Los Angeles, California, 1964).
18. Augustine, *De civitate Dei*, xii.10, 12, 14, in Aurelii Augustini *Opera* curaverunt B. Dombart et A. Kalb (*Corpus Christianorum*, ser. Lat. xlvii–xlviii; Turnholti, 1955): chs 12–22 correspond to chs 11–21 in the older editions; including Migne.

theological point. In such a merry-go-round there was no room for the divinely promised hope of progress towards happiness through knowledge of God. We could not believe that Plato would endlessly recur teaching the same philosophy to the same disciples, or worse that Christ would die and die again upon the cross.[19] But we could believe from sound teaching that each individual was able to move on a unique course towards true happiness, and that God had created the world and the human race uniquely with a definite beginning, progressing through linear time towards a definite end at the Last Judgement. Thus in the ordered course of God's providential government every event was unique, every human decision responsible, and every action both of individuals and in the succession of ages at once a genuine novelty and the fulfilment of a purpose.[20]

Within this scheme of Creation, Fall and Redemption, of the unique passage through linear time of responsible individuals moving towards eternity, which Christianity gave to the Western vision of history, Augustine left no doubt that progress in the human sciences and arts was definitely secondary.[21] He set out an argument showing that Moses and the early prophets had ante-dated all other thinkers, so that prophetic authority took precedence over the vaunted philosophical learning taught to the Egyptians by Hermes Trismegistus after the time of Prometheus and Atlas the great astronomer, long after which came Thales and the philosophers of the Greeks.[22] The disagreements of the philosophers contrasted with the harmony of the Scriptures.[23] Yet in the last book of the *City of God* he gave an attractive account of the inventions and discoveries which God's mercy had allowed even sinful man to make in the course of history through his genius and industry. Some were useful and necessary, some dangerous and harmful, and all had to be seen within the complete picture of man's spiritual destiny. Yet within that destiny he made room for these exercises of the gift of prudent intelligence, for the investigation by mind and hand of the natural creation from the circling stars and the ratios of music through the varieties of living species to the hidden parts of the body studied by anatomists even in dying men, and for the intellectual admiration of the beauty and utility of nature, and of the senses and inventive speech and arts of man himself.[24] In his final paragraphs, Augustine outlined a parallel between the six days of creation and the six ages of universal history, the first being that from Adam to the Flood and the sixth that in which he lived. This, at some unknown

19.　*Ibid.*, 14.
20.　*Ibid.*, 20–22; *cf.* lib. xv–xvi.
21.　*Ibid.*, xxii.24.
22.　*Ibid.*, xviii.37–39; *cf.* viii. 2, 12, 23-24. For this view of intellectual history, taken from the Hermetic *Asclepius*, see A. D. Nock et A. G. M. Festugière, *Corpus Hermeticum*, ii (Paris, 1945), 259, 264 seq.; *cf.* F. A. Yates, *Giordano Bruno and the Hermetic tradition* (London, 1964), 9 seq.; below ref. 52.
23.　*Ibid.*, 41.
24.　*Ibid.*, xxii.24.

time, would be followed by the Sabbath age of rest and then eternity.[25]

It seems to me that the simplicity of Christian certainty about the origin, purpose and end of the world and of man provided a powerful, though not of course sufficient, disposition towards the development of scientific thought. The conception of the natural world as the product of a rational and benevolent Creator and of man as made in his image was an invitation to use the gifts of reason and the senses to follow his thoughts. Kepler was to say just that.[26] At any rate, this view both of history and of nature was projected by Augustine on to the Latin West where natural science did eventually rise to become a major element of intellectual and practical culture. Augustine dominated Western medieval thinking on these subjects until the thirteenth century and was a powerful influence for centuries later. The conception of a benevolent destiny provided for responsible man within the ups and downs of his six historical ages was elaborated three centuries later, in the midst of the barbarian invasions of Christendom, by that distinguished historian the Venerable Bede in his lucid scientific essays on the measure of time, written in the oasis of Northumbria.[27] Four centuries later again, when the intellectual reconstruction of the West had got under way, philosophers described twelfth century achievements in the arts and sciences with naive confidence. The sources of their knowledge were but a modest part in Latin of the full riches of ancient thought: Boethius, Cicero, Augustine, Chalcidius's version of Plato's *Timaeus* on which they based scientific explanations of the formation of the world over the six days of creation. On these small foundations philosophers centred in the new schools of northern France developed a sense of mastering the past and of progressing forward in rational knowledge. One of them, Bernard of Chartres, famously compared his contemporaries to "dwarfs standing on the shoulders of giants", able to see more and farther than them "because we can raise ourselves up thanks to their giant stature".[28] Another, Adelard of Bath, translator of Euclid's *Elements* of geometry from Arabic into Latin, demanded for reason

25. *Ibid.*, xxii.30.
26. *E.g.*, Kepler to Herwart von Hohenburg, 9/10 April 1599, *Gesammelte Werke*, xiii, ed. M. Casper (München, 1945), 309, *Dissertatio cum nunceo sidereo* (1610; in Galileo Galilei, *Opere*, ed. naz. da A. Favaro *et al.*, 2a ed. (Firenze, 1968), iii, 123); *cf.* Whitehead, *Science and the modern world* (Cambridge, Mass., 1926), ch. 1.
27. Beda, *Opera de temporibus*, ed. C. W. Jones (Cambridge, Mass., 1943), 201-2, 303, 307–15; R. W. Southern, "Aspects of the European tradition of historical writing: 2. Hugo of St Victor and the idea of historical development", *Transactions of the Royal Historical Society*, xxi (1971), 161–2.
28. Ioannis Saresberaensis Episcopi Carnotensis, *Metalogicon libri iiii*, ed. C. C. J. Webb (Oxford, 1929), iii.4; John of Salisbury, *The Metalogicon: a twelfth century defense of the verbal and logical arts of the trivium*, transl. D. D. McGarry (Berkeley and Los Angeles, California, 1962), 167.

precedence over authority.[29] Yet another, enlarging on William of Conches in looking for collaboration by rational art with the natural powers given to things by their Creator, declared that the "dignity of our mind is its capacity to know all things".[30]

Yet we must see these quotations in context. The philosopher of this group with the most pronounced sense of both historical occasion and historical development, Hugh of St Victor, appealed to history to show how the restoration of the divine likeness in fallen man commenced with the recovery of his natural powers and integrity through the arts and sciences.[31] Hugh wrote a universal history on Augustinian lines of man's fall and subsequent long return from divine alienation,[32] in which he gave due place to the origins of both the mechanical and the liberal arts and sciences. Both began with artifice imitating nature.[33] Arts such as agriculture, building and language itself were invented under the spur of practical necessity and reduced to rule by reason. For, he wrote, as "the proverb says: 'Ingenious want has mothered all the arts'. Want it is that has devised all that you see most excellent in the occupations of men. From this the infinite varieties of painting, weaving, carving and founding have arisen, so that we look with wonder not at nature alone but at the artificer as well".[34] Later came the theoretical sciences invented under the draw of free inquiry into truth: theological, mathematical and physical.[35] As the rules of the arts controlled the manipulation of matter, so, in the theoretical sciences, logic and mathematics controlled rational argument into what was in existence and what must or could be. Before "art joined logic to philosophy, crude discourse handled the secrets of wisdom with common and vulgar simplicity".[36] But thereafter scientific knowledge developed, and could develop into what seemed to be an optimistic future. Yet in the final account Hugh saw all these investigations within the scheme of man's destiny as a fallen creature returning to his Creator, from knowledge of whom and of himself they must not become a distraction.[37]

It was the end of man that primarily concerned my final examples of

29.   Adelardus von Bath, *Die Quaestiones naturales*, c.6, ed. M. Müller (*Beitrage zur Geschichte der Philosophie des Mittelalters*, xxxi.2; Münster, 1923); L. Thorndike, *A history of magic and experimental science*, ii (New York, 1923), 28–29.
30.   R. W. Southern, *Medieval humanism and other studies* (Oxford, 1970), 40–42, 79–80.
31.   Hugo de Sancto Victore, *Didascalicon de studio legendi*, ed. C. H. Buttimer (Washington, D.C., 1939), i.5, 8, ii.1; English transl., with introduction and notes by J. Taylor (New York and London, 1961), 18 seq., 28–30; Southern, *op. cit.* (ref. 27), 163 seq.
32.   *De sacramentis*: see Southern, *op. cit.* (ref. 27), 166 seq.
33.   Hugh of St Victor, *Didascalicon*, ii.1, 20; i.9, 11, *cf.* 4–5.
34.   *Ibid.*, i.9; transl. Taylor, 56.
35.   *Ibid.*, ii.1, 17, 30.
36.   *Epitome Dindimi in philosophiam*: see *Didascalicon*, transl. Taylor, 12.
37.   *Didascalicon*, transl. Taylor, 12 seq.; 18 seq.; 28 seq.

medieval philosophers of history, Joachim of Fiore and Roger Bacon. About half a century after the northern philosophers had set out their optimistic thoughts, Joachim, by sober biblical studies in his monastery in Calabria, reached the alarming conclusion that Antichrist and the last age of the world were not just future prospects but immediately at hand. Elaborating and modifying Augustine's scheme of history by means of his own peculiar insights into the meaning of Scripture, he began to see imminent signs of the approaching consummation in the darkening external scene. These he expounded first to the Pope who approved his studies, and a few years later in the winter of 1190–91 at Messina to Richard I of England and his crusaders on their way to Palestine. Jerusalem had fallen in 1187 to Saladin, whom he identified with the penultimate persecutor, the abomination in the holy places. He collected information confirming old Christian fears of Islam; the Gospel had been preached to the ends of the Earth; the nations were at war and false prophets at large. Antichrist had already been born and had only to seize power.[38]

The date first predicted, 1260, passed without event and was to be deferred regularly in Joachite prophecies for the next three centuries.[39] But new signs, the Tartar menace from outside Christendom and social unrest within, were to catch the eye of Roger Bacon and lead him during 1266–68 to prepare for another Pope his great scheme for dealing with the situation by educational reform and scientific preparation.[40] This he saw as a matter of urgency. The Church must become forewarned by studying the prophecies of the Bible, the Sibyls, Merlin, Joachim and so forth, and by truly scientific astrology.[41] The Tartars had terrified the western nations by carrying their invasion across the Danube in 1241. Bacon gathered information about them, especially from the Franciscan William of Rubruck who had travelled among them a decade later. It seemed that they had already burst through the Caspian gates of the Caucasus and were about to spread across Christendom acclaiming Antichrist. He was convinced from such disasters as the Children's Crusade of 1212, and the so-called Shepherds Revolt which he had seen himself in 1251, that the Tartars and Saracens were sending their agents to sow discord likewise within Christendom. After the law of

38. M. Reeves, *The influence of prophecy in the later Middle Ages: a study of Joachimism* (Oxford, 1969), 3–14; Southern, "Aspects of the European tradition of historical writing: 3. History as prophecy", *Translations of the Royal Historical Society*, xxii (1972), 173–7.

39. Reeves, *op. cit.* (ref. 38), 48–59, 82–95, 227–8, 242–7, 308–16, 322–4, 367–9.

40. He set this out in the *Opus maius, Opus minus* and *Opus tertium*. For a summary of Bacon's life and writings, with bibliography, see A. C. Crombie and J. D. North, "Bacon, Roger", in *Dictionary of scientific biography*, i (New York, 1970), 377–85; see also Thorndike, *History of magic* (ref. 29), ii, 616 seq.; S. C. Easton, *Roger Bacon and his search for a universal science* (Oxford, 1952).

41. Roger Bacon, *Opus maius*, iv, "Mathematicae in divinis utilitas", "Judicia astronomiae", ed. J. H. Bridges, i (Oxford, 1897), 268–9.

Mahomet would come that of Antichrist, who would use the same foul methods of magical scientific 'fascination'. Christendom must be not only forewarned but also forearmed.[42]

It was clear to Bacon (stream-lining Augustine) that God had revealed to the patriarchs and prophets from the beginning of human life, to Abraham, Moses, Noah and their successors, one true wisdom entirely adequate for man's needs. This comprised not only theology and the moral law but also the full principles of philosophy without which the sciences and arts could never have been acquired. But because, through evil, unbelieving philosophers, Zoroaster, Prometheus, Hermes Trismegistus and the like, abused this pristine wisdom, God darkened the foolish hearts of the multitude and knowledge gradually disappeared. It was revived by Solomon, again lost through sin and revived again by the Greek philosophers from Thales to Aristotle, but these had learnt everything from the original Hebrew source.[43] Bacon made a great point of the wise being always apart from the multitude. Hence they concealed the precious and fragile truth gained through revelation and true reason in obscure or figurative language to preserve it from the incomprehension or misapprehension of the vulgar.[44] For this reason Bacon saw the recent and future progress of scientific knowledge as the product as much of the recovery of ancient texts and their true meaning, as of the discovery of knowledge by the experimental and mathematical study of nature. When he sketched the sciences and uses of agriculture, medicine or geography, or described ever-burning lamps, explosive powders, and the wonderful future machines for flying, lifting weights or driving carriages, ships and submarines, he believed that these had already been known to the ancients in a wiser past.[45] We had to recover that past in order to advance into a happier future, and this we would do only when we were restored to that one true wisdom founded on the scriptures and developed by reason and experience.

Bacon's criticisms of his contemporaries and his positive proposals fol-

42. *Ibid.*, "Geographia", 303 seq., 356–66, "Astrologia", 398 seq.; *cf. ibid.*, vi, "De scientia experimentali", ed. Bridges, ii (1897), 221–2; vii, "Moralis philosophia", i, 234 seq., iv. 1, 367 seq.
43. *Ibid.*, ii, "Philosophiae cum theologia affinitas", c.9, vol. i, 44–49; c.14, vol. iii (London, 1900), 67–68; *cf.* i, "Causae erroris", c.14, vol. i, 28 seq., vol. iii, 30 seq.
44. *Ibid.*, i, "Causae erroris", c.4, vol. i, 9–11.
45. See the three main works mentioned above, ref. 40; the *Communia naturalium* and *Communia mathematica* published in *Opera hactenus inedita*, ed. R. Steele, ii, xvi (Oxford, 1905–40), and the *Epistola de secretis operibus artis et naturae*, in *Opera quaedam hactenus inedita*, ed. J. S. Brewer (London, 1859), 532 seq.; Thorndike, *op. cit.* (ref. 29), ii, 654 seq., 688 seq. *Cf.* A. G. Molland, "Roger Bacon as magician", *Traditio*, xxx (1974), 445–60; *idem*, "Nicole Oresme and scientific progress", *Miscellanea mediaevalia veröffentlichungen des Thomas-Instituts der Universität zu Köln*, ix (1974), 206–20. This volume is devoted to "Antiqui und Moderni".

lowed from this historical vision. Writing acidly that our intellects were feeble enough in themselves without putting extraneous obstacles in their way, he identified four main current obstacles to the grasping of truth. These were respect for misleading or unworthy authority, as distinct from the well-founded authority of the Church and of scientific experts; the habits of long custom; uninstructed popular prejudice; and above all donnish vanity concealing ignorance under a false display of knowledge.[46] Despite his fundamentalism, he took a liberal view of the openness of knowledge, of the need to study the newly available Islamic philosophers, to accept the Scriptures and their traditional interpretations as the work of sometimes fallible men open to revision,[47] and to try to show the truth to unbelievers by argument and example, not by force as in some Christian operations against the Saracens and by the Teutonic knights east of Germany.[48] Above all he felt the infinite smallness of what we understood compared with what we did not know or believed but did not understand. Anyone who boasted of knowledge must be out of his mind.[49]

But, again looking back in order to look more confidently forward, he quoted with approval Seneca's combined respect for the ancients and belief in intellectual progress. Later ages corrected and added to the earlier. For "the study of wisdom can always increase in this life, because nothing is perfect in human discoveries. Hence we of a later age should supply what the ancients lacked, because we have entered into their labours, by which, unless we are asses, we can be aroused to better things; since it is wretched to be always using and never making discoveries".[50] This was indeed a Christian duty, as it was a duty to turn the science of unbelievers to Christian ends, and to spread the truth to them in a world where they were many and Christians few.[51] His reform of natural philosophy was to be based (following Robert Grosseteste) on the study of languages, of mathematics and especially such mathematical sciences as optics, astronomy and geography, and of *scientia experimentalis*. The last included among its functions those of natural magic, the uncovering of the hidden powers of nature, which like all these sciences could usefully be applied for the defence, improvement and expansion of Christian life. Of them all, theology remained the queen.

I have chosen to concentrate on the earlier rather than the last stretch of these two thousand years because there we are more likely to find illuminating contrasts with ourselves, treating the history of thought as a kind of

46. Roger Bacon, *Opus maius*, i.1–10, vol. i, 1 seq.
47. *Ibid.*, i.9, 12, vol. i, 17–21, 24–26.
48. *Ibid.*, iii, "De utilitate grammaticae", vol. i, 92, vol. iii, 115, continued 119–25, vii.iv. 1. vol. ii. 375–7.
49. *Ibid.*, i.10, vol. i, 21–23.
50. *Ibid.*, ii.15, vol. iii, 69–70; *cf.* i.5–6, vol. i, 12–13, citing Seneca, *Naturales quaestiones*, vi.5, vii.25.
51. As above refs 48, 50; *Opus tertium*, ed. Brewer, in *Opera quaedam hactenus inedita* (ref. 45), 3–4.

intellectual anthropology, as a study of intellectual and moral behaviour in a variety of different circumstances. By this I do not mean of course that European intellectual life from the thirteenth to the seventeenth century is for us an open tapestry. Simply I have no space to go into it. But let me in conclusion weave my pattern a little closer to the present.

Historians over the last half century have made familiar many forward-looking passages from sixteenth and seventeenth century observers of current advances in scientific and technical knowledge. Where Horace had symbolically reflected on the art of navigation as an unnatural hazard beyond man's normative limits, Rabelais acclaimed the triumph of ocean sailing which had brought into communication peoples whom nature had kept apart.[52] It might with some justice be concluded that the particular European experience of this period was sufficient to generate a new general philosophy. An accelerating expansion of European cultural experience was seen as it were in three dimensions: internally, in the intellectual and material mastery of nature through the power of mathematics and experiment, as in the arts of perspective and machines and the sciences of astronomy and physiology; temporally, in the recovery of ancient science and philosophy through scholarship; and spacially, in the growth of knowledge of the world beyond Christendom through exploration and conquest in Asia, Africa and America. Haunting fears that the world was in decrepitude, and consequently unable to produce men of the ancient genius, were quietened in the 1560s and 1570s by Jean Bodin and Louis Leroy in their universal histories, on the evidence both of the uniformity of nature and of modern performance.[53] This ancient

52.   Horace, *Odes*, i.3; Rabelais, *Pantagruel*, iii.51 (1546); Bury, *op. cit.* (ref. 1), 18; Alex Keller, "Mathematical technologies and the growth of the idea of technical progress in the sixteenth century", in A. G. Debus (ed.), *Science, medicine and society in the Renaissance*, i (1972), 14. See also H. Weisinger, "Ideas of history during the Renaissance", *Journal of the history of ideas*, vi (1945), 415–35, *idem*, "The idea of the Renaissance and the rise of modern science", *Lychnos* (1946–7), 11–35; E. Zilsel, "The genesis of the concept of scientific progress", *Journal of the history of ideas*, vi (1945), 325–49; W. K. Ferguson, *The Renaissance in historical thought: Five centuries of interpretation* (Cambridge, Mass., 1948); A. C. Keller, "Zilsel, the artisans and the idea of progress in the Renaissance", *Journal of the history of ideas*, xi (1950), 235–40; E. Garin, *Medioevo e Rinascimento* (Bari, 1954); R. F. Jones, *Ancients and moderns: A study of the rise of the scientific movement in seventeenth century England*, 2nd ed. (St Louis, 1961); A. C. Crombie, "Historians and the scientific revolution", *Physis*, xi (1969), 167–80. *Cf.* for the Hermetic-Platonist view of intellectual history, B. Kieszkowski, *Studi sul platonismo del Rinascimento in Italia* (Firenze, 1936); D. P. Walker, *The Ancient Theology: studies in Christian Platonism from the fifteenth to the eighteenth century* (London, 1972); above ref. 22.

53.   See especially Jean Bodin, *Methodus ad facilem historiarum cognitionem*, c. 7 (Parisiis, 1572; *Oeuvres philosophiques*, texte établi, traduit et publié par P. Mesnard, Paris, 1951; 1st ed. 1566); Loys Leroy, *Considérations sur l'histoire universelle* (Paris, 1567); *idem*, *De la vicissitude ou variété des choses en*

ghost was to walk and walk again over the next century before it was finally laid to rest by science.[54] Meanwhile Bodin, Leroy and later authors, revising Europe's place in universal history, renewed the conception of the unity of mankind in its diversity of races, customs, languages and approaches to nature.[55] It was soon suspected that the most famous of the new inventions, the mariners' compass, cannon and printing, came from China.[56] Nevertheless modern Europe was seen to be outstanding in its exploits of human intelligence, recently and for the future. Writers on science and technology, the educational reformer Peter Ramus,[57] the editor of Vitruvius and practical perspectivist Daniele Barbaro,[58] the philosophers Antonio Persio[59] (to whom Galileo was to show the planets through his telescope) and Tommaso Campanella[60] (who compared his discoveries to those of Columbus), and eventually Francis Bacon,[61] all delivered the same message.

By the seventeenth century the essential certainties of human purpose were still for the most part simple and clear. No one believed more in the power of ideas to influence action than the philosophers of Renaissance art, science and technology who acclaimed the power of reason first through geometry and then through mathematics and experiment. The reforming philosophers of history moreover, whether cultural or political, all treated their subject in a way recalling Roger Bacon: they offered analyses of past progress or regress that carried with them formulae for future advance. It was the age of method, of new or revitalized formulae for true philosophy,

l'univers, x–xii (Paris, 1576), 96[v] seq., 115[v]; Bury, *op. cit.* (ref. 1), 33, 37–41; Rossi, *op. cit.* (ref. 1), 70–72, 79–81.

54. *Cf.* Jones, *op. cit.* (ref. 52); G. Williamson, "Mutability, decay and seventeenth century melancholy", *Journal of English literary history*, ii (1935), 121–50; R. W. Hepburn, "George Hakewill: the virility of nature", *Journal of the history of ideas*, xvi (1955), 135–50; C. Hill, *Intellectual origins of the English revolution* (Oxford, 1965), 137 seq., 200 seq.

55. Leroy, *Considérations* . . . (ref. 53), 8–9, *De la vicissitude* . . . (ref. 53), i, ff.9[v] seq., xi, f.112[rv]; Bury, *op. cit.* (ref. 1), 43–49; Rossi, *op. cit.* (ref. 1).

56. Alex Keller, *op. cit.* (ref. 52), 23–24; *cf.* Francisco Sizi, *Dianoia* (Venetiis, 1611; in G. Galilei, *Opere*, iii, 2a ed. (Firenze, 1968), 239–40).

57. Petrus Ramus, *Scholarum mathematicarum, libri unus et triginta* (Basileae, 1569).

58. *I dieci libri dell' architettura di M. Vitruvio*, tradutti et commentati da Monsignor Barbaro Eletto Patriarca d'Aquileggia (Vinegia, 1556); *cf.* V. P. Zoubov, "Vitruve et ses commentateurs du xvie siècle", in *La science au xvie siècle: colloque de Royaumont 1957* (Paris, 1960), 69–90.

59. Antonio Persio, *Trattato dell'ingegno dell'huomo* (Vinetia, 1576), ff. 3, 8–10; *cf.* Galileo, *Opere*, ed. naz. iii, 366; A. C. Crombie, and A. Carugo, *Galileo's Arguments and Disputes in Natural Philosophy* (forthcoming).

60. *E.g.*, Campanella to Galileo, 13 January 1611, Galileo, *Opere*, ed. naz. xi, 24; below ref. 65.

61. For Bacon see P. Rossi, *Francesco Bacone: dalla magia alla scienza* (Bari, 1957, English translation, London, 1968); B. Farrington, *The philosophy of Francis Bacon* (Liverpool, 1964).

science, art, theology, government.[62]

But we must see these reflections of European experience in their context of current philosophical debate, mediated through contemporary commitments and expectations. Leroy saw all the achievements he admired going the way of other civilizations unless rescued by the hand of Providence, nations strange in complexion and costume overwhelming Europe, destroying all learning and beauty, ending in a confusion of profanity and famine.[63] Benito Pereira, a sober Spanish Jesuit philosopher of the Collegio Romano who was to become a source for several of Galileo's natural philosophical writings, saw the discovery of new peoples for conversion to Christianity as one of the 'prosperities' of the last Joachite age of the saints in which he believed he lived.[64] The much quoted Campanella based his predictions of future discoveries on astrology and his conception of science in his utopian *City of the sun* (1602) on magic.[65] Galileo still looked for the true ancient model for the true new science, finding it in Archimedes.[66] Marin Mersenne first became interested in science and mathematics as an antidote to the scepticism introduced in the sixteenth century from Sextus Empiricus by Montaigne, as evidence that man was capable of some rational knowledge and hence of knowledge of God.[67] Descartes was similarly motivated.[68]

Doubts were to find their most eloquent expression in Pascal. About 1647,

62. *Cf.* the commonplace repeated in the phrase used by Sir Walter Raleigh, *History of the world*, ii.21.6 (London, 1614), 537, that it was "the end and scope of all Historie, to teach by example of times past, such wisdome as may guide our desires and actions", and see the preface; Crombie, *op. cit.* (ref. 52).

63. Leroy, *De la vicissitude*... (ref. 53), xi, ff. 114^v–115; Bury, *op. cit.* (ref. 1), 46–47.

64. Benedictus Pererius, *Tertius tomus selectarum disputationum in Sacram Scripturam*, continens... *Disputationes super libro Apocalipsis B. Ioannis Apostoli*, prolegomena, disp. 5, marginal no. 30 (Lugduni, 1606), 21–22, *cf.* c. 1, disp. 20, marg. no. 82, p. 58. In *De Antichristo* included in this volume he rejected the idea that Mahomet was Antichrist. See Reeves, *op. cit.* (ref. 38), 283–4; A. C. Crombie, "Sources of Galileo's early natural philosophy", in *Reason, experiment and mysticism in the scientific revolution*, ed. M. L. Righini Bonelli and W. R. Shea (New York, 1975); Crombie and Carugo, *ibid.* (ref. 59), ch. 2 ii.

65. Campanella, *La Città del Sole*, ed. A. Seroni (Milano, 1962); Bury, *op. cit.* (ref. 1), 62–63; Yates, *Bruno*, 360–70; Alex Keller, *op. cit.* (ref. 52), 24–25.

66. See Crombie and Carugo, *ibid*, ch. 2 iii.

67. See R. Lenoble, *Marin Mersenne, ou la naissance du mécanisme* (Paris, 1943); A. C. Crombie, "Mersenne, Marin", *Dictionary of scientific biography*, ix (New York, 1974), 316–22; Crombie and Carugo, *ibid.* (ref. 59), ch. 8.

68. *Cf.* Descartes, *Discours de la méthode*, texte et commentaire par E. Gilson (Paris, 1947), 29, 267 seq.; and his correspondence with Mersenne in 1630 discussed by N. Kemp Smith, *New studies in the philosophy of Descartes* (London, 1952), 178 seq.

when he was twenty-five, Pascal compared the progressive education of humanity through the succession of ages to the education of an individual man: "De là vient que, par une prérogative particulière, non seulement chacun des hommes s'avance de jour en jour dans les sciences, mais que tous les hommes ensemble y font un continuel progrès à mesure que l'universe vieillit, parce que la même chose arrive dans la succession des hommes que dans les âges différents d'un particulier. De sorte que toute la suite des hommes, pendant le cours de tous les siècles, doit être considérée comme un même homme qui subsiste toujours et qui apprend continuellement".[69] Later, in the *Pensées*, after his disillusionment with Cartesian rationalism, Pascal moved closer to St Augustine's view of the same comparison, which appears in the *City of God*: "There is a process of education, through the epochs of a people's history, as through the successive stages of a man's life, designed to raise them from the temporal and the visible to an apprehension of the eternal and the invisible".[70] Even at a time when visible rewards were promised, Augustine had continued, man was commanded to concentrate his mind on the one, omnipotent Creator and Master of his soul. He should see in the lilies of the field, in the graceful harmony of natural forms and in the material blessings necessary for his own transitory life, expressions of that eternal, intelligible design. Pascal in maturity came likewise to give scientific reason second place in mankind's paramount approach to the *Deus absconditus*.[71]

When I began these comments by saying that during these two thousand years progress was not a concept foremost in men's minds, I meant in J. B. Bury's sense of conceiving "that civilization has moved, is moving, and will move in a desirable direction", and that it does so as a "necessary outcome of the psychical and social nature of man", independent of any notion of divine or natural providence.[72] For this as a systematic view of history I suppose we have to look first to Voltaire.[73] Long after Voltaire, progress in both knowledge and virtue was still conceived as occurring within a providential design, implicitly even by Charles Darwin.[74] But in Darwinian thinking the major modern shift was also present, from a conception of progress in some direction seen as desirable, to a conception of time and history as merely a

69. Pascal, "Préface sur le Traité du vide", *Oeuvres complètes*, ed. L. Lafuma (Paris, 1963), 232.
70. Augustine, *De civitate Dei*, x. 14.
71. Pascal, *Pensées*, no. 427, ed. Lafuma (= no. 194, ed. L. Brunschvicg).
72. Bury, *op. cit.* (ref. 1), 2, 5.
73. F. Diaz, "Idea del progresso e giudizio storico in Voltaire", *Belfagor*, ix (1954), 21–45; J. H. Brumfitt, *Voltaire historian* (Oxford, 1958); *cf.* A. Cento, *Condorcet e l'idea di progresso* (Firenze, 1956).
74. Darwin, *Origin of species* (1859), end; *cf.* C. C. Gillispie, *Genesis and geology* (Cambridge, Mass., 1951); H. M. Jones and I. B. Cohen (eds), *Science before Darwin* (Boston, Mass., 1963).

meaningless, open-ended, interminable succession.[75] We have lost the sense of both cosmological and historical design. This post-progress outlook contrasts in a way strangely with the evangelical desire, deeply embedded in Western scientific culture, to discover and spread true knowledge towards some better future.

Turning again to Louis Leroy's reflections on the possible devastation of his sixteenth century Europe, "si la memoire et cognoissance du passé est l'instruction du présent, et l'advertissement de l'advenir",[76] I may finish by secularizing the historical message. The greatest gift of scientific reason to the material arts of civilization has surely been to liberate mankind from a purely or nearly biological existence and to provide possibilities of choice. This in turn has arisen and grown from the commitment in our Western traditions of thinking and of society to deciding questions by free argument and evidence. For most of Western history nature has been accepted as already designed. Now in many parts of matter we ourselves can become the designer: "Heaven's not safe from man's desire".[77] The unknown incalculable powers in nature no longer haunt our uneasiness, but rather those in man himself and the consequences of our mastery in such occurrences as the explosions of populations and above all of industrial consumption and pollution. To these there have been perhaps historically predictable, though never predicted, responses: for minorities, moves to return to an over-simple life, not always in the woods virtuously feeding on nuts; or the urban cult of the irrational, neither primitive nor innocent; or violence. The majority just carries on. Most of mankind is or wants to be committed to the arts of civilization. How then does history teach us to conserve the physical and mental ecology of our civilization against devastation? By holding to its defining rational sense of the soluble and of the humane? By the design for which most people can look now only in ourselves?

Further references: W. K. C. Guthrie, *The Sophists* (Cambridge, 1971); E. Jeauneau, "'Nani gigantum humeris insidentes': essai d'interprétation de Bernard de Chartres", *Vivarium*, v (1967), 77-99, "Nains et géants" in *Entretiens sur la renaissance du xiième siècle*, publiés sous la direction de M. de Gandillac et E. Jeauneau (Paris, 1968), 21-52; R. Klibansky, "Standing on the shoulders of giants", *Isis*, xxvi (1936), 147-9; A. G. Molland, "Medieval ideas of scientific progress". *Journal of the History of Ideas*, xxxix (1978), 561-77; R. Nisbett, *History of the Idea of Progress* (New York, 1980).

75. B. Glass, O. Temkin and W. L. Straus Jr (eds), *Forerunners of Darwin: 1745–1859* (Baltimore, Maryland, 1959); F. C. Haber, "The Darwinian revolution in the concept of time", *Studium generale*, xxiv (1971), 289–307; A. C. Crombie, "Historical commitments of biology", *The British journal for the history of science*, iii (1966), 97–108.

76. Leroy, *De la vicissitude . . .* (ref. 53), xi, f. 114ᵛ; Bury, *op. cit* (ref. 1), 46.

77. Horace, *Odes*, i. 3.

3

THE RELEVANCE OF THE MIDDLE AGES
TO THE SCIENTIFIC MOVEMENT

IN THE FIRST VOLUME of his *Science and Civilisation in China*, Joseph Needham asks the question: "Why . . . did *modern* science, the tradition of Galileo, Harvey, Vesalius, Gesner, Newton, universally verifiable and commanding universal rational assent . . . develop round the shores of the Mediterranean and the Atlantic, and not in China or any other part of Asia?"[1] "China," he writes, "produced no Aristotle";[2] and no Euclid or Bacon or Descartes. Why?

The year before the publication of Dr. Needham's first volume, the same question put in a letter to a well-known scientist elicited the now famous reply:

Dear Sir, The development of Western Science has been based on two great achievements, the invention of the formal logical system (in Euclidean geometry) by the Greek philosophers, and the discovery of the possibility of finding out causal relationships by systematic experiment (Renaissance). In my opinion one need not be astonished that the Chinese sages have not made these steps. The astonishing thing is that these discoveries were made at all. Sincerely yours, A. Einstein.[3]

[1] Joseph Needham, *Science and Civilisation in China* (Cambridge, 1954), I, 19.

[2] *Ibid.*, p. 18.

[3] See D. J. de S. Price, *Science since Babylon* (New Haven, Conn., 1961), p. 15, n. 10.

The historical problems raised both by the origins of modern scientific thinking in the West and by the existence in the old civilizations of the East of corresponding scientific origins that somehow failed to develop have a topical interest for us now as we watch the appropriation, at ever increasing pace, of Western science by the modern peoples of Asia and Africa. Modern science itself began by an earlier act of appropriation of Aristotelian and Euclidean Greek science and of Arabic science by the peoples of Western Europe whose culture was based on the Latin language. The history of the scientific movement both in antiquity and in medieval and modern times shows natural science to be, not simply part of the natural heritage of mankind (whatever that would mean), but an invention of intellectual art, transmitted by cultural diffusion.

I shall take as the central theme for this paper an examination of the consequences of this medieval act of appropriation in generating the second great achievement indicated by Einstein, the methods by which cogent experimentation was introduced into scientific argument. But I shall also try to show that its topicality and relevance for us extend far beyond this austerely scientific achievement. Together with rational experimental science were generated intellectual attitudes still characteristic of the West. And the appropriation of the superior Arabic and Byzantine intellectual cultures by the barbarous peoples of the medieval Latin West offers a case history with many parallels today in the mental and social transformations brought about by the invasion by Western science and technology, and by their accompanying philosophy of secular reason, of societies guided until recently largely by religion and custom.

From the parochial point of view of modern historical scholarship, the study of the origins of modern science has suffered some very curious consequences from coming last in the studies of the historical movements that are held to have made modern Western civilization. It is a commonplace among the sophisticated that the terms "Renaissance," "Reformation," and "Scientific Revolution" refer to purely conventional divisions of periods and must not be given any causal or even descriptive significance. Yet it seems that this critical sophistication does not always go very deep, for there is still much history being written as if the advent of effective science was one of a succession of stages in a single movement of the liberation of the European intellect from whatever is held to have bound it—ignorance, dogma, custom, superstition. . . . When we recall the origin of this periodization itself, the apparent difficulty of being liberated from *it* becomes understandable. It is the cumulative product of a series of historical judgments made at different times and in differing circumstances in order to define a position in relation to the immediate past with a view to contemporary action. The picture presented of the past became an essential element in a formula of reform being offered as necessary for present and future progress.

As everyone knows, the concept of a renaissance was developed in the fifteenth century itself by admirers of the republican political virtues of ancient Rome, of Cicero's Latin style, and of the naturalistic ideal of ancient sculpture and painting, all of which they saw being revived in Italy and especially in Florence. By the end of the fifteenth century, the humanist historians had established the standard division of European history into antiquity, a period of barbarism for which Nicholas of Cusa coined the term "middle age,"[4] and a recent revival for which the term *la rinascita* was first used by the art historian Vasari.[5] To these already different political, literary, and artistic elements in this concept of a renaissance, a fourth was added in the sixteenth century: Erasmus' conception of a close causal connection between the revival of learning and that of religion.[6] Science was brought into the concept in the seventeenth century, first by such reformers of philosophy as Francis Bacon and Descartes, who used their picture of past stagnation as a means of promoting their new experimental and mathematical methods, and second by such writers as George Hakewill,[7] William Wotton,[8] and Fontenelle,[9] who produced the recent scientific successes as the trump card with which they completed the triumph of the Moderns over the Ancients and replaced a past classical ideal with a vision of future progress as the goal for action.

As a framework into which to fit an account of the origins of modern science, the obvious disadvantage of this historical scheme has come from its linking of these different events in politics, literature, art, religion, and science causally in a single series. The linkage between the revival of classical learning, the Protestant Reformation, and the liberation of the intellect to pursue scientific inquiry can be found, for example, in Bayle's *Dictionary* and in the writings of the

[4] P. Lehman, "Vom Mittelalter und von der lateinischen Philologie des Mittelalters", *Quellen und Untersuchenden zur lateinischen Philologie des Mittelalters*, V. i (1914).

[5] Wallace K. Ferguson, *The Renaissance in Historical Thought* (Cambridge, Mass., 1949), pp. 59–67.

[6] *Ibid.*, p. 54.

[7] *An Apologie or Declaration of the Power and Providence of God in the Government of the World* (Oxford, 1635).

[8] *Reflections upon Ancient and Modern Learning* (London, 1964).

[9] *Entretiens sur la pluralité des mondes: Digressions sur les anciens et les modernes*, ed. R. Shackleton (Oxford, 1955).

American author Cotton Mather.[10] Voltaire used it for his own sophisticated purposes as a stick with which to beat those whom he saw as the enemies of enlightenment in his time. The disadvantage of allowing it to survive any longer in our time is that it is a framework that can no longer accommodate the known facts.

The two important facts established by the scholarship of the last seventy or eighty years are, first, that the period during which the Latin West reappropriated the scientific thought of antiquity came *before* the humanist literary revival. From early in the twelfth century, Western scholars sought out and translated into Latin the scientific and philosophical learning in Greek and Arabic as eagerly as any humanist scholar, with the difference that they were primarily interested in scientific and philosophical writings for their content and not in literary and historical writings for their style. They traveled like Adelard of Bath to Sicily and Syria, they worked in places recovered from Islam like Gerard of Cremona in Toledo, or like William of Moerbeke they went to Greece. By the end of the thirteenth century they had made available in Latin the bulk of the Greek science that has come down to us, and had met and mastered the challenge of the superior Arabic learning of the theological and political enemy who occupied the southern shore of the Mediterranean. The later, humanist contribution to knowledge of ancient science was to produce better editions and translations. Nor does the view survive inspection that the medieval scholars merely accepted these new authorities. "We of later ages should supply what the ancients lacked," Roger Bacon wrote, "since we have entered into their labours. And by these, unless we are asses, we can be aroused to better things, because it is most miserable always to use old discoveries and never to be on the track of new ones. Christians should . . . complete the paths of the unbelieving philosophers, not only because we are of a later age and should add to their works, but so that we may also bend their labours to our own ends."[11]

The second fact that our account of the origins of modern science must accommodate is the more or less continuous technological progress observable in the West, beginning in the period of the invasions and proceeding throughout the Middle Ages in broad independence of political and cultural events, apart from some specific connections with science scarcely in evidence before the thirteenth century. Polit-

[10] *American Tears upon the Ruines of Greek Churches* (Boston, Mass., 1701); see A. C. Crombie, "Historians and the Scientific Revolution," *Endeavour*, XIX (1960), 9–13, *Physis*, xi (1969), 167-80.

[11] *The "Opus Majus" of Roger Bacon*, ed. J. H. Bridges (Oxford, 1897), I, 57. For the medieval view of Islam, see N. Daniel, *Islam and the West: The Making of an Image* (Edinburgh, 1960).

ical and cultural periodization is largely irrelevant for technology, yet medieval technology laid foundations for all subsequent technology and for science in several important ways. It developed power machinery based on water-, wind-, and ox- or horse-driven mills and such automatically self-adjusting machinery as the mechanical clock. It was inventive and active in applying inventions as shown by the clock, the compass, cartography, spectacles. It made a strong move toward precision, as in metallurgical assaying and in astronomical and mathematical instruments and computers, which provided the prototypes for scientific instrumentation.

That these facts of scientific and technological history should prove impossible to accommodate in a historical scheme designed by political and cultural historians in ignorance of them—or at least ignoring them—should not surprise us. What concerns me is that an a priori acceptance of the scheme should make the facts indigestible to historians who know them well. Let me give an example from an essay by an eminent medievalist published in 1951 and entitled "Why Was Science Backward in the Middle Ages?" His argument is distinguished by a fearless drawing of the conclusion from a major and a minor premise standing in apparent contradiction. After giving a sketch of medieval scientific and technological achievements, he concludes as follows:

In this way the very achievement of the late twelfth and thirteenth centuries merely underlines the verdict about the Middle Ages as a whole. The men of the Middle Ages were unable to do more than they did because they were lacking in scientific incentive. What they achieved in advancing the practical arts of humanity or in preserving and transmitting ancient learning, they did in so far and as long as they were not typically medieval.

In syllogistic form the argument runs:

Major premise a priori: There was no medieval science.
Minor premise from evidence: But there was medieval science.
    Conclusion: Therefore medieval science was not medieval.

The premises could yield an alternative conclusion:

    Therefore medieval science was not science.

This alternative was chosen by another medievalist in 1961. But I want to draw another conclusion altogether: that the time has come to forget this historical scheme supplying this nonsensical major premise and to look again at the facts.

To understand the development of scientific thought in the Middle Ages or in any other period we do indeed need to consider its linkage with the intellectual and social motives and opportunities that may have stimulated it in certain directions and blocked it in others. I shall devote the rest of this paper to a brief examination of some of the effects of the internal intellectual needs and external social pressures acting on scientific thinking in the Middle Ages in relation to three questions:

(1) scientific cosmology in face of theology;
(2) *scientia experimentalis* as a method of inquiry;
(3) quantification in science and in technology.

In each case I shall also consider the relevance of the medieval position to later developments of the scientific movement. I shall aim to illustrate the thesis that we must look in the later medieval West for the origins of certain essential methods of inquiry and of habits and attitudes of mind characteristic of the modern scientific movement, even when these were based on motives and conceptions of nature that we no longer accept.

(1) *Scientific cosmology in face of theology.* The encounter between what we may call the cosmologies of reason and of revelation in the thirteenth and fourteenth centuries is one of the most interesting episodes in Western intellectual history. It led to positions being taken up that have been formally repeated again and again when there has been a similar conflict between doctrines and intellectual loyalties derived from different sources. In Christian thinking, the first such encounter was that between pagan philosophy and Christian belief in late classical times, and the broad intellectual policy to be followed by medieval Christian philosophers was that laid down by St. Augustine in *De Genesi ad litteram.* Beginning with the basic principle that truth is self-consistent, St. Augustine had ruled out a priori any real contradiction between the data of divine revelation, true by definition in the light of their source, and the equally true data of observation and conclusions of valid reasoning. Any apparent contradiction must arise, he said, out of our incomplete understanding of the true meanings of the conflicting statements and would be resolved when these were correctly interpreted in the light of their different purposes. The Hebrew Scriptures expounding spiritual and moral doctrine need not necessarily be taken literally when they referred to a flat earth and a domed sky, in contrast to the globe and spheres of the Greek astronomers. The way was similarly opened for recognizing that expositions of physical and philosophical doctrines need not all be taken literally either. But a possibility of conflict remained, depending on the amount of irreducible core insisted upon on each side. The intellectual positions taken up when this debate arose once more in the thirteenth century were to be repeated in the controversy over the Copernican sys-

tem in which Galileo found himself engaged and again in that over Genesis and geology and evolution in the nineteenth century. They were paralleled also in the debates provoked by the use of Nature as a guide to human morality by nineteenth-century Romantic political philosophers and Darwinian sociologists, in the intellectual situation created by the Soviet concept of a Marxist science, and in some respects in the history of twentieth-century positivism.

In the thirteenth century the primary encounter was not directly of theological doctrine based on revelation with natural science as such, but with rational philosophical doctrines with which some scientific doctrines were associated. Purely technical science had no part in the encounter at all. Indeed, in the twelfth century, philosophical theologians had used their new learning to follow St. Augustine's advice and offer a rational exegesis of Scripture, as Thierry of Chartres used Plato's *Timaeus* to give a rational account of the days of creation described in Genesis. The conflict arose over specific metaphysical doctrines contained in Latin translations of Aristotle's philosophical writings and of Arabic exegeses of them, especially by Avicenna and by Averroës, which went into circulation in the early thirteenth century. The Western response to these texts was, first, local prohibitions against their use in teaching institutions and then, that failing, the taking-up of intellectual positions. I am concerned only with the effect of this encounter on philosophy of science. We can see this best by looking at some of the effects on one science—astronomy—of positions taken up in relation to one philosophical doctrine: that the universe is not a creation in time of God's free will but an eternal emanation of his intellect, and that it is possible for the human reason to know that intellect in such a way as to discover not only how the world is constituted but why it must necessarily be so constituted and not otherwise.

According to Averroës' followers in the thirteenth century, Aristotle had long ago discovered this necessary constitution of the universe. In *De Caelo* (ii. 3), Aristotle himself had in fact argued in a brilliant tour de force that the cosmology he described was the only possible system that could follow from God's known essence. This required that the heavens, aspiring to imitate God's eternal activity, should move uniformly in a circle; this in turn required the existence of earth at rest at the center; and so on. We have evidence of the use of this argument by Averroïsts in the list of propositions recorded in the *Chartularium Universitatis Parisiensis*[12] as having been condemned by the Bishop of Paris, Stephen Tempier, in 1277. These include:

[12] *Chartularium Universitatis Parisiensis*, ed. H. Denifle and A. Chatelain, i (Paris, 1889), pp. 546–49.

"Quod Deus non possit movere celum motu recto. Et ratio est, quia tunc relinqueret vacuum" (49). "Quod Deus non potest irregulariter, id est, alio modo, quam movet, movere aliquid, quia in eo non est diversitatis voluntatis" (50). "Quod theologi dicentes quod celum quandoque quiescit, arguunt ex falsa suppositione; et, quod dicere, celum esse, et non moveri, est dicere contradictoria" (100). The example of Paris was followed in the same year by the Archbishop of Canterbury, Robert Kilwardby. The theologians condemned these propositions in order to affirm God's absolute, omnipotent freedom. It has been claimed that the effect on natural philosophers was that they felt free to explore in scholastic exercises the consequences of God's having created the universe according to various hypothetical possibilities, for example, with the earth in motion instead of the heavens, or with infinite space containing several world like our own.

Astronomy at this time was already in purely scientific difficulties. There were in existence three different mathematical systems: the concentric spheres of Eudoxus, whose operation Aristotle had explained physically but which were known not to fit the facts, and Ptolemy's two systems of epicycles and eccentrics, which fitted the facts but were inexplicable by any system of physics. The interest of the moves now made in the search for the true system of astronomy is that they involved two different types of argument that were to reappear again in the Copernican debates and are indeed involved in some form in almost every search for scientific explanation.

The first move was to throw all existing systems open to doubt by the use of the argument that any attempt to infer a cause from an effect involves the logical fallacy of affirming the consequent in a conditional proposition. For example, "if p (epicycles) then q (observed motions of planets), but q therefore p" is logically invalid unless we know that the effect can have come about in only one possible way. But how can we be sure of this unique cause? This situation was pointed out by Thomas Aquinas for mathematical theories in astronomy and was to be used again by Osiander in his preface to Copernicus' *De Revolutionibus*, by Cardinal Bellarmine against Galileo, by Francis Bacon, and as an act of prudence (after Galileo's condemnation) by Descartes, to argue that all such theories are simply convenient calculating devices.[13] They were all equally disqualified from giving a true account of the world. The theological motive during the Copernican debate was, of course, to save Scripture from

[13] The best survey of these arguments is still Pierre Duhem's "Essai sur la notion de théorie physique de Platon à Galilée," *Annales de philosophie chrétienne*, 4th ser., VI (1908).

contradiction by science. A theological motive can also be seen in the subtle and powerful arguments by which William of Ockham denied the possibility of any rational knowledge of the world and reduced the order of natural events to an order of fact, depending on God's inscrutable will, which science can simply organize in convenient ways. The theological origins of positivism would repay further investigation by historians of philosophy. For astronomy, arguments of this type loosened the bonds of existing theories, but, by making the choice between rival theories of equal accuracy simply one of convenience, they did little to help the positive search for something better.

The positive advances in astronomical theory were made by an altogether different argument, making range of application the main distinguishing criterion of a true theory. I do not know of anyone before Kepler[14] who explicitly shrugged off the fallacy of affirming the consequent as simply part of all inductive scientific reasoning and offered this different criterion as the serious one, but this policy had in effect been stated in antiquity by Geminus in asserting that the choice between rival mathematical theories in astronomy must be made by physics. Ptolemy had tried to make the geostatic assumptions of his system plausible by empirical and physical arguments. In the fourteenth century Jean Buridan introduced in his theory of impetus a dynamical explanation of the motion both of projectiles and falling bodies and of the celestial spheres. Here was the beginning of a single physical criterion for distinguishing between theories requiring possible and impossible motions over the entire range of moving bodies, terrestrial and celestial.

Later in the fourteenth century Nichole Oresme, in his French commentary on Aristotle's *De Caelo* commissioned by Charles V of France, used a modified version of the impetus theory to argue that, Aristotle notwithstanding, the daily rotation of the earth on its axis was a possible motion. He argued that mathematical astronomy based on this assumption would be able to account for all the phenomena much more economically than on the geostatic assumption. Hence, since "God and Nature do nothing in vain,"[15] it would be reasonable to assume that God had in fact created the universe with the earth and not the spheres in motion. He systematically met the observational and physical objections to the earth's rotation by arguments that Copernicus was to parallel closely two centuries later. In reply to the

[14] Cf. N. Jardine, *The Birth of the History and Philosophy of Science: Kepler's 'A defence of Tycho against Ursus"* (Cambridge, 1984).

[15] *Le livre du ciel et du monde* (Book II, chap. xxv), ed. A. D. Menut and A. S. Denomy, *Medieval Studies*, III–V (1941–43), 278, with transl. (Madison, Wisc., 1968).

objection that it was the heavens that appear to rotate, he pointed out that all motion as observed is relative; and against Aristotle's physical requirement of a static earth as the unique gravitational center of the universe, he argued that gravity, spatial directions, and motion are all relative only to each particular world among all the possible worlds that God may have created in infinite space. Following St. Augustine's methods, Oresme also met objections from such biblical texts as that describing Joshua's miracle, implying that the heavens are in motion and the earth at rest, by pointing out that Scripture simply "conforms in this part to the manner of common human speech."[16]

In the end, Oresme recognized that his arguments had not positively proved the earth's rotation but had simply shown that the contrary had not been proved either. So he accepted the text, "Deus enim firmavit orbem terrae, qui non commovebitur" (Vulgate, Psalm 92), as the literal truth and treated his whole argument as an intellectual exercise. Yet it was a repetition of the same exercise in the seventeenth century that was to provide Newton with his decisive criterion. Within the system of classical mechanics, confirmed over the whole tested range of moving bodies, only some motions are possible, and these do not include those required by a geostatic system. So Newton distinguished the true system of astronomy as that which treated a planet as a projectile moving in one of a family of conic sections and made the earth a sputnik in orbit round the sun.

While range of application has become established as the most powerful criterion for choosing the most acceptable theories, the other arguments used in these medieval discussions have also left their mark on scientific thinking. Both the theological argument that the universe is a contingent product of God's free will, and the logical argument that all inference from effects to unique causes involves a logical fallacy, make knowledge of ultimate causes of the type envisaged by Aristotle effectively unattainable. Aquinas had drawn a distinction between two ways of establishing theoretical principles. In one, "sufficient reason could be brought to prove the principle,"[17] and he gave as an example the uniformity of the heavenly movements. "In the other way, reasons may be adduced which do not sufficiently prove the principle, but which may show that the effects which follow agree with it." He gave as an example the eccentric and epicycle systems and pointed out that the fallacy of affirming the consequent makes the proof insufficient. This same distinction was to be made again by Newton, Huygens, and other scientific thinkers in the seventeenth century and again many times since. The difference

16 *Ibid.*, p. 276.
17 *Summa theologicae*, Pt. I, q. 32, art. 1.

is that Newton and Huygens saw clearly that the "sufficient reason" for accepting a principle was not to be drawn from some principle of ontological "fitness" such as Aquinas used, but from a theory of wider application, as Newtonian dynamics gave sufficient reason for accepting Kepler's elliptical planetary orbits. So these distinct types of argument used in medieval astronomy have in combination very powerfully helped to clarify what is meant by a true theory in science.

(2) Scientia experimentalis *as a method of inquiry*. In all scientific inquiry there are two distinct elements: a concept of the nature of the world being investigated, and methods of carrying out the investigation. In any growing science these two elements continually interact with each other, and the methods of inquiry may eventually help to create an entirely new conception of the world. I shall discuss now some of the types of argument and method used by academic natural philosophers in the thirteenth and fourteenth centuries. I want to emphasize the need, in trying to understand early science, to pay attention to the arguments and methods as such, even when the conception of the world with which they were associated is one we no longer accept. We should also remember the circumstances in which scientific inquiries were carried out in the medieval universities and religious teaching orders. These institutions performed a function, without parallel on the same scale in antiquity, in providing for continuity of knowledge from one generation to the next so that a genuine philosophical community with generally accepted aims, methods, and standards could come into being. This medieval philosophical community has survived in the professional scientific community of our own times. The surprising historical phenomenon—surprising anyhow in the view of history I discussed in my introduction—may seem to be that a community of scholars whose normal method of working was commenting on Aristotle and other standard texts should have been interested in original scientific inquiry at all. Even more interesting as an historical problem is to find at the heart of this medieval academic culture, aiming primarily to train servants of church and state, both an intense interest in the logic of experimental science and a few experimental inquiries actually carried out.

Any attempt to estimate the meaning of the medieval *scientia experimentalis* has to take account of the fact that this covered a much wider range than the modern "experimental science." For example, Roger Bacon in his treatise *Scientia experimentalis*[18] uses in his claim for the rank and dignity of the subject the fact that theology is

[18] *Opus majus*, Part VI, *ed. cit.* II, and III (London, 1900); see M. Schramm, "Aristotelianism: Basis and Obstacle to Scientific Progress in the Middle Ages," in *History of Science*, ed. A. C. Crombie and M. A. Hoskin (Cambridge, 1963), Vol. II.

founded on the same basis. The distinguishing mark of *scientia experimentalis* seems to be that it is based on singular experiences, and these include the whole range of possible experiences from observations by means of the external senses to mystical experiences through divine illumination of the internal senses. In this range perhaps we have a reason for the intense medieval interest in this subject.

It is important to note also the natural scientific fields of inquiry in which the medieval conception of *scientia experimentalis* was developed. There were two main fields. One was medicine, including physiology and the investigation of the causes of diseases and of the properties of drugs. The other was "natural magic," which from the days of Roger to those of Francis Bacon included a definite set of subjects: optics, magnetism, machines for producing theatrically or practically astonishing effects by the harnessing of hidden sources of power, perpetual motion, alchemy, and astrology. This collection of subjects had accumulated since antiquity in Greek, Arabic, and Latin writings around the common idea of discovering the hidden powers of nature and harnessing them for a variety of theatrical or useful purposes. It was to convince the pope of the intellectual and practical usefulness of science that Roger Bacon sent him his *Opus majus* and other writings urging the need to promote better scientific education in the West. Bacon objected to the forcible conversion of conquered peoples such as he said was practiced by the knights of the Teutonic Order; science was part of the intellectual apostolate leading men to contemplate intelligently the work of the Creator known to Christians through revelation and, through this, leading unbelievers to the true Christian faith. It could also be put to immediate practical use by providing the rulers of Christendom with arms for protection against the forces of subversion within (directed by Antichrist, on whose agents he blamed the strange episode of the revolt of the *Pastoureaux* in France in 1251) and of Islam and the Tartars (under the successors of Genghis Khan) threatening from without. Bacon set great store by optics as a means of providing military intelligence and weapons. He wrote that Julius Caesar was said to have erected mirrors in Gaul with which he had observed what was happening in Britain; and he argued for the use of great burning mirrors to set enemy cities and camps on fire and of lenses to terrify those ignorant of their operation by making the sun and moon seem to fall down upon their heads —an early example of psychological warfare.

These associations of *scientia experimentalis* with "natural magic" explain why Roger Bacon might have found in his contemporary Pierre de Maricourt, the pioneer of the modern science of magnetism

acknowledged by William Gilbert, his ideal of the "dominus experi-
mentorum." It may help to explain also why experiment is so conspicuously absent from the normal methods of inquiry used in the
academic natural sciences based on Aristotelian texts, notably from
medieval dynamics and kinematics. Bacon described his conception
of *scientia experimentalis* in the *Opus tertium* in 1267:

And this science certifies all natural and artificial things in the particular and in the proper discipline by perfect experience; not by argument,
like the purely theoretical sciences, nor by weak and imperfect experiences like the practical sciences. And therefore this science is the master
of all the preceding sciences, and the end of all theoretical argument. . . .
One man I know, and only one, who can be praised for his achievements
in this science. Of discourses and battles of words he takes no heed: he
follows the works of wisdom, and in these finds rest. What others strive
to see dimly and blindly, like bats in twilight, he gazes at in the full light
of day, because he is a master of experiments. Through experiment he
gains knowledge of natural things, medical, chemical, and indeed of everything in the heavens or earth. He is ashamed that things should be known
to laymen, old women, soldiers, ploughmen, of which he is ignorant.
Therefore he has looked closely into the doings of those who work in
metals and minerals of all kinds. He knows everything relating to the art
of war, the making of weapons, and the chase; he has looked closely into
agriculture, mensuration, and farming work; he has even taken note of
the remedies, lot-casting, and charms used by old women and by wizards
and magicians, and of the deceptions and devices of conjurors, so that
nothing which deserves inquiry should escape him, and that he may be
able to expose the falsehoods of magicians. If philosophy is to be carried
to its perfection and is to be handled with utility and certainty, his aid
is indispensable. As for reward, he neither receives nor seeks it. If he fre-
quented kings and princes, he would easily find those who would bestow
on him honours and wealth. Or, if in Paris he would display the results
of his researches, the whole world would follow him. But since either of
these courses would hinder him from pursuing the great experiments in
which he delights, he puts honour and wealth aside, knowing well that his
wisdom would secure him wealth whenever he chose. For the past three
years he has been working at the production of a mirror that shall produce
combustion at a fixed distance; a problem which the Latins have neither
solved nor attempted, though books have been written upon the subject.[19]

Within this scientific context, the complex of terms *experimentum,
experientia, experimentalis* had a range of meanings extending from
simple observation to deliberately contrived experiment. I shall give

[19] *Opus tertium*, cap. xiii, ed. J. S. Brewer (London, 1859), pp. 46–47; see A. C.
Crombie, *Robert Grosseteste and the Origins of Experimental Science, 1100–1700*
(Oxford, 1953, 1971), pp. 205-6.

some examples to illustrate the theory and practice of *scientia experimentalis* as a method of analytical inquiry.

In the essentially Aristotelian physical world that they accepted, the natural philosophers of the thirteenth and fourteenth centuries looked for explanations of phenomena in a particular way. They envisaged the inquiry as a process of breaking down a complex observed phenomenon into the elements or principles involved in its production and then showing that these elements or principles provided the conditions necessary and sufficient to produce this phenomenon. This double process of argument had been known from its dual source in Greek mathematics and medicine as "analysis and synthesis" and was known from the time of Robert Grosseteste to that of Newton as "resolution and composition." In the thirteenth and fourteenth centuries the necessary and sufficient conditions were envisaged in terms of the four Aristotelian causes. To posit the four causes was to posit the caused phenomenon. Their commitment to the development of this approach logically and in experimental practice illustrates very clearly both the achievements and the limitations of the medieval natural philosophers.

There were two parts to the enterprise: first, to define what the phenomenon and its causal conditions were, and, second, to show how these causes brought the phenomenon about. For the first part, Grosseteste developed one characteristic type of argument, the *modus tollens* leading to a *reductio ad impossibile* for choosing between possible definitions and causes. The argument runs: "if p then q, but not q therefore not p." Grosseteste used it, in the short treatises he wrote on the nature of the stars, comets, the sun's heat, the rainbow, and other subjects, to eliminate certain explanations by showing that they led to consequences contradicted either by experience or by what he held to be established physical principles. For example, he rejected the explanation of the rainbow as a reflection of the sun's rays by a cloud acting as a large concave mirror because this would not produce either a bow or the reciprocal relation observed between the elevations of bow and sun. Grosseteste used the *modus tollens* to choose between a limited set of possible explanations—a closed world of theoretical possibilities—mostly taken from earlier writers, and his invariable acceptance of the one remaining uneliminated explanation exposed him to the fallacy of affirming the consequent. It also considerably limited the use of experiment for the *exploration* of nature and exposed him to Newton's celebrated strictures on similar arguments used in the controversies over his new theory of color. This theory, Newton wrote, "was evinced by me, not by inferring ' 'tis thus because not otherwise,' that is, not by deducing it only from a

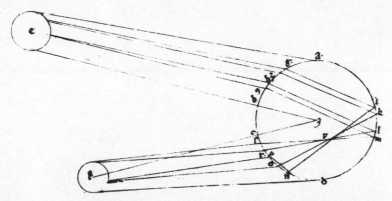

Fig. 1.—The paths of the rays inside a transparent sphere, from Theodoric of Freiberg's *De Iride*, II, cap. xviii–xx, Basel University Library MS F. IV. 30, fol. 21r (14th cent.). We may follow one "column" of light coming from the sun, *e*, and (incorrectly shown diverging) striking the sphere on the arc *qh*. On entering the sphere it is refracted to the opposite surface at *lm*, and thence is reflected internally. The reflected rays *lr* and *ms* intersect at *t*, and at *s* and *r*, respectively; the rays are refracted again on passing out into the air and so go (incorrectly shown converging) to the eye at *f*. In a raindrop the ray *hlr* is red and the ray *qms* is blue. (Figs. 1, 2, and 3 are reprinted from A. C. Crombie, *Robert Grosseteste*, with permission of the Clarendon Press.)

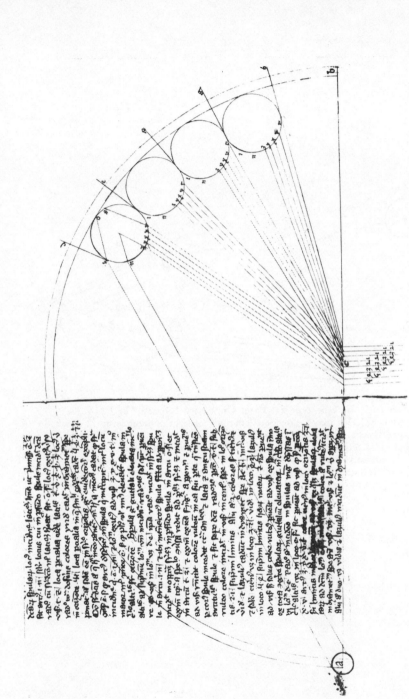

FIG. 2.—The formation of the primary (lower) rainbow, from Theodoric of Freiberg's *De Iride*, II, cap. xxxviii, fols. 33v–34r. The sun, *a*, and the four raindrops all lie on the "meteorological sphere" indicated by the large semicircle. The paths of the individual rays after entering each drop on the arc *ln* would be as drawn in Figure 1, with the four colors emerging from the drop on the following small arcs: *tv* red (corresponding to *r* in Fig. 1), *vx* yellow, *xy* green, *yz* blue (corresponding to *s* in Fig. 1). Each of the four drops sends a different color to the eye at *c*, thus producing four bands of color one below the other: *de* red, *ef* yellow, *fg* green, *gh* blue. From the optical point of view this diagram contains several mistakes: if the incident rays going from the sun to all four drops were drawn, they would not all be parallel as they should be; the different colored rays emerging from each individual drop should be diverging instead of parallel; and all the rays of a given color emerging from the different drops should be parallel.

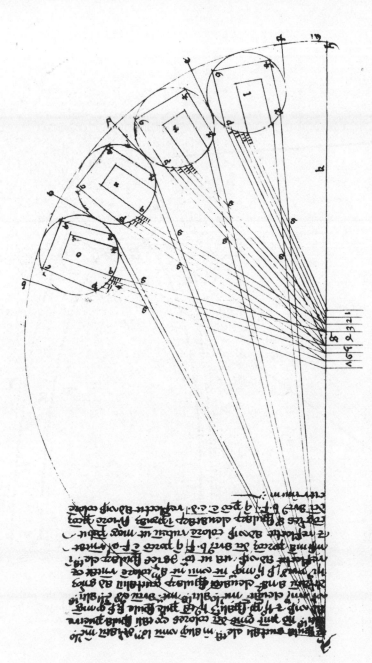

FIG. 3.—The formation of the secondary (upper) rainbow, from Theodoric of Freiberg's *De Iride*, III, cap. vi–vii, fol. 40r. The sun and four drops are shown on the "meteorological sphere," as in Figure 2. The incident sunlight *gg* enters each drop at *x* and is refracted; the colored rays (their individual paths not shown) are then reflected twice at *z* and at *c*, and refracted again on emerging into the air at *bd*. The four colors are marked: 1 red, 11 yellow, 111 green, 1111 blue. Each drop sends a different color to the eye at *g*, producing four bands of color in reverse order to those of the primary bow: *be* blue, *ad* green, *de* yellow, *ef* red. The emerging colored rays are here correctly shown diverging, but the diagram contains the other two optical mistakes in Figure 1.

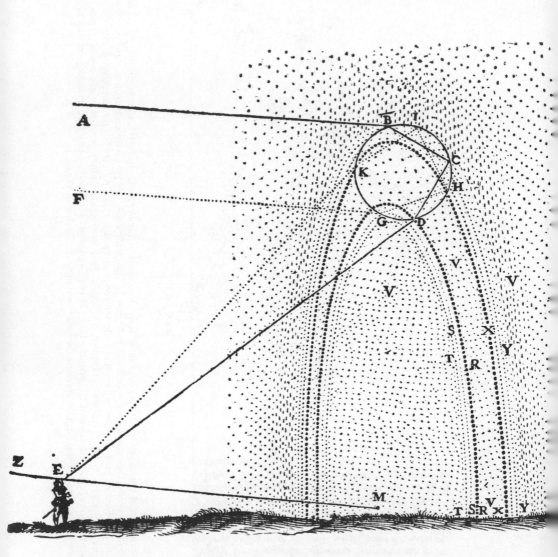

Fig. 4.—From Descartes's *Les Météores* (Leiden, 1637), Discours viii, showing the paths of the rays forming the primary (*A B C D E*) and secondary (*F G H I K E*) rainbows. The raindrop is enlarged. Note that here the sun's rays are correctly shown parallel.

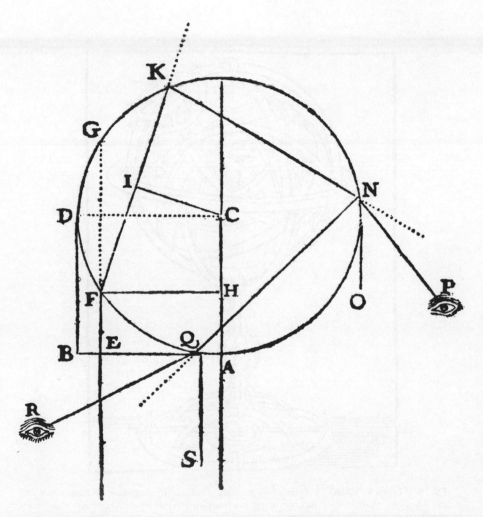

Fig. 5.—Descartes's diagram from *Les Météores*, Discours viii, used in calculating the paths of individual rays through a raindrop. A ray of sunlight incident at *F* passes through *F K N P* to form the primary bow and *F K N Q R* to form the secondary bow.

Fig. 6.—From J. Taisnier's *Opusculum perpetua memoria dignissimum, de natura magnetis et eius effectibus* (Cologne, 1562), showing his version of Pierre de Maricourt's automatic armillary operated by a lodestone.

FIG. 7.—From Christine de Pisan, "Epistre d'Othea," Bodleian Library, Oxford, MS Laud. Misc. 570, fol. 28v (1450), showing Temperance adjusting the clock, indicating the place of moderation in human affairs. Below sit four virtues. This manuscript was executed for Sir John Fastolf in 1450.

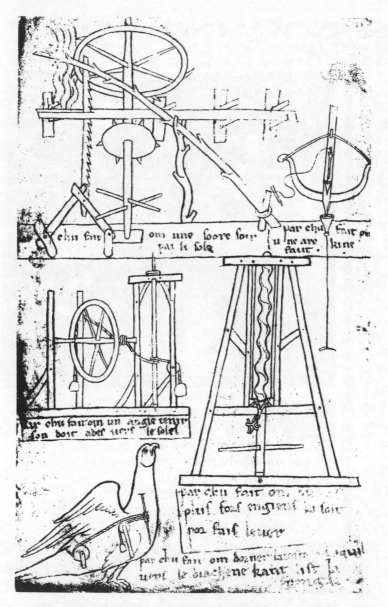

Within the illustration, the following text appears:

chu fin · om une soore soir / par chu fait om
par le sole / u ne avo kine
fait

ar chu fait om un angle tenir / on dort ader ner le solet

par chu fait om · / pluf soif msint le soir / pos fail leuer

par chu fait om doner ia... qui / uent le biackene kant ist le

Fig. 8.—From the album of Villard de Honnecourt, Bibliothèque Nationale, Paris, MS français 19093 (13th cent.). *Top left*, a water-driven saw executing two movements, one to work the blade and the other to push along the plank being cut. *Center left*, is a device operated by weights for moving an angel set on the spike so that its finger follows the sun; this is the earliest known diagram of an escapement mechanism such as was used in mechanical clocks. *Bottom left*, a mechanical eagle. (Reprinted from A. C. Crombie, *Medieval and Early Modern Science*, Vol. I, with permission of Harvard University Press.)

confutation of contrary suppositions, but by deriving it from Experiments concluding positively and directly."[20]

But another type of argument was used in the thirteenth and fourteenth centuries for discovering causal connections by the exploration of nature. This was the "medical inductive argument" known through the writings of Galen and Avicenna and used by them to investigate the curative properties of drugs. Roger Bacon and others used it to define the rainbow as belonging to the species of phenomena including colors seen in dew and in sprays made by mill-wheels, squirting water from the mouth with the back to the sun, and other artificial means involving water drops, and to define the colors produced by a hexagonal crystal as a different species of the same genus (distinguished by not being circular) and the colors produced by iridescent feathers as belonging to a different genus. The rainbow, then, belonged to the species of colors produced by the refraction of sunlight through transparent drops or spheres. For a bow to be seen, a large number of discontinuous drops was required. "For," wrote the fourteenth-century French physicist Themo Judaei after experimenting with sprays, "where such drops are absent, there no rainbow or part of it appears, although all the other requisite conditions are sufficient."[21]

I may quote now the logical rules defined by William of Ockham for establishing causal conditions; they sum up the medieval achievement in this direction (in a way very suggestive of J. S. Mill) in a work\ \now available in \a modern edition, his *Super quattuor libros sententiarum*. He wrote:

Although I do not intend to say universally what an immediate cause is, nevertheless I say that this is sufficient for anything being an immediate cause, namely, that when this particular thing (*res absoluta*) is posited the effect is posited, and when it is not posited, all other conditions and dispositions being the same, the effect is not posited. Whence everything that has such a relation to something else is an immediate cause of it, although perhaps not vice versa. That this is sufficient for anything being an immediate cause of anything else is clear, because if not, then there is no way of knowing that something is an immediate cause of something else. For if from the proposition, that this being posited the effect follows and this not being posited the effect does not follow, it does not follow that this is the cause of this effect, then there is no way of knowing that fire is the immediate cause of heat in wood, because it would be possible

[20] *Philosophical Transactions*, July 8, 1672, p.\5004. Mersenne had said that some philosophers seemed to think that they had established an explanation as true because it had not been proved false, like a murderer whose claim to innocence has not been disproved (*L'optique et la catoptrique*, II, Prop. IV [Paris, 1651], 88–90).

[21] Crombie, *Robert Grosseteste*, p. 265.

to say that there is some other cause of this heat, which however does not act except in the presence of fire.

From this other consequences follow. One is that, when a universal cause is removed and the ⟨effects do not occur, this cause is an immediate cause just like a particular cause. Therefore, because in the absence of the sun generable and corruptible things are not produced, which however are produced by the mediation of particular causes, it follows that the sun is the immediate cause of them; unless perhaps you say that the sun is the cause of something else which is the immediate cause of them, but always that the sun is the immediate cause of something, namely either the effect or the cause of this effect, and this is enough for the proposition. Another consequence is that if, when either the universal or the particular cause is removed, the effect does not occur, then neither of them is the total cause, but rather each a partial cause, because neither of those things from which by itself alone the effect cannot be produced is the efficient cause, and consequently neither is the total cause. Another consequence is that every cause properly so-called is an immediate cause, because that cause which can be removed or posited without having any influence on the effect, and which when posited in other circumstances does not produce the effect, cannot be considered a cause; but this is how it is with every other cause except the immediate cause, as is clear inductively.[22]

Ockham restricted the immediate causes to the formal, material, and efficient, remarking that the "special characteristic of a final cause is that it is able to cause when it does not exist."[23]

To this "medical inductive argument" for establishing causal connections Roger Bacon had added a further important notion, that of prediction, taken from another element in this complex of fields in which medieval experimental science developed. This notion came from astrology:

One can examine history in past times and study the effects of the heavens from the beginning of the world, as in floods, earthquakes, pestilences, famines, comets, prodigies, and other things without number, which have occurred both in human affairs and in nature. After one has collected these facts, one should consult the tables and canons of astronomy, and one will find that there are appropriate constellations corresponding to the particular effects. One should then study with the help of tables similar constellations in the future, either near or remote as one wishes; and one will then be able to make predictions of effects, which will be similar to those in the past, since if a cause be posited, so is the effect.[24]

Bacon held that such predictions could not presume to certainty in particular instances and that men were not compelled to act against

---

[22] *Super quattuor libros sententiarum* (Lyons, 1495), Book I, distinction 45, q. 1, D,
[23] *Ibid.*, Book II, q. 3, G.   ed. Gal. et al. (1967-82).
[24] *Opus Majus*, ed. Bridges, I, 389.

their will, but he said that astrology could throw light on the future by discovering general tendencies in the influence of the stars acting through the body on human dispositions as well as on nature at large.

Having discovered the formal definition of a phenomenon and of the conditions for its production, the second part of the inquiry aimed to discover the material and efficient   causes   by which it is produced. The best achievements of the medieval natural philosophers and the limitations imposed by their formulating of their problems in terms of the Aristotelian causes are exemplified by the remarkable treatise by Theodoric of Freiberg, *De iride et radialibus impressionibus*. A German Dominican who held high administrative office in the German Province, Theodoric tells us that he wrote this treatise at the request of the Master General, who spoke to him at the General Chapter held at Toulouse in 1304 and asked him to put the results of his researches into writing.[25] He seems to have died shortly after 1310, so its composition lies between these dates. Before *De iride*, Theodoric had written a treatise on physical optics entitled *De luce et eius origine*, which opens with the question put by God to Job: "By what way is light spread and heat divided upon the earth?" (Job 38). Theodoric said that the Lord had asked a difficult question if he was asking for the *causes* of the behavior of light, but that he would try to find them. He offered his explanation of the rainbow and other optical phenomena, as Descartes and Newton were to do, within the scheme of a general theory of light and color.

Theodoric began by citing Aristotle's *Posterior Analytics* to the effect that "it is the function of optics to determine what the rainbow is, because, in doing so, it shows the reason for it, insofar as there is added to the description of the rainbow the manner in which this sort of concentration [of rays] may be produced in the light going from any luminous heavenly body to a determined place in a cloud, and then by particular refractions and reflections of rays is directed from that determined place to the eye."[26] He recognized two main problems: first, how the colors were formed in each raindrop; and, secondly, how they were sent back to the observer in a definite number and order in an arc at a definite angle. Roger Bacon and Witelo (among others) had already tackled these problems and had given the angle of elevation of the radius of the bow as 42°, measured with an astrolabe. Witelo had also shown experimentally that, when sunlight was

---

[25] See William A. Wallace, *The Scientific Methodology of Theodoric of Freiberg* (Freibourg, Switzerland, 1959), p. 12; Crombie, *Robert Grosseteste*, pp. 242-43.

[26] *De iride*, I, cap. ii, in Crombie, *Robert Grosseteste*, p. 240; for the text of *De iride*, see J. Würschmidt's edition, *Beiträge zur Geschichte der Philosophie des Mittelalters* (Münster, 1914)), XII, 5–6.

passed through a hexagonal crystal or a spherical flask filled with water and the emerging colors thrown onto a screen, red was refracted least and blue most. In this way he explained the formation of colors, supposing that greater refraction progressively weakened the light so that it received progressive darkening from the medium. To explain the formation of the rainbow, he supposed that the colors emerging from one raindrop were reflected back to the observer by the convex external surfaces of the drops behind. The bow was an arc because the drops were spherical. The incident rays of sunlight were refracted and reflected through the same angle in each drop; Witelo had described a repetition of Ptolemy's experiments measuring the relation between the angles of incidence and refraction between air and water and other transparent media. The observer of the rainbow received rays of each of the colors from a set of drops standing in one of a set of concentric arcs one outside the other. If he moved his position, the observer would receive the colors from a wholly different set of drops.

Theodoric's mode of attack on the problem is notable, first, for his use of the *modus tollens* to reject Witelo's geometrical theory of the rainbow because this would not in fact yield the observations as claimed, and, second, for his systematic analysis of the formation of the colors and the paths of the rays in each drop by means of experiments with a hexagonal crystal and with a spherical glass flask of water and a crystal sphere used as "scale" models of a raindrop. These led him to a fundamental discovery: that the light was reflected back not from the convex external surfaces of the drops but from the concave internal surface of the same drop in which the colors were formed by refraction (see Fig. 1). He wrote:

Let the radiation enter the oft-mentioned transparent body and pass through it to the opposite surface and from that be reflected internally back to the first surface by which it originally entered, and then after passing out let it go to the eye; such radiation, I say, in as much as it is produced by a transparent spherical body, serves to explain the production of the rainbow. . . . Moreover, since, as was said above, any incident ray or radiation is not linear and indivisible but has depth and breadth like a column, therefore in any diagrams in the present work a light stream is represented by two lines bounding the light stream on either side.[27]

Using this discovery, Theodoric showed experimentally, by raising and lowering his model "raindrop" and covering now one and then another part of its surface, where the rays forming the primary and the secondary bows entered and emerged from the drop, and he

[27] *De iride*, II, cap. xviii; Crombie, *Robert Grosseteste*, p. 249.

worked out the geometrical paths of the colored rays inside. The order of the colors seen was the order of the drops sending them to the eye. He showed that the secondary bow was produced by two internal reflections and appeared about 11° above the primary (Figs. 2 and 3).

Theodoric's achievement was to discover the *mechanism* by which rainbows were produced. It was an achievement of the medieval method proceeding by a "resolution" of the complex phenomenon into the elements providing the formal, material, and efficient causes necessary and sufficient to bring it about. The limitations of this method of formulating and attacking a problem can be seen in Theodoric's failure to explain why the colors appeared only in narrow arcs of a definite size.[28] He fell back on saying that the position from which the rays returned to the eye was "in a place determined by nature."[29] He tried to account for the size in terms of the ratio between the distances from sun to raindrop and raindrop to eye, on the assumption that the sun and the drops forming the bow lay on a "meteorological sphere" centered at the observer's eye. For some reason, he used the value 22° instead of 42° for the angle of elevation of the radius of the primary bow. He also tried to connect this macroscopic ratio with the microscopic geometry of the raindrop through the size of the arc between the incident and emerging rays (n z in Fig. 2) and by means of this to account for the formation of the different colors.

Exactly where Theodoric failed in dealing with this problem can be seen, as Carl B. Boyer has shown, by comparing his approach with that of Descartes. Ignoring the "meteorological sphere," Descartes saw that the key to the problem lay in the angle between the rays incident upon and emerging from the raindrops. The fundamental difference in approach is that Descartes then *calculated* the paths of rays falling at different angles on a raindrop and showed that in each case there is a clustering of rays emerging from the drop in almost the same direction, at about 41° for the primary bow and about 51° for the secondary (Figs. 4 and 5). Descartes used the law of refraction for his calculations, but Theodoric could in fact have made them using Ptolemy's figures relating angles of incidence and refraction, which Witelo had published. The fundamental difference between their approaches is that in defining the necessary and sufficient conditions for the occurrence of the phenomenon Theodoric concentrated

[28] See Carl B. Boyer, "The Theory of the Rainbow: Medieval Triumph and Failure," *Isis*, XLIX (1958), 378–90, *The Rainbow* (New York, 1959).

[29] *De iride*, II, cap. xxvi, xxx.

on the particular initial conditions whereas Descartes began with the general law.

The limitation on Theodoric's ability to deal with the problem of the rainbow was not technical but conceptual. The same limitation, imposed in different ways by Aristotelian natural philosophy on the best (as well as the worst) medieval science, can be seen in almost every field of inquiry. Two fundamental changes can be distinguished in methods of physical inquiry between Theodoric and Descartes. The first was a change in the concept of nature making the object of inquiry the discovery not simply of the causal conditions defining particular phenomena, but of universal quantitative "laws of nature." This meant a change from the logic of subject and predicate to that of relations expressed as algebraic functions. The second change was to make measurement essential to all physical research. These two changes seem to have had independent origins respectively in the theoretical quantification of academic science and in the practical quantification of technology.

(3) *Quantification in science and in technology*. Some hints that we have regarding the different intellectual needs and social pressures affecting quantification in science and in technology open a field of research bearing directly on the question of continuity and innovation in the origins of the modern scientific movement. I can only indicate some of them briefly.[30]

From the thirteenth century on, there are hints scattered widely through natural philosophical writings of the formation of a new concept of nature as a machine acting according to quantitative laws. For example, Grosseteste, Roger Bacon, Witelo, Theodoric of Freiberg, and other students of optics and related sciences made a distinction, amounting to that between primary and secondary qualities, between the physical activity by which such forms of efficient causality as light, heat, and sound are propagated and the sensations they produce when they act on the appropriate sense organs of a sentient being. This distinction came from the Greek atomists; but in the thirteenth century it marked a significant departure from Aristotle by conceiving the world of physical science as something removed from direct observation and something capable of mathematical characterization. Bacon made another move toward a new concept of nature by using the term *leges naturae* to refer to the "laws of reflection and refraction"[31] in a recognizably modern sense and by his development of the idea of a *natura universalis*, constituted by such laws, superimposed upon the system of particular natures making up the Aristo-

30 See A. C. Crombie, "Quantification in Medieval Physics," *Isis*, LII (1961), 143–60.

31 *Un fragment inédit de l'"Opus tertium*," ed. P. Duhem (Quaracchi, 1909), p. 90.

telian universe. It was this "universal nature" that prevented the water from running out of the clepsydra, when the hole at the top was closed, by the "ordinatio corporum universi et mundi machinae congruentia."[32] Again, we find Pierre de Maricourt describing a perpetual motion machine made of a globular lodestone which, if mounted frictionlessly parallel to the celestial axis and inscribed with a map of the heavens, would by its daily rotation serve as a perfect clock (Fig. 6); and Pierre's contemporary Jean de St. Amand wrote: "Dico quod in adamante est vestigium orbis."[33] Later, after Buridan had ascribed the motion of the celestial spheres to the impetus originally given to them by God, which continued undiminished because there was no resistance, Oresme compared the celestial machine to a clock. For, he concluded his argument, "it is without a doubt like a man making a clock and letting it go and be moved by itself."[34] This analogy was on the way to becoming as much part of the conception of the universe as the mechanical clock erected by Henri de Vick on the Palais Royal in 1370, seven years before Oresme wrote his *Livre du ciel*, was becoming part of the daily lives of Parisians (see Fig. 7).

By far the most systematic medieval attempt at the theoretical quantification of physics was that known as the "intension and remission of forms." Behind this lay the assumption that differences in all other categories could be expressed as differences in the category of quantity. The method then aimed to represent, for example, a change in the intensity of a quality such as heat in the same way as a change in a quantity such as length. The graphical and algebraic methods developed for representing amounts and rates of change, and the kinematical concepts and theorems developed by these methods, are among the most striking medieval contributions to physics. But even in this direction, medieval natural philosophers failed to break completely out of the Aristotelian concept of nature as expressed in the logic of subject and predicate, as distinct from that of functional relations, which they were beginning to develop. This whole development took place within a world of academic discussions that made stringent demands on logic, was mainly concerned with the method as such, and applied it to degrees of divine grace as well as of local motion; but it neither made a serious demand for measurement nor exposed any measurements that were made to more than a remote

[32] *Quaestiones supra libros quatuor physicorum Aristotelis*, ed. F. Delorme, in *Opera hactenus inedita Rogeri Baconi*, VIII (Oxford, 1928), 200–201; see Schramm, *op. cit.*

[33] L. Thorndike, "John of St. Amand on the Magnet," *Isis*, XXXVI (1946), 156.

[34] *Livre du ciel*, Book II, chap. ii.

chance of being checked by repetition. Moreover, at the root of this medieval quantification of natural philosophy lay two great inherited inconveniences: the use of the Greek pairs of opposite qualities (hot –cold, heavy–light, etc.) before the establishment of single linear scales, and the development of the mathematical methods in the Greek language of proportions.

The contrast between this academic world of theory and the demands made wherever a practical problem arose throws considerable light on the needs and pressures among which modern science grew up. In practical life it mattered if one was given short measure or the wrong product, was subjected to incompetent surgery, or arrived at an unintended destination. Measurement was essential to meeting the demand for accurate, repeatable results. So we find that measurement became a regular part of the procedure of an academic science like astronomy on which a practical demand was made for the calendar, for telling the time of day, and for navigation. The whole development of practical fields like navigation, surveying, cartography, gunnery, instrument making, commercial arithmetic and bookkeeping, architecture, painting by linear perspective, painting and sculpture from nature, assaying of ores and precious metals, prescribing of drugs of known properties, and diagnosis and control of disease depended on the growing technical ability to specify the conditions for producing the desired result; and these conditions became increasingly quantitative.

The discovery of the specific causal conditions that produced the effect was likewise the essential aim of the experimental science, just as the specification of the premises capable of yielding a given conclusion was that of logic and mathematics. In all these fields, the logic, mathematics, and natural and experimental science of the academic community and the technology of the skilled craftsmen, there was a growing sense of precision throughout the later Middle Ages. Medieval technical writings and the whole early history of instrumentation are still relatively unexplored, yet it is surely here that one must chiefly look for those habits essential to experimental science that were developed by the demand for quantitative accuracy made by the problems themselves. The existence not only of instruments but of medieval technical *writings*, the productions of literate men, is evidence of interested contacts between scholars and craftsmen from at least the early twelfth century. Two historical movements encouraged the further growth of contacts from that period: the rise in the social scale of such specialized craftsmen as the *architectus*, and the enlargement of the scientific curricula of the universities. By the thirteenth century the result can be seen in such figures as Villard de Honnecourt (Fig. 8) and Pierre de Maricourt. Their successors were the "artist-engineers" of the Renaissance like Leo Battista Alberti and Leonardo da Vinci. I do not think that it was these men who created what was called in the seventeenth century the "new experimental-mathematical *philosophy*." This was the work of the successors of Robert Grosseteste and Nicole Oresme educated as natural philosophers and mathematicians in the universities. Their philosophical vision of an intellectual mastery through which nature could be subjected to human understanding and use descended from Roger Bacon's. But Roger Bacon's contemporaries could not solve many scientific problems, and they conspicuously lacked established standards of scientific cogency. The hints that we have suggest that the technical tradition of the late Middle Ages and the Renaissance played a decisive part in establishing the standards of modern experimental science. This is an open problem calling for historical investigation. Perhaps in these standards we have the real message of Western science to the world, for, in an intellectual tradition that has developed since Greek antiquity on the basis of the principle of noncontradiction, one distinction that has shone through all confusion is that between what one may want to believe and what is possible.

I have given examples of the ideological (theological), logical, and technological preparation of the Western mind for its development of science and technology. If we are to include vision as well as problem-solving in the history of science, we really have no choice but to take seriously someone like Roger Bacon when he sets out as a "persuasion" (in the *Opus majus*) a program for acquiring intellectual and practical power over nature by mathematics and experiment. The later history of the origins of modern science is the history of the diversification of methods by which this program was deployed by Western Europeans in their aggressive attacks on nature and on the rest of mankind.

Further references: Guilielmi de Ockham, *Opera philosophica*, i-vi, ed. G. Gál et al. (St. Bonaventura, N.Y., 1967-82); Villard de Honnecourt, *Carnet*, présenté et commenté par A. Erlande-Brandenburg, R. Pernoud, J. Gimpel, R. Bechmann (Paris, 1986); L. Bianchi, *L'errore di Aristotle: La polemica contro l'eternità del mondo nel xii secolo* (Firenze, 1984), "Omnipotenza divina e ordine del mondo fra xiii e xiv secolo", *Medioevo*, x (1984) 105-53, *L'inizio dei tempi* (Firenze, 1987); A. C. Crombie and J. D. North, "Bacon, Roger (c. 1219-c. 1292)" in *Dictionary of Scientific Biography*, i (1970) 377-85; G. S. Gordon, *Medium Aevum and the Middle Ages* (Oxford, 1925); J. M. G. Hackett, "*Scientia experimentalis*: from Robert Grosseteste to Roger Bacon" in *Proceedings of the Warburg Institute Grosseteste Symposium (1987)*, ed. J. McEvoy (in press); R. Hisette, *Enquête sur les 219 articles condamnés à Paris le 7 mars 1277* (Paris & Louvain, 1977); M. L. M. McLaughlin, "Humanist concepts of renaissance and middle ages in the tre- and quattrocento", *Renaissance studies*, ii (1988) 131-42; R. W. Southern, *Medieval Humanism and other Studies* (Oxford, 1970); see also chs. 2 p. 40, 4 p. 90, 5 p. 114, 6 p. 137, 7 p. 160, 9.

4

QUANTIFICATION IN MEDIEVAL PHYSICS

A WORTH-WHILE discussion of quantification in medieval physics requires particular care in deciding what is to be talked about. The whole question is obviously much less clear and much more equivocal in this period than it became later. So it is important to begin with some distinctions. I shall distinguish first between quantified procedures and quantified concepts, and I shall take a quantified procedure in science to be one that aims at measurement, that is, any procedure that assigns numbers in a scale. To be complete such a procedure must comprise both mathematical techniques for operating the scale theoretically and measuring techniques for using it to explore the world. Technology need contain little more than procedures of these kinds, which provide for the measurements and calculations with which it is concerned. But most sciences aim beyond these at providing explanations by means of a system of theory. So a quantified science, as distinct from quantified technology, comprises not only quantified procedures but also quantified explanatory concepts, each applicable to the other within a theoretical system. The development of a science then takes place through a dialogue between its theories and its procedures, the former offering an exploration of the expected world through predictions and explanations made by means of the technical procedures, and the latter confronting these theoretical expectations with the test of quantified data.

A dialogue of this kind requires that both sides should speak the same language. We are so familiar with the close and precise adaptation of conceptual and procedural language to each other in modern physics that it may come as a surprise to find authentic scientific systems in which this is not the case. Yet we do not have to look very far to find examples. In the contemporary social sciences and in psychology, they are notorious. We do not have to go many decades back in the history of modern genetics to find a very incomplete and interrupted dialogue between theories and procedures. Somewhat earlier, in the eighteenth century, we find the same situation in chemistry. The main interest of medieval physics in this context seems to me to be that it provides the earliest example in the development of modern science in which we can study the state of affairs when the dialogue between concepts and procedures was incomplete or absent. Then we can study the difference it made when clear and exact communication was opened, as it was in the seventeenth century. I shall assume that it is my brief to discuss medieval physics as a case history of a general problem. At the same time, I shall assume that this case history has a special historical interest because of its bearing on the particular question of the origins of modern scientific thinking.[1]

I propose to pursue the inquiry through two general questions. First, what internal intellectual needs and external practical and professional pressures were felt, leading to the quantification of theoretical concepts and theoretical procedures? Secondly, what internal intellectual needs and external practical and professional pressures were felt, leading to the collecting of quantitative factual data and to the confronting of theoretical analysis with exact and repeatable measurements?

All the information about medieval physics that has been brought to light recently shows that a far greater need was felt that concepts and theoretical and mathematical procedures should be quantified than that actual measurements should be made. The choice between different possible theoretical formulations was often decided on purely theoretical grounds within a theoretical system. When we look at how the scientific and philosophical problems concerned developed historically, this distribution of interest seems natural enough. Yet it appears as something of a paradox. We seem to be dealing with philosophical decisions that did not immediately yield much in the way of quantified physics that was empirically true, yet with decisions that may seem to have been necessary for the later development of such a physics. The paradox appears when we ask ourselves, on the one hand, what the medieval physicists themselves thought they were doing, and on the other, what we ourselves may judge their contribution to have been to the later development of quantified science. So we must consider this further question: to what extent did medieval natural philosophical ideas, in advance of factual knowledge and often also of much deep understanding of the scientific use to which they could be put, suggest physical problems and methods of conceptualizing physics in what turned out to be a fruitful direction? This question must be faced by any historian of a tradition of developing truth such as Western science. I do not think that

[1] I have based my discussion in this paper on information taken from the following sources, which should be consulted for further details and bibliography: Guy Beaujouan and Emmanuel Poulle, "Les origines de la navigation astronomique aux XIVe et XVe siècles" in *Le Navire et l'économie maritime du XVe au XVIIIe siècle: travaux du colloque tenu le 17 mai 1956 à l'Académie de Marine* présentés par Michel Mollat avec la collaboration d'Olivier de Prat, Paris, 1957; D. A. Callus (ed.), *Robert Grosseteste, Scholar and Bishop* (Oxford, 1955), chapter by A. C. Crombie; Marshall Clagett, *The Science of Mechanics in the Middle Ages* (Madison, Wisc., 1959); Marshall Clagett (ed.), *Critical Problems in the History of Science* (Madison, Wisc., 1959), paper by A. C. Crombie and commentary by I. E. Drabkin and Ernest Nagel; A. C. Crombie, *Robert Grosseteste and the Origins of Experimental Science 1100-1700* (Oxford, 1953), and *Medieval and Early Modern Science* (New York, 1959) (2 vols. Doubleday Anchor Books); E. J. Dijksterhuis, *Die Mechanisering van het Wereldbeeld* (Amsterdam, 1950) (German translation, 1955); Pierre Duhem, *Le Systeme du monde* (Paris, 1913-16) I-V, (1954-58) VI-VIII; C. W. Jones (ed.), *Bedae Opera de Temporibus* (Cambridge, Mass., 1943); Anneliese Maier, *Die Vorläufer Galileis im 14, Jahrhundert* (Rome, 1959), *Zwei Grundprobleme der Scholastischen Naturphilosophie*, 2nd ed. (Rome, 1951), *An der Grenze von Scholastik und Naturwissenschaften*, 2nd ed. (Rome, 1952), *Zwischen Philosophie und Mechanik* (Rome, 1958); E. A. Moody and Marshall Clagett, *The Medieval Science of Weights* (Madison, Wisc., 1952); Charles Singer *et al.* (eds.), *A History of Technology* (Oxford, 1957), III—chapters by Sir Harold Spencer Jones, H. Alan Lloyd, Derek J. Price, Charles Singer, Cyril Stanley Smith and R. J. Forbes, and E. G. R. Taylor; René Taton (ed.), *Histoire générale des sciences* (Paris, 1957), I

we should be bothered by the suggestion of teleology this question carries. It can be dealt with by trying first to determine what problems the natural philosophers of the past were aiming to solve in their own period and what their intentions and preoccupations were, and by trying then to see what difference their work made in the short and in the long run. It will cause no surprise that ideas and habits of thought may come to have applications undreamed of at an earlier stage of their history—so much so that an idea may generate a completely different one with a change of context.

Some intellectual need to produce some kind of quantified conceptualization of physics can be seen as early as the twelfth century, for example, in the Chartres school. The sources of this are a form of neoplatonic philosophy derived from St. Augustine and from Plato's *Timaeus,* and such scriptural texts as that from the *Wisdom of Solomon* stating that God had "ordered all things in measure and number and weight." Vague as it is, this notion suggested kinds of explanation to look for. For example, Thierry of Chartres, in attempting to give a rational analysis of the formation of the world at the creation, replaced Plato's demiurge with the Christian God. He said that God had created space or chaos and then had ordered it so as to form the universe in accordance with the mathematical ideas in His mind. So Thierry concluded that in order to understand the story of *Genesis* rationally, it was necessary to master the mathematics of the *quadrivium,* for mathematics was the key to all rational explanation of the physical world. We might perhaps call Thierry's programme "proto-quantitative." It included such elements as attempting to account for differences between qualities as observed, in terms of geometrical differences between Plato's geometrical particles. It is hopeful and for us suggestive. But it involves no numbers or measurements. It is hardly what we regard as science.

The first more seriously scientific moves towards the quantification of concepts and procedures in medieval physics were made in the course of a controversy that arose in the thirteenth century over the Aristotelian categories of "quantity" and "quality." In effect the origin of the controversy was a critique of Aristotle's qualitative physics from two other points of view also derived from Greek sources. These were first, the Pythagorean or Platonic physical concept that qualitative differences might be reducible to differences in geometrical structure, number and movement, that is to differences in quantities; and secondly, certain mathematical concepts and procedures.

The characteristics of Aristotle's conception of physics that strike us now as most alien to the thought of modern quantified physics are not only that it was explicitly qualitative, but also that it looked for its explanations in terms of a direct classification of immediate experience. Thus Aristotle's distinctions between motion up, down, and in a circle, and between natural and violent motion, were based on a direct classification of what bodies are actually seen to do. The cosmological system in which such motions were supposed to find their explanation was built up simply as a classification of these and similar directly observed distinctions. The "natures" that were supposed to be the explanatory sources of the behavior of different things were characterized simply by a direct description of what things actually did. Thus they gave no further information beyond that already obtained from direct observation. Their characterization included both quantitative and qualitative attributes. But these were irreducibly different. Certainly Aristotle's physics made use of some quantitative relationships, such as when he said that a body would move twice the distance in a given time when acted on by twice the power. But it did not aim except incidentally at measurement, calculation, and quantitative prediction. It aimed at *episteme, scientia*, true and certain rational knowledge. Aristotle held that he had found such knowledge when he had discovered the "nature" through direct observation.

The medieval critique of this conception of the aims of physics as a science certainly fell a good way short of the position Galileo was to take up. Galileo did his best to drop all the questions to which Aristotelian physics was the answer and to ask new kinds of questions. But the new elements by means of which both the medievals and Galileo introduced a new conception of physics were analogous. On the one hand, in certain fields medieval "Platonists" looked, like Galileo, for explanations not in immediate experience but in theoretical concepts at a remove from it and capable of quantification. On the other hand, both reduced the sharp distinction made by Plato and Aristotle between *episteme* and *techne, ars*, the manipulative skills, including mathematics.

This last distinction seems to me to supply one of the various keys that historians can offer to an understanding of what happened in the Scientific Revolution. Thus in Greek scientific thought Ptolemy's mathematical astronomy, which could predict the celestial motions but could not explain them, was supposed to be a distinct field of inquiry from Aristotle's physics, which was held to explain these motions. The technical mathematical devices of astronomy were *techne*. So it was possible to hold that alternative technical devices, for example, in the middle ages those of Eudoxus and Ptolemy and in the sixteenth and early seventeenth centuries those of Ptolemy, Copernicus, and Tycho Brahe, could be combined with the same system of physics, the same *episteme*. The dynamical analysis of terrestrial and celestial motion finally brought out into the open by Kepler, Galileo, and eventually Newton showed that this was a very superficial view of the matter. It showed that in so far as the "physics" of motion was left untouched by calculation and measurement, it could be disregarded. It was irrelevant. And it showed that in so far as "physics" was exposed to calculation and measurement it was subject to the same quantitative tests as the mathematical devices used in making predictions. The essence of the seventeenth-century revolution in physics can thus be seen, from this point of view, as the using of *techne*, "art," in fact the "new experimental-mathematical philosophy," to yield a true science of nature. This was not the certain rational knowledge of Plato's and Aristotle's *episteme*, but as Pascal, Huygens, and Newton pointed out it was the nearest to the physical truth that we could get.

In medieval physics the distinction between the science of "natures" and the art of applying mathematics to physical problems was certainly not abolished or reorganized as it became in the seventeenth century. But mathematical art, the so-called *scientia media*, was introduced into the science of nature far beyond Aristotle. So at the same time there were at least some quantified physical concepts, and others that were not yet quantified but were capable of being so. The weakest of the elements that have become essential to physics since the seventeenth century was measurement. I shall now consider some examples of these elements in the quantification of medieval physics.

An example of the "proto-quantification" of physical concepts, aiming to show how to express qualitative differences in terms of differences in quantities, but without yet assigning any quantities, is provided by thirteenth-century optics. Much of this is better described as a speculative program than as theory. The deductive machinery for making calculations from theory to data is largely missing. But medieval natural philosophers were certainly aware that such machinery should be supplied in a scientific system, and in optics they made some attempt to supply it. In some problems they reached a state of primitive quantification by assigning numbers.

Consider first the conception of optics as a physical science developed in the thirteenth century by Robert Grosseteste and Roger Bacon. Grosseteste conceived the "nature" that was the cause of given events as something, not open to direct inspection, in which the event was prefigured. The ultimate physical "nature" or substance in which all physical events were prefigured he held to be light (*lux*). This had the fundamental property of self-propagation which he characterized geometrically from two points of view: (1) *super lineas et angulos,* that is along straight lines that may change direction by reflection and refraction; and (2) *super figuras,* that is in a sphere from a centre or in a cone. Thus characterized, Grosseteste described how this light, from an originally created point, generated the dimensions of space and the spheres of the universe, and operated as the efficient cause in all motion. So for Grosseteste optics became the fundamental physical science, and in order to make it work as an explanatory system he said that it was essential to operate it by means of mathematics. "Hence," he wrote, "these rules and principles and fundamentals having been given by the power of geometry, the careful observer of natural things can give the causes of all natural effects by this method. And it will be impossible otherwise, as is already clear in respect of the universal, since every natural action is varied in strength and weakness through variation of lines, angles and figures. But in respect of the particular this is even clearer, first in natural action upon matter and later upon the senses."[2]

With Grosseteste, the Aristotelian "nature" or "form" thus became mathematically characterized. Roger Bacon, continuing Grosseteste's description of this program, wrote: "All categories (*praedicamenta*) depend on a knowledge of quantity, concerning which mathematics treats, and therefore the whole power of logic depends on mathematics."[3] He then used language indicating a further shift towards a quantified physics looking for its explanations not in definitions of essences or "natures" but in mathematically expressed laws. Bacon is the first writer I know to have used the term "law of nature" (*lex*

[2] "De Natura Locorum," in *Die Philosophischen Werke des Robert Grosseteste,* ed. L. Baur (*Beiträge zur Geschichte der Philosophie des Mittelalters,* IX, Münster, 1912), pp. 59-60.

[3] *Opus Maius,* ed. J. H. Bridges (Oxford, 1897), I, 103.

naturae) in the scientific sense familiar since the seventeenth century. Thus he wrote: "That the laws of reflection and refraction are common to all natural actions I have shown in the treatise on geometry,"[4] and he claimed to have demonstrated "by the law of refraction" how the image was formed in the eye.

As a piece of speculation this mathematicizing program has a number of features suggestive and interesting for us because we know what happened in the long run. In his account of *multiplicatio specierum*, Grosseteste distinguished between the physical activity by which visible light, heat, sound, and other forms of efficient causality were propagated through the medium, and the sensations they produced when they acted on the appropriate sense organs of a sentient being. This is not of course an original distinction; it was made by the Greek atomists. But in the thirteenth century it made a significant departure from Aristotle by conceiving the world of physical science as something removed from direct observation and something capable of mathematical characterization. Grosseteste himself attempted to formulate a geometrical, almost mechanical conception of the rectilinear propagation of light and of sound as a succession of "pulses" or "waves" transmitted from part to part. He tried to use this to account for reflection and refraction, and he offered a quantitative law or "rule" for determining the angle of refraction.[5] Roger Bacon, and later Witelo and Theodoric of Freiberg, made a similar distinction between directly perceived visible qualities and light as a geometrically conceived physical activity producing these qualities. They proposed that different visible qualities were effects produced by quantitative differences in the physical activity of light. Thus Witelo and Theodoric of Freiberg developed along these lines a suggestion made by Averroes giving a quasi-quantitative account of Aristotle's explanation of colour as a mixture of light and darkness. They observed experimentally that the colours of the spectrum were in an order of increasing amounts of refraction from red to blue. They attributed this to a progressive weakening of white light by refraction, so that progressively larger amounts of darkness became mixed with it. Similarly Grosseteste correlated intensity of illumination and of heat with the angle at which the rays were received and with their concentration. In the fourteenth century another Oxford natural philosopher, John of Dumbleton, speculated with the formulation of a quantitative law relating intensity of illumination to distance from the luminous source.

We might consider these speculations as part of the pre-history of a quantified conceptualization of the science of optics. If now we ask for their cash value in quantified procedures and firm scientific knowledge, we get another side to the story. In the whole conceptual development of optics following Grosseteste, there was almost no attempt at precise mathematical definition, at expressing the amounts of change quantitatively in numbers, or at measurement. One reason for this was certainly that these speculations carried the subject far beyond not only the facts but also the available mathematical

[4] *Un fragment inédit de l'Opus Tertium*, ed. P. Duhem (Quaracchi, 1909), p. 90; cf. p. 78.
[5] Cf. C. M. Turbayne, "Grosseteste and an ancient optical principle," *Isis*, 1959, *50*: 467-472.

techniques and concepts, which did not go farther than those of elementary geometrical optics. But if we descend from high speculation closer to the world of fact and of *techne*, we still find a gap between promise and fulfillment. We find ourselves in a scientific milieu in which certainly some natural philosophers had a more or less clear idea of how to proceed in science and in which some discoveries were made. For example, Roger Bacon's analysis and classification of the refractive properties of different curved interfaces, and his use of a geometrical model of the eye to analyze how the different refracting media focused the image, are highly intelligent examples of proto-quantitative scientific procedures. But in the milieu of medieval academic science neither intellectual need nor social pressure for consistent quantitative accuracy seems to have been felt strongly enough to produce reliably consistent results. In the academic science of the universities the chances of data being challenged by repetition must have been small. It was only where investigations had some definite practical value, such as astronomical observations had for the calendar, astrology and navigation, and chemical assaying had for commercial metallurgy, that there was a strong enough demand to ensure exact and repeatable measurements.

Some further examples from optics will illustrate this unreliability in measurement characteristic of medieval academic science in practice, however much quantitative procedures may have been advocated in principle. One of the most impressive pieces of quantitative academic science in the thirteenth century is Witelo's account of the measurement of the values of the angles of refraction of light passing between air, water and glass, with angles of incidence increasing by 10 degrees to a maximum of 80 degrees. Witelo described in detail the construction and use of an apparatus for making these measurements, set out the results in tables showing concomitant variations between angles of incidence and amounts of refraction, generalized these in a set of rules assigning greater or lesser amounts of refraction but not numbers, and offered a physical explanation in terms of the densities of the refracting media. But did Witelo ever actually make these measurements? Two facts raise doubts. First, the values in the tables showing refraction from air into water and into glass, and from water into glass, which are fairly accurate, are identical with those in Ptolemy's tables for similar experiments. Secondly, Witelo's tables show very inaccurate or impossible reciprocal values.[6] (Ptolemy did not include these.) It seems that Witelo derived these values from a misapplication of the law that the paths of the rays are the same whether we are considering the light passing, for example, from air into water or from water into air. He did not know that at the higher angles of incidence, all the light striking the under surface of the water will be reflected and none will be refracted into the air. If Witelo had actually made these experiments, he would have discovered this phenomenon, but it was not discovered until the fourteenth century.

Another revealing example is provided by the studies of the rainbow.[7] According to the conception of scientific methodology developed in the thirteenth

[6] Crombie, *Robert Grosseteste*, pp. 223-225.
[7] *Ibid.*, pp. 64-66, 124-127, 155-162, 196-200, 226-277, 290-292.

and fourteenth centuries, the explanation of an event was to be sought through an analysis of the conditions necessary and sufficient to produce it. The conditions producing a rainbow were stated in the form that if there be postulated a certain refracting medium, namely rain drops, at a position at which the incident sunlight makes an angle of 42 degrees with the line connecting the rain drops and an observer, then the observer will see a rainbow. Roger Bacon states that he measured with an astrolabe this angle subtended by the radius of the rainbow. Later investigators, especially Witelo and Theodoric of Freiberg, proceeded most intelligently to try to find out what happened to the light when it struck the rain drops. They set up geometrical models, rejected models that did not yield the observed results, and Theodoric finally carried out a successful analysis showing, by means of spherical flasks of water used as model raindrops, how the sunlight, by refraction and internal reflection, produced the order and shape of the colours seen in both the primary and the secondary bows. He stated correctly that the angle between these two bows is 11 degrees. But he also stated that he had measured with an astrolabe the angle subtended by the radius of the primary bow and had found it to be 22 degrees. It is obvious that he could not have obtained by measurement this value for an angle that is approximately 42 degrees. Theodoric's work is characteristic of a large part of medieval optics and medieval physics as a whole. He had an intelligent analytical procedure. Neither his procedure nor his conceptualization of the problem was explicitly quantified, but both were a preliminary to the quantification that Descartes, for example, was to give to the problem of the rainbow by assigning numbers by means of the newly discovered law of refraction. But Theodoric was unreliable in his alleged measurements.

It is obvious that when they were dealing with problems in academic science, the kinds of problems that might be discussed in commentaries on texts of Aristotle and other authors used in the arts faculties of universities, medieval natural philosophers suffered not simply from a lack of quantified procedures for dealing with their speculation, but also from a lack of firm intention to apply such procedures in experimental measurement. The dialogue in their own minds between concepts and procedures for measurement had not become properly established. The fact is that however much some of them may have discussed the methodology of experimental quantitative science and advocated putting it into practice, nearly all medieval natural philosophers were primarily theoreticians. They made consistent *measurements* only when some *practical* need demanded it. But they found the development of a dialogue between concepts and quantified *theoretical* procedures something that followed naturally from their academic problems. To this aspect of medieval physics, to the development of quantified theoretical and mathematical procedures and related concepts without measurement, I must now turn.

This theoretical quantification of academic medieval physics was developed out of an attempt to provide the same procedures for representing changes of any kind, quantitative or qualitative. Behind this was the conception that all real differences could be expressed as differences in the category of quantity, for example, that a change in the intensity of a quality such as heat could be expressed as a magnitude in the same way as could a change in a quantity such as length. The question was opened in a theological context by Peter Lombard's assertion that the virtue of charity could increase and decrease in an individual and be more or less intense at different times. How was this to be understood? Two schools of thought developed and their divergent principles were taken over into physics.

The conservative school supported Aristotle's principle that since quality and quantity belonged to absolutely different categories, the one could not be reduced to the other. Examples of changes in quantity were changes in length or number, which were brought about by the addition or subtraction of either continuous or discontinuous homogeneous parts. That was all the change involved. But a change in a quality such as heat was quite different. Heat might exist in different degrees of intensity, but a change in intensity was not brought about, for example, by adding one homogeneous part of heat to another. The heats of two bodies brought into contact did not make a greater heat, as the lengths of two bodies made a greater length. So Aristotle and his supporters considered that each degree of intensity of heat was a different quality, and that a change in the intensity was brought about by loss of one quality of heat and the acquisition of another. The same went for every change in quality.

The radical school aiming at quantifying physics had to make several moves in order to deal with these opposing arguments and achieve their goal. Some philosophers distinguished between a body and its qualities and said that, for example, if the heat or the weight of one body were abstracted from it and then added to another, the latter would become hotter or heavier in amounts capable of expression in numerical degrees. Following this line of thought, definitions and distinctions of quantities were sharpened. For example, in the fourteenth century the expression "specific weight" was used to distinguish density, or intensity of weight proportional to volume, from gross weight. Another problem that arose concerned the characterization of scales. Greek writers conceived of qualities as existing in pairs of opposites: hot-cold, wet-dry, heavy-light, bright-dark, and so on. Thus Galen had suggested representing both heat and cold in numerical degrees. This conception of pairs of opposites was a major obstacle to the quantification of physics until the general introduction of linear scales from the seventeenth century. For example, when Buridan, in developing the dynamical concept of *impetus,* proposed as a measure of "quantity of motion" the product of "speed" multiplied by "quantity of matter," this applied only to "heavy" and not to "light" bodies.

In the end, whatever view they took of the real nature of qualities and of qualitative change, natural philosophers and mathematicians made two important contributions to the quantification of physics in the fourteenth century. They created concepts for quantifying space, time, speed, and other magnitudes. And they devised procedures for *representing* any kind of change numerically and for manipulating the quantities concerned. The best illustration of this is found in kinematics and dynamics.

The theoretical quantification of the science of local motion began with a critique of those parts of Aristotle's treatment of the subject that had themselves some implied quantification. The technical procedures were derived in the first place from the theory of proportions expounded by Euclid and Archimedes. Consider first the stages in the critique of the Aristotelian relationship making speed (v) directly proportional to the motive power (p) and inversely proportional to the resistance (r) of the medium: $v \propto p/r$. The first thing that had to be done was to put the relationship into this form, which was impossible for the Greeks because they did not consider speed (v) to be a magnitude. According to the Greek conception, a magnitude could result only from a "true" proportion, that is from a ratio of two "like" quantities such as two distances (s) or two times (t).[8] So Aristotle could express the relationship only by considering it in separate stages. Thus

$$\frac{s_1}{s_2} = \frac{t_1}{t_2}, \quad \text{i.e. speed is uniform, when } p_1 = p_2 \text{ and } r_1 = r_2;$$

$$\frac{s_1}{s_2} = \frac{p_1}{p_2} \qquad \text{when } t_1 = t_2 \text{ and } r_1 = r_2;$$

$$\frac{s_1}{s_2} = \frac{r_2}{r_1} \qquad \text{when } t_1 = t_2 \text{ and } p_1 = p_2.$$

A metric definition of speed as a magnitude determined by the ratio between two "unlike" quantities, distance and time, i.e. $v = s/t$, was foreshadowed in the thirteenth century by Gerard of Brussels but made explicit only in the fourteenth century by Thomas Bradwardine and other mathematicians at Oxford.

Bradwardine was now in a position to propose an alternative to the Aristotelian expression $v \propto p/r$, which could not apply to cases where $p = r$ and $v = o$. After considering some other proposals, he came to the conclusion that the relationship was one which we would now call exponential and which we can express as $v = \log(p/r)$. Since $\log 1/1 = o$, the condition is satisfied that when $p = r$, $v = o$, and the relationship gives a continual gradual change in v as p/r approaches 1. It is clear that Bradwardine was concerned with obtaining a relationship consistent within his theoretical system that would also describe actual motions. He also made the important and influential move of shifting the ground of the discussion from the causal "why" to the mathematical "how," that is, from the physical causes of movement to the spatiotemporal effects of movement. But he does not seem to have thought of making experimental measurements to decide whether his expression did in fact describe actual motions.

Following Bradwardine, the theoretical quantification of the science of motion was carried several stages further at Oxford and Paris, but all without experimental measurement. Bradwardine's analysis had related velocity to instantaneous changes. At Merton College, William Heytesbury, Richard Swineshead, and John of Dumbleton went on to develop a concept of instantaneous velocity and with it an analysis of various kinds of acceleration, which Heytesbury defined as "the velocity of a velocity." (I use "velocity" in this context nonvectorially as synonymous with "speed.") This analysis grew out

---

[8] See Clagett, *The Science of Mechanics in the Middle Ages*, pp. 165ff.

of the problem of representing the amounts and rates of change of any quality or quantity, which was known as "the intension and remission of forms," or "the latitude of forms." A "form" in this context was any variable quality or quantity. The "intensity" or "latitude" of a form, for example velocity, was the numerical value that was assigned to it, and thus it was possible to speak of the rate at which the intensity of the variable form, velocity, changed in relation to an invariable form known as the "extension" or "longitude," such as distance or time. Velocity was said to be "uniform" when equal distances were covered in equal successive intervals of time, and "difform" when unequal distances were covered as in accelerated or retarded motion. Further distinctions were made between "uniformly difform" motion, that is uniform acceleration or retardation, "difformly difform" motion, and so on. A very important definition was that of uniformly accelerated movement as one in which equal increments of velocity were acquired in equal intervals of time.

The problem of the relationship between the categories of quality and quantity that is behind this analysis is reflected in the distinction of the intensity of a velocity as its "quality," in contrast to the distance covered which was its "quantity." In cases of acceleration, the quality of velocity was said to vary from instant to instant. Thus instantaneous velocity was the intensity or quality of a velocity at an instant. It was measured numerically by the distance that *would* be covered by a point if it were allowed to move for a given time at the velocity it had at that instant. In Paris Nicole Oresme applied a graphical method to this analysis, using two-dimensional figures to represent changes of variable forms in relation to invariable ones. Thus he represented the "extension" of time by a horizontal straight line and the intensity of velocity at each instant by a perpendicular raised at a corresponding point on the horizontal. The height of the perpendicular represented the intensity or "quality" of the velocity, whereas the area of the whole figure, which is dimensionally equivalent to the distance covered in the movement, was its "quantity" or "total" velocity.[9]

Out of this theoretical quantification and analysis of motion came a number of interesting and valuable procedures and theorems. The most significant procedures occur in the associated development of the concept of functional dependence. The best known theorem is the so-called Mean Speed Rule of Merton College. This makes an approach that has become characteristic of modern kinematics, seeing as the basic objective of analysis the representation of nonuniform velocities by uniform velocities. The Merton theorem states that a uniform acceleration produces the same "quantity of motion," as measured by distance travelled in a given time, as a uniform velocity equal to the instantaneous velocity at the middle instant of the time of the acceleration. This theorem has application to the motion of freely falling bodies, which in the fourteenth century was discussed as a case of uniform acceleration. Yet none of these academic mathematical philosophers cleared up the question whether the velocity of falling bodies increased in proportion to distance fallen or to the time. That had to wait until the sixteenth century. And none of them checked the mathematical analysis against measurements made with fall-

[9] Cf. Clagett, *op. cit.*, pp. xxv-xxvi.

ing bodies. The analysis of the problem within the framework of the Greek theory of proportions made measurement largely inapplicable. That had to wait until Galileo's experiments with a ball rolling down an inclined plane. The reason for these omissions is undoubtedly that these mathematical philosophers were primarily theoreticians, interested in philosophical method and mathematics. They felt no compelling intellectual need or social pressure to take a particular interest in falling bodies or any other particular phenomena in nature.

By far the most sophisticated and exact part of physical science in the thirteenth and fourteenth centuries was based on concepts quantified in this way for theoretical and mathematical manipulation, without thought of actual experimental measurements. As a general phenomenon arising in the arts faculty, this kind of approach to physical problems represented a union of the philosophical approach of Aristotle with the mathematical approach of Archimedes. Another example is the work in statics, where, for example, in the treatises associated with the name of Jordanus Nemorarius, trajectories and levers were analyzed into the effective quantities involved—vertical rectilinear displacement, horizontal distance from the fulcrum, "gravity according to position," and so on. This analysis made implicit use of the important new principle of virtual displacements. A further example is Jean Buridan's move towards the quantification of dynamics through the concept of impetus. This was put forward as a solution of the problem, arising within Aristotelian physics, of providing a cause for the continual motion of projectiles and for the accelerated motion of falling bodies. But by giving a quantitative measure of impetus as the quantity of matter in the moving body multiplied by its velocity, Buridan provided a measure of the *effect* of motion clearly analogous to the definition of quantity of motion or momentum used in seventeenth century mechanics. Similarly his account of the production of acceleration in falling bodies by the continuous action of a *constant* gravity has analogies with Newton's definition of force. Theoretical quantification was thus taking physics out of the irreducible Aristotelian categories. Metaphysical or "physical" restrictions, for example to considering velocity a magnitude or to comparing linear and circular motion, began to be put on one side.[10] In a quantified physics, mathematics treats all quantities as belonging to the same category.

The notion of proportions used in medieval science does not lead to measurement; hence measurements were not appropriate to the inquiry being undertaken. Nevertheless the investigation of proportions in the fourteenth century did lead to the formulation of important mathematical and logical definitions and theorems that were *later* taken over into seventeenth-century mathematical physics—for example, velocity, acceleration, instantaneous velocity, the Mertonian Mean Speed Rule. Thus, although the scholastics did not have precisely the same aims and intentions as seventeenth-century physicists, they did produce results which became part of the main history of physics—especially in kinematics. But we must not forget that medieval writers on "latitude of forms" applied their quantitative methods not only to physical

---

[10] Cf. Clagett, *op. cit.*, p. 181.

problems such as motion, but also to degrees of divine grace, sin and other qualities. The fact that they considered such a wide range of questions by means of their method marks an important difference between their focus of attention and that of seventeenth-century physicists. The same is true of medieval work in the field of optics. A writer might consider within the same general framework the propagation not only of the light but also of influences from the stars and even of divine grace. Yet at the same time valuable work was done in optics strictly speaking, for example on refraction and the rainbow and on the analysis of the eye as an optical instrument by imposing a geometrical model on anatomy. Some of the numerical figures given can have been obtained only by actual measurement, for example 42 degrees for the radius of the rainbow. Yet we may doubt whether many of the figures given as if they were the results of measurements were really obtained in actual experiments. Until *after* Galileo such figures were in fact usually derived from mathematical theory.

Yet although the main development of quantification in academic medieval physics was in theory divorced from actual experiment, it would be mistaken to suppose that these philosophers were totally uninterested in the application of their theoretical analysis to the observable world and in checking it by reference to observations. Buridan, for example, continually invoked common-sense observations to illustrate his conclusions. At the same time there is evidence of a general move in practical life to quantify space, time, weight, and other aspects of the world as experienced and used. For example, by the time Henri de Vick's mechanical clock, divided into 24 equal hours, had been set up on the Palais Royale in Paris in 1370, the time of practical life was on the way to becoming the abstract mathematical time of units on a scale that belongs to the world of science. King Charles V ordered all churches in Paris to ring the hours and quarters according to the time by de Vick's clock. The division of hours into 60 minutes and of minutes into 60 seconds also came into general use in the fourteenth century. Space also became abstractly quantified. In painting, the symbolic arrangements and size of subjects according to their importance in the theological hierarchy began to give way in the fourteenth century to the division of the canvas into an abstract checkerboard according to the rules of perspective. And besides maps arranging the world symbolically round a heavenly Jerusalem, there appeared maps by cartographers in which a terrestrial traveler or mariner could find his position on an abstract system of co-ordinates of latitude and longitude. Similarly in commerce and fiscal administration, exchanges and obligations were estimated in abstract units of money and bills of exchange and regulated by standardized units of weight and measure. In theoretical academic science the relating of quantified theory to measurement could remain a matter of private, internal interest. But in practical life exact and repeatable measurements are of the essence and are consequently subject to external demand. My final set of examples will show that when a similar external demand was made from science, it likewise produced exact measurements. But since the demand was primarily practical and utilitarian in its bearing, its effect upon scientific theory was far less intimate than that of contemporary theoretical discussions.

The hypothesis that in the medieval period it was normally external practical demand rather than an internal feeling of intellectual need that led to the development and use of procedures and instruments for obtaining accurate and consistent measurements, and that such measurements were lacking when such a demand was absent, whatever the field, can be tested by means of some quantities that appear in more than one context. Consider the treatment of three such quantities, time, space and weight, in academic natural philosophy and the practical crafts.

Time was the principal practical concern of astronomy, a science belonging to the academic *quadrivium*. Until the seventeenth century, astronomy was far ahead of all other theoretical sciences in the extent to which it was accurately and systematically quantified with actual measurements. For the medieval astronomers, Ptolemy's writings provided an example not only of quantified mathematical theory and procedures but also of systematic numerical observational data. The reason for the early development of astronomy in these respects was certainly that from remote antiquity the various regular movements of heavenly bodies had provided the standard measures and divisions of time regulating practical affairs, and also that since the main divisions into the solar year and day and the lunar month are all incommensurable, their relation to each other in the mathematical calendars and systems available required periodic checking by fresh measurements.

There were two main practical problems in the middle ages: to get an accurate perpetual calendar, relating especially the lunar year used in calculating the date of Easter to the solar year; and to devise means for telling the time of day at different times of year and different latitudes by observing the elevation of the sun or some other heavenly body. From the time Bede wrote on the subject early in the eighth century, these problems taught medieval scholars to think in numbers and to measure, calculate, and check against further measurements. They created a demand for mathematical knowledge and skill and for measuring instruments. Thus Bede gave a table for use with a sundial showing the length of a 6-ft. gnomon at noon, 9 a.m., and 3 p.m. at intervals of about a fortnight throughout the year, at a latitude of 55°, corresponding to that of his monastery at Jarrow.[11] From the period when the full influence of Greek and Arabic astronomy was felt in the thirteenth century, a variety of instruments for making astronomical measurements and telling the time were manufactured and put into use in the West. The most important were the astrolabe, the quadrant, and the sundial, which were improved in various ways for greater accuracy and range. At the same time improvements were made in mathematical techniques for making numerical calculations. The "Arabic" numerals and positional arithmetic introduced in the thirteenth century came into wide use first in calendars and astronomical tables and then in commercial transactions. In both fields it had an obvious practical advantage over the Roman system. The development of modern trigonometry dates from mathematical work done in Oxford and France in the fourteenth century in connection with astronomy.

The practical demand for an accurate knowledge of time put a premium on

---

[11] See D. J. Price, in *History of Technology*, III, 595.

the precision of instruments and calculations. For observations made with the naked eye, the limit of accuracy is about 5 minutes of arc for angle-measurements, 20 seconds of time estimated by the earth's daily rotation, and 2½ degrees of terrestrial longitude estimated by means of eclipses and other methods involving lunar positions.[12] Ptolemy's mathematical astronomical theory had in most particulars reached this degree of accuracy. But an angle of 5 minutes subtends a distance of only 1 millimetre on a divided circle of 1½ metres in diameter. So to attain the precision required by the interaction of theory and measurement, instrument makers had to develop a very refined skill. Precision was achieved by the accuracy and closeness of the divisions, by making instruments large, and by paying attention to jointing and stability. There were considerable difficulties. For example, there was no method of geometrical construction for angles less than 15 degrees; below that divisions were made by eye. Yet with an ordinary thirteenth-century astrolabe the time could be told to within 2-5 minutes. The precision attained was well sufficient to enable astronomers to recognize by the end of the thirteenth century that Ptolemy's mathematical astronomy was much more accurate than Aristotle's. For example, in 1290 Guillaume of St. Cloud determined the latitude of Paris correctly as 48° 50′ and the obliquity of the ecliptic as 23° 34′, which compares well with the modern value of 23° 32′ for the obliquity at that date.

Thus the practical demands made on them forced astronomers to achieve an accuracy that enabled them to make a choice between theories on grounds of measurement. Compared with the systematic and regular method of observing introduced in the sixteenth century by Tycho Brahe, using instruments of measured degree of error, the irregular observations made by the medieval astronomers still allowed many discrepancies between theory and fact to pass undetected. But they made measurements to a degree undreamed-of in fields of contemporary academic physics that had no immediate practical applications. Demands made by such applications could lead the same scholar or group of scholars, for example, those beginning with Grosseteste who for over a century were concerned with the reform of the Julian calendar, to recognize the decisive importance of numerical measurements in a practical problem while showing no such awareness in their work in purely academic physics.

The same contrast appears in a comparison of academic treatment of space and distance, for example in discussions of motion, with the treatment given in contemporary methods of surveying, navigation, cartography, and later of gunnery. Here again practical demands forced an attention to numerical measurement and calculation and led to the development of instruments and mathematical techniques. Surveying methods were being taught in the *quadrivium* by the twelfth century, and in the whole practical quantification of space scholarly mathematics played an essential part in supplying mathematical procedures to the empirical methods of mariners, instrument makers, and other craftsmen. One example will suffice. In the sixteenth century the compass-charts or *portolani* used in navigating gave two essential pieces of information: the route to follow and the angle it must make with the North-South axis as given by a magnetized needle; and the distance to run in the direction

12 *Ibid.,* pp. 583-584

thus determined. Ideally the navigator went on a line at a constant angle from the line of the magnetized needle until he reached his destination. If this was impossible or if he went off course for a time, rudimentary trigonometrical tables, called *martelogio,* showed how to return to his original route. These seem to have been the product of scholarly mathematics. An early indication of them is given by Raymond Lull in his *Ars Magna* (1305-1308), where he wrote: "When a ship runs eight miles towards the south-east, these eight miles are equivalent to only six miles towards the east."[13] In modern terminology, $8 \cos 45° = 5.6466$. This provided for numerical measurements and calculations such as were not found in contemporary academic discussions of motion.

The quantification of weight by measurement likewise occurred only when there was a practical demand, but here this was felt almost entirely in the field of the practical crafts and not in academic science. For example, practical metallurgists wanted to be able to produce alloys of desired and repeatable properties, coins of known and honest value, and so on. The earliest physical property of metals to be quantitatively measured was density. A table dating from the eleventh or twelfth century gives a list of weights relative to wax to show the founder how much metal to melt.[14] But it was in assaying that quantitative methods based on measuring weight with a balance were most extensively developed. Ores were assayed for economic value and coins or jewelry to determine their quality and to detect fraud. The product was put through various processes, and weighing was carried out at appropriate stages with balances of various degrees of sensitivity. The most sensitive showed about 0.1 milligram.[15] There were beam-lifting devices to protect the knife-edge from shock, and in the course of time these became more accurate with further refinements, just as was happening with other scientific instruments. In quantitative factual knowledge, practical chemistry was far ahead of theory in the middle ages and remained so until the eighteenth century. The assayer excelled the alchemist in all but the desire for a systematized philosophy. But a dialogue between them and between the two sides of chemistry they represented was virtually impossible. The assayer concentrated his attention on changes in weight, the alchemist on changes in color and appearance. The former had no theory and the latter a theory based on the wrong concepts. The predicament of medieval chemistry is the most extreme case of the whole medieval scientific predicament of intellectual aspiration failing to get into communication with practical demand and so with quantified fact.

No claim could be made that this analysis is anything more than a preliminary exploration that may raise some questions for discussion and suggest some comparisons with problems of quantification in other periods and branches of science. But this I take to be the purpose of the papers prepared for this symposium. To give openings for discussion I will conclude by set-

---

[13] See Beaujouan and Poulle, *op. cit.,* pp. 106-107.
[14] See C. S. Smith and R. J. Forbes, in *History of Technology,* III, 59.
[15] *Ibid.,* p. 60.

ting out the main answers, suggested by my analysis, to the questions asked at the beginning.

1. The primary internal, intellectual need felt by medieval natural philosophers was for rational, theoretical clarification and understanding rather than for knowledge acquired through observation. This need arose in a desire to understand rationally and clarify (a) the features of cosmogony and cosmology accepted as having been revealed, and (b) the system of natural philosophy presented in the Latin translations of Aristotle and the other Greek and the Arabic philosophers and mathematicians.

2. Consequently, medieval natural philosophers discussed quantification and other problems of scientific method primarily as theoretical problems without systematic reference to actual scientific measurement. They directed their intellectual effort towards quantifying theoretical concepts and procedures, especially in response to problems arising within Aristotelian philosophy and out of its relationship with concepts and procedures presented by Greek mathematics. As a result, they made some useful progress with theoretical problems. But, although they made some measurements, their intellectual interests did not by themselves provide an intellectual need strong enough to ensure that measurements in academic science were in fact accurate and that decisions between different theoretical principles or concepts were always made on grounds of actual measurements.

3. This theoretical emphasis in intellectual interests was supported and maintained by the aims, content, and methods of the education provided by the medieval universities, where the basis of both the arts course and of the higher courses in theology, law, and medicine was the making of a critical study and commentary on theoretical problems raised by standard texts.

4. Departure from this purely theoretical emphasis occurred only when there was a strong external, practical demand for exact measurements. When this was present, theoretical concepts and procedures became quantified in such a way that measurement was applicable, accurate measurements were made and used to test and decide between different theories, and instruments were developed to get increasing precision. The effect of such external, practical pressure appears in both theoretical science and the practical crafts, and in the work of both scholars and craftsmen, but because of its strongly practical, utilitarian character it did not have a profound influence on the accepted theoretical concepts of physics. Medieval academic science and medieval technology were in fact two almost completely independent monologues.

5. Thus there was in medieval physics a very incomplete dialogue between theoretical concepts and procedures on the one hand, and practical quantifying procedures in contact with the data of observation on the other. As a result, medieval physics never escaped from its Aristotelian framework. Interesting quantified procedures and conclusions were formulated within these general limits, and some of these were taken over into seventeenth-century physics, but the framework of physics as a whole was never completely rethought and reconstructed by the medieval philosophers.

6. The establishment of a complete dialogue between quantified theory and quantified theoretical and experimental procedures, between *episteme* and *techne,* is one of the principal changes that occurred in the seventeenth century. Systematic measurement became the procedure both for collecting exact data and for testing theories or challenging whole systems of theory. As this complete dialogue developed it was both felt as an internal, intellectual need and also demanded by external, practical pressure. Thus it became an intellectual and practical requirement for the new scientific profession that grew up with aims that had important differences from those of the medieval scholars. Intellectual, professional, and practical pressures all now demanded a quantified study of nature and not simply of theory.

7. This case history of medieval physics seems to suggest certain analogies in other fields and periods in the history of science, which seems to be an especially suitable subject for the comparative method of analysis.

Further references: G. Beaujouan, *L'intérdependance entre la science scolastique et les techniques utilitaires (xiie, xiiie et xive siècles)* (Paris, 1957), "Motives and opportunities for science in the medieval universities" in *Scientific Change*, ed. A. C. Crombie (London, 1963) 219-36, "Reflexions sur les rapports entre théorie et pratique au moyen âge" in *The Cultural Context of Medieval Science*, ed. J. E. Murdoch and E. D. Sylla (Dordrecht, 1975) 437-84; W. Bergmann, "Innovation im Quadrivium des 10. und 11. Jahrhunderts", *Sudhoffs Archiv*, Beiheft xxvi (1975); B. Gille, "Les développements technologiques en Europe de 1100 à 1400", *Cahiers d'histoire mondiale*, iii (1956) 63-108, *Esprit et civilisation technique au moyen âge* (Paris, 1957), "Le moyen âge en occident" in *Histoire générale des techniques*, publiée sous la direction de M. Daumas, i (Paris, 1962) 431-598, "Les xve et xvie siècles en occident", ii (1965) 7-139, *Histoire des techniques*, pub. sous la direction de B. Gille (Paris, 1978); J. Gimpel, *The Medieval Machine* (London, 1988); D. S. Landes, *Revolution in Time* (Cambridge, Mass., 1983); J. Le Goff, *Pour une autre moyen âge* (Paris, 1977); F. R. Maddison, "Early astronomical and mathematical instruments", *History of Science*, ii (1963) 17-50, "Medieval scientific instruments", *Rivista da Universidade de Coimbra*, xxiv (1969) 3-60; J. D. North, *Richard of Wallingford* (Oxford, 1976), *Chaucer's Universe* (Oxford, 1988), *The Universal Frame* (London, 1989), *Stars, Minds and Fate* (London, 1989); N. Pevsner, "The term 'architect' in the middle ages", *Speculum*, xvii (1942) 549-62; E. Poulle, *Les instruments astronomiques du moyen âge* (Paris, 1983); P. Sternagel, *Die artes mecanicae im Mittelalter* (Regensburg, 1966); L. White jr., *Medieval Technology and Social Change* (Oxford, 1962), *Medieval Religion and Technology* (Berkeley & Los Angeles, 1986); see also chs. 3 p. 71, 5 p. 114, 6 p. 137, 7 p. 160, 9.

AVICENNA'S INFLUENCE ON THE MEDIEVAL
SCIENTIFIC TRADITION

"Aristotle . . . purged away the errors of preceding philosophers, and enlarged philosophy, aspiring to that full measure of this subject possessed by the ancient patriarchs, although he was not able to perfect each of its parts. For his successors have corrected him in some particulars, and have added many things to his works, and additions will continue to be made until the end of the world, because there is no perfection in human discoveries. . . . But the larger portion of the philosophy of Aristotle received little attention either on account of the concealment of the copies of his work and their rarity, or on account of their difficulty, or unpopularity, or on account of the wars in the East, till after the time of Mahomet, when Avicenna and Averroes and others recalled it to the light of full exposition. Although some of his works on logic and certain others have been translated from Greek by Boethius, yet from the time of Michael Scot, whose translations with authentic expositions of certain parts of Aristotle's works on nature and metaphysics appeared in the year of our Lord 1230, the philosophy of Aristotle has grown in importance among the Latins. But in comparison with the vastness of his wisdom contained in a thousand books, only a very small portion up to the present time has been translated into Latin, and still less is in common use among students. Avicenna in particular, the imitator and expositor of Aristotle, and the man who completed philosophy as far as it was possible for him to do so, composed a threefold volume on philosophy . . . The Latins have the first in certain parts . . ., that is the book of *Sufficiency*. After him came Averroes, a man of sound wisdom, . . . though he must be corrected in some particulars and completed in many others."[1]

THIS passage from the brief history of philosophy which Roger Bacon included in 1266-7 in his *Opus Maius* neatly places Avicenna in the Western scientific tradition. He was the first of the two great Arabic Commentators whose exposition and

[1] Roger Bacon, *Opus Majus*, II, 13, ed. J. H. Bridges, Oxford, 1897, I ; English trans. by R. B. Burke, Philadelphia, 1928, I, 63.

extension of Aristotle's thought helped to bring about the first phase of the Scientific Revolution, which effectively began in the 13th century, and without which the dramatic progress of the second, 17th-century phase would have been utterly impossible. My purpose in this paper will be to draw attention to some of the more important lines of original research to which the Latin translations of Avicenna's writings gave rise ; in other words, to try to estimate his influence in that process of bringing the natural world within the grasp of our understanding and of our use which is the dominant characteristic of the civilisation that has grown up in the West since the 12th century.

In a famous passage, Whitehead characterised " the novelty of our present society " by the " union of passionate interest in the detailed facts with equal devotion to abstract generalisation ", by the marriage of the interests of " practical men " with those of " men of philosophic temperament ".[2] By the mid-12th century, when the first of Avicenna's writings were put into Latin, this marriage of interests was already becoming apparent, and it helps to explain the passionate interest in the recovery of the scientific learning of the Greeks and Arabs that dominated the intellectual life of that period.

After the collapse of the Roman Empire in the West, almost all that remained to the Latin world of the brilliant achievements of Greek science was Pliny's encyclopædia, bearing in every chapter and phrase the marks of its composition by a civil servant, and Boethius' translations and elementary treatises on logic and mathematics. In contrast with this meagre intellectual equipment, which put any original science out of the question until the 12th-century translators had' done their work, the period following the barbaric invasions showed a degree of technical activity and invention which is one of the most remarkable ever seen.[3] If modest by modern standards, the achievements of the period between about 800 and 1200 already in some directions surpassed anything done in the Classical world, and they were to go on with increasing

---

[2] A. N. Whitehead, *Science and the Modern World*, Cambridge, 1926, ch. 1.
[3] See Lefebvre des Noëttes, " La ' Nuit ' du Moyen Age et son Inventaire ", *Mercure de France* (Paris), CCXXXV (1932), 572 *sqq.* ; Lynn White, Jr., " Technology and invention in the Middle Ages ", *Speculum* (Cambridge, Mass.), XV (1940), 141 *sqq.* ; A. C. Crombie, *Augustine to Galileo*, London, 1959, 1979.

speed to produce the technological age in which we now live.

Of the outstanding technical achievements of these first centuries, down to the time when the translation of the bulk of the known corpus of Greek and Arabic scientific writings, including those of Avicenna, was nearing completion, I may perhaps mention, for example, the wheeled plough and the new methods of harnessing draft animals, the new methods of building, the beginnings of the mechanisation of industry by the use of driving-wheels worked by wind or water, the progress of chemistry and metallurgy seen in glass making, distilling and bell founding, and the beginnings, however crude they may appear to us, of an improvement in methods of surgery and the diagnosis of disease.

For the history of science, the most important result of this technological activity was that it produced in men of learning a mentality interested in finding exact experimental answers to practical questions, and so predisposed them to temper their " devotion to abstract generalisation " by observation and measurement. For example, as early as the 7th century Bede wrote what is still one of the best elementary treatises on the calendar.[4] The need for an accurate calendar to determine the date of Easter was the chief reason for the early interest taken in astronomy and we find Canute, Earl Harold and William the Conqueror all importing astronomers and mathematicians from the new scientific centre of Lotharingia.[5] Among the earliest Arabic writings to be translated into Latin were treatises on the astrolabe and, in fact, a large proportion of the translations made before 1200 were of writings on astronomy, the abacus, the new Hindu arithmetic, chemistry, medicine, and other practical subjects.[6] In the 12th century this practical tendency began to affect the teaching of the seven liberal arts. We find, for example in the *Didascalicon*

[4] Bedae *Opera de Temporibus*, ed. C. W. Jones, Cambridge (Mass.), 1943.
[5] M. C. Welborne, " Lotharingia as a center of Arabic and scientific influence ", *Isis* (Cambridge, Mass.), XVI (1931), 188 *sqq.*
[6] C. H. Haskins, *Studies in the History of Mediaeval Science*, 2nd ed., Cambridge (Mass.), 1927 ; A. van der Vyver, " Les premières traductions latines (10e–11e siècles) de traités arabes sur l'astrolabe ", I*er Congrès International de Géographie Historique, Bruxelles*, 1931, *Mémoires*, II, 266 *sqq.*, " Les plus anciennes traductions latines médiévales (10e–11e siècles) de traités d'astronomie et d'astrologie ", *Osiris* (Cambridge, Mass.), I (1936), 658 *sqq.*, " L'évolution scientifique du haut moyen âge ", *Archeion* (Roma), XIX (1937), 12 *sqq.*

of Hugh of St. Victor,[7] the *Heptateuchon* of Thierry of Chartres[8] and a list of textbooks in use in Paris as given in a Caius MS,[9] that the mathematical subjects of the *quadrivium* were being extended and specialised to include various kinds of technical knowledge, and that newly-translated works on medicine also were given a prominent place in the curriculum.

In the 12th century we can see the time when the begetting of modern science by philosophy out of technology became a possibility, the time when " men of philosophic temperament " began to turn away from the vision, given them by St. Augustine, of the natural world as a symbol of another, spiritual world, and to see it as a world of " natural causes " open to investigation by observation and hypothesis. What made this new scientific vision possible was the new logical and mathematical equipment and the new systems of scientific explanations provided by the translators of the Greek and Arabic scientific writings. Of these, by far the most important in determining how this vision was to be exploited were Aristotle's " new logic " and physical works, together with works by Euclid, Ptolemy and Galen and by the principal Arabic commentators. Of the last, as Roger Bacon has told us, the first was Avicenna.

Avicenna's principal contributions to science are contained in the Kitab al-Shifa, or *Book of the Remedy*, an encyclopædic commentary on the works of Aristotle, and in the *Canon of Medicine*, an encyclopædia of medicine based principally on the writings of Galen, though including also the work of other Greek and Arabic doctors. The first of Avicenna's writings to appear in Latin was a partial translation of the *Kitab al-Shifa* made in Toledo during the second quarter of the 12th century. Toledo had been reconquered from the Muslims in 1085 by Alfonso VI of Castile and, some half-century later, Raymond, first Archbishop of Toledo, set up there a school of translation

[7] Ed. J. P. Migne, *Patrologia Latina*, CLXXVI, Paris, 1854 , and C. H. Buttimer, Washington (D.C.), 1939, trans. J. Taylor (New York, 1961).

[8] A. Clerval, " L'enseignement des arts libéraux à Chartres et à Paris dans la première moitié du XIIᵉ siècle d'après l'Heptateucon de Thierry de Chartres ", *Congrès scientifique international des Catholiques, Paris, 1888*, Paris, 1889, II, 277.

[9] *Sacerdos ad altare accessurus*, Cambridge MS Gonville and Caius 385 (605), 13 c., ff. 7–61 ; see Haskins, *op. cit.*, pp. 356 *sqq.*

which became the most famous in all Christendom. It seems that, in their intellectual relations with the Muslims left in the newly occupied territories, the Christian conquerors had not only betrayed some of that bluffness of manner expected from the military mind, but had also stooped to the most vulgar propaganda against Islam.[10] Raymond wanted to substitute for this an apostolate of the intellect, the first stage of which was to read and master Mohammedan thought. Books were brought north from Cordova where, it is interesting to recall, the last great Arabic commentator, Averroes, was born in the year Raymond became archbishop of Toledo, 1126. Within a short time the Toledo school had established relations with Chartres, and soon its translations were providing the whole of Western Christendom with entirely new intellectual horizons.

Scientifically the most important of the first sections of the *Kitab al-Shifa* to appear in Latin were the commentaries on Aristotle's logic, on *De Anima* and on the *Physics*, the so-called *Sufficientia Physicorum* referred to by Roger Bacon. These sections were translated by the Archdeacon of Segovia Dominicus Gundissalinus, in collaboration with a converted Spanish Jew, John of Spain or Ibn Daud.[11] The latter has left an account of how the collaboration was made: " I in a loud voice put the [Arabic] text into the vulgar tongue [Castilian], and the Archdeacon translated each phrase separately into Latin."[12] This phonetic method, in which the original had to pass into the language of the translation through an intermediate language, had its drawbacks and was to be severely criticised by Roger Bacon[13] and others in the 13th century. Even when the translation was made by a scholar who knew and read both Arabic and Latin, as with other sections of the *Kitab al-Shifa* and the *Canon of Medicine*, the result was often excessively literal. Of the remaining sections of the former work, part of the commentary on the *Meteorology* was translated and paraphrased about 1200 by an Englishman,

[10] G. Théry, " Notes indicatrices pour s'orienter dans l'étude des traductions médiévales ", in *Mélanges Joseph Maréchal*, Bruxelles, 1950, II, 305 *sqq.*
[11] H. Bédoret, " Les premières versions tolédans de philoscphie. Oeuvres d'Avicenne ", *Revue Néoscolastique* (Louvain), XLI (1938), 374 *sqq.*
[12] Théry, *op. cit.*, p. 310.
[13] See C. B. Vandewalle, *Roger Bacon dans l'Histoire de la Philologie*, Paris, 1929.

Alfred of Sareshel, under the title *De Mineralibus*,[14] and the commentary on *De Animalibus* was translated about 1230 by Michael Scot while he was at the court of the Emperor Frederick II in Sicily.[15] A complete translation of the *Canon of Medicine* was made at Toledo before 1187 by Gerard of Cremona.[16]

Of the lines along which Avicenna's writings assisted the exploitation of the new science provided by the whole corpus of translations from Greek and Arabic, the first to be noted is the process by which the logical method of forming definitions was related to experimental procedure.[17] Broadly speaking, in the Greek and Arabic science which grew up within the framework of Aristotle's philosophy, an event was held to be explained when it was shown to be the product of the nature of some substance. The task of the investigator was therefore to define the different " natures " found in the world and to distinguish one from another, rather in the same way as in a modern elementary text-book of inorganic chemistry different substances are defined and distinguished by the enumeration of characteristic properties. Quite apart from any other limitations, this Greek conception of explanation kept too close to the model of geometry, in which, for example, the fact that the three internal angles of a triangle added up to two right angles could be shown to follow from the definition of a triangle, but that definition itself, once grasped, required no further investigation. The principal contribution of 13th-century Christendom to scientific method was to convert this search for " natures " into an inductive and experimental procedure for isolating the conditions necessary and sufficient to produce a given event. The experimental argument developed by logicians and natural philosophers from the 13th century was

[14] M. Alonso Alonso, "Homenaje a Avicenna e su milenario. Las traducciones de Juan González de Burgos y Salomón", *Al-Andalus* (Madrid), XIV (1949), 291 *sqq.* ; Avicennae *De Congelatione et Conglutinatione Lapidum, being sections of the Kitab al-Schifa.* The Latin and Arabic texts ed. with Engl. trans. of latter by E. J. Holmyard and D. C. Mandeville, Paris, 1927 ; A. Mieli, *La Science Arabe*, Leyden, 1938, pp. 104 *sqq.*

[15] Haskins, *op. cit.*, p. 261 ; G. Lacombe, *Aristoteles Latinus*, Roma, 1939, p. 81 ; G. Sarton, *Introduction to the History of Science*, Baltimore, 1931, II 579 *sqq.*

[16] Sarton, *op. cit.* II, 343.

[17] In this paper I have not discussed aspects of Avicenna's work which seem to have had no influence on the Latin world ; see Sarton, *op. cit.* I, 709 *sqq.*

something original in the history of science, and it must be ranked, along with the Greek idea of geometrical proof and the mathematics of motion perfected in the 17th century, as one of the three great methodological inventions that made modern science possible.

The classical writer, apart from Aristotle, who had the most concern for induction was Galen, and Avicenna, inspired by Galen,[18] made his contribution to the experimental method in his *Canon of Medicine*. At the beginning of the section on drugs, which is itself of considerable pharmacological and botanical interest,[19] he laid down seven rules defining the conditions for a reliable experimental investigation of the causes of the effects of drugs administered to cure diseases in man. In effect, he was trying to relate the effects of drugs to their chemical constitution as this was then understood: that is, to the proportions of the four primary qualities which they possessed. It was thought, for example, that a drug which reduced the excess of heat in a fevered person must have a cold nature. Avicenna's rules may be summarised as follows[20]:

[18] *Cf.* the important, recently discovered text, known only in the Arabic version : Galen, *On Medical Experience*, ed. with Engl. trans. by R. Walzer, Oxford, 1944.
[19] E. Kremers and G. Udang, *History of Pharmacy*, Philadelphia, 1940, pp. 19 *sqq*; E. H. F. Meyer, *Geschichte der Botanik*, Königsberg, 1856, III, 201-3.
[20] The Latin trans. is worth quoting *in extenso* : " Medicinarum cognoscuntur virtutes ex duabus viis, una earum est semita experimenti, et altera est ratiocinationis semita. Nos vero in experimento sermonem praemittamus. Dicimus ergo, quod experimentum ad cognitionem virtutis medicinae cum fiducia non perducit, nisi post observationem septem conditionum. Una earum est, ut sit medicina vacua a qualitate acquisita ex caliditate accidentali, aut a frigiditate accidentali, aut qualitate, quae accidat ei cum alteratione in sua substantia, aut vicinitate alterius. Aqua enim quamvis frigida sit natura, tamen quum calefit, calefacit, dum permanet calida. . . . Et secunda est ut illud, in quo experitur, aegritudinem habeat singularem, nam si aegritudo est composita, et in ea sunt duae res significantes duas curationes contrarias et experiatur in ambobus medicina, et conferat, nescimus causam in illo vere. Verbi gratia, quum homo habet febrem phlegmaticam et datur ei in potu agaricus et removetur febris eius, non oportet ut iudicemus agaricum esse frigidum, quoniam confert aegritudini calidae, quae est febris ; immo forsitan non confert, nisi propterea quod resolvit materiam phlegmaticam et evacuat eandem, et quum deficit materia removetur febris phlegmatica. Et hoc quidem vere est iuvamentum per se, permistum iuvamento per accidens, per se quidem cum comparatione ad materiam, sed per accidens cum comparatione ad febrem. Et tertia est ut medicina sit experta iam in [duobus] contrariis, ita ut quum utrique eorum simul conferat, non iudicetur, quod sit contraria complexioni alicuius eorum, et fortasse confert uni eorum per se, et alteri per accidens, sicut scamonea, si experiamur ipsam in aegritudine frigida, non est longinquum quin conferat, et calefaciat. Et quum experimur ipsam in aegritudine calida, sicut est febris tertiana, non elongatur quin

1. The drug must be free from any extraneous, accidental quality; for example, we must not test the effect of water when it is heated, but wait until it has cooled down.

2. The experimentation must be done with a simple and not a composite disease, for in the second case it would be impossible to infer from the cure what was the curing cause in the drug.

3. The drug must be tested with two contrary types of disease, because sometimes a drug cured one disease by its essential qualities and another by its accidental ones. It could

conferat in evacuando choleram. Quum ergo ita sit, non acquirit nobis experimentum fiduciam caliditatis, aut frigiditatis, nisi postquam scimus quod unam duarum rerum efficit per se, et efficit alteram per accidens. Et quarta est ut sit virtus, quae est in medicina opposita ei, quod aequatur ei de potentia aegritudinis. Sunt enim medicinae quaedam, quarum caliditas minoratur a frigiditate aegritudinis alicuius, quare penitus in eam non agit. Et quandoque, quum administratur in infrigidatione aliqua leviore illa, facit calefactionem. Oportet ergo ut experiatur prius in debiliori, et secundum gradus fiat processio paulatim, donec sciatur virtus medicinae, non dubitetur. Et quinque est ut observetur tempus, in quo apparet eius impressio, et operatio, nam si in primis, quum administratur, apparet, confidere facit quod efficit illud per se. Et si fuerit operatio quae in primis apparet ex ea, contraria ei, quae apparet in fine aut in principio rei non apparet ex ea operatio, deinde in fine rei apparet ex ea operatio; tunc erit locus ambiguitatis, et dubietatis; forsitan enim efficit illud, quod operatur per accidens, quando efficit in primis operationem occultam, quam sequitur per accidens haec operatio alia apparens; et haec quidem dubietas est, et ambiguitas, et haesitatio in virtute medicinae. Existimatio vero, quod eius operatio non sit, nisi per accidens, quandoque vigoratur, quum eius operatio non apparet, nisi post separationem obviationis membri; nam si per se efficeret, operaretur dum obviaret; impossibile enim est ut deficiat dum obviat, et operetur dum non obviat, et hoc quidem est iudicium plurimum sufficiens. Quandoque vero conveniens est, ut in quibusdam corporibus efficiat suam operationem, quae est per se, post operationem suam, quae est per accidens, et illud est quum iam aquisierit virtutem extraneam vincentem virtutem naturalem, sicut aqua calida; in praesenti enim calefacit, in die vero secundo, aut in hora, in qua removetur ab ea eius impressio accidentalis, facit pervenire in corpore frigus, procul dubio propter conversionem partium [perviarum] ad dispositionem naturalem frigoris, quod debet habere. Et sexta est, ut observetur processus operationis eius secundum assiduationem, aut secundum plurimum; nam si non fuerit ita, tunc processio operationis ab ea est per accidens; quoniam res naturales procedunt a principiis suis, aut semper, aut secundum plurimum. Et septima quidem est, ut experimentum sit in corpore hominis. Nam si experiatur in corpore non hominis, possibile est, ut fallat duobus modis. Unus eorum est, quoniam possibile est, ut sit medicina comparata ad corpus hominis calida, et comparata ad corpus leonis, et equi frigida, quum haec medicina est calidior homine, et frigidior equo, vel leone. . . . Et secundus, quoniam quandoque comparata ad unum duorum corporum habet proprietatem, quam non habet comparata ad corpus secundum. . . . Isti ergo sunt canones, quos observare oportet in cognitione virtutum medicinarum ex via experimenti." (Avicennae *Canon Medicinae*, II. i. 2, Venetiis, 1608, I, 245–6). He went on to speak of the *via rationis*, which depended on the theory of the four qualities and elements (ibid., c. 3, p. 247). For similar conditions described in the second half of the 13th century by Petrus Hispanus and Jean de Saint Amand, see L. Thorndike, *A History of Magic and Experimental Science*, New York, 1923, II, 508–13.

not be inferred, simply from the fact that it cured a certain type of disease, that a drug necessarily had a given quality.

4. The quality of the drug must correspond to the strength of the disease. For example, there were some drugs whose " heat " was less than the " coldness " of certain diseases, so that they would have no effect on them. The experiment should therefore be done first with a weaker type of disease, then with diseases of gradually increasing strength.

5. The time of action must be observed, so that essence and accident are not confused. For example, heated water might temporarily have a heating effect because of an acquired extraneous accident, but after a time it would return to its cold nature.

6. The effect of the drug must be seen to occur constantly or in many cases, for if this did not happen it was an accidental effect.

7. The experimentation must be done with the human body, for testing a drug on a lion or a horse might not prove anything about its effect on man.

Passing over the work of the 13th-century writers, particularly in Oxford,[21] on the logic of experimental investigation and the outstanding practical studies made at the same time in zoology, magnetics, optics[22] and other sciences, I will quote a passage from William of Ockham to show how Avicenna's rules had become refined by more than a century's experience. This passage is in effect the first expression of what J. S. Mill was to call the Method of Agreement and Difference, and it is worth mentioning that this method was explicitly used in a contemporary 14th-century experimental study of the cause of the rainbow.[23] Ockham wrote :

" This is sufficient for anything being the immediate cause, namely, that when it is present the effect follows and when not present, all other conditions being the same, the effect does not follow. . . . That this is sufficient for anything to be the immediate cause of anything else is clear, because if not there is no way of knowing that anything

[21] See A. C. Crombie, *Robert Grosseteste and the Origins of Experimental Science*, Oxford (1953, 1971).

[22] See Crombie, *op. cit.*, and *Augustine to Galileo*.

[23] Thimonis *Super Quatuor Libros Metheororum*, III. 14, Venetiis, 1522, f. 117ᵛ.

is the immediate cause of anything else. . . . All causes properly so-called are immediate causes."[24]

The *Canon of Medicine* was by far the most popular of Avicenna's writings, and both in the Arabic and Latin worlds he was known not only as a philosopher and scientist, but also as the prince of physicians. It was between the two greatest doctors of antiquity that Dante placed him in Limbo along with other noble souls who had not received the Christian revelation :

> " Euclide geomètra e Tolomeo,
> Ipocrate, Avicenna e Galïeno,
> Averroìs, che'l gran comento feo."[25]

Chaucer included him among the authorities used by his " Doctour of Physic " :

> " Wel knew he the olde Esculapius
> And Deyscorides, and eek Rufus,
> Olde Ypocras, Haly and Galyen,
> Serapion, Razis and Avycen,
> Averrois, Damascien and Constantyn,
> Bernard and Gatisden and Gilbertyn."[26]

In the *Canon* Avicenna codified the whole of ancient and Arabic medical knowledge as he knew it, for example basing his account of anatomy and physiology largely on Galen and the botanical section on Dioscorides.[27] Thus his book remained the most popular medical text-book for six centuries, and this perhaps has obscured the value of the many important and methodical observations that it contains. Of particular interest are the clinical observations on diseases of all kinds, from skin troubles and diseases of the lungs to disorders of the nervous system and types of insanity. I will quote two passages : they show an order of mind which, in the lesser

[24] Magistri Guilielmi di Ockam. . . . *Super Quattuor Libros Sententiarum,* I. xlv, q. 1, D, Lugduni, 1495, ed. Gal et al, as ch. 3 above.

[25] *Inferno,* IV, ll. 142 *sqq.*

[26] *Canterbury Tales,* Prologue, ll. 429 *sqq.*

[27] For Avicenna's position in the history of Arabic medicine, see L. Leclerc, *Histoire de la Médecine Arabe,* Paris, 1876, I ; E. G. Browne, *Arabian Medicine,* Cambridge, 1921 ; C. L. Elgood, *A Medical History of Persia and the Eastern Caliphate,* Cambridge, 1951. See also the text in P. de Konig, *Trois Traités d'Anatomie Arabe,* Leiden, 1903.

men who were influenced by Avicenna, no doubt became a substitute for observation, but without which observations by themselves are practically useless. The first passage is headed:

"*The signs of disease.* 1. Some signs are characteristic of diseases—thus : rapid pulse-rate, in fever, itself indicates fever. 2. Other signs indicate the *position* of the disease. Thus a hard pulse denotes diaphragmatic pleurisy ; undulant pulse denotes inflammation in the substance of the lung. 3. Other signs indicate the *cause* of the disease. For instance, the signs of plethora, or of depraved states in their various forms.

" 4. Some symptoms are essential to the illness, as they begin and end with it. (For instance, acute fever, piercing pain, difficult breathing, cough and serrine pulse—essential to pleurisy.) Other symptoms show no time-relation of this kind ; they sometimes coincide with the disease and sometimes not (e.g. headache in fever). Other symptoms appear only towards the close of the illness—as for instance, the symptoms of crisis, of maturation, of delayed maturation ; the signs of death. These symptoms are often associated rather with acute illness.

" 5. Other symptoms concern the state of the members. Some of them are discernible by the special senses—colour, hardness, softness, heat, cold, and the like. Others are discernible by all senses together—the form of the member, its position (posture, attitude), its size, its movements or stillness. Some symptoms point to an interior state, as when tremor of the lower lip reveals nausea. Changes in measure and number reveal internal states ; for instance, shortness of fingers denotes small liver.

" 6. Morbid states are discernible by the special senses. Thus a black or yellow colour of the excrement reveals a morbid state. Black or yellow jaundice of the whole body reveals an obstruction in the biliary passages.

" 7. States manifested to the sense of hearing.—Belching reveals an upset stomach and defective digestive power.

" 8. Odours and tastes also enable one to recognise morbid states.

" 9. Other visible evidences ; curved nails denote ulceration of the bronchi, pulmonary tuberculosis and ' hectic '. Redness of the cheek-bones suggests inflammatory deposit in the lung."[28]

[28] Quoted, with alterations, from O. Cameron Gruner, *A Treatise on the Canon of Medicine of Avicenna, incorporating a translation of the first book,* London, 1930, pp. 258-9 (*Canon Medicinae,* I. ii. iii. 1, Venetiis, 1608, I, 130).

The second passage is headed :

> " *Transmission of disease from person to person.*
> " A.—*Transmission by infection.* (i) From one house
> to an adjoining one. Here belong lepra, scabies, variola,
> pestilential fever, septic inflammatory swellings and ulcers;
> (ii) from a house in the wind-track to another ; (iii) when
> one person gazes closely at another (e.g. ophthalmia) ;
> (iv) fancy : e.g. when a person's teeth chatter because he
> thinks of something sour ; (v) such diseases as pulmonary
> tuberculosis, impetigo, leprosy.
> " B.—*Hereditary transmission.* Vitiligo alba ; prema-
> ture baldness ; gout ; pulmonary tuberculosis ; lepra.
> " C. *Racial* transmission.
> " D.—*Endemic* transmission. The sweating sickness of
> Anglia ; elephantiasis in Alexandria ; aurigo in Apulia ;
> endemic goitre, and many the like."[29]

Another passage on types of pain certainly does show some
of the dangers of too much devotion to classification. In this
Avicenna distinguished fifteen varieties of pain : boring, com-
pressing, corrosive, dull, fatigue, heavy, incisive, irritant, itch-
ing, pricking, relaxing, stabbing, tearing, tension, throbbing.[30]

In the West, the *Canon* first began to have an influence from
the end of the 12th century, when it helped to produce a
branching out of surgery with Roger of Salerno, Roland of
Parma, and other members of the Salerno school.[31] In fact,
the translation of the *Canon* put the whole of Western medicine
on a new footing, although its influence was not always good.
For example, it advocated the theory that wounds should not
be cleaned but left to " suppurate ",[32] and it supported the
tendency to regard surgery as an inferior branch of medicine,
fit work for unlettered barbers and cutters for the stone. Both
these points were severely attacked by certain Western doctors at the end of the 13th century,[33] but unfortunately they

[29] Gruner, *op. cit.* p. 171 (*Canon*, I. ii. i. 8, I, 95).
[30] Gruner, *op. cit.* p. 249 (*Canon*, I. ii. ii. 20, I, 127).
[31] See D. Campbell, *Arabian Medicine and its Influence on the Middle Ages*, London, 1926, I, 124 *sqq.* ; C. Singer, *The Evolution of Anatomy*, London, 1925, p. 68.
[32] *Canon*, IV. iv. i. 3, II, 140.
[33] *E.g.* by Henri de Mondeville : see Sir T. C. Allbutt, *The Historical Relations of Medicine and Surgery to the End of the Sixteenth Century*, London, 1905, pp. 37 *sqq.* ; J. J. Walsh, *Medieval Medicine*, London, 1920, pp. 116 *sqq.* ; Sarton, *Introduction*, III, 865–73.

continued to find advocates for another three hundred years. At the end of that period the *Canon* was issued in many printed editions in Latin, fifteen during the last thirty years of the 15th century and a further twenty during the 16th century. Several more were printed in the 17th century.[34]

The complicated influence of so universal a work, acting over so long a period on so chancy an art as medicine cannot be stated in a few sentences. I would merely point out that although even the hours wasted in a National Health waiting-room might seem well spent in comparison with what would probably be the result of spending the same period in a 14th-century surgery, nevertheless, we find by that time, in medicine, the same spirit of enterprise and innovation as we find in the other practical arts on the borders of science, and in science itself. For example, 14th-century physicians made accurate diagnostic descriptions of a large number of common diseases, including bubonic and pneumonic plague, diphtheria, leprosy, rabies, diabetes, gout, cancer and epilepsy[35]; they advanced a theory of infection by " traces " left by the diseased person and introduced the practice of quarantine[36]; they extended the use of such metallic drugs as mercury and of opium and other mild anæsthetics[37]; they mastered such difficult operations as those for hernia and cataract[38]; and they filled teeth with gold leaf[39] and prescribed spectacles for defective sight.[40]

To the experimental spirit that produced these results the general emphasis of Avicenna's teaching undoubtedly con-

[34] Max Meyerhof, " Science and medicine ", in *Legacy of Islam*, ed. Sir Thomas Arnold and A. Guillaume, Oxford, 1931, pp. 329–30 ; Sarton, *Introduction*, I, 711.

[35] See Walsh, *op. cit.* pp. 80 *sqq.*, 128 *sqq.*; P. Diepgen, " Die Bedeutung des Mittelalters für den Fortschritt in der Medizin ", in *Essays on the History of Medicine Presented to Karl Sudhoff*, ed. C. J. Singer and H. E. Sigerist, Oxford and Zürich, 1924, pp. 109–10 ; Sarton, *Introduction*, III, 271 *sqq.*, 881 *sqq.*, 1651–68, 1683, 1691, 1703.

[36] A. M. Campbell, *The Black Death and Men of Learning*, New York, 1931, pp. 56–63, 112 *sqq.*; Diepgen, *op. cit.* pp. 111–2.

[37] Walsh, *op. cit.* pp. 96 *sqq.*, 120 *sqq*; Diepgen, *op. cit.* pp. 114–5 ; Guthrie, *A History of Medicine*, Edinburgh, 1945, pp. 107–8 ; Sarton, *Introduction*, III, 883.

[38] Allbutt, *op. cit.* pp. 73 *sqq.*; Guthrie, *op. cit.* p. 124 ; Sarton, *Introduction*, III, 844, 1235.

[39] Walsh, *op. cit.* pp. 138 *sqq.*

[40] For bibliography, see : Sarton, *Introduction*, II, 1024 *sqq.*, 1040 ; III, 873 *sqq.*, 1199, 1235, 1708 ; chapter 9 below.

tributed, and in two important physiological investigations his influence can be more specifically indentified. The first was that which led to the formulation of the theory of the circulation of the blood. Avicenna himself had simply accepted Galen's theory that the blood and " spirits " ebbed and flowed between the respective halves of the heart and the veins and arteries, a connection between the venous and arterial systems being established through pores supposed to pass through the interventricular septum.[41] In the 13th century Avicenna's account of this theory was criticised in a commentary on the *Canon* by an Egyptian physician, Ala al-Din Ibn al-Nafis, who asserted that these pores did not exist and that the blood passed from the right to the left sides of the heart via the lungs. This theory, the first statement of the theory of the lesser or pulmonary circulation, Ibn al-Nafis advanced on purely logical grounds ; for example, if such pores did exist the blood in the left side of the heart would not be able to remain pure.[42] In fact, one of his biographers said he was better at theory than as a practitioner and told a story which illustrates his method of work :

> " The Master Ala ad-Din once went to the public bath which is situated at Bab az-Zuhuma. While he was washing himself he went suddenly to the dressing-room of the bath, asked for ink, pens and paper and wrote down a treatise on the pulse from beginning to end. Thereupon, he returned to the bath and finished his ablutions.
> " It is told that he once said : ' If I did not know that my works will last for ten thousand years after me, I should not have written them.' But the responsibility for this must be assumed by the man who related it about him. In sum, he was a great *Imam* and many excellent men said: ' He is a second Ibn Sina.' "[43]

The theory of the pulmonary circulation seems to have been forgotten until the 16th century. Ibn al-Nafis' commentary was first published in the West in a Latin edition of Avicenna's *Canon* which appeared at Venice in 1547, though the section on the pulmonary circulation was omitted. A few years

---

[41] *Canon*, III. xi. i. 1, I, 669–70.

[42] M. Meyerhof, " Ibn Al-Nafis (XIIIth century) and his theory of the lesser circulation ", *Isis*, XXIII (1935), 116–7.

[43] *Ibid*. p. 109.

later this theory was published by a Spaniard, Miguel Serveto (1553), and by a pupil of Vesalius, the Paduan physiologist Realdo Colombo (1559), who supported it by experiments. There is at present no evidence that either of these two writers knew of Ibn al-Nafis' manuscripts.[44] Whether they did or not, this Egyptian commentator on Avicenna's *Canon* was the first to state the theory which Harvey was to generalise into his theory of the general circulation of the blood, thereby laying the foundations of modern physiology.

The second physiological investigation stimulated by Avicenna was into the nature of vision. Different Greek writers had argued the point whether vision was effected by rays going forth from the eye and making contact with the object seen, or by light entering the eye after coming from the object.[45] In his *De Anima* Avicenna rejected the theory that material rays went forth from the eye and asserted that objects were seen by light entering the eye ; but he said that a sort of psychological act of looking went forth from the eye.[46] This distinction was taken up by Robert Grosseteste[47] and Roger Bacon [48], and was developed by them into a distinction between the subjective sensations received through sight and the external physical activity that produced those sensations. The latter they conceived of as a succession of waves or pulses travelling through a transparent medium, a theory of which we also find a suggestion in Avicenna's *De Anima*.[49] Here, then, are the beginnings of two doctrines that came to have a profound influence in the 17th century : the distinction between so-called primary and secondary qualities and the wave theory

[44] See H. P. Bayon, "William Harvey, physician and biologist : his precursors, opponents and successors. Part III." *Annals of Science* (London), III (1938), 448 ; Part IV, *ibid.* IV (1939), 88.

[45] E. Wiedemann, "Zur Geschichte der Lehre vom Sehen", *Annalen der Physik und Chemie* (Leipzig), Neue (Dritte) Folge, XXXIX (1890), 470 *sqq.*

[46] *De Anima*, I. 5, f. 5, III. 1, f. 10ʳ, in Avicennae . . . *Opera in lucem redacta*, Venetiis, 1508 ; see E. Wiedemann, " Ibn Sina's Anschauung vom Sehvorgang ", *Archiv für die Geschichte der Naturwissenschaften und der Technik* (Berlin), IV (1912–13), 239–41.

[47] *De Lineis, Angulis et Figuris, De Iride,* in *Die Philosophischen Werke des Robert Grosseteste*, ed. L. Baur (*Beiträge zur Geschichte der Philosophie des Mittelalters*, IX), Münster, 1912, pp. 59–60, 73 ; Roberti Linconiensis *Commentaria in Libros Posteriorum Aristotelis*, II. 4, Venetiis, 1494, f. 29. See Crombie, *Robert Grosseteste*, ch. 5, § 2.

[48] *Opus Maius*, V. i. vii. 2–4, ed. Bridges, II, 49–53.

[49] II. 6, *ed. cit.* f. 9ᵛ.

of light.[50]   Besides these, Avicenna's account in the *Canon* of
the anatomy and physiology of the eye was one of the sources
which Roger Bacon used for his own work on the formation of
the image of behind the lens.   Among other things Avicenna
taught Bacon that the lens was not spherical but flattened.[51]
Bacon's was the first important Western study of this problem,
and it led directly on to the more satisfactory accounts of vision
given in the 17th century.[52]

Of Avicenna's other scientific writings, by far the most
influential was the so-called *De Mineralibus* in the version by
Alfred of Sareshel.   This contains passages on alchemy and
on geology which are among the most important he ever wrote.
In the first of these passages he demolished the claim by
alchemists to be able to transform base metals into gold by
fusion and other chemical processes.   An account of his views
on metals was given by a later Arabic writer, Al-Jildaki,
according to whom

> "Avicenna considered that each of the six metals was
> a distinct species of one genus, just as the genus plant
> included different species, and the genus animal likewise.
> And in the same way that it is impossible to convert a horse
> into a dog or a bird into a horse, or a man into a bird, so
> it is impossible to convert silver into gold or copper into
> silver or lead into iron."[53]

On this subject, Avicenna himself wrote :

> "As to the claims of the alchemists, it must be clearly
> understood that it is not in their power to bring about any
> true change of species.   They can, however, produce excel-
> lent imitations, dyeing the red [metal] white so that it
> resembles silver, or dyeing it yellow so that it closely re-
> sembles gold.   They can, too, dye the white [metal] with
> any colour they desire, until it bears a close resemblance
> to gold or copper ; and they can free the leads from most
> of their defects and impurities.   Yet in these [dyed metals]
> the essential nature remains unchanged ; they are merely

[50] See Crombie, *Robert Grosseteste.*
[51] *Canon*, III. iii. i. 1, p. 530b ; *Opus Maius*, V. i. iii. 3, ed. Bridges, II,
24.   For a diagram, see British Museum MS Royal. 7. F. viii, ff. 54ᵛ, 61ᵛ
[52] See Crombie, *loc. cit.*
[53] See Holmyard and Mandeville's edition of Avicennae *De Congelatione
et Conglutinatione Lapidum*, p. 7.

so dominated by induced qualities that errors may be made concerning them, just as it happens that men are deceived by salt, *qalqand*, sal-ammoniac, etc.

" I do not deny that such a degree of accuracy may be reached as to deceive even the shrewdest, but the possibility of eliminating or imparting the specific difference has never been clear to me. On the contrary, I regard it as impossible, since there is no way of splitting up one combination into another. Those properties which are perceived by the senses are probably not the differences which separate metals into species, but rather accidents or consequences,[54] the specific differences being unknown. And if a thing is unknown, how is it possible for anyone to endeavour to produce it or to destroy it ?

" . . . It is likely that the proportion of the elements which enter into the composition of the essential substance of each of the metals enumerated is different from that of any other. If this is so, one metal cannot be converted into another unless the compound is broken up and converted into the composition of that into which its transformation is desired.[55] This, however, cannot be effected by fusion,[56] which maintains the union and merely causes the introduction of some foreign substance or power."[57]

This passage was widely quoted by 13th-century and later writers, including Albertus Magnus.[58] They used it to combat the persistent claims of alchemists to have made gold, just as they used other parts of *De Mineralibus* for its useful classification of chemical substances.[59]

The geological sections of *De Mineralibus* are concerned with the formation of mountains and rocks, and of fossils. Greek writers had advanced two general types of theory to account for mountains. One type allotted the predominant role in their formation to the action of water, which built them up by sedimentation and carved them into valleys by

---

[54] *E.g.* " such accidental properties as odours and densities ", *ibid.* p. 42.

[55] Alfred of Sareshel's Latin translation reads : " Hec compositio in aliam mutari non poterit compositionem nisi forte in primam reducantur materiam et sic in aliud quam prius erat permutatur ", *ibid.* p. 55.

[56] A method used by alchemists.

[57] *Ibid.* pp. 41–2.

[58] J. R. Partington, "Albertus Magnus on alchemy", *Ambix* (London), I (1937), 3 *sqq.*

[59] *De Congel.* . . . . ed. Holmyard and Mandeville, pp. 33 *sqq.* ; see also Holmyard, *Makers of Chemistry*, Oxford, 1931, pp. 68 *sqq.*

erosion ; the presence of marine shells on mountains was regarded as evidence for the occurrence of temporary deluges.
According to the other type of theory the most important
cause of the raising of mountains was the thrusting up of soil
by imprisoned gas ; water and wind then caused erosion.[60]

Avicenna adopted a compromise between those two types
of theory, though giving the greatest importance to the " plu-
tonic " forces described in the second. He thought that the
raised earth would be transformed into rock partly by the
hardening of clay in the sun and partly by the " congelation "
of water, either in the way stalactites and stalagmites are
formed, or by some form of precipitation brought about by
heat or by some unknown " mineralising, solidifying power ".[61]

As evidence for the first method, he recalled how " In my
childhood I saw, on the bank of the Oxus, deposits of clay
which people use for washing their heads ; subsequently I
observed that it had become converted into a soft stone, and
that was in the space of approximately 23 years."[62] Similarly,
he went on, mountains become " petrified in the course of ages,
the limits of which history has not preserved[63] " and, he
added, it is because some mountains are formed from earth
raised from the sea floor " that in many stones, when they are
broken, are found parts of aquatic animals, such as shells,
etc."[64] Only two Greek writers, Anaximander and Diogenes
of Apollonia, had recognised fossils as the remains of animals
which had once lived where their fossils were found.[65] Avicenna
accounted for them as follows :

> " Stones are formed, then, either by the hardening of
> agglutinative clay in the sun, or by the coagulation of
> aquosity by a desiccative earthy quality, and by reason
> of a desiccation through heat. If what is said concerning
> the petrifaction of animals and plants is true, the cause
> of this [phenomenon] is a powerful mineralizing and petrify-
> ing virtue which arises in certain stony spots, or emanates
> suddenly from the earth during earthquakes and sub-

[60] P. Duhem, *Etudes sur Léonard de Vinci*, Paris, 1909, II, 283 *sqq.*
[61] *De Congel.* . . . p. 20.
[62] *Ibid.* p. 19.
[63] *Ibid.* p. 28.
[64] *Loc. cit.*
[65] Duhem, *op. ciɩ.* p. 289.

sidences, and petrifies whatever comes in contact with it. As a matter of fact, the petrifaction of the bodies of animals and plants is not more extraordinary than the transformation of waters."[66]

This theory he supported by the following observation :

" In Arabia there is a tract of volcanic earth which turns to its own colour everyone who lives there and every object which falls upon it. I myself have seen a loaf of bread in the shape of a round, flat cake—baked, thin in the middle, and showing the marks of teeth—which had petrified but still retained its original colour, and on one of its sides was the impression of the lines in the oven. I found it thrown away on a mountain near Jajarm, a town of Khurasan, and I carried it about with me for a time. These things appear strange only on account of their infrequent occurrence ; their natural causes, however, are manifest and well-known."[67]

These passages represent the origin of the modern theory of fossils, which was advanced for the first time in the West by Albertus Magnus in his commentary on *De Mineralibus*[68] and from him went to Leonardo da Vinci and other 16th- and 17th-century writers.[69] Albertus used other Greek and Arabic authorities besides Avicenna and he avoided Avicenna's hesitation between the two types of explanation of mountains. He definitely asserted that the only major cause of the raising of mountains was the eruption of the earth, and he rejected the theory of temporary deluges in which the ocean overflowed on to the continents. He showed, by some observations made near Bruges and at Cologne, that the main action of the sea was limited to forming littoral deposits and sand dunes.[70] Of the formation of fossils, he gave the following account. It is an excellent example of how the translation of a Greek or Arabic text led the 13th-century writer to make original observations of his own. The description of such observations, in fact, forms a large proportion of all Albertus' scientific commentaries.

" There is no-one who is not astonished to find stones

---

[66] *De Congel.* . . . p. 22.
[67] *Ibid.* pp. 22–3.
[68] Duhem, *op. cit.* pp. 309 *sqq.*
[69] *Ibid.* pp. 318 *sqq.* ; and for Avicenna, pp. 305 *sqq.*
[70] *Ibid.* **pp. 310, 313.**

which, both externally and internally, bear the impression
of animals. Externally they show their outline and, when
they are broken open, there is found the shape of the
internal parts of these animals. Avicenna teaches us that
the cause of this phenomenon is that animals can be entirely
transformed into stones and particularly into salt stones.
Just as earth and water are the usual matter of stones, he
says, so animals can become the matter of certain stones.
If the bodies of these animals are in certain places where a
mineralising power (*vis lapidificativa*) is being exhaled, they
are reduced to their elements and are seized by the qualities
peculiar to these places. The elements which the bodies of
these animals contained are transformed into the element
which is the dominant element in them : that is the terrestrial element mixed with the aqueous element ; then the
mineralising power converts the terrestrial element into
stone. The different external and internal parts of the
animal keep the shape which they had beforehand."[71]

" Evidence of this ", he went on in another work, *De
Causis Proprietatum Elementorum*,[72] " is that parts of
aquatic animals . . . are found in the rocks in hollows on
mountains, where without doubt the water deposited them
enveloped in sticky mud, and they were prevented by the
cold and dryness of the stone from putrefying completely.
Very strong evidence of this kind is found in the stones of
Paris, in which one very often comes across round shells
the shape of the moon."

Duhem has traced the history of these ideas down to the
16th century, and it is interesting to remember that when
Cuvier brought about his reform of palæontology in the early
years of the 19th century, he based many of his conclusions
upon fossils found in those Parisian building-stones which had
caught the eye of Albertus Magnus.

Another branch of science in which Avicenna's genius for
the important is shown is his development of the so-called
theory of *impetus*, which was designed to explain the movement
of projectiles. The particular problem involved, arose only
within the Aristotelian system of physics but, Duhem has
argued,   the attempts to solve it supplied some of the basic
concepts which, by an intellectual twist, Galileo converted into

[71] *De Mineralibus*, I. ii. 8, in Alberti Magni . . . *Opera Omnia*, ed. Petri
Jammy, Lugduni, 1651, II, 222.
[72] II. iii. 5, ed. Jammy, V, 327 ; Duhem, *op. cit.* pp. 311-2.

the theory of inertial motion on which 17th-century mechanics rests.[73] According to Aristotle, any body was kept in motion only by the continuous operation of an efficient cause.[74] What then kept a stone in motion after it had left the hand of the person who threw it ? Aristotle said it was the air,[75] but the 6th-century Alexandrian commentator, John Philoponos, said that the air resisted motion and that the projectile was kept in motion by a quality or power of movement impressed upon the projectile itself.[76]

The first Arabic writer known to have taken up this theory of Philoponos was Avicenna,[77] who defined this power[78] as " a quality by which the body pushes that which prevents it moving itself in any direction ".[79] He called it also a " borrowed force ",[80] a quality given to the projectile by the projector, as heat was given to water by a fire. Avicenna modified Philoponos' theory in two important directions which brought it nearer the modern theory of inertia. First, whereas Philoponos had held that even in a void, if that were possible, the impressed force would gradually disappear and the projectile come to rest, Avicenna argued that in the absence of any obstacle this force, and the so-called " violent " motion which it caused, would persist indefinitely. Secondly, he tried to express moving power quantitatively. He said, in effect, that bodies moved by a given power would travel with velocities inversely proportional to their weights, and that bodies moving with a given velocity would travel (against the resistance of the air) distances directly proportional to their weights.[81]

A further approach towards the modern theory of inertia was made by a 12th-century follower of Avicenna, Abu al-Barakat al-Baghdadi, who tried to explain the acceleration of

[73] See Duhem, *op. cit.* 1913, III ; A. Maier, *Zwei Grundprobleme der Scholastischen Naturphilosophie,* Roma, 1951; M. Clagett, "Some general aspects of physics in the Middle Ages ", *Isis,* XXXIX (1948), 30 *sqq.*

[74] *Physics,* VIII. 4, 254b 7 *oqq.*

[75] *Ibid.* c.10, 267a 4.

[76] Duhem, *op. cit.* II, 189 *sqq.,* III, 34, 62 ; Philoponos used the words δύναμις ἐνδοθεῖσα: : S. Pines, " Les précurseurs musulmans de la théorie de l'impétus ", *Archeion,* XXI (1938), 299.

[77] Pines, *op. cit.* pp. 300 *sqq.*

[78] *Mail qasri,* that is ροπή or ὁρμή.

[79] Pines, *op. cit.* p. 301.

[80] *Quwwa mustafada, ibid.* p. 302.

[81] *Ibid.* pp. 302–3.

falling bodies by the accumulation of successive increments of power with successive increments of velocity.[82] This, in effect, substituted for Aristotle's theory of motion the principle that a constant force produced not merely velocity but acceleration.

Although the known manuscript and printed copies of the Latin translation of Avicenna's *Sufficientia Physicorum* do not contain the section of his commentary in which he discussed this theory of projectiles,[83] precisely the same theory was advanced in the West in the late 13th and early 14th centuries. The phrase used for the moving power by Peter Olivi (*c.* 1248–98),[84] the first Latin writer known to have discussed it, was *inclinatio violenta*, which is the etymological equivalent of the Arabic phrase, *mail qasri*.[85] For *inclinatio violenta* the 14th-century Parisian physicist, Jean Buridan, used the phrase *impetus impressus*, which he defined quantitatively as equal to weight multiplied by velocity. This will be recognised as the modern definition of *momentum*, and Galileo, who introduced this definition into 17th-century mechanics, used the words *impeto* (taken probably from Buridan) and *momento* as synonyms.[86] The twist by which Galileo transposed the whole theory and made it something quite new was to regard *impeto* not as an efficient cause of motion, but simply as a means of giving a mathematical description and measure of it.[87]

Even allowing, then, for the temptation to exaggerate, which all contributors to a millenary celebration must feel, I think we can agree with Roger Bacon's judgment that, in its natural branches, Avicenna was " the man who completed philosophy as far as it was possible for him to do so ". Certainly many of the subjects he touched proved to be some of

[82] *Ibid.* pp. 303–5.

[83] *Ibid.* pp. 305–6.

[84] B. Jansen, " Olivi, der älteste scholastische Vertreter des heutigen Bewegungsbegriffs ", *Philosophisches Jahrbuch der Görres-Gesellschaft* (Bonn), XXXIII (1920), 137 *seq.*

[85] Pines, *op. cit.* p. 305.

[86] Duhem, *op. cit.* III, 35 *sqq.*, 53 *sqq.*, 116 *seq.* ; Clagett, *Isis*, XXXIX (1948), 40–1 ; Galileo Galilei, *Discorsi e Dimostrazioni Matematiche intorno a Due Nuove Scienze*, III, ed. naz. (*Opere*, VIII), Firenze 1898, pp. 202–3.

[87] See A. Mieli, " Il tricentenario dei ' Discorsi e dimostrazioni matematiche ' di Galileo Galilei ", *Archeion*, XXI (1938), 193 *sqq.*, espec. p. 239 ; A. Koyré, *Etudes Galiléennes*, I–III (*Actualités Scientifiques et Industrielles*, Nos. 852–4), Paris, 1939 ; E. A. Moody, 'Galileo and Avempace', *Journal of the History of Ideas* (Lancaster, Pa. and New York), XII (1951), 163–93, 375–422 ; Crombie, *Augustine to Galileo*.

the most important in the later history of science, even though a 12th-century Arabic doctor described his *Canon of Medicine* as " wastepaper " and a 13th-century Spaniard called it " scribblings ".[88]

No account of Avicenna's influence would be complete which did not contain some mention of his contribution to an activity more graceful than natural science, yet no less characteristic of the world in which we now live. In medieval education, this activity formed part of the *quadrivium*, and perhaps it was sent by Providence to mitigate the technological rigours introduced by the other mathematical sciences: I mean music. In the history of musical technique Avicenna is interesting for his accounts of ' organising', the earliest form of harmony, and of " mensural music " in which, instead of the fluid time-values persisting, for example, in plainchant, the durations of the notes have an exact ratio among themselves.[89] There is no trace in Latin of the musical section of Avicenna's *Kitab al-Shifa*, but it was almost certainly through Arab contacts, mainly in Spain, that the West began to learn organising in the 10th century and mensural music in the 12th. The use of harmony and rhythm in the Western manner has been achieved by realising the possibilities of these two techniques.

Avicenna's interest in the technique of music was merely the preliminary to what he regarded as the serious function of the art, to bring the soul of the listener into relation with the harmony of the spheres.[90] He was particularly interested in the therapeutic value of music and in the effect of different compositions on mood. Above all, music was one of the ways in which the soul was made ready to see wisdom, and Roger Bacon quotes him as comparing the man who had no " particular and definite " knowledge of eternal life with " a deaf man who has never heard in his privation of the power of imagining the delight of harmony, although he may be certain of the reality and nature of its sweetness."[91]

---

[88] Guthrie, *History of Medicine*, p. 92.

[89] H. G. Farmer, " Clues for the Arabian influence on European musical theory ", *Journal of the Royal Asiatic Society* (London), 1925, pp. 61 *sqq.* See also G. Reese, *Music in the Middle Ages*, New York, 1940 (London, 1941).

[90] H. G. Farmer, *The Influence of Music : From Arabic Sources*, London, 1926, pp. 11, 23.

[91] *Opus Maius*, VII. 1, ed. Bridges, II, 242.

Perhaps, if we are to look to music to take the edge off science, we shall not in the 20th century expect it to lead us to a Pythagorean communion with the celestial spheres. Our characteristic form of wisdom is perhaps our recognition that, as Roger Bacon put it, " there is no perfection in human discoveries ". To music we may assign the more modest and domestic role of helping to keep us human. Possibly this has always been so. A player before a gathering, described in about the year of Avicenna's birth, played the strings

> " in a kind of way that made everyone in the assembly laugh for the merriment and pleasure, joy and gladness, which entered their souls. Then he altered them and played them in another way, and made them all weep from the sadness of the mode and grief of heart. Then he altered them again, and played them again, and made everyone go to sleep."[92]

Further references: Albertus Magnus, *Book of Minerals*, transl. D. Wyckoff (Oxford, 1967); Accademia Nazionale dei Lincei, *La diffusione delle scienze islamiche nel medio evo europeo* (Roma, 1987); J. Agrimi, C. Crisciani, *Edocere medicos* (Napoli, 1988); P. O. Kristeller, *Studi sulla scuola di Salerno* (Napoli, 1986); R. W. Southern, *Medieval Humanism and other Studies* (Oxford, 1970); G. Whitteridge, *William Harvey and the Circulation of the Blood* (London, 1971); see also chs. 3 p. 71, 4 p. 90, 6 p. 137, 7 p. 160.

[92] Farmer, *Influence of Music*, p. 22.

6

GROSSETESTE'S POSITION IN THE
HISTORY OF SCIENCE

'ALL the wise men of antiquity', Roger Bacon wrote in the fourth book of his *Opus Maius*, 'worked in mathematics so that they might know all things, as we have seen in some scholars of our own times, and as we have heard of in others who learned all knowledge through mathematics, which they knew well. For there have been some famous men, such as Robert, Bishop of Lincoln, and Brother Adam Marsh and many others, who have known how, by the power of mathematics, to unfold the causes of all things and to give a sufficient explanation of human and Divine phenomena. This is assured by the writings of these great men, for example by their works on the impression [of the elements], on the rainbow, on comets, on the generation of heat, on the investigation of the places of the world, on celestial things, and on other questions appertaining both to theology and to natural philosophy. And so it is obvious that mathematics is absolutely necessary, and useful, to the other sciences.'

It was characteristic of thirteenth-century science as a whole, but especially of that part of it showing Grosseteste's direct influence, to stress the importance of scientific method. The works cited by Roger Bacon as evidence of the effectiveness of the mathematical method, respectively *De Impressionibus Elementorum, De Iride, De Cometis, De Calore Solis, De Natura Locorum*, and *De Sphaera*, contained some of Grosseteste's most interesting contributions to mathematical physics. Bacon claimed in his *Compendium Studii* that 'before all other men' Grosseteste 'wrote about science'. For the historian of science Grosseteste's special importance is that he seems to have been the first Western writer to go systematically into the logic of experimental argument in scientific inquiry. It was for his conception of experimental and mathematical science that his followers, both in Oxford and on the Continent, chiefly valued his work. The main purpose of this essay will be to show what innovations Grosseteste introduced into the conception of scientific method inherited from the Greeks and Arabs, how he investigated some physical problems found in available texts, and what influence he had upon his immediate followers and upon the later history of science in the West.[1]

For about half a century before Grosseteste was born (*c.* 1168), one of the most important activities of Western scholars interested in science had been to translate Greek and Arabic scientific writings into Latin. Grosseteste himself took part in this work, encouraging the study of Greek and Hebrew, both at Oxford and at Lincoln, and including among his own translations from the Greek part of Artistotle's *De Caelo* and of Simplicius's commentary on it, and the pseudo-Aristotelian *De Lineis Indivisibilibus*. By the year of Grosseteste's death (1253), Latin versions had been made of most of the important Greek and Arabic scientific works of which knowledge has survived. All these were not available to him, but certainly his greater knowledge of Greek and Arabic science was one of the reasons for the marked superiority of his own scientific work over that of his immediate predecessors, for example that of Alexander Neckam and Alfred of Sareshel in England. Belonging to an earlier generation when the work of translation was far less complete, these writers were still concerned largely with putting the original texts into Latin and with mastering their contents. Grosseteste's was the earliest generation in a position to put this new literary knowledge to original scientific use on any considerable scale. He stands out from his contemporaries as something more than a translator and encyclopaedist because he, before anyone else, was able to see that the major problems to be investigated, if science was to progress, were those of scientific method.

The corpus of translations known in Grosseteste's time contained scientific writings of two main types. First, there was a large number of purely practical treatises, for example on the astrolabe, the calendar and other astronomical subjects, surveying, chemistry, and medicine. The West had been the scene of considerable technical activity at least since the ninth century, when the new wheeled plough and new methods of harnessing draught animals came into use. These were followed by further improvements in power-driven machinery; water-mills and windmills were used for numerous industrial purposes, from corn-grining and fulling to mining and the working of bellows for metallurgy. Chemistry, medicine, surgery, practical mathematics, and other technical subjects closely related

[1] See for a fully documented account of these subjects my *Robert Grosseteste and the Origins of Experimental Science*, Oxford, at the Clarendon Press, 1953, 1971; below p. 137.

to science developed considerably during the thirteenth century; the compass and astrolabe were improved, spectacles and the mechanical clock invented. Scholars took an active interest in various aspects of this new technology and, from the middle of the twelfth century, the technical subjects in school and university courses began to be elaborated. As a result, scholars began to develop a mentality interested in finding exact experimental answers to practical questions.

There is ample evidence to show that many scholars in the twelfth century observed things for themselves and were conscious of the need for experiment. But for a long time their methods remained *ad hoc* and rule-of-thumb, aimed at dealing only with a particular problem. They had no conception of how to generalize problems and how to establish general proofs and explanations. A good example is the use, in works on surveying, of the conclusions of Euclid's theorems, which the authors were quite incapable of proving.

The conception of generalized scientific explanation, with definite canons for accepting one explanation and rejecting another, was introduced into science from the second type of scientific writing to be translated into Latin during the twelfth century. For the present discussion, the main works falling into this category are Euclid's *Elements*, probably first translated in full by Adelard of Bath, who used an Arabic original, and Aristotle's logical writings, especially the *Posterior Analytics*, translated in three versions during the second half of the twelfth century. At first these books had little effect on science itself, but they completely revolutionized philosophy and philosophical theology, and law. Philosophers learnt from them to structure their arguments on the distinction between experimental knowledge of particulars and 'rational' or 'scientific' knowledge of their cause. By this they meant some prior principles from which the particulars thus could be deduced. Surveyors could discover experimentally that a triangle inscribed in a semicircle was right-angled; Euclid provided the 'explanation' of this fact by proving that it followed by deduction from his axioms, postulates, and definitions. For twelfth-century philosophers like Peter Abelard, mathematics became the model science; they attempted to formulate theological arguments according to the mathematical-deductive method. Aristotle provided a generalized account of the method within the structure of his syllogistic logic, with rules for distinguishing between valid and invalid syllogisms. Gratian used the same local method to reform canon law.

The application of the new conception of rational, or scientific, explanation to natural science was simply the last of the achievements of a general intellectual movement of the twelfth century. By the end of the century the formal structure of the new method had been filled in by material examples from the many specialized scientific writings translated from Greek and Arabic. Prominent among those who discussed these new texts were some English scholars working in centres in which Grosseteste was himself to work: Roger of Hereford, Daniel of Morley, and, possibly, Alfred of Sareshel in Hereford; Alexander Neckham, a Master Hugh, John of London, and John Blund in Oxford. One reference suggests that Grosseteste studied not only mathematics and philosophy, but also medicine, and perhaps law. Certainly his writings show a wide grasp of contemporary science, ranging from the logic of science and pure mathematics, through theoretical speculations about cosmology and the nature of light, to the application of scientific theories to such practical problems as the reform of the calendar and the improvement of sight. Thus he was well equipped for the role for which he was cast in the history of science, that of the founder of the Oxford school, whose major achievement was its contribution to a fresh conception of experimental and mathematical argument.

(2)

Grosseteste's conception of the logic of science, of the goal of a scientific inquiry, and of the explanation that was the achievement of the goal, was based in the first place on Aristotle's *Posterior Analytics*. He gave the most systematic account of his ideas on scientific method in his commentary on this work. It seems likely, from specific references in his other writings and from their contents, and from references to external events and to him, that he wrote this commentary over a long period, finishing it perhaps about 1225, by which time he had begun his treatises on optics and astronomy and other special scientific problems. These exemplified his scientific vision and methodology. This methodology may be considered under two headings: first, induction and experiment; and secondly, mathematical physics.

Grosseteste's conception of the role of induction and experiment in scientific inquiry was based on the conception of scientific explanation expounded by Aristotle. The aim of a scientific inquiry, Aristotle asserted, was to discover premisses from which something already known as a fact could be deduced or 'demonstrated'. When this had been done, the investigator had acquired knowledge not only of 'the fact' (τὸ ὅτι), but also of 'the reason for the fact' (τὸ διότι). These two types of knowledge were distinguished in medieval Latin by the terms, respectively, *demonstratio quia* and *demonstratio propter quid* (or *quare*). The whole effort of Greek natural science had been directed towards getting knowledge of the physical world such that propositions about observed facts could be demonstrated from general principles or theories, in just the same way as the conclusions of Euclid's theorems were demonstrated from his axioms, postulates, definitions, and the conclusions of prior theorems. The Greeks had addressed the question of how to discover true premisses for demonstrated knowledge and to test their truth within two main scientific contexts, mathematics and medicine. The method in the mathematical sciences (astronomy, optics, acoustics, mechanics) was primarily postulational, controlled by reference to observation but proceeding primarily by unfolding the consequences of the principles postulated, as Euclid did in his optics. The more complex subject-matter of the biomedical sciences required a more inductive, observational approach, as exemplified for Grosseteste and his contemporaries by Aristotle himself, with Galen and Avicenna.

A scientific inquiry began, Grosseteste followed Aristotle in asserting, with an observed phenomenon, 'the fact'; the purpose of the inquiry was to discover 'the reason for the fact'. Taking up a discussion in the first chapter of Aristotle's *Physics*, Grosseteste said, in his commentary on this work that the phenomena perceived through the senses were composite. The first stage of an inquiry was to break up the composite phenomenon into the principles or elements of which it was formed. This inductive process he called 'resolution'. Having isolated the separate principles involved, the next stage of an inquiry was, by recombining them, to reconstruct the phenomenon theoretically. This process he called 'composition'. The truth of the principles was tested by comparing the composite of theory, deduced from them, with the composite of observation.

A scientific inquiry thus proceeded by the alternation of the argument in two opposite directions, one going inductively from effect to cause, the other deductively from cause to effect. Aristotle had described the argument from effect to cause as a process of abstraction going from composite observed phenomena 'more knowable to us' (πρὸς ἡμᾶς γνωριμώτερα), to abstract principles prior in the order of nature but at first less knowable to us. In his commentary on Aristotle's *Physics*, Grosseteste described the procedure as follows:

> The natural way for us to arrive at knowledge of principles is to go from ... whole objects which follow from the principles themselves, to the principles themselves ... The way of knowledge is ... from confusedly known whole complete objects ... into the parts themselves by which it is possible to define the whole object itself, and from the definition to return to determinate knowledge of the whole object.

The essentials of the method of 'resolution and composition' for discovering and defining the causal principles, or 'forms', from which the observed phenomena could be deduced, were briefly described by Aristotle in the thirteenth chapter of the second book of the *Posterior Analytics*. Grosseteste made the method the centre of his logic of inductive inquiry. In effect, the definition of the form stated the conditions necessary and sufficient to produce the phenomenon. The first problem was to investigate as exhaustively as possible the various correlations of happenings present in the phenomenon, so that their common formula could be discovered; that is, so that they could be expressed as a generalization, or statement of a regularity. Grosseteste gave a formal description of the method in his commentary on the *Posterior Analytics*, and applied it to some specific problems. Thus he argued that 'all scammony of its nature withdraws red bile'. This part of his method like Aristotles was taxonomic. He commented on one example:

> If, therefore, we wish to define this accidental natural thing, 'having horns', we will say that 'having horns' is 'not having teeth in the upper mandible in those animals to which Nature does not give other means of preservation in place of horns', and we reach this definition by the division of the accidental natural thing into co-accidents.

The method of 'resolution and composition' can best be illustrated by means of research into the cause of the rainbow, begun by Grosseteste, carried on by Albertus Magnus, Roger Bacon, and Witelo, and completed in the first decade of the fourteenth century by Theodoric of Freiberg. The first three writers were directly influenced in their method by Grosseteste, the last possibly indirectly.

The inquiry began with a resolution of different kinds of spectrum, including the colours seen in the rainbow, into their elements, so that their common formula, or formulae, could be discovered. A large number of examples of coloured spectra were examined and classified according to their common attributes. For example, the spectra seen in rainbows, in the spray made by mill-wheels, by the oars of a rowing-boat, and by squirting water from the mouth, and in sunlight passed through a spherical glass flask full of water on to a screen, all shared the attributes of being associated with transparent spheres or drops in which, it was found, the different individual colours were refracted through different angles and the colours always formed a circle or part of a circle. Members of a second group, the spectra produced by sunlight shining through a glass prism or hexagonal crystal, shared the common attribute of being formed by colours refracted through different angles, but differed from the members of the first group by not being circular. Members of a third group, the spectra produced by different kinds of iridescent feathers, shared the common attributes of being formed by reflected, not refracted, colours, which changed in a special manner with changing incidence of light: these attributes distinguished the members of this group from those of the preceding ones. The common formula of the first two groups was: colours of the spectrum produced by differential refraction. The common formula of all these groups was furnished by an hypothesis supposing that both refraction and reflection by a dense medium weakened white light; according to the angle through which it was bent, it absorbed different degrees of darkness from the medium, and thereby became differentiated into the colours of the spectrum: colours of the spectrum produced by the weakening of white light.

To the question: What are the conditions necessary and sufficient to produce a rainbow? the investigator had now given a partial answer by defining the species of spectrum to which the rainbow belonged, and by distinguishing this from the species to which it did not belong. From the separate elements, or attributes, discovered by resolution, the rainbow could then be reconstituted theoretically by composition. This genus: colours of the spectrum, of one species of which the rainbow was a member, was divided according to successive *differentia*, and those applicable to the rainbow combined to form an aggregate defining the rainbow itself. As Grosseteste said in his commentary on the *Posterior Analytics*: 'the whole aggregate becomes convertible with [i.e. equivalent to] the thing to be defined, though each of the parts of that aggregate has a wider application'. For example, the genus was divided according to whether the colours were produced by refraction or reflection; colours produced by refraction were then divided according to the nature of the refracting medium; and so on. Eventually an aggregate of *differentia* was formed which specifically defined the rainbow itself: colours of the spectrum produced by the differential refraction of sunlight in spherical drops in large numbers, the refracted colours emerging at approximately 42° to the incident light and forming part of a circle, etc.

The definition reached by resolution and composition showed the cause of the phenomenon under investigation, in the sense that it showed the conditions necessary and sufficient to produce it. This was the formal definition, or formal cuase, of the phenomenon; it showed what it was. It led immediately to a further question: How do the elements described in the formal definition bring the phenomenon about? To explain this, Grosseteste said, we must consider not only the formal cause (defining what the phenomenon is), but also the material, efficient, and final causes. 'Thus,' he said in his *De Statu Causarum*, 'we have four genera of causes, and from these, when they exist, there must be a caused thing in its complete being.'

In natural science, except to characterize the biological function of organs, Grosseteste did not include consideration of final causes. Material and efficient causes he introduced into the explanation by showing the rearrangements of material parts that would have to take place in time, in order to bring about the consequences required by the formal cause. In the case of the phenomenon 'having horns', Grosseteste described the movements of 'earthy matter' taking place in the head in order to produce teeth in some animals, horns in others. A fruitful device which he and his successors adopted to explain the formation of a rainbow was to propose, on the basis of the discovered relations between the limited number of elements defining the species to which the rainbow belonged, a theoretical model from which this phenomenon could be deduced. The purpose of the model was to show in detail how the elements were related, for example exactly how the light behaved in passing through the drops where a rainbow was seen; in this manner it provided the demonstrated knowledge which was the goal of the inquiry.

The special significance of this use of theoretical models in an investigation was that it made it possible to bring a remote and intractable phenomenon like the rainbow down, so to speak, from the clouds and into the laboratory, where it could be studied by deliberately arranged experiments. Grosseteste proposed a theoretical model in which he tried to deduce the appearance of a rainbow from an independently developed rule governing the refraction of light at the junction of two transparent media. He supposed that the rainbow was produced by the refraction of sunlight through successive layers of moist atmosphere forming a cloud, which acted as a single compound lens; he thought the rainbow was seen on a second cloud, acting as a screen on to which the colours were thrown. In his analysis of refraction Grosseteste gave an account of the behaviour of light passing through a spherical glass flask full of water. Albertus Magnus, taking Grosseteste's explanation of the rainbow as his point of departure, used such a flask as a model to show the action of a cloud acting as a single lens. Roger Bacon, Witelo, and, finally, Theodoric of Freiberg, departing radically from Grosseteste's theory, showed that the rainbow was produced, not by the whole cloud acting as a single lens, but by the *individual* drops of water of which the cloud was composed. Witelo and Theodoric built up their theories of the rainbow by using spherical glass flasks full of water as model rainbows.

A problem encountered in the construction of a theory that took account of material and efficient causes, as well as the formal cause (or definition), was that such a theory, or theoretical model, could not be reached by a continuous inductive argument in the same manner as the conclusions of a theory could be demonstrated by a deductive argument. Following Artistotle, he asked in his commentary on the *Posterior Analytics*:

Can the cause be reached from knowledge of the effect with the same certainty as the effect can be shown to follow from its cause? Is it possible for one effect to have many causes? If one determinate cause cannot be reached from the effect, since there is no effect which does not have some cause, it follows that an effect, when it has one cause, may have another, and so that there may be several causes of it.

After the resolutive-compositive method had done its work of separating, describing, and classifying the elements of a phenomenon, there was a logical gap to be crossed only by the investigator's scientific imagination. On the basis of the facts discovered by induction, the investigator tried to construct a theory from which those facts could be deduced. This may be seen as a scientific interpretation of Aristotle's νοῦς, perhaps 'intuition'. Grosseteste adapted the logical form of the *reductio ad impossible* or *ad contradictionem* explicitly to empirical investigations. The causal premisses proposed lead either to contradiction or to agreement with *ratio et experimentum*, that is established theory and observation. In *De cometis* he criticized 'those who form their opinion from their observations without the necessary foundation of theory' for then theories would vary with every observation. But the test as he wrote in *De calora solis* was that opinions were either 'clear from both theory and observation' or 'false, as observation shows'.

Two metaphysical assumptions on which Grosseteste based his procedure for choosing between possible theories were long to play a role in discussions of the use of experiment in science. Both he derived from statements by Aristotle. The first was the principle of the uniformity of nature. As he said in *De Generatione Stellarum*: 'Things of the same nature are productive of the same operations according to their nature'; 'the same cause, provided it remains in the same condition, cannot produce anything but the same effect.' The second assumption was of the principle of economy. 'Nature operates in the shortest way possible', he said in *De Lineis, Angulis et Figuris*. And in his commentary on the *Posterior Analytics* he said: 'that demonstration is better, other circumstances being equal, which necessitates the answering of a smaller number of questions for a perfect demonstration, or requires a smaller number of suppositions and premisses from which the demonstration proceeds . . . because it makes us know more quickly.' This pragmatic form of the principle of economy has become consecrated in the logic of science under the name Ockham's Razor. It was widely used in the thirteenth and fourteenth centuries, especially in astronomy.

An important consequence of Grosseteste's analysis of the logic of experimental science, a consequence of which he was himself aware though it was fully discussed first by Ockham, was to give a special significance to the principle of economy. It followed, from the fact that the same observations could be deduced from more than one theory and that it was impossible to discover all the possible theories from which given observations could be deduced, that the experimental verification of a particular theory did not exclude the possibility that another theory might be true in the same sense. Moreover, the experimental verification of a theory was no guarantee that it would not one day be falsified. Therefore, experiemental science showed, as it was put, that some theories were sufficient to 'save the appearances' and others were not; it did not show that a theory was necessarily true in the sense of being a necessary conclu-- sion from the analysis of the observed facts, a unique and final statement of how nature was actually constructed. A theory could be shown to be probably true to a greater or less degree; it could not be shown to be necessarily and ontologically true. Demonstrations in natural science, Grosseteste said in his commentary on the *Posterior Analytics*, were 'probable rather than strictly scientific . . . Only in mathematics is there science and demonstration in the strictest sense.' In his use of the principle of economy Ockham showed that the choice between two theories, both of which were logically coherent and fitted the facts, could only be a matter of convenience, and that it was convenient to use the simpler.

In the work on the rainbow done between Grosseteste and Theo- doric of Freiberg, use was made both of experimental tests, and of the principle of economy, to reject false theories and construct true ones. After the theories of Grosseteste, Albertus Magnus, Roger Bacon, and Witelo had all been shown to be inadequate, Theodoric eventually hit upon one which gave the right results. Before him, investigators had been led astray by the analogy of the rainbow colours seen when sunlight passes through a spray or through a single spherical flask of water and falls on to a screen; they thought that in the rainbow itself the light was refracted right through each raindrop, acting as a spherical lens, and was reflected back to the eye by other drops behind. Theodoric showed that this model would not produce anything like the observed rainbow; for example, the colours would be in the reverse of the order seen. He hit upon the original idea that each part of the sunlight, sent back from the rain- drops to be seen as a rainbow, was refracted and reflected within the *same* individual drop. This model, he said, had the additional advantage over the previous one of being simpler. From it he built up and tested, by means of a classical series of experiments with crystals and glass flasks, a theory which explained both the primary and the secondary rainbow. His work completed a line of research which Grosseteste began; above all it is an example of the fruitfulness of a conception of scientific method. All these writers on the rainbow con- ceived of the investigation of this particular problem as an opening into an indefinitely extended inquiry of which the purpose was to construct a general theory giving demonstrated knowledge of all the phenomena produced by light. **Grosseteste himself** put forward the earliest known form of the wave theory of light. Witelo, Theodoric, and the mid-fourteenth-century French writer, Themon Judaei, acting on a suggestion by Grosseteste, first stated that each of the colours seen in a spectrum produced by passing sunlight through a prism or hexagonal crystal was a different species of ray, generated by the modification of white light by differential refraction. This work was not forgotten.

A detailed illustration of Grosseteste's method of scientific procedure is given in the translation of one of his short treatises printed as the Appendix to this chapter. Before coming to this, it will be convenient to discuss briefly the second heading under which his scientific methodology is being considered: mathematical physics.

(3)

Of the means whereby demonstrated knowledge could be obtained of the physical world, Grosseteste gave special importance to mathematics. He had two main reasons for this, one methodological, the other metaphysical.

The method by which Grosseteste used mathematics to provide demonstrated knowledge of observed facts was Aristotle's principle of 'subordination'. Some sciences, Aristotle said, were logically 'subordinate' to others, in the sense that statements made in them could be shown to be particular consequences of more general statements made in a 'superior' science. For example, particular statements made in astronomy about the observed movements of the heavenly bodies could be deduced from a purely geometrical theory; statements made in optics about the behaviour of light could be deduced from geometrical laws; statements about musical harmony could be deduced from arithmetical laws. This relationship of subordination could hold only between sciences making univocal statements about the same subject, 'as number-related sound is number-related' as Grosseteste put it in his commentary on the *Posterior-Analytics*. He went on:

> With such sciences, of which one is under the other, the superior science provides the reason (*propter quid*) for that thing of which the inferior science provides the fact (*quia*).
>
> But one must know that an inferior science always adds the condition by which it appropriates to itself the subject and also the characteristics of the superior science, and they are in the conclusions of the subordinate science like two natures, namely, the nature which it receives from the superior and

its own nature which it superadds of itself. And so the superior science does not speak of the causes of the thing that is superadded . . . but treats of the causes of the subject which the inferior science receives from it. And so the subordinating science treats of the causes of a conclusion that has been appropriated into the subordinate science, and it does this not in itself but in its universal, for the conclusion of an inferior science is in the superior science only in its universal. For this reason mathematicians very often know the reason for a conclusion of an inferior science, but they do not know the fact, because they do not know the cause of the conclusion in itself but in its universal and from the mathematical aspect. And these sciences are subordinate to mathematics which consider forms existing in the subject, but not as being in the subject but as abstract. The inferior sciences appropriate these forms in some way to the subject; just as a science sometimes subordinates, sometimes is subordinated, so the same science may be subordinated to one and subordinate another to itself. For example, optics falls under geometry, and under optics falls the science concerned with the rays of the sun refracted in a concave watery cloud. It is optics that provides the causes of the rainbow simply speaking, that is according to the condition of radiation which optics appropriates over and above the geometrical subject.

Precisely how he regarded the relationship between mathematics and the subordinate, physical sciences, in explaining the observed phenomena described by the latter, Grosseteste made clear in his discussion of the law of reflection of light. Having given what he regarded as a satisfactory geometrical demonstration of the law, he said in his commentary on the *Posterior Analytics*:

Yet the cause of the equality of the two angles made on a mirror by the incident ray and the reflected ray is not a middle term taken from geometry, but is the nature of the radiant energy generating itself according to the rectilinear progress, which, when it is generated on an obstacle having in itself this kind of spiritual nature, becomes there as a principle regenerating itself along a path similar to that along which it was generated. For, since the operation of nature is finite and regular, the path of regeneration must be similar to the path of generation, and so it is regenerated at an angle equal to the angle of incidence.

Geometry could provide 'the reason for the fact' in the sense that it could describe what happened; it could provide the formal cause. But it could not provide the material and efficient causes, from which it was explicitly an abstraction. The material and efficient causes were the 'nature' which the inferior science, optics, 'superadds of itself'. 'This is more physical than mathematical,' Grosseteste said in his commentary on the *Physics*, 'and perhaps astronomy in certain

parts of its conclusions is like this.' In discussing astronomy Grosseteste pointed out that the geometrical theory of epicycles and eccentrics, with which Ptolemy 'saved the appearances', could not provide
the material and efficient causes of the heavenly movements; for
these he relied on Aristotle's 'physical' cosmology. From the embar-
rassment he was one of the first to feel at the contradictions between
the two theories, later astronomers were to begin the reform of the
whole subject completed by Copernicus, or, indeed, by Newton.

Grosseteste's second, metaphysical reason for giving special
importance to mathematics in attempting to provide scientific
explanations of the physical world was based on an ontological
theory about the nature of physical reality. He held that the fundamental physical substance, the ultimate identity persisting through
all change and the original physical cause of all change, was light. In
his short treatise, *De Luce seu De inchoatione Formarum*, he described
how in the beginning of time God created unformed matter and a
point of light, which, propagating itself in a sphere, produced the
dimensions of space and, subsequently, all other physical beings. By
its expansion light gave corporeal form to the unformed primitive
matter. Into the complicated derivation of this Neoplatonic theory
from Greek, Arabic, and Latin sources, and into the details of
Grosseteste's cosmogony of light, it is impossible to enter here. The
importance of the theory for the history of science is, first, that it convinced Grosseteste himself that optics was the fundamental physical
science; and secondly, because optics could not be studied without
mathematics, that Grosseteste's influence committed a growing
body of scientists to the use of mathematical theories, not only in
optics but in all possible branches of science. 'All causes of natural
effects have to be expressed by means of lines, angles and figures,'
Grossetest said in *De Lineis*, 'for otherwise it would be impossible to
have knowledge of the reason (*propter quid*) concerning them.' He
went on, in *De Natura Locorum*: 'these rules and principles and fundamentals having been given by the power of geometry, the careful
observer of natural things can give the causes of all natural effects by
this method.' These phrases echo through the writings of later
'careful observers' on whom Grosseteste's influence can be proved:
Roger Bacon, John Pecham, John of Dumbleton in Oxford, Albertus
Magnus, Witelo, Themon Judaei on the Continent, and many
others. In the achievements of later experimental physics we may
hear their distant echo still.

(4)

Grosseteste's influence on later generations of scientists was greatest in his own University of Oxford. He established in the university a tradition of scientific inquiry which gave it a leadership in Western science for over a century. Among the first to show his influence was his friend, and successor as lecturer to the Franciscans, Adam Marsh. Other scientific writers influenced by him in his lifetime were the Fransiscans Thomas of York, Thomas Docking and Bartholemew the Englishman; later there was Robert Kilwardby, who became Archbishop of Canterbury. Most prominent among his immediate disciples was Roger Bacon who may not have known Grosseteste in person. Bacon's discussion of the use of induction, experiment and mathematics in science, and his detailed work on optics and the calendar, directly and explicitly followed the lines of inquiry laid down by Grosseteste. Among later Oxford writers, the unknown author of the *Summa Philosophiae* formerly attributed to Grosseteste himself, John Peckham, John of Dumbleton, and Simon Tunsted continued his work on optics; Duns Scotus, Walter Burley, and William of Ockham cited him on scientific method; Thomas Bradwardine, Henry of Harclay, William of Alnwick, and Robert Holcot took up his discussions of measurement and of the summation of infinite aggregates; John of Eschenden cited him in connexion with weather prediction, Thomas Werkwoth in connexion with astronomical observations. On the Continent Albertus Magnus, the first important scientific teacher in Paris, quoted at length from Grosseteste's writings on scientific method and on optics; Witelo began his treatise on optics with an account of the theory of 'multiplication of species' by which Grosseteste and Roger Bacon had explained the propagation of light; Giles of Lessines quoted him on comets, Themon Judaei on the rainbow. Directly, and indirectly through Roger Bacon, he also influenced the Parisian astronomers of the later thirteenth century. From the end of the fifteenth century several editions were printed of his commentary on the *Posterior Analytics* and of his astronomical writings. Editions of his optical tracts were published in 1503 and 1514. In the second half of the sixteenth century Dr. John Dee made a collection of manuscripts of works by Grosseteste and Roger Bacon as an explicit part of a programme for reviving science in England; Robert Recorde, in his *Castle of Knowledge*, recommended him in a list of astronomical books among 'Dyvers Englyshe menne [who] have written right well in that argument'. All this shows that Grosseteste was remembered as a founder of an enduring scientific tradition.

A good example of Grossetest's persisting influence is that of his work on the reform of the calendar. On this subject he wrote four separate treatises: an elementary early first *Compotus* followed by a *Calendarium* and a revised *Compotus* both correcting the first; then later the much more scientific *Compotus Correctorius* written perhaps between 1215 and 1220 (printed in Roger Bacon's *Opera*, 1926). The theoretical astronomical basis of these writings Grosseteste expounded in the *De Sphaera*, which may be dated also perhaps between 1215 and 1220.

The inaccuracy of the calendar used in the West was noted at the end of the eleventh century by a chronicler who pointed out that the paschal new moon was falsely predicted. About a century later Roger of Hereford tried to get an accurate reckoning of the mean lunar month. By the beginning of the thirteenth century a fuller knowledge of Greek, Jewish, and Arabic systems of chronology brought to the fore the need to reform the Latin calendar and provided the knowledge by which this could be done.

The basic difficulty in the Latin calendar was the need to combine reckonings based on the length of the solar year with those based on the movements of the moon, since the day, the lunar month, and the solar year are incommensurable. No number of days can make an exact number of lunar months or solar years, and no number of lunar months can make an exact number of solar years. An accurate calendar must therefore include a system of *ad hoc* adjustments.

The immediate practical interest in the reform of the calendar was that its inaccuracy produced gross errors in the date of Easter and thus in the whole series of movable feasts of the Church. Moreover, it was obvious to the eye that the calendar was wrong. In the Julian calendar, long established in the West, the length of the year was reckoned as 365¼ days. The relationship between the lunar month and the solar year was determined by means of the nineteen-year cycle, according to which nineteen solar years were considered equal to 235 mean lunar months. But these times were not exactly equal, and an error remained even after further systems of adjustment had been introduced. Grosseteste showed that, with the system in current use, in every 304 years the moon would get 1 day, 6 minutes, 40 seconds older than the calendar showed. He pointed out, in the tenth chapter of the *Compotus Correctorius*, that by his time the moon was never full when the calendar said it should be, and that this was especially obvious during an eclipse. As Roger Bacon, who continued Grosseteste's work for calendar reform, scathingly put it in the fourth part of his *Opus Maius*: 'every computer knows that the beginning of lunation is in error 3 or 4 days in these times, and every rustic is able to see this error in the sky.'

Easter Day was always the first Sunday after the full moon on or after the spring equinox. Grosseteste pointed out that in the contemporary reckoning of Easter there were two errors. First, because the solar year was not exactly 365¼ days, the true equinox then fell on an earlier date than that indicated by the Julian calendar; this is clear, he said, from observations with instruments and from the more accurate *Toletan Tables* made by the Arabs. The second source of error was the inaccuracy of the nineteen-year cycle for the moon. It was generally supposed that the current method of reckoning Easter had been laid down by the Council of Nicaea. Though appreciating the understandable conservation of ecclesiastical authorities, Grosseteste said that there was an undoubted need for reform.

Grosseteste's plan for reforming the calendar was threefold. First, he said that an accurate measure must be made of the length of the solar year. He knew of three estimates of this: that of Hipparchus and Ptolemy, accepted by the Latin computists, that of Al-Battani, and that of Thābit ibn Qurra. He discussed the systems of adjustments that would have to be made in each case to make the solstice and equinox occur in the calendar at the times they were observed. Al-Battani's estimate, he said in the first chapter of his *Compostus Correctorius*, 'agrees best with what we find by observation on the advance of the solstice in our time.' The next stage of the reform was to calculate the relationship between this and the mean lunar month. For the new-moon tables of the *Calendarium* Grosseteste had used a multiple nineteen-year cycle of seventy-six years. In the *Compotus Correctorius* he calculated the error this involved, and proposed the novel idea of using a much more accurate cycle of thirty Arab lunar years, each of twelve equal months, the whole occupying 10,631 days. This was the shortest time in which the cycle of whole lunations came back to the start. He gave a method of combining this Arab cycle with the Christian solar calendar and of calculating true lunations. The third stage of the reform was to use these results for an accurate reckoning of Easter. In the tenth chapter of the *Compotus Correctorius*, he said that even without an accurate measure of the length of the solar year, the spring equinox, on which the date of Easter depended, could be discovered 'by observation with instruments or from verified astronomical tables.'

Grosseteste's writings on the reform of the calendar, especially his correction of the lunar calendar, inspired subsequent work for two centuries. Sacrobosco's *Computus*, written probably a few years after Grosseteste's, gives the same (erroneous) figure for the difference between the earlier calendars of Gerland and of Dionysius. Roger Bacon, in his *Computus* and in the sections on the calendar in the *Opus Maius* and *Opus Tertium*, repeated Grosseteste's criticisms of the contemporary calendar and his remedies, though he also offered new ones based on the Jewish method of reckoning. John Campanus of Novara relied directly on Grosseteste for his *Compostus Major*, copying parts of his section on the moon almost word for word. Cardinal Pierre d'Ailly based his *Exhortatio ad Concilium Generale Constantiense super correctione kalendarii* almost entirely upon Grosseteste's writings. Institutional conservatism blocked these early attempts at reform; nevertheless, Grosseteste can be said to be the original architect of the Gregorian Calendar of 1582, a calendar, ironically, not accepted in his own country for another 170 years.

Grosseteste can truly be claimed as the first great English scientist and philosopher of science. At a time when guidance was essential, he provided England's young university with a creative understanding of science that made it for a time a leading scientific centre in Christendom, and enabled it to contribute to the modern world something entirely new. Stern and intellectual by nature, he called his disciples to high intellectual tasks, yet at the same time inspired a strong personal devotion. He was 'the true teacher who interiorly illuminates the mind, and shows the truth'. In his writings are found to a high degree those characteristics of empiricism, inspired by the imagination and guided by the reason, that have marked the English achievement not only in science, but in many other aspects of practical and intellectual life.

APPENDIX

THE modes of argument used by Grosseteste in his method of experimental verification and falsification are called, respectively, the *modus ponendo ponens* and the *modus tollendo tollens*. The first takes the following syllogistic form:

If A is B, it is C,
A is B,
∴ A is C.

The second takes the form:

If A is B, it is C,
A is not C,
∴ A is not B.

We have a good illustration of his use of these forms of argument in his treatise, *De Calore Solis*. As in every period of the history of science, he worked within a framework of existing theory, for example of Aristotle's cosmology with its distinction between natural and violent motions and its assertion that bodies in the inferior, sublunary region could undergo all kinds of change, whereas the heavenly bodies, composed of the fifth element, could change only by local motion. The book, *On Mirrors*, to which he refers, is Euclid's *Catoptrica*. Though not remarkable for its observations, *De Calore Solis* contains the essential elements of the logical procedures used in experimental verification and falsification. The following is a translation from the Latin text printed in Baur's edition of his philosophical writings (pp. 79–84).

On the Heat of the Sun

As our main purpose is to discuss whatever may be the principle of generation of the heat of the sun, we may ask universally: How many principles of generation are there? Since there are three principles from which heat is generated, namely a hot body, motion and a concentration of rays, we should realise that the heat in these is of a single nature (*univocum*); from this single nature an effect of a single nature is produced in them. And since they have an effect of a single nature, it follows that in all these principles there is a cause of a single nature: for, of every effect of a single nature there is a cause of a single nature. That the heat in all of them is of a single nature is clear, because, from whichever of them it is generated, it has the same powers and produces the same effects. Therefore it is univocally, not equivocally, named.

Let us, then, look for this univocal cause. In all of them the proximate cause of heat is scattering (*disgregatio*). Whence, since a hot body generates heat, this is by the scattering of materials. But how this explanation fits motion and a concentration of rays it is difficult to see.

Local motion, from which heat is generated, is divided into natural and violent motion, natural motion again into rectilinear and circular motion. First let us discuss violent motion, or a heavy body violently moved. A heavy body can be moved violently in three ways, up, down, or down but not directly towards the centre of the earth. In all cases it is clear that in the violent motion there is scattering because of the motion. For in violent motion there is a two-fold motive power, one part natural, the other violent, and these move every part of the moving body in different directions. As a result of this tendency to go in different directions, scattering takes place. Because of the violent motion, the moving body must be scattered part from part, and so heat results. Since, in the first way of moving violently, there is the greatest amount of opposition between the tendencies of the moving powers (they are moving in completely opposite directions), this produces the most scattering and the most heat; the second and third ways produce only moderate heat. This is in the highest degree clear from both theory (*ratione*) and from observation (*experimento*).

The same thing is shown in the case of natural motion. For heat is generated during motion in anything moving naturally downwards. Acting on every part there is actually a two-fold motive power, partly natural, partly violent. It is obvious that a natural power is operating here. That a violent power is also operating I show as follows:

Everything that is heavy and is moved downwards not directly towards the centre of the earth, is moved violently. But all heavy parts are moved downwards not directly towards the centre. Therefore all heavy parts are moved violently. The minor premiss I prove thus: The parts of a heavy body always keep the same distance apart in the whole. Therefore, since they are moved downwards with the motion of the whole, they move along lines which remain a constant distance apart. But lines which remain a constant distance apart when extended to infinity in either direction never meet. Therefore the parts of a naturally moved heavy body are moved downwards along non-intersecting lines. Therefore they are not moved directly towards the centre of the earth, because, if they were, they would be moved along lines running directly together there. So the principle is evident, namely that acting on every part of a body moved naturally down there is a two-fold power tending in different directions. But the opposition between these tendencies is weaker than the opposition between the tendencies of the parts in violent motion; so, of all agencies generating heat, natural motion generates the least natural heat in motion. Thus it is plain that from natural rectilinear motion, and from violent motion, heat is generated, and from a hot body heat is generated by a univocal cause.

The same can be shown, by similar reasoning, of the third principle of generation of heat. That some heat may be generated, from a univocal cause of heat, by the concentration of rays is shown by *On Mirrors*; rays from a concave mirror directed towards the sun produce combustion, and this is on account of scattering. A ray in a denser transparent medium is more incorporated than in a less dense one (and we are not speaking of total incorporation, like heat, but of a certain partial incorporation). Because of this incorporation, the incorporated parts of the air fly apart when the rays are concentrated at one point, each part, at the point itself, going along its own straight line. As a result there will be, round this point, the greatest dispersion of the air into different directions, and so there will be a scattering and heat will result. Thus it is evident that in these three genera heat is present from a cause of a single nature.

If, then, the sun generates heat, it will do so either as a hot body does, or as motion does, or as a concentration of rays does. That the sun does not generate heat in the manner in which a hot body does is evident from the following: It is proved in the seventh book of the *Physics* that an agent producing a change of quality, and the subject undergoing change, must be in immediate contact. Hence, if there were a medium between the original agent of change and the ultimate changed subject, that medium would first have to be changed by the heat of the hot sun, rather than the ultimate subject; otherwise the original agent and the first subject to be changed would not be in immediate contact. Therefore, since there are several media between the sun and the air, and next to the sun (which produces change according to the heat it possesses) is the fifth element or part of the fifth element, it must follow that the heat of the sun must first bring about a change of heat in the fifth element, rather than in the air. But this is impossible, because if the fifth element can undergo change of quality, it is corruptible. Therefore the first premiss is impossible, namely that the sun generates heat in the manner in which a hot body does. Perhaps some would say that heat is present in the sun virtually, as it is in pepper. But this is not to the point, because, in so far as heat is present in pepper virtually and not actually, it cannot produce movement unless it is moved by something else, nor qualitative change unless it is changed by something else. And similarly for the sun. But this is impossible; so therefore is the first premiss.

That heat is not generated from the motion of the sun is shown as follows. Now motion does not generate heat, unless there are, in every part of the moved thing, different tendencies moving the part in different directions. But in everything that is moved circularly and not violently, any part has the same tendency as the whole; there is no difference: the tendency of every part is to move in a circle. Therefore no heat is generated by circular motion. You might perhaps say that although there is no intrinsic cause of heat in anything moving in a circle, nevertheless there is an extrinsic cause, as there is with inferior bodies from the resistance of the medium. But this is false for two reasons: one reason is that in these inferior bodies the resistance of the medium is not the source of the heat produced by motion. If it were, since the medium resists equally things moving with natural and with violent motion, the same amount of heat should be generated by violent and by natural motion. But this is false, as observation shows; therefore so is the first premiss. The other reason why it is false is that the sun and stars have no resistance to their motion, because they are not moved by motors of their own. But since they are fixed in their spheres, they are moved by the motion of their spheres, like a ship in a river, which is moved by the motion of the river, as the Philosopher [Aristotle] shows in the second book of the *De Caelo et Mundo*.

There remains therefore only the theory that the sun generates heat by the concentration of rays. This is shown as follows: The sun's rays in the transparent medium of the air are, through the nature of the dense body, to some extent incorporated in it. Rays falling downwards on to the plane, concave, or convex surface of the earth are reflected at equal angles, as shown by the last of the principles taught in *On Mirrors*. Therefore, if they fall perpendicularly, they are reflected perpendicularly; and so the incident and the reflected rays go along the same line in totally opposite directions, and there is a maximum of scattering. This is the case on the equator, when the sun is at the zenith of this region, and at any place south or north of the equator at a distance from it less than that of the tropic of cancer or of the tropic of capricorn. In these regions the sun's rays must fall perpendicularly twice a year. But at a place on the tropic of cancer or the tropic of capricorn, the sun can reach the zenith only once, and only once send rays perpendicularly to this place. When this happens there is a maximum of scattering and of heat in these places. This is a violent scattering, such as is brought about by a concentration of rays refracted through a spherical body or reflected from a concave mirror, though in it the rays go in totally opposite directions, whereas in the case of the spherical refracting body and the concave mirror they do not.

In regions at greater distances from the equator than the tropic of cancer, since the sun does not come north far enough to reach the zenith, the rays fall at an angle less than a right angle, and are reflected at the same angle and so not in a totally opposite direction. The further the place from the equator, the more obtuse the angles at which the solar rays fall and are reflected, and the less opposed the directions in which the incident and reflected rays go, the less the scattering, and the less the heat generated. This is shown by observation.

If it is asked why heat is not generated from the rays of the sun in the fifth element, two replies can be given: first, that reflected rays do not intersect there; secondly, even if they did intersect after being reflected in a totally opposite direction [to the incident rays], heat would not be generated. For, since in this transparent medium there is no dense nature, the solar rays are not in any way incorporated in it, and so cannot scatter the parts of matter. In the uppermost layer of air, where the air is thinnest, the least amount of heat is generated, as observation shows. For there are more clouds on the summit of mountains, where the solar rays are brightest, than in valleys, though, nevertheless, rays are reflected there, just as they are in a valley; but, because of the thinness of the air there, the density of the air is small, so is the incorporation of light with it, and hence so also is the scattering of the parts of the air in the concentration of rays. In a valley there is a greater incorporation of rays and therefore more scattering and more heat.

Further references: Robert Grosseteste, *Die philosophischen Werke*, ed. L. Baur (*Beiträge zur Geschichte der Philosophie des Mittelalters*, ix; Münster, 1912), *Commentarius in viii libros Physicorum Aristotelis*, ed. R. C. Dales (Boulder, Col., 1963), *Commentarius in Posteriorum analyticorum libros*, ed. Pietro Rossi (*Firenze, 1981*); Roger Bacon, *Opera hactenus inedita*, ed. R. Steele, vi (*Oxford, 1926*); S. H. Thomson, "The text of Grosseteste's *De cometis*", Isis, xix (1933) 19-25; A. C. Crombie, "Grosseteste, Robert (c.1168-1253)" in *Dictionary of Scientific Biography*, v (1972) 548-54 and *Styles . . .* ch. 3.i..; R. C. Dales, "Robert Grosseteste's scientific works", *Isis*, lii (1961) 381-402; S. Gieben, "Bibliographica universa Roberti Grosseteste ab anno 1473 ad anno 1969", *Collectanea Franciscana*, xxxix (1969) 362-418; J. H. Lesher, "The meaning of *nous* in the *Posterior Analytics*", *Phronesis*, xviii (1973) 44-68; J. McEvoy, *The Philosophy of Robert Grosseteste* (Oxford, 1982), "The chronology of Robert Grosseteste's writings on nature and natural philosphy", *Speculum*, lviii (1983) 614-55, ed. *Proceedings of the Warburg Institute Grosseteste Symposium* (1987) (in press); J. D. North, "The Western calendar" in *The Universal Frame* (London, 1989) 39-77; R. W. Southern, *Robert Grosseteste* (Oxford, 1986); see also chs. 3, 7.

7

THE SIGNIFICANCE OF MEDIEVAL DISCUSSIONS OF SCIENTIFIC METHOD FOR THE SCIENTIFIC REVOLUTION

We all know Kant's famous comment on the Scientific Revolution, his declaration in the preface to the second edition of the *Critique of Pure Reason* that with the conception and methods of science put into practice by Galileo and his contemporaries "a new light flashed upon all students of nature" and "the study of nature entered on the secure methods of a science, after having for many centuries done nothing but grope in the dark." Kant's view of the Scientific Revolution, which he shared in broad outline with eighteenth-century historians of civilization like Voltaire and Hume, was essentially that of the seventeenth-century scientists and philosophers of science themselves. Certainly Francis Bacon asserted vigorously that the methods used in the study of nature *should* make a clean break with the past and a fresh start, and the scientific innovators of the period, conscious of doing something new, were no less emphatic in declaring that they had in fact done so. Moreover, the leaders of the scientific movement stated very clearly and explicitly their views of the nature of the changes in scientific thinking and methods they were bringing about. It scarcely needs to be said that for the historian, attempting himself to chart the course of those changes, these statements are indispensable evidence. Until about half a century ago the conception they presented of the immediate past was by and large accepted at its face value.

It was the heroic adventures of Pierre Duhem in medieval science, following the campaigns in which in the last three decades of the last century Denifle and Ehrle and their followers brought back into the realm of scholarship such wide new territories of medieval thought and removed so many previously accepted features from the landscape, that made the first general challenge to the conception of the Scientific Revolution as a clean break with the immediate past and made what may be called the "medieval question" a major historical issue. Duhem and the scholars who have followed him have in the first place discovered and put in order an imposing amount of factual data, so that the broad outlines of the history of scientific thought can now be traced with some confidence from the end of the classical period into the seventeenth century. But even when these have been accepted by both sides in the debate, the problem of the relation of seventeenth-century science to medieval science still remains a *questio disputata*.

If we formulate the problem as the discovery of the origins of modern science, it is clear that we immediately introduce some conception, explicit or implied, of the essential characteristics of the modern science whose origins we have set ourselves to discover. In other words a philosophical interpretation of the nature of modern scientific methods and thinking enters into our historical interpretation of the course of events. We place ourselves in a position similar to those taken with such confidence by Francis Bacon and by Kant. There are obvious dangers in this position, for it is a temptation to read history backwards, to regard as significant in the scientific thought of the past only those features that seem to resemble the features favored by our own conception of what science should be and to discount everything else as simply mistaken; at the crudest, it is a temptation to see the past as so many anticipations of, contributions to, or recessions from the present. We do not have to be told that these temptations are essentially anti-historical. Yet the nature of science is such that the historian must at every stage of his historical inquiries ask questions that are non-historical, though not anti-historical. He must for example ask, as an historian, whether something is good or bad science, thereby introducing a non-historical evaluation, based on his own superior scientific knowledge, that is nevertheless essential for his historical judgment of the course of events. In other words, if it is the first duty of an historian of science to see the problems as they were seen in a given period by those who were then facing them, it may be argued that it is equally essential to his understanding for him to appreciate the aspects of the problem that have been revealed only later and that perhaps could not have been seen in the period in question. In this way the development of science itself can continue to shed new light upon history.

It seems evident that a large part of the debate over the significance of medieval thought for the origins of modern science turns on questions of philosophical interpretation rather than of historical fact. Granting, for example, that the two and a half centuries from the *floruit* of Adelard of Bath to the death of Oresme saw the re-education of Western Europe in the sophistication of Greek philosophical thinking, it may be argued that the relatively poor showing in immediate scientific results indicates that scientifically the West had made a false start, and that this is proved by a closer examination of the irresolution with which experimentation was practiced after lengthy discussions of scientific method or of the ultimately ineffective manner in which conceptions like *impetus* or "the intension and remission of forms" were formulated. Their purpose, it may be argued, was clearly not scientific in the seventeenth-century sense. We must ask then what we are to accept as scientific thinking and methods, or at least as relevant to the development of scientific thinking and methods? What were the medieval conceptions of the aims, objects and methods of science, how do they compare with those of the seventeenth century, and what is the historical connection between them? These are our problems.

I should say at the outset that I regard natural science as a highly sophisticated form of thinking and investigating and one that has been learnt only through a tradition. I do not think that the opinion that science is organized common sense or generalized craftsmanship and technology survives comparison with the actual scientific tradition, a tradition which seems to me to be essentially Western and to begin with the Greeks. Impressive as are the technological achievements of ancient Babylonia, Assyria, and Egypt, of ancient and medieval China and India, as scholars have presented them they lack the essential elements of science: generalized conceptions of scientific explanation and of mathematical proof. It seems that it was the Greeks who invented natural science as we know it, by their assumption of a permanent, uniform, abstract order and laws by means of which the regular changes observed in the world could be explained by deduction, and by their brilliant idea of the generalized use of scientific theory tailored according to the principles of non-contradiction and the empirical test. It is this essential Greek idea of scientific explanation, "Euclidian" in logical form, that has introduced the main problems of scientific method and philosophy of science with which the Western scientific tradition has been concerned. These seem to me to be of three general kinds.

First there are those concerning the character of the natural order by means of which events are explained, for example, whether it consists of substances determined teleologically and qualitatively or whether all changes are reducible to quantitative changes of matter in motion, whether action at a distance is conceivable or whether space must be filled with a continuous medium. It is these "concepts of nature," or "regulative beliefs" as we may call them after Kant, that determine the kinds of abstract entities that are used in a theory; they are the investigator's presuppositions about what he expects to find by his analytical methods; they control the form his explanations will take, the questions he will ask and the problems he will discover; and by suggesting certain types of hypotheses but not others they may assist inquiry in some directions but limit or prevent it in others. They are essentially unfalsifiable by observation; changes in them are brought about by re-thinking.

Secondly, there are the problems concerning the relation of theories to the data explained, the classical problems of "scientific method" as such. They concern, for example, the inductive rules for collecting and ordering data and for establishing causal connections, the conception of causation, the processes of discovery, the use of hypotheses, the criteria according to which a theory is to be accepted or rejected or one theory preferred to another, the questions of the existence of theoretical entities and of the place of concepts of nature in scientific explanation.

Thirdly, there are the problems of scientific procedure, the experimental and mathematical techniques.

It is natural that problems of scientific method should have a special importance in times of great intellectual change when the direction, objectives and forms of scientific inquiry are still being determined or redetermined. The re-introduction of the scientific tradition into the Latin West through the translations from Greek and Arabic made the twelfth, thirteenth, and fourteenth centuries such a time. This is certainly one reason, though not the only reason, why the natural philosophers of the period felt it necessary to become philosophers of science first and scientists only secondly. It is as philosophers that I think we should most justly consider them, and it is as such that the development of their ideas finds an intelligible center and that their differences from seventeenth-century scientists become reasonable. We may then ask what place they have in the scientific tradition. We can provide an answer, I think, by looking at scientific thought in the middle ages and in the seventeenth century from the point of view of the three aspects of scientific method which I have just distinguished.

The influence of the translation into Latin of Euclid's *Elements* and of Aristotle's logic in the twelfth century is an excellent illustration of the transmission of science by a learned tradition. Before these works were mastered, a number of twelfth-century scholars wrote of the investigation of nature as being in principle empirical and even experimental—*nihil est in intellectu quod non prius fuerit in sensu*—and showed that they were aware of the possibility of mathematical proofs. But neither in natural science nor in mathematics were scholars able to transcend the rule-of-thumb methods of the practical crafts; a pathetic example from the eleventh century may be read in the correspondence published by Tannery and Clerval between Ragimbold of Cologne and Radolf of Liège, who vainly tried to outdo each other in attempting to prove that the sum of the internal angles of a triangle equals two right angles, and in the end suggested verifying the proposition experimentally by cutting out pieces of parchment.[1] It is important for the scientific tradition that scholars

---

1 P. Tannery and M. l'Abbé Clerval, "Une correspondance d'écolâtres du XIe

should have held so strongly in mind a theory of empiricism, but it was not until they had learnt from Greek sources the idea of a theoretical scientific explanation and of a geometrical proof, and had been shown many examples, that they were in a position to begin to possess themselves of the whole tradition. If we turn from the writings of, for example, Adelard of Bath or Hugh of St. Victor to those of Fibonacci or Robert Grosseteste or Jordanus Nemorarius, we have a measure of the difference these sources made.

We may take Robert Grosseteste and Roger Bacon as examples of what thirteenth-century philosophers made of the scientific tradition. In their writings we find a systematic attempt to determine what natural science should be, as distinct for example from mathematics or metaphysics or other kinds of inquiry of which the new translations brought instances. I do not question that it was possible at that time to produce excellent science simply by carrying on with the problems and techniques the Greeks and Arabs had developed from the point where they left off, without bothering with methodology at all. Indeed some of the best work of the period, that attributed to Jordanus or of Gerard of Brussels or Peter of Maricourt, was produced in just this way. But it is essential to the scientific tradition that its representatives should have sought to possess themselves not only of "know how" but also of understanding of what they are doing. At times and in problems in which there is uncertainty about what a scientific explanation should be and how a scientific investigation should be made, methodological inquiries become indispensable and may change the course of what is done.

I have argued at length elsewhere[2] that the contribution of Grosseteste and Roger Bacon and their successors to the scientific tradition of their time was to formulate, from the theoretical empiricism of the twelfth century and the deductive form of scientific explanation learnt from Euclid and from Aristotle's logic, a conception of science that was experimental, mathematical, and deductive. From one point of view we can see their work as an attempt to combine the form of scientific thought imposed by Greek geometry and expounded by Plato with the empirical requirements insisted upon by the other great tradition in Greek methodology, that of medicine and of Aristotle. The medieval philosophers were searching for a model and a method of scientific thought applicable to

siècle," *Notices et extraits des manuscrits de la Bibliothèque Nationale*, XXXVI (1899), 498.

2 *Robert Grosseteste and the Origins of Experimental Science, 1100–1700* (Oxford, 1953, 1971).

natural science, to physics, distinct from the geometrical model. It is relevant to look at some details. First, Grosseteste saw that the problem of discovering and identifying the causes of events was a sophisticated problem, and with the aid of Aristotle he began to develop the logical procedures of "resolution and composition" for analyzing a complex phenomenon into its elements and for discovering the "common nature" of a group of events. He conceived of the cause of an event as something, the "nature," in which the event was prefigured, but the cause was hidden from our direct inspection, and the results of our analysis might leave us with an ostensible plurality of causes. Here he contrasted natural science with mathematics, in which premises and conclusion (cause and effect) were reciprocal. In natural science we may never be able to reduce the ostensible plurality to one actual cause in which the effect is univocally prefigured, but in order to eliminate false causes and so far as possible to identify true causes, he proposed a method of "verification and falsification" whereby proposed causes were tested by comparing consequences deduced from them with observation.

It seems to me that the discussion of the form of natural science and of these inductive procedures by Grosseteste and Roger Bacon, by various optical writers and astronomers, and by Duns Scotus and Ockham, are an important contribution to the history of scientific method. They insisted on the *a posteriori* and probable character of natural science, the dependence of its conclusions on sense experience, its difference from the model of geometry.[3] They came to understand that experimental tests applied

---

3 E.g. concerning physics: "videndum est de modo procedendi, considerandi et demonstrandi in hac scientia. Circa quod dico: esse sciendum quod, licet in hac scientia sint demonstrationes propter quid, sicut in ceteris scientiis, tamen ordine doctrine qui incipere *debet* a notioribus et facilioribus communitati, cui tradenda est scientia, procedendum est ab effectu ad causam . . ." (William of Ockham, *Summulæ in libros Physicorum,* [Rome, 1637], I, 5). "Cum ergo scientia naturalis habeat considerare de compositis, sequitur quod ad considerationem eius pertinent partes compositi et causae eiusdem. Iste autem partes componentes per se sunt materia et forma. . . . Primo dicendum est quod sint a posteriori, quia a priori hoc probare non possumus." (*Ibid.,* I, 7.) Cf. Grosseteste: "Similiter in naturalibus est minor certitudi propter mutabilitatem rerum naturalium." He places natural science with other disciplines in which we can reason rather "probabiliter quam scientifice, licet in his sint scientia et demostratio sed non maxime dicta. In solis enim mathematicis est scientia et demonstratio maxime et particulariter dicta. . . . In doctrinis [i.e. mathematics] autem est facilior et brevior resolutio usque ad principia quam in dyalecticis vel aliis . . . quia in doctrinis magis convertuntur termini" (sc. premisses and conclusions). (*Commentaria in libros Posteriorum Aristotelis,* I, 11; see my *Robert Grosseteste,* p. 59, n. 2, p. 82, n. 4.)

to the consequent enable us to deny the postulated conditions, but not to affirm them as more than probable. For choosing between different hypotheses of equal empirical standing they gave a fundamental importance to the principle of economy which could lead to a radically conventional conception of theories. In effect, they reached the idea of a cause as the conditions necessary and sufficient to produce an event. A clear statement was given by Ockham in his commentary on the *Sentences* (book I, distinction xlv, question 1, D):

Although I do not intend to say universally what an immediate cause is, nevertheless I say that this is sufficient for something being an immediate cause, namely that when it is present the effect follows, and when it is not present, all the other conditions and dispositions being the same, the effect does not follow. Whence everything that has such a relation to something else is an immediate cause of it, although perhaps not *vice versa*. That this is sufficient for anything being an immediate cause of anything else is clear, because if not there is no other way of knowing that something is an immediate cause of something else. . . . It follows that if, when either the universal or the particular cause is removed, the effect does not occur, then neither of them is the total cause but rather each a partial cause, because neither of those things from which by itself alone the effect cannot be produced is the efficient cause, and consequently neither is the total cause. It follows also that every cause properly so called is an immediate cause, because a so-called cause that can be absent or present without having any influence on the effect, and which when present in other circumstances does not produce the effect, cannot be considered a cause; but this is how it is with every other cause except the immediate cause, as is clear inductively.[4]

A large amount of excellent scientific research has always been carried out at the somewhat "Francis Baconian" or "John Stuart Millian" level indicated by the analysis of the observable conditions necessary and sufficient to produce an event. In the thirteenth and fourteenth centuries the production of rainbows and allied phenomena were explicitly investigated in these terms, and the results were stated in the form that if, for example, you postulate a certain refracting medium, rain drops, at a position at which the incident sunlight makes an angle of 42° with the line connecting the raindrops and an observer, then you will expect a rainbow to be seen. But science at this level remains merely descriptive. Any attempt to offer a general explanation connecting, for example, different optical phenomena and the conditions of their production will depend on postulating a general theory of light, and this will depend in turn on the

4 For the original Latin of this passage see my *Robert Grosseteste*, p. 173, n. 5.

conceptions we have of the basic entities and principles of which light consists and on our ability to formulate the mathematical laws according to which these behave. In other words a method that aims at finding explanations is of little use in science except in association both with a conception of the kinds of causes, principles and laws the method is expected to discover and with a knowledge of necessary mathematical and experimental techniques, and in fact all discussions of scientific method have presupposed such a "conception of nature" and such techniques.

A fundamental difficulty, as we can now see it, was made for the scientific philosophers of the middle ages by the conception of nature, and consequently of explanation, which they inherited from Aristotle. Indeed one can see the discussions from Grosseteste to Galileo as a long and finally successful attempt to escape from this aspect of Aristotle's conception of science. Aiming principally at establishing the definition of the "nature" or essence or "form" of a thing, Aristotle's conception of explanation meant that when this had been discovered the explanation had been given and so no further questions in this direction need be asked. The difficulty of escape into a new range of questions was enormously magnified by the logically connected series of answers Aristotelian philosophy could provide in terms of the well-elaborated concepts of matter and form, potentiality and actuality, efficient and final causality.

We all remember Galileo's comment on explanations of this kind, and his brisk assertion that they may be answers indeed, but not to the questions he wanted to ask. The definition of the "nature" or essence, as he pointed out in a famous passage on falling bodies in the *Dialogue concerning the Two Principal Systems of the World,* was merely a summary of observed behavior; as such it was useful for classification, but it could tell us no more than the observations it summarized. So "gravity" was not an explanation but merely "the name that has been attached to [the falling of bodies] by the many experiences we have of it a thousand times a day. We don't really understand what principle or what power it is that moves a stone downwards, any more than we understand what moves it upwards after it has left the projector, or what moves the moon round."[5] We all remember how Galileo himself attacked these problems, how, in another famous declaration, in the *Two New Sciences,* he rejected any

---

5 Galileo Galilei, *Le Opere di Galileo Galilei* (Edizione nazionale; Firenze, 1890–1909), VII, 260–61. Newton made the same point in his attack on specific qualities which "tell us nothing" (*Opticks,* Query 31. [4th ed.; reprinted London, 1931], p. 401), and so did Molière in his mockery of the "virtus dormitiva" in *Le Malade Imaginaire.*

consideration of the physical cause of the acceleration of freely falling bodies and turned to a purely kinematic approach, "to investigate and demonstrate some of the properties of accelerated motion, whatever the cause of this acceleration may be."[6] These passages indicate a major change in the objectives of scientific inquiry. Instead of searching for the essence, Galileo proposed to correlate certain accidents. He proposed moreover to measure them and to correlate them by in effect a mathematical function. The last was fundamental. The kinematic law of falling bodies was his personal triumph in this approach, and as he pointed out in connection with another of his mathematical laws, that describing the trajectory of a projectile, such a law extends our knowledge by enabling us to predict events we have not yet observed. But that was not the end of Galileo's conception of scientific explanation. We all recall yet another famous passage, from *Il Saggiatore* (question 48): "I hold that there exists nothing in external bodies for exciting in us tastes, odours and sounds except sizes, shapes, numbers and slow or swift motions." It was in terms of these "primary qualities" that he conceived of the ultimate composition of the physical world, and in terms of these and the *particelle minime,* the primary particles characterized by them, of which he held matter to consist, that he conceived of explanations of the phenomena described by the mathematical predictive laws. In other words, for Aristotle's conception of nature he substituted another in which all phenomena were to be reduced to matter in motion. Like Newton's his approach was to establish the descriptive mathematical laws before considering their causes, but the mechanical causes remained his ultimate objective in science.

I have given this brief sketch of Galileo's conception of the objectives of scientific inquiry because with him we find a confidently successful solution of a methodological problem that occupied Western scientific philosophers from the thirteenth century. The success of seventeenth-century physics depended on the adaptation to each other of a "mechanical" philosophy of nature, a methodology of experimental science with functional correlation as its aim, and effective algebraic and geometrical techniques. We can, I think, see the beginnings of this combination in the conception of science presented by Grosseteste and Roger Bacon: a conception of physical nature in which the essence or "form" itself is mathematically determined, and a conception of the immediate objective of

---

6 Galileo Galilei, *Opere,* VIII, 202. Kepler's photometric law, stating that intensity of illumination varies inversely as the square of the distance from the source, is a good contemporary example of a functional relationship. (*Ad Vitellionem Paralipomena,* I, 9 [Frankfurt, 1604], p. 10)

inquiry as mathematical and predictive laws instead of the Aristotelian essential definition. In the fourteenth century we find the development of mathematical techniques designed to take advantage of the new mathematical methodology and conception of explanation.

It was through his Platonically-inspired "metaphysics of light" that Grosseteste made his fundamental move towards the mathematicization of the concept of nature and the shift from the "form" to the "law" as the object of scientific inquiry. Since *lux* was the fundamental "corporeal form," the primary basis of the extension of matter in space and of all motion, it followed that optics was the fundamental physical science, and the study of optics was "subordinate" to geometry. Hence he could conclude:

The usefulness of considering lines, angles and figures is the greatest, because otherwise it is impossible to understand natural philosophy without these. They are completely efficacious in the whole universe and in parts, and in related properties, as in rectilinear and circular motion. They are efficacious also in action and in being acted upon, and this whether in matter or the senses. . . . For all causes of natural effects have to be expressed by means of lines, angles and figures, for otherwise it would be impossible to have knowledge of the reason (*propter quid*) concerning them. (*De lineis, angulis et figuris.*)[7]

Hence these rules and principles and fundamentals having been given by the power of geometry, the careful observer of natural things can give the

---

7 "Utilitas considerationis linearum, angulorum et figurarum est maxima, quoniam impossibile est sciri naturalem philosophiam sine illis. Valent autem in toto universo et partibus eius absolute. Valent etiam in proprietatibus relatis, sicut in motu recto et circulari. Valent quidem in actione et passione, et hoc sive sit in materiam sive in sensum. . . . Omnes enim causae effectuum naturalium habent dari per lineas, angulos et figuras. Aliter enim impossibile est sciri 'propter quid' in illis. Quod manifestum sic: Agens naturale multiplicat virtutem suam a se usque in patiens, sive agat in sensum, sive in materiam. Quae virtus aliquando vocatur species, aliquando similitudo, et idem est, quocunque modo vocetur; et idem immittet in sensum et idem in materiam, sive contrarium, ut calidum idem immittit in tactum et in frigidum. Non enim agit per deliberationem et electionem; et ideo uno modo agit, quicquid occurrat, sive sit sensus, sive sit aliud, sive animatum, sive inanimatum. Sed propter diversitatem patientis diversificantur effectus. In sensu enim ista virtus recepta facit operationem spiritualem quodanmodo et nobiliorem; in contrario, sive in materia, facit operationem materialem, sicut sol per eandem virtutem in diversis passis diversos producit effectus. Constringit enim lutum et dissolvit glaciem." *Die Philosophischen Werke des Robert Grosseteste*, ed. L. Baur. (*Beiträge zur Geschichte der Philosophie des Mittelalters*, IX [Münster, 1912], pp. 59–60.)

causes of all natural effects by this method. And it will be impossible otherwise, as is already clear in respect of the universal, since every natural action is varied in strength and weakness through variation of lines, angles and figures. But in respect of the particular this is even clearer, first in natural action upon matter and later upon the senses . . . (*De natura locorum*.)[8]

There is no need to insist that Grosseteste's execution of this program, and the theory of the "multiplication of species" which it had in view, made little contribution to the permanent body of science. It is the program itself that is significant. And it is relevant to draw attention to a further aspect of it. In developing his theory of the multiplication of species we find him distinguishing between the physical activity by which the *species* or *virtus* were propagated through the medium and the sensations of sight or heat which they produced when they acted on the appropriate sense organs of a sentient being. His geometrization or mechanization of physical nature in effect involved him in distinguishing between primary and secondary qualities. This distinction became methodologically significant in physics when the primary qualities were conceived, as in his suggestions that light was a series of pulses and heat a motion of particles, as a physical activity that need not be directly observable but whose nature physics had to discover. A number of optical writers in the thirteenth and fourteenth centuries, for example Witelo and Theodoric of Freiberg, proposed explanations of the qualitative differences observed in light in terms of quantitative differences in the light itself, for example relating color to angle of refraction. One, John of Dumbleton, was even to attempt to formulate a photometric law relating intensity of illumination to distance from the source.

With Roger Bacon the program for mathematicizing physics and the conception of laws of nature in a nearly seventeenth-century sense become explicit. He wrote for example:

All categories (*praedicamenta*) depend on a knowledge of quantity, concerning which mathematics treats, and therefore the whole power (*virtus*) of logic depends on mathematics.[9]

---

8 "His igitur regulis et radicibus et fundamentis datis ex potestate geometriae, diligens inspector in rebus naturalibus potest dare causes omnium effectuum naturalium per hanc viam. Et impossibile erit aliter, sicut iam manifestum est in universali, quando variatur omnis actio naturalis penes fortitudinem et debilitatem per varietatem linearum, angulorum et figurarum. Sed in particulari magis est manifestum istud idem, et primo in actione naturali facta in materiam et postea in sensum, ut complete pateat veritas geometriae." *Ibid.*, pp. 65–66.

9 Roger Bacon, *Opus Maius,* ed. J. H. Bridges (3 vols.; Oxford, London, 1900), Vol. I, p. 103; cf. pars iv, C. 3: "In quo probatur per rationem quod omnis scientia requirit mathematicam."

In the things of this world, as regards their efficient and generating causes, nothing can be known without the power of geometry.[10]

The language he uses in a discussion of the "multiplication of species" seems to relate this general program unequivocally to a shift in inquiry from forms to laws. He wrote for example: "That the laws (*leges*) of reflection and refraction are common to all natural actions I have shown in the treatise on geometry."[11] He claimed to have demonstrated the formation of the image in the eye "by the law of refraction," remarking that the "species of the thing seen" must so propagate itself in the eye "that it does not transgress the laws which nature keeps in the bodies of the world." Here the "species" of light were propagated in straight lines, but in the twisting nerves "the power of the soul made the species relinquish the common laws of nature (*leges communes nature*) and behave in a way that suits its operations."[12]

10   *Ibid.*, Vol. I, p. 143–44.
11   "Que vero sint leges reflexionum et fractionum communes omnibus actionibus naturalibus, ostendi in tractatu geometrie, tam in Opere Tertio quam Primo; sed principaliter in Opere separato ab his, ubi totam generationem specierum, et multiplicationem, et actionem, et corruptionem explicavi in omnibus corporibus mundi." (Roger Bacon, *Un fragment inédit de l'Opus Tertium*, ed. P. Duhem [Quaracchi, 1909], p. 90.) Grosseteste used the word "regulae" for the "laws" of refaction which he proposed: see *De natura locorum*, ed. Baur, p. 71 and *De lineis*, p. 63.
12   "Deinde quia tolleretur visio, nisi fieret fractio speciei inter pupillam et nervum communem, in quo est communis sectio nervorum, de qua superius dixi; et dextra videretur sinistra, et e converso; ideo demonstro hoc per legem fractionum, in geometricis expositam, ut sic salvetur visio. Et nichilominus tamen oportet quod species rei vise multiplicet se novo genere multiplicationis, ut non excedat leges quas natura servat in corporibus mundi. Nam species a loco istius fractionis incedit secundum tortuositatem nervi visualis, et non tenet incessum rectum, quod est mirabile, sed tamen necesse, propter operationem a se complendam. Unde virtus anime facit speciem relinquere leges communes nature, et incedere secundum quod expedit operationibus ejus." Roger Bacon, *Un fragment inédit de l'Opus Tertium*, ed. Duhem, p. 78. I am indebted to Dr. M. Schramm of the Johannes Wolfgang Goethe University, Frankfurt, for drawing my attention to this passage. *Opus Maius*, Vol. I, p. 151, Vol. II, p. 49). The following passage occurs in a Constitution of the Emperors Theodosius, Arcadius, and Honorius: "Sufficit ad criminis molem naturae ipsius leges velle rescindere, inlicita perscrutari, occulta recludere, interdicta temptare." (James Bryce, *Studies in History and Jurisprudence* [Oxford, 1901], II, p. 119, n. 2.) For further late classical references, especially in Stoic, Jewish and Christian writers, see Marshall Clagett, *Greek Science in Antiquity* (New York, 1956), pp. 122–23, 137–44, 148. Francis Bacon sometimes used "form" and "law" as synonyms, writing in the *Novum Organum*, II, 2: "Licet enim in natura nihil vere existat praeter corpora individua, edentia actus puros individuos ex lege; in doctrinis tamen, illa ipsa

It is characteristic of these medieval philosophers that Grosseteste and Bacon should not have combined the methodological insight which they showed in their fundamental notion of the multiplication of species with any attempt at precise mathematical definition, at expressing the amounts of change quantitatively in numbers, or at measurement. One reason for this was no doubt that they had at their disposal no other mathematical concepts beyond those occurring in elementary geometrical optics, but clearly they were also uncertain about how to make another move beyond the position they had reached.

The final stage in the new medieval conception of science is marked by the methodological criticism of Ockham and the methodological and technical attempts by mathematicians in the fourteenth century to express different kinds and rates of change in mathematical form. One of the principal objects of Ockham's logical inquiries was to define the criteria by which something could be said to exist. He concluded that nothing really existed except what he called *res absolutae* or *res permanentes,* individual things determined by observable qualities. This led him, in the debate over the physical cause of motion, to cut the ground from under the feet of all the other parties, for he declared in effect that the problem was illusory. He recognized nothing real in motion beyond

lex, ejusque inquisitio, et inventio, atque explicatio, pro fundamento est tam ad sciendum, quam ad operandum. Eam autem *legem,* ejusque *paragraphos,* formarum nomine intelligimus; praesertim cum hoc vocabulum invaluerit, et familiariter occurrat." There is a similar linguistic inertia in Galileo's use of the word "definizione" for his mathematical law of free fall: below, n. 15. Francis Bacon's conception of "form" presupposed the explanation of all physical phenomena in terms of matter in motion; similarly Robert Boyle in *The Excellency and Grounds of the Mechanical Hypothesis:* "The philosophy I plead for . . . teaches that God . . . establish'd those rules of motion, and that order amongst things corporeal, which we call the laws of nature. Thus, the universe being once fram'd by God, and the laws of motion settled . . . the phenomena of the world, are physically produced by the mechanical properties of the parts of matter." (*Works,* abridged by Peter Shaw [London, 1725], I, 187.) An interesting collection of further quotations is given under "Law" in J. A. H. Murray, *New English Dictionary* (Oxford, 1908). Newton used "axiomata seu leges motus" in the *Principia Mathematica,* and he made a sharp distinction between experimentally established laws and hypotheses advanced to explain them by mechanical causes: see A. Koyré, "Pour une édition critique des oeuvres de Newton," *Rev. d'hist. des sciences,* VIII (1955), 19–37; I. Bernard Cohen, *Franklin and Newton* (Philadelphia, 1956), Appendix 1. For a sociological interpretation see E. Zilsel, "The Genesis of the Concept of Physical Law," *The Philosophical Review,* LI (1942), 245 ff., and the comment by M. Taube, *ibid.,* LII (1943), 304 ff.

the observable bodies that were moving; to say that a body was moving was to say no more than that from moment to moment it was observed to change its spatial relations with other observable bodies. He held that the abstract terms of the debate were misleading. "If we sought precision," he declared, "by using words like 'mover,' 'moved,' 'movable,' 'to be moved,' and the like, instead of words like 'motion,' 'mobility,' and others of the same kind, which according to the way of speaking and the opinion of many are not seen to stand for permanent things, many difficulties and doubts would be excluded. But now, because of these, it seems as if motion were some independent thing quite distinct from the permanent things."[13]

This is not the occasion to discuss the relevance of Ockham's conception of motion to the formation of the concept of inertia; I will say only that I think that the theory of *impetus* was at least as relevant. Nor is it the occasion to discuss the advantages or disadvantages of "nominalism" for science. But I think that it is extremely relevant that Ockham, and others like him, should have so explicitly shifted the ground of the discussion of motion, and of physics in general, from "why" to "how." The scientific treatment of motion was reduced to giving an accurate description of how bodies changed their observable spatial relations with neighboring bodies. The same move that he made as a logician was made contemporaneously by Bradwardine as a physicist, in his attempt to produce an algebraic law relating velocity, power and resistance. The two great technical developments in the fourteenth-century treatment of motion, Bradwardine's "word-algebra" and the algebraic, geometrical, and graphical treatment of "intension and remission of forms" in Oxford and Paris, had origins separate from "nominalist" or Ockhamist methodology,

---

13 "Propter autem modum loquendi multe sunt difficultates que mihi videntur secundum principia Aristotelis de motu magis vocales quam reales. Si enim uteremur precise istis vocabulis: movens, motivum, mobile, moveri et huiusmodi, et non talibus: motus, motio et consimilibus, quæ secundum modum loquendi et opinionem multorum pro rebus permanentibus non videntur supponere, multæ difficultates et dubitationes essent exclusæ. Nunc autem propter talia videtur quod motus sit alia res secundum se tota distincta a rebus permanentibus." Ockham, *Summulae in lib. Physicorum* (Rome, 1637), III, 7. Cf. *The Tractatus de Successivis attributed to William Ockham,* ed. P. Boehner, Franciscan Institute Publications, i [St. Bonaventura, New York, 1944], p. 47.) In the *Summa Logicae,* I, 49, ed. Boehner (Franciscan Inst. Publ., Text Series ii), St. Bonaventura, 1951, I, 141, Ockham wrote: "praeter res absolutae, scilicet substantias et qualitates, nulla res est imaginibilis, nec in actu nec in potentia." Cf. *Tractatus de Successivis,* p. 33: "Omnis res una vel est substantia vel qualitas, sicut alibi est ostensum et nunc suppositum."

but there is evidence that it was under the influence of the latter, as well as of Bradwardine, that Oxford mathematicians like Richard Swineshead and Dumbleton specifically rejected dynamical explanations of motion and confined themselves to kinematic mathematical description. This was a limited objective which their technical equipment gave them some hope of reaching, and in pursuing it they showed considerable sophistication and mathematical skill. They showed a complete mastery of the technique, perhaps learned from Archimedes, of posing problems and theorems *secundum imaginationem* as possibilities for purely theoretical analysis, without immediate empirical application. In pursuing their object of giving quantitative and mathematical expression to change and to the factors producing it, they grasped the fundamental idea of functional dependence and, especially in Oresme's graphical method, made notable progress in the treatment of variable quantities, which the Greeks had never exploited. In finding expressions for rates of change, they formulated sophisticated concepts like those of acceleration and instantaneous velocity, used infinitesimals, and reached important results like the Mertonian Mean Speed Law.

I have attempted to show how it is possible to trace in the thirteenth and fourteenth centuries the development of a conception of natural science similar in several fundamental respects to that found in the seventeenth century. Following the recovery of the "Euclidean" form of science, the medieval theory of science embraced three broad aspects. First, there was the analysis of the logical relationship between theories and the data explained and of the criteria and methods for testing and accepting or rejecting a theory. These included the empirical principle of verification and falsification or exclusion and the rational or conventional principle of economy, as exemplified in "Ockham's razor." Secondly, there was the conception, neoplatonic in inspiration, that nature was ultimately mathematical and could be explained only by mathematical laws. This introduced, in place of the Aristotelian "form" with its irreducible qualitative differences between different substances and their movements and behavior, a new concept of universal "laws of nature" as the proper object of scientific inquiry. And thirdly there were the new techniques, especially mathematical techniques, introduced in exploiting this program and ultimately to transform it.

It may seem at first sight that what I have just said would leave no room for any important changes in scientific method between the fourteenth and the seventeenth centuries. A glance at the results obtained in the two periods would be sufficient to warn us against any such conclusion. The manner in which many medieval scientific investigations were

actually carried out and the results obtained often seem absurdly inadequate in comparison with the intelligence displayed in discussing principles. One often has the impression that one might have missed the point.
If one were expecting simply a seventeenth-century point I think that one's
impression would be correct. The difference seems to me to mark a major
change in the center of philosophical interest between the fourteenth
and the seventeenth centuries, a change of which the immensely superior
technical equipment and efficiency of seventeenth-century science is at
least partially a consequence.

A striking example of this change and of its consequences for scientific method, an example which has been rather thoroughly studied by
historians, can be seen in the treatment of motion. The fourteenth-century scholars who worked out the mathematical functions and kinematic
theorems for motion combined a truly impressive mathematical skill and
resource with an apparent lack of interest in finding means to apply their
results to actual motions. They went through the whole discussion without making a single measurement, although certainly leading scholars
like Bradwardine and Albert of Saxony were looking for true laws of
motion, and although they formulated their problems mathematically in
such a way that they could find the answer only by measuring the concomitant variations in the parameters involved.

Buridan himself commented on the work of Bradwardine and Swineshead: "these rules are rarely or never made to be deduced to the effect"
(*quod istae regulae raro vel nunquam inventae sunt deduci ad effectum*).
But he added: "Nevertheless it is not necessary to say that such rules are
useless or artificial because, even if the conditions which they postulate
are not fulfilled in nature, it could happen that they will be realized by
the omnipotence of God."[14] These philosophers had before them examples of the measurement of concomitant variations in astronomy and in
the accounts by Ptolemy and by Witelo of the systematic increase in the
angles of refraction of light with increasing angles of incidence. They
even discussed measurement in theory and even units of measurement.
But something seems to have kept their gaze turned in a direction different from that which seventeenth-century science has taught us to seem
obvious. We can see what this was by looking at the context of the discussion, which was never simply mechanics in the seventeenth-century
sense, but problems of motion as they occurred within the more general
philosophical and methodological problem of how to find quantitative
expressions for changes of all kinds, quantitative or qualitative. The in-

14 See A. Maier, *Die Vorlaeufer Galileis im 14. Jahrhundert* (Rome, 1949), p. 101,
n. 41.

teresting mathematical and physical results that came out of the discussion of the "intension and remission of forms" were really by-products of an essentially philosophical and methodological inquiry.

The direction of interest is quite different when we turn to Galileo. Instead of methodological principles and mathematical possibilities for their own sake, he firmly took the motions actually found in nature as the object of his inquiries. "For anyone may invent an arbitrary type of motion and discuss its properties," he wrote in a famous passage in the *Two New Sciences*.[15] "But we have decided to consider the phenomena of bodies falling with an acceleration such as actually occurs in nature and to make this definition of accelerated motion exhibit the essential features of observed accelerated motions." Galileo's experiments with a ball rolling down an inclined plane to measure the relation between "space traversed in time passed" distinguish his discussion of free fall from all its predecessors. They illustrate a general change of interest between the fourteenth and the seventeenth centuries from scientific method as such to scientific method applied to the facts of nature. The faults of the medieval conception of scientific method are largely the faults of principles insufficiently tested by application. Systematic, technical application in the seventeenth century brought about a far-reaching change in the grasp and precision of the principles themselves. Surely it is significant that the idea of functional dependence and the measurement of concomitant variations, which were really as essential to the thirteenth- and fourteenth-century conception of a scientific law as to that of the seventeenth-century, were *explicitly* discussed as part of scientific method for the first time only by Galileo and Francis Bacon. At the same time several other fundamentally important aspects of scientific method came into the field of discussion, for example the role of hypotheses in predicting new knowledge and guiding research, the conception of controls and, on the technical side, the grasp of the need for precision in measuring instruments.

Although it is my purpose simply to chart the course of an intellectual change rather than to attempt to explain it, it is relevant to point to the institutional context of the medieval discussions. The central doctrines of medieval science were developed almost entirely within the context of academic discussions based on the books used in university teaching, especially in the faculty of arts.[16] It is true that the applications of aca-

15 Galileo Galilei, *Opere*, VIII, 197.
16 During the thirteenth and fourteenth centuries the scientific content of the arts course was expanded far beyond the four traditional mathematical subjects, geometry, astronomy, arithmetic and music, forming the *quadrivium*. Not only Euclid's *Elements* and Ptolemy's *Almagest*, but treatises on practical astronomy,

demic sciences, such as of astronomy in determining the calendar, of arithmetic in the work of the exchequer and of commercial houses, or of anatomy and physiology and chemistry in surgery and medicine, were put into practice outside the universities. It is true also that in other fields of technology, and in art and architecture with their increasing tendency to naturalism, developments took place that were to be of profound importance for science. But it was the clerics of the universities who were responsible for the main theoretical conceptions of science, and their interest in them was in general epistemological or metaphysical or logical rather than strictly scientific in the modern sense. Although it would be false to suggest that scientific problems were always discussed in a philosophical context in the Middle Ages, the ambience of the discussions and the habit of presenting them in commentaries on Aristotle or other philosophical or theological writers certainly put pressure in that direction. This would help to explain the striking contrast between the sustained interest in the logic and theory of experimental science from thirteenth-century Oxford to sixteenth-century Padua[17] and the comparative scarcity of actual experimental investigations. It also helps to explain the development of science, as distinct from merely philosophy of science, from the end of the sixteenth century in scientific societies outside the universities, even though the members were predominantly university men. And it gives point to the rejection by these new scientists of the purely philosophical academic methodology that had lost touch with the actual problems of science, and of the medieval discussions that lay behind it.

It may be asked whether the medieval conception of scientific method can really be claimed to have any more significance for the scientific tradition than the inadequate science with which it was associated, and also whether it did in fact have any influence in the sixteenth and seventeenth centuries. (So we might be tempted to give a double negative.) In answer to the first question there seems to me no doubt that a process of philosophical orientation was as necessary a preliminary to the scientific performance of the seventeenth century as it was to that of the Greeks. If

Aristotle's writings on natural science, Alhazen's and Witelo's optical treatises, and other scientific works found their way into the curricula of various universities.

17 See J. H. Randall, Jr., "The development of Scientific Method in the School of Padua," *Journal of the History of Ideas,* I (1940), 177ff.; P. O. Kristeller and J. H. Randall, Jr., "The Study of Renaissance Philosophy," *ibid.,* II (1941), 490ff. The medical faculty was important at Padua and arts was a preparation primarily for this instead of for theology as at Paris and Oxford.

this is true then the significance of this philosophical stage is clearly much greater than the immediate scientific results that it produced, although certainly this is not to say that the medieval philosophers appreciated the full significance of their methodological insights or saw all the problems which their seventeenth-century successors saw and solved. Indeed their very deficiency in performance shows that they did not. It is we, looking back on the whole story, who are in a position to judge the significance of its various episodes. Among these the renewed appreciation in the sixteenth and seventeenth centuries of the scientific performance of Archimedes was certainly something that allowed Galileo and his contemporaries to get scientific results far beyond the range of philosophical talk. The point of my argument is that the significance of Archimedes' methods, and of the mathematical-Platonic conception of nature, for scientific inquiry could be grasped because the preceding discussions of scientific method had shown, at least partly, what to look for. After the successes of the seventeenth century, philosophers were in a position to assess the actual achievements of science, and since then discussions of scientific method have been largely an analysis of scientific work already achieved. But before the middle of the seventeenth century the general lines of scientific thinking had not yet been firmly established by results, and it seems to me to be one of the most important characteristics of the whole period of the origins of modern science that it contained so many discussions and programs of scientific thinking, from those of Grosseteste and Roger Bacon to those of Galileo, Francis Bacon, Descartes, and Newton.

I have not in this paper dealt specifically with the important question of the actual influence, direct or indirect, of medieval writers which it is possible to trace in the scientific writings of the sixteenth and seventeenth centuries.[18] Certainly most of the principal medieval doctrines

18 For bibliographical studies of the medieval writings available in print see especially A. C. Krebs, "Incunabula scientifica et medica," *Osiris,* IV (1938), and G. Sarton, *The Appreciation of Ancient and Medieval Science during the Renaissance (1450–1600)* (Philadelphia, 1955). For some studies of special cases the following may be consulted: E. Gilson, *Etudes sur le rôle de la pensée médiévale dans la formation du système cartésien (Etudes de Philosophie Médiévale, XIII)* Paris, 1930; C. Boyer, *The Concepts of the Calculus* (New York, 1939); A. Koyré, *Etudes galiléennes (Actualités scientifiques et industrielles,* Nos. 852–54 [Paris, 1939]); A. Maier, *Zwei Grundprobleme der scholastischen Naturphilosophie* (2nd ed.; Rome, 1951), *An der Grenze von Scholastik und Naturwissenschaften* (2nd ed.; Rome, 1952); E. A. Moody, "Galileo and Avempace," *Journal of the History of Ideas,* XII (1951); and my *Robert Grosseteste.*

were available in printed editions and were taught in various universities, especially in Padua and Paris and in Germany, in the sixteenth century. But when one asks more specifically what, for example, Galileo or Descartes actually knew and what use they made of the dynamics of *impetus* or of fourteenth-century Oxford kinematics or of Oresme's graphical methods, the evidence becomes difficult and unsatisfactory. That they had some knowledge of the earlier work in these fields is beyond doubt, and we can trace it specifically in Galileo. Sometimes he uses old language in a new context, as when he uses *impeto* within his new "inertial" dynamics or when he describes an "Archimedean" procedure for establishing functional relationships in the language of the *metodo resolutivo e compositivo*. Linguistic inertia is evidence of continuity with earlier forms of thought, whatever changes the requirements of successful scientific practice may have brought about.

One of the profoundly influential and fruitful events that made up the scientific revolution of the seventeenth century seems to me to have been the restoration of full contact between science and scientific methodology. In spite of the promising conception of science that began in the thirteenth century, medieval scientists in the end succeeded only in revising some isolated sections of the physics and cosmology they inherited from the Greeks and Arabs. The successful revision by seventeenth-century scientists of the whole of the theoretical framework and assumptions of physical science was effected by a close combination of philosophical and technical maneuvers. The conception they formed of scientific method, of the counters available in terms of conceptions of nature, hypotheses, logical procedures and mathematical and experimental techniques, was closely measured by the technical success of the results and by their universality. It was proved by results that the mathematicization of nature, the "mechanical philosophy,"[19] the use of abstract theories, the experimental

19 The exploitation of the hypothesis or "regulative belief" that all forms of change could be reduced to matter in motion and therefore explained mechanically gave the seventeenth century a powerful guide to inquiry which combined exactly with the experimental and mathematical method. It could provide a foundation for explanations in a way that medieval concepts of nature, even Grosseteste's and Roger Bacon's "physics of light," could not. Cf. M. Boas, "The establishment of the mechanical philosophy," *Osiris,* X (1952), 412 ff. For a test-case of a leading scientist whose inquiries were hindered by the lack of a "mechanical philosophy" Harvey's lack of progress in understanding the functions of the blood and of respiration may perhaps be cited. In this respect Descartes' criticism in the *Discours* of Harvey's failure to account for the cause of the action of the heart is also to the point. When he allowed himself to advance beyond the experimental results Harvey's conception of explanation

method, the conception of functional dependence, the new algebra and geometry, were successful elements in a scientific method. It was proved by results that motion was the right problem in which to find the key to physics. It was for the very important reason that it succeeded, and this could only be discovered by trying, that seventeenth-century mechanics became the principal model for the methods of science as a whole. It seems to me that their ability to be good judges of scientific success, and to be impressed by it, is a measure of the distance between the natural philosophers of the seventeenth century and their medieval predecessors with whom they shared so many ideas and aspirations in common.

The forms and methods of modern science are the product of a long and complicated intellectual struggle but as in so many aspects of the Scientific Revolution the final stages, so long prepared, were taken rapidly by men of genius in the seventeenth century. But to become a good judge of science was something that required resolution and sophistication even after the main way was clear. Francis Bacon, heir in a sense to the empirical tradition of Greek medicine and Aristotle, and Descartes, heir in a sense to Euclid and Plato, both proposed versions of a second great model of scientific thought that was to replace the first great model, that of Greek geometry, or as Bacon mistakenly thought, of Aristotle's *Organon*. Galileo's version is nearer the mark in physics. But the polemics between the Cartesians and Newton show that even towards the end of the seventeenth century the proper relationship to be understood between observational data, laws, hypotheses, and mechanical explanations in terms of the reigning concept of nature was still a matter of dispute. The continuation of the debate down to the present moment, and the transformation of the seventeenth-century model itself as a result of more recent developments in physics, in non-Euclidian geometries, in the mathematical theory of probability, and in logical analysis, show with the most unequivocal directness that thought about the forms and methods of science is an inseparable part

was essentially Aristotelian. Nearly all the leading seventeenth-century scientists, for example Galileo, Kepler, Descartes, Boyle, Newton, were consciously preoccupied with scientific method, especially with the relationships between facts, laws, theories, and the mechanical philosophy, and to use Boyle's phrase, with the "requisites of a good hypothesis" (cf. M. Boas, "La Méthode scientifique de Robert Boyle," *Rev. d'hist. des sciences,* IX [1956], 120–21; R. S. Westfall, "Unpublished Boyle Papers Relating to Scientific Method," *Annals of Science,* XII [1956], 116–17; also E. A. Burtt, *The Metaphysical Foundations of Modern Physical Science* [2nd. ed.; London, 1932].) In the mainly descriptive sciences like botany and zoology there was an analogous methodological preoccupation with the relation of "natural" to "artificial" systems of classification.

of the progress of scientific thought itself. I have spoken only about the history of physics, because this has provided the leading model. If we complicated our inquiry by including in it, as indeed we should, other and especially the biological sciences, we would find other species of model (although recognizably of the same scientific genus) but a parallel story.

Further references: C. Burnett (ed.), *Adelard of Bath* (London, 1987); J. P. Anton (ed.), *Naturalism and Historical Understanding: Essays in the philosophy of J. H. Randall* (Albany, N.Y., 1967); A. C. Crombie and N. G. Siraisi (eds.), *The Rational Arts of Living (Smith College Studies in History*, vol. 50; Northampton, Mass., 1987) and Crombie, *Styles* . . . ch. 3.i, iii; *La Filosofia della natura nel medievo* (Milan, 1966); N. W. Gilbert, *Renaissance Concepts of Method* (New York, 1960); E. Grant (ed.), *A Source Book in Medieval Science* (Cambridge, Mass., 1974); D. C. Lindberg (ed.), *Science in the Middle Ages* (Chicago, 1978); A. Maier, *Metaphysische Hintergründe der spätscholastischen Naturphilosophie* (Rome, 1955), *Zwischen Philosophie und Mechanik* (Rome, 1958), *Die Vorläufer Galileis im 14. Jahrhundert* (2nd ed.; Rome, 1966), *Ausgehendes Mittelalter* (Rome, 1964-77), *Zwei Untersuchungen zur nachscholastischen Philosphie* (2nd ed.; Rome, 1968); J. E. Murdoch and E. D. Sylla (eds.), *The Cultural Context of Medieval Learning* (Dordrecht, 1975), J. E. Murdoch, *Album of Science: Antiquity and the Middle Ages* (New York, 1984); and for terminology, laws of nature and functions, A. C. Crombie, "Infinite power and the laws of nature; a medieval speculation" in *L'infinito nella scienza*, ed. G. Toraldo di Francia (Rome, 1987) 223-43; L. Lutz et al. (eds.), *Lexikon des Mittelalters* (Aachen, 1977-87); A. Maier, "Der Gesetzbegriff in der historischen Wissenschaften", *Studium generale*, xix (1966) 657-67; A Maierù, *Terminologia logica della tarde scolastica* (Rome, 1972); P. Michaud-Quantin, M. Lemoine, *Etudes sur le vocabulaire philosophique du moyen âge* (Rome, 1970); F. Oakley, *Omnipotence, Covenant, and Order* (Ithaca, N.Y., 1984); L. Olivieri (ed.), *Aristotelismo veneto e scienza moderna* (Padua, 1983), M. Schramm, "Aristotelianism", *History of Science*, ii (1963) 91-113, "Steps towards the idea of function", ibid., iv (1965) 70-102; C. Vasoli, *La dialattica e la retorica dell' Umanismo* (Milan, 1968); A. P. Youschkevitch, "The concept of function up to the middle of the nineteenth century", *Archive for History of Exact Sciences*, xvi (1976) 37-85; see also chs. 3 p. 71, 4 pp. 74, 90, 5 p. 114, 6 p. 137, 11-12.

8

SCIENCE AND THE ARTS IN THE RENAISSANCE:
THE SEARCH FOR TRUTH AND CERTAINTY, OLD AND NEW

"Man is to render praise to God"—so wrote Leon Battista Alberti in the mid-fifteenth century—"to satisfy him with good works for those gifts of excelling *virtù* that God gave to the soul of man, greatest and pre-eminent above all other earthly animals".[1] Works could satisfy their creator with those qualities of *virtù* in any kind of activity ranging from the conduct of family life to painting and architecture. All when they did so shared the common characteristic indicated by Alberti when he explained by the method of perspective for "the painter how he can represent with his hand what he has conceived with his mind".[2]

The term *virtù* in Renaissance Italian indicated a style of intellectual and consequently practical behaviour. A man of *virtù*, acting rationally in the image of his Creator, was a man with intellectual power (*virtù*) to command any situation, to act as he intended, like an architect producing a building according to his design, not at the mercy of fortuitous circumstances or *fortuna*. Whether in mind or matter, in the natural sciences or the constructive arts, in private or political life, a man of

---

1. Leon Battista Alberti, *I libri della famiglia*, ed. by C. Grayson (*Opere volgari*, i (Bari, 1960)), 133; *cf.* for full documentation of this paper with bibliographies A. C. Crombie, *Styles of scientific thinking in the European tradition*, especially chs 1: "Historiography of science: the variety of scientific methods", 2.iv: "Analysis and synthesis: the mathematical arts and sciences", 3.ii: "The rational artist and the rational experimenter", and 4: "Hypothetical modelling transposed from Renaissance art into early modern science"; and Crombie and A. Carugo, *Galileo's Arguments and Disputes in Natural Philosophy*, especially chs 1: "Introduction", and 3: "The Idea of mathematics in sixteenth century thought" (forthcoming); also Crombie, "Philosophical presuppositions and shifting interpretations of Galileo", in *Theory Change, Ancient Axiomatics, and Galileo's Methodology*, ed. J. Hintikka, D. Gruender and E. Agazzi, i (Dordrecht, 1981); and for guides to further bibliography, below, refs 3, and 13-19.

2. Alberti, *De pictura* (1435), i. 24, ed. by C. Grayson, in *On painting and on sculpture* (London, 1972), 58; *cf.* A. J. Close, "Commonplace theories of art and nature in classical antiquity and in the Renaissance", *Journal of the history of ideas*, xxx (1969), 467-86; C. W. Westfall, "Painting and the liberal arts: Alberti's view", *ibid.*, 487-506; J. S. Ackerman, "Alberti's light", in *Studies in late medieval and Renaissance painting in honor of Millard Meiss*, ed. by I. Lavin and J. Plummer (New York, 1978), 1-28; see below, ref. 17.

virtù aimed always to be in rational control of himself as a moral being and in relation to his fellow men and to nature, in control of what he did and what he made. He was the rational artist in all things.

The conception of the *virtuoso,* the rational artist aiming at reasoned and examined control alike of his own thoughts, intentions, and actions, and of his surroundings, seems to me to be of the essence of the European morality, meaning both habits and ethics, out of which the European scientific movement was generated and engineered. In this context the rational artist and the rational experimental scientist appear as exemplary products of the same intellectual culture. The rational perspective artist formed in his mind a conception of what he would represent by an antecedent analysis of visual clues organized optically by geometrical perspective; the rational experimental scientist proceeded likewise by an antecedent mathematical and conceptual analysis of his subject-matter. They shared an intellectual commitment to the cultivation of *virtù.* This common commitment offers an invitation, then, to relate the styles of scientific thinking in any period to contemporary styles of thinking in the arts, in philosophy and theology, and in practical affairs. It offers likewise an invitation to analyze the various elements that make up an intellectual style in the study and treatment of nature : conceptions of nature and of science, of scientific inquiry and scientific explanation, of the identity of natural science within an intellectual culture, and the intellectual commitments and expectations that affect attitudes to innovation and change. These questions again, asked comparatively of different cultures, offer a culturally integrated view of the historical problem of the unique origins of modern science in the society of Western Europe.

The scientific movement has been concerned with man's relations with nature as perceiver, as knower and as agent. If we can characterize the commitment to the ideal of deciding by argument and evidence all questions about what exists and about what should be done, we can see in the origins of modern science a series of Western responses to the recovery of ancient thought made by a new society with some different mental and moral commitments and expectations. Medieval and early modern Europe had a different view of nature and of man and his destiny, a different theology, a different economy, and a different view of technology. We may distinguish three broad stages of intellectual response and orientation, each developing a characteristic style of formulating and solving its problems.

With the first intellectual impetus given by the recovery of ancient texts from the twelfth century came a primary intellectual achievement. This was the grasp and critical elaboration by the philosophical community of the medieval schools and universities, of the construction of a demonstrative explanatory system on the models of Euclid's geometry and Aristotle's natural philosophy. Together with this came a critical elaboration of logical precision, from methods formalized by Aristotle, for the control of argument and evidence to decide a question, including decision by calculation, observation, and experiment. Secondly came a matching of this logical control of argument and calculation with a likewise theoretically designed and measured control of a variety of different materials and practical activities. Programmes towards this end already expressed from the twelfth century that urge towards rational analysis and ingenious contrivance for the material mastery of nature,[3] which was to be achieved in action by the practitioners of a diversity of arts. This group, working essentially outside the universities but not without university contacts, came to succeed by making rational and, where possible, quantitative analysis precede material construction or action. Thus they achieved control of the measured representation of visual space by perspective painting and sculpture, and of time by the mechanical clock, of music by measured temporal patterns of pitch and interval, of spatial location and transport by trigonometric surveying and cartographic coordinates, of building and machines by a search for rational mechanics, of commerce and administration by systematic book-keeping and numerical recording. The goals of the arts, whether technological or aesthetic, should not be confused with those of philosophy and the sciences, but it does not seem difficult to recognize in them all a common intellectual style in which each reinforced the others, and all came to contribute to the third stage of the origins of modern science. That was the confident establishment of the "new sort of philosophizing"[4] in the "physico-mathematical experimental learning"[5] of the seventeenth century. The intellectual approaches leading in this way to a conception both of scientific inquiry and of artistic composition as cognate arts of the soluble began with the recognition that theoretical analysis and rational design must precede material analysis and construction. They concluded with an experimental science that combined, with effective logical precision, a

3. *Cf.* Dominicus Gundissalinus, *De divisione philosophiae*, hrg. L. Baur (*Beiträge zur Geschichte der Philosophie des Mittelalters*, iv, 2–3 (Münster, 1903)), 10–33, 90–124, esp. 112–24; Adelard of Bath, *Quaestiones naturales*, hrg. M. Müller (*Beiträge . . .*, xxxi.2 (Münster, 1934)); also A. C. Crombie, *Augustine to Galileo: Science in the middle ages and early modern times*, 2 vols, new impression (London and Cambridge, Mass., 1979); *idem*, *Robert Grosseteste and the origins of experimental science 1100–1700*, 3rd ed. (Oxford, 1971), ch. 2; *idem*, "Quantification in medieval physics", *Isis*, lii (1961), 143–60; *idem*, "The relevance of the middle ages to the scientific movement", in *Perspectives in medieval history*, ed. by K. F. Drew and F. S. Lear (Chicago, 1963), 35–57; and *idem*, "Some attitudes to scientific progress: Ancient, medieval and early modern", *History of science*, xiii (1975), 213–30: all with further references.

4. William Gilbert, *De magnete* (London, 1600), preface.

5. *Journal Book of the Royal Society*, 28 November 1660, quoted by C. R. Weld, *A history of the Royal Society* (London, 1848), 65.

theoretical search for common forms of explanation with a practical demand for accurately reproducible results.

Some of the characteristics of this intellectual culture which produced the rational European movement of both science and the arts can be exemplified from that enterprize of the search for truth and certainty which became explicit in the middle stage of this intellectual orientation, during the fifteenth and sixteenth centuries. European intellectual life received a considerable stimulus in the late fifteenth and early sixteenth centuries from the recovery, publication and active use of a body of Greek philosophical and scientific writings hitherto either unknown or with little influence in the Latin West. These writings fell into two main groups, with some overlap, each producing a corresponding response, centred at the beginning in Italy.[6]

The first group of writings comprized philosophical texts, notably the extant works of Plato translated into Latin by the Florentine philosopher Marsilio Ficino together with then-associated Hermetic documents, and detailed reports of Greek atomism and scepticism provided especially by Lucretius, and by Sextus Empiricus and Diogenes Laertius. These were taken up by philosophers dissatisfied with established academic Aristotelianism, who saw them primarily as a means of finding other, more acceptable, rational criteria for knowledge in general and for religious knowledge in particular, and of bringing about moral improvement and educational reform. At the same time they introduced a complex intellectual and moral crisis: from Plato and the Hermetics as ambiguous alternatives to the Christian theology of creation with its integral moral doctrine of providence; from the atomists by the elimination of Providence altogether; and most pervasively from the sceptics whose arguments, launched into the republic of letters by Montaigne, produced a continuing intellectual insecurity to become, in the discriminating treatment of such as Marin Mersenne and Descartes and Pascal, an integral part of European thinking. The second group of writings comprized texts on the mathematical sciences and arts and their applications. Of these some came to exert a powerful general influence upon intellectual history, while others of greater specialization, about optics and mechanics and music and so on, supplied the theory used and developed by practical mathematicians and artists.

The intellectual commitments of the two groups of persons primarily interested in these writings can best be compared by looking at their conceptions of a common subject: the place of mathematics in intellectual culture. Such a comparison shows that they shared a very general outlook as members of the same integrated world, but that the uses they saw for mathematics and their conceptions of rational choice were poles apart. The debates and practical experience over all these questions promoted

6. *Cf.* Crombie, *Styles* (ref. 1), ch. 3. ii; Crombie and Carugo, *Galileo's ... Natural Philosophy* (ref. 1), chs 1 and 3.

in their specialized range a growth of the technical content of the sciences and arts, but more generally and more subtly they promoted shifts of intellectual style, most profoundly perhaps in the commitments and expectations of disagreement as well as agreement. The comparison illustrates again the need for us to understand the whole context of thought about true knowledge and its value, if we are to see how art and science as problem-solving activities fitted into the contemporary scheme of knowledge and existence.

The most striking characteristic shared by this intellectual inheritance was its mathematical rationalism, dominating the conception of a whole range of knowledge and practice from physics and the visual and musical arts to ethics and theology. The ultimate literary source of this rationalism was Plato, with behind Plato the Pythagoreans, notably Archytas of Tarentum. Platonic or Pythagorean rationalism had a long history in medieval thought, through Plato's *Timaeus,* through St Augustine, and also through Aristotle himself. It received a new life in the fifteenth century from Ficino's Latin versions and commentaries, and also from other contemporary scholarship, of which much the most important for the mathematical sciences and arts was that included in Giorgio Valla's great work *De expetendis et fugiendis rebus opus* (1501 : On things to be sought and to be shunned). In this Valla presented a compendium of all the sciences and arts, aimed at both intellectual enlightenment and moral education from a point of view which he shared both with the moral philosopher Ficino and with their contemporaries Leonardo da Vinci and Albrecht Dürer and other practical artists.

The point of view which they shared had been established in Platonic thought as a specific theory of nature and of man's relation to nature as perceiver, knower and agent. Nature had been designed by divine art on the analogy of human art with mathematical order and proportion perceptible by sight and hearing, but properly graspable only by the intellect. Conversely, Valla cited Archytas to the effect that man had first to conceive in his mind both what he wanted to explain, and what he wanted to make or do. Science was knowledge of stable universal principles such as mathematicians knew. The artist, before making something, by reason "fashions and forms it inwardly, and accordingly makes an image for himself of everything that is to be portrayed".[7] Valla saw both the experimental science of nature and the constructive arts (mechanical, plastic, visual, musical) as the imposition of reason by antecedent analysis, above all through mathematics.

In this view Valla was guided also by two other ancient authors whose works were to exert a powerful influence upon the intellectual history of the sixteenth century. The Roman architect Vitruvius insisted on the precedence of theory in any rational action, and in particular of

7. Valla, *De expetendis* . . . (Venetiis, 1501), i.3.

mathematical theory in a constructive art. The authors of the first Italian edition of *De architectura* (1521), begun by Cesare Cesariano and continued by Benedetto Giovio and Bono Mauro, developed this in a fascinating exegesis of the words 'machinatio' and 'machina' (which have in Greek and Latin the same range of meaning from mechanical contriving to political machination as they do in English and other modern European languages) into a view of inquiry into the operation of things as cunning intellectual contriving. Again they cited Archytas as a mechanic, famous for constructing a wooden dove which flew, to illustrate that intellectual contrivance must first find out by reasoning both what men wanted to explain and what they wanted to "put into practice through a burning desire to produce in sensible works with their own hands that which they have thought out with the mind".[8]

Valla's other general guide was the Hellenistic Greek philosopher Proclus. In his commentary on Euclid's *Elements of geometry*, Proclus set out a Platonic and Pythagorean scheme which was to offer probably the most influential programme for the mathematical sciences and arts in the sixteenth century. He saw mathematics as an intermediate science, generated by the mind but both stimulated by and projected upon the world of the senses. In one direction its reasoning replicated the complex material world with a world of ideas, and led the mind from the observable uncertainties of matter to the rational certainties of the highest abstractions. In the other direction, by descending into matter it delivered out of itself the principles both for scientific understanding of the material construction of the world and for the materially constructive mathematical arts. These sciences and arts included those to which in both theory and practice Renaissance Italy above all, but also the Netherlands and other European centres, made their major contributions to the intellectual history of the European scientific movement, by the development of rational mechanics, of cosmography and cartography, of optics applied to perspective painting and sculpture, and of measured music. All involved a rational inquisition, representation, and finally imitative manipulation of nature. The perspective artists made the geometrical optics they learnt from Euclid and his ancient and medieval successors yield a practical method of showing precisely what would be seen under specified conditions of angle of vision, distance, reflection and refraction, shadow and so on and of transfering this three-dimensional information to a two-dimensional surface. Albrecht Dürer's assertion, that "a good painter is inwardly full of figures", which pour forth "from the inner ideas of which Plato writes",[9] was

8. Marcus Lucius Vitruvius Pollio, *De architectura libri dece, traducti de latino in vulgari, affigurati, commentati* (Como, 1521), x.i, f.162v, cf. i.3, f.18; P. Galluzzi, "A proposito di un errore dei traduttori di Vitruvio nel '500", *Annali dell Istituto e Museo di Storia della Scienza di Firenze*, i (1976), 78–80.

9. *Cf.* E. Panofsky, *The life and art of Albrecht Dürer* (1955), 280, cf. 252-3.

made by an artist with technical experience in the practical mathematics of design, and should be so understood. Likewise, a precise technical bearing should be understood in the mathematical rationalism of Leonardo da Vinci's repeated assertions that all art must begin in the mind before it can issue through the hands, and that nature has necessary laws which art must follow but which, unlike nature, the artist is free to manipulate acording to his own design. Thus the rational artist was the exemplary man of *virtù*, always in control of what he made within the rationally examined limits of the possible. For "whatever exists in the universe through essence, presence or imagination he has first in the mind and then in the hands".[10] The inquisition of nature, for this master both of design and of the intellectual play of thought-experiments, was then a pursuit of intellectual contrivance and machination: "O speculator on things, I do not praise you for knowing the things that nature through her order naturally brings about ordinarily by herself; but I say rejoice in knowing the end of those things that are designed by your own mind."[11]

The philosopher Ficino shared this view which made man through his rational imitation and manipulation of God's designs nature's rival and master, alone among animals capable of inventive progress. But Ficino's attention was focussed on another aspect of Platonism. His was a rational artist's vision of man's moral principles of action. In imposing mathematical order and proportion on matter the Platonic God in both classical and Christian thought gave the world a morally as well as intellectually normative harmony. This harmony came to have various meanings such as simplicity, economy and fitness, which supplied a conception of sufficient explanation with profound influence in the history of science. Harmony was also the bond linking Renaissance science, the visual and musical arts, medicine, and ethics. For such a philosopher as Ficino, mainly interested in moral enlightenment, virtue, like painting, must likewise be designed first in the mind before it could issue in action. In this he reinforced with the new Platonism the essentially Aristotelian style conceived for the mastery of human nature, and the cultivation of the habit of virtue true to that nature, by practice guided by right reason. Beyond that he saw with Plato in mathematical ideas an efficacious means of leading the mind from the material world and its concerns upwards to theology and the contemplation of the divine creator. Within this Platonic scheme Ficino elaborated a complex system of correspondence between the macrocosm of the world and the microcosm of the human body and soul, and of the harmonious influence transmitted

10. Leonardo da Vinci, *Treatise on painting, Codex Urbinas Latinus 1270*, transl. by A. P. McMahon (Princeton, 1956), i, 35.

11. Leonardo da Vinci, *Les manuscrits . . . de la Bibliothèque de l'Institut*, Cod.G, f.47r, publiés . . . par . . . C. Ravaisson-Mollien (Paris, 1890).

through the primary media of light and sound. From this he developed a practical moral psychology for encouraging virtue by means of visual designs and music, which would draw down corresponding influence from the heavens.[12]

The contrast between the moral philosophers and the practical mathematicians and artists lay in their conception of rational choice. This is yet another illustration of the complexity of the intellectual landscape through which we must follow the scientific movement. It was for the role of mathematical ideas in moral and theological education that mathematics was encouraged by many philosophers of Platonic leanings during the sixteenth century. It is significant that in Italy there was a link between efforts to promote both Platonism and mathematics in universities, including Jesuit universities, persisting into the negotiations for appointments to chairs in each subject of Galileo's older contemporaries and of Galileo himself. Within this context the moral philosophers saw mathematics essentially as a stage in moral and theological education. Its certainty was for the religious an antidote to scepticism. Its use was to help to induce a general state of mind leading to virtuous action. The philosophers who saw mathematics thus rather as a means to moral and theological education, than to solving scientific or practical problems, were often notable too for their eclectic tolerance of apparently opposing systems. This was an ancient and widespread mental attitude, based on the optimistic belief that all great thinkers when correctly interpreted must be found to harmonize in truth. Hence the tradition that the proper work then for philosophers was to look for concordance between apparently opposing authorities, so that Plato and Aristotle and even the atomists, although probably not the sceptics, would be found to agree in essentials with each other and all with true theology.[13]

In sharp contrast was the brutal insistence of the practical mathematicians and artists that accurate thinking and precisely controlled action alike required the exact identification of specific problems, and that the solution of specific problems required an uncompromising choice. The sciences of nature and the contructive arts were at their cutting edge alike the products not of a general state of mind but of clear limited decisions. The practical mathematicians and artists found their problems in contemporary practices, illuminated by the newly edited and translated Greek works on the mathematical sciences. These were both general, like those of

12. *Cf.* D. P. Walker, *Spiritual and demonic magic from Ficino to Campanella* (London, 1958), ch. i.

13. *Cf.* Crombie, "Mathematics and Platonism in the sixteenth-century Italian universities and in Jesuit educational policy", in *Prismata: Naturwissenschaftsgeschichtliche Studien: Festschrift für Willy Hartner*, hrg. Y. Maeyama und W. G. Saltzer (Wiesbaden, 1977), 63–94, and Crombie and Carugo, *Galileo's ... Natural Philosophy* (ref. 1), ch. 3.

Proclus and Pappus, and specialized, like those of Euclid and Ptolemy on optics and on music, of Aristoxenus on music, and of Archimedes and the Aristotelian *Mechanica* on that subject. These subjects in Greek thought comprised *techne,* or art, as distinct from *episteme* or true science. But by the turn of the sixteenth century, the success of the mathematical and technical arts in solving limited problems had put them into a position for the claim to be made that they alone could discover the only true science of nature there was.[14]

The intellectual approaches leading through sixteenth century thought to this conception of science as an art of the soluble may be broadly summarized as follows. Recognition that theoretical analysis and rational design must precede material analysis and construction led to the conception of rational sciences of mechanics and optics and music and so on, all within the limits of the possible. "I have seene all enginiers deceiv'd", wrote Galileo in 1593, "while they apply their engines to works of their owne nature impossible; in the success of which both they them-selves have bene deceiv'd, and others also defrauded of the hopes they had conceiv'd upon their promeses". For effects could be obtained only "according to the necessary constitution of nature . . . . And . . . all wonder ceases in us of that effect, which goes not a poynt out of the bounds of natures constitution".[15] Art could not cheat nature, but by discovering, obeying and manipulating natural laws, with an increasing emphasis on quantification and measurement, art was seen to deprive nature of its mysteries and to achieve a mastery exemplified by rational prediction. This rational mastery was illustrated also by the growing popularity of the modelling and extension of the natural by artificial constructions, ranging from clockwork devices to perspective representations as imitative models of the natural clues for perception. In science the model was seen as a means of investigating and explaining the natural. So nature, envisaged in Platonic thought at the beginning of the century as an expression of divine geometry, had been given by the mathematical arts an extended image at the end. For Plato, wrote a French regius professor of these arts who was also a physician, in answering the question what God did, should not have stopped at "he always geometrizes" but should have added "and always mechanizes. For this world is a machine, and indeed the greatest, most efficacious, firmest and most shapely of

14. *Cf.* Crombie and Carugo, *ibid.* (ref. 1); Crombie, *Styles* (ref. 1), chs 3–4, also Crombie (ed.), *Scientific change* (London and New York, 1963); above refs 1 and 3, and below 17–19.

15. Galileo Galilei, *Le mecaniche* (undated), ed. naz., direttore A. Favaro (*Le opere,* ii (Firenze, 1968)), 155; transl. by Robert Payne (1636): transcribed from British Museum MS Harley 6796, f.317r, by A. Carugo: see Crombie and Carugo, *ibid.* (ref. 1), ch. 2. iii.

machines".[16]

Such words must be understood in their intellectual context and that context was certainly not yet that of Descartes. Yet without imposing a completely mechanistic conception of nature, the mathematical sciences and arts combined by the end of the sixteenth century to create within European intellectual culture an effective context for solving problems. I shall conclude with one example. The solution by Johannes Kepler in 1603/4 of the fundamental physiological problem of vision, that of how the eye formed an image on the retina, was the first major modern physiological discovery. With this demonstration, Kepler introduced a new conception of how to investigate the relation of perceiver to perceived in all the senses. It became as important as William Harvey's later demonstration of the circulation of the blood in opening new prospects for physiology in general. Before Kepler, developments in perspective painting and in the instrumentation of surveying and astronomy had created both a geometrical theory of visual space and a technique for demonstrating what would be seen under specified optical conditions and for representing this upon a plane surface. Two notable contributions prepared the ground for Kepler's solution. The first was Alberti's conception of a picture as a section of the pyramidal figure formed by the lines of vision connecting the object seen with the eye, and his demonstration of how to make the section correctly by viewing the object or scene through a checkered screen. The second was Leonardo da Vinci's use of another device, a camera obscura for throwing an inverted picture of the scene through a pinhole on to a screen. Leonardo compared the eye to a camera obscura with a lens in it, but assiduous attempts by both anatomists and mathematicians throughout the sixteenth century to explain how the eye effected vision all foundered on the same difficulty: the inverted image. The problem as inherited from Greek and medieval optics had been formulated to include questions of perception and causation which prevented a purely geometrical analysis of the formation of the image. Kepler succeeded by first isolating the geometrical optics of the eye as an answerable question to be treated apart from all other aspects of vision. He answered it by treating the living eye on the model of a camera obscura with a lens in it, and by reforming the optical geometry of how this device focussed the picture on to the retinal screen. This demonstration provided contemporaries both with a model of scientific method, and with a scientific basis for

16. Aristotelis, *Mechanica, Graeca emendata, Latine facta, et commentariis illustrata,* ab Henrico Monantholio medico et mathematicarum artium professore regio, Epistola dedicatoria (Parisiis, 1599); *cf.* P. Rossi, *I filosofi e la macchine 1400–1700,* 2a ed. (Milano, 1971); Crombie and Carugo, *ibid.* (ref. 1), ch. 3. ii, Crombie, *Styles* (ref. 1), ch. 4.ii: "The modelling of the senses".

reintroducing the investigation of the complexities of the perceptual process: for example, how to understand the retinal image as accurately symbolic rather than literally representative of the scene perceived. It provided at the same time a clear scientific basis from which to correct and extend the natural performance and range of the senses by means of artificial instruments.[17] Later in the century, from a similar background in the development of measured and instrumented music, the resonating strings of a lute were to be proposed as a model for the analysis of pitch by the ear.[18]

We may see then in the mathematical sciences and arts of early modern Europe one fecund cultural source of that conception of man's relation to nature as perceiver and knower and agent which came to characterize the European scientific movement and with it more generally European culture. In this context we may ask ourselves a question. The successes of the mathematical and technical arts in solving limited and clearly defined problems threw a critical light upon all claims to access to the true science of the nature of things. This intellectual experience was paralleled elsewhere in the scientific movement, for example in the search in biology and medicine for taxonomic criteria that would provide at once a practical classification of living organisms and their diseases and the true natural and causal system. We may ask then what is the comparative value, for scientific as for artistic creation and discovery, of precision with its limitation of risk risking a limitation of vision, as against a general state of mind? What is its value as against such intellectual commitments and expectations as likened reasoning towards mechancal design with that towards aesthetic and moral design, and

17. *Cf.* Crombie, "Kepler: de modo visionis", in *Mélanges Alexandre Koyré*, introd. de I. B. Cohen et R. Taton, i (Paris, 1964), 135–72; *idem*, "The mechanistic hypothesis and the scientific study of vision", *Proceedings of the Royal Microscopical Society*, ii (1967), 32–47; *Styles* (ref. 1), ch. 4.ii; M. Baxandall, *Painting and experience in fifteenth century Italy* (Oxford, 1972); S. Y. Edgerton, Jr, *The Renaissance rediscovery of linear perspective* (New York, 1975); and Alberti, above, ref. 2.

18. *Cf.* Crombie, "The study of the senses in Renaissance science", *Actes du Xe Congrès international d'histoire des sciences: Ithaca N.Y. 1962* (Paris, 1964), 93–114; *idem*, "Mathematics, music and medical science", *Actes du XIIe Congrès international d'histoire des sciences: Paris 1968*, iB (Paris, 1971), 295–310; *idem*, "Marin Mersenne (1588–1648) and the seventeenth-century problem of scientific acceptability", *Physis*, xvii (1975), 186–204; *idem*, *Galileo and Mersenne* (ref. 1), ch. 9; also C. V. Palisca, "Scientific empiricism in musical thought", in *Sevententh century science and the arts*, ed. H. H. Rhys (Princeton, 1961), 91–137; D. P. Walker, "Some aspects of the musical theory of Vincenzo Galilei and Galileo Galilei", *Proceedings of the Royal Musical Association*, c (1973–74), 33–47; *idem*, *Studies in musical science in the late Renaissance* (London and Leiden, 1978).

against the suggestive sources of the imagination which may yet yield
only verbiage?

Galileo enjoyed the habit of "speculative minds" in reading "the book
of nature, always open to those who enjoyed reading and studying it
with the eyes of the intellect. He said that the letters in which it was
written were the propositions, figures and conclusions of geometry, by
means of which alone was it possible to penetrate any of the infinite
mysteries of nature".[19] About this "book of nature, where things are
written in only one way" he "could not dispute any problem *ad utranque
partem*"[20] as in a scholastic exercise; for the book of nature was "the
true and real world which, made by God with his own hands, stands
always open in front of us for the purpose of our learning".[21] Galileo
aimed to define for his contemporaries the rational identity both of
nature, and of natural science in specific distinction from other diverse
forms of thinking within contemporary intellectual culture. He reminded
theologians sacred or profane of "the difference that there is between
opinable and demonstrative doctrines; so that . . . they might the better
ascertain themselves that it is not in the power of professors of demonstrative sciences to change opinions at their wish . . .; and that there is
a great difference between commanding a mathematician or a philosopher
and directing a merchant or a lawyer, and that the demonstrated
conclusions about the things of nature and of the heavens cannot be
changed with the same ease as opinions about what is lawful or not in a
contract, rent or exchange".[22] Again he wrote of a certain philosopher:
"Possibly he thinks that philosophy is a book and a fiction by some man,
like the *Iliad* or *Orlando furioso,* books in which the least important thing
is whether what is written in them is true. Well . . . things are not like
that."[23] It was scandalous "to allow people utterly ignorant of a science
or an art to become judges over intelligent men and to have power to
turn them round at their will by virtue of the authority granted to them—

19. Vincenzo Viviani, "Racconto istorico della vita di Galileo" (1654; *Le opere,*
    xix, 625); *cf.* R. Mondolfo, *Figure e idee della filosofia della Rinascimento*
    (Firenze, 1963), 117–59, 291–373; Crombie, "The primary properties
    and secondary qualities in Galileo Galilei's natural philosophy", in
    Saggi su Galileo Galilei (Firenze, preprint, 1969); *idem,* "Sources of
    Galileo's early natural philosophy", in *Reason, experiment and mysticism
    in the scientific revolution,* ed. by M. L. Righini Bonelli and W. R. Shea
    (New York, 1975), 157–75; *idem,* "Philosophical presuppositions . . ."
    (ref. 1).

20. Galileo, note of 1612, *Le opere,* iv, 248n.

21. Galileo, "Prima Lettera circa le Macchie Solari" (1612; *Le opere,* v, 96n.).

22. Galileo, *Lettera a Madama Christina di Lorena* (1615; *Le opere,* v, 326).

23. Galileo, *Il saggiatore,* q. 6 (1623; *Le opere,* vi, 232).

these are the novelties with power to ruin republics and overthrow states".[24]

Galileo's public controversies dramatized a subtle shift in the commitments and expectations of disagreement as well as agreement in the intellectual style of the early modern heirs at once of Aristotle and of Moses. His account of scientific objectivity is for us a brisk antidote to the naïver sociological relativism promoted (for whatever motives) by people evidently ignorant of the distinction between the history of science and the history of ideology. His arguments communicate the specific identity of the scientific movement, an identity requiring in its adequate historians, as in those of music or painting, a specific technical mastery of its content. He lays out for us an intellectual enterprize integrated by its explicit historic criteria for choosing between theories and investigations at different levels of the true, the probable, the possible, the fruitful, the sterile, the impossible and the false. By means of these criteria natural scientists have exercized a kind of natural selection of theories and investigations, which has directed scientific thinking as the history of solving problems while at the same time embodying them in ever more general explanations. Thus it is the history of objective progress in knowledge.

Galileo with his learned love of literature, music, and the visual and plastic arts, his eloquent baroque Italian and his matching skills as lutanist and as draftsman, his sense of scientific elegance and of cosmological design, his insistence on being both a philosopher and a mathematician, his desire to win an argument as well as to win the truth—Galileo belongs as recognizably as any of his literary or artistic or philosophical contemporaries to the Tuscan intellectual culture into which he was born. With his aggressive creative energy he too, as he described the musical interval of the fifth, "tempering the sweetness by a drop of tartness, seems at the same time to kiss and to bite".[25] He was an exemplary man of *virtù*, the rational experimenter, in all these sciences and arts of the Renaissance. In that we shall surely find no contradiction. In that context we seem most likely to see how the defining capacity of both art and science to solve specific problems drew in operation upon the suggestive sources alike of the analytical and the constructive imagination.

Further references: R. Lenoble, "Origines de la pensée scientifique moderne" in *Histoire de la science*, ed. M. Daumas (Paris, 1957), 367-534, *Esquisse d'une histoire de l'idée de nature* (Paris, 1969); J. W. Shirley and F. D. Hoeniger (eds.), *Science and the Arts in the Renaissance* (Washington, D.C., 1985); D. Woodward (ed.), *Art and Cartography* (Chicago, 1987); see also chs. 9-13.

24. Galileo, notes related to the *Dialogo sopra i due massimi sistemi del mondo* (1632; *Le opere,* vii, 540).
25. Galileo, *Discorsi e dimostrazioni matematiche intorno a due nuove scienze,* i (1638; *Le opere,* viii, 149).

9

THE MECHANISTIC HYPOTHESIS AND
THE SCIENTIFIC STUDY OF VISION

Toute la condition de notre vie dépend de nos sens, entre lesquels celui de la vue étant le plus universel et le plus noble il n'y a point de doute que les inventions qui servent à augmenter sa puissance, ne soient des plus utiles qui puissent être. (Descartes, *La dioptrique*)

I

THE contributions made by biological and psychological inquiries to the establishment of modern science have until very recently fallen in a curious way between two historical stools. An excessive enthusiasm for mathematical physics has led the majority of historians of science to neglect these subjects altogether. Historians of biology on the other hand have tended to neglect the problems posed for biology by the physical sciences. Yet the view of the physical world created by natural philosophy and mathematical physics in the sixteenth and seventeenth centuries, especially its reduction to a mechanism and the consequential emphasis on quantitative precision, provided new and powerful opportunities and techniques for investigating the living body. These came not simply from the use of analogies with physical and technological artifacts and machines to illuminate natural processes and functions, as in William Harvey's comparison of the heart with a force pump; analogies of this kind went back to antiquity. Nor did the new opportunities come simply from the fact that the progress of physical knowledge made it possible to find exact solutions to limited physiological problems. We may remind ourselves that the first major discovery in modern physiology was made not by Harvey but two decades earlier by a mathematical physicist, Johannes Kepler. The discovery by Harvey of the circulation of the blood provided a fact that necessitated the reconstruction of the theory of the exchange of energy and matter by the engine of the body. Kepler's discovery in 1603 of the dioptric mechanism by which the eye forms an image dealt with a problem more intimately part of a new approach to physiology, explicitly revolutionary in its ambitions and in its consequences[1]. This was to offer an exclusive and exhaustive programme for discovering answerable questions about living things and for finding their answers.

The natural philosophers of the seventeenth century who created the view of the whole of physical nature as nothing but a mechanism also put to themselves the question: how does a living and sentient being, the

---

1 For Kepler see below nn. 87-87; for the problem of dating of Harvey's discovery see Harvey, *Anatomical Lectures*, ed. Whitteridge, pp. xxviii-xxix Pagel, "An Harveyan prelude to Harvey", *History of Science*, ii (1963) 115. For 'models' in antiquity cf. Solmsen, *Aristotle's System of the World*, and "Nature as craftsmen in Greek thought", *Journal of the History of Ideas*, xxiv (1963) 473-96.

"animate and sentient body" as Galileo[2] called it, the *ingenium* of Descartes[3], receive information about this external world and what is the nature and validity of this information ? What is the relationship of the perceiving organism to the world perceived ? The question is fundamental, for an answer to it requires a characterization of both sides of the relationship. I want in this paper to discuss the role of this question in establishing effective scientific thinking at the heart of early modern biology. How did it come to be grasped that problems offered by the senses, first by vision and later by hearing and the other senses, could be formulated in such a way that contemporary physical and biological science could solve them exactly and definitively, after centuries of intelligent effort ? How did a new formulation come to be given to the further question of the co-ordination of information by the animate and sensitive body and its consequential behaviour, a question affecting the whole scope and method of the study of living things ? It is obvious that, in order to disentangle the history of these questions, it is more than ever necessary to look beneath the surface of immediate scientific results, and to ask what assumptions were being made about both the subject matter and the scope and method of the inquiry.

Before the microscope and telescope were invented as instruments for extending the unaided range of the senses, the most complicated optical system known was the eye itself. Hence it is appropriate that a discussion of historical aspects of microscopy should begin with an analysis of efforts to reach scientific understanding of vision and of their consequences. It is important to note the context of the inquiry. The basic documents before Kepler show distinctive approaches to the problems, related to their different provenances. Both in literary and intellectual derivation and in social and institutional context these were of four main kinds, overlapping on some essential issues : the writings of anatomists and physiologists belonging to medical schools; the writings of academic philosophers on vision; the writings of academic mathematicians and natural philosophers on geometrical and physical optics; and the writings of artists on perspective. Both inside and outside the universities mathematical and experimental optics belonged to the field of natural magic, comprising a set of subjects on the peripherae of the standard natural philosophy of the schools. This included optics, magnetism, cosmetics, alchemy, and the study of machines, all collected since antiquity in Greek, Arabic and Latin writings around the common idea of discovering the hidden powers in nature that could be harnessed to produce astonishing, theatrical, and useful effects. When the microscope and telescope were introduced into scientific research as artificial aids to the natural power of the eye, the association of optics with natural magic understandably threw doubt on the validity of the information they provided, as Galileo was to discover. This important aspect of the intellectual and social background to the invention of these instruments

2　*Il saggiatore* (1623) q. 48.
3　*Regulae ad directionem ingenii* (1628-29), xii; the *ingenium* was the whole body-mind equipment: see N. Kemp Smith, *New Studies in the Philosophy of Descartes*, pp. 22, 151.

has been discussed by Vasco Ronchi[4] and need not be treated again here. I propose to confine my attention to the intellectual moves by means of which Kepler made the fundamental discovery that established modern physiological optics[4a], and by which after him Descartes and others identified and distinguished further answerable questions that gave direction to the scientific study of the reception of information and the co-ordination and communication of information and behaviour in men, animals and machines.

The historical problem is to discover how the early modern investigators thought their way into a new view of questions they had inherited from Greek and medieval sources. Greek philosophers had offered formulations of ideas on two sets of basic issues. First: by what means do the different special senses mediate information about the external world to the animate being ? Plato and Aristotle brought one fundamental issue out into the open by asking how a relationship or interaction resulting in a sensation, that is between a sensitive body (*percipiens*) and a sensed object (*percipiendum*), differs from a merely physical relationship or interaction between insensitive bodies[5]. The problem became that of discovering what connected *percipiens* and *percipiendum* and how sensation was effected by means of this connection.

On how sensation was effected in the principal senses of vision and hearing in which the connection was made through a medium[6] there were two main contrasting views, which came to form the opposing poles of theorizing down to the seventeenth century. According to the view developed mainly by the Greek atomists, vision was effected in the first place by "images", "copies" or "representations"[7] continually thrown off objects as replicas of their shape and colour and passing through the air into the eye; hearing was effected by audible impressions or particles, corresponding in character to their source, passing from sounding objects

---

4 Ronchi, *Storia della luce,* revised as *Histoire de la lumière,*   *The Nature of Light* (London, 1979);   *Il cannocchiale di Galileo e la scienza del seicento.*

4a For the history of physiological optics much useful information can be found in the admirable historical discussions by Helmholtz, *Physiological Optics,* transl. Southall, and in Hischberg, *Geschichte der Augenheilkunde.* Polyak, *The Retina,* and *The Vertebrate Visual System* are also full of historical information, unfortunately not always accurate, and have extensive bibliographies; see below p. 258.

5 Plato, *Philebus* 33D-34A, *Timaeus* 64A-C, *Theaetetus* 156A; Aristotle, *De anima,* ii. 1-2, 5, 11-12, 412a1-414a28, 416b31-418a5, 424a5-b18; Beare, *Greek Theories of Elementary Cognition,* pp. 210-49; Ross, *Aristotle,* 5th ed., pp. 136-9.

6 Seeing, hearing and smelling were held to take place through a medium, as distinct from touching and tasting which most authors regarded as a different case, although Aristotle (*De anima,* ii. 11, 422b19-423b26; *De sensu,* i. 436b5-437a16) argued that these also had their internal, though not external media. For the Greek philosophical theories of the senses see Beare's standard work and Stratton, *Theophrastus and the Greek Physiological Psychology before Aristotle* (with a translation of Theophrastus, *De sensibus*).

7 The words used were *deikela* (Democritus) and *eidola* (Aristotle. Theophrastus); Beare, pp. 25, 29 n. 3; below n. 9. In Latin the words used were *Formae*(Latin Alhazen, Witelo, Maurolico), *imagines* (Roger Bacon), *species* (Roger Bacon, Leonardo da Vinci, Maurolico, Kepler), *simulacri, similitudini* (Leonardo da Vinci), *idola* (Leonardo da Vinci, Maurolico, Kepler), *picturae, illustrationes* (Kepler); see below.

into the ear[8]. But in addition to this passive reception of images or emanations or currents of particles that were presented to the soul as the immediate data of sense, there was in sensation also an active process by which, for example, the eye by its own effort looked at the object and selected from among the images continually striking it those to which it paid attention[9]. According to the alternative view developed in somewhat different ways mainly by Aristotle and the Stoics, sensation was effected not by anything passing through the medium, but by an " affection ", modification or movement of the medium itself connecting the sense organ with the object sensed[10]. In vision this did not provide an image in the eye; rather vision was primarily an active process by which in the presence of external light the soul perceived objects by means of the eye. The Stoic theory was that the soul effected vision by means of a specific " visual pneuma " sent from the brain along the optic nerve to the eye, where in the presence of light it " stressed " the adjoining air and so contacted the objects in the visual field. Each was reported by a cone of stressed air with its base on the object and its apex at the pupil, a construction derived

---

8   Beare, op. cit. pp. 25-37, 99-102; Bailey, *The Greek Atomists and Epicurus*, pp. 165-72, 404-7.

9   Empedocles had explained sensation by emanations (*aporroiai*) streaming off objects and entering the pores of the sentient organ; vision was effected in addition by the agency of fire issuing from the eyes (Beare, op. cit. pp. 14-23; Kirk and Raven, *The Presocratic Philosophers*, p. 343). Plato offered a similar explanation of vision by a visual current of fire issuing from the eyes, which, in the presence of daylight, met in the line of vision and united with a current of fire-particles streaming off the object seen. Neither Empedocles nor Plato held that the incoming emanations were images in the sense of pictures of the object seen. For both, the proper object of vision was colour. Plato related the sensible qualities of objects to the elements composing them: " nothing can be visible without fire, or tangible without something solid, and nothing is solid without earth " (*Timaeus* 31B). He made colours as seen a consequence of the interaction of the sentient being with the different shapes, sizes and motions of the fire-particles streaming off the coloured object (*Timaeus* 45B-46A, 67C- 68E, translated with commentary by Cornford, *Plato's Cosmology;* Beare, op. cit. pp. 42-56; and *Theaetetus*, 153-7, translated with commentary by Cornford, *Plato's Theory of Knowledge*). Theophrastus (*De sensibus* § 5, in Stratton, op. cit.) gave this account of Plato's views: " [The organ of] vision he makes to consist of fire; (and this is why he regards colour also as a flame given off from bodies, having particles commensurate with the organ of vision); assuming then that there is this effluence and that [effluence and organ] must unite, he holds that the [visual stream] issues forth for some distance and coalesces with the effluence, and thus it is we see. His view, consequently, may be said to lie midway between the theories of those who say that vision falls upon [its object] and of those who hold that something is borne from visible objects to the [organ of sight] ". It was Leucippus and Democritus who conceived the emanations as images (*deikela, eidola*) of the object's form. Democritus seems to have found the key to vision in the image that we can see reflected in the pupil of someone else's eye. He proposed the peculiar theory that emanations from both the object and the eye met and formed an impression in the air like that of a mould on wax; this went to the pupil as the visual image (*emphasis*) (see Aristotle, *De sensu*, ii, 438a 5-16 and Theophrastus, *De sensibus* §§ 49-83 in Stratton, op. cit.; and on these sources Beare, op. cit. pp. 23-37, Kirk and Raven, op. cit. pp. 421-4). Epicurus modified and developed the atomist theory of incoming images, with a sophisticated account of the active visual process of 'looking' with attention (see Bailey, op. cit. pp. 167-70, 406-11). Democritus and the other

atomists made colours subjective 'secondary qualities' produced by the interaction of the sense organs with the 'primary properties' of the order, position, size and shape of the atoms. Plato's geometrical shapes antecedent to the four elements acted as primary properties, and to the atomist's list he added numbers and variations in motion, but his discussions of the nature of the sensible qualities have to be related to the philosophical problem in hand. In some passages (e.g. *Timaeus* 80E, *Republic* 508C) he makes colours something actually existing in things, whereas in others (especially *Theaetatus* 153-7) he seems to make them exist only in the interaction between our seeing and the object seen. Theophrastus (§§ 60-1, in Stratton, op. cit.) wrote on this: " Democritus and Plato, however, are the investigators who go into the question most fully, for they define the object of each sense; although [Plato] never robs these objects of their external reality, whereas Democritus reduces them one and all to effects in our sensuous faculty. Where the truth itself lies, is not the question we are now discussing. Let our aim be rather to report the range of each author's treatment and the precise definitions he gives, stating by way of preface his general method. Democritus has no uniform account of all [the sensory objects]: some he distinguishes by the size [of their atoms], others by the shape, and a few by the [atomic] order and position. Plato, on the other hand, refers nearly all of them to effects in us, and to our perceptive faculty. Consequently each of these authors would seem to speak directly counter to his own postulate. For the one of them, who would have sensory objects to be but effects in our perceptive faculty, actually describes a reality resident in the objects themselves; while the other, who attributes the objects' character to their own intrinsic being, ends by ascribing it to the passive change of our perceptive faculty". The following passage from the *Theaetetus* (153-7, transl. Cornford) is of particular interest for the subject of this essay: " First, to take the case of the eyes, you must conceive that what you call white colour has no being as a distinct thing outside your eyes nor yet inside them, nor must you assign it any fixed place. Otherwise, of course, it would have its being in an assigned place and abide there, instead of arising in a process of becoming. . . . On that showing we shall see that black or white or any colour you choose is a thing that has arisen out of the meeting of our eyes with the appropriate motion. What we say 'is' this or that colour will be neither the eye which encounters the motion nor the motion which is encountered, but something which has arisen between the two and is peculiar to each several percipient. Or would you be prepared to maintain that every colour appears to a dog or any other creature just such as it appears to you ? . . . Or to another man ? Does anything you please appear to him such as it appears to you ? Are you quite sure of that ? Are you not much rather sure that it does not even appear the same to yourself, because you never remain in the same condition ? . . . As soon, then, as an eye and something else whose structure is adjusted to the eye come within range and give birth to the whiteness together with its cognate perception — things that would never have come into existence if either of the two had approached anything else — then it is that, as the vision from the eyes and the whiteness from the thing that joins in giving birth to the colour pass in the space between, the eye becomes filled with vision and now sees, and becomes, not vision, but a seeing eye. . . . And so, too, we must think in the same way of the rest — 'hard', 'hot' and all of them — that no one of them has any being just by itself . . . but that it is in their intercourse with one another that all arise in all their variety as a result of their motion . . .".

10   Like Plato, Aristotle held that the proper object of vision was colour (*De anima*, ii. 7, 418a26 sqq.); see Beare, op. cit. pp. 56-92 for Aristotle's account of "the diaphanous" as the medium of light, theory of colour as the actualization of potentialities both in the object seen and in the seeing eye, and theory of the visual function. An eye was a seeing eye; a dead eye was only an eye in name (*De anima*, ii. 1, 412b19-413a3; *Meteorologica*, iv. 12, 390a 10-15). He discussed colours at length in his account of the rainbow in the *Meteorologica* (iii. 2-5, 371b18-377a28), where he also used the conception of visual rays.

from Euclid's geometrical analysis of perspective (fig. 9)[11]. Hearing was mediated by means of a wave motion propagated from the sounding body through the air in spheres, just as waves spread in circles over the surface of water struck by a falling stone; according to the modifications of its motions the air conveyed different information, in the form of auditory sensations, to the soul through the "auditory pneuma" sent to the ears[12]

Prop. II. Theor.

:ει μϑύων τὰ ραγ.

Æqualium magnitudinum inæqualiter diſtantium, quæ propius poſitæ ſunt accuratius cernuntur.

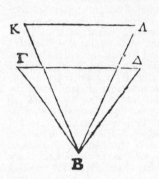

SIT oculus B, aſpectabiles vero magnitudines ΓΔ & ΚΛ, quæ æquales & parallelæ cogitandæ ſunt; propior autem oculo ſit ΓΔ quam ΚΛ, & emittantur ab oculo radii ΒΓ, ΒΔ, ΒΚ, ΒΛ. nunquam dicemus fieri poſſe, ut radii, à B oculo ad ΚΛ tendentes, tranſeant per Γ,Δ puncta: alioqui [ex ſchol. ſeq.] trianguli ΒΛΚ latus ΚΛ majus eſſet latere ΓΔ [trianguli ΒΔΓ.]

ἰ ΓΔ ὑπὸ atqui ΚΛ poſita eſt æqualis ipſi ΓΔ : quare ΓΔ

Fig. 9.   From Euclid, *Optica,* in *Opera Omnia* (Oxford, 1703): illustrating the principle that the apparent size of an object is proportional to the angle of vision (i.e. the angles ΚΛ and ΓΔ subtended at the eye at B)   ; cf. props. 6-8.

11   For details see Sambursky, *Physics of the Stoics,* pp. 21-9, 44; Pohlenz, *Die Stoa,* i, 87 sqq., ii, 51 sqq.; Brehier, *Chrysippe,* pp. 164 sqq. Chrysippus discussed both of the famous analogies to be used by Descartes (*Regulae,* xii; *Traité de l'homme* and *La dioptrique,* i, iv). He rejected the theory of some of his predecessors that the "presentation" (*phantasia*) of objects to the soul was like the impression of a seal on wax; rather it was a "modification (*heteroiosis*) of the soul" (Sextus Empiricus, *Adversus mathematicos,* vii. 228-30, 372; *Pyrrhoniarum hypotyposeon,* ii. 7, 70-8). But according to Diogenes Laertius (vii. 157) he was one of those who held "that we see when the light between the visual organ and the object stretches in the form of a cone. . . . The apex of the cone in the air is at the eye, the base at the object seen. Thus the thing seen is reported to us by the medium of the air stretching out towards it, as if by a stick"; cf. below n.25. For Euclid see *Optica,* def. 2; Lejeune, *Euclide et Ptolémée,* pp. 42-3.
12   Diogenes Laertius, vii. 158; Sextus Empiricus, *Adversus mathematicos,* vii. 228; Sambursky, op. cit. pp. 23, 26. As in the seventeenth century, consideration of hearing seems to have undermined belief in the visual model of impressions or images as the effectors of sensation; below n. 132.

The second set of issues arose from trying to explain the operation of the animate body as a whole: how is the information received through the different senses both differentiated and co-ordinated to give a single consistent view of the world and consistent behaviour in relation to it ? The opposing views on the mode of operation of the special senses led to a corresponding polarization of opinion on the basis of their differentiation. On the atomist view, the different special senses reported different information because each was constructed to receive different kinds of external stimulus or " image " from the environment. On the Stoic view, accepted and developed by Galen, the differentiation depended primarily on the internal response of the specific pneuma sent by the soul to each sense organ effecting contact with its proper object in the environment. Each special sense was designed to respond normally to its proper object, but each would give the same specific response to any form of stimulation[13].

Some most interesting formal physiological problems were raised, largely for the future, by the attempts both of the atomists and of the Stoics to account for the co-ordination of information and behaviour by means of the corporeal action and being acted upon of a purely corporeal " soul "[14]. But in these philosophies physiological problems were subordinate to the main purpose of offering a theory of human nature in keeping with their basic principle that everything capable of interaction is corporeal. Aristotle was more empirical in recognizing the need to explore the distinction between human awareness and animal co-ordination[15]. To a large extent in late antiquity, and certainly in medieval and early modern times, the basis of discussion, even for the mechanistic explanations of the seventeenth century, was laid down by his account of two general aspects of the sensitive faculty of the soul. One was the *sensus communis* as the mental power by which we distinguish and compare the information received through the different special senses, perceive the " common sensibles " (motion and rest, shape, number, magnitude, time) proper to no special sense, perform acts of recognition, and are conscious of ourselves perceiving. The other was the power of the soul to effect movements; this he explored in detail through his comparative studies of the adaptive movements of the animate body[16].

Besides these ideas of the philosophers, Greek mathematicians and anatomists offered a sufficient technical basis for a successful scientific attack at least upon the question of how the eye operates as a receptor of external stimuli. The classical analysis of the geometry of visual space initiated by Euclid; its development by Ptolemy to include the experimental determination of the correlation between the angles of refraction and of incidence at the plane surface between air and water, air and glass, and water and glass, the mathematical determination of the location of the refracted image (fig. 10) and a physical conception of the visual ray[17]; the

---

13 Galen, *De placitis Hippocratis et Platonis*, vii. 4-5.
14 Bailey, op. cit. pp. 194 sqq., 396 sqq.; Sambursky, op. cit. pp. 21 sqq.; Pohlenz, Brehier, op. cit.
15 cf. Balme, *Aristotle's Use of the Teleological Explanation*.
16 Cf. Ross, *Aristotle*, 5th ed., pp. 139-46; Beare, op. cit. pp. 215 sqq., 276 sqq.
17 Euclid, *Optica*, definitiones; Ptolemy, *L'optique de Claude Ptolémée*, v, éd. Lejeune; see Lejeune, *Euclide et Ptolémée*, and *Recherches sur la catoptrique grecque*.

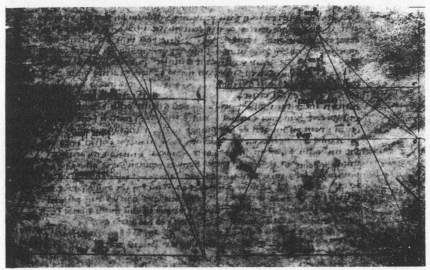

Fig. 10. From Roger Bacon, *Opus maius,* v. iii. ii. 2, Oxford MS Bodley 874 (15 cent.) f.60ʳ: illustrating the construction given by Ptolemy (*Optica,* v. 3, 70-81, ed. Lejeune) for the location of the image after the refraction of the visual cone at plane surfaces.
Left diagram: with the eye (*oculus*) in the rarer medium (*corpus subtilius*), the visual rays to the thing seen (*res visa*) are refracted at the interface (*m h*) so that the angle of vision is increased (*o g p*) and the image (*imago rei*) appears larger (*m* at left margin has been truncated in photographing). Right diagram: with the eye in the denser medium (*corpus densius*) the refraction decreases the angle of vision (*d g b*) and the image appears smaller. Looking at the right side of the left diagram, this construction locates the image (*d*) at the intersection of the projection of the refracted ray (*g p d*) with the perpendicular or *cathetus* (*f h*) dropped from the thing seen to the refracting surface.

conics of Apollonius; and the accounts of the anatomy and physiology of the eye given by Rufus of Ephesus and Galen[18] — these provided all that was technically necessary to solve the crucial problem of the dioptric mechanism of the eye. Similarly, a basis at least for the quantitative study of the physical conditions for auditory distinctions was provided by Greek works foreshadowing the correlation of pitch with frequency of vibrations or pulsations of the air[19]. Can we say why the Greeks did not find scientific solutions of problems technically within their grasp ? The difficulty seems to me to have been not technical but conceptual, and this continued in the interesting Arabic and Latin work on vision down to Kepler. But whether or not we can explain sensibly why something did *not* happen in history, we can I think discover an essential condition for the success of the seventeenth-century scientists if we look below the

18   Rufus d'Ephèse, *Oeuvres,* pub. Daremberg et Ruelle; Magnus, *Die Anatomie des Auges bei den Griechen und Römern, Die Augenheilkunde;* below nn. 22-32. Rufus, followed by Galen, described the lenticulate 'lens', flattened more anteriorly than posteriorly, and the optic chiasma.
19   Politzer. *Geschichte der Ohrenheilkunde,* i; and see my book, *Marin Mersenne and the Science of Music.*

surface of immediate results and observe the commitments with which they carried out their attacks upon these detailed problems.

I want to argue that it was the 'mechanistic hypothesis' that made it possible to formulate and, so far as was technically possible, to solve the problems of the sensory mechanisms and to make a fresh approach to those of perception in the early modern period, and that for two reasons. The first was that its ruthless commitment, in advance of making any observations, to asking only one kind of question provided the initial key to success by isolating problems that would open to it. Thus it allowed an old question to be approached in a new way by clearly defining the immediate problem for research: in a world that was assumed to be simply a system of mechanisms, this was to discover the particular mechanisms concerned in each case. The second reason was that this commitment forced a clear recognition, as nothing less ruthless could, of its own limits. Once the full extent of the mechanistic commitment had become clear in the seventeenth century, it became comparatively easy to see that there were several different *kinds* of question involved in the inquiries into sensation and perception. The general terms of the new inquiry were as old as Democritus's distinction between 'primary' properties and 'secondary' qualities which Galileo, Descartes and other contemporaries repeated. In the external world there were only " sizes, shapes, numbers and slow or fast movements "; these excited in us through our " ears, tongues and noses " the sensations of different qualities of " sounds, tastes, and odours "[20]. Through our eyes the differences in the shapes and motions of the physical constituents of light were sufficient to excite in us all the different qualities of colour[21]. But it became clear at this time, as it had not been seen clearly before, that the physiological part of the inquiry was limited to discovering the strictly physical changes excited in the sense organs by the external physical influences acting upon them. How these quantitative physical changes were translated into the corresponding sensory information received by the sentient animal was another problem. By the end of the seventeenth century clear distinctions had been made between three quite different kinds of question:

(i) *Physical and physiological:* by what mechanisms are the external physical motions providing the stimulus mediated into internal physical motions of the sense organs, nerves and brain of the body? It was recognized that physiological progress depended on progress in physical knowledge of optics, acoustics, etc.

(ii) *Physico-psychological:* how do these physical motions of the sense organs, nerves and brain effect sensations in the animate and sensitive body, or provide it with the means of having different sensations and making perceptual distinctions? Here a distinction came to be drawn between what are now called (a) the philosophical or logical question of physico-psychological interaction or causation and (b) the empirical question of physico-psychological parallelism or correlation.

(iii) *The empirical psychological problem of perception:* how as a matter of independent observation do we see, hear, etc., that is, what information do we receive in visual, auditory, etc. perception and what

20   Galileo, *Il saggiatore*, q. 48.
21   Descartes, *Regulae*, xii; **below nn. 121-2, 133.**

sensory clues are necessary for us to have the perceptions we do ? (We are not of course concerned here at all with the kind of philosophical problem of *what* we see, hear, etc., involved, for example, in the recent theory of ' sense data '.)

My argument is then that the mechanistic hypothesis, used as an instrument of research, became the instrument of seventeenth-century success because it transformed, not the techniques or even at the start most of the essential facts, but the formulation of the inherited problems so that these different questions could be distinguished and made separately answerable. The new scientific advances thus began with and, as they developed, made clearer the explicit recognition that these different kinds of problem required different modes of attack, which came up against different kinds of frontier of knowledge. I shall use as illustrations the study of vision and of the co-ordination of information and behaviour.

II

No doubt because of their deep general theoretical interest in the geometry of space, the Greeks had developed the study of vision far in advance of that of the other senses. In fact it retained this position and remained a model for the inquiries into other senses, especially hearing, until the nineteenth century. But the Greeks developed optics in a special way. They were primarily interested in the problem of *how we see*. Euclid founded the science of geometrical optics and perspective as a geometrical theory of visual perception, taking the eye as the point of origin of lines of vision (fig. 9). Ptolemy developed this physically by taking the eye as the point of origin of visual rays emitted from the eye (fig. 10)[22]. This geometrical approach raised no physiological problems, but when these were discussed the treatment of the *physiology of the eye* and of the means by which *vision is effected* were invariably made to serve as an immediate explanation of *how we see*. Mathematicians and physiologists of all philosophical schools, even the atomists, all stressed the character of sensation as an active process. An eye was a living eye through which we looked and saw; a dead eye was not an eye at all. The difference between the three kinds of question involved was clearly recognized by no one.

This common aim of all ancient analyses of vision is evident in the most impressive and influential of the physiological theories, that of Galen. In three different works Galen discussed philosophical theories of vision, and the anatomy and function of the eye[23]. He rejected the atomist theory that vision is effected by images entering the eye because it could not explain either the perception by one person of large objects like a mountain of which the image would not fit into the pupil, or the perception of the same thing by several persons each of whom would have to receive its image. As for the alternative theory of an outgoing visual spirit or emanation as envisaged by Plato, he could not believe that the eye could

---

22   Lejeune, *Euclide et Ptolémée*, pp. 35-44, 85 sqq.; *Recherches sur la catoptrique grecque*, pp. 57, 153-66.
23   Galen, *De placitis Hippocratis et Platonis*, vii. 3-7; *De anatomicis administrationibus*, x, 1-4; *De usu partium*, viii. 5-6, x. I should like to thank Mr. T. M. Brown for lending me a paper with an interesting discussion of Galen.

emit enough to surround all objects[24]. All through Galen's physiology there is strong Stoic influence and it is not surprising that he fell back on a version of the Stoic theory that vision is effected by the extromission not of an emanation, but of an alteration, in the presence of light, of the air extending to the object seen[25]. The aim of his analysis becomes clear when he proceeds to develop it in anatomical and optical detail.

On grounds of location and structural fitness he concluded that " the *crystallinus* [crystalline body, our lens] is the essential organ of vision "[26], and he argued that this was confirmed by the fact that vision was obstructed by " suffusions " (*hypochymata*) between the *crystallinus* and the cornea and restored when the suffusion was removed (fig.11). Galen was working half a century after Ptolemy and he shows a useful working knowledge of geometrical optics. " In connection with this matter ", he began his optical analysis of how vision is effected, " I must touch upon mathematical theory — an unknown subject to the majority of educated persons, and one that makes even experts therein hated and unacceptable "[27]. He introduced the Euclidean visual or ' perspective ' cone by inviting the reader to consider a circular object forming its base to be connected with the pupil at its apex, first by a large number of thin gossamer threads such as spiders make, and then more abstractly by " visual lines " replacing the threads (fig.12). Anything placed in front of the pupil would obscure the part of the circle on its line of vision, and so, he concluded:[28]

. . . one will easily perceive that it is not without reason that mathematicians have constructed the proposition that all vision occurs in straight lines. We will, then, in the future, call these straight visual

24 Galen, *De placitis . . .*, vii. 5-7; trans. De Lacy (1978-80).
25 Ibid. vii. 5, 7. Sambursky (*Physics of the Stoics*, p. 127) translates relevant passages from these chapters respectively: " Since of all the sensations only the sense of vision receives the perception of the object by transmission through the medium of air, not as from a stick but as some part kindred to and coalescing with it, and only by this and by the incidence of light does it get the speciality of seeing, it stands to reason that it needs the luminous pneuma which flows from above, strikes the surrounding air and assimilates it to itself (c. 5). . . . That we see through the medium of air is obvious and agreed by all. However, the question is whether this happens as if something comes to us along a path from the object, or if the air serves us as an organ of cognition for an object seen just as the nerves do for an object touched. Most people believe that the modification produced by the things that reach us is transmitted by the nerve to the ruling part of the soul, and thus the object is perceived. But these people do not realize that the sensation of pain could not arise in a limb cut or broken or burned, if the limb itself did not hold the faculty of sensation. But actually the opposite of their opinion is true. The nerve itself namely is part of the brain, like a branch or offshoot of a tree, and this part into which the nerve is rooted fully receives the faculty of sensation and thus becomes able to distinguish the object touching it. Something similar happens to the air surrounding us. When illuminated by the sun it becomes an organ of vision precisely as the pneuma arriving (in the eye) from the brain, but before the illumination occurs which produces a modification through the incidence of the sun's rays the air cannot become such an affected organ " (c. 7).
26 Galen, *De usu partium*, viii. 5, x. 1.
27 Ibid. x. 12; cf. c. 14.
28 Ibid. x. 12.

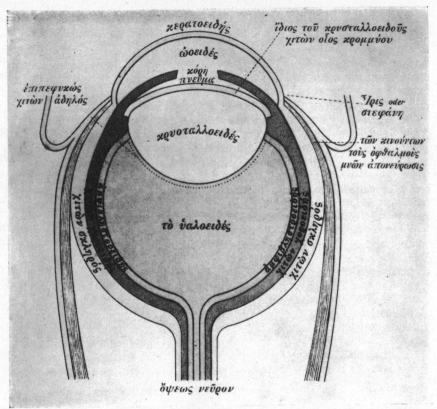

Fig. 11. Galen's anatomy of the eye, according to Magnus, *Die Augenheilkunde der Alten* (Breslau, 1901). Reading down the vertical axis the parts are: cornea, aqueous humour, pupil, capsule, crystallinus, vitreous humour, retina, choroid, sclerotic. The vitreous humour continues into the hollow optic nerve (cf. fig.14).

lines and the delicate gossamer threads that run from the pupil to the periphery of the circle, not 'spider-threads' but 'visual lines', bearing in mind that the periphery of the circle is seen by virtue of these lines, and the centre by virtue of one other line, namely that one that runs in the axis of the cone, and that the entire upper surface of the circular area is seen by virtue of a still greater number of lines that run to it from the pupil.

He went on to explain with the aid of geometrical diagrams the effect on the field seen of using either eye separately and both together (fig. 12). He gave an account of the double vision produced by pushing the eyeball slightly out of place and of the phenomena of the horizontal and vertical squint. He explained the normal occurrence of single vision with two eyes by the placing of their axes in the same plane effected by their anatomical union at the junction of the optic nerves[29]. Finally he gave geometrical

29 Ibid. x. 12-14. Euclid did not discuss binocular vision. For Ptolemy's account of how the two visual axes intersect at the object see Ptolemy, *Optica*, ii. 27 sqq., iii. **25 sqq.**, éd Lejeune; Lejeune, *Euclide et Ptolémée*, pp. 130 sqq. Ptolemy was **offering an** analysis of spatial relations seen with two eyes.

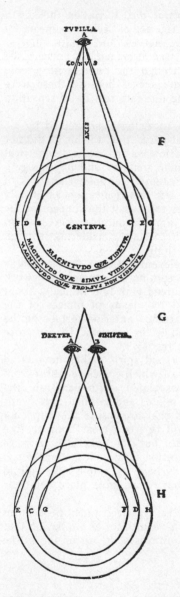

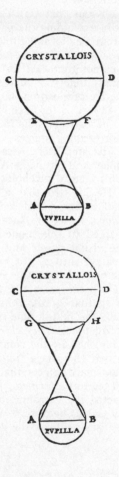

Fig. 12.
From Galen, *De usu partium*, x. 12 (Venice, 1556): illustrating the visual cone (cf. fig. 9). Top figure: every object (the circle BC) is seen within a specific area of peripheral vision (extending to DE but not FG). Bottom figure: the position of an object against its background appears slightly different according to whether it is seen with the right or left eye or both eyes.

Fig. 13.
From Galen, *De usu partium*, x. 15 (Venice, 1556): illustrating the greater area of the *crystallinus* directed towards objects seen through the pupil by a flatter anterior surface (bottom diagram GH as compared with top diagram EF).

reasons for the anterior flattening of the *crystallinus*. It was in this organ that the visual faculty of the brain effected the act of seeing by means of the visual pneuma sent out along the optic nerves, and so its anterior surface directed towards the outer world was designed to present the greatest possible area of communication, through the pupil, with visible objects (fig.13)[30]. Sensation could arise in the nerves because these were extensions of the brain, but the brain was the ultimate seat of all sensation and perception[31].

It is obvious that Galen's whole approach to vision was directed by his interest in explaining the phenomena of visual perception. In this he did not differ from Euclid and Ptolemy; his contribution was to relate geometrical and physical optics to certain aspects of ocular anatomy and physiology[32]. The apparent total lack in antiquity of any geometrical-optical analysis of the atomist theory of images seems to have left this theory a scientifically unattractive proposition, but it seems obvious to us that the concept of the eye as an organ for receiving images is a more favourable concept than any of the extromission theories from which to start considering it as an organ for *forming* images — a very different thing.

This first step was envisaged early in the eleventh century by the Arabic philosopher and physician Avicenna. While accepting the general framework of Galen's faculty psychology, Avicenna disagreed with him radically about vision. He insisted that vision was effected by means of images of the shapes of coloured bodies formed on the flattened anterior surface of the *crystallinus,* or as the Latin translator called it the *glacialis*. Its structure was adapted to this mode of operation (cf. fig.14): [33]

> The visual power and material of the visual spirit makes its way to each eye through the two hollow nerves of which you have learnt from anatomy. When the nerves and the associated coats penetrate the eyeball, the extremity of each of them dilates and is filled and swells up so that it can contain the humours that are inside the pupil. Of these the middle one is the *glacialis,* and this is a clear humour, like a hailstone. The *glacialis* is spherical, but its spherical form is diminished by the compression of its anterior surface. It is compressed so that the image (*informatio*) on it may have an ample size, and so that small objects that are seen may have a suitable place for their images to be formed (*informentur*).

He rejected the extromission theory (which he criticized in its Stoic form used by Galen) because it would lead to such absurdities as supposing that a power issuing from the diminuitive eye compresses the air as far as the

---

30   Galen, *De usu partium,* x. 15.
31   Ibid. x. 14; *De placitis . . .,* vii. 4-5. Galen held that we come by habit to locate objects outside us, so that we do this even with specks floating in the eye and in states of delirium.
32   Above nn. 17, 22.
33   Avicenna, *Liber canonis de medicinis cordialibus,* iii. iii. i. 1 (Venetiis, 1555). An influential earlier ninth-century Arabic work on ocular anatomy and physiology was Hunain ibn Isḥāq, *The Book of the Ten Treatises on the Eye.* ed. Meyerhof. A Latin version became a standard work in the West during the thirteenth century; Hunain was not always a reliable guide to Galen's views; for bibliography see Sarton, *Introduction to the History of Science,* i. 611-3.

stars. Through the forms passively imprinted in the eye objects were faithfully represented to the external visual sense located in the optic nerve; there they were actively perceived, and then fully recognized by the interior soul. He wrote of the external senses : [34]

One of them is sight, which is a faculty located in the concave nerve; it perceives the image of the forms of coloured bodies imprinted on the vitreous humour. These forms are transmitted through actually transparent media to polished surfaces. The second is the sense of hearing, which is a faculty located in the nerves distributed over the surface of the ear-hole; it perceives the form of what is transmitted to it by the vibration of the air which is compressed between two objects, one striking and the other being struck, the latter offering it resistance so as to set up vibrations in the air which produce the sound. This vibration of the air outside reaches the air which lies motionless and compressed in the cavity of the ear, moving it in a way similar to that in which it is itself moved. Its waves touch that nerve, and so it is heard. . . . The forms of all the sensibles reach the organs of sense and are imprinted on them, and then the faculty of sensation perceives them. This is almost evident in touch, taste, smell, and hearing. But concerning sight, a different view has been maintained, for some people have thought that something issues from the eye, meets the object of sight, takes its form from without — and that this constitutes the act of seeing. . . . But . . . sight is not due to something issuing from us towards the sensed object. It must therefore be due to something' coming towards us from the sensed object; since this is not the body of the object, it must be its form. If this view were not correct, the creation of the eye with all its strata and humours and their respective shape and structure would be useless.

Avicenna offered no explanation of how the eye operated as an image-forming device; such an explanation was the masterly and presumably independent contribution of his slightly older Arabic contemporary, the physicist Alhazen. Well known in the West from the thirteenth century both in a Latin translation and through the expositions of Roger Bacon in the *Opus maius* (1267) and of Witelo (c. 1270), Alhazen provided with Witelo the standard optical textbook and the most widely accepted explanation of vision before Kepler's. Alhazen ranks with Ptolemy and Kepler as an architect of scientific optics. In his explorations of the physics, physiology and psychology of vision he stands comparison intellectually with Descartes and Helmholtz. He stands apart from the common habit of both Arabic and Latin medieval natural philosophers of looking for means to reconcile apparently conflicting explanations; instead he set out to solve a problem, and accepted the consequences of his solution. He made an

---

34 Quoted from Rahman, *Avicenna's Psychology. An English translation of Kitāb-al-Najāt, book ii, chapter vi*, pp. 26-9; cf. pp. 30-31 on the distinction, for example, between the presentation, to the internal senses of a sheep, of the shape and colour of a wolf, and the recognition of this as a wolf in all its meaning for the sheep. For his discussion of vision see also Avicenna, *De anima*, i. 5, iii. 1 (Venetiis, 1508); cf. Wiedermann, *Archiv für die Geschichte der Naturwissenschaften und der Technik*, iv (1912-13) 239-41; Crombie, "Avicenna's influence on the medieval scientific tradition", in *Avicenna: Scientist and Philosopher*, ed. Wickens, p. 95.

advance of major proportions in attempting to develop a physical theory of the propagation, reflection and refraction of light as distinct from vision[35], and in attempting a geometrical-optical analysis of how images are not simply received but formed in the eye. But an investigation of his brilliant insight that the eye itself must be treated as an optical system shows that even he, like all before him, failed to recognize the need to separate the essentially different kinds of question involved in the act of sight.

Alhazen began by assuming a version of the Greek atomist theory that vision was effected by "images" or "copies" (*idola, species, forma*) propagated from the visible object to the eye. Following Euclid and Ptolemy, he supposed that a visual cone of rays extended from the object, as its base, to its apex at the eye (figs. 15, 16: object *al*, image *cd*)[36]. From Galen he accepted the belief that the *crystallinus* or *glacialis* was the sensitive organ, and he then proposed the original theory that the image of the object was propagated by physical rays sent from each point on it to a corresponding point on the sensitive anterior surface of the *glacialis*, which thus effected a perception of the whole object through the separate perceptions of each of its points. The rays carried the colours as well as the other visual qualities of the object, so that all were represented in the pattern of point-sensations. Each perception of a point was accompanied by a distinct, innate sense of direction, and he gave an interesting account of how the eye effected perception of the whole object by means of movements by which it explored or 'scanned' an object or field of vision[36a]

Alhazen's geometrical treatment of image-formation enabled him to offer at once a geometrical solution of the ancient and puzzling problem of how the images of large objects (houses, camels) got through the diminutive pupil. But it also raised some difficulties. First, if each sensitive point on the *glacialis* was stimulated by every ray reaching it from all points on the object, the *glacialis* would not be able to distinguish different colours coming from different parts of the object. To overcome this difficulty he introduced the hypothesis that only rays striking the *glacialis* perpendicularly and without weakening by refraction stimulated it fully. This agreed with a mechanical analogy: a weapon struck deepest when it struck perpendicularly to the surface of its target[37]. But it made necessary the further anatomical assumption that in the optical system of the eye the centres of curvature of the cornea, the aqueous humour (*albugineus*) and the anterior surface of the *glacialis* all coincided at the centre of the eyeball (figs. 15, 16 : *b*).

35 Alhazen, *Opticae thesaurus libri septem*, vii (Basiliae, 1572). See Bauer, *Die Psychologie Alhazens;* Schramm, *Ibn Al-Haythams Weg zur Physik,* and "Ibn Al-Haythams Stellung in der Geschichte der Wissenschaften ", *Fikrun Wa Fann,* No. 6 (1965) 1-22; and for earlier bibliography, especially of Wiedemann's publications, see Sarton, *Introduction . . .,* i, 721-3. An Arabic text of Alhazen with English translation is published by Sabra (1983), (1988); below, p. 258.

36 Alhazen, *Opticae thesaurus,* i. 5, theorems 14-20, 23-7; see translations in Appendix.

36a Ibid. ii. 2, theorems 42-4.

37 Ibid. vii. 2, theorum 8, where he also used to explain refraction the ballistic model of an iron ball thrown at various angles against a thin penetrable screen; cf. vii. 6, theorem 37, i. 5, theorems 14-18, 30.

A second difficulty shows even more clearly how Alhazen's thinking was kept on to the wrong track by his attempt to make the mechanism by which the image is formed explain immediately how we see. He agreed with Galen that vision was not completed in the *glacialis* but that " vision is completed when the visual form (*forma visibilis*) received by the *crystallinus* passes through to the optic nerve " [38]. He also described an experiment with a *camera obscura* in which, when a number of candles were set up " opposite an opening leading into a dark place, with a wall or opaque body opposite the opening, the lights (*luces*) of these candles appear on the body or that wall, separately and corresponding in number to the candles . . ."[39]. But he used this experiment simply to show that the " lights " all passed in straight lines through the same hole unaffected by each other and this " is to be understood for all transparent bodies, including the transparent coats of the eye ". His difficulty was that he knew

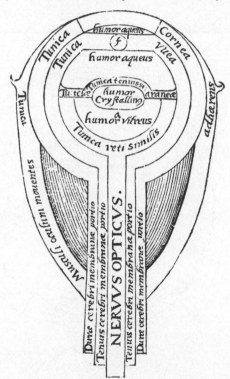

Fig. 14. The anatomy of the eye, from a contemporary illustration inserted by Risner in editing Alhazen, *Opticae thesaurus*, i, 4 (Basel, 1572); see Witelo, *Opticae*, iii. 4, same edition, p. 87; cf. fig. 3.

38 Ibid. i. 5, theorem 25.
39 Ibid. i. 5, theorem 29.

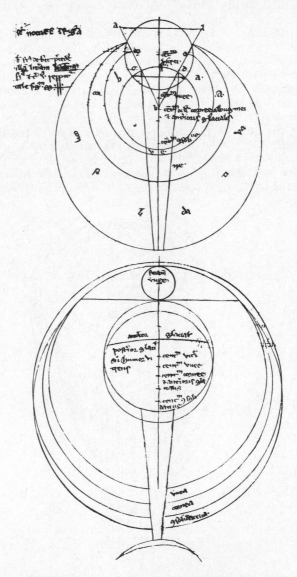

Fig. 15. From Roger Bacon, *Opus maius,* v. i. iii. 3, British Museum MS Royal 7.
F. viii (13 cent.) f. 54ᵛ: illustrating the geometrical optics of the eye
according to Alhazen. Bacon wrote in this chapter: "I shall draw, therefore,
a figure in which all these matters are made clear as far as is possible on a
surface, but the full demonstration would require a body fashioned like the
eye in all the particulars aforesaid. The eye of a cow, pig, and other
animals can be used for illustration, if anyone wishes to experiment".
His intention was to draw simply a geometrical diagram showing the
various curvatures of the ocular media; *centrum* meant centre of curvature.
"Let *al* be the base of the cone, which is the visible object, whose image
(*species*) penetrates the cornea under the conical form and enters the opening, and which tends naturally to the centre of the eye, and would go there
if it were not met first by a denser body by which it is bent, namely, the

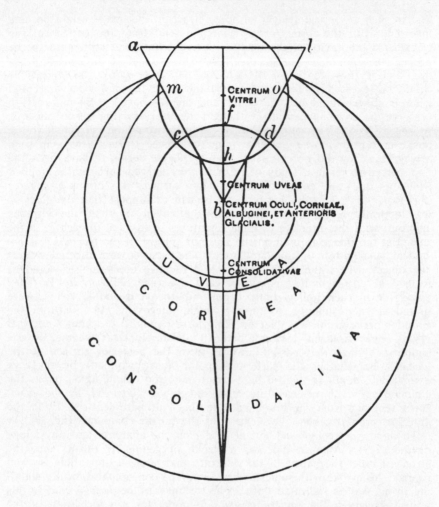

Fig. 16. From *The "Opus Majus" of Roger Bacon,* v. i. iii. 3, ed. Bridges, ii, 24 (Oxford, 1897): top diagram of fig. 15 redrawn. The diagram is not anatomical, but a geometrical model showing the curvatures of the different refracting media according to Alhazen's optical theory of the eye. The "centre of the eye" (*centrum oculi, b*) coincides with the centres of curvature of the cornea, the aqueous humour (*albugineus*) and the anterior surface of the *glacialis*. In front of this are the centres of the vitreous humour and the choroid (*uvea*), and behind it is the centre of the sclerotic (*consolidativa*). The object *al* sends rays which pass perpendicularly through the cornea at *m, o* and strike the anterior surface of the *glacialis* perpendicularly at *c, d,* thus passing through without refraction. At the posterior surface of the *glacialis* the rays are refracted away from the centre so that they do not intersect; thus an erect image of the object reaches the entrance of the optic nerve at the back of the eye.

vitreous humour, *c h d "*. In the top diagram the refraction should be shown not as drawn, but at the interface between the convex *posterior* surface of the *glacialis* and the concave anterior surface of the vitreous humour (*c h d; h* is missing); see figs. 16, 17.

that in such an optical system without refraction the image would become inverted. "But the form (*forma*) cannot extend from the surface of the *glacialis* to the cavity of the nerve in straight lines and still preserve the proper positions of its parts. For all these lines meet at the centre of the eye, and if they continued straight on past the centre their positions would be reversed: what is right would become left and vice versa, and what is above would become below and below above "[40]. So in order to preserve the erect image that he thought necessary for the eye to cause us to see as we do, he supposed that the rays would be refracted at the posterior surface of the *glacialis* — now conceived to be a lens — in such a way that they did not intersect (figs. 16, 17). He seems to have been the first person to make a study of refraction by curved surfaces; he applied Ptolemy's rules and constructions for plane surfaces to sections of spheres (figs. 10, 17, 19)[41]. To solve his problem he had to suppose that the *glacialis* was optically rarer (more transparent he called it) than the vitreous humour, with the interface of their curvatures in front of the centre of the eye. But the image formed on the anterior surface of the *glacialis* was not optical, but a pattern of stimulated points. The two eyes were directed towards the object, where their axes met so that the two erect images would be formed at corresponding points in each eye (fig. 10: *hrf, lte*)[41a]. They passed down each hollow optic nerve and, to avoid double vision, were united at their junction to form a single image (fig. 18: *kad*). In the common nerve vision was effected. This corresponds to Avicenna's external visual sense. Alhazen does not make it absolutely clear whether it was simply an image that passed inwards from the posterior surface of the *glacialis,* or whether the pattern of point-sensations made by the rays extended in depth through a light-sensitive region extending as far as the common nerve. In any case the single image was conveyed, by the visual spirit sent out from the brain, back to the "ultimate sentient "[41b] in the anterior cerebral cavity, the location of the *sensus communis* (fig. 39).

To impose a geometrical-optical model on the anatomy and physiology of the eye as Alhazen did was a stroke of genius. It throws into the strongest relief the nature of the difficulty that made it impossible for him to make his stroke with sufficient brutality. The conceptual difficulty standing in his way is indicated both by his treatment of the *glacialis*, and by his failure to see in the *camera obscura* a model for the formation of the image in the eye. It is easy for us to recognize now that the first, necessary though not sufficient, condition giving Kepler success where Alhazen failed was conceptual: complete willingness to apply the mechanistic hypothesis to this case. In addition he had to discover how to carry out the optical analysis correctly. How did this conceptual change come about ?

40 Ibid. ii. 1, theorem 2.
41 Ibid. vii.7.44-50. Alhazen (vii. 3, theorem 9) was interested in magnification, not simply refraction by a ' burning glass '.
41a Ibid. i. 5, theorem 27, iii. 2, theorems 2-10, vii. 6, theorem 36; cf. Witelo, *Opticae libri decem,* iii, theorems 32-50 (Basileae, 1572).
41b Ibid. i. 5, theorems 16, 26-7; ii. 1, theorem 2.

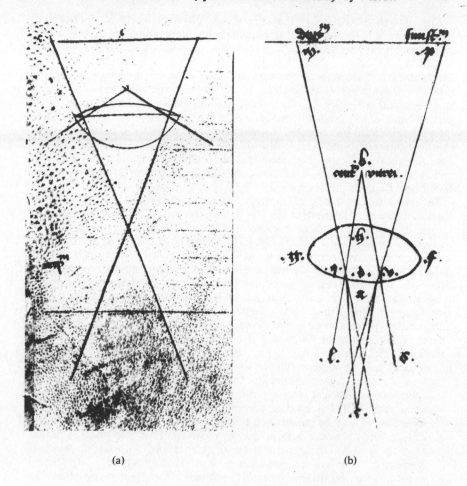

(a)   (b)

Fig. 17.   From Roger Bacon, *Opus maius*, v. i. viii. 1: (a) British Museum MS Royal
7. F. viii (13 cent.) f. 61ᵛ, showing the shape of the *glacialis*, flatter anteriorly;
(b) Oxford MS Bodleian Library, Digby 234 (15 cent.) f. 247ʳ. The rays
from the right (*dextrum m*) and left (*sinistrum p*) ends of the visible
object pass perpendicularly through the anterior surface of the flattened
glacialis (*g f*), and are refracted at its posterior surface (*q, u*) so that instead
of intersecting (below *a*) they reach the optic nerve (*c*) with image
correctly orientated. The rays passing into the vitreous humour (held to
be optically denser than the *glacialis*) are refracted according to Ptolemy's
rules towards the perpendiculars (*bl, bs*) meeting at its centre of curvature
(b); cf. figs. 10, 19.

The growth of the belief that the whole physical world is a system of mechanisms is a broad cultural phenomenon, depending on a wide range of philosophical and technological interests, activities and inventions. Why it should have been a belief that grew and became increasingly accepted in early modern Europe is a question that asks for an investigation of the intellectual sociology of the beliefs associated with the various philosophical and technical activities of this period, in comparison with those of other periods and other civilizations. It would be valuable, if enough suitable information could be collected, to make such a comparison between China, classical antiquity, the Arabic world, and the early modern West. In any case the question has no easy answer. I shall simply indicate some scientific and technical discoveries, inventions, attitudes and proposals that may have facilitated Kepler's strategic move.

Several different kinds of interest in optics developed as the work of Euclid, Ptolemy, Galen, Hunain ibn Ishāq, Avicenna, Alhazen and other Greek and Arabic authors became available in Latin. Beginning in the thirteenth century with Robert Grosseteste at Oxford, natural philosophers saw in optics an eminent example of Aristotle's theory of demonstration in natural science. In exploring the subject they made a number of relevant proposals and advances, in particular towards physical explanations of the propagation, reflection and refraction of light and in their work on lenses. Grosseteste distinguished clearly between the physical properties of light, and similar powers propagated from their sources or agents, and their effects on the organs of vision and the other senses. He wrote in one of the essays in which, on the basis of his cosmology of light, he tried to establish geometrical and physical optics as the fundamental natural science:[42]

> . . . a natural agent propagates its power from itself to its recipient (*patiens*), whether it acts on the senses or on matter. This power is sometimes called a species, sometimes a similitude, and is the same whatever it may be called. . . . For it does not act by deliberation and choice, and therefore acts in one way, whatever it may meet, whether something with sense perception or something without it, whether something animate or inanimate. But the effects are diversified according to the diversity of the recipient. For when received by the senses this power produces an operation in some way more spiritual and noble; on the other hand when received by matter, it produces a material operation, as the sun by the same power produces diverse effects in different subjects, for it cakes mud and melts ice.

In spite of this Grosseteste made a somewhat eclectic use of the sources available to him and gave his account of vision in terms of extromitted visual rays. His most relevant discussion of optics was on refraction, which he said had been "untouched and unknown amongst us until the present time"[43]. He almost certainly did not know Alhazen's study of refraction by spherical surfaces, but he used Ptolemy's rules (*regulae*) and construction with plane surfaces to give an explanation of the refraction

42 Grosseteste, *De lineis*. ed. Baur, p. 60; see Crombie, *Robert Grosseteste and the Origins of Experimental Science*, p. 110, cf. pp. 113-5.
43 Grosseteste. *De iride*. ed. Baur. p. 73; Cromble. op. cit. p. 119.

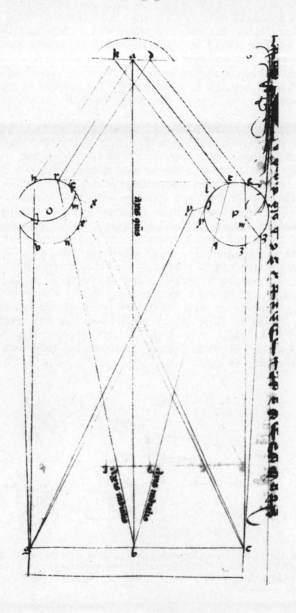

Fig. 18.   From Witelo, *Opticae,* iii. 37, Oxford MS Bodleian Library, Ashmole 424
(late 14 cent.) f 78ᵛ: illustrating Alhazen's theory of binocular vision.
Rays from points *g b c* on the object are sent respectively to *h r f* and
l t e at the entrance of each optic nerve; the two erect images unite at
k a d in the optic chiasma.

of light by a spherical burning-glass (fig. 18)[44]. He also used Ptolemy's construction for locating the refracted image with a plane surface, proposed an original 'law' of refraction[45], and described the application of these, with Euclid's rule that apparent size is proportional to the visual angle, in order to make objects appear nearer or larger by means of refraction. This was a proposal not only to use a lens for the purpose of magnification as distinct from burning, but to do so on the basis of scientific optics. He wrote:[46]

> This part of *Perspectiva,* when well understood, shows us how we may make things a very long distance off appear as if placed very close, and larger near things appear very small, and how we may make small things placed at a distance appear any size we want, so that it may be possible for us to read the smallest letters at incredible distances, or to count sand, or grains, or seeds, or any sort of minute objects. . . . It is obvious from geometrical reasons, given a transparent body (*diaphanum*) of known size and shape at a known distance from the eye, how a thing of known distance, size and position will appear in place, size and position. The same geometers will find it obvious how transparent bodies can be shaped so that they receive the rays issuing from the eye making an angle at the eye as large as they like, and constrict the rays as much as they like on the visible objects, large or small, far away or near. In this way all visible objects may be made to appear to them in any position and of any size they like; and they can make very large objects appear very small, and contrariwise very small and remote objects as if they were large and easily discernible by sight.

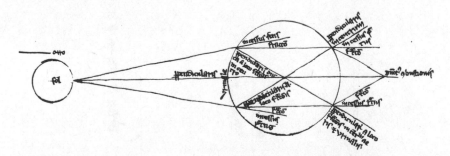

Fig. 19. From Roger Bacon, *Opus maius,* iv. ii. 2, British Museum MS Royal 7. F. viii (13 cent.) f. 25ʳ: illustrating the explanation of a burning glass given according to Ptolemy's rules for refraction by Grosseteste, *De natura locorum.*

44 Grosseteste, *De natura locorum,* ed. Baur, p. 71, cf. *De lineis,* p. 63; Ptolemy, *Optica,* v. 3, 70-81, éd. Lejeune, pp. 224-5, 262-6. See Crombie, op. cit. pp. 120-3, and pp. 116-7 for Grosseteste's sources.

45 Grosseteste, *De iride,* ed. Baur, pp. 74-5. On these pages he gives first the 'law' of refraction, and then the construction for locating the image based on Ptolemy, *Optica,* v. 3, éd. Lejeune, pp. 224-5; cf. Baur, *Philosophie des Robert Grosseteste,* pp. 117-8; Crombie, op. cit. p. 123; below n. 47.

46 Grosseteste, *De iride,* ed. Baur, pp. 74-5; Crombie, op. cit. p. 119.

Later in the thirteenth century Grosseteste's disciple Roger Bacon carried further these inquiries of the master he admired so much, but with the advantage of knowing Alhazen. Bacon seems to have made an original advance on Alhazen by giving constructions, based on those of Ptolemy for plane and of Alhazen for convex refracting surfaces, providing rules (*canones*) classifying the properties of convex and concave spherical surfaces with the eye in various relationships to the refracting media (fig. 20)[47]. He went on in a well-known passage to apply these rules to the proposal made by Grosseteste:[48]

> If the letters of a book or any minute objects be viewed through a lesser segment of a sphere of glass or crystal, whose plane base is laid upon them, they will appear far better and larger. Because, by the fifth canon about a spherical medium whose convexity is towards the eye and the object is placed below it and between the convexity and its centre, all things concur to magnify it. For the angle under which it is seen is greater, and its image (*imago*) is also greater, and nearer to the eye than the object itself; because the object is between the centre and the eye. And therefore this instrument is useful to old men and to those that have weak eyes. For they may see the smallest letters sufficiently magnified. But if the medium be the larger segment of a sphere, or but half of one, then by the sixth canon, the apparent visual angle will be greater than the true, and the image also greater than the object; but the place of it will be beyond the object; because the centre of the sphere is between the eye and the object. And therefore this instrument is not so powerful in magnifying as a lesser segment of a sphere. Also instruments made of crystal bodies with plane surfaces, by the first canon about planes, and with concave surfaces, by the first and second canons about spherical surfaces, will perform the same thing. But the lesser of two segments of a sphere magnifies more manifestly than any of them all, by reason of all the three causes. . . . Greater things than these may be performed by refracted vision. For it is easy to understand by the canons above mentioned, that the greatest things may appear exceedingly small, and on the contrary; also that the most remote objects may appear just at hand, and on the contrary. For we can give such figures to transparent bodies, and dispose them in such order with respect to the eye and the objects, that the rays shall be refracted and bent towards any place we please; so that we may see the object near at hand or at a distance, under any angle we please. And thus from an incredible distance we may read the smallest letters, and may number the smallest particles of dust and sand, by reason of the greatness of the angle under which we may see them; and on the contrary we may not be able to see the greatest bodies just by us, by reason of the smalness of the angles

47   Bacon, *Opus maius*, v. iii. ii. 3, ed. Bridges. Bacon's diagrams illustrating his different cases were reproduced in printed editions of Pecham (1556) and Bacon (1614).

48   Ibid. v. iii. ii. 4, v. iii. iii. 4; translated from Jebb's edition of 1733 by Robert Smith, *A Compleat System of Opticks*, ii, Remarks Nos. 84, 113. Smith quoted these passages to refute the opinion of William and Samuel Molyneux that Bacon was the inventor of spectacles and of the telescope (Remarks Nos. 84-90, 111-21).

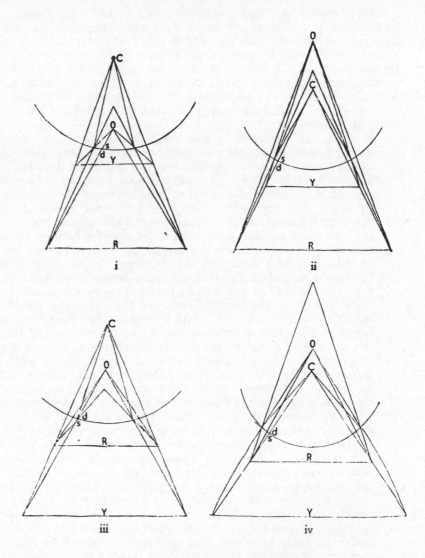

Fig. 20. From Roger Bacon, *Opus maius*, v. iii. ii. 3, British Museum MS Royal 7. F. viii (13 cent.) ff. 91ʳ-94ᵛ (re-lettered): illustrating his classification of the properties of curved refracting surfaces. Rays go from each end of the object (*res, R*), are refracted at the curved surface separating the optically rarer (*subtilior, s*) and denser (*densior, d*) media, for example air and glass, and meet at the eye (*oculus, o*). The image (*ymago, Y*) is seen, according to Ptolemy's construction (fig. 10), at the intersection of the projection of these refracted rays entering the eye with the perpendicular going from the object (R) to the centre of curvature (*centrum*, C). It is

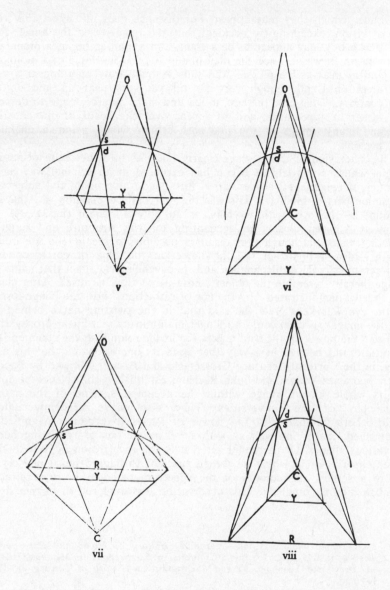

magnified or diminished according to whether the concave (i-iv) or convex (v-viii) surface is towards the eye, whether the eye is on the rarer (i, ii, v, vi) or denser (iii, iv, vii, viii) side of the curvature, and whether the eye is on the side of the centre of curvature (C) towards (i, iii) or away from (ii, iv) the object, or the centre of curvature is on the side of the object towards (vi, viii) or away from (v, vii) the eye. He recommended a convex lens forming a hemisphere (vi) or less than a hemisphere (v) to aid weak sight.

under which they may appear. For distance does not affect this kind of vision, excepting by accident, but the quantity of the angle. And thus a boy may appear to be a giant, and a man as big as a mountain, forasmuch we may see the man under as great an angle as a mountain and as near as we please. And thus a small army may appear a very great one, and though very far off yet very near us, and on the contrary. Thus also the sun, moon and stars may be made to descend hither in appearance, and to appear over the heads of our enemies; and many things of the like sort, which would astonish unskilled persons.

The conclusion of this passage clearly takes us into the realm of natural magic, whose potentialities Bacon had explored in an original way in his account of *scientia experimentalis*[49]. But Bacon also made the subject of refraction part of medicine. His was the first Latin exposition of Alhazen's account of the eye, with its lens, as an optical system (figs. 15, 16). He followed Alhazen closely in accounting for the structure and function effecting vision, although perhaps it is possible to see in one apparently original idea a break in the insistence on the type of correspondence between physiological mechanism and its psychological effect that made the image literally resemble the object whose perception it caused. After claiming to have demonstrated " by the law of refraction " how the image formed in the eye was kept erect, he said that in the twisting nerve behind the eye the image (*species*) could no longer maintain its rectilinear propagation; and so " the power of the soul makes the image relinquish the common laws of nature and behave in a way that suits its operations "[50]. Be this as it may, in the thirteenth century Grosseteste and Bacon, followed by Bacon's contemporaries Witelo and John Pecham, established the science of optics in its whole known range within the accepted scheme of the natural philosophy of the universities. They also made academic natural philosophers familiar with the power of lenses to produce magnified or diminished images, as well as with other properties of refracting bodies of various shapes. Of particular interest is the recognition by Witelo that, in an experiment in which he passed sunlight through a hexagonal crystal on to a screen, the colours of the spectrum emerged in rays refracted through different angles[51]. This observation was explored in further detail

---

49   Bacon, *Opus maius*, vi; cf. Thorndike, *History of Magic and Experimental Science*, ii, 649 sqq., 751 sqq.; Crombie, in *Perspectives in Medieval History*, ed. Drew and Lear, pp. 45 sqq.; Schramm, in *History of Science*, ii (1963) 104 sqq.

50   Bacon, *Un fragment inédit de l'Opus tertium*, ed. Duhem, p. 78, cf. p. 90. For Bacon's account of ocular physiology, the union of the images in the optic chiasma, and the " ultimate sentient " see *Opus maius*, v. i. iii-iv, v. i. v. 1-3, v. i. vii. 1-2; cf. Crombie, *Robert Grosseteste . . .*, pp. 152-5. Bacon's main anatomical sources were Hunain Ibn Ishāq and Avicenna. For *lex naturae* cf. Wolfson, *Philo*; Clagett, *Greek Science in Antiquity*, pp. 137-45; Crombie in Clagett (ed.), *Critical Problems in the History of Science*, pp. 89, 98-9; Schramm, in *History of Science*, ii (1963) 106-9.

51   Witelo, *Opticae libri decem* (1572); Bäumker, *Witelo*; Pecham, *Perspectiva communis*. Cf. Crombie, *Robert Grosseteste . . .*, pp. 165-7 (Pecham), 216-8, 230-1 (Witelo); Lindberg, *Archives internationales d'histoire des sciences*, xviii (1965) 37-53 (Pecham).

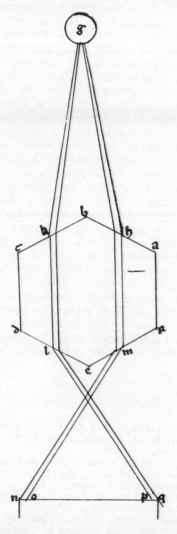

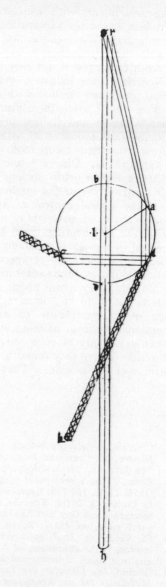

Fig. 21.
From Theodoric of Freiberg, *De iride*, ii. 23, Basel MS Oeffentliche Bibliothek der Universität, F. IV. 30 (14 cent.) f. 24ʳ: illustrating the projection on to a screen of colours produced by passing sunlight through a hexagonal crystal. Two spectra are formed with red at *o* and *p*, blue at *n* and *q*, respectively.

Fig. 22.
From Theodoric of Freiberg, *De iride*, ii. 8, Basel MS Oeffentliche Bibliothek der Universität, F. IV. 30 (14 cent.) f. 15ᵛ: illustrating the formation of colours (crosshatched) in light passed through a spherical transparent ball.

in the experiments with a spherical crystal or glass on which Theodoric of Freiberg based his explanation of the form and colours of the rainbow (figs. 21, 22)[52]. What connection the academic study of lenses may have had with the introduction of eyeglasses in northern Italy at the end of the thirteenth century it is not easy to say. The invention was associated with the Venetian glass industry, and it gradually made at least part of the medical profession familiar with the lens as an aid to natural vision[53].

During the fourteenth century natural philosophers in the English, French, German and Italian universities became increasingly drawn into epistomological problems of vision[54], but in the fifteenth century quite a different interested group took up scientific optics for its own purposes. The group that Olschki[55] characterized as 'artist-engineers' were a product of Italian urban society and essentially practical in their outlook. Their contribution to the intellectual context of European science was to add to the logical control of argument achieved by the philosophers, a rational control of materials of many different kinds in painting, sculpture, architecture, engineering, canal building, fortification, gunnery, music. The leaders of this group increasingly came to have training in anatomy and the theoretical sciences of perspective and mechanics as well as in such practical skills as bronze-casting and masonry. The artists of the Italian *quattrocento* who wrote about their work came to define their aim, as Ghiberti put it, to be " imitare la natura quanto a me fosse possibile "[56]; which meant specifically to give a convincing presentation of three-dimensional space in painting and sculpture. They turned for help to the geometrical theory of perspective developed by Euclid, Ptolemy, Alhazen and Witelo, where they found a sophisticated means of gaining theoretical control over visual space. They found a method of quantifying the visual

52 Crombie, *Robert Grosseteste . . .*, pp. 248-50, and in *Perspectives in Medieval History*, ed. Drew and Lear, pp. 51-4; Boyer, *Isis*, xlix (1958) 378-90; Wallace, *The Scientific Methodology of Theodoric of Freiberg*.

53 Rosen, " The invention of eyeglasses ", *Journal of the History of Medicine*, xi (1956) 13-46, 183-218; Crombie, *Robert Grosseteste . . .*, pp. 151, 353, *Augustine to Galileo*, i, 231-2. The earliest known medical writer certainly to mention spectacles was Guy de Chauliac, *La Grande chirurgie*, revue et collationnée . . . par Nicaise, pp. 491-2; Rosen, op. cit. p. 203; below n. 77.

54 Cf. Vescovini, *Studi sulla prospettiva medievale*. Of particular philosophical interest is the discussion of " species " and other concepts by Ockham, *Super quattuor libros sententiarum annotationes*, ii. 18, 26.

55 Olschki, *Die Literatur der Technik und der angewandten Wissenschaften vom Mittelalter bis zur Renaissance*, pp. 35 sqq.; cf. below n. 73.

56 Ghiberti, *Commentarii*, hrg. Schlosser, i, 48; Krautheimer, *Lorenzo Ghiberti*, pp. 14, 229. For discussions of the history of perspective painting see especially Krautheimer, op. cit. pp. 229-53; Parronchi, *Paragone*, lxxxix (1957) 3 sqq., xcv (1957) 3 sqq., cvii (1958) 3 sqq., cix (1959) 3 sqq., cxxxiii (1961) 18 sqq., *Studi Danteschi*, xxxvi (1959) 5 sqq.; Panofsky, " Die Perspektive als symbolische Form ", *Vorträge der Bibliothek Warburg, 1924-25*, pp. 258-330; Wieleitner, *Repertorium für Kunstwissenschaft*, xlii (1920) 249-62. See also Antal, *Florentine Painting and its Social Background*; Bunim, *Space in Medieval Painting and the Forerunners of Perspective*; Chastel, *Art et humanisme à Florence au temps de Laurent le Magnifique;* Francastel, *Peinture et société;* White, *Journal of the Warburg Institute*, xii (1949) 58 sqq., xiv (1951) 42 sqq.

field that enabled them to calculate and predict what would be seen, in particular relations of distance, size, order and shape. Brunelleschi, followed by Alberti, explained the new technique by means of optical instruments. Alberti's was a 'peep-show', not quite a *camera obscura* but more likely a box in which a scene painted on a screen was viewed through a pin-hole[57]. To some extent these artists, and others such as Piero della Francesca and Leonardo da Vinci, were offering a theoretical justification of methods learnt mainly by practice, but this itself is an interesting phenomenon and it shows a characteristic attitude towards the nature that was to be imitated by artifice and mathematical science. It was an active, rationally aggressive attitude to nature. Thus Leonardo wrote:[58] " O speculator on things, do not boast of knowing the things that nature ordinarily brings about; but rejoice if you know the end of those things that you yourself devise ".

If Ptolemy and Galen, to say nothing of Alhazen, had all the scientific knowledge necessary to solve the problem of the dioptric mechanism of the eye, then Leonardo was even better placed. He had available all they knew and in addition the theory of lenses, experience with eyeglasses[59], and the model of the *camera obscura*. He gave a brilliant illustration of the theory of perspective in painting by means of his famous ' window', in which he showed how a three-dimensional scene was depicted on a two-dimensional sheet of glass that cut off a plane section of the " cone " of light rays going from the scene to the eye[60]. He was a skilled experimental anatomist : he described a method of embedding an eye for sectioning by placing it in white of egg and boiling solid (cf. figs. 23-25)[61]. He introduced what may be

57 See the anonymous Life of Alberti in Muratori, *Rerum Italicarum Scriptores,* xxv. cols. 299C-300A; and Alberti, *On Painting,* i, transl. Spencer, pp. 28-9, 50-1,57,05-6. Alberti finished *De pictura* in Latin in 1435; the date of the Italian version is 1436. For Brunelleschi see Manetti, *Vita di Filippo Brunelleschi*; Argan, *Journal of the Warburg Institute,* ix-x (1946-47) 96 sqq.; Parronchi, *Paragone,* cvii (1958) 3-32, cix (1959) 3-31; Sanpaolesi, *Belle Arti,* ii (1951) 25-54; Wittkover, *Journal of the Warburg Institute,* xvi (1953) 275 sqq. A form of *camera obscura* was known in Byzantium in the sixth century; see Huxley, *Anthemius of Tralles,* pp. 6-8, 44-6. In the form described by Alhazen (above n. 39) it was also known to Roger Bacon, John Pecham and other Latin successors: cf. Duhem, *Système du monde,* iii, 499-529, iv, 10-19, 580-1; Sarton *Introduction to the History of Science.* i, 721-3, ii, 762, 966, 990, 1029; Polyak, *The Retina,* pp. 132-4; see below p. 258.

58 Leonardo da Vinci, *Literary Works,* ed. Richter, ii, 250, No. 1206; *Les manuscrits de Léonard de Vinci,* publié . . . par Ravaisson-Mollien, Codex G, f. 47r.

59 Leonardo da Vinci, *Codice Atlantico,* transcrizione . . . di Piumati, f. 244r; *The Notebooks,* arranged . . . MacCurdy, i, 249; cf. Hofstetter,' *American Journal of Optometry,* xxx (1953) 41-4.

60 Leonardo da Vinci, *Les manuscrits* . . . pub. . . . Ravaisson-Mollien, Cod. A, ff. 1v, 37v; cf. Pirenne, *The British Journal for the Philosophy of Science,* iii (1952) 169 sqq. The 'window' had been used to illustrate the same point by Alberti, *On Painting,* i, transl. Spencer, p. 51.

61 Leonardo da Vinci, *Les manuscrits* . . . pub. . . . Ravaisson-Mollien, Cod. K, f. 119r; *Selections from the Notebooks,* ed. Richter, p. 160. Leonardo's numerous anatomical drawings provide a striking record of his own progress in knowledge; compare for example his conventional drawing of the three cerebral ventricles in Leonardo da Vinci, *Quaderni d'anatomia,* pub. da

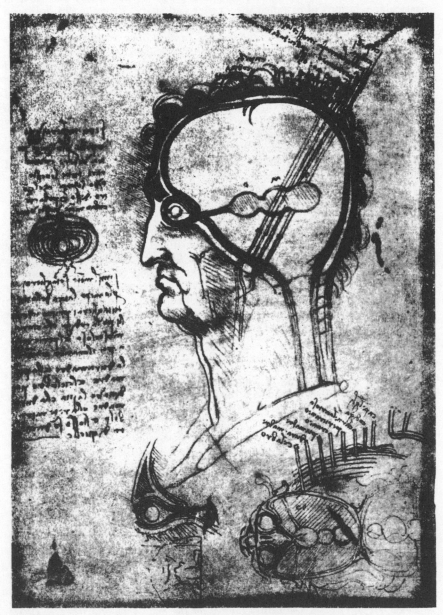

Fig. 23.   From Leonardo da Vinci, Royal Library, Windsor MS, Clark
No. 12603ʳ; *Quaderni d'anatomia,* v, f. 6 (c. 1490): illustrating
vertical and cross sections of the skull and eyes. The three
cerebral ventricles accommodating respectively the *sensus
communis* with fantasy and imagination, thought and judgement, and memory, are represented conventionally; cf. figs.
24, 39). Reproduced by gracious permission of Her Majesty
the Queen.

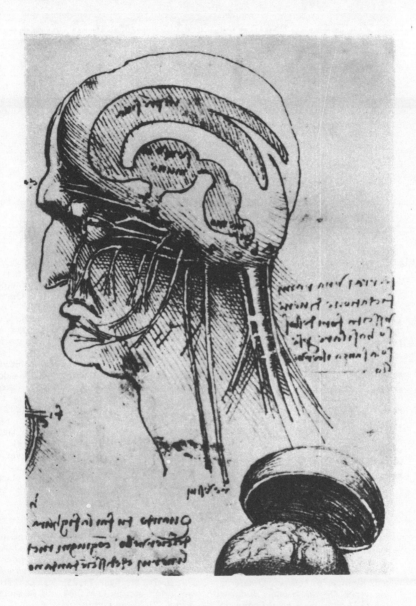

Fig. 24. From Leonardo da Vinci, MS Weimar (*Dessins anatomiques,* . . . par Huard, planche xiv): illustrating the dissection of the cranial nerves and of the cerebral ventricles after injection with wax.

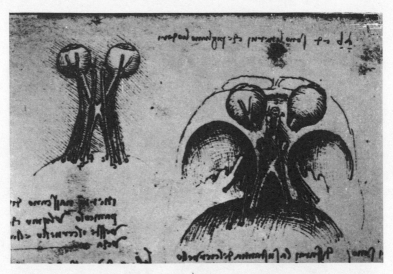

Fig. 25.   From Leonardo da Vinci, Royal Library, Windsor MS, Clark No. 19052ʳ;
            Dell 'anatomia fogli B, f. 35ʳ (c. 1504-6): dissections of the optic nerves
            showing the chiasma, and also of the oculo-motor, trigeminus and olfactory
            nerves. Reproduced by gracious permission of Her Majesty the Queen.

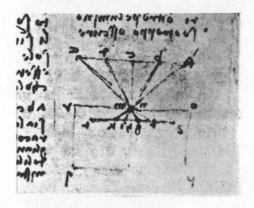

Fig. 26. From Leonardo da
Vinci, Codex D, f. 8ʳ:
i l l u s t r a t i n g his
account   of   the
c a m e r a   obscura.
Reading   Leonardo's
mirror-writing   from
right   to   left,   the
visible object (*a b c
d   e*)   sends   rays
through   the   small
window (*n   m*) to
form   a   reversed
image   (*k-f*) on the
screen   (*s-t*) placed
inside the dark box
(*o r p q*).

Vangensten, Fonahn, Hopstock, v, f. 6ᵛ (fig. 23; cf. fig. 39) with his drawings
based on his method of anatomical investigation by injecting melted wax with
a syringe into the ventricles (Clark, *A Catalogue of the Drawings of Leonardo
da Vinci . . . at Windsor Castle*, No. 19127ʳ; *Selections from the Notebooks*,
ed. Richter, p. 160; cf. *Quaderni . . .*, v. ff. 7r, 8ᵛ; figs. 24, 25); cf. Leonardo
da Vinci, *On the Human Body*, with translation etc. by O'Malley and Saunders,
pp. 142 sqq. See also Leonardo da Vinci, *Dell' anatomia fogli A, B, . . .
transcritti . . . da Piumati*; *Dessins anatomiques*, choix et présentation par
Huard. For the chronology of Leonardo's manuscripts see Calvi, *I manoscritti
di Leonardo da Vinci . . .*, Clark, op. cit., O'Malley and Saunders, op. cit.,
Pedretti, *Studi vinciani*, pp. 264-89, Leonardo da Vinci, *Fragments at Windsor
Castle . . .*, ed. Pedretti, pp. 19-28, *On Painting. A lost book . . .* reassembled
. . . by Pedretti, pp. 95 sqq., 252-9; and for their later history and publication
see Leonardo da Vinci, *Literary Works*, ed. Richter, i, 5 sqq., ii, 393 sqq. and
Panofsky, in *The Renaissance*, ed. Ferguson, pp. 148-51, cf. below n. 73.

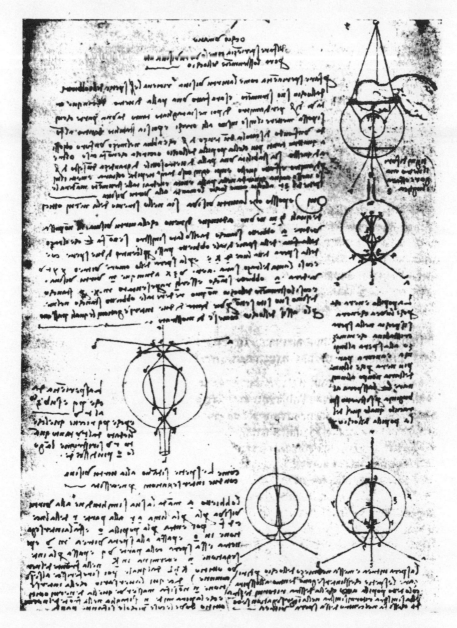

Fig. 27.   From Leonardo da Vinci, Codex D. f. 3ᵛ. The middle left diagram
illustrates his modification of Alhazen's ocular dioptrics so that the rays
entering the pupil from each end of the visible object intersect but are
restored by the lens to their original order before reaching the optic nerve.
The bottom right diagrams show the slightly bulging cornea. The top
right diagram illustrates Leonardo's model with a small glass ball inside a
larger one filled with water

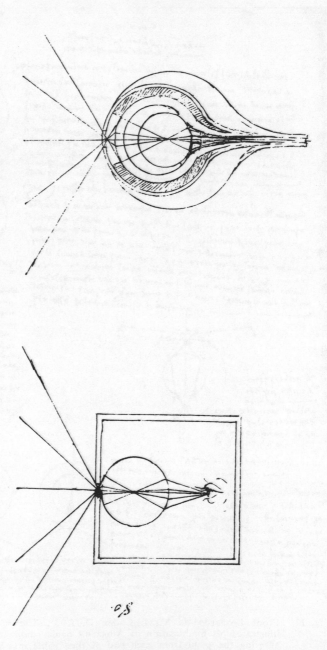

Fig. 28.   From Leonardo da Vinci, Codex Atlanticus, f. 337ᵛ:
illustrating his comparison of the eye with a *camera
obscura*. In this construction the rays intersect for a
second time in the centre of the lens in order to
preserve the correct orientation of the image at the
optic nerve. The ocular anatomy is peculiar, showing
the aqueous humour extending all round inside the
dark choroid (*uvea*), and the vitreous humour in front
of the spherical *crystallinus*.

called an engineering approach to the investigation of function by constructing models out of glass. Above all, it was he, so far as we know, who first compared the image-forming operation of the eye to that of a *camera obscura*. Grosseteste and Roger Bacon had discussed the magnification and diminution of images by lenses, and Witelo and Theodoric of Freiberg the coloured shapes thrown on a screen by refracting light through a crystal; the *camera obscura* unequivocally introduced the image as a picture on a screen[62].

But Leonardo did not solve the dioptric problem of the eye, for reasons that are clear in all his accounts and constructions. His analysis of vision was based on Alhazen's, and for the same reason as Alhazen he found it necessary to look for a physical arrangement that would produce an image that was erect and correctly orientated right and left. In this he showed a firm grasp of the need to explain optically what happened to the image as it passed through the various refracting media as far as the optic nerve. He supposed that the rays, after intersecting on entering the eye as in a *camera obscura,* would fall inverted on the anterior surface of the *crystallinus;* there they would be refracted and intersect again in the *crystallinus,* thus restoring them to their original order (figs. 26-28). In this order the image entered the optic nerve. It is evident that while Leonardo had gone a long way towards treating the eye simply as a physical instrument, he too found it impossible to escape from the main purpose of making the eye's mechanism provide an immediate cause of how we see, by delivering to the seat of the visual power an image representing the object essentially as we see it. It is evident also that a contributory reason for his failure was that he lacked the scientific equipment to carry out an adequate optical analysis. But Leonardo's discussions have the freshness given by practical needs. As a painter he pointed out that the image could not literally represent the proportions of its object unless all the parts of the object were equidistant from the eye; and he drew attention to ungeometrical clues such as tone and shade representing distance and scaling in a visual field[63]. His recurring experiments and the speculations accompanying his progress in anatomical knowledge show a restless concern with the operation of the eye and with the location of the sensitive organ of vision and its relation to the brain[64]. The following passages are from his most sustained discussion; the accompanying diagrams give three of his constructions for ocular dioptrics :[65]

Why nature made the pupil convex, namely protruding like part of a

62   Above n. 57; cf. Leonardo da Vinci, *Literary Works*, ed. Richter, i, 27. Leonardo (ibid. i, 230) described the spectrum thrown on a wall or floor by passing sunlight through a glass flask of water; cf. above nn. 51-2.

63   Cf. Leonardo da Vinci, *Treatise on Painting*, i. 5, transl. McMahon; *Literary Works*, ed. Richter, i, 32-33.

64   Leonardo's speculations indicate a mechanistic conception both of the transmission of sensory information and images to the brain, and of the operation of the motor function and of muscles; cf. *Literary Works*, ed. Richter, i, 259, ii, 89-90, 100-2. I am grateful to Dr. K. D. Keele for a discussion of this subject.

65   Leonardo da Vinci, *Les manucrits . . .* pub. . . . Ravaisson-Mollien, Cod. D. The following passages are from the translation by Dr. Nino Ferrero, *American Journal of Ophthalmology*, xxxv (1952) 507-21, with some changes; cf. *Literary Works*, ed. Richter, i, 140-6. Leonardo's three constructions for ocular dioptrics are illustrated in figs. 27, 28 and 29.

ball: Nature made the surface of the opening of the eye convex in order to allow the surrounding objects to imprint their images (*similitudini*) at greater angles, which could not happen if the eye were flat [fig. 27]. . . . *Whether the objects send their images* (simulacri) *to the eye with the parts in their identical proportion:* The objects do not send their images to the eye with the parts proportioned as they are in the object itself. This is proved by the ninth proposition and as between things of the same size the farthest will appear the smallest. Let *a* be the eye and *b, c, d* be the object. For the ninth proposition I state that *b-d,* parts of this object, will appear smaller than the part *c* because they are farther from the eye than *c*. . . . *How the images* (spetie) *of any object that reach the eye through a hole, imprint themselves upside-down on its pupil and the visual sense sees them upright:*[65a] The pupil of the eye which gets through a very small round hole the images of the bodies situated beyond the said little hole, always gets them upside-down, but always the visual power sees them upright as they are. And this happens because said images pass through the centre of the crystalline sphere situated in the middle of the eye : in this centre they converge in one point, then they spread out over the opposed surface of this sphere without bending, and over the said surface the images become upright like the objects from which they come. From there they are received by the visual power and transmitted to the mind where they are perceived. . . . (Necessity has provided that all the images of objects in front of the eye shall intersect in two places. One of these intersections is in the pupil, the other in the crystalline lens; and if this were not the case the eye could not see so great a number of objects as it does. . . . No image, even of the smaller object, enters the eye without being turned upside down; but as it penetrates into the crystalline lens it is once more reversed and thus the image is restored to the same position within the eye as that of the object outside the eye [fig. 27])[65b]. . . . *How objects on the right side would not appear right to the visual virtue, if their images did not pass through two intersections:* . . . In this way the instrument of the eye shows to the extremity of the optic nerve as right is right and as left is left [fig. 27]. . . . *About the way to make the experiment to show how the visual sense uses the eye as an instrument:* In order to make the experiment on how the visual sense gets the image of the objects from its instrument — the eye — a ball of glass will be made with a diameter of five eighths of a *braccia*[65c]; from one side of it a piece should be cut out so that a face might be put into it to the ears. Then let us fix to the bottom of it a box, one third of a *braccia* in size; with a hole in the middle which is four times larger than the pupil of the eye — or approximately so, it does not matter. Besides this, let us make a ball of thin glass with a diameter of one sixth of a *braccia* and let us fill everything with clear lukewarm water. Then put

65a By *popilla* Leonardo meant the part of the eye in depth from the anterior surface of the cornea to that of the lens; cf. below n. 67. The word *idolo* for image occurs on f. 2^r.

65b The passage in brackets has been inserted from *Literary Works*, ed. Richter, i, 144; Windsor MS, Clark, op. cit., No. 19150^v.

65c The Florentine *bracchia* was about 54 cm.

your face into the water and look into the ball and observe: you
will see that this instrument sends out the images of *s-t* to your
eye, as the eye sends them to the visual sense. Assuming that the
visual power is at the end of the optic nerves of which *h-m* is one,
then we affirm that the visual power *m* cannot see a left object from
its left part if the ray of the image of said object does not pass
through the centre of two spheres, namely through the sphere of the
cornea *d-k* and through the sphere of the vitreous humour *xytv*.
Then *m*, the visual virtue, will see a left object, to be represented in *x*
left; the instrument of the eye cannot see the left object where it is
located but through two intersections which pass through the axis
of the eye as demonstrated [fig. 27]. . . . The visual power is distributed
all over the pupil of the eye and every point of it can conceive the
nature of the objects put before the eye. . . .

*How the pupil receives the images of the things situated before the
eye only from the opening and not from the object:* The pupil of the
eye receives the images of the objects through the surface of the
openings and not from the object. This is proved partly by means of
the glasses, by which the images of the objects are magnified or
reduced depending on the major or minor curving of the external
surfaces of the glasses. Then it is proved by the quality of the internal
and external angles made by the rays of the images, which enter the
surface of the eye itself. . . . *Why the right object does not appear left
to the eye:* The images of the objects in the eye on entering the eye
bend the straightness of their rays, as it happens in perspective when
images pass from the density of the water to the thinness of the air.
But going back to the question that the right object does not appear
left to the eye, we see clearly from the experiment that the images
entering the albugineous humour through the pupil of the eye meet
together in the sphere of the crystalline humour, and here we have two
chances, namely: the visual power resides in the crystalline humour or
it widens at the extremity of the optic nerve, which gets these images
and then transmits them to the common sense, as the olfactory
nerves do. If such power resides in the centre of the crystalline
humour, it receives the images over the surface and they are referred
there from the surface of the pupil, where the objects are mirrored or
reflected from the surface of the uvea which bounds and closes the
albugineous humour, which has darkness behind its transparency, like
transparent glass which is provided with the opacity of lead in order
that objects may be better reflected over the surface of the glass
[fig. 29][65d]. If the visual power is in the centre of the crystalline sphere,
then all the objects sent to it from the surface of the pupil of the eye
will be seen in the right spot where they are and will not change
from the right to the left and will appear bigger, as shown in
perspective. And if the crystalline sphere gets images reflected from
the concavity of the uvea, they will be upright, although the uvea is a
concave mirror, and they will be upright because the centre of the
crystalline sphere is concentric with the centre of the sphere of the

---

65d In this curious construction the *uvea* acted as a spherical mirror reflecting
   images to the *crystallinus*.

uvea. But it is true that images reaching the uvea from outside of the eye pass through the centre of the crystalline sphere and become upside-down on reaching the uvea, and the same happens to those that reach the uvea without passing through the humour. Therefore, we might say, admitting the visual power to be at the extremity of the optic nerve, that it is clear that all the objects are straightened by the crystalline sphere, because those that were inverted in the uvea are taken and inverted a second time by the crystalline sphere, which presents upright the images that were given to it inverted. . . . *How the images of the objects received by the eye in its albugineous humour intersect:* The experiment, showing how objects send their images or resemblances intersected inside the eye in the albugineous humour, is made by images of illuminated objects entering a completely dark room through some very small round hole. If you get these images on a sheet of white paper held rather close to the small hole from inside this room, you will see on this paper all the aforesaid objects with their own shapes and colours but smaller and upside-down because of the said intersection. When these images come from a place illuminated by the sun they will have the appearance of actually being painted (*dipinti*) on the paper, which has to be very thin and seen from behind, and the little hole has to be made in a very thin sheet of iron. Let *abcde* be the objects illuminated by the sun. Let *o-r* be the wall of the dark room with the little hole *n-m,* and *s-t* be the sheet of paper whereon the rays of the objects strike. They will be inverted because their rays being straight, *a* right becomes left in *k* and *e* left becomes right in *f.* The same things happen within the pupil [fig. 26]. . . . *About the proportions of the position of the images that imprint themselves over the eye:* The proportion of the position of the objects dispersed over fields placed before the eye is never the same as the proportion of same images over the eye itself, unless the said objects are equidistant from the curve of the eye. This is proved : let *aec* be the surface of the eye and *desrf* be the objects spread over the field. I maintain that *desf,* the objects equidistant from the surface of the eye, will be spread over the surface of the eye with the same proportion with which they are spread in this field. And this is proved with the ninth rule of this treatise which reads : " The similar and equal triangles cut equidistant from their bases, will have the cuttings in the same proportion among themselves as the bases of the triangles have among themselves. But if these cuttings are not equidistant from their bases, then they will not follow the same proportion as in the bases ". . . . The eye will never acknowledge the true contour of the shape of any object situated in the far distance. . . . I maintain that it is not possible to ascertain in what part of this background the extremity of said object terminates. And this is proved by means of the third rule of this treatise which reads : " The visual power is not in a point alone, as the painters who deal with perspective maintain, but it is all over the pupil through which the images of the objects enter the eye into a space larger than the pupil itself. These images, the nearer they are to the centre of the visual power situated in this space, the better they will be acknowledged, and the farther they are the less they will be acknowledged ".

Against this background the ocular models used by the two leading sixteenth-century mathematical writers on optics acquire a particular interest. Both were Italians. In his manuscript, finished in 1554, Francesco Maurolico of Messina gave as his starting-points the ocular anatomy of Vesalius and the optics of Roger Bacon and Pecham[66]. Like these he accepted the lens as the seat of the " visual power ", but he added that " on its shape depends the quality of vision whether short or long "[67]. The nature and limits of his achievement follow precisely from his approach to the operation of the eye through a particular artificial model : the properties of artificial lenses of various shapes of which he had made a study. He went on to say that whereas the flattened anterior surface of the lens of the eye was designed to receive the images (*species*) of objects, the posterior surface was designed to transmit them. He discussed ocular

Fig. 29. From Leonardo da Vinci, Codex K, f. 119ᵛ: illustrating the construction in which the rays entering from the right and intersecting in the pupil were reflected by the choroid (*uvea*), acting as a concave mirror, on to the *crystallinus*.

66 Maurolico, *Diaphanorum partes, seu libri tres* (1611) pp. 72-3.
67 " Inter ea, quae ad visum spectant, dignitatis arcem obtinent glacialis sive chrystallinus humor, quem et pupillam appellare meo iudicio possumus: in qua visiva virtus, tamquam in sede consistit; haec utrinque convexa, sed non sphaerica, verum compressa, et a parte anteriori compressior, quo latiori susciperet formas rerum visibilium spatio. Hic in organo humorum nobilissimus medium sortitur locum. Ab huius forma dependet qualitas visus sive brevis, sive longi, caeteris passionibus exclusis, ut postea dicemus. Hic itaque humor in visione recipit species, receptasque per opticum nervum ad communis sensus iudicium defert: hic ergo facit ad recipiendum. Qui autem facit ad transmittendum, is est humor albugineus, sive aqueus, per quem traijciuntur species . . . Ad nutrimentum servit humor vitreus, a quo glacialis nutritur. Item retina, sive retiformis pellicula ex visorio nervo progrediens, et vitreo alimentum suppetens " (ibid. pp. 69-70). Cf. Roger Bacon, *Opus maius*, v. i. ii, 3 : " Et humor crystallinus vocatur pupilla, et in ea est virtus visiva, sicut in subjecto quod primo immutatur, licet non radicaliter, quoniam nervus communis est organum radicale, et ibi completur visio, quantum potest virtus visiva, ut sequentia demonstrabunt ". Like Bacon, Maurolico used the three terms *glacialis, crytallinus humor* and *pupilla* synonymously for the lens; the *humor albugineus* must be a mistake for *vitreus* through which the *species* were transmitted, as on pp. 74, 76 (below n. 69); the *retina* served for nutrition (cf. p. 71; below n. 81).

dioptrics as an application of the properties of artificial lenses, under the heading: " *On spectacles.* How visual rays passed through a transparent body convex on both sides converge more quickly, and how they diverge when passed through a body concave on both sides " (fig. 30)[68]. Adapted to the functioning of the eye, the lens was double convex and the surrounding coats of the cornea, choroid (*uvea*), aqueous and vitreous humour and retina similarly almost spherical.

Hence the lens (*pupilla*), placed in the middle of the eyeball and the receptable of the images (*species*), must be globular, but not spherical lest the perpendicular visual rays should pass through the centre of the sphere, intersect, and carry to the optic nerve an altered, that is inverted orientation (*situs*) of the thing seen, so that the things seen appear inverted. But the lens must be compressed and as it were made from two portions of spheres, which Roger Bacon well realized; unless the vitreous humour makes up part of this globe. So it happens that the visual rays falling on the anterior surface of the lens and carried through its depth without meeting, that is before coinciding, are carried in their own proper orientation to the optic nerve and present (*repraesentent*) the image (*species*) in its proper position. But it was appropriate that this most excellent humour should be transparent for admitting images, soft and delicate for suffering affection (*ad patiendum*), damp for sensation (*ad sentiendum*), somewhat compact for retention, with a very smooth and uniform convex face, so that with the central axis of the visual cone admitted perpendicularly through the centre, and the other rays refracted at equal angles of inclination, they make the form (*forma*) of the thing seen without alteration. As has been said the lens was made up of two convex faces, so that the anterior can receive the images (*species*) of visible things and the posterior transmit them to the *sensus communis.* . . . But how vision is effected, whether under some law of refraction or of spirits, was by no means easy to decide. Would that this account could be taken from natural philosophy (*physica*) or from mathematics alone; because we would reach the goal of truth by following either the one or the other, whether by borrowing the sensitive power from natural philosophy or the law of the refraction of rays from mathematics. . . .

He went on to make use of Alhazen's construction for the point-point transmission of rays from object to image in order to show how the visual cone entered the eye, and to explain central and peripheral vision. He argued that the anterior face of the lens was more flattened, that is a portion of a larger sphere, than the posterior face, because this enabled it to receive the lateral rays refracted through the cornea on a larger visual cone. " Thus ", he concluded, " the directness of the visual axis and the obliquity and refraction of the surrounding rays are clearly established. From these is made up as one whole the radiant cone of which the axis is the primary and central visual ray but the base is the area seen; before it converges into the apex, the image (*species*) of this base, most exactly preserving a similar form (*figura*), is transported through the cornea,

68   Ibid. pp. 73-4.

aqueous humour, lens (*glacialis humour*) and vitreous humour to the visual nerve "[69]. This analysis led him to criticize his predecessors Roger Bacon and Pecham for their account of the transmission of the rays, for he argued that this account must lead to intersection in the lens: " Which was inconsistent with nature, both because of its discordance with the lenticulate form, and so that the images (*idola*) should not be presented inverted through the intersection of the rays ".

By considering the image at the optic nerve Maurolico was able then to offer an explanation of short and long sight by relating these defects to the shape of the lens, and to prescribe convex and concave eyeglasses for their correction. But if this seems a notable feat, it must be admitted that his optical analysis shows little real scientific progress. He was simply completing, by the best technical means he knew, an analysis that he thought that Alhazen's Western successors had not carried out correctly. He worked within the old framework, still accepted the lens as the sensitive organ, and was still bound by the spell of the erect and correctly orientated image.

Maurolico's writings on this subject, like Leonardo's[69a], did not enter the public domain of letters until after Kepler had published his solution. We are told in the biography by his nephew that Maurolico gave a large number of his scientific manuscripts to Christopher Clavius when this

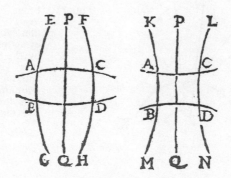

Fig. 30. From Maurolico, *Diaphanorum partes seu libri tres* (Lyon, 1613) p. 73: illustrating his account of the convergence of rays in a double convex lens and their divergence in a double concave lens.

69 Ibid. p. 76.
69a Cf. above n. 61, below n. 73.

respected Jesuit mathematician visited him in Messina in 1574[70]; and we are told in the dedication to the volume in which his optical work was first published in 1611 that his manuscripts had long been in circulation[71]. The known evidence does not tell us whether or not Kepler knew anything about them or their contents, for example through his acquaintances among the German and Austrian Jesuits to whom Clavius might well have sent information[72]. Whoever may have known of Maurolico's analysis of vision, his conclusions did not appear in the public domain before 1611. But Kepler certainly did know and treat with respect the work of his other leading sixteenth-century mathematical and experimental predecessor, the Neapolitan Giambattista della Porta. To us Kepler's respect may seem scarcely deserved, for Porta's work was scientifically well below the first rank and he developed his optical ideas half within that field of natural magic aiming not to discover but to astonish and entertain. But in this field he found a model for the eye, and this is what he provided for Kepler. The nature and limits of Porta's achievement follow like Maurolico's precisely from the model he used. He seems to have been the first to publish, in the 1558 edition of *Magia naturalis,* a comparison of the eye with a *camera obscura.* After describing the inverted scenes that can be projected on to the screen of a *camera*

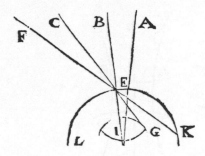

Fig. 31.   From Porta, *De refract-ione,* iii. 3 (Naples, 1593): illustrating the refraction of peripheral rays (F E G) by the cornea (L E K) so that they fall on the anterior surface of the *crystallinus* (I G), where they form an erect image (see text).

70   His nephew Francesco della Foresta published his *Vita dell' Abbate . . . D. Francesco Maurolyco* in Messina in 1613; see p. 17. For critical discussion see Scaduto, *Archivum historicum societatis Iesu,* xviii (1949) 133-40; Rosen, *Proceedings of the American Philosophical Society,* ci (1957) 179, 187-8.

71   Maurolico, *Photismi de lumine et umbra . . . Diaphanorum partes, seu libri tres* (Neapoli, 1611). The volume was published after the appearance of Galileo's *Sidereus nuncius* (1610), in order to establish Maurolico's rights and avoid plagiarism; cf. Ronchi, *Storia della luce,* pp. 93-4.

72   See Rosen in the discussion of Ronchi, " L'optique au xvie siècle ", in *La science au XVIᵉ siècle. Colloque international de Royaumont, 1-4 juillet 1957* (Paris, 1960) 65; cf. Scaduto, op. cit. But it is difficult to see how Kepler could have got much help from Maurolico in making his fundamental conceptual revision of the problem of vision; Ronchi (ibid. p. 56; *Storia della luce,* pp. 101-6) appears too optimistic.

obscura, and how these can be made clearer and restored upright by placing suitable lenses inside the small window, he went on:[73]

I have often shown this spectacle to admiring friends delighted with such an illusion; and I could scarcely dislodge them from their opinion by natural reasons and optics even after explaining the device (*artificium*). From this it may be clear to philosophers and students of optics where vision is effected; and if the question of intromission discussed for so long is broken off, both can be demonstrated by no other device. The image is sent in through the pupil, as by the opening of a window, and the part of the crystalline sphere located in the middle of the eye takes the place of the screen; something that I know will greatly delight ingenious people. It is described more fully in our optics.

In applying this model of the *camera obscura* to the eye in his optical work, *De refractione*[74], Porta maintained explicitly that, for us to see as we do, the image had to be erect and correctly orientated. He argued with support from Galen that the *crystallinus* was the prime instrument of vision and full seat of the visual power[74a], and that Alhazen's theory that vision was completed by images transmitted beyond this point was impossible because the optic nerves were anatomically unadapted for such a purpose[74b]. He went on to argue that, in order to receive a correctly orientated image, the screen of the anterior surface of the *crystallinus* had to be in front of the point of intersection of the rays in the centre of the eyeball[74c]. While he broke some fresh ground in his optical account of the role of the cornea in refracting the peripheral rays so that they fell on to

---

73 Porta, *Magia naturalis* (1589) xvii. 6. Porta (ibid. xvii. 10) also first published an account of combinations of lenses for magnification in this, the principal Latin edition. Before that accounts had been published of a *camera obscura* with a glass lens inside the pin-hole by Cardano, *De subtilitate* (1550) iv, and by Daniele Barbaro, *La practica della prospettiva* (1568) ix. 5. The English translation of Porta's *Natural Magick* (London, 1658) distorts the meaning of the passage given here. For Porta see Ronchi, *Storia della luce*, pp. 59 sqq. Porta (*De refractione*, 1593, lib. i. 12, ix. 17, 20) cited *De subtilitate*, and Cardano (ibid. xvii) knew at least the anatomical work of Leonardo da Vinci: " Quae vero solum iuvantur, etsi non illustrentur, artes sunt, militaris, magia, chymistica, machinatoria quae sub architectura continentur. Pictura non solum iuvatur, sed etiam illustratur. Est enim pictura mechanicarum omnium subtilissima, eadem vero et nobilissima. Nam quicquid plastices aut sculptura conatur, mirabilius pictura fingit, addit umbras et colores, et opticen sibi iungit, novis etiam additis quibusdam inventionibus: nam pictorem omina necesse est scire, quoniam omnia imitatur. Est philosophus pictor, architectus, et dissectionis artifex. Argumento est praeclara illa totius humani corporis imitatio, iam pluribus ante annis inchoata a Leonardo Vincio Florentino, et pene absoluta: sed deerat operi tantus artifex ac rerum naturae indagator, quantus est Vessalius "; cf. Panofsky, in *The Renaissance*, ed. Fergerson, pp. 148-51, above nn. 61, 62, 65.

74 Porta, *De refractione* (1593) iv. 1-2 continues the comparison of the eye with a *camera obscura*; cf. the comparison published by Benedetti (1585): below p. 258.

74a Ibid. iii. 1, 13, 15.

74b Ibid. vi. 1; in iii. 6 he rejected the theory of Alhazen and Witelo that the ocular refracting media formed concentric spheres; cf. Maurolico, above n. 69. His frequent references to Roger Bacon and Pecham are further evidence of their position as standard optical authors in the sixteenth century; cf. above n. 66.

74c Ibid. iii. 14; cf. vi. 1, pp. 144-5 on preventing inversion in binocular vision, on which in lib. vi he offered a new theory; below n. 106.

the *crystallinus* (fig. 31)[75], he ignored the optical properties of the eye beyond this organ altogether. This was a limitation from his model on which Kepler was to comment.

Contemporary with this work the anatomists of the medical schools developed another characteristic approach to vision and the eye. They represent among Kepler's predecessors a further distinctive interest, whose detachment from that of the mathematicians appears strange unless we remember the insulation that can be established by the institution of a powerful profession, reinforced perhaps by Galen's warnings against the suspicion aroused in medical practice by too much mathematical knowledge. This insulation of the medical profession is apparent in the leading four-teenth-century anatomical textbooks by Mondino[76] and Guy de Chauliac which essentially follow Galen, although the latter is the earliest medical text known for certain to prescribe eyeglasses[77]. The 'restorers' of anatomy in the Italian medical schools in the first half of the sixteenth century set out simply to establish by dissection an accurate descriptive ocular anatomy. The great Vesalius declared himself silenced by the question of the functions of the parts he had exhibited; he refused to discuss their optical properties; the whole issue was a question for philosophical and medical dispute outside his present purpose[78]. He took the same attitude to the ossicles of the middle ear, which he helped to discover, " since thus far the duties and uses of all of them lie hidden from me; I can understand them no more than the visual and olfactory instruments "[79]. His successor at Padua, Realdo Colombo, corrected a mistake repeated by Vesalius by showing that the *crystallinus* is located forward from the central position in the eyeball traditionally given to it; but his discussion of its function as the principal instrument of vision scarcely goes beyond Galen's[80].

Later in the century a fundamental contribution to the elucidation of visual function was made by an anatomist, Felix Plater, professor of medicine at Basel, when in 1583 he published the assertion that the retina is the sensitive visual receptor. Listing the contents of the eye he wrote

---

75 Ibid. iii. 3, 14, iv. 9. On refraction at the cornea cf. Leonardo da Vinci, above n. 65, fig. 19. Porta broke new ground also by offering in lib. viii a new theory of spectacles.

76 Mondino, *Anatomia;* several editions, some with woodcuts and some with commentaries, were published at the end of the fifteenth century and in the first half of the sixteenth. The most original commentary was by Berengario da Carpi, *Commentaria* (1521).

77 Guy de Chauliac, *La Grande chirurgie*, revue et collationnée . . . par Nicaise, pp. 491-2. Guy finished his work in 1363.

78 Vesalius, *De humani corporis fabrica* (1543) vii. 14, pp. 649-50. He referred here to Galen, *De usu partium* on the *crystallinus.*

79 Vesalius, *Anatomicarum Gabrielis Falloppii observationum examen* (1564) p. 29; cf. O'Malley and Clarke, *Bulletin of the History of Medicine*, xxxv (1961) 424-5.

80 Colombo, *De re anatomica* (1559) x. He accused Vesalius of basing his description on dissections of animals, not human bodies.

that through the pupil:[81] " The illumination of external things irradiating the cornea is sent into the dark chamber of the eye ". This led him to the item (fig. 32): " The principal organ of vision, namely the optic nerve dilated into the grey, hemispherical retina (*retiformis*) after it enters the eye: which catches and discriminates the forms and colours of external things that flow with the illumination into the eye through the aperture of the pupil and are presented to it by its eyeglass, as will be described. . . . It has affinity with the substance of the brain, with which through the nerve it is continuous ". But after setting up this apparently promising ocular system he showed only the vaguest understanding of its optical properties. Going through the parts of the eye he came to: " Three very clear humours, which in distinct situations fill the cavity of the eye and assist the act of vision. . . . First, the crystalline humour, which is the eyeglass of the visual nerve: placed facing this nerve and aperture of the pupil, it collects the images (*species*) or rays flowing into the eye and, spreading them over the area of the whole retiform nerve, it presents (*repraesentat*) these magnified, acting like an internal eyeglass (*perspicillum*), so that the nerve can take possession of them more easily ". The question of an inverted image evidently did not arise.

An important detail of retinal anatomy was clarified in 1587 by Giulio Cesare Aranzi, professor of medicine at Bologna, when he pointed out that in horses and cattle the optic nerve enters the eyeball not centrally as

---

81 Plater, *De corporis humani structura et usu* (1583) pp. 186-7. In his remarks on Averroës's medical encyclopaedia *al Kullïyät* (which became in the thirteenth-century Latin translation *Colliget*) Sarton. (*Introduction* . . ., ii, 356, 360) wrote: " He understood the function of the retina ". Sarton (op. cit. p. 361) seems to have taken this opinion from an article by Fukala, *Archiv für Augenheilkunde*, xlii (1900) 203 sqq. As one of those who have helped to perpetuate what is in fact an error (it occurs also in Polyak, *The Retina*, pp. 134-5), I take this opportunity of correcting it. The essential Latin passage from the *Colliget*, ii. 15 (Venetiis, 1553) f. 15ᵛ is printed in my *Robert Grosseteste* . . ., p. 153, n. 3. This follows a passage in which Averroës said that the function of the choroid (*tunica quae dicitur ferina*) was to nourish and supply natural heat to " the so-called net (*dicta retina*) ". In translation he continued: " But the first use of the retinal coat (*tela retina*) is to convey through its nerves the visual spirit, that is the natural heat whose complexion has been tempered in the brain and through the two nerves going to the eyes; it also nourishes the crystalline humour (*crystallina humiditas*) by means of distillation and gives it natural heat through its arteries. But Galen acknow-ledges that the web (*aranea*) is extremely clear and transparent, because the colours and forms are imprinted upon it; hence this coat (*tela*) is the proper instrument of vision, either by itself or with the aid of the *crystallina* ". The error was started by Fukala's gratuitous identification of the *tela retina*, the retina, with the *aranea*, the capsule of the lens (*crystallina*). In fact Averroës was making no new point; his account of vision was essentially the same as Avicenna's (above nn. 33-34). In opening this chapter on vision and the eye he wrote: " It appears that the proper instrument for this sense is either the round humour (*humiditas rotunda*) called *crystallina* or *glacialis* or the reticulate web (*reticula aranea*) that is placed on this humour ". Dr. A. I. Sabra informs me that the Latin gives a good literal rendering of Averroës's Arabic text; I am grateful to him for checking this for me and for his help in putting the matter straight. For the variations in terminology for the parts of the eye cf. above n. 67, below n. 99e.

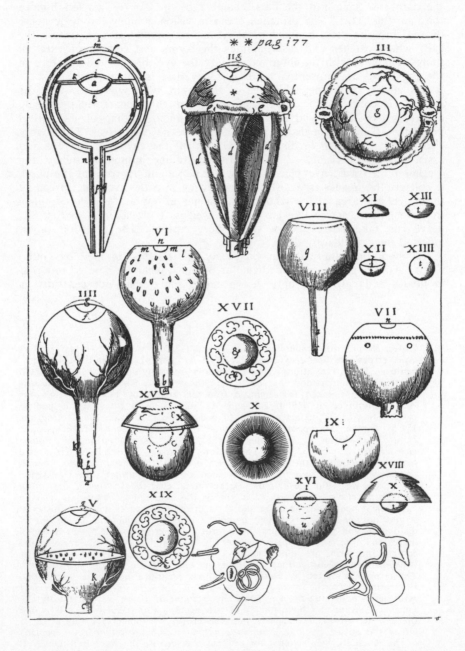

Fig. 32. From Kepler, *Ad Vitellionem paralipomena*, v. 2 (Frankfurt, 1604), after
Plater, *De corporis humani structura et usu*, tabula xlix (Basel, 1583).
The two unshaded diagrams at the bottom right are of the middle ear.
Kepler follows Plater in giving the following explanation:

I: A line drawing showing a projection of the membranes and fluids (*humores*) as found in the actual eye. Where: A, lens; B, vitreous humour; C, aqueous humour; D, related coat; E, opaque part of the sclerotic (*crassa tunica*); F, choroid (*uvea*); G, retina (*retiformis*); H, hyaloid (*hyaloides*); I, lens capsule; K, ciliary processes of the choroid coat; L, boundary of the choroid on the sclerotic; M, corneal part of the sclerotic, of which the convex bulge noticed by others is indicated by a dotted line; N, N, eye muscles; O, optic nerve; P, thin membrane of the nerve; Q, thick membrane [sclerotic] of the nerve.

II: The eye intact with the muscles, taken out of the skull and with the eyelids removed.

III: The eye-ball seen from the front.

IIII: The sclerotic with part of the optic nerve.

V: The sclerotic, cut transversely.

VI: The choroid with part of the optic nerve.

VII: The inverted interior surface of the same.

VIII: The retina with the substance of the optic nerve.

IX: The hyaloid coat.

X: The ciliary processes, radiating from the front of the hyaloid coat.

XI: The lens capsule.

XII: The lens in its capsule.

XIII: The naked lens, seen from the side.

XIIII: The lens seen from the front.

XV: The three humours together, aqueous, vitreous and lens, partly shaded.

XVI: The vitreous humour with the lens.

XVII: The vitreous humour alone seen from the front.

XVIII: The aqueous humour shown in position over the lens.

XIX: The aqueous humour above seen from the front.

A, II, III, VI, VIII: Visual or optic nerve.

B, II, IIII, VI: Thin coat covering the nerve.

C, II, IIII, V: Sclerotic surrounding the nerve.

DDD, II: The eye muscles on one side.

EE, II, III: Part of the related coat extending under the eyelids.

*,II, III: Expanded part of the same, intact.

F, II, III, IIII, V: Dark part or iris of the eye, which the white surrounds.

G, II, III, IIII, V: Black pupil or centre of the eye, in the middle of the iris. Note in II, IIII, V at G the arc, indicated by a dotted line, rising from the sides of the iris and forming part of a smaller circle than the globe of the eye. This was added by me from the observations of others. Note also the bulge of the cornea rising from the white.

H, II, III: Little piece of flesh at the corner of the eye.

I, II, III: Tear ducts.

K, IIII, V: Vessels dispersed over the sclerotic.

LL, V, VI: Fibres by which the choroid is attached to the sclerotic.

MM, VI: Boundary of the choroid, where it stops at the cornea.

N, VI, VII: Opening in the choroid, or pupil.

OO, VII: Beginning of the ciliary processes.

P, VII: Beginning of the choroid, extending from the thin coat.

Q, VIII: Dimensions of the retina extending above the middle of the eye.

R, IX: Pocket of the hyaloid coat holding the lens.

S, XI, XII: Width of the lens capsule.

T, in XII, XIII, XVIII: Spherical posterior part of the lens (according to others protruding in a cone, but according to me hyperbolic).
in XIIII, XVI: Flattened anterior part of the same.

V, XV, XVI: Dimensions of the vitreous humour.

X, XV, XVIII, XIX: Dimensions of the aqueous humour.

Y, XV: Region at which the vitreous humour is separated from the aqueous by the hyaloid coat.

Z, XV, XVIII: Region in which the choroid is bathed by the aqueous humour.

&, XVII: Cavity remaining in the vitreous humour after the lens has been removed.

§, XIX: Corresponding cavity in the aqueous humour.

hitherto believed, but at one side (cf. fig. 35)[82]. But the culmination of this great sixteenth-century effort towards an accurate ocular anatomy was the superbly illustrated treatise published in 1600 by   Girolamo Fabrici   da Aquapendente. Possibly the most original anatomist of the whole Italian school,   Fabrici   is also a telling example of the insulation of medical optics before Kepler from any real understanding of the mathematical physics of the problem. Fabrici discussed ancient philosophical theories of vision, Galen, and the optical account of Alhazen, Witelo and Pecham[83]. But he evidently did not see the point of the physical conception of light developed by the mathematicians. His long argument aimed to establish an account of the physiology of perception in which the *species* or *formae* entering the eye were to be understood in the Aristotelian sense as modifications of the diaphanous medium in the presence of illumination, and as Galen had said the seat of vision was the *crystallinus*[83a]. He used Alhazen and Witelo simply to show, like Porta, how refraction at the cornea allowed larger objects to be seen by drawing into the eye a larger visual cone[84]. Refraction also occurred in the aqueous humour, and these ocular refractions strengthened light and vision, as could be seen in a burning glass and in the action of spectacles " in which art excels   nature " by restoring youth to the eyes[84a]; but in so far as the *crystallinus* resembled a refracting glass or crystal the function of its bulging posterior surface was to stop the further transmission of light, not to project an image[85]. He rejected any transmission of images beyond the *crystallinus* as both anatomically and optically impossible. As he treated the subject, the *crystallinus* had the full power of perception, by means of a visual cone, without any problem of an inverted image[85a]. With some concessions to later optical knowledge, he stood in his formulation of the problem of vision firmly with the accepted medical authorities Aristotle and Galen.

Kepler, as indicated by the title of his work, *Ad Vitellionem paralipomena quibus astronomiae pars optica traditur,* undertook his study of optics, as Ptolemy had undertaken his, in the first place to understand and counteract the errors arising from the conditions of observation: first from vision

82   Aranzi, *Anatomicarum observationum liber* (1587) c. 18. The fact that in man the point of entry of the nerve forms a 'blind spot' displaced to one side was discovered by Edme Mariotte and published in 1668; below n. 115. Aranzi (op. cit. c. 21) also carried out an experiment in which he removed the back of an ox's eye and looked from behind through the vitreous humour, *crystallinus* and cornea at objects placed in front of the pupil; cf. below nn. 100, 129.

83   Girolamo   Fabrici, *De visione, voce, auditu* (1600), " De oculo visis organo ", i (on ocular anatomy, where he cited principally Rufus of Ephesus and Galen), ii. 1-5 (on the theories of the Stoics, Epicureans, Aristotle, Plato and Galen). He cited Pecham as " Auctor Perspectivae communis " (pp. 64, 80, 95, 97; above n. 51) and Witelo with Alhazen (pp. 41, 70, 72); he also referred to Cardano and Porta (p. 44). He gave accurate drawings of the lens (p. 35) and other parts, but still drew the nerve entering the eyeball centrally (p. 105).

83a Ibid. ii. 3, 6-7, pp. 40-2, 49-54; iii. 7, pp. 96 sqq.

84   Ibid. iii. 1, 2, pp. 61, 73-8; cf. above nn. 65, 75.

84a Ibid. iii. 5, pp. 80-4; quotation on p. 83.

85   Ibid. iii. 7, 10-11, pp. 102-3, 106-12; on p. 103 he likened this action of the *crystallinus* to that of a refracting glass in preventing the passage of the light which it unites.

85a Cf. ibid. iii. 5, p. 82, where he discussed the avoidance of intersection and inversion of rays.

which he said were " to be sought in the structure and functioning of the eye itself "[86], and secondly from astronomical instruments which he went on to discuss. He wrote most of *Ad Vitellionem paralipomena* in 1603, when Imperial Mathematician at Prague, as an interlude in the work on Mars that yielded his first two laws of planetary motion; he presented the completed manuscript to the Emperor Rudolf II on New Year's Day 1604[87]. The text that provided his title was undoubtedly the combined Latin edition of Alhazen and Witelo published in 1572[88], and in continuing the subject of this comprehensive work Kepler established his approach to vision by discussing first the purely physical properties of light. He characterized his physical conception of light by the assertions that light radiates from any luminous source as a two-dimensional spherical surface moving " not in time, but in a moment "[89], and that " a ray of light is nothing but light itself in motion "[90]. Since, he held, the intensity of light remained constant along each ray but decreased in the spherical surface in proportion to its distance from the source, these ideas led him to the discovery of the fundamental law of photometry[91]. He went on to discuss the operation of the *camera obscura* described by Porta[92], the localization of images in mirrors[93], and the measurement of refraction, where he improved on Ptolemy's tables as published by Witelo and gave as an approximation that, for angles less than 30°, the angle of refraction was approximately proportional to the angle of incidence[94]. Finally he came to his treatment of vision, eyeglasses and the errors of astronomical observa-

86 Kepler, *Ad Vitellionem paralipomena* (1604) v (*Gesammelte Werke*, hrg. von Dyck, Caspar und Hammer, ii) 143. For an English translation of Kepler's chapter v. 2-3 and related passages see Crombie, " Kepler: de modo visionis ", in *Mélanges Alexandre Koyré*, i, 135-72; and for historical discussion of Kepler's optics see Ronchi, *Storia della luce*, and *Atti della Fondazione G. Ronchi*, xi (1956) 189-202. Kepler discussed the optics of astronomical observation in *Ad Vitellionem paralipomena*, ii, and v. 5.; see below p. 258.
87 Caspar, transl. and ed. Hellman, p. 144. Kepler published the two astronomical laws, stating that each planet moves in an elliptical orbit, of which the radius vector sweeps out equal areas in equal times, in *Astronomia nova aitiologetos, seu physica coelestis tradita commentariis de motibus stellae Martis ex observationibus G. V. Tychonis Brahe* (1609; *Ges. Werke*, iii).
88 Above nn. 35, 51.
89 Kepler, *Ad Vitellionem paralipomena*, i, prop. v.
90 Ibid. i, prop. viii.
91 i.e. that the intensity of light is in inverse proportion to the square of the distance (i.e. the radius). For his refusal to apply the inverse-square law to the motive force exerted by the sun on the planets see Koyré, *La révolution astronomique*, 198 sqq.; cf. Crombie, *Augustine to Galileo*, ii (1979), 200-1.
92 Kepler, *Ad Vitellionem paralipomena*, ii, prop. vii.
93 Ibid. iii.
94 Ibid. iv. For the discovery c. 1601 of the sine law of refraction by Thomas Harriot, using Witelo's tables relating angles of incidence and refraction, see Lohne. *Sudhoffs Archiv*, xlvii (1963) 151-72. Witelo gave almost exactly the same figures as Ptolemy; cf. Crombie, *Robert Grosseteste . . .*, pp. 221-5. The sine law was also formulated but not published by Willebrord Snell some time before his death in 1626, and again probably independently by Descartes, who published it for the first time in *La dioptrique*, ii (1637), but without the sine notation: see Kramer, *Abhandlungen zur Geschichte der Mathematik*, iv (1882) 233 sqq.; Kortweg, *Revue de métaphysique et de morale*, iv (1897) 489 sqq.; Straik (1975), Costabal (1982) below p. 258.

tion. For the eye his anatomical authorities were Plater and his friend Johannes Jessenius, who had based his ocular anatomy on Fabrici but in physiological optics followed Alhazen and Witelo[95].

While useful, none of this new knowledge was strictly necessary for Kepler's solution of the dioptric problem of the eye. He succeeded by seeing the problem in a new way, as he himself clearly shows in carefully defining his relationship to his predecessors. Thus he wrote:[96] "Compare the true mode of operation (*modus*) of vision as given by me with that given by Plater, and you will see that this famous man is no farther from the truth than is compatible with being a medical man who deliberately does not treat mathematics". Of Porta he wrote that it was he who in *Magia naturalis* "first proposed the mechanism (*artificium*) of that process of which I have set out a formal demonstration"; he went on to say that if Porta had included in his account the way in which the inverted image is thrown by the lens on to the retina, "clearly you would have unravelled the mode of operation (*modus*) of vision "[97]. Kepler and his immediate predecessors all had at their disposal the same necessary scientific knowledge, the same conception of the eye as an image-forming device, and the same two artificial models: the *camera obscura* and the glass or crystal lens. Kepler succeeded in solving the strictly technical problem of ocular dioptrics because he alone satisfied both the conditions separately necessary and together sufficient for technical success: like some of his predecessors he used these models to explain the functions of the parts of the eye, but unlike any of them he discovered how to execute the optical analysis correctly. But Kepler's scientific achievement in the analysis of vision went beyond this important discovery. Unlike any of his predecessors, when he applied the mechanistic hypothesis to this case, he did so as an explicitly strategic decision enabling him in the first place to restrict the analysis of vision simply to discovering how the eye operates as an optical instrument like any other, in fact as a dead eye; then, having discovered this, he faced the now clearly distinguished problem of how the indisputably inverted and reversed image in the living eye mediates perception. His intellectual behaviour in facing this question of the relationship of the perceiving organism to the world perceived is recognizably of a piece with that exhibited in confronting his early astronomical speculations with Tycho Brahe's data.

About this time Kepler wrote of his scientific programme for astronomy and celestial physics:[98] "My aim in this is to show that the celestial

95   Johannes Jessenius, *Anatomia Pragae* . . . (1601) ff. 123ᵛ-126. Kepler (*Ad Vitellionem paralipomena*, v. 1, 2; *Ges Werke*, ii, 150-1, 159-61) argued against Jessenius that its posterior surface was hyperbolical rather than conical; cf. above n. 83. Jessenius was in 1603 professor of medicine at Wittenberg. In 1600, while in Prague, he had acted as intermediary in the negotiations that led to Kepler's going there to work with Tycho Brahe and become appointed Imperial Mathematician; see Casper, *Kepler*, ed. cit. pp. 105, 121, 166, 257.

96   Kepler, *Ad Vitellionem paralipomena*, v. 4 (*Ges. Werke*, ii) 187; in this section he gave a valuable account of his anatomical and optical predecessors and sources.

97   Ibid. p. 189; *crystallinus* is translated below as lens.

98   Kepler an Herwart von Hohenburg, 10 Feb. 1605 (*Ges. Werke*, xv) 146; cf. above nn. 87, 91.

machine is to be likened not to a kind of divine living being but rather to a clockwork . . ., in so far as nearly all the manifold movements are carried out by means of a single simple magnetic corporeal force, just as in a clockwork all motions come from a simple weight. Moreover I show how this physical conception is to be presented through calculation and geometry . . .". In keeping with this philosophical commitment he demonstrated the physiological mechanism of the eye conceived, as far as the retina as a screen receiving images, as part of the same dead world as the physical light that entered it. He banished from this passive mechanism any active power to look at an object, and solved the optical problem of how it forms an image by a new geometrical construction reversing Alhazen's. Of the physical rays going in all directions from a luminous or illuminated object, some fell on to the pupil (fig. 33). He demolished Alhazen's construction based on Euclid's ' perspective cone ' extending from a base on the object seen to an apex at the eye (figs. 9, 16), and with it finally the surviving influence of the assumption that an actual image of the object itself travelled to the eye. Instead he demonstrated how an inverted and reversed image was formed in the eye by means of a construction showing a multitude of radiant cones of light rays going from apices at every point on the object (fig. 34 : VXY) to a common base on the lens, whence each point was brought to a focus on the retina (fig. 34: RST). To account for how we see by means of this inverted and reversed image or picture on the retina he offered a simple geometrical rule relating it to the world outside. But at the retina the light rays ended and were succeeded by a different kind of motion; how the visual faculty of the soul effected vision by means of this retinal image and subsequent motion he put outside his mathematical-optical solution as a problem for natural philosophy. The following gives the essence of his analysis : [99]

I say that vision occurs when the image (*idolum*) of the whole hemisphere of the world in front of the eye, and a little more, is formed on the reddish white concave surface of the retina (*retina*). I leave it to natural philosophers to discuss the way in which this image or picture (*pictura*) is put together by the spiritual principles of vision residing in the retina and in the nerves, and whether it is made to appear before the soul or tribunal of the faculty of vision by a spirit within the cerebral cavities, or the faculty of vision, like a magistrate sent by the soul, goes out from the council chamber of the brain to meet this image in the optic nerves and retina, as it were descending to a lower court. For the equipment of opticians does not take them beyond this opaque surface which first presents itself in the eye. I do not think that we should listen to Vitellio (book III, Proposition xx)[99a], who thinks that these images of light (*idola lucis*) go out further through the nerve, until they meet at the junction half-way along each optic nerve, and then separate again one going to each cerebral cavity. For by the laws of optics (*leges optices*), what can be said about this

99 Kepler, *Ad Vitellionem paralipomena*, v, 2 (*Ges. Werke*, ii) 151-7: Crombie in *Mélanges Alexandre Koyré*, i, 147-58.

99a Witelo, *Opticae libri decem*, iii, prop. xx: " Vision is not completed until the form received by the surface of the *glacialis* arrives in due order at the common nerve ".

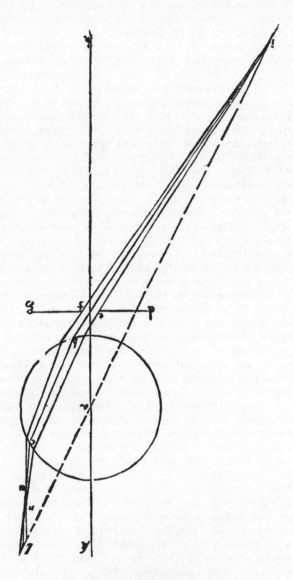

Fig. 33.   From Kepler, *Ad Vitellionem paralipomena*, v. 3,
prop. xxiii (Frankfurt, 1604): illustrating his
model for demonstrating ocular dioptrics using
for simplicity a spherical lens made of a flask
of water (*a*) placed inside the small window (*e f*)
of a *camera obscura*. Kepler explained how rays
from each point (*i*) of the object were brought
together through *n m* to form in this model a
somewhat indistinct image on the screen placed
at *k l*.

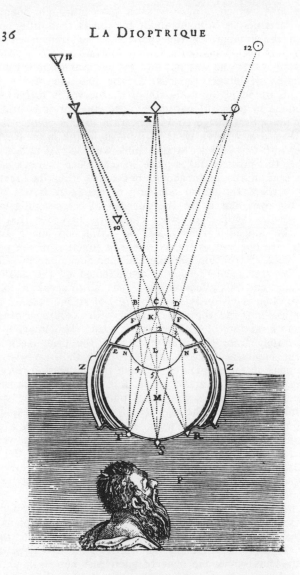

Fig. 34. From Descartes, *La dioptrique*, v (Leiden, 1637): illustrating Kepler's ocular dioptrics. Rays from each point on the object (VXY) are refracted through the cornea (BCD) and lens (L) to foci (RST) on the retina where they form an inverted image of the object. The man looking at the eye, with its back removed, set in a *camera obscura* would see the inverted image on the translucent retinal screen.

hidden motion[99b], which, since it takes place through opaque and hence dark parts and is brought about by spirits that differ in every respect from the humours of the eye and other transparent things, immediately puts itself outside the field of optical laws ? . . . Hence in III, Proposition lxxiii[89c] he was put into by no means minor difficulties over this union of images (*species*) at the junction of the nerves. Because if this union in the mid-path of the nerves is to be asserted, it must be done in terms of natural philosophy. For it is undeniably certain that no optical image could penetrate to this point. It seems then clear that, if any nerve went to its seat in the brain freely in a straight line, with two eyes we would think we saw two things instead of one. Either this junction takes place so that when one eye is closed this hidden seat in the brain should not cease from its function of judging. Or perhaps the actual doubling of the seats is not only on account of the eyes, but is for the purpose of correct judgement of distances, as with the pair of eyes. Therefore, in order that visible things may be judged correctly and a distinction made between what is seen with one and with two eyes, this junction of the passages must take place. Here this one optical conclusion from the first chapter can be stated :[99d] the spirits are affected by the qualities of colour and light, and this affection (*passio*) is, so to speak, a colouring and a lighting. For in vision images (*species*) of strong colours remain behind after looking, and these are united with colours printed by a fresh look, and a mixture of both colours is made. This image (*species*) existing separately from the presentation of the thing seen is not present in the humours or coats of the eye, as shown above; hence vision takes place in the spirits and through the impression (*impressio*) of these images (*species*) on the spirit. But really this 'impression' does not belong to optics but to natural philosophy and the study of the wonderful. But this by the way. I will return to the explanation of how vision takes place. Thus vision is brought about by a picture of the thing seen being formed on the concave surface of the retina[99e] That which is to the right outside is depicated on the left on the retina, that to the left on the right, that above below, and that below above. Green is depicted green, and in general things are depicted by whatever colour they have. . . .

So that I may go on to treat this process of depiction and prepare for a demonstration of it, I say that this picture consists of as many **pairs of cones**　　　　as there are points in the thing seen, in pairs always with the same base, namely the width of the lens (*crystallinus*) or part of it. Thus while one cone of each pair has its apex at the point seen and its base on the lens (somewhat altered by refraction through the cornea), the other has the same base on the lens as the

99b See below, n. 117.

99c Witelo, op. cit. iii, prop. lxxiii.

99d Ibid. iii, prop. i: "Hence vision receives the form of the colour of the thing seen only from light admixed with the form of colour ".

99e Kepler sometimes used two terms for the same thing: *retina* and *retiformis, crassa tunica* and *sclerode, uvea* and *choroidea, foramen uveae* and *pupilla, hyaloides* and *tunica hyalina;* cf. fig. 32, and above n. 67.

first one and the apex at a point in the picture depicted on the retina; this cone undergoes refraction on passing out of the lens (figs. 33, 34). All the outer cones meet in the pupil, so that they intersect in that space, and right becomes left. . . . In fact more or less the same thing happens as we showed in Chapter II in a closed chamber [i.e. *camera obscura*]. The pupil (*pupilla*) corresponds to the window and the lens to the screen opposite it, provided that the pupil and lens are not so near that intersection is incomplete and everything is confused. . . . Finally the sensory power or spirit diffused through the nerve is more concentrated and stronger where the retina meets direct cones : . . . from that point it is diffused over the sphere of the retina, gets further from the source, and hence becomes weaker . . . so the sides of the retina do not usurp for themselves its sensory capacity, but whatever they can, they bring into the perfection of direct vision. Thus, when we see a thing perfectly, we see it within the whole surrounding area of the visible hemisphere. For this reason oblique vision satisfies the soul least and only invites the turning of the eyes in that direction so that they may see directly. . . . Everything said so far about the lens can be observed in everyday experiments with crystal **balls** (*pilae crystallinae*) or glass urinary flasks filled with clear water[99f]. For if one stands at the glazed window of a room with a globe of this kind of crystal or water, and arranges a sheet of white paper behind the globe at a distance equal to half the diameter of the globe, the glazed window with the fluted wooden or leaden divisions between the lights will be very clearly depicted on the paper, but inverted (fig. 33). The same effect can be obtained with other things, if the place is darkened a little. Thus, using a globe of water set up in a chamber opposite a small window, as we described above in Chapter II, Proposition vii, everything that can reach the globe through the width of the small window or opening will be depicted very clearly and delightfully on the paper opposite. . . Since the lens is convex and is denser than the surrounding humours, just as the water in the glass flask is denser than the air, therefore whatever we have demonstrated in this way with the globe of water, and using these media, will have been proved also for the lens, except in so far as it has a different convexity from the globe. So let us proceed with the demonstration of matters belonging to the crystalline or glass globe. . . .

The sensation of vision follows the action of illumination, in manner and proportion. (*Passio visionis sequitur actionem illustrationis, in modo et proportione.*) The retina is illuminated distinctly point by point from individual points of objects, and most strongly so at its individual points. Therefore in the retina, and nowhere else, can distinct and clear vision come about. This is so much the more evident

---

99f The section to the end of this paragraph is from *Ad Vitellionem paralipomena*, v. 3 (*Ges. Werke*, ii) 162: "Demonstration of the conclusions stated concerning how vision takes place through the lens". For simplicity Kepler used a spherical model lens for his demonstration; on the true shape see above n. 95. The reference to ii, prop. vii, is to his chapter on the *camera clausa* or *camera obscura*.

because distortion of the proportions of the picture leads to faults of vision. . . . And so if you are bothered by the inversion of this picture and fear that this would lead to inverted vision, I ask you to consider the following. Just as vision is not an action (*actio*), because illumination is an action but sensation (*passio*) is the contrary of action, so also, in order that the positions may correspond, the sensing things [*patientia*, i.e. the retinal images] must occur opposite to the agents that bring them about. Now the positions are perfectly opposite when all the lines connecting opposite points run through the same centre, which would not have been so if the picture had been erect. And so in the inverted picture, although right and left are interchanged everywhere and with respect to any common line, none the less with respect to themselves the right-hand parts of the object are perfectly opposed to the right-hand parts of the picture, and the upper parts of the object to the upper parts of the picture, like a hollow to a hollow. . . . Therefore none of that absurdity is perpetrated by the inverted picture, from which Vitellio so assiduously ran away, and in which Jessenius followed him. . . .[99g]

Kepler's dioptrical solution was convincing. An immediate effect of his achievement, made by an initial restriction of the analysis of vision to a problem in dioptrics followed by a simple mathematical rule relating the result to how we see, was to stimulate the formulation of numerous further problems of vision purely physiologically. Again it was the mathematical natural philosophers rather than medical schools that made physiological optics burst into this fresh flower. Kepler's own analysis was amplified. Christopher Scheiner directly observed the formation of the image on the retina of freshly dead animal and human eyes from which he had removed the backs (cf. figs. 34, 36)[100]. Descartes corrected Kepler's optical analysis by

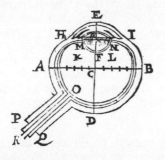

Fig. 27. From Scheiner, *Oculus*, i. i. 9 (Oeniponti, 1619): showing the structure of the eye, with the refracting media of the cornea (E) and lens (MN), and the optic nerve (O) entering the eyeball to one side of the point of central vision on the retina (D).

99g This paragraph is from ibid. v. 4 (*Ges. Werke*, ii) 184-5.
100 Scheiner mentioned carrying out these experiments with some collaborators, in Rome in 1625, in *Rosa ursina* (1630) ii. 23. In *Oculus* (1619) ii. i. 5-12, ii. ii. 9, iii. i. 1-5, 12-18, 27-32, he had described a model eye consisting of a *camera obscura* with a cornea, lens, spherical retina and two glass chambers corresponding to the aqueous and vitreous humours. He studied refraction in the different parts of the eye, and applied his model to show that in the eye an inverted image was thrown on to the retina and that this and not the lens was the sensitive organ. Aguilonius (*Opticorum libri tres*, 1613, i. i, 27, pp. 2-5, 26-7) had still argued for the lens capsule (*aranea*), which he held to be an extension of the retina and optic nerve. Cf. Rohr, *Zeitschrift für ophthalmologische Optik*, vii (1919) 129, *Archiv für Augenheilkunde*, lxxxvi (1920) 254-5; above nn. 81, 82. On the established model of the *camera obscura* cf. Kohlhans, *Tractatus*

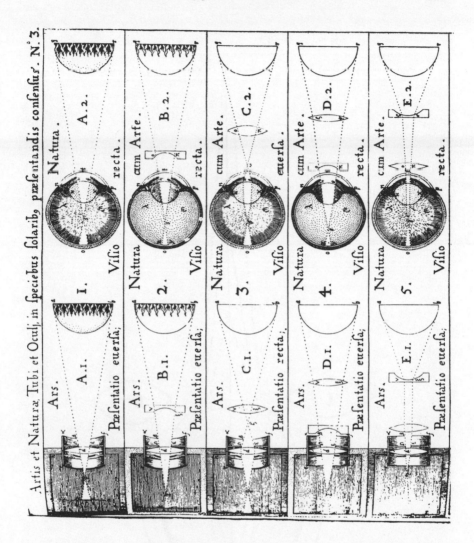

Fig. 36.   From Scheiner, *Rosa ursina,* ii. 23 (Bracciani, 1630): illustrating his comparison between the eye and a *camera obscura* with a lens system, and the effects on each of using further lenses.

opticus (1663) ii. ii. 3, p. 257: " De applicatione camerae ad oculum. E Scheinero ", and p. 501: " Artis et Naturae mira est conspiratio: ita ut oculus camera sit obscura naturalis, et camera obscura oculus artificialis "; Sturm, *Collegium Experimentale* (1676) ii, p. 7: " . . . vii. Denique oculum nihil aliud esse, quam parvam cameram obscuram . . .".

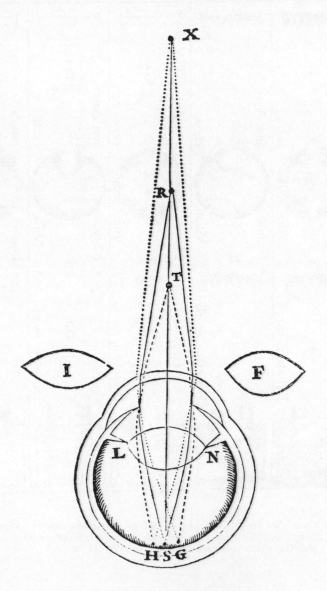

Fig. 37. From Descartes, *Tractatus de homine* (Paris, 1664): illustrating the accommodation of the eye so that it can focus objects at different distances (X, R, T) by changes in the shape of the lens (LN, I, F). In this way a single eye gives clues to perception of distance.

making use of his new knowledge of the sine law of refraction and treating the lens in its actual lenticulate shape instead of simplified as a sphere[101]; with Scheiner he is responsible for the accepted explanation of accommodation by changes in the shape rather than the position of the lens as Kepler had proposed (fig. 37)[102]. New scientific understanding was reached both of the technical defects of normal vision and their correction by appropriate lenses, parallel with that of the more complicated instruments of the telescope and microscope extending the normal power of the eye, and also of phenomena lying across the boundaries of psychology with physiology and the physics of instruments. Kepler and Scheiner in their analyses of direct and indirect vision made the important suggestion that eye movements should be taken into account in the design of optical instruments[103].

Even more interesting in the new approaches it elicited was the problem of finding something more satisfactory than the inherited explanation of how the two eyes give vision of a single field. Alhazen had supposed that the axes of the two eyes met at a point on the object seen, making the two images coincide so that they could unite at the optic chiasma where, according to Galen, the two nerves were connected (figs. 12, 18)[104]. The difficulty in this theory of anatomical union was that it gave no means of representing physiologically the difference between the fields of vision from the two eyes, though this had been well known since antiquity. Leonardo da Vinci[105] had insisted that a painting could not imitate the effect of binocular vision. Porta[106] had tried to get round the difficulty by supposing that we saw with only one eye at a time, and Kepler[107] by supposing that there was a mental interpretation of the binocular sensations. It was Porta's suggestion that received the most interesting development, especially by Descartes[108], Gassendi and Mersenne, in the first half of the seventeenth century. Mersenne tried to discover experimentally whether the axes of the two

101 Descartes, *Traité de l'homme* (1633; *Oeuvres*, publiées par Adam et Tannery, xi) 152-3, *La dioptrique*, v; below n. 129; cf. above nn. 94, 95, 99f.

102 Kepler, *Dioptrice* (1611; *Ges. Werke*, iv) prop. lxiv; Scheiner, *Oculus*, i. ii. 1, p. 31, iii. i. 12, p. 163; Descartes, *Traité de l'homme* (*Oeuvres*, xi) 155-6, *La dioptrique*, vii. Scheiner accepted Kepler's proposed mechanism, but suspected that the lens also changed in shape.

103 Kepler, *Ad Vitellionem paralipomena*, v. 5, cf. *Dioptrice*, prop. lxxv sqq.; Schiener, *Oculus*, iii. ii, pp. 245-8; cf. Helmholtz, *Physiological Optics*, transl. Southall, iii, 119-20.

104 Above nn. 29, 41a.

105 Leonardo da Vinci, *Treatise on Painting*, ii. 220, transl. McMahon; cf. above n. 63, figs. 15-17.

106 Porta, *De refractione*, vi. 1, pp. 142 sqq.

107 Kepler, *Dioptrice*, prop. lxii; cf. *Ad Vitellionem paralipomena*, iii, props. viii-xiv. Another version of the so-called projection theory was proposed by Aguilonius, *Opticorum libri sex* (1613) ii, def. 11, props. xlvii-1; he supposed that the visual images were always projected on a certain plane, which he called the *horopter*, passing through the point of fixation: cf. Helmholtz, *Physiological Optics*, transl. Southall, iii, 483; and on Ptolemy, Lejeune, *Euclide et Ptolémée*, pp. 124-8, 144-53, 169-71; above n. 29.

108 Descartes recognized central vision with a small part of the retina, consequent scanning by means of eye movements (cf. above n. 36a), and perception of depth with only one eye (above n. 102, below n. 137), but he made single binocular vision a result of the two images forming at corresponding points in each eye and coming together in the pineal gland: *Traité de l'homme* (*Oeuvres*, xi) 157-63, 174-6, *La dioptrique*, v-vi; cf. figs. 40, 42, 43, 45.

eyes met at the point being looked at, or remained parallel while each eye looked at the point alternately. In agreement with Gassendi[109] he decided for the second account, concluding:[110] " . . . it is only one eye that ever sees the object; . . . since the parallelism of their axes does not allow them to meet at this point . . . they must look at it alternately. . . . Hence, after trying this with our own eyes, we have to conclude that the nerve and muscles of one eye relax, and more or less cease to operate, while the axis of the other is fixed on the object". This explained the phenomena of rivalry between the two visual fields. He envisaged a 'scanning' of the field by movements of the eyes, and following Hobbes he suggested that the fact of our actually seeing, at any one time, only particular objects in the whole visual field focused on the retina, could be explained by supposing that the act of attention was in some way effected by a return of rays "which the eyes project out on to the object"[111]. For so conservative a radical, this was a satisfactory way of reconciling the two chief ancient conceptions of the visual act. Mersenne was unusual among the academic natural philosophers of this period in giving his actual measurements; of interest is his determination that the least angle an object must subtend at the eye in order to become visible is 15″[112]. Later in the century Christiaan Huygens specified the conditions for single binocular vision in more precise detail[113], and demonstrated the optical system of the eye by means of a simplified eye reduced to a single spherical refracting surface (fig. 38), and of a model constructed with a cornea, lens and diaphragm in a *camera obscura*[114].

This catalogue of researches following, though not all occasioned by, Kepler's successful mode of attack, could be greatly extended. Serious puzzles and, in a period when natural philosophers knew what they meant by demanding that a scientific theory had to come within the technical range of testability, scientific uncertainty remained. A good example is the controversy provoked by Edme Mariotte by questioning whether his discovery of the 'blind spot' allowed the retina still to be regarded as the

109 Gassendi, *Syntagma philosophicum*, Physica, iii. ii. vii. 7 (*Opera*, ii, 1658) 395; cf. William Briggs, *Philosophical Collections* (1682) 167-78, *Philosophical Transactions*, xiii (1683) 171-82.

110 Mersenne, *L'optique et la catoptrique* (1651) i, prop. xxvi, pp. 65-66: he referred here to Porta (above n. 106) and to Gassendi's letters on the subject; Mersenne died in 1648 and this work was published posthumously.

111 Mersenne, *L'optique et la catoptrique*, i, prop. xxv, p. 61; cf. *Universae geometriae . . . synopsis* (1644) vii, Hypotheses and prop. iii, pp. 567-71. Lib. vii is Hobbes's " Opticae ", reprinted in *Opera . . . latine*, v, 215-48; see Lenoble, *Mersenne*, pp. xxviii, 318, 370--1; below n. 140. For Hobbes's interest in optical manuscripts by Grosseteste and Roger Bacon see Pacchi, *Rivista critica di storia della filosofia*, xx (1965) 499 sqq.; cf. Crombie, *Robert Grosseteste . . .*, pp. 278-80.

112 Mersenne, *L'optique et la catoptrique*, i, prop. xxx, p. 72. Cf. on *minima perceptibiles* Ptolemy, *Optica*, ii. 47 sqq., éd. Lejeune; Lejeune, *Euclide et Ptolémée*, pp. 116-21; Hooke, " A general scheme . . . ", ii and " Lectures of light . . . ", iii, *Posthumous Works* (1705), pp. 12, 97.

113 Huygens, " De l'oeil et de la vision ", *Oeuvres complètes*, xiii, 790-9.

114 Huygens, *Dioptrica*, prop. xxxi (*Opera posthuma*, 1703) 112-6; probably written 1667-91 (*Oeuvres complètes*, xiii, pp. iii sqq., cxliii-cl, 128-34, 787-802). Huygens's simplified eye was similar to the 'reduced eye' introduced by J. B. Listing in 1851; see Helmholtz, *Physiological Optics*, transl. Southall, i, 91, 95-6; Southall, *Journal of the Optical Society of America*, vi (1922), 839-42.

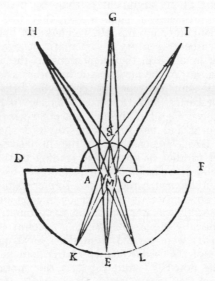

Fig. 38.| From Huygens, *Dioptrica*, prop. xxxi (Louvain, 1703): illustrating his simplified eye reduced to a single spherical refracting surface ABC.

sensitive organ of vision; he proposed the choroid[115]. Even so, by the end of the century the work of these researchers, of Isaac Newton himself[116] and of many others, had established physiological optics as a science in which the competent were confident of how to proceed.

115 See *Nouvelle découverte touchant la veüe* (1668), and the revised edition in Mariotte, *Oeuvres*, ii (1740) 495-534, with his original letter and replies by Jean Pecquet and Claude Perrault; the controversy can be followed through the *Histoire de l'Académie royale des Sciences*, i, 102-5 (1669), and Année 1704, pp. 269-71; *Le journal des sçavans*, iii (1668) 402-10; *Philosophical Transactions*, iii (1668) 668-71, v (1670) 1023-42, xiii (1683) 265-7; and *Acta Eruditorum*, Anno 1683, pp. 67-73; cf. Grmek (1985), below p. 258.

116 Newton, *Opticks*, 4th ed. (1730), queries 12-16, 23-4; cf. *Quaestiones quaedam philosophicae*, Cambridge MS University Library Additional 3996 (? 1664-5) ff. 104-5, 122-4; Westfall, *British Journal for the History of Science*, i (1962) 171 sqq. Attention was drawn to the importance of this notebook by Hall, *The Cambridge Historical Journal*, ix (1949) 238 sqq. On physiological optics cf. also Newton, Cambridge MS University Library Additional 3975 (*c.* 1665-93) ff. 15-22; Hall, *Annals of Science*, xi (1955) 27 sqq.

III

The second part of my argument is that, by first successfully defining the physiological problems in such a way that they could be solved in isolation by contemporary physics, the mechanistic hypothesis also brought about in the seventeenth century a systematic recognition of the different kinds of question involved in the phenomena of the animate and sensitive body. The chief author of the mechanistic hypothesis as a total characterization of the relationship between the perceiving organism and the world perceived was Descartes, and Descartes was led to this commitment not simply through physiology but through his more general inquiries into the nature of the world and our knowledge of it. I shall confine myself to showing briefly how, largely through the initiative of Descartes, three different kinds of frontier of knowledge leading to three separate fields of autonomous inquiry came to be distinguished.

When in *Ad Vitellionem paralipomena* Kepler explicitly put on one side the problem of how vision is effected by means of the body's sensory apparatus, because this was not a problem for geometrical optics, and when he rejected as optically impossible Witelo's account of how the " images " (*species, idola lucis*) were carried from the eye through the hollow optic nerve to the seat of the visual faculty of the soul in the nerves or brain, he added the side note:[117] " And yet it is this motion that brings about vision, from which the name optics is derived; and so it is wrong to exclude it from the science of optics simply because, in the present limited state of our knowledge, it cannot be accommodated in optics ". He had liberated physiology from psychology and philosophy to the extent of being able to solve his dioptric problem, but he still supposed that the vision we experienced required the delivery to the visual faculty of an image resembling the object as a picture, made up of points corresponding in order if not in orientation. He also explained the turning of the eyes towards an object by the concentration towards the centre of the retina of " the sensory power or spirit diffused through the nerve "[118]. In his *Dioptrice* (1611) he tried to deal more specifically with this problem:[119]

> *Vision is the sense of the stimulated retina* (affectae retiformis) *filled with visual spirit; or, To see is to be aware to the extent that the retina is stimulated.* The retina is painted with the coloured rays of visible things. This picture or representation (*pictura seu illustratio*) is a kind of affection (*passio*), but not superficiary[119a], as when chalk is rubbed on a wall or light shines on it, but a qualitative affection penetrating the spirits. . . . But this picture does not complete the act of vision until the image (*species*) so received by the retina passes through the continuity of the spirits to the brain, and is there delivered to the threshold of the faculty of the soul. This happens as follows: all external sense is accomplished by a reception and impression (*impressio*), that is by an affection (*passio*), when the image (*species*) of an external thing is impressed on that which feels,

---

117   Kepler, *Ad Vitellionem paralipomena*, v. 2 (*Ges. Werke*, ii) 152; above n. 99b.
118   Ibid. p. 156; above n. 99.
119   Kepler, *Dioptrice*, prop. lxi (*Ges. Werke*, iv) 372-3.
119a *superficiaria*, a term in Roman law meaning situated on another man's land.

and this affection is called sensation (*sensio*). But inside within the brain is something, whatever it may be, which is called the *sensus communis,* on which is impressed the image (*species*), effecting the visual affection, that is painted by the light from the visible thing. Thus these images fall on the instrument of vision outside the seat of the *sensus communis;* then by means of an immaterial image (*species immateriata*) descending from the instrument affected or painted and carried to the threshold of the *sensus communis* they are impressed on the *sensus communis.* But this impression is hidden from our understanding. . . .

He suggested that the retinal image might be transmitted through the visual spirit filling the optic nerve like a wave across water, and so be imprinted on the *sensus communis* in the brain.

In applying the mechanistic hypothesis to one particular organ, leaving its functioning in relation to the whole system of the body untouched, Kepler stands to Descartes in the same relationship as does Harvey. Descartes was critical of Harvey not only because he disagreed with his particular explanation of the heart's action on the model of a force pump, but also because Harvey had not related this mechanism to a general physiology itself based on physics reduced to the laws of matter in motion[120]. However one may judge Descartes's efforts to put Harvey right, it was his commitment to the total mechanistic hypothesis of nature, organized and inanimate, that enabled him to revolutionize the question of how the perceiving organism is related to the world perceived. His first account in the *Regulae ad directionem ingenii* (completed by 1629) suggests that he came to his belief that the body was a sheer mechanism like its environment through precisely this question, and perhaps through Kepler's analysis of vision[121]. Afterwards he developed in detail his mechanistic physiology and his strictly mechanical theory of physical light, using three not wholly reconcilable models: pressure through the medium as in his adoption of the Stoic analogy of the stick to account for vision, Alhazen's missile in the shape of a tennis ball to account for reflection and refraction, and an original explanation relating colours to the speeds of rotating globules[122]. His primary contribution was to show that two quite distinct questions were confused in the traditional formulation such as Kepler had given the question: what happens beyond the retina (or similarly beyond the receptors of hearing, etc.) in the nerves and brain to give us sensations ? He began by distinguishing the case of animals from that of men. Mersenne, at least to some extent independently, made the same distinction[122a].

120 Descartes, *Discours de la methode,* v (*Oeuvres,* vi) 50; cf. Crombie *Robert Grosseteste* . . ., pp. 312-4, *Augustine to Galileo,* ii (1979) 243-8, and in *Actes du 2ème Symposium international d'Histoire des Sciences. Pise-Vinci 16-18 Juin 1958,* pp. 192-201, for discussion and references; also *Styles...,* chs. 3.v, 4. ii-iii.
121 Descartes, *Regulae,* xii; cf. Kemp Smith, *New Studies in the Philosophy of Descartes,* pp. 21 sqq. The *Regulae* were published first in Descartes, *Opera posthuma* (1701); cf. trans. Marion (1977), below p. 258.
122 For these models see respectively Descartes, *Traité de l'homme* (*Oeuvres,* xi) 160-1, *La dioptrique,* i, iv (cf. above nn. 11, 25); *La dioptrique,* i, ii (cf. above n. 37); and *Les météores,* viii.
122a See my forthcoming book on Galileo, Mersenn'

(i) *The animal-machine: how is a body considered to be without sensation stimulated to co-ordinated behaviour?* Kepler had treated the living eye as far as the surface of the retina as a dead optical instrument. Starting with a purely physical ' image ' impressed on the senses, Descartes in the *Traité de l'homme* and *La dioptrique*[123], and Mersenne in *Harmonie universelle*[124], generalized this programme physiologically on the basis of their mechanistic philosophy of nature by treating the whole living. animal body as a dead machine, ruthlessly allowing only one kind of question : what physical motions follow each preceding physical motion ? So the motion of light or sound impressed a physical image in the eye or ear, this was transmitted through a purely physical " animal spirit " to the brain, and eventually through the physical structure of the neuro-muscular system a response took place co-ordinated with other built-in responses (figs. |40-1, 43-5).| Thus the study of animal behaviour became the study of the co-ordination of physiological states without sensation. As Mersenne put it in discussing animal responses to sounds :[125] " Animals have no knowledge of these sounds, but only a representation, without knowing whether what they apprehend is a sound or a colour or something else; so one can say that they do not act so much as are acted upon, and that objects make an impression on their senses from which their action necessarily follows, as the wheels of a clock necessarily follow the weight or spring that drives them ".

This machine body that was neither animate nor sensitive, and had no organizing principle separate from its parts, received ' information ' only in the sense of a twentieth-century computer; its *sensus communis* was simply the product of engineering design. It was in fact a ' natural ' machine constructed by God, just as artificial machines were constructed by men, as a solution to an engineering problem. The co-ordinated behaviour of the animal machine in response to external stimuli received through its different sense organs was God's solution to the problem of designing a machine that would preserve and propagate itself by pursuing the beneficial and avoiding the harmful aspects of its environment. The only difference between ' natural ' and ' artificial ' from the inquirer's point of view was that we did not know in advance the construction of natural machines but had to discover it, and since the ultimate parts were usually invisible this required special research[126]. But the research dealt only with purely physiological questions, separate from all questions about sensation. In this way the mechanistic hypothesis made the physiology of the senses **explicitly** autonomous in face of distinctively scientific and

123 Descartes seems to have started writing both these works in Holland in 1629: cf. Kemp Smith, *New Studies . . .*, pp. 23-5; Descartes, *Correspondance, publiée . . . par Adam et Milhaud*, i, 83, 135-6, 170-1. *Traité de l'homme* was published posthumously first in Latin in 1662 and in French in 1664.
124 Published in two parts in 1636-37; see Lenoble, *Mersenne*, pp. xxi sqq. I have discussed the dates of composition and printing of Mersenne's writings and the origins of the theory of the animal-machine in my forthcoming |*Styles ...*, chs. 3.iv, 4 and *Mersenne.*
125 *Harmonie universelle*, Seconde partie (1637), Traitez de la voix et des chants, i, prop. lii, p. 79: this was finished by 1635; for the same point cf. Mersenne, *Les préludes de l'harmonie universelle* (1634), question vi, pp. 157-9; Lenoble, *Mersenne*, p. 319; below ch. 15.
126 Descartes, *Principia philosophiae* (1644), iv. 203-4.

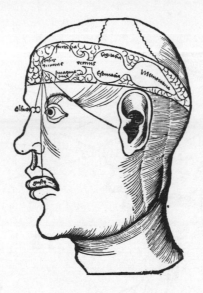

Fig. 39.   From Reisch, *Margarita philoso-phica* (Strasbourg, 1504); illustrating the traditional division of the brain into three ventricles each with a localized function: in the first is the *sensus communis*, connected by nerves to the eye, nose, tongue and ear, with fantasy and imagination; in the second, thought and judgement; in the third, memory.

technical frontiers concerning in this case only what happens materially and physically behind the retina and the corresponding receptors of sounds and other stimuli.

Descartes's animal machine was an attempt, for want of any better knowledge, to get a view across this scientific frontier by means of an hypothetical model. It was a ' relational model ', offering a formal correspondence with the actual body without identity of parts. The potential value of such a model is like that of any theoretical analysis in advance of experimentation : it may pose new questions and show a phenomenon to be explicable as an example of some other kind of phenomenon. It may suggest the form of the answer to be found as the scientific frontiers advance, though there is always the danger that an answer may be found too soon. The test of the actual value of such speculations is made by nature itself — meaning by ' nature ' what the late Alexandre Koyré once aptly described as something unknown except that it falsifies our hypotheses. Descartes's mechanistic model made biology literally research in engineering. In this way he made formal anticipations of some very important discoveries, including the reciprocal innervation of antagonistic muscles (of the eye : fig. 41), brain

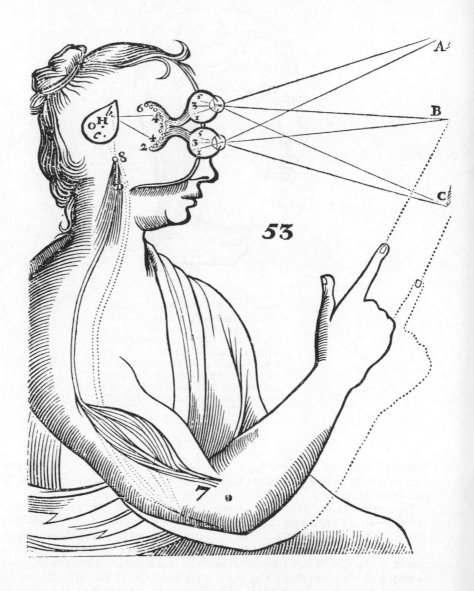

Fig. 40.   From Descartes, *Tractatus de homine* (Paris, 1664): illustrating the purely
mechanistic transmission of the stimulus of the light going from the
object (ABC) to form the visual images (135), thence of the 'sensory'
stimulus to the endings of the optic nerves in the cerebral ventricle (246),
and thence through the 'animal spirit' filling the ventricles to the pineal
gland (H). From there the motor stimulus (i.e. animal spirit) passes
through the opening (8) of the nerve to the arm muscle (7) which it
causes to contract by blowing it up: cf. figs. 41, 42, 45.

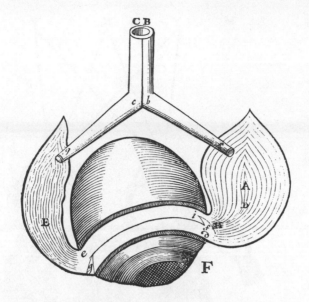

Fig. 41. From Descartes, *Tractatus de homine* (Paris, 1664): illustrating his model of the antagonistic muscles of the eye, innervated so that when one (A) contracted, the other (E) relaxed. According to his pneumatic neuromuscular model, muscles contracted when animal spirit sent down the hollow nerves (CB) blew them up like balloons, and relaxed when it was shut off by suitably arranged valves; cf. fig. 40.

patterns of sensory impressions (fig. 42), and the beginning of the concept of the reflex[127]. Descartes's hypothetical hydraulic or pneumatic neuromuscular physiology was replaced by electrical and chemical engineering as a guide, but still formally with the Cartesian approach. Advance was restricted only by a technical frontier limiting ability to answer answerable physiological questions. In fact real advances in knowledge of what happens physiologically behind the retina and the cochlea were made technically possible only in the nineteenth century by the preceding advances in physical optics and acoustics, in histology following the improved achromatic microscope and new chemical stains, and in electrophysiology with the work of Johannes Müller's pupils in Berlin, above all of Helmholtz.

(ii) *How does the animate body receive and differentiate information through its senses?* Having defined the physiological frontier in the study of the animal body, Descartes then had no difficulty in arguing that the question of how sensations were caused in men was quite a different kind of question encountering a different kind of frontier. He argued in *La*

127   cf. Kemp Smith, *New Studies . . .*, pp. 53-4, 145-55; Canguilhem, *La formation du concept du réflexe*, pp. 27 sqq.

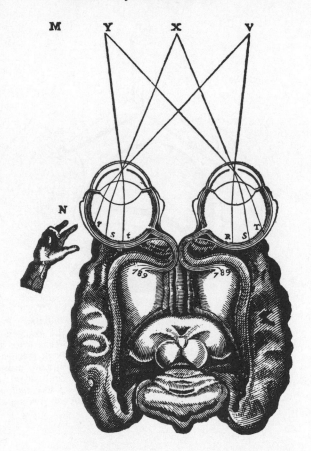

Fig. 42.   From Descartes, *La dioptrique*, v (Leiden, 1637):
illustrating the transmission of light from the
object (VXY) to form a visual image in each eye
(RST, *rst*), and then of these images through
the optic nerves to form corresponding patterns
(789) in the cerebral cavities; cf. figs. 40, 45.

dioptrique (1637) that an account of the 'representative image' type, such
as Kepler's, did not touch the central problem (recognized clearly since
Plato) of passing from a physical motion or image, produced by external
physical stimuli in the sensory mechanisms, to a sensation in the sentient
being. He wrote:[128] "In order to facilitate the explanation of the special
sense of sight, I must at this point say something about the nature of the
senses in general. First, we know for certain that it is to the soul that sense
belongs, not to the body. . . . Again, we know that sensation occurs,
properly speaking, not in view of the soul's presence in the parts that serve

128   Descartes, *La dioptrique*, iv.

as external sense-organs, but only in view of its presence in the brain, where it employs the faculty called *sensus communis*. . . . Finally, we know that it is through the nerves that the impressions made by objects upon the external organs are transmitted to the soul in the brain ". He introduced his account of ocular dioptrics by comparing it with the formation of images in a *camera obscura* with a lens, and continued (fig. 34)[129] :

> Take the eye of a newly dead man or, failing that, of an ox or some other large animal; carefully cut away the three enveloping membranes at the back, so as to expose a large part of the humour (M) without shedding any; then cover the hole with some white body, thin enough to let daylight through, for example a piece of paper or eggshell (RST). Now put this eye in the opening of a specially made window (Z), so that its front (BCD) faces a spot where there are a number of objects (V, X, Y) lit up by the sun, and the back, where the white body (RST) is, faces the inside of the room (P) you are in. No light must enter the room except through the eye, of which you know that all the parts from C to S are transparent. If you now look at the white body (RST), you will see, I dare say with surprise and pleasure, a picture representing in natural perspective all the objects outside (VXY), in due proportion to their distance. You must of course see that the eye keeps its natural shape, for if you squeeze it never so little more or less than you ought, the picture becomes less distinct. And it should be noticed that the eye must be squeezed a little more, and made proportionately a little longer, when the objects are very near than when they are farther away. . . . Now when you have seen this picture in a dead animal's eye, and considered its causes, you cannot doubt that a quite similar picture is produced in a living man's eye. . . . Further, the images of objects are not only produced in the back of the eye but also sent to the brain (fig. 42), as you can easily understand if you suppose that, for example, the rays going to the eye from the object V touch at the point R the end of one of the small fibres of the optic nerve that takes its origin at the location 7 on the interior surface of the brain 789. . . . From which it is clear that once more a picture 789 is formed, sufficiently similar to the objects VXY, this time on the interior surface of the brain. . . . And from there I can again transport it to a certain small gland located about the middle of the concavities of the brain; this is the proper seat of the *sensus communis*.

But, he went on :[130]

> While this picture, in thus passing into our head, always retains some degree of resemblance to the objects from which it proceeds, yet we need not think, as I have already sufficiently shown, that it is by means of this resemblance that the picture makes us perceive the objects, as though we had inside our brain yet another pair of eyes to see it; rather, we must hold that the movements that go to form the picture, acting immediately on our soul inasmuch as it is united to our body, are so ordained by nature as to give it such sensations.

129   Ibid. v; cf. above n. 100.
130   Ibid. vi.

With this *reductio ad absurdum* Descartes's main argument against the
'representative image' theory was that it was irrelevant because it took
the physiological image as the object instead of as the means of sensing.
The frontiers involved in his position should be distinguished with some
care. He behaved then as if he recognized that the question : how do
physiological motions cause sensations ? belonged to a type to be explicitly
classified by John Locke[131] as in principle unanswerable because it concerns
relations between different categories of subject. He simply avoided the
frontier that Kepler had attempted to cross from motions to sensations, a
philosophical, logical frontier of knowledge established by what we cannot
know. Instead he directed his attack again wholly towards a quite different,
empirical and scientific frontier, reached by asking a different, answerable
question : what physical and physiological clues determine different
sensations ? He pointed out that even in vision the image was not a
strict representation of the object but more like a two-dimensional sketch
that could suggest with a few strokes many different qualities, including
many that were not visual at all; still less was the image strictly representative in hearing and the other senses. Once the other senses were taken
seriously into consideration it became obvious that the pictorial resemblance
of the retinal image to its object was accidental in effecting sensations; the
'image' of sound could mean only its formal ordered correspondence with
its source[132]. So, he wrote :[133]

> The perceived qualities of seen objects can all be brought under six
> main heads : light, colour, position, distance, size and shape. First,
> then, as regards light and colour, the only qualities belonging specially
> to the sense of sight : it must be held that our soul is of such a nature
> that a sensation of light is determined by the strength of the
> disturbance that occurs at the points of origin of the optic nerve-
> fibres in the brain; and one of colour, by the kind of disturbance. In
> the same way, the disturbance of the nerves that supply the ears
> determines the hearing of sounds; the disturbance of the nerves in the
> tongue determines the tasting of flavours; and in general, disturbance
> of nerves anywhere in the body determines, if it is moderate, a feeling
> of enjoyment, and if it is too violent, a pain. But there need be no
> resemblance here between the ideas conceived by the soul and the
> disturbances that cause them. You will readily believe this if you
> observe that people hit in the eye think they see a great number of
> fiery flashes in front of them, in spite of shutting their eyes or being
> in a dark place; this sensation can be ascribed only to the force of the
> blow, which sets the optic nerve-fibres in motion as a strong light
> would do. The same force might cause one to hear a sound, if
> applied to the ears, or to feel pain, if applied to other parts of the
> body.

Embodied inside its "statue or machine of clay"[134], the soul knew

---

131 *Essay on the Humane Understanding* (1690), i. 9, iv. 3.
132 Cf. above nn. 8, 9, 12; Crombie, in *Proceedings of the Tenth International
     Congress of History of Science*, pp. 99-100, on Volcher Coiter **and others; below**
133 Descartes, *La dioptrique*, vi.   ch. 14.
134 Descartes, *Traité de l'homme* (*Oeuvres*, xi) 120.

objects only symbolically through the motions they set up in the nervous system. It was in a position analogous to ourselves finding our way about in the dark by means of a stick or to men born blind who had made such use of tactile sensations all their lives and " one might almost say that they see with their hands ". The " very rapid and lively movement or activity transmitted to our eyes "[134a] as light, like the movement or resistance communicated by the stick, gave the soul its " occasions " or clues for its sensations and perceptions. So :[135]

> . . . the only question we need raise is that of knowing how the images can supply to the soul the means of sensing all the diverse qualities of the objects to which they stand related, and not how in themselves they bear resemblance to them. When our blind man touches bodies with his stick, they certainly transmit nothing to him beyond merely setting his stick in motion in different ways, according to their different qualities; by this means they set in motion the nerves of his hand, and the points of origin of these nerves in his brain; and this is what occasions the soul's perception of various qualities in the bodies, corresponding to the various sorts of disturbance that they produce in the brain.

By following this approach Descartes and Mersenne opened up a new field of empirical inquiry into the correlations of our sensations with states of our nervous systems and of the external world as conceived by current physiological and physical theory. Descartes tried to show how different sensations of colour could be determined by the different speeds of rotation of the corpuscles of light[136]; perception of distance by motions set up in the brain by movements of accommodation in each eye (fig. 37) and of the convergence of the axes of the two eyes relative to each other (fig. 43), by the " force " of light striking the eye (hence haziness), and by the apparent sizes of objects whose actual sizes we know[137]; perception of magnitude by the magnitude of the retinal image and the angle of vision subtended at the eye, coupled with knowledge of the distance of the object; perception of shape by the shapes of the retinal images coupled with knowledge of the actual relationships between the parts of objects — thus the images may be ovals and lozenges but they make us see circles and squares[138]. Mersenne pioneered the exploration and quantitative specification of the physical motions of sounding bodies and of the air correlated with the sensations and emotions induced by music[139]. After this they could with genuine scientific knowledge distinguish the study of perception and recognition as an autonomous field of psychology, separate from that of mere sensation and from the optical physiology of image-formation and its equivalent in the other senses.

134a Descartes, *La dioptrique*, i.
135 Descartes, *La dioptrique*, iv; cf. *Traité de l'homme* (*Oeuvres*, xi) 143-4, 174-7, *Meditationes de prima philosophiae* (1641) vi, *Principia*, iv. 189, *Les passions de l'âme* (1649), cc. 23, 36; Kemp Smith, *New Studies . . .*, pp. 212-9.
136 Descartes, *Les météores*, viii; cf. above n. 122.
137 Descartes, *Traité de l'homme* (*Oeuvres*, xi) 157-61; *La dioptrique*, vi; cf. above nn. 63, 102, 108.
138 Ibid.
139 Mersenne, *Harmonie universelle*, Traitez de la nature des sons et des mouvemens de toutes sortes de corps, i, props. i-ii; cf. above nn. 124-5. Mersenne published the main results of his inquiries at length in *Harmonie universelle* (1636-37), *Harmonicorum libri* (1636), and *Cogitata physico-mathematica* (1644).

Fig. 43. From Descartes, *Tractatus de homine* (Paris,
1664): illustrating the perception of distance
through binocular vision by means of the
angle at which the axes of the two eyes
converge on the object (bottom diagram),
just as a blind man perceives distance by
means of the angle of convergence of his
two sticks (top diagram).

The influence of the mechanistic hypothesis in its total form, laying out a programme for research and explanation extending far beyond the technical frontier of testable theory, raises a question of historical judgement. Descartes's chronic over-confidence in the success of his hypotheses in achieving the total reduction of the physical world to matter in motion, in believing too soon that by defining the form an answer should take he had discovered the answer in each particular case, could be fatal to his weaker followers. But just because this programme was both so complete in its claims and so fruitful in the questions it put to the subject-matter of the animate and sensitive body, it became a challenge to the stronger to consider explicitly what contemporary science had achieved, and could and could not achieve. The mechanistic hypothesis became a challenge at once to explore the subject-matter of the animate and sensitive body through ideas capable of generating scientifically testable theories, and to recognize the conjectural status of ideas precisely because they were still beyond the technical range of experimental test. Naturally the nature of the challenge was not grasped in the same way by all concerned and understanding of it developed with scientific experience.

Contemporary with Descartes and Mersenne the critical speculations of Hobbes and Gassendi offered alternative accounts of the mediation of sensory information and the co-ordination of behaviour. Hobbes's published and unpublished work on optics is in special need of historical analysis relating it to his sources and to his model for a purely corporeal psychology[140]. Gassendi, taking the Greek atomists as his starting-point, argued like Descartes that no literal representation of an object was conveyed to the brain, but that the objects of the senses were represented symbolically by the motions they produced there. In his critique of Descartes's device of the pineal gland, and his frankly conjectural alternative model, he brought out with great clarity the need to find an appropriate formulation of the problem of correlating sensory and physiological states[141]. Malebranche, becoming so excited after chancing to take up the *Traité de l'homme* that he was forced by the palpitations of his heart to put it down for a while, followed a different lead given by Descartes in pursuing this problem empirically[142].

---

140 Cf. Hobbes, *A Minute or first Draught of the Optiques*, Brit. Mus. MS Harley 3360, *Tractatus opticus*, Brit. Mus. MS Harley 6796, ff. 193-266, *English Works*, vii, 467-71, *Opera . . . latine*, ii, 7 sqq. (" De homine "), v, 215-48 (" Opticae ", here called *Tractatus opticus;* above n. 111), 308-18 (" Praefatio in Mersenni Ballisticam "), *The Elements of Law*, ed. . . . Tönnies; Jacquot, *Thales*, viii (1952) 36-86, *Notes and Records of the Royal Society*, ix (1952) 188 sqq.; Alessio, *Rivista critica di storia della filosofia*, xvii (1962) 393 sqq.; Pacchi, *Convenzione e ipotesi nella formazione della filosofia naturale di Thomas Hobbes*, pp. 15-41.

141 Gassendi, *Syntagma philosophicum. Physica*, III. II. III. 1-4, vi. 2, viii. 2-4 (*Opera*, ii, 1658) 237 sqq., 338 sqq., 402 sqq.; Descartes *Meditationes . . . Objectiones . . . cum responsionibus authoris*, objectiones v; Brett, *The Philosophy of Gassendi*, pp. 106-35. In *Objectiones . . .* v Gassendi criticized Descartes's theory of the pineal gland logically on the grounds that the unextended thinking substance of the soul was excluded by definition from contact with an extended unthinking substance of the body; for anatomical criticisms cf. below n. 151.

142 Malebranche, *La recherche de la verité* (1674), texte établi par Lewis; below n. 159. He read the 1664 edition of the *Traité de l'homme* in 1664; see André, *La vie du R. P. Malebranche*, pub. . . . par Ingold, pp. 11-16.

Another example of exploration through speculation designed to be fed back into testable science is the renewed discussion of the question: what determines the specificity of the different senses, so that some physical and physiological motions produce sensations of seeing, others of hearing, and so on ? Speculation polarized round ancient hypotheses, but with more physical and physiological knowledge and franker recognition of their hypothetical status. In refuting the 'representative image' theory of vision Descartes had shown that the motions giving rise to the other kinds of sensation did not literally resemble their sources. The mechanisms of the special sense organs were so designed that they normally responded to, and mediated to the nerves, different kinds of external physical movements. But arguing that " it is the soul that sees, not the eye "[143], and correspondingly hears, smells, tastes and touches through the mediation of the brain, he agreed with the principle of Galen's specific pneuma, that the different kinds of sensation resulting from external stimulation were determined not by the character of the stimulus but by the part of the brain in which the consequential motions were set up. Hence a blow or pressure on the eye produced sensations of bright flashes, and these in turn confirmed for Descartes his theory that light was simply one kind of mechanical pressure among many others, producing different sensations of colour according to the different motions set up in a particular nerve[144]. It followed that the same sensation could be produced by an external stimulus to the outer end of the nerve at the sense organ and by an internal stimulus to the inner end at the brain. Mersenne argued that an angel could make us see and hear objects outside us by moving our internal nerves[145]. Then how do we come to locate the objects of the senses outside us ? Descartes replied that we could only suppose that a perfect God would not make the lives of his creatures an eternal hallucination and had given us besides perception a sort of innate geometry that enabled us to locate the objects of perception in space[146].

This theory of the differentiation of the senses led to speculations about the physiological causes of after-images, hallucinations, noises in the head,

143 Descartes, *La dioptrique*, vi.
144 Ibid. vi and j; cf. Hobbes, " Opticae ", in Mersenne, *Universae geometriae . . . synopsis*, vii, prop. iii; above nn. 111, 140. For Galen's 'specific pneuma' see above nn. 11-13; and cf. the theory of 'specific nerve energies' developed by Johannes Müller, in his *Handbuch der Physiologie des Menschen* (1838-40), transl. Baly as *Elements of Physiology*, iii. 5, Preliminary Considerations, vol. ii (1842) 1065 : " V. Sensation consists in the sensorium receiving through the medium of the nerves, and as the result of the action of an external cause, a knowledge of certain qualities or conditions, not of external bodies, but of the nerves of sense themselves; and these qualities of the nerves of sense are in all different, the nerve of each sense having its own peculiar quality or energy. The nerves of the senses have assuredly a specific irritablity for certain influences; for many stimuli, which exert a violent action upon one organ of sense, have little or no effect upon another: for example, light, or vibrations so infinitely rapid as those of light, act only on the nerves of vision and common sensation; slower vibrations, on the nerves of hearing and common sensation, but not upon those of vision; odorous substances only upon the olfactory nerves ".
145 Mersenne, *Harmonie universelle*, Tr. de la voix, i. prop. lii, p. 81; cf. Ockham, *Super quattuor libros sententiarum annotationes*, ii. 4-5, R.
146 Descartes, *Principia*, ii. 1; *Meditationes* vi; *La dioptrique*, vi; cf. Kemp Smith, *New Studies . . .*, pp. 155-9, 213-4; above nn. 31, 135, 137.

and the cerebral localization of brain function, which the French physiologist Du Verney proposed to investigate by the study of diseases acting as natural experiments in extirpation[147]. The alternative theory of the Greek atomists, making the specificity of the senses depend primarily on the nature of the external stimulus rather than the internal response of the nerves, also had the support of some of the best physiological opinion. Thus Thomas Willis, under the influence of Gassendi, held that the senses were different only because each received a different kind of external physical stimulus or particle and could receive no other; those "proportionate to one sense organ are incommunicable to the others "[148]. One of the most important consequences of his speculations was his comparative anatomical study of the variety of solutions, shown by the sensory equipment of animals ranging down the scale of nature, to the engineering problems of their information systems. He argued that the five external senses of man and the higher animals were constructed to respond to the five kinds of influence or stimulus in the environment of which perception was most necessary for survival, but that God could have given us further senses responding to yet further influences. In the lower animals the number of different senses might be less than five, in oysters and limpets perhaps reduced only to touch. He wondered what kind of different appearances these different creatures must be given of their common world[149].

The role of the Cartesian model of the animal machine in the intellectual history of biology was attractively portrayed by one of Descartes's astutest critics, the Danish anatomist Nicholas Steno, in his *Discours sur l'anatomie du cerveau* given at a gathering in Paris in 1665[150]. Steno shared in the stimulation given by the Cartesian mechanistic programme to all natural philosophy in the middle decades of the seventeenth century. But he was provoked by the use of the Cartesian hypotheses in physiology, as Newton was to be in his critique of Cartesian optics and mechanics[150a], into insisting on defining what had been and could be actually established: in particular instances and not just in terms of a general rule of scientific validity. Steno pointed out the difference between modelling functions with artefacts and research into living systems themselves: the frontier of actual knowledge could be crossed only by direct experimentation on the actual animal body. Beginning his discussion of the brain with a disarming "sincere and public confession that I know nothing about it ", he went on to say that some people "will give you an account of the brain and of the disposition of its parts with an assurance as if they had been present at the construction of this marvellous machine and had penetrated all the designs of its great

147   Du Verney, *Traité de l'organe de l'ouïe* (1683) troisieme partie, pp. 188-207; cf. Crombie, in *Proceedings of the Tenth International Congress of History of Science,* pp. 107-11, where Du Verney's contribution to the resonance theory of hearing is discussed.
148   Willis, *De anima brutorum* (1672) i. 10, p. 159; cf. i. 11-15 on the special senses, and i. 1 on previous authors; Cranefield, *Bulletin of the History of Medicine,* xxxv (1961) 291 sqq; Crombie, op. cit. pp. 104-7.
149   Willis, op cit. i. 1-3, 10.
150   Steno, *Discours . . . sur l'anatomie du cerveau . . .* (Paris, 1669); *Opera philosophica,* ed. Maar, ii, 1 sqq. 313.
150a For Newton's use of Descartes see Koyré, *Newtonian Studies*; above n. 116.

Architect "[151]. He congratulated Descartes on the beautiful machine he had described to imitate a man; in this he had surpassed all other philosophers: no one else had explained all our actions mechanically. But, he said, Descartes knew too well the deficiencies of existing knowledge to describe the true composition of the human body. His machine did not agree with actual dissection and anatomy, but some people had taken it for an account of the actual body. He described the proper method of approach: [151a]

> There are only two ways of reaching knowledge of a machine: one is that the master who made it should show us its construction; the other is to dismantle it down to its smallest springs, and examine them separately and together. These are the true means of knowing the construction of a machine; and nonetheless most people have . . . been content to observe its movements, and on these observations alone have built systems which they have offered as the truth when they believed that they could explain in this way all the effects coming to their knowledge. They have not taken into consideration that the same thing can be explained in different ways and that it is only the senses that can assure us that the idea that we have formed conforms to nature. Now the brain being a machine, we cannot hope to discover its construction in any other way than those by which we discover the construction of other machines. There is then nothing to do but what is done with all other machines: I mean to dismantle piece by piece all its springs, and consider how they can act separately and together. It is just in this research that one can say with reason that the number of those who have shown the ardour of true curiosity is very small indeed. . . .

He went on to say that most anatomical research was done by physicians and surgeons, but when they became established in practice they could no longer spare the time. Professors of anatomy in the medical schools did not feel obliged to do research. "The demands of research giving us the truth requires a whole man, with nothing to do but that "[151b]. But theoretical investigators who themselves do not dissect would also have greatly assisted others

> . . . if they had made an exact report of what anatomists had written on the brain, or if they had set out according to the laws of analysis all the ways of explaining animal actions mechanically, or if they had drawn up an exact catalogue of all the propositions they have found in which it would be necessary to distinguish carefully those based on fact and observation from those based only on reasoning. But so far no one has done anything of the kind; that is why we need pay attention almost solely to those who have worked themselves. The first thing to consider is the account of the parts, in which we must decide what is true and certain in order to distinguish this from propositions that are false or uncertain. It is not even enough to be able to clarify one's own mind: the evidence of the demonstration

---

151   Steno, *Opera*, ed. Maar, p. 3. He went on to discuss the contemporary anatomical critique of the Cartesian machine, especially that relating to the brain and pineal gland (pp. 7-12, 20-21).

151a   Ibid. p. 16.

151b   Ibid. p. 17.

must oblige everyone else to agree; otherwise the number of controversies will grow instead of diminishing. . . .[151c]

I try to follow the laws of philosophy which teach us to search for truth while doubting its certainty, and not to be content until one is confirmed by the evidence of the demonstration.· . . . I have said nothing so far about the functions of parts or of the actions called animal, because it is impossible to explain the movements made by a machine if one does not know the construction of its parts. Reasonable people must find these confident anatomists very funny when, after having discoursed on the functions of parts of which they do not know the structure, they bring in as a justification for the functions they assign to them that God and nature do nothing in vain. But they deceive themselves in this application of this general maxim; what God, according to their reckless judgement, has destined for one purpose turns out later to have been made for another. So it is much better to confess ignorance, to be more reserved in coming to a decision, and not to undertake so lightly to explain by simple conjectures something that is so difficult[151d].

Steno gave practical advice about pursuing this inquiry. He pointed out that different methods of dissection could produce different and sometimes false results, so more than one method should be used : if a structure was natural it would remain the same. A good artist was needed to draw the dissections accurately. Some structures were easier to examine in some animals than in others, so a comparative study of the brain should be made in different species of animal and in different states of the same species : foetal and adult, healthy and diseased. There were considerable differences between the brains of different animals and some differences from our own brains even " in the animals nearest to ourselves "[151e]. His scheme of research included a systematic study of the action of the brain not only through the effects of wounds, medicines and diseases in man, but also by experiments on living animals. He suggested opening their skulls in order to investigate the peripheral effects of direct stimulation of different parts of the brain mechanically and by applications of drugs and injections of drugs and foods into the vessels. In all this he said that there was little to be learnt from predecessors and the books of ancients. He was proposing an attack on the technical and scientific frontier by asking further questions of the same kind as Descartes had asked, but looking for answers by direct research into living things; a programme for " the infinity of researches that must be made on men and on animals, and in all the different states in which they must be studied "[151f].

When Steno gave his lecture part of this programme was already being actively carried out in England by Willis, whose illustrations of the brain, some of which were by Wren, he said were the best available (cf. fig. 44)[152]. In 1667 a systematic comparative study of the structures and functions of all the organs of animal bodies was proposed in the Académie des Sciences

151c Ibid. p. 19.
151d Ibid. pp. 23-5.
151e Ibid. pp. 25-6; on methods of dissection etc. see pp. 5-6, 12, 19-20, 23-4.
151f Ibid. p. 26.
152 Ibid. p. 12; cf. Willis, *Cerebri anatome* (1664) praefatio. on Wren's illustrations for this edition.

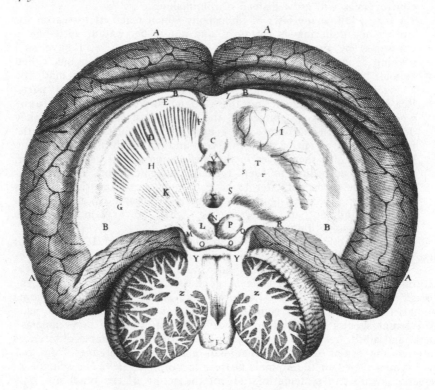

Fig. 44. From Willis, *De anima brutorum*, c. 7, tabula viii (Oxford, 1672): vertical
section of the human brain showing the cerebral hemispheres (AA)
separated to display among other structures the *corpus callosum* (B),
corpus striatum (DEFGHI), optic thalamus (K), fornix (C), pineal gland
(N), the process (Y) from the *medulla oblongata* to the cerebellum (Z),
and the beginning of the spinal cord.

by Claude Perrault[153]. The study made of the sense organs is of particular
interest because it was accompanied by a systematic attempt to relate
arguments from structure to function to known physics. Perrault, Du
Verney, Mariotte and their colleagues re-explored the foundations of ocular
and auditory anatomy and physiology with a grasp as firm as Steno's both
of the role and of the nature of scientific conjecture[154]. Like Willis, Perrault
argued that the human senses were differentiated not by the nerve stimulated
but by the external stimulus; he argued that if the optic nerve was
inserted in the tongue it would carry impressions of taste, just as the
nerves of the tongue if provided with the receptors of the eye would serve
for vision[155]. In this as in the other scientific conjectures about what might
happen in the nerves as conductors and the brain as co-ordinator of

153 *Historie de l'Académie royale des Sciences*, i, 18; cf. pp. 117, 223.
154 Above nn. 115, 147; cf. Perrault, *Essai de physique*, i (1680) preface.
155 Perrault, ibid. ii, 217-33.

information and behaviour, speculative exploration met in this period a narrow technical frontier limiting the possibility of experimental exploration and test. But we may see in them a stage of scientific ideas preceding and, through the formulation given to its questions, helping to generate the stage of scientifically testable theories. It was a major scientific achievement of the seventeenth century to try to recognize the precise degree to which these physiological questions could and could not be answered.

The contribution that I should claim for the mechanistic hypothesis in the scientific study of the senses is, first, that it made explicit the separation of the answerable questions of physiology and psycho-physiological correlation from unanswerable questions in the inherited approach. We need not accept the exact lines of the separation between what was claimed in the seventeenth century as known in fact, unknown but capable of being found out by asking questions appropriate to the subject-matter, and in principle unknowable. But we have to accept that these distinctions mark a major step in scientific thinking. The mechanistic hypothesis in its total, Cartesian form brought out into the open the exact lines both of the scientific frontier of potentially testable propositions, and of the technical frontier of then actually testable propositions; and so it offered a clear view of what to do next to extend the area of scientific knowledge. The pushing back of these scientific and technical frontiers by the direct study of living things led in turn to the recognition of the diversity of answerable questions to be discovered in the subject-matter of the animate and sensitive body.

This was in effect an empirical recognition that, in extending its area, scientific knowledge encountered not simply a technical frontier limiting ability to answer one kind of question, but also a methodological frontier calling for a different kind of question to be addressed to living things because in fact they were living and not dead. Frontiers of this kind lay in two main directions, both polarized during the century after Descartes in opposition to the mechanistic hypothesis in its brutal form. One is indicated by the discovery that the co-ordination of behaviour took place at different levels not easily fitted into a single mechanistic scheme, by the superceding of the simple Cartesian automaton with the experimental exploration of these levels, and by the insistence expressed by Albrecht von Haller that organic behaviour as observed had its own regularities not immediately reducible to physico-chemical laws[156]. Total commitment to the mechanistic hypothesis eliminated biology in the division of the field of living things between physics and psychology; the recognition of this frontier was a factual re-assertion of an autonomous biology. We may be inclined now to try to absorb this frontier into the technical one; my point is simply that it was the mechanistic hypothesis that made the problem. Matching this declaration of the *de facto* autonomy of the physiology of behaviour, the other methodological frontier arose from a new insistence that, in perception likewise, sentient organisms did not simply respond by built-in mechanisms to external influences, but actively initiated the organizing of a meaningful world. The sentient organism principally considered was of course man.

156 Cf. Canguilhem, " La physiologie animale ", in *Histoire générale des sciences, publiée sous la direction de Taton*, ii, 593 sqq.; Crombie and Hoskin, " The scientific movement and its influence (1610-1650) ", *New Cambridge Modern History*, iv, " The scientific movement and the diffusion of scientific ideas (1688-1751) ", ibid. vi (both 1970).

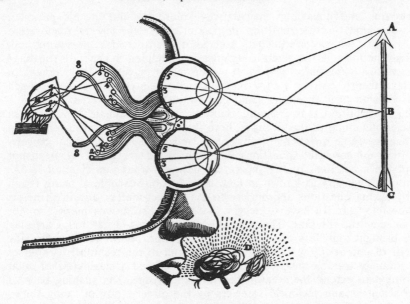

Fig. 45. From Descartes, *Tractatus de homine* (Paris, 1664): illustrating his purely mechanistic and neurological conception of the co-ordination of the senses so that, e.g., the visual stimulus, going from the arrow (ABC) through the images (135,246) uniting in the pineal gland (H) at *a b c*, prevents attention being paid to the olfactory stimulus going from the flower (D) through the olfactory nerve (8) to the pineal gland at *d*; cf. figs. 39, 40, 42.

(iii) *How does the animate body co-ordinate the information received through the different senses?* While side-stepping the question of the causation of sensations by physiological motions, Descartes had nevertheless (in accordance with his general reductive programme) tried to show that the sensations and perceptions we have are not only correlated with, but can in consequence also be derived from physiological states of our nervous systems. He tried to show that how we see can be derived immediately from the body's optical apparatus, and he simply assumed that the co-ordination of the information received through the different senses was built into the inheritance of the animate and sensitive body (fig. 45)[157] In this way men were given one consistent view of the world and animals consistent behaviour in relation to it. Thus he supposed it self-evident that a blind man groping about with two sticks would form a conception of the geometry of space exactly as a sighted man did (fig. 43) [157a]. Leibniz[158] made the same assumption. Malebranche[159] did not, and he made the co-ordination of the senses a question for empirical research. The most

157   Descartes, *Traité de l'homme* (*Oeuvres*, xi) 185-90.
157a Above nn. 134a-35, 137.
158   Leibniz, *Nouveaux essais sur l'entendement humain* (1704) ii. 9.
159   Malebranche, *De la recherche de la vérité*, i; Smith, *British Journal of Psychology*, i (1905) 191-204.

famous denial of the Cartesian assumption arose out of the problem put by William Molyneux to Locke : whether a man born blind and given sight would be able at once to recognize differences in shape by sight because he had already learnt to do so by touch[160]. Molyneux and Locke held that he would not. Berkeley[161] agreed with them, pointing out that current physiological theory could not tell us what the man would see. He argued more generally that in this case, as in judging distance and magnitude, we should assume that we learn these things for each sense separately and also learn by experience to co-ordinate the information received through the different senses. The co-ordination could not be assumed to be built into the sensory mechanism; the *sensus communis* was a power that the mind exercised actively. The results of operations for congenital cataract have confirmed Berkeley's basic contentions[162]. The interest of his manoeuvre for my argument is that by questioning a methodological commitment, he assisted at the birth of an independent field of empirical inquiry. He showed in his *New Theory of Vision* (1709) that the co-ordination of perception must be studied first as a problem independent of that of the co-ordination of physiological states; their correlation was a separate problem. And so he pointed the way to an explicitly autonomous psychology of perception as an empirical science exploring its data independently both of current theories of physical clues and the body's apparatus, and of the logical problem of the causation of sensation.

The effect of total commitment to the mechanistic hypothesis in the scientific study of the senses emerges as a paradox. It was as fruitful in the opposition it provoked as in the acceptance it commanded, and in the research it generated as in the clarification of thought it made necessary. These ideas manipulated in the background were certainly not a necessary condition for the technical invention of the microscope and telescope, but they were nevertheless a genuine part of the same scientific world. " The whole conduct of our life depends on our senses ", Descartes began *La dioptrique,* " among which vision being the noblest and most universal, there can be no doubt that inventions serving to increase its power are the most useful there can **possibly** be "[163]. He claimed to have taken up the scientific study of vision in this elegant work in order to construct a telescope on scientific principles. To do so rationally meant first acquiring scientific knowledge both of light, by which we see, and of the eye and associated nervous system, which are the natural instruments of sight. This was an introduction to his concluding technical study of lenses. We know now that the passive, camera-like features of the eye that took such intellectual efforts to discover and are so fundamental to its optical system, nevertheless raise the least interesting questions about vision. It is the active searching for meaningful information that recent science and

---

160   Locke, *Essay* . . ., ii. 9.
161   Berkeley, *An Essay towards a New Theory of Vision* (1709), and **Theory** *of Vision . . . Vindicated* (1733).
162   Von Senden, *Space and Sight.*
163   Descartes, *La dioptrique,* i; cf. viii-x on means of improving vision, lenses, telescopes and their construction, and his correspondence from 1629 with the optician Guillaume Ferrier in *Correspondence, publiée* . . . par Adam et Milhaud, i-iii.

engineering have revealed as the most interesting characteristic both of the variety of solutions to their problems shown by the comparative study of animal sensory systems, and of the artifacts with which we model them or extend their natural range in precision and in detecting new kinds of physical clue. In this more recent history the distinctive lines of the technical and conceptual frontiers are no less interesting than in the more distant past, when scientific thinking first charted a course through the problem of relating the perceiving organism to the world perceived.

Further references: (1) Al-Hasan ibn al-Haytham, *Kĭtab-al-Manazir, Books i-iii (On direct vision)*, ed. A. I. Sabra (Kuwait, 1983), and transl. (London, 1989); Roger Bacon, *Philosophy of Nature (De multiplicatione specierum* and *De speculis comburentibus)*, ed. and transl. D. C. Lindberg (Oxford, 1983); Giovanni Battista Benedetti, *Diversarum speculationum mathematicarum et physicarum liber*, "De visu" (Taurini, 1585) 296-7; Descartes, *Règles utiles et claires pour la direction de l'esprit*, transl. with notes by J.-L. Marion and mathematical notes by P. Costabel (La Haye, 1977); Galen, *On the Doctrines of Hippocrates and Plato*, ed., transl. and commentary by P. H. De Lacy, 2 vol, (Berlin, 1978-80); Leonardo da Vinci, *Corpus of the Anatomical Studies in the Collection of Her Majesty the Queen*, ed. K. D. Keele and C. Pedretti, 3 vol. (New York), 1978-80), and K. Clark, *A Catalogue . . .* (below p. 261), 2nd ed. with the assistance of C. Pedretti, 3 vol. (London, 1968-69); Witelo, *Perspectiva* Book i, ed. and transl. S. Unguru (Wroclaw, etc., 1977), Book v, ed. and transl. A. M. Smith (1983); (2) in full in A. C. Crombie, "Expectation, modelling and assent in the history of optics, i: Alhazen and the medieval tradition, ii: Kepler and Descartes", *Studies in History and Philosophy of Science*, xxi (1990) and *Styles . . .* chs. 2.i, 3.i, 4.ii; M. R. Cohen and I. E. Drabkin, *Source Book in Greek Science* (New York, 1948); P. Costabel, *Démarches originales de Descartes savant* (Paris, 1982); S. Y. Edgerton jr., *The Renaissance Rediscovery of Linear Perspective* (New York, 1975), and in Shirley and Hoeniger (1985) and Woodward (1987) above p. 173; J. V. Field, "Two mathematical inventions in Kepler's *Ad Vitellionem paralipomena*", *Studies in History and Philosophy of Science*, xvii (1986) 449-68; T. Frangenberg, "Il 'De visu' di G. B. Benedetti" in *G. B. Benedetti*, ed. A. Ghetti (Venezia, 1985) 271-82; E. Grant (ed.), *Source Book in Medieval Science* (Cambridge, Mass., 1974); R. L. Gregory, *The Intelligent Eye* (London, 1970); M. D. Grmek, "Un débat scientifique exemplaire: Mariotte, Pacquet et Perrault à la recherche du siège de la perception visuelle", *History and Philosophy of the Life Sciences*, vii (1985) 217-55; K. D. Keele, *Leonardo da Vinci's Elements of the Science of Man* (New York, 1983); M. Kemp, *Leonardo da Vinci* (London, 1981); H. M. Koelbing, "Felix Platters Stellung in der Medizin seiner Zeit", *Gesnerus*, xxii (1965) 59-67, *Renaissance der Augenheilkunde 1540-1630* (Bern, 1967), "Ocular physiology in the seventeenth century and its acceptance by the medical profession", *Analecta medico-historica*, iii (1968) 219-24; D. C. Lindberg, *Theories of Vision from Al-Kindi to Kepler* (Chicago, 1976), *Studies in the History of Medieval Optics* (London, 1986); M. H. Pirenne, *Optics, Painting and Photography* (Cambridge, 1970); R. Rashed, "Le *Discours de la lumière* d'Ihn al-Haytham (Alhazen)", *Revue d'histoire des sciences*, xxi (1968) 197-224, "Optique

(continued on p. 284)

REFERENCES

1. ORIGINAL SOURCES, WITH CATALOGUES AND TRANSLATIONS

(a) *Manuscripts*

Roger Bacon, *Opus maius*, British Museum MS Royal 7.F. vii (13 c.).
Roger Bacon, *Opus maius*, British Museum MS Royal 7.F. viii (13 c.).
Roger Bacon, *Perspectiva et de speculis* R. Baconis, Oxford MS Bodley 874 (15 c.). *Opus maius* v.
Rogeri Bacon *Opus majus*, Oxford MS Bodleian Library Digby 235 (15 c.).
Thomas Hobbes, *A Minute or first Draught of the Optiques in two parts, The first of Illumination, [The] second [of] Vision*, by Thomas Hobbes at Paris 1646, British Museum MS Harley 3360.
Thomas Hobbes, *Tractatus opticus*, and *A Short Tract on First Principles*, British Museum MS Harley 6796, ff. 193-266, 297-308. Extracts printed in Thomas Hobbes, *The Elements of Law*, ed. F. Tönnies (Cambridge, 1928) 152-81. See nn. 111, 140.
Isaac Newton, *Questiones quaedam philosophicae*, Cambridge MS University Library Add. 3996 (?1664-5).
Isaac Newton, Cambridge MS University Library Add. 3975 (c. 1665-93).
John Pecham. *Perspectiva Fratris Johannis de Pecham*, Oxford MS Bodleian Library Ashmole 1552 (14 c.) ff. 148ʳ-175ᵛ.
Theodorici Teutonici de Vriburgo, *De iride*, MS Öffentliche Bibliothek der Universität Basel, F. IV. 30 (14 c.).
Magistri Witelonis Poloni *De perspectiva magnum opus*, Oxford MS Bodleian Library Ashmole 424 (late 14 c.).

(b) *Printed works*

Henrici Cornelii Agrippae . . . *De occulta philosophia libri* (Antverpaie, *artium, atque excellentia verbi Dei declamatio* (Parisiis, 1531).
Henrici Cornelii Agrippae . . . *De occulta philosophia libri tres* (Antverpiae, 1531).
Francisci Aguilonii e Societate Iesu *Opticorum libri sex* (Antverpiae, 1613).
L. B. Alberti, *De pictura*, in M. Vitruvii Pollionis *De architectura libri decem* . . . (Amstelodami, 1649) 165 sqq.
L. B. Alberti. *Leone Battista Albertis kleinere kunsttheoretische Schriften* (*Della pittura libri tre; De statua; I cinque ordini architettonici*) im Original-text herausgegeben, übersetzt, erläutert . . . von H. Janitschek (*Quellenschriften für Kunstgeschichte*, xi; Wien, 1877).
L. B. Alberti, *On Painting*, translated with an introduction by J. R. Spencer (London, 1956).
Alhazeni Arabis *Opticae thesaurus libri septem*, nunc primum editi. . . . *Item* Vitellionis Thuringopoloni *libri* x. Omnes instaurati, figuris illustrati et aucti, adiectis etiam in Alhazeni commentariis, a Federico Risnero (Basiliae, 1572).
G. C. Aranzi. Iulii Caesaris Arantii Bononiensis . . . *Anatomicarum observationum liber* . . . (Venetiis, 1587).
Aristotle, *One the Soul*, and *On Sense and Sensible Objects*, with an English translation by W. S. Hett; *Meteorologica*, with an English translation by H. D. P. Lee (Loeb Classical Library; London and Cambridge, Mass., 1935, 1952).

Aristotle, *Complete Works,* translated into English under the editorship of J. A. Smith and W. D. Ross, 11 vol. (Oxford, 1908-31).

Averrois Cordubensis *Colliget libri vii* cum quibus etiam nunc primum in quinto libro impressimus translationem trium illorum . . . a Jacob Mantino. . . . Addidimus itidem post antiquam translationem tres illas sectiones Collectaneorum tribus Colliget libris, Secundo scilicet, Sexto et Septimo respondentes, a Iohanne Bruyerino Campegio, elegantissime latinitate donatas (Venetiis, 1553).

Avicenne perhypatetici philosophi ac medicorum . . . primi *Opera in lucem redacta . . . Logyca. Sufficientia. De caelo et mundo. De anima. De animalibus. De intelligentiis.* Alpharabius *De intelligentiis. Philosophia prima* (Venetiis), 1508.

Avicennae *Liber canonis de medicinis cordialibus et cantica,* iam olim quidem a Gerardo Carmonensi ex arabico sermone in latinum conversa, postea vero ab Andrea Alpago Bellunensis . . . infinitis pene correctionibus ad veterum exemplarium arabicorum fidem in margine factis . . . (Venetiis, 1555).

Avicenna : see also F. Rahman.

Rogerii Bacconis Angli, viri eminentissimi *Perspectiva* . . . nunc primum in lucem edita opera et studio Iohannis Combachii . . . (Francofurti, 1614). *Opus maius* v.

Fratris Rogeri Bacon . . . *Opus majus ad Clementem Quartum, Pontificem Romanum,* ex MS codice Dubliniensi, cum aliis quibusdam collato, nunc primum edidit S. Jebb (Londini, 1733).

Roger Bacon. *The ' Opus Majus' of Roger Bacon,* ed. J. H. Bridges, vols. i-ii (Oxford, 1897), vol. iii (London, 1900). Vols. ii and iii contain also *Tractatus* Rogeri Baconi *de multiplicatione specierum.*

Roger Bacon. *Un fragment inédit de l'Opus tertium de Roger Bacon précédé d'une étude sur ce fragment,* [par] P. Duhem (Quarracchi, 1909).

Daniel Barbaro, *La practica della perspettiva* (Venetia, 1568).

Berengario da Carpi. *Carpi commentaria cum amplissimis additionibus super Anatomia Mundini* una cum textu eiusdem in pristinum et verum nitorem redacto (Bononiae, 1521).

G. Berkeley, *Essay towards a New Theory of Vision* (Dublin, 1709).

G. Berkeley. *The Theory of Vision, or Visual Language, showing the immediate presence and providence of a Deity. Vindicated and Explained* (London, 1733).

G. Berkeley, *Works,* edited by A. A. Luce and T. E. Jessup, 9 vol. (London and Edinburgh, 1948-57).

William Briggs, "A new theory of vision, communicated to the Royal Society ", *Philosophical Collections* [of the Royal Society, ed. R. Hooke], No. 6 (London, 1682) 163, 167-78.

William Briggs, "A continuation of a discours about vision, with an examination of some late objections against it ", *Philosophical Transactions,* xii (1683) 171-82.

Hieronymi Cardani Mediolanensis *De subtilitate libri xxi* (Parisiis, 1550).

Hieronymi Cardani Mediolanensis, *De propria vita liber.* Ex Bibliotheca Gab. Naudaei (Parisiis, 1643).

Guy de Chauliac, chirurgien, maistre en médicine de l'Université de Montpellier, *La grande chirurgie composée en l'an 1363*, revue et collationnée sur les manuscrits et imprimés latins et français ornée de gravures, avec des notes . . . par E. Nicaise (Paris, 1890).

K. Clark, *A Catalogue of the Drawings of Leonardo da Vinci in the collection of His Majesty the King at Windsor Castle* (Cambridge, 1935).

Realdi Colombi Cremonensis . . . *De re anatomica libri xv* (Venetiis, 1559).

F. M. Cornford, *Plato's Theory of Knowledge. The Theaetatus and the Sophist of Plato translated with a running commentary* (London, 1935).

F. M. Cornford, *Plato's Cosmology. The Timaeus of Plato translated with a running commentary* (London, 1937).

A. C. Crombie, "Kepler: de modo visionis", in *Mélanges Alexandre Koyré*, ed. I. B. Cohen and R. Taton, i (Paris, 1964) 135-72.

R. Descartes, *Discours de la méthode pour bien conduire sa raison, et chercher la vérité dans les sciences. Plus La dioptrique, Les météores et La géometrie, qui sont des essais de cete méthode* (Leyde, 1637).

R. Descartes, *Discours de la méthode*, texte et commentaire par E. Gilson (Paris, 1947).

Renati Des-Cartes *Meditationes de prima philosophia . . . Objectiones doctorum aliquot virorum in praecedentes Meditationes cum responsionibus authoris* (Parisiis, 1641). Secunda editio septimis objectionibus antehac non visis aucta (Amstelodami, 1642).

Renati Des-Cartes *Principia philosophiae* (Amstelodami, 1644).

René Des Cartes, *Les passions de l'ame* (Amsterdam, 1649).

Renatus Des Cartes, *De homine* . . . (Lugduni Batavorum, 1662).

Descartes, *Le monde ou Traité de la lumiere, et des autres principaux objets des sens* . . . (Paris, 1664).

R. Des-Cartes, *Opuscula posthuma physica et mathematica* (Amstelodami, 1701).

R. Descartes, *Oeuvres*, publiées par C. Adam et P. Tannery, 12 vol. (Paris, 1897-1913).

Descartes, *Correspondance*, publiée avec un introduction et des notes par C. Adam et G. Milhaud, i-viii- (Paris, 1936-63-).

Laertii Diogenis *De vitis dogmatis et apophthegmatis eorum qui in philosophia claruerunt libri x*, Thoma Aldobrandino interprete (Roma, 1594).

Diogenes Laertius, *Lives of Eminent Philosophers*, with an English translation by R. D. Hicks, 2 vol. (Loeb Classical Library; London and Cambridge, Mass., 1925).

A. Dürer, *Underweysung der Messung, mit dem Zirckel und richtschent in Linien Ebnen und ganzen Corporen* . . . (Nürenberg, 1525).

Joseph Guichard Du Verney, *Traité de l'organe de l'ouïe* (Paris, 1683).

Euclidis *Optica et catoptrica,* nunquam antehac Graece aedita, eadem Latine reddita per Ioannem Penam Regium Mathematicum (Parisiis, 1557).

Euclidis quae supersunt omnia, ed. David Gregory (Oxford, 1703).

Euclidis *Optica, Opticorum recensio theoris, Catoptrica cum scholiis antiquis*, edidit I. L. Heiberg (*Opera omnia*, vii, Teubner; Lipsiae, 1895).

Euclid: see also P. Ver Eecke.

Euclid. "The Optics of Euclid", transl. by H. E. Burton, *Journal of the Optical Society of America*, xxxv (1945) 357-72.

Hieronymi Fabricii ab Aquapendente *De visione, voce, auditu* (Venetiis, 1600).

N. Ferrero, "Leonardo da Vinci: of the eye. An original new translation from *Codex D*", *American Journal of Ophthalmology*, xxxv (1952) 507-21.

Baron Della Foresta, *Vita dell' Abbate parto D. Francesco Maurolyco* (Messina, 1613).

Piero dei Franceschi, *De prospectiva pingendi,* edizione critica a cura di G. Nicco Fasola . . .2 pt. (Firenze, 1942).

K. Freeman, *Ancilla to the Pre-Socratic Philosophers.* A complete translation of the fragments in Diels, *Die Fragmente der Vorsokratiker* (Oxford, 1948).

Galeni *Omnia quae extant in Latinum sermonem conversa,* ex tertia Iuntarum editione (Venetiis, 1556).

Galeni *Opera* ex sexta Iuntarum editione (Venetiis, 1586).

Claudi Galeni *Opera omnia,* editionem curavit . . . C. G. Kühn, ii-v (Lipsiae, 1821-3).

Galen, *De usu partium,* x. English translation in *The American Encyclopaedia and Dictionary of Ophthalmology,* ed. Casey A. Wood, xi (Chicago, 1917) 8590-8621.

Galen, *On Anatomical Procedures,* translation of the surviving books with introduction and notes by C. Singer (London, 1956). Books i-ix.5, surviving in Greek.

Galen, *On Anatomical Procedures. The later books,* a translation by the late W. H. L. Duckworth edited by M. C. Lyons and B. Towers (Cambridge, 1962). Books ix.6-xv, surviving in Arabic translation.

Galileo Galilei, *Il saggiatore* (Roma, 1623).

Galileo Galilei, *Le opere,* edizione nazionale; direttore A. Favaro, coadiutore, I. del Lungo, 20 tom. (Firenze, 1890-1909).

Petri Gassendi Diniensis . . . *Opera,* 6 tom. (Lugduni, 1658).

Lorenzo Ghiberti, *Denkwürdigkeiten (I Commentarii),* zum ersten Male nach der Handschrift der Biblioteca nazionale in Florenz vollständig herausgegeben und erläutert von J. von Schlosser, 2 Bde. (Berlin, 1912).

Robert Grosseteste, *Libellus* Linconiensis *de phisicis lineis angulis et figuris per quas omnes actiones naturales complentur* (Nurenberge, 1503).

Robert Grosseteste, Bischofs von Lincoln, *Die philosophischen Werke,* zum erstenmal vollständig in kritischer Ausgabe besorgt von L. Baur (*Beiträge zur Geschichte der Philosophie des Mittelalters,* ix; Münster, 1912).

Albrechtus von Haller, *Elementa physiologiae corporis humani,* 8 tom. (Lausannae, 1757-8).

William Harvey, *Lectures on the Whole of Anatomy,* an annotated translation of *Praelectiones anatomiae universalis* by C. D. O'Malley, F. N. L. Poynter, K. F. Russell (Berkeley and Los Angeles, 1961).

William Harvey. *The Anatomical Lectures of William Harvey. Prelectiones anatomie universalis; De musculis,* edited, with an introduction, translation and notes by G. Whitteridge (Edinburgh and London, 1964).

H. von Helmholtz, *Treatise on Physiological Optics,* translated from the 3rd German edition, edited by J. P. C. Southall, 3 vol. (Menasha, Wisc., 1924-25).

Thomas Hobbes, *English Works* . . . edited by Sir W. Molesworth, vii (London,1845).

Thomae Hobbes, *Elementorum philosophiae,* secunda sectio, " De homine "; and *Tractatus opticus* and " Praefatio in Mersenni Ballisticam " (*Opera philosophica quae latine scripsit omina* . . . collecta . . . Gulielmo Molesworth, ii, v; Londini, 1839-45). See nn. 111, 140.

Thomas Hobbes, *The Elements of Law, Natural and Polite,* edited . . . by F. Tönnies (Cambridge, 1928).

Robert Hooke, *Posthumous Works, containing his Cutlerian Lectures and other Discourses* . . . published by R. Waller (London, 1705).

Hunain ibn Ishâq. *The Book of the Ten Treatises on the Eye ascribed to Hunain ibn Is-Hâq (809-877 A.D.). The earliest existing systematic text-book of ophthalmology,* the Arabic text edited from the only two known manuscripts, with an English translation and glossary by Max Meyerhof (Cairo, 1928).

Christiani Hugenii . . . *Opera posthuma, quae continent Dioptricam* . . . (Lugduni Batavorum, 1703).

Christiaan Huygens, *Oeuvres complètes,* publiées par la Société Hollandaise des Sciences, xiii (La Haye, 1916).

Iohannis Jessenii a Iessen, *Anatomiae Pragae anno MDC abs se solenniter administratae historia* (Witebergae, 1601).

Ioannis Keplerus, *Ad Vitellionem paralipomena, quibus astronomici pars optica traditur* (Francofurti, 1604). See also A. C. Crombie.

Ioannis Kepleri . . . *Dioptrice* . . . (Augustae Vindelicorum, 1611).

Johannes Kepler, *Gesammelte Werke,* herausgegeben im Auftrug der Bayerischen Akademie der Wissenschaften . . . Unter der Leitung von W. von Dyck und M. Caspar . . . F. Hammer, 18 Bde. (München, 1937-59). See below p. 107.

J. Ch. Kohlhans, *Tractatus opticus* (Lipsiae, 1663).

Phillipe de La Hire, *Reflexions sur la dissertation de Mr de la Hire touchant la conformation de l'oeil, envoyée à l'autheur du Journal des Sçavans* (Paris, 1685).

Phillipe de La Hire, *Mémoires de mathématique et de physique contenant:* . . . *Une dissertation des differences des sons de la corde de la trompette marine. Un traité des differens accidens de la vûe* (Paris, 1694).

A. van Leeuwenhoek. " A letter from Mr. Anthony Leeuwenhoeck Fellow of the Royal Society, dat. Apr. 14, 1684, containing observations about the cristallin humor of the eye, etc.", *Philosophical Transactions,* xiv (1684) 780 (wrongly numbered 790)-789. An account of the retina seen under the microscope, including the blood vessels and rods and cones, which he first observed in 1674 : *Philosophical Transactions,* viii (1674) 178-82. See *Collected Letters,* edited, illustrated and annotated by a committee of Dutch scientists, iv (Amsterdam, 1952) 208-51.

G. W. von Leibniz. *Nouveaux essais sur l'entendement humain* (1704), in *Oeuvres philosophiques latines et françoises de* . . . *Mr. de Leibnitz* tirées de ses manuscrits qui se conservent dans la Bibliothèque Royale à Hanovre, et publiées par . . R. E. Raspe . . . (Amsterdam, Leipzig, 1765).

G. W. Leibnitz, *New Essays concerning Human Understanding* . . . translated from the original Latin, French and German, with notes by A. G. Langley (New York, 1896).

Leonardo da Vinci : see also K. Clark and N. Ferrero.

Leonardo da Vinci. *Les manuscrits de Léonard de Vinci,* publiées en fac-similés phototypiques avec transcriptions littérales, traductions françaises, avant-propos et tables méthodiques par M. C. Ravaisson-Mollien, 6 tom. (Paris, 1881-91). Codices A, B & D, C., E & K, F & I, G, L & M, H, Ash. 2037 & 2038.

Leonardo da Vinci. *Das Buch von der Malerei, nach dem Codex Vaticanus (Urbinas) 1270* herausgegeben, übersetzt und erläutert von H. Ludwig, 3 Bde. (*Quellenschriften für Kunstgeschichte und Kunsttechnik des Mittelalters und der Renaissance,* xv-xvii; Wien, 1882).

Leonardo da Vinci, *Il Codice Atlantico nella Biblioteca Ambrosiana di Milano* . . . trascrizione diplomatica e critica di G. Piumati, 8 tom. (Milano, 1894-1904).

Leonardo da Vinci. *I manoscritti di Leonardo da Vinci della reale biblioteca di Windsor. Dell' anatomia fogli A, B,* . . . transcritti e annotati da G. Piumati, con traduzione in lingua francese (Parigi, 1898; Torino, 1901).

Leonardo da Vinci, *Quaderni d'anatomia,* pubblicati da O. C. L. Vangensten, A. Fonahn, H. Hopstock, 6 vol. (Christiana, 1912).

Leonardo da Vinci. *The Notebooks of Leonardo da Vinci,* arranged, rendered into English and introduced by E. MacCurdy, 2 vol. (London, 1938).

Leonardo da Vinci, *Literary Works,* ed. and transl. J. P. and I. A. Richter, 2nd ed., 2 vol. (Oxford, 1939); C. Pedretti, *Commentary* (1977).

Leonardo da Vinci. *Selections from the Notebooks of Leonardo da Vinci,* edited with commentaries by I. A. Richter (Oxford, 1952).

Leonardo da Vinci, *On the Human Body. The anatomical, physiological and embryological drawings of Leonardo da Vinci,* with translations, emendations and a biographical introduction by C. D. O'Malley and J. B. de C. M. Saunders (New York, 1952).

Leonardo da Vinci, *Treatise on Painting, Codex Urbinas Latinas 1270,* translated and annotated by A. P. McMahon, 2 vol. (Princeton, 1956).

Leonardo da Vinci. *Fragments at Windsor Castle from Codex Atlanticus,* edited by C. Pedretti (London, 1957).

Léonard de Vinci, *Dessins anatomiques (anatomie artistique, descriptive et fonctionelle),* choix et présentation pas P. Huard (Paris, 1961).

Léonard de Vinci, *Dessins scientifiques et techniques,* choix et présentation par P. Huard et M. D. Grmek (Paris, 1962).

Leonardo da Vinci, *On Painting. A lost book (Libro A),* reassembled from the Codex Vaticanus Urbinas 1270 and from the Codex Leicester by C. Pedretti (Berkeley and Los Angeles, 1964).

John Locke, *An Essay concerning Humane Understanding* (London, 1690).

Nicolas Malebranche. *De la recherche de la verité* . . ., 4 tom. (Paris, 1674).

Malebranche, *De la recherche de la vérité* . . . introduction et texte établi par Geneviève Lewis, 2 tom. (Paris, 1946).

Antonio Manetti. *Vita di Filippo Brunelleschi* [ed. E. Toesca] (Firenze, 1927).

E. Mariotte; J. Pecquet. *Nouvelle découverte touchant la veüe* (Paris, 1668).

E. Mariotte. " A new discovery touching vision ", *Philosophical Transactions,* iii (1668) 668-71.

E. Mariotte. "Nouvelle découverte touchant la veuë", *Le journal des sçavans*, iii (1668) 402-10.

E. Mariotte; J. Pecquet; Cl. Perrault. "Sur l'organe de la vision " (1669), *Histoire de l'Académie royale des Sciences*, i (1733) 102-3.

E. Mariotte; Cl. Perrault. " An account of two letters of Mr. Perrault, and Mr. Mariotte, concerning vision ", *Philosophical Transactions*, xiii (1683) 265-7.

E. Mariotte; J. Pecquet; Cl. Perrault. "Letters escrites sur le sujet d'une nouvelle decouverte, touchant la veuë, faite par M. Mariotte ", *Acta Eruditorum*, Anno 1683, pp. 67-73.

E. Mariotte; J. Pecquet; Cl. Perrault. *Nouvelle découverte touchant la vûe, contenue en plusieurs lettres écrites par Messrs. Mariotte, Pecquet & Perrault, de l'Académie Roïale des Sciences*, nouvelle edition, revûe & corrigée (*Oeuvres de Mariotte*, nouvelle edition, La Haye, 1740, ii) 495-534.

Abbatis Francisci Maurolyci Messanensis *Photismi de lumine et umbra ad perspectivam et radiorum incidentiam facientes, Diaphanorum partes, seu libri tres* . . . (Neapoli, 1611; Lugduni, 1613).

Marin Mersenne. *Les préludes de l'harmonie universelle, ou questions curieuses* (Paris, 1634).

F. Marini Mersenni . . . *Harmonicorum libri* . . . *Harmonicorum instrumentorum iv* . . . (Lutetiae Parisiorum, 1636).

F. Marin Mersenne de l'Ordre des Minimes, *Harmonie universelle, contenant la theorie et la pratique de la musique* (Paris, 1636-37).

F. M. Mersenni M. *Universae geometriae, mixtaeque mathematicae synopsis, et bini refractionum demonstratarum tractatus* (Parisiis, 1644).

F. Marini Mersenni Minimi *Cogitata physico-mathematica* (Parisiis, 1644).

Marin Mersenne. *Novarum observationum physico-mathematicarum* F. Marini Mersenni Minimi *tomus iii*, quibus accessit Aristarchus Samius *De mundi systemata* (Parisiis, 1647).

Marin Mersenne. *L'optique et la catoptrique du Reverend Pere Mersenne Minime*, nouvellement mise en lumiere après la mort de l'autheur (Paris, 1651).

J. Méry, " Des mouvemens de l'iris, et par occasion la partie principale de l'organe de la vûe ", *Histoire de l'Académie royale des Sciences*, Année 1704 (Paris, 1722) 261-71.

Mondino dei Luzzi. *Anothomia* Mundini *totius corporis humani*, in Joannes de Ketham, *Fasciculus medicine* (Venetiis, 1495).

Mondino dei Luzzi; Guido de Vigevano. *Anatomies de Mondino dei Luzzi et de Guido de Vigevano* [facsimile edited by] E. Wickersheimer (Paris, 1926).

Johannes Müller, *Handbuch der Physiologie des Menschen für Vorlesungen*, 2te Aufl., 2 Bde. (Coblenz, 1835-40).

Johannes Müller, *Elements of Physiology*, transl. from the German with notes by W. Baly, 2 vol. (London, 1838-42).

L. A. Muratori, *Rerum Italicarum scriptores*, xxv (Milano, 1751).

M. C. Nahm (editor), *Selections from Early Greek Philosophy*, 3rd ed. (New York, 1947).

Sir Isaac Newton, *Opticks: or, a Treatise of the Reflections, Refractions, Inflections and Colours of Light*, 4th edition (London, 1730).

Isaac Newton, *Unpublished Scientific Papers*. A selection from the Portsmouth Collection in the University Library, Cambridge, chosen, edited and translated by A. Rupert Hall and M. Boas Hall (Cambridge, 1962).

Magistri Guilhelmi di Ockam, *Tabule ad diversas huius operis, super quattuor libros Sententiarum annotationes et ad Centilogii theologici eiusdem conclusiones facile reperiendas apprime conducibles* (Lugduni, 1495); ed. Gal et al. (1967-82): above p. 71.

Guillelmus de Occam O.F.M., *Opera plurima*, 4 vol. (Lyon, 1494-96; réimpression en fac-similé, London, 1962).

John Pecham. *Perspectiva tribus libris succinctis denuo correcta, et figuris illustrata*, per Pascalium Hamellium mathematicum regum (Lutetiae, 1556).

Jean Pelerin. Viator, *De artificiali perspectiva* (Tulli, 1505).

Claude Perrault, *Essais de physique ou recueil de plusieurs traitez touchant les choses naturelles* (i-iii, Paris, 1680; iv, 1688).

Felicis Plateri archiatri et profess. Basil., *De corporis humani structura et usu libri iii* (Basileae, 1583).

Plato, *Theaetetus, Philebus,* with English translations by H. N. Fowler; *Timaeus,* with transl. by R. G. Bury; *Republic,* with transl. by P. Shorey, 2 vol. (Loeb Classical Library; London and Cambridge, Mass.. 1921-30). See also F. M. Cornford.

Io. Bapt. Portae Neapolitani *Magiae naturalis libri xx* (Neapoli,1558, 1589).

John Baptista Porta, a Neapolitane, *Natural Magick* (London, 1658).

Ioan. Baptistae Portae Neap., *De refractione optices parte libri novem* (Neapoli, 1593).

Ptolemy, *L'Ottica di Cl. Tolomeo* da Eugenio Ammiraglio di Sicilia — scrittore del secolo xii — ridotta in latino sovra la traduzione araba di un testo greco imperfetto, ora per la prima volta conforme a un codice della Biblioteca Ambrosiana . . . publicata da G. Govi (Torino, 1885). This is the first printed edition of a work known in the West from the 13th century and copied several times in manuscript in the 16th and 17th centuries.

Ptolemy. *L'Optique de Claude Ptolémée dans la version latine d'après l'arabe de l'émir Eugène de Sicile,* édition critique et exégétique par A. Lejeune (Louvain, 1956).

F. Rahman, *Avicenna's Psychology. An English translation of Kitāb al-Najāt,, book ii, chapter vi,* with historico-philosophical notes and textual improvements on the Cairo edition (Oxford, 1952).

G. Reisch, *Margarita philosophica* . . . (Argentinae, 1504).

Rufus d'Ephèse, *Oeuvres,* . . . publication commencée par le Dr. Ch. Daremberg, continuée et terminée par Ch. E. Ruelle (Paris, 1879).

Christophorus Scheiner, *Oculus, hoc est, fundamentum opticum* . . . (Oeniponti, 1619).

Christopherus Scheiner, *Rosa ursina* . . . (Bracciani, 1630).

Sexti Empirici . . . *Adversus mathematicos,* Gentiano Herveto Aurelio interprete. Eiusdem Sexti *Pyrroniarum hypotyposeon libri tres* . . . (Parisis, 1569).

Sexti Empirici *Opera quae extant* . . . *Pyrrhoniarum hypotyposeon libri iii* . . . Henrico Stephano interprete: *Adversus mathematicos,* Gentiano Herveto Aureliano interprete (Genevae, 1621).

Sexti Empirici *Opera,* recensuit H. Mutschmann et J. Mau, indices collegit K. Janáček (Teubner; Lipsiae, 1958-62).

Sextus Empiricus, *Outlines of Pyrrhonism* and *Against the Professors,* with an English translation by R. G. Bury, 4 vol. (Loeb Classical Library; London, 1939-49).

Robert Smith, *A Compleat System of Opticks,* 2 vol. (Cambridge, 1738).

Nicolaus Steno, *Discours . . . sur l'anatomie du cerveau, a messieurs de l'Assemblée, qui se fait chez Monsieur Thevenot* (Paris, 1669).

Nicolai Stenonis *Opera philosophica,* edited by V. Maar, 2 vol. (Copenhagen, 1910).

G. M. Stratton, *Theophrastus and the Greek Physiological Psychology before Aristotle* (London, 1917).

Joh. Christoph. Sturmius, *Oculus, de visionis organo et ratione genuina, dissertatio physica, . . .* (Altdorffi, 1678).

Johannes Christophorus Sturmius . . . *Collegium Experimentale sive Curiosum . . .* (Norimborgae, 1676).

Theodoricus Teutonicus de Vriberg, *De iride et radialibus impressionibus* (Dietrich von Freiberg *Ueber den Regenbogen und die durch Strahlen erzeugten Eindrücke*), zum ersten Male nach den Handschriften herausgegeben und mit einer Einleitung versehen von J. Würschmidt (*Beiträge zur Geschichte der Philosophie des Mittelalters,* xii. 5-6; Münster, 1914).

Theophrastus : see G. M. Stratton.

Constantii Varolii, . . . *Anatomiae, sive de resolutione corporis humani . . . libri iv . . .* a J. B. Cortesio . . . nunc primum editi . . . Ejusdem Varolii et H. Mercurialis *De nervis opticis . . . epistolae* (Francofurti, 1591).

P. Ver Eecke, *Euclide, l'optique et la catoptrique,* oeuvres traduites pour la première fois du grec en français avec une introduction et des notes (Paris et Brughes, 1938; 2nd ed. 1959).

Andreae Vesalii Bruxellensis, scholae medicorum Patavinae professoris, *De humani corporis fabrica libri septem* (Basileae, 1543).

Andreae Vesalii *Anatomicarum Gabrielis Falloppii observationum examen* (Venetiis, 1564).

Richard Waller, " Concerning the burning-glasses of the ancients, from the History of the Academie Royale des Sciences, for the year 1708, with some remarks ", in *Philosophical Experiments and Observations of the late eminent Dr. Robert Hooke, S.R.S., . . . and other eminent virtuoso's in his time,* publish'd by W. Derham, F.R.S. (London, 1726) 348-61.

Thomas Willis, *Cerebri anatome, cui accessit nervorum descriptio et usus* (Londini, 1664). With illustrations by Christopher Wren.

Thomas Willis, *De anima brutorum quae hominis vitalis ac sensitiva est, exercitationes duae* (Oxonii 1672).

Thomas Willis. *The Remaining Medical Works of that famous and renowned physician Dr. Thomas Willis . . .* Englished by S. P[ordage] (London, 1681).

Thomas Willis, *Two Discourses Concerning the Soul of Brutes, which is that of the vital and sensitive of man,* Englished by S. Pordage, (London, 1683).

Thomas Willis. *Dr. Willis's Practice of Physick, being the whole works of that renowned and famous physician* (London, 1684).

Witelo. Vitellonis Thuringopoloni *Opticae libri decem*, instaurati . . . a Federico Risnero (Basiliae, 1572).

Christopher Wren. *Parentalia: or, Memoirs of the Family of the Wrens; viz. of Mathew Bishop of Ely, Christopher Dean of Windsor, etc., but chiefly of Sir Christopher Wren,* . . . compiled by his son Christopher . . . (London, 1750).

2. MODERN WORKS

R. I. Aaron, *John Locke,* 2nd ed. (Oxford, 1955).

J. S. Ackerman, " Ars sine scientia nihil est ", *Art Bulletin,* xxxi (1949) 84-111.

F. Alessio, " ' De homine ' e ' A minute or first draught of the optiques ' di Hobbes ", *Rivista critica di storia della filosofia,* xvii (1962) 393-410.

F. Alessio, " Questioni inediti di ottica di Biagio Pelacani da Parma ", *Rivista critica di storia dell filosofia,* xvi (1961) 79-110, 188-221.

F. Alessio, " Per uno studio sull'ottica del trecento ", *Studi medievale,* 3ª serie, ii.2 (1961).

A. Ames, K. N. Ogle and G. H. Gliddon, " Corresponding retinal points, the horopter and size and shape of ovular images ", *Journal of the Optical Society of America,* xxii (1932) 538-631.

F. H. Anderson, " The influence of contemporary science on Locke's methods and results ", *University of Toronto Studies: Philosophy,* ii.1 (1923).

P. André, *La vie du R. P. Malebranche, prêtre de l'Oratoire, avec l'historie de ses ouvrages,* publiée par le P. Ingold (Paris, 1886).

F. Antal, *Florentine Painting and its Social Background* (London, 1947).

G. C. Argan, " The architecture of Brunelleschi and the origins of perspective theory in the fifteenth century ", *Journal of the Warburg Institute,* ix (1946) 96-121.

D. Argentieri, " L'ottica di Leonardo ", in *Leonardo da Vinci,* editione curata dalla Mostra di Leonardo da Vinci in Milano (Novara, 1939) 405-36.

G. E. Arrington, Jr., *A History of Ophthalmology* (New York, 1959).

C. Baeumker, *Witelo, ein Philosoph und Naturforscher des xiii. Jahrhunderts* (*Beiträge zur Geschichte der Philosophie des Mittelalters,* iii.2; Münster, 1908).

C. Bailey, *The Greek Atomists and Epicurus* (Oxford, 1928).

D. M. Balme, *Aristotle's Use of the Teleological Explanation. Inaugural lecture at Queen Mary College* (London, 1965).

H. Bauer, *Die Psychologie Alhazens, auf Grund von Alhazens Optik dargestellt* (*Beiträge zur Geschichte der Philosophie des Mittelalters,* x.5; Münster, 1911).

L. Baur, " Der Einfluss des Robert Grosseteste auf die wissenschaftliche Richtung des Roger Bacon ", in *Roger Bacon Essays,* ed. A. G. Little (Oxford, 1914) 33-53.

L. Baur, *Die Philosophie des Robert Grosseteste* (*Beiträge zur Geschichte der Philosophie des Mittelalters,* xviii. 4-6; Münster, 1917).

J. I. Beare, *Greek Theories of Elementary Cognition from Alcmaeon to Aristotle* (Oxford, 1906).

S. A. Bedini, "The role of automata in the history of technology", *Technology and Culture*, v (1964) 24-42.

A. Bednarski, "Das anatomische Augenbild von J. Peckham", *Sudhoffs Archiv für Geschichte der Medizin*, xxii (1929), 352-6.

A. Bednarski, "Die anatomischen Augenbilder in den Handschriften des Roger Bacon, Johann Peckham und Witelo", *Sudhoffs Archiv für Geschichte der Medizin*, xxiv (1931) 60-78.

L. Belloni, "Schemi e modelli della machina vivente nel seicento", *Physis*, v (1963) 259-98.

G. Bergsträsser, *Ḥunain ibn Isḥāḳ und seine Schule* (Leiden, 1913).

H. G. Beyen, "Die antike Zentralperspektive", *Archäologischer Anzeizer (Beiblatt zum Jahrbuch des deutschen Archäologischen Instituts*, liv, 1939) 47-72.

A. Birkenmajer, "Etudes sur Witelo, i-iv", *Bulletin international de l'Académie polonaise des sciences et des lettres* (Cracovie), Classe d'hist. et de philos., Année 1918, pp. 4-6, 1920, pp. 354-60, 1922, pp. 6-9.

G. Bonno, *Les relations intellectuelles de Locke avec la France* (Berkeley and Los Angeles, 1955).

E. G. Boring, *Sensation and Perception in the History of Experimental Psychology* (New York, 1942).

E. G. Boring, *A History of Experimental Psychology*, 2nd ed. (New York, 1950).

C. B. Boyer, "The theory of the rainbow: medieval triumph and failure", *Isis*, xlix (1958) 378-90; *The Rainbow* (New York, 1959).

F. Brandt, *Thomas Hobbes' Mechanical Conception of Nature* (Copenhagen, 1928).

E. Bréhier, *Chrysippe et l'ancienne stoicisme* (Paris, 1951).

G. S. Brett, *The Philosophy of Gassendi* (London, 1908).

G. S. Brett, *A History of Psychology*, 3 vol. (London, 1912-21); edited and abridged by R. S. Peters (London, 1953).

A. M. Brizio, *Razzi incidenti e razzi refressi (del fo 94ᵛ ed altri del Codice Arundel) III lettura vinciana, Vinci, Biblioteca Leonardiana, 21 aprile 1963* (Firenze, 1964).

M. S. Bunim, *Space in Medieval Painting and the Forerunners of Perspective* (New York, 1940).

D. A. Callus (editor), *Robert Grosseteste, Scholar and Bishop* (Oxford, 1955).

G. Calvi, *I manoscritti di Leonardo da Vinci dal punto di vista cronologico, storico e biografico* (Bologna, 1925).

G. Canguilhem, *La formation du concept de réflexe au xviie et xviiie siècle* (Paris, 1955).

G. Canguilhem, "The role of analogies and models in biological discovery", in *Scientific Change*, edited by A. C. Crombie (London, 1963) 507-20.

G. Canguilhem, "La physiologie animale", in *Histoire générale des sciences*, publiée sous la direction de R. Taton, ii (Paris, 1958) 593-619.

M. Caspar, *Kepler*, translated and edited by D. Hellman (New York, 1959).

A. Chapuis et E. Gélis, *Le monde des automates: étude historique et technique*, 2 tom. (Paris, 1928).

A. Chapuis, E. Droz, *Automata. An historical and technological study*, translated by A. Reid (Neuchâtel and London, 1958).

A. Chastel, *Art et humanisme à Florence au temps de Laurent le Magnifique* (Paris, 1959).

M. Clagett, *Greek Science in Antiquity* (New York, 1956).

Sir Kenneth Clark, *Leon Battista Alberti on Painting* (London, 1944).

P. F. Cranefield, "A seventeenth-century view of mental deficiency and schizophrenia : Thomas Willis on 'stupidity or foolishness' ", *Bulletin of the History of Medicine*, xxxv (1961) 291-316.

A. C. Crombie, "Avicenna's influence on the medieval scientific tradition ", in *Avicenna: Scientist and Philosopher*, edited by G. M. Wickens (London, 1952),

A. C. Crombie, *Robert Grosseteste and the Origins of Experimental Science 1100-1700* (Oxford, 1953; 3rd impression 1971). With bibliography on medieval optics.

A. C. Crombie, "The significance of medieval discussions of scientific method for the scientific revolution ", in *Critical Problems in the History of Science*, ed. M. Clagett (Madison, Wisc., 1959) 79-101.

A. C. Crombie, *Augustine to Galileo. Medieval and Early Modern Science*, 2nd ed., 2 vol. (New York, 1959, 3rd ed. (Cambridge Mass. & London, 1979).

A. C. Crombie, "Some aspects of Descartes' attitudes to hypothesis and experiment ", *Actes du 2ème Symposium international d'Histoire des Sciences, Pise-Vinci 16-18 juin 1958* (Paris, 1960) 192-201.

A. C. Crombie (editor), *Scientific Change. Historical studies in the intellectual, social and technical conditions for scientific discovery and technical invention, from antiquity to the present* (London and New York, 1963).

A. C. Crombie, "The study of the senses in renaissance science ", *Proceedings of the Tenth International Congress of the History of Science: Ithaca, New York, 1962*, i (Paris, 1964) 93-114.

A. C. Crombie, "The relevance of the middle ages to the scientific movement ", in *Perspectives in Medieval History*, edited by K. F. Drew and F. S. Lear (Chicago, 1964) 35-57.

A. C. Crombie, "Early concepts of the senses and the mind ", *Scientific American*, ccx (May, 1964) 108-16.

A. C. Crombie and M. A. Hoskin, "The scientific movement and its influence, 1610-1650 ", and "The scientific movement and the diffusion of scientific ideas, 1688-1751 ", in *The New Cambridge Modern History*, iv, vi (1970).

E. J. Dijksterhuis, *The Mechanization of the World Picture*, transl. by G. Dikshoorn (Oxford, 1961).

K. Doehlemann, "Die Entwicklung der Perspektive in der altniederländischen Kunst ", *Repertorium für Kunstwissenschaft*, xxxiv (1911) 392-422, 500-35.

A. G. Drachmann, *Ktesibios, Philon and Heron; a study in ancient pneumatics* (Copenhagen, 1948).

A. G. Drachmann, *The Mechanical Technology of Greek and Roman Antiquity* (Copenhagen and London, 1963).

P. Duhem, *Le système du monde. Histoire des doctrines cosmologiques de Platon à Copernic*, 10 tom. (Paris, 1913-59).

W. Elsaesser, "Die Funktion des Auges bei Leonardo da Vinci", *Zeitschrift für Mathematik und Physik*, historisch-litterarische Abteilung, xlv (1900) 1-6.

John Field, H. W. Magoun and Victor E. Hall (editors), *Handbook of Physiology: Section 1: Neurophysiology*, 3 vol. (Washington, D.C., 1959-60).

P. Francastel, *Peinture et Societé* (Paris, 1952).

V. Fukala, "Der arabische Artz Averrhoës war der erste, welche die Netzhaut als den lichtempfindlichen Theil des Auges erkannte", *Archiv für Augenheilkunde*, xlii (1900) 203-14.

E. Garin, *La cultura filosofica del rinascimento italiano* (Firenze, 1961).

E. Garin, *Italian Humanism*, transl. by P. Munz (Oxford, 1966).

F. H. Garrison, *An Introduction to the History of Medicine*, 4th ed., revised (Philadelphia, 1929).

B. Gille, *Les ingénieurs de la renaissance* (Paris, 1964).

E. Gilson, *Etudes sur le rôle de la pensée médiévale dans la formation du système cartésien* (*Etudes de philosophie médiévale*, xiii; Paris, 1930).

D. Gioseffi, *Perspectiva artificialis. Per la storia della prospettiva* (Trieste, 1957).

E. Gombrich, *Art and Illusion, a study in the psychology of pictorial representation* (London, 1960).

R. L. Gregory, *Eye and Brain* (London, 1966).

W. de Grüneisen, "La perspective: esquisse de son évolution des origines jusqu'à la renaissance", *Mélanges d'archéologie et d'historie*, xxxi (1911) 393-434.

A. Haas, "Antike Lichttheorien", *Archiv für Geschichte der Philosophie*, xx (1907) 345-86.

A. Haas, "Die ältesten Beobachtungen auf dem Gebiete der Dioptrick", *Archiv für die Geschichte der Naturwissenschaften und der Technik*, ix (1922) 108-111.

G. D. Hadzsits, *Lucretius and his Influence* (London, 1935).

A. R. Hall, "Sir Isaac Newton's Note-Book, 1661-5", *The Cambridge Historical Journal*, ix (1949) 239-50.

A. R. Hall, "Further optical experiments of Isaac Newton", *Annals of Science*, xi (1955) 27-43.

D. W. Hamlyn, *Sensation and Perception. A history of the philosophy of perception* (London, 1961).

L. H. Heydenreich, *Leonardo da Vinci* (New York and Basel, 1954).

J. Hirschberg, *Geschichte der Augenheilkunde* (Graefe-Saemisch, *Handbuch der gesamten Augenheilkunde*, 2te Aufl., xii-xiv; Leipzig, 1899-1912).

J. Hirschberg and J. Lippert, *Die Augenheilkunde des Ibn Sina*, aus dem Arabischen übersetzt und erläutert (Leipzig, 1902).

H. E. Hofstetter, "Leonardo and contact lenses", *American Journal of Optometry*, xxx (1953) 41-44.

G. Huxley, *Anthemius of Tralles. A study of later Greek geometry* (Greek, Roman and Byzantine Monographs, i; Cambridge, Mass., 1959).

J. Itard, "Les lois de la réfraction de la lumière chez Kepler", *Revue d'histoire des sciences*, x (1957) 59-68.

W. M. Ivins, *On the Rationalization of Sight, with an examination of three renaissance texts on perspective* (New York, 1938).

W. M. Ivins, *Art and Geometry* (Cambridge, Mass., 1946).

W. Jablonski, " Die Theorie des Sehens im griechischen Altertum ", *Sudhoffs Archiv für Geschichte der Medizin*, xxiii (1930) 306-31.

J. Jacquot, " Un document inédit : les notes de Charles Cavendish sur la première version du De corpore de Hobbes ", *Thales,* viii (1952) 36-86.

J. Jacquot, " Notes on an unpublished work of Thomas Hobbes ", *Notes and Records of the Royal Society,* ix (1952) 188-95.

F. R. Johnson, *Astronomical Thought in Renaissance England* (Baltimore, 1937).

H. W. Jones, " Sir Christopher Wren and natural philosophy : with a check list of his scientific activities ", *Notes and Records of the Royal Society,* xiii (1958) 19-37.

D. Kaufmann, *Die Sinne. Beiträge zur Geschichte der Physiologie und Psychologie im Mittelalter aus hebräischen und arabischen Quellen* (Leipzig, 1884).

K. D. Keele, *Leonardo da Vinci on movement of the heart and blood* (London, 1952).

K. D. Keele, " Leonardo da Vinci's physiology of the senses ", in *International Symposium on Leonardo da Vinci 2-8 May -1966* (University of California, Los Angeles; in press).

A. G. Keller, *A Theatre of Machines* (London, 1964).

G. J. Kern, *Die Grundzüge der linear-perspektivischen Darstellung in der Kunst der Gebrüder Van Eyck und ihrer Schule . . .* (Leipzig, 1904).

G. J. Kern, " Die Kritik der perspektivischen Zeichnung und ihre Bedeutung für die Kunstgeschichte ", *Sitzungsberichte der Kunstgeschichtliche Gesellschaft, Berlin,* vi (1905) 37-42.

G. J. Kern, " Perspektive und Bildarchitektur bei Jan van Eyck ", *Repertorium für Kunstwissenschaft,* xxxv (1912) 27-64.

G. J. Kern, " Die Anfänge der zentralperspektivischen Konstruktion in der italienischen Malerei des 14. Jahrhunderts ", *Mitteilungen des Kunsthistorischen Instituts in Florenz,* i (1912) 39-65.

G. J. Kern, " Die Entwicklung der zentralperspektivischen Konstruktion in der Europäischen Malerei von der Spätantike bis zur Mitte des 15. Jahrhunderts ", *Forschungen und Fortschritte,* xiii (1937) 181-4.

G. J. Kern, " Das Jahreszeitenmosaik der Münchner Glyptothek und die Skenographie bei Vitruv ", *Archäologischer Anzeiger (Beiblatt zum Jahrbuch des Deutschen Archäologischen Instituts,* lxxxiii, 1938) 245-65.

G. S. Kirk and J. E. Raven, *The Presocratic Philosophers. A critical history with a selection of texts* (Cambridge, 1957, 1983).

A. C. Klebs, " Incunabula scientifica et medica ", *Osiris,* iv (1938) 1-359.

R. Klein, " Les humanistes et la science ", *Bibliothèque d'humanisme et renaissance,* xxiii (1961) 7-16.

R. Klein, " Pomponius Gauricus on perspective ", *The Art Bulletin,* xliii (1961) 211-30.

D. J. Korteweg, " Descartes et les manuscrits de Snellius ", *Revue de métaphysique et de morale* iv (1896) 489-501.

A. Koyré, " L'oeuvre astronomique de Kepler ", *XVIIe Siècle,* Paris, No. 30 (1956) 69-109.

A. Koyré, *La révolution astronomique: Copernic, Kepler, Borelli* (Paris, 1961).

A. Koyré, *Newtonian Studies* (London, 1965).

A. Koyré, *Etudes d'histoire de la pensée scientifique* (Paris, 1966).

P. Kramer, "Descartes und das Brechungsgesetz des Lichtes", *Abhandlungen zür Geschichte der Mathematik*, iv (1882) 233-78.

W. Kranz, "Die älteste Farbenlehre der Griechen", *Hermes*, xlvii (1912) 126-40.

R. Krautheimer, *Lorenzo Ghiberti* (Princeton, 1956). With bibliography on linear perspective.

J. Laird, *Hobbes* (Oxford, 1934).

E. H. Land, "Experiments in color vision", *Scientific American*, cc (May 1959) 84-99.

G. Leisegang, *Descartes Dioptrik* (Meisenheim-am-Glan, 1954).

A. Lejeune, *Euclide et Ptolémée. Deux stades de l'optique géométrique grecque* (*Université de Louvain, Recueil de travaux d'histoire et de philosophie*, iii. 31; Louvain, 1948).

A. Lejeune, *Recherches sur la catoptrique grecque d'après les sources antiques et médiévales* (*Académie royale de Belgique. Classe des lettres et des sciences morales et politiques, Mémoires*, lii, Brussels, 1957).

R. Lenoble, *Marin Mersenne, ou la naissance du mécanisme* (Paris, 1943).

Léonard de Vinci et l'expérience scientifique au xvi siècle (*Colloques internationalaux du Centre national de la Recherche Scientifique, Sciences humaines*, Paris 4-7 juillet 1952; Paris, 1953).

J. Y. Lettvin, H. R. Maturana, W. S. McCulloch and W. H. Pitts, "What the frog's eye tells the frog's brain", *Proceedings of the Institute of Radio Engineers*, xliii (1959) 1940-51.

D. C. Lindberg, "The 'Perspectiva communis' of John Pecham: its influence, sources and content", *Archives internationales d'histoire des sciences*, xviii (1965) 37-53.

A. G. Little (editor), *Roger Bacon, Essays contributed by various writers on the occasion of the commemoration of his birth* (Oxford, 1914).

H. A. Lloyd, "Mechanical timekeepers", in *A History of Technology*, edited by C. Singer, E. J. Holmyard, A. R. Hall and T. I. Williams, iii (Oxford, 1957) 648-75.

J. Lohne, "Thomas Harriott (1560-1621). The Tycho Brahe of optics", *Centaurus*, vi (1959) 113-21.

J. Lohne, "Zur Geschichte des Brechungsgesetzes", *Sudhoffs Archiv für Geschichte der Medizin und der Naturwissenschaften*, xlvii (1963) 151-72.

D. Odon Lattin, *Psychologie et morale aux xiie et xiiie siècles*, 4 tom. (Louvain, 1942-54).

A. A. Luce, *Berkeley and Malebranche* (Oxford, 1934).

H. Magnus, *Die Anatomie des Auges bei den Griechen und Römern* (Leipzig, 1878).

H. Magnus, *Die Augenheilkunde der Alten* (Breslau, 1901).

H. Magnus, *Die Anatomie des Auges in ihrer geschichtlichen Entwicklung* (Breslau, 1906).

C. Maltese, "Per Leonardo prospettico", *Raccolta vinciana*, xix (1962), 303-14.

P. Mesnard, "L'ésprit de la physiologie cartésienne", *Archives de philosophie*, xiii, No. 2 (1937) 181-220.

J. Mesnil, "Masaccio et la théorie de la perspective", *La Revue de l'art ancien de moderne*, xxxv (1914) 145-56.

J. Mesnil, "Die Kunstlehre der Frührenaissance im Werke Masaccios", *Vorträge Bibliothek Warburg, 1925-26* (Leipzig, Berlin, 1928) 122-46.

M. Meyerhof, "New light on Ḥunain ibn Isḥāq", *Isis*, viii (1926) 685-724.

G. Nicco Fasola, "Svolgimento del pensiero prospettico nei trattati da Euclide a Piero della Francesca", *Le arti*, v (1942-43) 59-71.

K. N. Ogle, "An analytical treatment of the longitudinal horopter", *Journal of the Optical Society of America*, xxii (1932) 666-728.

L. Olschki, *Geschichte der neusprachlichen wissenschaftlichen Literatur: i, Die Literatur der Technik und der angewandten Wissenschaften vom Mittelalter bis zur Renaissance* (Heidelberg, 1919); ii, *Bildung und Wissenschaft im Zeitalter der Renaissance in Italien* (Leipzig, 1922); iii, *Galilei und seine Zeit* (Halle a.s., 1927).

C. D. O'Malley and E. Clarke, "The discovery of the auditory ossicles", *Bulletin of the History of Medicine*, xxxv (1961) 419-41.

C. D. O'Malley, *Andreas Vesalius of Brussels 1514-1564* (Berkeley and Los Angeles, 1964).

A. Pacchi, "Ruggero Bacone e Roberto Grossatesta in un inedito hobbesiano del 1634", *Rivista critica di storia della filosofia*, xx (1965) 499-502.

A. Pacchi, *Convenzione e ipotesi nella formazione della filosofia naturale di Thomas Hobbes* (Firenze, 1965).

W. Pagel, "An Harveyan prelude to Harvey", *History of Science*, ii (1963) 114-25.

E. Panofsky, "Das perspektivische Verfahren Leone Battista Albertis", *Kunstchronik*, xxvi (1915) 506-15.

E. Panofsky, "Die Perspektive als symbolische Form", *Vorträge der Bibliothek Warburg, 1924-25* (Leipzig, Berlin, 1927) 258-330.

E. Panofsky, *Early Netherlandish Painting, its origins and character*, 2 vol. (Cambridge, Mass., 1953).

E. Panofsky, "Artist, scientist, genius: notes on the 'Renaissance-Dämmerung'", *The Renaissance; Six Essays*, edited by W. K. Ferguson jr. (New York, 1962).

A. Parronchi, "Le fonti di Paolo Uccello", *Paragone*, lxxxix (1957) 3-32, xcv (1957) 3-33. With bibliography on linear perspective.

A. Parronchi, "Le due tavole prospettiche di Brunelleschi", *Paragone*, cvii (1958) 3-32, cix (1959) 3-31.

A. Parronchi, "La perspettiva dantesca", *Studi Danteschi*, xxxvi (1959) 5-103.

A. Parronchi, "Le 'misure dell'occhio' secondo il Ghiberti", *Paragone*, cxxxiii (1961) 18-48.

Pauly-Wissowa, *Paulys Real-Encyclopädie der classischen Altertumswissenschaft*, neue Bearbeitung . . . von G. Wissowa . . . W. Kroll . . . K. Mittelhaus . . . K. Ziegler (Stuttgart, 1893-1963-).

C. Pedretti, *Studi vinciani: documenti, analisi e inediti leonardeschi* (Genève, 1957).

J. Pelseneer, "Gilbert, Bacon, Galilée, Kepler, Harvey et Descartes: leurs relations", *Isis*, xvii (1932) 171-208.

G. Perrod, "La diottrica oculare di Leonardo da Vinci", *Archivio do ottalmologia*, xiv (1907) 369-81. With text of Leonardo, Codex D.

R. S. Peters, *Hobbes* (London, 1956).

N. Pevsner, "The term 'architect' in the middle ages", *Speculum*, xvii (1942) 549-62.

F. Pick, *Joh. Jessenius de Magna Jessen, Artz und Rektor in Wittenberg und Prag* . . . (*Studien zur Geschichte der Medizin* . . . xv; Leipzig, 1926).

M. H. Pirenne, " Descartes and the body-mind problem in physiology", *The British Journal for the Philosophy of Science,* i (1950) 43-59.

M. H. Pirenne, " The scientific basis of Leonardo da Vinci's theory of perspective ", *The British Journal for the Philosophy of Science,* iii (1952) 169-85.

M. Pohlenz, *Die Stoa; Geschichte einer geistigen Bewegung,* 2 Aufl., 2 Bde. (Göttingen, 1955).

A. Politzer, *Geschichte der Ohrenheilkunde,* 2 Bde. (Stuttgart, 1907, 1913).

S. L. Polyak, *The Retina* (Chicago, 1941).

S. L. Polyak, " The history of our knowledge of the structure and functioning of the eye ", in P. C. Kronfeld, *The Human Eye in Anatomical Transparencies* (New York, 1944).

S. L. Polyak, *The Vertebrate Visual System* (Chicago, 1957).

John Pope-Hennessy, *The Complete Work of Paolo Uccello* (London, 1950).

D. J. de S. Price, " Automata and the origins of mechanism and mechanistic philosophy ", *Technology and Culture,* v (1964) 9-23.

D. J. de S. Price, " Precision instruments to 1500 ", and " The manufacture of scientific instruments from *c* 1500 to *c* 1700 ", in *A History of Technology,* edited by C. Singer, E. J. Holmyard, A. R. Hall and T. I. Williams, iii (Oxford, 1957) 582-647.

L. Reti, " Francesco di Giorgio Martini's treatise on engineering and its plagiarists ", *Technology and Culture,* iv (1963) 287-98.

G. M. A. Richter, " Perspective, ancient, mediaeval and renaissance ", *Scritti in onore di Bartolomeo Nogara* . . . [ed. R. Paribeni] (Città del Vaticano, 1937) 380-8.

W. Riese, *A History of Neurophysiology* (New York, 1959).

W. Riese and G. E. Arrington, " The history of Johannes Müller's doctrine of the specific energies of the senses: original and later versions ", *Bulletin of the History of Medicine,* xxxvii (1963) 179-83, 281.

M. von Rohr, " Ausgewählte Stücke aus Christoph Scheiners Augenbuch, übersetzt und erläutert ", *Zeitschrift für ophthalmologische Optik,* vii (1919) 35-44, 53-64, 76-91, 101-13, 121-33.

M. von Rohr, " Zur Wurdigung von Scheiners Augenstudien ", *Archiv für Augenheilkunde,* lxxxvi (1920) 247-63.

M. von Rohr, " Auswahl aus der Behandlung des Horopters bei Fr. Aguilonius um 1613 ", *Zeitschrift für ophthalmologische Optik,* xi (1923) 41-59.

M. von Rohr, " Der Sehvorgang und seine Unterstützung durch Brillengläser nach Maurolycus im Jahre 1554 ", *Zeitschrift für ophthalmologische Optik,* xii (1924) 14-28.

M. von Rohr, " Zur Entwicklung der dunklen Kammer (*camera obscura*) ", *Zentral-Zeitschrift für Optik und Mechanik,* xlvi (1925) 233, 255, 272, 286, 303.

M. von Rohr, " Kepler und seine Erklärung des Sehvorganges ", *Die Naturwissenschaften,* xviii (1930) 941-5.

V. Ronchi, *Storia della luce,* 2ª ed. (Bologna, 1952); revised French transl., *Histoire de la lumière* (Paris, 1956, *The Nature of Light* (London, 1970).

V. Ronchi, "L'ottica del Keplero e quella di Newton", *Atti della Fondazione G. Ronchi,* xi (1956) 189-202.

V. Ronchi, *Il cannocchiale di Galileo e la scienza del seicento* (Torino, 1958).

V. Ronchi, "L'optique au xvie siècle", in *La science au xvie siècle. Colloque international de Royaumont, 1-4 juillet 1957* (Paris, 1960) 49-65.

E. Rosen, *The Naming of the Telescope* (New York, 1947).

E. Rosen, "Did Roger Bacon invent eyeglasses ? ", *Archives internationales d'Histoire des Sciences,* xxxiii (1954) 3-15.

E. Rosen, "The invention of eyeglasses", *Journal of the History of Medicine and allied Sciences* xi (1956) 13-53, 183-218.

E. Rosen, "Maurolico's attitude toward Copernicus", *Proceedings of the American Philosophical Society,* ci (1957) 177-94.

Sir W. D. Ross, *Aristotle,* 5th ed., revised (London, 1949).

P. Rossi, *I filosofi e le macchine (1400-1700)* (Milano, 1962).

G. Ryle, *The Concept of Mind* (London, 1949).

S. Sambursky, *Physics of the Stoics* (London, 1959).

S. Sambursky, "Philoponus' interpretation of Aristotle's theory of light", *Osiris,* xiii (1958) 114-26.

P. Sanpaolesi, "Ipotesi sulle conoscenze matematiche statiche e meccaniche del Brunelleschi", *Belle Arti,* ii (1951) 25-54.

G. de Santillana, "The role of art in the scientific renaissance", and "Commentary" by A. C. Crombie, in *Critical Problems in the History of Science,* ed. Clagett (Madison, Wisc., 1959) 33-78.

G. Sarton, "The scientific literature transmitted through the incunabula," *Osiris,* v (1938) 41-245.

G. Sarton, *Introduction to the History of Science,* 5 vol. in 3 (Baltimore, 1927-47).

M. Scaduto, "Il matematicc Francesco Maurolico e i Gesuiti", *Archivum historicum societatis Iesu,* xviii (1949) 126-41.

M. Schramm, "Zur Entwicklung der physiologischen Optik in der arabischen Literatur", *Sudhoffs Archiv für Geschichte der Medizin und der Naturwissenschaften,* xliii (1959) 289-316.

M. Schramm, *Ibn al-Haytham's Weg zur Physik* (Wiesbaden, 1963).

M. Schramm, "Aristotelianism: basis and obstacle to scientific progress in the middle ages", *History of Science,* ii (1963) 91-113.

M. Schramm, "Steps towards the idea of function: a comparison between Eastern and Western science in the middle ages", *History of Science,* iv (1965) 70-102.

M. Schramm, "Ibn Al-Haythams Stellung in der Geschichte der Wissenschaften", *Fikrun Wa Fann,* No. 6 (Hamburg, 1965) 1-22.

J. F. Scott, *The Scientific Work of René Descartes* (London, 1952).

H. J. Seemann, "Eilhard Wiedemann (1852-1928)", *Isis,* xiv (1930) 166-86. With a bibliography of his writings.

M. von Senden, *Space and Sight. The perception of space and shape in the congenitally blind before and after operation* (London, 1960).

R. E. Siegel, "Theories of vision and color perception of Empedocles and Democritus; some similarities to the modern approach", *Bulletin of the History of Medicine,* xxxiii (1959) 145-59.

O. von Simson, *The Gothic Cathedral* (London, 1956).

C. Singer, "Steps leading to the invention of the first optical apparatus ", *Studies in the History and Method of Science,* ed. C. Singer, ii (Oxford, 1921).

C. Singer, E. J. Holmyard, A. R. Hall, and T. I. Williams (editors), *A History of Technology,* 5 vol. (Oxford, 1954-58).

N. Smith, "Malebranche's theory of the perception of distance and magnitude", *The British Journal of Psychology,* i (1905) 191-204.

Norman Kemp Smith, *New Studies in the Philosophy of Descartes* (London, 1952).

F. Solmsen, *Aristotle's System of the World, a comparison with his predecessors* (Ithaca, N.Y., 1960).

F. Solmsen, "Nature as craftsman in Greek thought", *Journal of the History of Ideas,* xxiv (1963) 473-96.

J. Soury, *Le système nerveux central, structure et fonctions. Histoire critique des théories et des doctrines,* 2 vol. (Paris, 1899).

J. P. C. Southall, "The beginnings of optical science", and "Early pioneers in physiological optics", *Journal of the Optical Society of America,* vi (1922) 292-311, 827-42.

P. H. Spettmann, *Die Psychologie des Johannes Pecham* (*Beiträge zur Geschichte der Philosophie des Mittelalters* xx. 6; Münster, 1919).

K. Sudhoff, *Tradition und Naturbeobachtung in den Illustrationen medizinischer Handschriften und Frühdrucke vornehmlich 15. Jahrhunderts* (*Studien zur Geschichte der Medizin . . .* i; Leipzig, 1907).

K. Sudhoff, *Ein Beiträg zur Geschichte der Anatomie im Mittelalter, speziell der anatomischen Graphik, nach Handschriften des 9. bis 15. Jahrhundert* (*Studien zur Geschichte der Medizin . . .* iv; Leipzig, 1908).

K. Sudhoff, "Die Lehre von den Hirnventrikeln in textlicher und graphischer Tradition des Altertums und Mittelalters ", *Archiv für die Geschichte der Medizin,* vii (1913) 149-205.

K. Sudhoff, "Weitere Beiträge zur Geschichte der Anatomie im Mittelater, ii " *Archiv für die Geschichte der Medizin* vii (1913) 363-78.

R. Taton (editor), *Histoire générale des sciences,* 4 tom. (Paris, 1957-64).

Eva Tea, "Witelo, prospettico del secolo xiii ", *L'Arte,* xxx (1927) 3-30.

G. ten Doesschate, "Uit de geschiedenis der oudste stadia van de perspectiesleer ", *Nederlandsch Tijdschrift voor Geneeskunde,* lxxxii (1938) 3341-53, 3856-67.

G. ten Doesschate, "Oxford and the revival of optics in the thirteenth ventury ", *Vision Research,* i (1962) 313-42.

L. Thorndike, *A History of Magic and Experimental Science,* 8 vol. (New York, 1923-58).

C. M. Turbayne, "Berkeley and Molyneux on retinal images ", *Journal of the History of Ideas,* xvi (1955) 339-55.

C. M. Turbayne, "Grosseteste and an ancient optical principle ", *Isis,* l (1959) 467-72.

G. Federici Vescovini, "Le Questioni di ' Perspectiva ' di Biagio Pelacanı da Parma ", *Rinascimento,* xii (1961) 163-243.

G. Federici Vescovini, *Studi sulla prospettiva medievale* (Torino, 1965).

S. Vogl, *Die Physik Roger Bacos* (Erlangen, 1906).

S. Vogl, "Roger Bacons Lehre von der sinnlichen Spezies und vom Sehvorgange ", in *Roger Bacon Essays* ed. A. G. Little (Oxford, 1914) 205-27.

J. A. Vollgraff, "Snellius' notes on the reflection and refraction of rays", *Osiris,* i (1936) 718-25.

W. A. Wallace, *The Scientific Methodology of Theodoric of Freiberg* (Fribourg, 1959).

J. Walsh, "Galen's writings and influences inspiring them", *Annals of Medical History,* vi (1934) 1-30, 143-9, vii (1935) 428-37, 570-89, viii (1936) 65-90, ix (1937) 34-61.

R. S. Westfall, "The foundations of Newton's philosophy of nature", *The British Journal for the History of Science,* i (1962) 171-82.

J. White, "Developments in renaissance perspective", *Journal of the Warburg Institute,* xii (1949) 58-79, xiv (1951) 42-69.

J. White, *The Birth and Rebirth of Pictorial Space* (London, 1957).

Lynn White jr., "Natural science and naturalistic art in the middle ages", *The American Historical Review,* lii (1947) 421-35.

Lynn White jr., *Medieval Technology and Social Change* (Oxford, 1962).

G. M. Wickens (editor), *Avicenna: Scientist and Philosopher* (London, 1952),

E. Wiedemann, "Zur Geschichte der Lehre von Sehen", *Annalen der Physik und Chemie,* Neue (dritte) Folge, xxxix (1890) 470-4.

E. Wiedemann, "Ueber das Sehen durch Kugel bei den Arabern", *Annalen der Physik und Chemie,* Neue (dritte) Folge, xxxix (1890) 565-76.

E. Wiedemann, "Optische Beobachtungen", *Sitzungsberichte der physikalisch-medizinischen Societät in Erlangen,* xxxvi (1904) 332-9.

E. Wiedemann, "Ibn al Haiṯam ein arabischer Gelehrter", in *Festschrift J. Rosenthal . . . gewidmet,* i (Leipzig, 1906) 147-77.

E. Wiedemann, "Eine Zeichnung des Auges bei dem Bearbeiter der Optik von Ibn al Haiṯam, Kamāl al Dīn al Fārisī und Merkverse über den Bau des Auges", *Centralblatt für praktische Augenheilkunde,* xxxiv (1910) 204-8.

E. Wiedemann, "Ueber die erste Erwähnung der Dunkelkammer durch Ibn al Haiṯam", *Jahrbuch für Photographie . . .,* xxiv (1910) 12-13.

E. Wiedemann, "Ueber die Erfindung der Camera obscura", *Verhandlungen der Deutschen physikalische Gesellschaft,* xii (1910) 177-82.

E. Wiedemann, "Uber die Brechung des Lichtes in Kugeln nach Ibn al Haiṯam und Kamāl al Dīn al Fārisī", *Sitzungsberichte der physikalisch-medizinischen Societät in Erlangen,* xlii (1910) 15-58.

E. Wiedemann, "Zu Ibn al Haiṯams Optik", *Archiv für die Geschichte der Naturwissenschaften und der Technik,* iii (1910-11) 1-53.

E. Wiedemann, "Zur Optik von Kamāl al Dīn", *Archiv für die Geschichte der Naturwissenschaften und der Technik,* iii (1910-11) 161-77.

E. Wiedemann, "Zu den optischen Kenntnissen von Quṭb al Dīn al Schīrāzī", *Archiv für die Geschichte der Naturwissenschaften und der Technik,* iii (1910-11) 187-93.

E. Wiedemann, "Ibn Sīnās Anschauung vom Sehvorgang", *Archiv für die Geschichte der Naturwissenschaften und der Technik,* iv (1912-3) 239-41.

E. Wiedemann, "Ueber die Camera obscura bei Ibn al Haiṯam", *Sitzungsberichte der physikalisch-medizinischen Societät in Erlangen,* xlvi (1914) 155-69.

E. Wiedemann, "Roger Bacon und seine Verdienste um die Optik", in *Roger Bacon Essays,* ed. A. G. Little (Oxford, 1914) 185-203.

H. Wieleitner, "Zur Erfindung der verschieden Distanzkonstructionen in der malerischen Perspektive", *Repertorium für Kunstwissenschaft,* xlii (1920) 249-62.

W. P. D. Wightman, *Science and the Renaissance. An introduction to the study of the emergence of the sciences in the sixteenth century,* 2 vol. (Edinburgh and London, 1962).

W. P. D. Wightman, "Science and the renaissance", *History of Science,* iii (1964) 1-19.

H. J. J. Winter, "The optical researches of Ibn al-Haitham", *Centaurus,* iii (1954) 190-210.

John Wisdom, *Problems of Mind and Matter* (Cambridge, 1934).

R. Wittkover, "Brunelleschi and 'proportion in perspective'", *Journal of the Warburg Institute,* xvi (1953) 275-302.

G. Wolff, "Neue Perspektiven für die Geschichte die Perspektive", *Zeitschrift für mathematischen und naturwissenschaftlichen Unterricht,* xlvi (1915).

G. Wolff, "Mathematik und Malerei", *Mathematicische Bibliothek,* xx-xxi (1916).

G. Wolff, "Zu Leon Battista Albertis Perspectivlehre", *Zeitschrift für Kunstgeschichte,* v (1936) 47-54.

H. A. Wolfson, *Philo,* 2 vol. (Cambridge, Mass., 1947).

J. Würschmidt, "Ueber die Brennkugel", *Monatschafte für den naturwissenschaftlichen Unterricht,* iv (1911) 98-113.

J. Würschmidt "Roger Bacons Art des wissenschaftlichen Arbeitens, dargestellt nach seiner Schrift *De speculis*", in *Roger Bacon Essays,* ed. A. C. Little (Oxford, 1914) 229-39.

J. Würschmidt, "Zur Theorie der Camera obscura bei Ibn al Haitam", *Sitzungsberichte der physikalisch-medizinischen Societät in Erlangen,* xlvi (1914) 151-4.

J. Würschmidt, "Zur Geschichte, Theorie und Praxis der Camera obscura", *Zeitschrift für mathematischen und naturwissenschaftlichen Unterricht,* xlvi (1915) 466.

W. Wundt, "Zur Geschichte der Theorie des Sehens", *Zeitschrift für rationelle Medizin,* vii (1859) 279-317.

Robert M. Young, "Scholarship and the history of the behavioural sciences", *History of Science,* v (1966) 1-51.

Addenda: the following are translations of Kepler's optical works into German:

J. Kepler, *Dioptrik oder Schilderung der Folgen, die sich aus der unlängst gemachten Erfindung der Fernrohr für das Sehen und die sichtbaren Gegenstände ergeben,* in deutscher Uebersetzung von F. Plehn (Ostwalds Klassiker der exakten Wissenschaften, No. 144; Leipzig, 1904).

"J. Keplers Behandlung des Sehens nach den Paralipomena vom Jahre 1604", übersetzt von F. Plehn, *Zeitschrift für ophthalmologische Optik,* viii (1920) 154-7, ix (1921) 13-26, 40-54, 73-87, 103-9, 143-52, 177-82 (*Ad Vitellionem paralipomena,* v).

J. *Keplers Grundlagen der geometrischen Optik (im Anschluss an die Optik des Witelo),* in deutscher Uebersetzung von F. Plehn, herausgegeben von M. von Rohr (Ostwalds Klassiker der exakten Wissenschaften, No. 198; Leipzig, 1922) (*Ad Vitellionem paralipomena,* ii-iv).

APPENDIX

Alhazen, *The Treasure of Optics in seven books,* edited for the first time . . . by Friedrich Risner (Basel, 1572).

. . . Book i, ch. 5, theorem 25 : *Vision is completed when the visual form* (forma visibilis) *received by the crystalline humour passes through to the optic nerve* [figs. 6-8]. It has been shown (i. 4. 4.) that this humour is somewhat transparent and also somewhat opaque, and for this reason it is likened to ice (*glacies*). Because it is somewhat transparent it receives the forms (*formae*), and these penetrate it by virtue of its transparency (*diaphanitas*); and because it is also somewhat opaque it prevents the forms from passing right through it, doing this by virtue of its opacity (*spissitudo*). Thus the forms are fixed (*finguntur*) in its surface and body, but faintly. It is the same with any transparent body that is somewhat opaque : light illuminating it penetrates in so far as it is transparent and is fixed at its surface in so far as it is opaque. The *glacialis* is also disposed (*praeparatus*) to receive those forms and to sense them, so that the forms penetrate it by virtue of its receiving and sensing power (*propter virtutem sensibilem recipientem*). When the form reaches the surface of the *glacialis* it acts on it and the *glacialis* is affected (*patitur*) by it; because it is a property of light that it can effect vision (*ut operetur in visum*) and a property of the eye (*visus*) that it can be affected by light. This action (*operatio*) effected by light in the *glacialis* penetrates its body only along straight radial lines, because the *glacialis* is disposed to receive the forms of light perpendicularly on these lines. When light penetrates the body of the *glacialis* it is accompanied by colour, for colour is mixed with light and the *glacialis* receives this action and penetration. From this action and affection (*passio*) arises the sensation (*sensus*) effected in the *glacialis* by the forms of visible things reaching its surface and penetrating its whole body; and from the ordering of the parts of the form at its surface and in its whole body is effected its sensation of the arrangement (*ordinatio*) of the parts.

Theorem 26 : *Vision is in the same category as things causing pain.* This effect of light on the *glacialis* is of the same kind as pain. But some pains are tolerable and do not hurt the affected organ, and these are not felt or considered to be pains at all. In this connection it is significant that light causes pain, because strong lights manifestly disturb and hurt vision, as for example sunlight when the spectator (*aspiciens*) looks at the body of the sun itself or at sunlight reflected from smooth bodies to the eye, because these lights are manifestly painful to sight. The effect of all light in bringing about vision is of the same kind and varies only in greater or less degree; and since all are of one kind and the action of stronger lights is of the same kind as pain, it follows that the actions of lights are of the same kind as pain and vary only in greater or less degree. Because the effect of weak or moderate lights is slight, it does not appear to sense as pain. Hence the sensation in the *glacialis* from the action of light is of the same kind as the sense of pain. From there this sense occurring in the *glacialis* extends to the optic nerve and comes to the front of the brain; there resides the ultimate sensation and ultimate sentient (*ultimus sensus et sentiens ultimum*), the sensitive power in the front of the brain. This power apprehends the sensible things (*comprehendit sensibilia*), but the eye (*visus*) is only an instrument of this power; because the eye receives the forms of visible things and sends them to the ultimate sentient and this apprehends these forms and through them the visible things (*res visibiles*) in them. The form at the surface of the *glacialis* extends into its body, and thence into the thin substance in the cavity of the nerve until it reaches the common nerve, and with the arrival of the form at the common nerve vision is completed. By means of the form arriving at the common nerve the ultimate sentient apprehends the forms of visible things.

Theorem 27: *One visible form is usually seen with each eye* [fig.10]. The spectator apprehends seen things with two eyes and so the form of the thing seen must come to each eye. Hence from one seen thing two forms come to vision (*ad visum*), for the spectator apprehends a single thing. This happens because the two forms coming from a single seen thing to the two eyes run together on reaching the common nerve and are super-imposed one on the other and made into one form; and by means of this form made up of two forms the ultimate sentient apprehends the form of that thing. The two forms coming to the two eyes from the one seen thing are ordered and made into one form before the ultimate sentient apprehends them. That the ultimate sentient apprehends the form only after the union of the two forms is shown by the fact that, when a spectator changes the position of one eye while the other remains fixed, . . . he will see instead of one thing two, and if he opens one eye and closes the other, he will see only one. . . . Since a single seen thing is apprehended sometimes as one and sometimes as two, and in each case there are two forms in the two eyes, it follows that beyond the two eyes there is another sentient to which, from a single seen thing, come two forms as one when this is apprehended as one, and by which two forms are apprehended when the thing is apprehended as two. It follows that sensation is completed only in this sentient, and not in the eye. Sensation can extend from the parts to the ultimate sentient only in the nerves continuous with the brain. Hence the two forms extend from the eye along the nerve connecting it with the brain until they reach the ultimate sentient. These two forms extend from the two eyes and run together at the junction of the two nerves. The evidence that the forms of visible things extend through the cavity of the nerve and come to the ultimate sentient, at which vision is completed, is that an obstruction in this nerve destroys vision and that vision is restored when the obstruction is removed. Medicine testifies to this. The reason why the two forms sometimes run together, and sometimes do not, is that when the two eyes are in a natural position they are in corresponding positions in relation to a single seen thing, so that the form comes to corresponding positions in each eye; but when one eye is displaced the eyes are in different positions in relation to the seen thing, and so the two forms from it come to different positions in each eye. It has already been said, in discussing the structure of the eye (i. 4. 4.), that the common nerve has a corresponding position in relation to the two eyes, so that the positions of the two places correspond, the positions of the two eyes relative to the same place in the common nerve correspond, and the two hollow nerves become one in which the two visual forms are united. It could be said that the forms coming to the eye do not come to the common nerve, but sense (*sensus*) extends from the eye to the common nerve just as do the senses of pain and touch, and then the ultimate sentient apprehends that sensible thing. We say that the actual sensation (*sensus ipse*) coming to the eye certainly

comes to the common nerve, but the sensation that comes to the eye is not
so much a sensation of pain as a sensation acting in the manner of pain;
it is a sensation of light and colour and of the arrangement (*ordinatio*) of
the parts of the thing seen. But the sensation of different colours and
arrangements is not of the same kind as pain. We will show later how a
sensation of sight arises from all these things. Hence the sensation going to
the common nerve is a sensation of light and colour and arrangement,
and that by means of which the ultimate sentient apprehends light and
colour is some kind of form. . . .

Theorem 29 : *Light and colour penetrate transparent bodies separately.*
That lights and colours are not mixed in the air or in transparent bodies
is shown by the following. When in one place several candles are put at
various different points, all opposite an opening leading into a dark place
(*locus obscurus*), with a wall or an opaque body opposite the opening, the
lights (*luces*) of those candles appear on the body or that wall separately and
corresponding in number to the candles. Each one of them appears opposite
one candle on a line passing through the opening. If one of the candles is
screened off, only the light opposite that one candle disappears, and if the
screen is removed the light reappears. This can be tried at any time : for
if the lights intermixed in the air they would become intermixed in the
air in the opening and would have to pass through intermixed, and they
would not become separate later. But we do not find it so. Hence the lights
are not intermixed in the air, but each one of them extends on straight
lines. These straight lines are equidistant, intersecting each other, and
variously situated. The form of each and every light extends on all the
straight lines that can be extended into that air at that time, but they
do not intermix in the air, and the air is not tinged by them; they only
pass through its transparency and the air does not lose its own form.
What we say about light and colour and air is to be understood for all
transparent bodies, including the transparent coats of the eye (*visus*). . . .

Book ii, ch. 1, theorem 2 : *The crystalline and vitreous humours differ
in transparency, and so the visual form is refracted at the surface of the
vitreous humour* [figs. 7-9]. The ultimate sentient apprehends the positions
of the parts of the thing seen only in so far as they are on the surface of
this thing. If the positions of the parts of the form coming to the surface
of the *glacialis* have the same relation to each other as those of the parts
of the surface of the thing seen (i. 5. 18), and these forms extend as has
been described, and if everything is so, then vision is completed only after
the arrival of the form from the surface of the *glacialis* at the common
nerve and the placing of its parts as they are on the surface of the *glacialis*
without any admixture. But the form comes from the surface of the
glacialis to the common nerve only through its extension through the cavity
of the nerve on which the eye (*oculus*) or *glacialis* is constructed. If, therefore, the form does not reach the cavity of this nerve arranged as it is on
the *glacialis,* neither will it reach the common nerve with its proper arrangement. But the form cannot extend from the surface of the *glacialis* to the
cavity of the nerve in straight lines and still preserve the proper positions
of its parts. For all those lines meet at the centre of the eye (*visus*), and
if they continued straight on past the centre their positions would be
reversed : what is right would become left and vice versa, and what is
above would become below and below above. Thus if the form extended

on straight lines it would be collected at the centre of the eye and become as it were a single point. And since the centre of the eye (*visus*) is in the middle of the whole eye (*oculus*) and in front of the place of curvature of the hollow nerve, if the form extended from the centre of the eye (*oculus*) as a single point in one line, it would reach the place of curvature as a single point, and so the whole form would not reach this place. For it would be only one point, namely the end of the axis of the cone. If it extended on straight radial lines and passed through the centre, it would become reversed in accordance with the reversal of the intersecting lines along which it extended. Therefore the form can come from the surface of the *glacialis* to the cavity of the nerve with its parts in their proper positions only on refracted lines, cutting across the radial lines. And since this is so, it follows that vision will be completed only after the refraction of the form coming from the surface of the *glacialis* and extending on lines cutting the radial lines. This refraction must occur before it reaches the centre, because if the lines were refracted after passing through the centre they would be reversed. It has been shown (i. 5. 18) that this form passes through the body of the *glacialis* on straight radial lines, and since it can come to the cavity of the nerve only after refraction on lines cutting the radial lines, it follows that the form is refracted only by its passage through the body of the *glacialis*. It has been said (i. 4. 4) in discussing the structure of the eye (*in forma visus*) that the body of the *glacialis* is of unequal transparency and that its posterior part, called the vitreous humour, has a different transparency from the anterior part. There is no body in the *glacialis* different in constitution (*forma*) from the anterior body except the body of the vitreous. It is a property of the forms of light and colour that are refracted when they meet another body of different transparency from the first. Therefore the forms are refracted only at their entry into the vitreous humour. This body has a transparency different from that of the body of the anterior *glacialis* only so that the forms can be refracted in it. Its surface must be in front of the centre of the eye so that the forms are refracted at this surface before they pass through the centre. This surface must also be correspondingly ordered, because if it was not the form would appear distorted after refraction. . . .

Book iii, ch. 2, theorem 2: *The axes of the visual cones passing through the centre of the pupil* (foramen uveae) *of each eye always meet at a single point on the visible object* (visibilis), *and are perpendicular to the surface of the eye* (visus) [fig. 10]. It has been shown in the first book (i. 5. 18) that the eye apprehends visible objects only on refracted perpendicular radial lines, and that the order of visible objects and of their parts is apprehended only by means of the arrangement (*ordinato*) of the radial lines. It has been said also (i. 5. 27) that a single seen thing, apprehended at the same time by the two eyes, is apprehended as one only when it has a corresponding position in relation to the two eyes, and that if the position is different then one thing is apprehended as two. But any normal visible objects, which are always seen with two eyes, are always apprehended as one. Hence we must show how a single seen thing is seen with two eyes as one thing for most of the time and in most positions, and how a single seen thing has a corresponding position in both eyes for most of the time and in most positions. It will be shown also how a single seen thing has different positions in relation to both eyes, and how this happens. We have already discussed this in the first book (i. 5. 27) in general but not definitively. Hence we say that when a spectator looks at some seen thing, each eye faces this thing; and when the spectator directs the pupil (*pupilla*) towards the thing, each eye directs the pupil towards it in a like direction. When vision (*visus*) is moved on to a thing seen, both eyes (*visus*) are moved on to it; and when the eye directs the pupil towards it, the axes of the two eyes come together at that thing and unite in some point on its surface. If the spectator moves the eye over the thing seen, these two axes move together over its surface and over all its parts. In general the two eyes are in all respects disposed in the same way, the sensitive power (*virtus sensibilis*) in them is the same, and their action and affection (*actio et passio*) is always and entirely the same. If one eye is moved towards a visible object, the other moves immediately towards that object with the same motion, and if one eye comes to rest, so does the other. It is impossible for one eye to be moved towards a visible object and for the other to remain at rest unless restrained. It has been shown earlier (i. 5. 19) that between any seen thing and the centre of the eye there may be imagined a visual cone, of which the apex is at the centre of the eye and the base on the surface of the seen thing which the eye apprehends, and this cone contains all the perpendiculars by means of which it apprehends that thing. Therefore when the axes of the two eyes unite in some point on the surface of the seen thing, this surface is the common base of the two radial cones formed between the centres of the two eyes and that thing. Then the axes join each eye at a point in a corresponding position, because it is opposite the middle of each eye, and the two axes connecting the thing seen with the two eyes are perpendicular to the surface of each eye. . . .

(continued from p. 258)

géometrique et doctrine optique chez Ibn al-Haytham", *Archive for History of Exact Sciences*, vi (1970) 271-98; G. A. Russell, "The emergence of physiological optics" in *Science in Islamic Civilisation*, ed. R. Rashed and R. Morelou (London, 1990); A. I. Sabra, *Theories of Light from Descartes to Newton* (London, 1967), "Ibn al-Haytham (965-c.1040)" in *Dictionary of Scientific Biography*, vi (New York, 1972) 189-210, "The physical and the mathematical in Ibn al-Haytham's theory of light and vision" in *Commemoration volume of Biruni International Congress* (Tehran, 1976) 439-78; G. Scherz (ed.), *Nicolaus Steno and his Indice* (Copenhagen, 1958), *Steno and Brain Research in the Seventeenth Century* (*Analecta Medico-Historica*, iii; Oxford, 1968); J. W. Shirley, "An early experimental determination of Snell's law", *American Journal of Physics*, xix (1951) 507-8, ed. *Thomas Harriott* (Oxford, 1974), ed. *A Source Book for the Study of Thomas Harriott* (New York, 1981); S. M. Straker, *Kepler's Optics* (Indiana Univ. Thesis 1971; Ann Arbor, Mich., 1980), "Kepler, Tycho, and the 'Optical part of Astronomy'", *Archive for History of Exact Sciences*, xxiv (1981) 267-93; D. J. Struik, "Snel, Willebrord (1580-1626)" in *Dict. Sci. Biog.* xii (1975) 499-502; K. H. Tachau, *Vision and Certitude in the Age of Ockham* (Leiden, 1988); see also chs. 3, 8, 10, 14, 15.

10

KEPLER: *DE MODO VISIONIS*

A translation from the Latin of Ad Vitellionem Paralipomena, *V, 2, and related passages on the formation of the retinal image*

In his latest work Dr. Koyré has given us a further analysis of Kepler's contribution to astronomical thought in the seventeenth century. I offer here an English translation, so far as I know the first to be published, of the Latin text in which Kepler describes the fundamental contribution which his astronomical investigations led him to make to a different science, physiology. I have translated from *Ad Vitellionem paralipomena quibus astronomiae pars optica traditur* the whole of Chapter V, Section 2, together with the introduction to this chapter, the introductions to Sections 1 and 3, and the Propositions in Section 3 demonstrating the main conclusions about the formation of the retinal image described in Section 2. Space does not permit the inclusion of a translation of Kepler's very interesting critical discussion in Section 4 of the analysis of vision made by earlier « opticans and anatomists », or of his account of the anatomy of the eye in Section 1. I have translated the text published in the edition by Walther von Dyck, Max Caspar and Franz Hammer [1], but the illustrations are reproduced from the first edition of 1604.

Kepler wrote most of *Ad Vitellionem paralipomena* during 1603

---

1. *Gesammelte Werke*, II (Munich, 1939). The pagination of this edition is printed in the margin. For a modern account of the mechanism of the eye, see M. H. PIRENNE, *Vision and the eye* (London, 1948; 2nd ed., 1967).

while he was Imperial Mathematician at Prague, interrupting his work on Mars (later published in the *Astronomia nova,* 1609) to do so, and presented the completed manuscript to the Emperor, Rudolf II, on New Year's day, 1604[2]. Witelo (or Vitellio) had completed his text, itself based largely on Alhazen's, about 1270, and Kepler undoubtedly used the Latin edition of both writers by Friedrich Risner published in 1572 as *Alhazeni Arabis Opticae thesaurus libri septem... Vitellonis Thuringopoloni Opticae libri decem.* This was the most comprehensive treatise on optics then available. Kepler began his treatise with a discussion of the nature of light, asserting that light radiated from any luminous source as a two-dimensional spherical surface travelling « not in time, but in a moment[3] », and that « a ray of light is nothing but light itself in motion[4] ». The intensity of light remained constant along each ray but decreased in the spherical surface in inverse proportion to the square of its distance from the source, a conclusion by which he discovered the fundamental law of photometry. He went on to apply these conceptions in Chapter II to the operation of the *camera obscura,* or 'pin-hole camera', of which a description had recently been published by Giambattista della Porta[5]; in Chapter III to the localization of images in mirrors; and in Chapter IV to the measurement of refraction. Here he improved on Ptolemy's table given by Witelo, but made no further progress towards a general law than the approximation that, for angles less than 30°, the angle of refraction was proportional to the angle of incidence. This foregoing analysis of light put Kepler into a position to proceed in Chapter V with his analysis of vision and, besides his discovery of the formation of the retinal image, this chapter is important for his discussion of binocular vision and of convex and concave specta-

---

2. Max CASPAR, *Kepler,* transl. and ed. by Doris Hellman (New York, 1959), 144.
3. *Paralipomena,* I, Proposition v. For an historical discussion of Kepler's optics, see V. RONCHI, *Storia della luce* (2nd ed., Bologna, 1952), and « L'ottica del Keplero e quella di Newton », *Atti della Fondazione G. Ronchi,* XI (1956), 189-202.; and above ch. 9 with references on p. 258.
4. *Paralipomena,* I, Prop. VIII.
5. In *Magia naturalis,* book XVII, c. 6 (Naples, 1589).

cles in Section 3, and finally for his application of his conclusions to errors of astronomical observation in Section 5.

The analysis of visual perspective given by Alhazen and Witelo was based on the postulates of geometrical optics laid down by Euclid, according to which « visual rays » extend from the eye in a cone with its vertex at a point in the eye and its base on the object seen. Alhazen[6] adopted the theory that vision is brought about by light sent out, from the object seen, along this « visual cone » (or « pyramid ») to the eye[7]. Following Galen in believing that the lens was the seat of vision, he attempted to give an analysis of the mechanism of vision by combining these ideas with the geometrical optics developed in the treatise by Euclid and in that attributed to Ptolemy. He assumed that rays were sent to the eye from every point on the object seen; those meeting the cornea perpendicularly passed unrefracted through it to the lens; and those falling perpendicularly on the anterior surface of the lens gave rise to sensation by producing there an « image » made up of points corresponding to points on the object seen (cf. fig. 46). Since such impressions were produced in both eyes, to avoid his theory leading to double vision, Alhazen introduced a further hypothesis that vision was not completed at the anterior surface of the lens, but in the optic nerve. But first he had to avoid what he saw as a further difficulty. The normal incident rays passing through the anterior surface and body of the lens into the vitreous humour would intersect at the common centre of curvature of this surface and of the cornea, change sides, and so produce an inverted image on the nerve at the back of the eye. Alhazen could not accept this inverted image, so he supposed that the rays converging towards the centre of curvature were, before they intersected, refracted away from

6. *Alhazeni Opticae*, ed. cit., I, cap. 5. Cf. Matthias SCHRAMM, « Zur Entwicklung der physiologischen Optik in der arabischen Literatur », *Sudhoffs Archiv*, XLIII (1959), 289-316; *Ibn Al-Haythams Weg zur Physik*, Wiesbaden, 1963.
7. « Omnes formarum visibilium distincta visio fit secundum pyramidem, cuius vertex est in centro oculi, basis vero in superficii rei visae. Ex quo patet, omne quod videtur, sub angulo videri. Euclides 2 hypothe. opt. Alhazen 19 n 1. » *Vitellonis Opticae*, ed. cit., III, XVIII.

each other at the posterior surface of the lens, and so reached
the nerve without crossing (at *hrf* and *lte* in fig. 46). Ptolemy
had shown that oblique incident rays were refracted towards

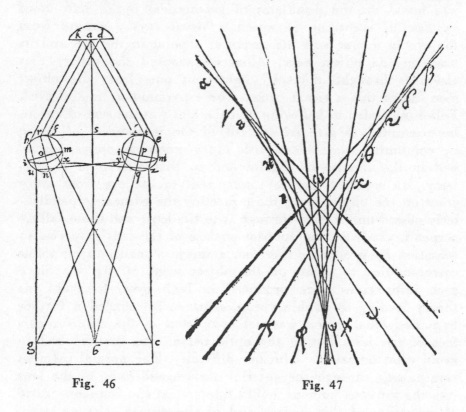

Fig. 46   Fig. 47

the perpendicular drawn to the interface when passing from
a rarer into a denser medium, and away from the perpendicular when passing from a denser into a rarer medium. To bring
about the refraction of the rays in the direction he required,
Alhazen had to assume that the lens was optically rarer than
the vitreous humour. Following Galen, he supposed the optic
nerves to be hollow. He then proposed the hypothesis that
in each eye the image (*forma*, or *species*) enters the hollow
optic nerve and passes down to where the two nerves meet in
what is now called the *optic chiasma*, and that there the two
images unite to form a single image (*kad* in fig. 46). The *chiasma*
was the seat of the *sensus communis* of visual judgement.

Witelo[8] followed Alhazen's theory of vision in all essentials. Kepler took it as the point of departure from which, after showing that it was optically impossible, he launched his entirely new theory in the passages translated below.

Besides Witelo and Alhazen, Kepler consulted a number of other authors for information both about optics and vision, and about the anatomy of the eye. He gave details of his sources in Section 4 and in the introduction to Section 2 of Chapter V. His principal source for the anatomy of the eye was the Swiss anatomist Felix Plater's *De corporis humani structura et usu*, first published at Basel in 1583 and reprinted in 1603. Vesalius' successor at Padua, Realdo Colombo, had already corrected one mistaken accepted notion about the lens by showing that it is located forward from the central position in the eye-ball given it by Alhazen and Witelo. Plater described the lens anatomically (as Alhazen, Witelo and Roger Bacon had geometrically) as flattened, with the anterior surface more flattened than the posterior. More important was Plater's assertion that the seat of vision is not the lens but the retina. He held that the lens stood to the retina as a convex spectacle lens stood to an eye with weak sight : both magnified the object seen. Kepler wrote of Plater's explanation of vision : « Compare the true mechanism of vision as given by me with that given by Plater, and you will see that this famous man is no farther from the truth than is compatible with being a medical man who deliberately does not treat mathematics[9]. »

The other main anatomical authority mentioned by Kepler, Johannes Jessenius, was at that time professor of medicine at Wittenberg[10]. In 1600, while in Prague, Jessenius had acted as intermediary in the negotiations that led to Kepler's coming there to work with Tycho Brahe and be appointed Imperial Mathematician. Jessenius was later to become Rector of the

---

8. *Vitellonis Opticae*, ed. cit., III. Cf. C. Baeumker, *Witelo, ein Philosoph und Naturforscher des XIII. Jahrhunderts (Beiträge zur Geschichte der Philosophie des Mittelalters*, III, 2, Münster, 1908); and A. C. Crombie, *Robert Grosseteste and the origins of experimental science* (Oxford, 1953; 3rd impression 1971). 213-218, also 151-155.

9. *Paralipomena*, V, 4, *Ges. Werke*, II, 187. For Bacon see *Opus Maius*, V, I, III, 3.

10. Caspar, *Kepler*, pp. 105, 166, 257.

University of Prague, and to be put to death publicly in the
market place for his Calvinistic leanings in the « Prague execution » of 21st June, 1621. In his *Anatomia Pragensis* (Wittenberg, 1601), which Kepler used, he followed essentially the description of the eye given by the great Paduan anatomist Girolamo Fabrici da Aquapendente in his *De oculo visis organo*
(Venice, 1600). Fabrici's were the most accurate drawings of
the eye and its structures so far published, showing the shape
of the lens correctly, although Kepler disagreed with the account
given by Jessenius, holding that the posterior surface was hyperbolical and not a cone. He arrived at this conclusion by geometrical reasoning and gave a drawing of the lens as he saw
it in Chapter V, Section 2. But Fabrici, followed by Jessenius, still held to the old view that the lens was the seat
of vision.

Another medical authority cited by Kepler is Jean Fernel,
presumably his *De naturali parte medicinae* (1542) or the revised edition published as the *Physiologia* (1554). On the mechanism of vision he cited Aristotle's *De sensu et sensilibus* and
the views of Empedocles and Democritus described and refuted
there by Aristotle; Macrobius' *Saturnalia*; Cornelius Gemma's
Cosmocritices (*i.e.* book I of *De naturae divinis characterismis*,
Antwerp, 1575), essentially following Witelo on vision; and
della Porta's *Magia naturalis*, of which the principal Latin
edition was that published at Naples in 1589. In this entertaining
work, Porta, while accepting the old view that the lens was the
seat of vision, likened the eye to a *camera obscura*, with the
pupil acting as the small window or 'pin-hole' throwing the
image on to the lens as the screen. Kepler wrote of Porta that if
he had added to his account the mechanism by which the inverted
image is thrown by the lens on to the retina, « clearly you
would have unravelled the mechanism of vision[11] ».

Among earlier optical investigations not cited by Kepler, two
whose writings were available only in manuscript are of particular interest. Leonardo da Vinci, while not departing essentially
from Witelo's account of vision, is significant for making what
might be called an engineering approach to the problem, com-

11. *Paralipomena*, V, 4, *Ges. Werke*, II, 189.

paring the mechanism of the eye to that of a *camera obscura* long before Porta and proposing to investigate the functions of the parts of the eye by making glass models[12]. The second writer, Francesco Maurolico, had in his *Photismi* solved the problem of the focussing of the *camera obscura* and in *Diaphanorum* ... made a detailed study of lenses, but he again could not understand correct vision with an inverted and reversed image. Following Vesalius and Roger Bacon he described the lens as flattened, more in front than behind, and attempted an optical analysis of its operation. Dated 1554, this work by Maurolico was published only in 1611, edited by Christopher Clavius with other writings as *Photismi de lumine et umbra ... Diaphanorum partes, seu libri tres.* The publisher explained in the preface that Maurolico's manuscripts had long been in circulation, but there is no evidence that Kepler had any knowledge of them[13].

Kepler's discovery of how the retinal image is formed was the first thorough and successful solution of an important physiological problem to be made in modern times. Like Harvey's discovery of the circulation of the blood, which it precedes, it dealt with a physiological problem capable of solution by means of the physical science available. Kepler's solution was not complete. Having failed to discover the law of refraction, he had to rely on an approximation. He was content to use a spherical lens as a model for his analysis in Section 3, although he knew that the lens of the eye is not spherical and in fact described its shape in terms of conic sections, of which his treatment in Book III of the *Paralipomena* has considerable mathematical interest. Moreover he supposed that the optic

12. *The Notebooks of Leonardo da Vinci*, ed. and transl. by E. MacCurdy (London, 1938), I, 119, 241-245, 266; *Literary Works*, ed. J. P. and I. A. Richter (2nd ed., London, 1939), I, 140-146; N. Ferrero, « Leonardo da Vinci : of the eye; an original new translation from Codex D », in *American Journal of ophthalmology*, XXXV (1952), pp. 507-521.— Alhazen, *op. cit.*, I, c. 5, théorem xxix, had described an experiment with a *camera obscura* but his theories did not fit with using this model to solve the dioptric mechanism of the eye.
13. First ed. Naples, 1611; 2nd ed. Lyons, 1613. Cf. RONCHI, *Storia della luce*, pp. 92-106; and above pp. 218, 258.

nerve entered the eye-ball in the centre exactly opposite the pupil, although as early as 1587 Giulio Cesare Aranzi had already observed and pointed out in his *Anatomicarum observationum liber* that in horses and cattle the optic nerve enters laterally. The fact that in man the point of entry forms a « blind spot » displaced to one side was discovered by Mariotte and published in 1668 in his *Nouvelle découverte touchant la veüe*.

The whole study of vision has considerable general scientific interest, from Alhazen's attempt to discover the mechanism of vision by means of a geometrical optical model, through the mechanical models using a *camera obscura* and lens developed by Kepler's more immediate predecessors. Kepler's strategic move was to separate the physical problem of the formation of the retinal image \ initially ' from the psychological problem of sensation and perception, and to restrict his attention to the former. Optics could deal only with this. Then he solved his problem by seeing that the formation of the retinal image must be analysed, not in terms of the « perspective cone » used by Alhazen and Witelo with its base on the object seen and its vertex at the eye (cf. fig. \46), but in terms of a multitude of cones of rays coming to the eye from vertices at every point on the object seen (cf. fig.\49, \51). In this way he showed that vision came about when a picture of the object seen, or of the whole visible world extending to slightly more than 180 degrees (slightly more than a hemisphere, as he put it) standing in front of the eye, was thrown upon the retina. Thus, he wrote[14] :

« The sensation of vision follows the action of illumination, in manner and proportion. (*Passio visionis sequitur actionem illustrationis, in modo et proportione.*) The retina is illuminated distinctly point by point from individual points of objects, and most strongly so at its individual points. Therefore in the retina, and nowhere else, can distinct and clear vision come about. This is so much the more evident because distortion of the proportions of the picture leads to faults of vision... And so if you are bothered by the inversion of this picture and fear that this would lead to inverted vision, I ask you to consider

14. *Paralipomena*, V, 4, *Ges. Werke*, II, 184-185.

the following. Just as vision is not an action (*actio*), because illumination is an action but sensation (*passio*) is the contrary of action, so also, in order that the positions may correspond, the sensing things [*patientia*, i.e. the retinal images] must occur opposite to the agents that bring them about. Now the positions are perfectly opposite when all the lines connecting opposite points run through the same centre, which would not have been so if the picture had been erect. And so in the inverted picture, although right and left are interchanged everywhere and with respect to any common line, none the less with respect to themselves the right-hand parts of the object are perfectly opposed to the right-hand parts of the picture, and the upper parts of the object to the upper parts of the picture, like a hollow to a hollow... Therefore none of that absurdity is perpetrated by the inverted picture, from which Vitellio so assiduously ran away, and in which Jessenius followed him... »

This conclusion led Kepler to his rule (stated below, p. 300) for relating the retinal image to the world seen.

Kepler continued his analysis of vision in his *Dioptrice* (1611), among other things attempting to account for accomodation by changes in the position of the lens. Later the study of the retinal image was taken up by Christopher Scheiner in his *Oculus* (1619) and in *Rosa Ursina* (1630), where he mentions experiments in which he removed the backs of human and animal eyes and observed the formation of the image on the retina. Descartes describes a similar experiment with the eye of an ox in discours V of the *Dioptrique* (1637), where his knowledge of the law of refraction discovered by himself and Snell allowed him to amplify Kepler's optical analysis. Scheiner and Descartes are also responsible for the accepted explanation of accommodation by changes in the shape of the lens. Finally Huygens in his *Dioptrica*[15], Proposition XXXI, demonstrated the formation of the image and other phenomena by means of an artificial model of the eye which he had constructed. Even then Kepler's discovery did not cease to be challenged or to leave serious puzzles. Mariotte provoked a long con-

15. *Opera posthuma* (Leiden, 1703), 112-116. See, on T. Harriot's discovery of the sine law about 1601, J. Shirley, *American Journal of Physics*, xix (1951), 507-8.

troversy by questioning whether the 'blind spot' allowed the
retina to be regarded as in fact the sensitive organ of vision,
and such problems as those of the relation between direct and
indirect vision, and of how a single visual field can be seen
with two eyes, raised once more the psychological aspects of the
subject.

Kepler wrote about this time of his scientific programme for
cosmology : « My goal is to show that the heavenly machine
is not a kind of divine living being but similar to a clockwork [16]. »
His analysis of vision demonstrated a physiological mechanism in
separation from all other non-mechanistic elements. Because of
its function in the engine of the body, Harvey's discovery of
the circulation of the blood brought about a more profound
reorganization of physiology as a whole. But when one considers
the relation of Descartes' optics to his mechanistic physiology,
the influence of the mechanistic programme, and the whole
development of theories of perception in the seventeenth century
and later, Kepler's discovery is scarcely less interesting in its
consequences.

Kepler was an inelegant and sometimes obscure latinist, and
although I have attempted to keep my translation as close as
possible to his original language, I have not hesitated to depart
from it when necessary in order to translate his sense rather
than his words. I should like to thank my friend Dr. O.R. Gur-
ney for his kindness in reading my translation and restraining
some of my bolder departures, and both him and Dr. D.T. Whi-
teside for making a number of valuable suggestions, most of
which I have adopted. I have translated *crystallinus* as lens throughout.

Chapter V

DE MODO VISIONIS

143   Whilst the diameters of the planets and the amounts of
       eclipses of the sun are recorded by astronomers as basic

16. Letter to Herwart von Hohenburg, 10th feb. 1605, *Gesammelte Werke*,
XV, 146.

values, some deception of vision arises partly from the instruments of observation, as we discussed above in Chapter II, and partly just from vision itself; and this, as long as it is not counteracted, makes considerable trouble for investigators and detracts from scientific judgement. The source of the errors in vision is to be sought in the structure and functioning of the eye itself. Had the opticians Alhazen and Vitellio, or after them the anatomists, dealt with this clearly, lucidly and without danger of uncertainity, they would have released me from this task of continuing the Things Omitted from Vitellio in this chapter. But to procede methodically with the matter : First I shall put together, as it were as principles, an account of the relevant parts of the eye based on the most approved anatomists; for the account given by Vitellio is false and confused. Se-

144 condly, /I shall sketch in summary the way vision takes place. Thirdly, I shall demonstrate each particular point. Fourthly, I shall lay bare the points that escaped the reasonings of the opticians and medical men concerning the functioning of the eye. And lastly I shall explain deceptions of vision arising from instruments, and apply this to astronomical practice.

1. ON THE ANATOMY OF THE EYE

It favours reliability of demonstration that I am going to bring forward not observations on the eye by myself, but an account combining those published by the most outstanding medical men. For what if anyone were to accuse me of bad faith and of trying to establish my own views, or of unskilfulness in dissections which I have never seen or taken part in ? So, men of accepted authority in a field of which they have the best knowledge may speak for me; I will give an account of the subject to the limits of my own professional knowledge. For then they will scarcely grudge

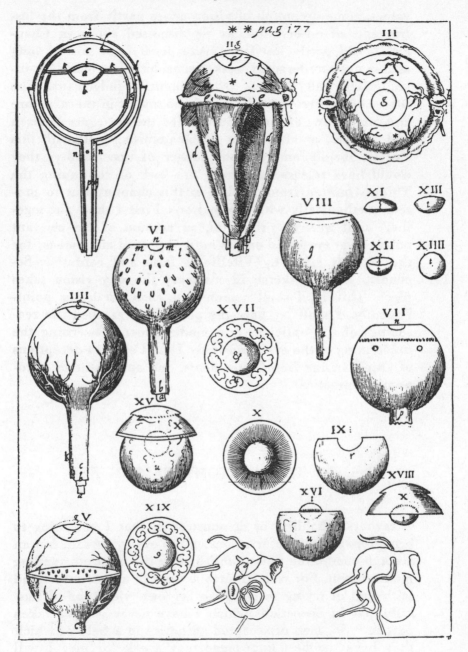

Fig. 48

yielding place to me in mathematics in so far as I may be properly well-regarded by expert judgment.

I consulted chiefly the illustrations in Felix Plater's *De corporis humani structura et usu*, which were published in 1583 and reprinted this year, 1603 [see below pp. 311-314 and fig. 48]. With these I compared the *Anatomia Pragensis* of my friend Johannes Jessenius of Jessen, not so much because he was able above all to profit by following Aquapendentius, but because the fortune of war gave him considerable anatomical experience himself. If, mathematician as I am, I have passed over anyone of greater worth in this discipline, I hope they will treat me with indulgence...

151   2. HOW VISION TAKES PLACE

Although the forehead, the eyelashes, the eyebrows and the sockets play a part in the process of vision, they do not play a principal part. So I have dealt with their function in advance, while I was describing them[17]. The parts I have included below all belong to the eye-ball itself and contribute to its principal function. I have described how vision takes place in such a way that the functions of each separate part can be seen, these, so far as I know, having been investigated and discovered by no one else. And I ask mathematicians to study this carefully, so that something certain about this noblest of functions may at last take its place in philosophy.

I say that vision occurs when the image (*idolum*) of the whole hemisphere of the world which is in front of the eye, and a little more, is formed on the reddish white concave surface of the retina (*retina*). I leave it to natural philosophers to discuss the way in which this image or picture (*pictura*) is put together by the spiritual principles of vision

17. *Paralipomena*, V, 2, *Ges. Werke*, II, 146-147.

residing in the retina and in the nerves, and whether it is
made to appear before the soul or tribunal of the faculty
of vision by a spirit within the cerebral cavities, or the
152   faculty of vision,/ like a magistrate sent by the soul, goes
out from the council chamber of the brain to meet this image
in the optic nerves and retina, as it were descending to a
lower court. For the equipment of opticians does not take
them beyond this opaque surface which first presents itself
in the eye. I do not think that we should listen to Vitellio
(book III, Proposition XX) [18], who thinks that these images
of light (*idola lucis*) go out further through the nerve, until
they meet at the junction half-way along each optic nerve,
and then separate again one going to each cerebral cavity.
For, by the laws of optics (*leges optices*), what can be said
about this hidden motion [19], which, since it takes place
through opaque and hence dark parts and is brought about
by spirits which differ in every respect from the humours
of the eye and other transparent things, immediately puts
itself outside the field of optical laws ? So, whereas Vitellio argues thus in book III, Proposition XX : the images
(*species*) must be united, therefore (Proposition XXI)
refraction must take place at the back of the vitreous
humour, and (Proposition XXII) the spirits must be pellu-
cid, I reverse this argument : spirits are not an optical body,
and their thin hollow nerve is not optically in a direct
line [20]. Even if it were, it would immediately become bent

18. « Visio non completur, nisi cum ordinatio formae recepta in superficie
glacialis, ad nervuum pervenerit communem. » The Latin Alhazen and
Witelo use « forma » where, for example, Roger Bacon uses « species » and
Kepler « species » or « idolum ».
19. And yet it is this motion that brings about vision, from which the
name Optics is derived; and so it is wrong to exclude it from the science
of Optics simply because, in the present limited state of our science, it cannot be accommodated in Optics (*Kepler's note*).
20. Cf. Roger BACON : « Nam species a loco istius fractionis incedit secundum tortuositatem nervi visualis, et non tenet incessum rectum, quod est
mirabile, sed tamen necesse, propter operationem a se complendam. Unde
virtus anima facit speciem relinquere leges communes naturae, et incedere
secundum quod expedit operationibus ejus. » *Un fragment inédit de l'Opus
tertium*, ed. P. Duhem (Quaracchi, 1909), 78.

by the movements of the eye and the opaque parts of the nerve would become opposed to the light entering the tiny opening or door of the passage. Hence light neither passes through the posterior surface of the vitreous humour nor is refracted there, but falls upon it. And indeed how could images (*species*) entering perpendicularly be refracted ? It is strange that this did not occur to Vitellio when he was writing book III, Proposition XXXI[21]. Hence in III, Proposition XXXIII[22] he was put into by no means minor difficulties over this union of images (*species*) at the junction of the nerves. Because if this union in the mid-path of the nerves is to be asserted, it must be done in terms of natural philosophy. For it is undeniably certain that no optical image could penetrate to this point. It seems then clear that, if any nerve went to its seat in the brain freely in a straight line, with two eyes we would think we saw two things instead of one. Either this junction takes place so that when one eye is closed this hidden seat in the brain should not cease from its function of judging. Or perhaps the actual doubling of the seats is not only on account of the eyes, but is for the purpose of correct judgement of distances, as with the pair of eyes. Therefore, in order that visible things may be judged correctly and a distinction made between what is seen with one and with two eyes, this junction of the passages must take place. Here this one optical conclusion from the first chapter can be stated[23] : the spirits are affected by the qualities of colour and light, and this affection (*passio*) is, so to speak, a colouring and a lighting. For in vision images (*species*) of strong colours remain behind after looking, and these are

21. « Uno puncto rei visae, superficiebus amborum visuum perpendiculariter incidente : necesse est axes radiales in centris foraminum gyrationis nervorum concavorum angulariter refringi. »
22. « Virtus sensitiva comprehendit quantitatem anguli, quem in centro visus respicit superficies rei visae solum ex comprehensione partis superficiei visus, in qua figuratur forma rei visa. »
23. « Visus ergo non recipit formam coloris rei visus, nisi ex luce admixta cum forma coloris. » (*Vitellonis Opticae*, III, 1). Cf. : « Formae ergo lucis et coloris cuiuslibet rerum visibilium, oppositarum visui, in eodem tempore venient ad superficiem visus. » (*Alhazeni Opticae*, I, c. 5, XIV).

united with colours printed by a fresh look, and a mixture of both colours is made. This image (*species*) existing separately from the presentation of the thing seen is not present in the humours or coats of the eye, as shown above; hence vision takes place in the spirits and through the impression (*impressio*) of these images (*species*) on the 153 spirit. But really this « impression »/does not belong to optics but to natural philosophy and the study of the wonderful. But this by the way. I will return to the explanation of how vision takes place.

Thus vision is brought about by a picture of the thing seen being formed on the concave surface of the retina. That which is to the right outside is depicted on the left on the retina, that to the left on the right, that above below, and that below above. Green is depicted green, and in general things are depicted by whatever colour they have. So, if it were possible for this picture on the retina to persist if taken out into the light by removing the anterior parts of the eye which form it, and if it were possible to find someone with sufficiently sharp sight, he would recognize the exact shape of the hemisphere compressed into the confined space of the retina. For a proportion is kept, so that if straight lines are drawn from separate points on the thing seen to some determined point within the eye, the separate parts are depicted in the eye at almost the same angle as that at which these lines meet. Thus, not neglecting the smallest points, the greater the acuity of vision of a given person, the finer will be the picture formed in his eye.

So that I may go on to treat this process of depiction and prepare for a demonstration of it, I say that this picture consists of as many   pairs   of cones 'as there are points in the thing seen, in pairs always with the same base, namely the width of the lens (*crystallinus*) or part of it. Thus while one cone of each pair has its vertex at the point seen and its base on the lens (somewhat \ altered by refraction through the cornea), the other has the same base on the lens as the first one and the vertex at a point in the picture depicted on the retina; this cone undergoes refrac-

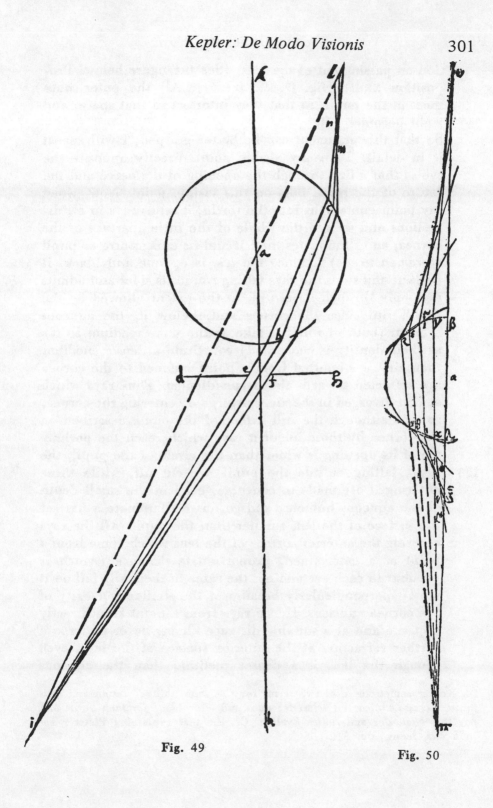

Fig. 49

Fig. 50

tion on passing out of the lens. (See the figure below, Proposition XXIII) [fig. 49; cf. fig. 51]. All the outer cones
meet in the pupil, so that they intersect in that space, and
right becomes left.

So that this argument can be better grasped, I will repeat
it in detail. Take any visible point directly opposite the
eye so that a line through the opening of the nerve and the
centre of the pupil falls on this visible point. Now, when
any point emits light into the world, it sends rays in all directions and so into the whole of the little aperture of the
cornea, and illuminates the iris and its dark centre or pupil
(*foramen uveae*) [24]. Since the iris is opaque and black, it
deflects and stops the rays falling round its sides and admits
rays only through its centre, to the extent allowed by the
pupil. But since the cornea and, below it, the aqueous
humour (both of which I take as the same medium so far
as their density is concerned) constitute a denser medium
than air, rays emitted from a point inclined to the cornea
are refracted towards the perpendicular. Thus rays which
at first diverged in the air, converge on entering the cornea,
so that although the full extent of the circle described on
the cornea by those incident rays which reach the perime-
ter of its opening is wider than the circle of the pupil, the
154   rays / falling outside the pupil are cut off, while those
entering it are made to converge, even in the small depth
of the aqueous humour, and go on to illuminate a part of
the surface of the lens smaller than the pupil. All the rays
entering the anterior surface of the lens which come from a
point at a determined, proportionate distance (which is
peculiar to each eye and not the same in them all) fall on it
almost perpendicularly because of the similar convexity of
the cornea and lens. Hence rays from a point seen directly
opposite and at a suitable distance almost never undergo a
further refraction at the anterior surface of the lens, even
though the lens is a denser medium than the aqueous

24. Kepler sometimes uses two terms for the same thing : *retina* and *retiformis*; *crassa tunica* and *sclerode*; *uvea* and *choroidea*; *foramen uveae* and
pupilla; *hyaloides* and *tunica hyalina*. Cf. the text explaining Plater's Tabula xlix, below, pp. 312-314.

humour. Again here I ascribe the same density as concerns refraction to the lens and its capsule *(aranea)*, as also below to the vitreous humour and the hyaline coat *(tunica hyalina)*. Hence as many of these rays emitted by a single point as are admitted through the pupil descend through the whole depth of the lens, converging more and more as they go, until they reach its hyperbolic posterior surface. Thus if it were possible to represent a series of these rays in a section through the eye, that going from the top of the cornea to the bottom of the lens would make one and the same conical surface, of which the width is determined by the position of the pupil, and the vertex reaches to a point somewhere behind the eye. These rays having then proceeded in a cone through the posterior surface of the lens into the vitreous humour, which is a rarer medium than the lens, are refracted away from the perpendiculars drawn to the surface at the point of refraction, so that the refracted rays run together towards the axis. Thus they terminate in a shorter and blunter cone than that by which they came. Thus all these rays coming from one visible point finally meet in another point, the very centre and extremity of the optic nerve, where this is joined to the retina [S in fig. 51; directly above O in fig.48, I]. For nature has measured the depth of the vitreous humour between the lens and the retina according to this density of the lens and the magnitude of these refractions.

The most distinct vision occurs only when all the light from the same point, however much dispersed by the width of the cone admitted through the pupil, is brought by two refractions, one in the cornea and the other at the posterior surface of the lens, to a bright focus at one point on the retina, the very opening of the nerve carrying the visual faculty or spirit. To this point no other rays from any other luminous point can come, because of the blackness and opacity of the choroid *(uvea)*, the narrowness of the pupil, the ciliary processes, and the other things mentioned above. So far we have spoken of the visible as a point, not a body, so that it had no parts, and no distinction of right from 155 /left, above from below. But this is not really what is visible, but an element or rather limit of the thing seen. Thus vision of a point as just explained is not to be taken as the completion of vision but as one element in it. For as in the thing seen there are many points, so there are many as it were elements in the vision of that thing. Vitellio III, xix, remains nevertheless true [25] : nothing is seen unless with some magnitude proportionable to it. Thus let there be some point near the first one, side by side with it, and to the right of it [corresponding to *i* in fig. 49 and Y in fig. 51, the point directly opposite the pupil being *h* and X respectively]. This point also sends light to the cornea and the underlying iris, and it looks towards the pupil obliquely. So rays entering the circle of the pupil form a kind of scalene cone which at the pupil intersects the upright cone from the first point, and after intersection goes to the left within the choroid, falling on part of the surface of the lens illuminated by the first point and on part not illuminated by it, but more to the left. In fact more or less the same thing happens as we showed in Chapter II in a closed chamber [*i.e. camera obscura*]. The pupil (*pupilla*) corresponds to the window and the lens to the screen opposite it, provided that the pupil and lens are not so near that intersection is incomplete and everything is confused. Hence at the anterior surface of the lens the cone going to the left is refracted towards the upright cone, and, although still passing through the lens obliquely, falls so much the more upright on the hyperbolic [posterior] surface of the lens. There again, though not enough, it is refracted towards the direct first cone, so that it is separated from the cone less in the vitreous humour than in the lens, but still remains separated, and so goes to the left side of the retina. But Nature has found an admirable way of preventing the disturbance of the proportions of the visible hemisphere which would occur if points outside in the air, mutually opposite to those on the retina on a line through the centre of the eye, were deflected from

25. « Corpus visibile oportet ut sit alicuius quantitatis respectu superficiei visus, ad hoc, ut actu videatur. »

LA DIOPTRIQUE

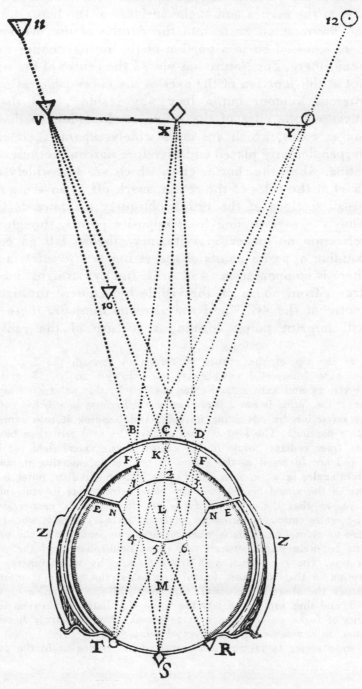

Fig. 51

an opposite position through the threefold refraction of the ray, at the cornea and at the surfaces of the lens, and passed down at an angle into the depths of the eye and so were focussed on to a portion of the retina smaller than a hemisphere. For Nature has placed the centre of the retina, not at the junction of the axes of the cones penetrating the vitreous humour but a long way inside[26], and she has advanced the edge of the retina at the sides, so that the longer cones, which are more widely separated, intercept perpendicularly placed and therefore narrow sections of the retina, while the shorter ones, which are less widely separated at the sides of the retina, mark off at an acute angle broad sections of the retina obliquely set towards them. Thus the rays coming from opposite points, though after refraction no longer opposite, nevertheless fall on corresponding opposite points of the retina (*retiformis*), and so there is compensation. And so if, finally, straight lines are drawn from points on the visible hemisphere through the centre of the eye[27] and the vitreous humour, these lines will imprint points forming a picture of the radiating

26. i.e., at the tip of the caustic of refraction through the lens, where the cones have intersected completely; cf. below n. n. 36, 38, and Propositions xix, xx and xxii, xxiv. Kepler goes on in this passage to say that the shape of the retina is not a true hemisphere because nature has compensated for refraction by advancing its sides and bending it into something more like a parabola. The longer cones (within the eye) will then be those that come from radiant points in the centre of the visual field (or hemisphere) and are focussed at the centre of the retina, meeting it more or less at right angles (e. g., at S in fig. 51). The farther a radiant point is from the centre of the visual hemisphere, the more refracted is its cone of rays in the eye, so that the point of focus on the retina is proportionately nearer the centre (*minus divaricantur ad latera retinae*) than it would be if there were no refraction. This is what requires compensation if the proportion is to be maintained between the visual hemisphere and the picture on the retina. The compensation is brought about by advancing the sides of the retina so that the more lateral a cone is, the sooner it meets the retina (hence the shorter the cone), the more oblique the angle at which it meets it, and thus proportionately the wider the distances between successive points of focus on the elongated as compared with a truly hemispherical retina, so counteracting the effect of refraction.
27. The sense seems to require *oculi*, instead of *retinae* as in the printed texts.

points on the retina opposite. If this did not happen the
size of things seen indistinctly to the side would keep
changing when the eyes were turned, as happens when
156 spectacles / are worn. For these, although fixed immovably
in relation to the eye, if they are moved round with it
represent things at rest as having some motion, because
of the varying amount of the hemisphere appearing at the
sides.

Now we must go further into the difference between direct
and lateral vision. First, the cone of direct vision is boun-
ded simply by the choroid, so that it falls wholly on the
cornea, whereas some of the oblique cones are displaced to
the side of the cornea itself. They may be too wide for the
choroid, so that light is badly measured out to the retina.
The direct cone is circular or upright, the oblique ones
compressed or scalene. The axis of the direct cone is not
refracted at the cornea, whereas the axes of the oblique
ones are refracted there. All the lines of the direct cone are
almost perpendicular in the lens, but none of the oblique
ones. The direct cone is cut equally by the anterior surface
of the lens; the oblique ones are cut unequally because,
where the anterior surface of the lens slopes more, it cuts
an oblique cone lower down. The direct cone cuts the hyperbolic surface or convex bulge of the lens circularly and
equally; the indirect ones cut it unequally. All the rays of
the direct cones are focussed at one point on the retina,
which is essential in this matter; the lines of the indirect
ones cannot all be focussed only at one point, for the causes
already given, and so they form a less distinct picture. The
direct cone comes to a point at the centre in the middle of
the retina, the oblique ones do so to the sides. The direct
cone falls upright on the retina; the lateral ones fall obliquely because, as already described, the centre of the retina
is below the intersection of the axes of the cones in the
vitreous humour. Finally, the sensory power or spirit diffused through the nerve is more concentrated and stronger
where the retina meets direct cones, because of its source
and where it has to go : from that point it is diffused over
the sphere of the retina, gets further from the source, and

hence becomes weaker. But as in a funnel and in a fishing net with a sack which were likened above to the retina[28] the sides all send the liquid or the fishes into the canal or sack; so the sides of the retina do not usurp for themselves its sensory capacity, but whatever they can, they bring into the perfection of direct vision. Thus, when we see a thing perfectly, we see it within the whole surrounding area of the visible hemisphere. For this reason oblique vision satisfies the soul least and only invites the turning of the eyes in that direction so that they may see directly. This is how Vitellio III, xvii, should be interpreted[29]. For by the perpendicular alone nothing is seen distinctly. But direct and properly distributed, or distinct, vision is brought about by all the rays from the same point (from which a perpendicular can be drawn through the centre of the pupil and of the humours) being collected at the very centre of the opening of the nerve (as in Vitellio, III, xxix)[30].

157 The colour of the retina is neither dark nor black, in case it should tint the colours of things, nor dazzling white, in case too much brightness should pour into the vitreous humour and the things appearing white and bright above this / should be made to seem too coloured. See the corollary to Chapter i, Proposition xxx and xxxi. The shape of the retina is larger than a hemisphere. It must in the first place be a hemisphere, thus proportionate to the picture received of things, as already said. Beyond that, the border extends as far as the ciliary processes so that when the eye-ball is filled with the vitreous humour the retina is kept stretched with the collar narrower than the belly. It cannot be tied on because of the softness and subtlety of the visual spirit, for which indeed there are canals through the nerve,

28. V, 2, *Ges. Werke*, II, 149.
29. « Visio distincta fit solum secundum perpendiculares lineas a punctis rei visae ad oculi superficiem productas. Ex quo patet, omnem formam visam sic ordinari in oculi superficie, sicut est ordinata in superficie rei visae. »
30. « Omnem punctum formae incidentem superficiebus visuum per axes radiales, ad centrum foraminis gyrationis nervi concavi pertingere est necesse. »

contrary to the nature of the rest of the nerves, so that the substance of the nerve does not impede it. Now if the retina did not occupy more than a hemisphere, it could become easily wrinkled and slip back on to the junction of the nerve. In any case the gap between the hemisphere and the ciliary processes had to be filled, so otherwise this would have had to have been done with the choroid or with the vitreous humour. How much better that it should be done with the retina! This extends the visual function into the border. Although none of the cones formed by the lens reach this border, nevertheless slits appear formed by the ciliary processes, so that some light can enter from the sides through the ciliary processes and be received by this co-pious border of the retina. For a line drawn from the extreme edge of the cornea through the adjacent edge of the pupil almost falls on to the junction of the lens with the ciliary processes; one drawn through the opposite edge of the pupil almost touches the origin of the ciliary pro-cesses from the choroid. By this machinery Nature has brought it about that we see more than a hemisphere with the eyes fixed, or at any rate as much as is admitted through the corner of the eye[31], with a minimum of movement. Indeed with a little wider vision you would be able to see your ears, especially if they were long, with the eyes on the same side. I have often been surprised at seeing the sun and my shadow both appearing as if in front, instead of being opposite each other. It seems to be Nature's pre-caution to protect the eyes that, when they are not actually turned away, things approaching come immediately into view wherever the eyes are looking. And this preserves the whole living thing, for certainly it takes care to pre-serve itself and this adaptation helps it to look after its body.

The vitreous humour has a skin, so that it is not weakened and made flaccid by the moisture of the nerves or the retina, and so that it does not run into the aqueous humour

31. Cf. V, 1, *Ges. Werke*, II, 146, ll. 25-26; VIRGIL, *Eclogues*, III, 8 : I am grateful to Mr. Colin Hardie for this reference.

at the front through the fissures in the ciliary processes. It must differ in density from the lens and from the aqueous humour because of refraction. For unless it was rarer than the lens, the rays would not be bent away from the perpendicular and brought together to the axis of each cone. Since the vitreous is denser than the aqueous humour, the rays entering through the ciliary slits can fall more deeply through it and draw near the outermost cones formed through the lens.

158   The lens also has a coat so that, soft as it is, it does not run into the aqueous humour. But the lens does not reach as far as the sides of the retina, so that in this space the rays of the cones may be focussed to a point. Hence, to be supported and connected with the supply of nutriment, it has to be attached by the ciliary processes to the choroid (*choroidea*). These are wholly black, so that they do not admit light; and dense, so that the lower chamber of the vitreous humour may, as it should, be dark, and so that an illuminated vitreous humour should not dilute the images (*species*); which will doubtless come about by their becoming inflated and swelling up in bright light and shrinking when the light is reduced, like the choroid (*uvea*). The posterior surface of the lens is of hyperbolic or similar shape, so that the rays passing down through the hyperbola and converging in the same upright cone may be focussed at a nearer point on the same axis. That this is not possible with any other shape is demonstrated below[32]. The anterior surface of the lens bulges so that when a radiant point shines obliquely on to the pupil, this surface is cut more at a slant by the scalene cone, and so the amount intercepted by the cone is kept the same so far as possible. And in order that it may meet perpendicularly all the rays (coming from the same given point) which are refracted by the cornea, and are brought together towards a single point after refraction, I assume this anterior surface of the lens to be simply circular or spherical.

The whole choroid with the ciliary processes is present to

32. Proposition xxiv, below.

produce sufficient darkness, in case too much light should be harmful. It does nothing towards the formation of the image (*species*) or picture, nor if it did would it ever complete or perfect it, because the pupil is too wide for the size of the eye. Indeed in darkness it dilates to three times its width in sunlight, so that in darkness most of the surface of the lens is uncovered in order to let more of the weak light focussed to a point through the lens (focussing itself not being affected by the pupil) stimulate the sense so much the more clearly. The more light there is, on the contrary, the narrower the pupil, in order to exclude more light in case too strong a light should injure the sense. Thus the position of this pupil is where the rays intersect, and it exists for the sake of the lens itself. But this intersection does not take place in a point, but is spread out over a long cone because of the circular surface of the lens. So the position of the pupil forms the base of this cone of intersections. For between the pupil and the lens there is no intersection, and if anything were exposed to vision there it would be seen inverted and indistinct. The inner side of the choroid is rough, lest if it were smooth it should reflect the rays reflected to it from the surface of the lens. In fact it surrounds the retina with a totally black coat of similar substance. For the retina gets its nutriment through the choroid to which it owes the blackness of its anterior parts. Supposing the retina itself to be transparent, the black cancels this.

159 The aqueous humour is necessary to fill the chamber and to provide a single continuous medium as far as the lens for transmitting the rays refracted at the cornea. The cornea itself is seen to be a small part of a spheroid, so that rays falling perpendicularly on the anterior surface of the lens can be focussed to one point. Nothing prevents the roundness of the cornea from being perfect, as explained below.

160 To help the reader who does not have anatomical illustrations to hand, I include here a copy of Felix Plater's Tabula xlix [fig. 48]. I wish I had put this selection at the beginning of the work, for then I could have adapted the text to it. There was no need to add explanation of letters and signs

beyond that of Plater himself. I have added only the references to my text [33].

There are 19 figures, for the engraver added the last two (of the organs of hearing) without instructions.

I. A line drawing showing a projection of the membranes and fluids (*humores*) as found in the actual eye. Where : A, lens; B, vitreous humour; C, aqueous humour; D, related coat; E, opaque part of the sclerotic (*crassa tunica*); F, choroid (*uvea*); G, retina (*retiformis*); H, hyaloid (*hyaloides*); I, lens capsule; K, ciliary processes of the choroid coat; L, boundary of the choroid on the sclerotic; M, cornea part of the sclerotic, of which the convex bulge noticed by others is indicated by a dotted line; N, N, eye muscles; O, optic nerve; P, thin membrane of the nerve; Q, thick membrane [sclerotic] of the nerve.

II. The eye intact with the muscles, taken out of the skull and with the eyelids removed.

III. The eye-ball seen from the front.

IV. The sclerotic with part of the optic nerve.

V. The sclerotic, cut transversely.

VI. The choroid with part of the optic nerve.

VII. The inverted interior surface of the same.

VIII. The retina with the substance of the optic nerve.

IX. The hyaloid coat.

X. The ciliary processes, radiating from the front of the hyaloid coat.

XI. The lens capsule.

XII. The lens in its capsule.

XIII. The naked lens, seen from the side.

XIV. The lens seen from the front.

XV. The three humours together, aqueous, vitreous and lens, partly shaded.

XVI. The vitreous humour with the lens.

XVII. The vitreous humour alone seen from the front.

33. I have omitted these references. (A.C.C.)

XVIII. The aqueous humour shown in position over the
lens.

XIX. The aqueous humour above seen from the front.

161 *A*, in II, IV, VI, VIII.	Visual or optic nerve.
B, in II, IV, VI.	Thin coat covering the nerve.
C, in II, IV, V.	Sclerotic surrounding the nerve.
DDD, II.	The eye muscles on one side.
EE, II, III.	Part of the related coat extending under the eyelids.
*, II, III.	Expanded part of the same, intact.
F, *II*, *III*, *IV*, *V*.	Dark part or iris of the eye, which the white surrounds.
G, *II*, *III*, *IV*, *V*.	Black pupil or centre of the eye, in the middle of the iris.
	Note in II, IV, V at *G* the arc, indicated by a dotted line, rising from the sides of the iris and forming part of a smaller circle than the globe of the eye. This was added by me from the observations of others. Note also the bulge of the cornea rising from the white.
H, II, III.	Little piece of flesh at the corner of the eye.
I, II, III.	Tear ducts.
K, IV, V.	Vessels dispersed over the sclerotic.
LL, V, VI.	Fibres by which the choroid is attached to the sclerotic.
MM, VI.	Boundary of the choroid, where it stops at the cornea.
N, VI, VII.	Opening in the choroid, or pupil.
OO, VII.	Beginning of the ciliary processes.
P, VII.	Beginning of the choroid, extending from the thin coat.

Q, VIII.	Dimensions of the retina extending above the middle of the eye.
R, IX.	Pocket of the hyaloid coat holding the lens.
S, XI, XII.	Width of the lens capsule.
T, in XII, XIII, XVIII.	Spherical posterior part of the lens (according to others protruding in a cone, but according to me hyperbolic).
in XIV, XVI.	Flattened anterior part of the same.
V, XV, XVI.	Dimensions of the vitreous humour.
X, XV, XVIII, XIX.	Dimensions of the aqueous humour.
Y, XV.	Region at which the vitreous humour is separated from the aqueous by the hyaloid coat.
Z, XV, XVIII.	Region in which the choroid is bathed by the aqueous humour.
&, XVII.	Cavity remaining in the vitreous humour after the lens has been removed.
§, XIX.	Corresponding cavity in the aqueous humour.

162   3. *Demonstration of the conclusions stated concerning how vision takes place through the lens*

Everything said so far about the lens can be observed in everyday experiments with crystal   balls (*pilae crystallinae*) or glass urinary flasks filled with clear water. For if one stands at the glazed window of a room with a globe of this kind of crystal or water, and arranges a sheet of white paper behind the globe at a distance equal to half the diameter of the globe, the glazed window with the fluted wooden or leaden divisions between the lights will be very clearly depicted on the paper, but inverted. The same effect can be obtained with other things, if the place is darkened a little. Thus, using a globe of water set up in a chamber opposite a small window, as we described above in Chapter II, Proposition VII [34], everything that can reach the globe through the width of the small window or opening will be depicted very clearly and delightfully on the paper opposite. Since the picture is clear at this one distance (namely with the paper a semi-diameter of the globe away from it), it will become indistinct at positions in front of or behind this one. But the direct opposite happens using the eyes. For if the eye is placed at a distance of a semi-diameter of the globe behind the glass, where before the picture of the thing represented through the glass had been clearest, it is now most indistinct. For the glass appears either all white, or all red, or all dark, etc. If the eye is moved nearer the globe, it sees things opposite erect and magnified, where they were indistinct on the paper, but if it is moved away from the globe to a distance greater than a semi-diameter of the globe, it sees them as distinct images, inverted, reduced in size, and lying on the surface of the globe itself. In the former experiment, with the paper in this position, the picture disappeared entirely. All this happens with a globe of water, because of the refractions and shape, since it has a convex shape. Since the lens is convex and is denser than the surrounding humours, just as the water in the glass flask is denser than the air, therefore whatever we have demonstrated in this way with the globe of water, and using these media, will have been proved also for the lens, except in so far as it has a different convexity from the globe. So let us proceed with the demonstration of matters belonging to the crystalline or glass globe...

34. On the *camera clausa*, or *camera obscura*.

174   DEFINITION

Whereas up to now the image has been an entity of reason
(ens rationale), *the shapes of things really present on the
paper, or on any other screen, will now be called pictures.*

175   PROPOSITION XIX

What happens using the eye with an aqueous sphere has
been described [35]. I shall now show how the direct opposite
happens with a piece of paper. First,

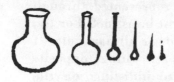

the following can be deduced directly from what has been said : *namely, the reason why, if the paper
almost touches the globe, the shape
of the globe (if it is a urinary flask,
with a long collar [fig.|52])* is de-

Fig. 3

picted *on the paper, by sunlight radiating into the sphere,
with a bright border.* For whatever rays enter the globe
do not yet in that position intersect with the axis. Since
the paper touches the globe, all the rays that could
pass through the globe are here. *Then the border is brightest* because the most concentrated rays intersect with each
other in a circle (but not yet in the axis), as is seen
in α, б, γ, δ, in the figure [fig. 47] and as agrees with
the previous demonstrations. When the paper is moved
away a twentieth of the diamenter of the globe from the
glass (although the illumination comes from far off) some
rays in the middle of the figure now begin to intersect
with the axis, here at ω, *and the middle of the figure
becomes brighter. The figure becomes smaller as the pa-*

35. What is seen when the eye is placed behind a sphere is analysed in
the preceding Propositions.

per is moved farther away, but the cone formed by these lines does not alter in section in a swiftly changing succession of circles, for it does not decrease proportionately, but quickly at first and then slowly. The genuine cause of this is the succession of rays. For, of the rays that intersect in the axis and then separate, the outer ones first form the boundary at α, 6, γ, δ; these are succeeded by the inner ones forming the boundary at ε, ζ, η, θ. If this cone formed by refracted and intersecting rays were to appear intact in the air, it would be seen as a figure generated by an arc with one end rotated in a circle and the other remaining aloft, the arc curving inwards; for the cone is slender in the middle and very sharp-pointed[36]. Where the paper meets the point of the cone, at ψ, *the illumination is strongest, so that with a hot sun it can burn « fire dust »* (*pulvis pyrius*)[37] in cold water. For, by Proposition xv, not indeed all but nevertheless most of the rays intersect there/in one central point. The remaining rays τφαυ, which have already intersected, are dispersed round this point, and *form a set of rays going towards one centre.* When the paper is moved beyond the last point ψ, *the inside of the figure disappears with the intersection of all the rays.* Thus we can understand how great the burning powers would be if all the rays that can pass through the globe came together.

176

PROPOSITION XX

Through a globe of denser medium than the surroundings, any point beyond the intersections of the parallels[38] *depicts itself strongly on a piece of paper placed at the last point of intersection of the rays, but not in front of or behind*

36. Kepler is describing the caustic, i. e. the envelope of the refracted cone of light, formed by a spherical lens refracting parallel rays : cf. Proposition XXIV, fig. 50.
37. Gunpowder; cf. J. R. PARTINGTON, *A History of Greek Fire and Gunpowder* (Cambridge, 1960), 170, 162.
38. The *intersectiones parallelorum* is the caustic of refraction formed by a spherical lens refracting parallel rays. The *ultimus terminus refractionum*

this point, and the picture made up of all the points appears inverted. The cause of its depicting itself strongly is that the globe brings together to one point a large number of rays going out from a given point which are near the perpendicular, as demonstrated above. This does not happen with the rays intersecting more rapidly at ω, because the more rapid intersection at ω is effected by the rays αω, βω, sent in more weakly from the sides because more refracted. Indeed the place of intersection ω on the paper is occupied by other rays (passing through the globe from the same luminous point) which have not yet intersected, but which have been focussed and are bright and thus obliterate the rays intersecting at ω. Again, cones coming from other points of the luminous thing are still too wide apart, as here ιχ, and produce confusion by partly overlapping.

By contrast, at the final intersection ψ, a large number of rays coming from the same luminous point and lying near the ultra-powerful perpendicular ψ, ω run together at one point, as shown in Proposition xv, and because the cones taper to a sharp point they occupy no other region. Thus single points are depicted separately and distinctly. Only a few rays from other points on the visible thing arrive, but by now intersected and weaker, as would happen if one of the cones terminated in υ; then the vertex of the new cone would fall on the intersection η υ with the old one, which is how whatever confusion there is in this picture is brought about. For the image is inverted, not because of the intersections already described of the rays in front of the glass, but because every point of the thing seen, radiating perpendicularly into a sphere, depicts itself in a very strong cone behind the glass. Thus the axes of

is the tip of the caustic, in the case of parallel rays the last point at which the incident rays would intersect on passing through the globe or, conversely, the greatest distance at which a radiant point placed there sends rays that would emerge from the globe parallel. Kepler is saying that a radiant point (emitting diverging rays) must be at a greater distance from the lens than this, if it is to produce a caustic of refraction through the lens : cf. Propositions xv-xvi.

the cones ψω intersect in the centre of the sphere, these
having undergone no refraction. This is the genuine cause
of the inversion of the picture brought about by a sphere
denser than the surroundings, when it is not covered up by
anything solid but an opening is left...

177 PROPOSITION XXIII

*When a screen with a small window is placed in front of
the globe within the limit of the sections of the parallels* [39],
*and the window is smaller than the globe, a picture of the
visible hemisphere is projected on to the paper, formed by
most of the rays brought together behind the globe at the
limit of the last intersection of the rays from a luminous
point. The picture is inverted, but purest and most distinct
in the middle* [40]. So great is the uncertainty in this matter
and indeed such its novelty that unless we take the greatest
care, it may easily become confused. Indeed I was held up
myself for a long time, until I convinced myself that all the
different effects had the same explanation. Let *a* be the
centre of a globe of water *bc*, in front of which is placed
an opaque screen *dg* with a small window *ef* smaller than
the globe [fig.49]. Let the visible thing be *hi*. The paper
is at *k*, where the final intersection of the radiation from *h*
takes place. It the screen were absent, by Proposition XX,
i would depict itself at the final intersection of its rays at *l*,
178 and the point *h* at the point *k*./ But they would project

39. i. e. within the caustic; see n. 38.
40. Thus we may seek some light from Method. There is a form of refraction through a globe by which vision is deceived by imagining to itself
simulacra which are not real (we said *imagines*), on which see Propositions VII, and XVII and XVIII. Again there is another form of refraction by which
real pictures of things are formed; and this can happen in two ways : in
one the pictures are formed by a naked globe, as in Propositions XIX, XX,
XXI, XXII, in the other by a globe covered except for a small window, as
in Proposition XXIII. For there is different apparatus for these forms of
refraction. Propositions VIII to XVI are concerned with refraction through a
globe in general (*Kepler's note*).

the lateral rays of the cones so that they intersect each
other and overlap. But with the screen in position, no more
of the rays from *h* can enter the sphere than can pass
through *ef* and then nearly all meet at *k*, and this cone is
reduced as if by pruning, so that no rays can be projected
so as to intersect at *l* and cause confusion there. Again,
the brightest part of the radiation going in the cone *il*,
namely the radiation through the centre *a*, is clearly cut
off by the screen *de*, and the very bright tapering apex *l*,
which could produce confusion at *k*, is absent. In fact no
more of the radiation from *i* is left than can go through *ef*.
This consists of the rays that successively intersect in the
width *mn*, by Proposition XIX, and after intersection cut
al and fall on the paper placed at *k*; they fall on the near
side of *l*, and not at a point but spread out because they
have already intersected at *m*. Hence the picture is dark
and indistinct at the sides. Thus if you move the sides of the
paper nearer they are depicted better, but still not quite
accurately, because the intersections are spread out not only
in depth at *mn* (which would not matter much) but also
laterally.

Since the intersection takes place through *ef*, after *ie* and *if*
have been cut by *hk*, the rays pass through *mn* before meeting *al*, by Proposition XIX. Therefore the rays leaving *i* on
the right leave *mn* on the left, nor can there be another
intersection by which they could return to be right.

The small window *ef* must be narrow because if it were
wider it would not perform its functions. And it must be
near the globe, because if it were too far away the rays
entering from the visual hemisphere would be too few
and more confused.

COROLLARY

*Here is seen the function of the pupil in the eye; also why
the sides of the retina are nearer the lens than the bottom.*

Proposition XXIV

Rays converging within a medium denser than the surroundings, towards any given point, are brought together, in a hyperbolical conical surface [i.e. a caustic] *enclosing the medium, to a point nearer than this point.* Let α be the centre of the globe βζ, forming the denser medium, in which βλ, γϰ, δι, εθ, ζη converge at π [fig. 50]! And let βαπ be the axis. Therefore, by the foregoing, ζη will be refracted to ηο, εδ to δξ, δι to ιν and γϰ to ϰμ. I want all the rays to be brought together to one point. Hence I must obtain more refraction at ιϰ, so that ϰμ, ιν meet απ more quickly, and less refraction at θη, so that ηο, θξ meet απ farther down, and thus |οξνμ become one point. Refraction will be greater at ϰ if γϰ falls more 179 obliquely, and/less at η if ζη falls more perpendicularly on the surface. But because γϰ, ζη rest in the surface, therefore ηθιϰλ must be moved, so that the slope to η is less than ζη and the slope to ϰ more than γϰ. This is done in both cases not by means of one and another circle but by conic sections. Any of these can cut any circle in the four points. See Apollonius Book IV, Proposition xxv. Hence there will be two in this semicircle, and two in the other. Thus, intersecting at η so that it enters the circle there, it will fall more perpendicularly than ηζ, and cutting the same circle again at ϰ, on emerging it will fall more obliquely than γϰ. Further, the only conic section that measures the refractions is the hyperbola or some very similar curve, as shown in Chapter IV, Proposition v. Indeed it is demonstrated there that the surface enveloping all the emerging parallel rays is a hyperbolic conic section and nothing else.

Corollary

Thus is seen the design of Nature concerning the posterior surface of the lens in the eye. She wants all the rays ente-

*ring the pupil from a visible thing to come together at one
point on the retina, both so that each point of the picture
will be so much the clearer, and so that the other points of
the picture will not be accidentally confused with other,
unfocussed or focussed rays.*

*It is also seen that the expansion of the pupil has no other
purpose than that which I said above* [41], *nor does it confuse
the picture but only makes it clearer.*

41. V, 2, *Ges. Werke,* II, 158 : above, p. 311.

11

THE PRIMARY PROPERTIES AND SECONDARY
QUALITIES IN GALILEO GALILEI'S
NATURAL PHILOSOPHY*

1. - Introduction.

When in 1610 Galileo was negotiating his return from Padua to his native Florence, he requested that in « the title and function » of his service the Grand Duke should add the name « philosopher » to that of « mathematician » [1].

He was the leader of the scientific movement in the early seventeenth century who, by his private researches and public actions, was most responsible for establishing the enduring identity of modern science in relation to other fields of learing. He saw natural science as an autonomous field of dependable knowledge, with open frontiers, acquired by asking specific and answerable questions. He battled for two essential elements of an effective strategy for scientific thinking: principles of explanation applicable to the whole of nature, and methods of research by which to find accurate and convincing solutions to limited problems. An essential criterion for accepting the first was their strict and technical applicability to the second. He approached the new philosophy at once as a Renaissance artist-engineer, taking nature to pieces and reassembling it from known principles, and as a humanist debating the best ancient model for true philosophy.

Galileo's natural philosophy and its permanent interest cannot be understood unless we see him as he saw himself: first, as the heir to antiquity who transformed the questions of the philosophers to make them capable of technical answers; and secondly as the heir to the issue of the relation of belief to reason put at heart of Western intellectual history by

---

* The subject of this paper will be discussed with full documentation in A.C. Crombie and A. Carugo, *Galileo's Arguments and Disputes in Natural Philosophy* (forthcoming).

[1] Galileo, *Opere*, ed. maj., X, 353; henceforth designated as *G.G.*

Christianity. The challenge of Copernican cosmology repeated the encounter between Aristotelian philosophy and Christian theology in the thirteenth and fourteenth centuries, an encounter to be repeated in form again and again between doctrines and intellectual loyalties coming from radically different sources. Galileo's public controversies and condemnation transformed him in his life-time into an historical symbol of this issue, both within the minds of individuals and externally in the relation of free inquiry to the habits of society and the institutions of church and state.

Galileo decided his philosophical attitudes early. As a lecturer at Pisa he had been initiated into the opposing accounts given by Aristotle, and by Plato and the atomists, of fundamental questions that he was to make his own: the validity of mathematics in physical science, the nature of the elementary constituents of matter, the nature and validity of the information received through the senses. But characteristically he made his first declaration of independence from the Aristotelian conception of physics, in his earliest original writings, in the light not of the natural philosophers but of the mathematicians. Geometry confirmed his acceptance of Aristotle's theory of scientific demonstration, on which he wrote an unprinted treatise [2] and on which to the end of his life he tried to base all his claims to finding true explanations. But Archimedes supplied his first and enduring model for a scientific method of discovery, and brought him firmly down on the side of Plato's conception of the validity of mathematics in physics.

In his writings *De motu* of uncertain date he specifically attributed to « the superhuman Archimedes » [3] his method of approaching physical problems by means of an antecedent theoretical analysis that remained the most powerful instrument of his mature work. Archimedes taught him to simplify physical problems for mathematical solution by postulating idealised abstractions — perfectly frictionless planes, spherical bodies, parallel lines — that could be applied to concrete situations; to manipulate these in a theoretical world of thought-experiments; and in this way to define the role of actual experiments precisely to deciding by measurement whether the ideal world of his theoretical constructions was the actual world in which he lived. Archimedes also set him on his first steps towards the cosmological revolution to which he devoted his scientific life, by showing that this actual world discovered only by reason, and even contradicted by immediate observations, must comprise the whole of

[2] *Disputationes de praecognitionibus et de demonstratione*, BNC di Firenze, Manoscritti Galileiani, 27, ff. 4ʳ-31ᵛ; A. PROCISSI: *La collezione galileiana della Biblioteca Nazionale di Firenze*, Roma, 1959, p. 106.

[3] *G. G.*, I. 300; cf. A. KOYRÉ: *Études Galiléennes*, Paris, 1939, I, p. 72.

nature in a uniform mathematical scheme. He used Archimedes's analysis of floating bodies as a model to make the positions and motions of the elements in the universe likewise simply a problem of hydrostatics. In this way he could reject Aristotle's teleological cosmology and make the arrangement of the universe instead simply the resultant of mechanical forces. At the same time he began the replacement of the unworkable Greek scheme of pairs of contrary qualities with the scheme of linear, quantitative scales used in modern physics.

Galileo was in fact demonstrating by means of this terrestrial experimental model the relativity of gravity postulated in the cosmology of the *Timaeus* and already exploited by Copernicus, and before him by Nicole Oresme, as an alternative to Aristotle's. During his last years at Pisa he seems to have been encouraged by the Platonist philosopher Iacopo Mazzoni to give further specifically Platonic content to his conception of the real theoretical world existing behind immediate appearances. Mazzoni devoted a substantial section of his *De comparatione Platonis et Aristotelis* (1597) to the question « whether the use of mathematics brings profit or loss to physics » [4]. Plato, he wrote, « believed mathematics to be especially fitted for physical investigations, which was the reason why he himself always had recourse to mathematics in dealing with physical mysteries ». He illustrated this by the power of theories postulating geometrical figures or atoms as the elementary constituents of matter to explain the physical properties and sensible qualities arising from them. Writing in 1597 from Padua to congratulate him on his book, Galileo reminded him of their Pisan discussions of Plato « under whose discipline it seems that all who dedicate themselves to search for truth do and must gather together » [5]. These ideas of the elementary constituents and primary properties of matter, and of their relation to the secondary qualities of sensation, matured in Galileo's mind during his years at Padua while, as he wrote to Kepler also in 1597, he tried to follow a true « method of philosophizing » [6]. Archimedes provided the method of exploring the one true world; Plato and the atomists showed him what he expected to find. Their methods and principles came into their own in the creative years 1610-1616 following his return to Florence when, in his four great controversies over the telescope, floating bodies, the sunspots and the

---

[4] IACOBI MAZONII CAESENATIS, in Almo Gymnasio Pisano Aristotelem ordinarie Platonem vero extra ordinem profitentis, *In universam Platonis et Aristotelis philosophiam praeludia, sive de comparatione Platonis et Aristotelis*, Venetiis, 1597, sectio IV, lib. XVIII, pp. 187-189. Cf. A. KOYRÉ: *Galileo and Plato* in *Journal of the history of ideas*, IV (1943), pp. 420-421.

[5] Galileo to Mazzoni, 30 May 1597 (*G. G.*, II, 197-198).

[6] Galileo to Kepler, 4 August 1597 (*G. G.*, X, 68).

Copernican system, he developed all the main characteristics of his natural philosophy.

« Galileo ... », he wrote of himself at this time, « being used to study in the book of nature, where things are written in only one way, would not be able to dispute any problem *ad utranque partem* or to maintain any conclusion not first believed or known to be true » (*G. G.*, IV, 248). He flourished on disputes and had no inhibitions in arguing to win, as well as to win the truth. His natural philosophy reflects his extraverted personality, his clear common sense, his realism and attachment to concrete illustrations of abstract theories, his combative intolerance of confusion and obscurity. He was the diametrical opposite of the introverted, mystical type like Kepler. But if he enjoyed controversy, he waged it to establish the identity of the true science of « the true and real world, which, made by God with his own hands, stands always open in front of us for the purpose of our learning » (*G. G.*, V, 96). Galileo put in a fresh way the fundamental question of the relationship of the observer to this world observed. I shall illustrate his conception of the identity of natural philosophy through his treatment of three problems.

2. - The nature and validity of the information received through the senses and their relation to the external world.

The publication of the *Sidereus nuncius* (1610) raised two kinds of doubt about the validity of observations made through the telescope. The first arose from technical objections to the available lenses which Galileo met with technical answers. The second arose from the association of optical devices with « natural magic » aimed at illusion and deceit, and the belief that only direct vision, certified by touch, could show the world as it really was. [7] Galileo's discussions of the physical nature of light and of the physiology and psychology of vision, in trying to meet this kind of doubt, are a good example of his firm grasp of the fact that a necessary condition for success in scientific inquiry was the selection of soluble problems and valid evidence. He tried to find technical answers to questions cited from current authorities as philosophical puzzles. This is clear in the comments elicited by Giulio Cesare La Galla's validation of the telescope in *De phoenomenis in orbe Lunae* (1612). Galileo dissociated himself from La Galla's kind of argument and linked the validation of

---

[7] Cf. L. GEYMONAT: *Galileo Galilei: a biography and inquiry into his philosophy of science*, translated from the Italian with additional notes and appendix by S. DRAKE, New York, 1965, pp. 35-51; V. RONCHI: *Il cannocchiale di Galileo e la scienza del Seicento*, Torino, 1958; ID.: *Storia del cannocchiale*, Città del Vaticano, 1964.

the senses, aided or unaided, with the fundamental question of the relationship of mathematics to physics in the investigation of nature. His attitude appears neither as Platonist nor as Aristotelian but rather as a pragmatic one, with which he had no objection to associating famous philosophical names.

La Galla had assumed in an introductory chapter, « By what method the discussion should be undertaken » (*G. G.*, III, 323-325), the traditional Aristotelian view that the certainty of mathematical demonstrations held only in the abstract subjects of geometry and arithmetic and was stripped from the subjects of the senses:

« and although mathematics does sometimes descend to physical quantities, as in optics and harmonics, nevertheless physical and natural quality does not affect the theory (*contemplatio*) of it at all, since it considers it only by accident; as is obvious to anyone who studies these subjects only theoretically and scientifically, but not practically and mechanically ».

Galileo commented:

« it is asked whether mathematical considerations about the heavens are physical or mathematical: for if they are mathematical — the times of eclipses, conjunctions etc. — they will not agree with sensible and real conjunctions. It is no less ridiculous to say that geometrical [considerations] do not apply in materials, and if anyone were to have said that aritmetical attributes (*passiones*) did not apply in sensible bodies; and, for example, that rules for training and coordinating an army do not apply as long as we deal with soldiers in the flesh ».

La Galla went on to say that Aristotle's arguments against Plato had made it superfluous for him to show further how prejudicial mathematics were to the investigation of natural things. But he related this question to a discussion of the « sensible forms and qualities », maintaining that « it is asserted by philosophers and known from experience » that « the senses are deceived over the common sensibles, namely motion, rest, number, size and shape; although they are normally either not at all or to the least degree at fault over the proper sensibles, such as colour or taste. For since the common sensibles are not attributes (*passiones*) of this or that fixed and determined quantity, as is necessary with the proper sensibles which go with certain dispositions, but they belong to quantity as quantity and as they are its attributes, so it happens that sense can judge nothing certain or settled about them ». He gave as an illustration the shape of a stick in water, which appeared bent to vision but straight to touch, and again straight to vision when taken out of the water. Galileo noted: « therefore the deception of the oar under water does not arise from shape being a common sensible but from the difference of the media ».

La Galla found in optics the best example of the prejudice to the investigation of nature introduced by mathematics because it dealt with the common sensibles:

« for if the question is purely mathematical it abstracts from sensible and particular conditions; but if a judgement of sense follows, it is deceived. We have a most certain proof of this: for large illusions and deceptions occur in practical optics and harmonics, not indeed on account of the [sense] organ or the medium, but on account of the object, such as we easily see in pictures painted according to perspective, in which the eyes certainly see a thing otherwise than it is, even giving proportionate distances to it all: for we see on a plane and entirely level surface many roughnesses, heights, depths, chasms ».

Galileo wrote:

« If these deceptions arise from perspective, who will correct and understand them better than the students of perspective (*perspectivi*) themselves? ».

La Galla continued:

« Therefore, so that we may avoid this occasion for deception, I have considered that it would be safer to undertake this discussion physically rather than mathematically and optically. But I say that the occasion for deception arises not on the part of the [sense] organ and of the telescopic glass, as some have said (for innumerable people including myself discovered with the greatest certainty that this does not deceive, when we looked at exactly the same thing with the glass making no change in the thing except just in this respect: namely that the thing that we were observing confusedly and obscurely and scarcely at all on account of the distance and remoteness, we saw with the aid of the instrument as distinctly and clearly as if we were near at hand) but on account of the object, which cannot be seen from so great a distance except by means of light and shadow, from the various combinations of which it is probable that there appear these phenomena in the globe of the moon which we have undertaken to discuss ».

Galileo again showed his impatience with philosophical discussions of problems that could be solved technically, noting:

« if the students of perspective themselves produce many deceptions from the various combinations of light and shadow, no one better than themselves will correct them ».

He went on later (*G. G.*, III, 396-397):

« ... Vision is deceived in judging a straight stick half in water, judging it bent because shape is a common sensible; but in the same way and for the same cause it is deceived also about colours by the refraction of rays in a triangular crystalline prism. ... You want to accuse the mathematicians of ignorance for not being alert to sense being deceived in the common sensibles, as if knowing whether it was deceived or not was a recondite and profound mystery and secret of philosophy. But who has made more, and more exact observations and theorizings (*speculazioni*) about the deceptions of vision than the mathematicians themselves? The deception that makes the straight stick appear bent to me does not consist in the colour, even less in shape being a common sensible belonging as much to vision as to touch, for if that were so it would have to deceive as much out of the water as in it. Hence vision remains deceived by the way of seeing, that is by the image (*specie*) being refracted through the two different transparent media. This refracted visual image (*specie visiva*), since it has nothing to do with moving the sense of touch, is therefore not a common sensible. Hence the deception is not in the common sensible but in the proper one. He does not perceive that to say that vision is deceived when it judges by colour that the straight stick is bent puts the deception in the proper sensible and not in the common one, colour being the proper sensible of vision. The eye is not deceived at all in receiving as broken the image of the stick put half in water, because it comes no less true and real from the water broken and bent than from the air straight; but the deception is in the inference (*discorso*), which does not know that the visible images (*spezie visibili*) are refracted in the different transparent media ».

Galileo's eventual answer was the account in *Il saggiatore* (1623) of the « primary and real properties » (shape, size, location in place and time, touching or not, number, slow or swift motion) which he found himself obliged to attribute to matter, as distinct from the secondary qualities of sensation these produced in the « animate and sensitive body » (*G. G.*, VI, 347-349). With one exception, these primary properties had been assembled by the Greek atomists and Plato and listed by Aristotle as quantities as distinct from qualities, and as the objects common to more than one sense as distinct from those proper to each sense [8]. The item not included in Aristotle's list was the correlation of different sensory qualities with *variations* in speeds of motion. This came from the musical theorists, from Archytas of Tarentum and Plato to Boethius, who had linked pitch with the speed of the motions producing sound [9]. From these identifiable sources Galileo was provided with all the essential items for his explanation of the production of different sensible qualities by variations in motion of external bodies, represented as objects of touch and characterized only

---

[8] Aristotle's « common sensibles » were « motion, rest, shape, size, number, unity »: *De anima*, III, 1, 425a, 15-17; cf. *De sensu*, c. 1, 437a, 4-16. To these he added space and time as quantities: *Categoriae*, c. 6, 4b, 20-6a, 35. For Aristotle's account of the reduction by the atomists of all the senses to touch and of the proper to the common sensibles see *De sensu*, c. 4, 442a, 30b-17; note continued on p. 343.

[9] PLATO: *Timaeus*, 67A-C; THEONIS SMYRNAEI philosophi Platonici *Expositio rerum mathematicarum ad legendum Platonem utilium*, recensuit E. HILLER, Lipsiae, 1878, pp. 47-72; ARISTOTELES: *De anima*, II, 8, 419b, 4-420a, 4; C. JANUS (K. VON JAN): *Musici scriptores Graeci*, Lipsiae, 1895-1899, below nn. 11-13.

by the common sensibles. By defining this stable relationship in the passage of information to the perceiving organism from the world perceived, he offered a programme of experimental research into the physical basis of distinctions of sensation and perception and so into the physiology and psychology of the senses.

The idea that sound was propagated spherically through the air, just as waves on water were propagated circularly over the surface, had been put forward by the Stoics [10]. When Boethius adopted this analogy in his *De musica* he followed the Stoics and the Aristotelian work *De audibilibus* [11] in treating sound as a propagation of impulses from one part of the air to the next, rather than a bodily forward movement either of a part of the air or of a stream of particles passing through the air as Plato, Aristotle and the atomists had conceived it [12]. That is, Boethius gave a physical account of sound not as a transport of matter, but as a propagation of a state of motion in the form of waves or impulses. He added the important refinement of relating the pitch of heard sounds explicitly to the frequency of these vibratory impulses [13]. In the sixteenth and early seventeenth centuries this conception of sound was developed by means of experiments with vibrating strings, and used to explain resonance, consonance and dissonance, and other auditory phenomena first by Girolamo Fracastoro [14], Giovanni Battista Benedetti [15] and Vincenzo Galilei [16],

[10] J. VON ARNIM: *Stoicorum veterum fragmenta*, Lipsiae, 1903, II, p. 140; DIOGENES LAERTIUS: *Lives of eminent philosophers*, « Zeno », VII, p. 158, with an English translation by R. D. HICKS, London and Cambridge Mass., 1925, II, p. 261 (Loeb Classical Library); M. VITRUVII POLLIONIS *De architectura libri decem*, cum commentariis D. BARBARO, Venetiis, 1567, V, 3, pp. 171-172; S. SAMBURSKY: *Physics of the Stoics*, London, 1959, p. 23.

[11] Ps. ARISTOTELES: *De audibilibus*, 800*a*, 1-10; 803*b*, 1-804*a*, 7; cf. ID.: *Problemata*, XI, 6, 899*a*, 33-899*b*, 6; XIX, 24, 919*b*, 15-19; c. 39, 921*a*, 1-30; c. 41, 921*b*, 1-13; c. 50, 922*b*, 35-923*a*, 4.

[12] For references to these views see above *notes* [9-10]; D. LAERTIUS: [*cit. n.* [10]], « Epicurus », X, pp. 52-53.

[13] A. M. T. SEVERINI BOETHII *De institutione musica libri quinque*, ed. G. FREIDLEIN, Lipsiae, 1867, I, cc. 3, 8-11, 14; C. G. W. (GUALTHERUS) MIEKLEY: *De Boethii libri de musica primi fontibus*, Jena, 1898.

[14] H. FRACASTORII *De sympathia et antipathia rerum*, Venetiis, 1546, cc. 4, 11, 14.

[15] I. B. BENEDICTI *Diversarum speculationum mathematicarum et physicarum liber*, Taurini, 1585, « De intervallis musicis », pp. 277-283; see C. V. PALISCA: *Scientific empiricism and musical thought*, in H.H. RHYS, editor: *Seventeenth century science and the arts*, Princeton, 1961, pp. 104-109.

[16] V. GALILEI: *Dialogo della musica antica et della moderna*, Fiorenza, 1581; ID.: *Discorso intorno all'opere di messer Gioseffo Zarlino da Chioggia*, Fiorenza, 1589, pp. 92-95, 103-105, 109, 116-118; ID.: *Discorso particolare intorno alla diversità delle forme del diapason* and *Discorso particolare intorno all'unisono*, Biblioteca Nazionale Centrale di Firenze, Ma-

and then by Isaac Beeckman [17], Marin Mersenne [18], and Vincenzo's more famous son Galileo Galilei himself [19]. The complicated problem of their relationships will be discussed elsewhere. Galileo's independent contribution to knowledge of the physical basis of hearing and music was in fact of much less importance than the programme within which he conceived the problem. His own work within this programme included also the study of the physical basis of vision. At the same time, by envisaging an organized body neither animate nor sensitive, he offered a programme of research into the animal machine. His pioneering contributions to the study of animal and vegetable structures and of animal locomotion [20] were continued in the work of his brilliant disciple Giovanni Borelli [21], followed in the next generation by Marcello Malpighi [22].

---

noscritti galileiani, 3, ff. 44ʳ-54ᵛ, 55ʳ-61ᵛ; A. PROCISSI: [*cit. n.* ²], pp. 4-5; C. V. PALISCA: [*cit. n.* ¹⁵], pp. 120-135.

[17] See especially I. BEECKMAN: *Journal tenu ... de 1604 à 1634*, publié avec une introduction et des notes par C. DE WAARD, La Haye, 1939, I, ff. 23ʳ-24ʳ (1614-1615); 100ʳ-101ʳ, 104ᵛ-105ʳ (1618); 108ʳ (1619). Cf. also R. DESCARTES: *Compendium musicae* (1618; first published 1650; see R. DESCARTES: *Oeuvres*, publiées par C. ADAM et P. TANNERY, Paris, 1908, X, pp. 79-150); J. KEPLER: *Harmonice mundi libri v* (1619), lib. III, v (see J. KEPLER: *Gesammelte Werke*, hrg. ... M. CASPAR, München, 1940, vi); below *nota* ¹⁸.

[18] Mersenne described his view of and contributions to the science of sound in a long series of works: especially M. MERSENNE: *Quaestiones celeberrime in Genesim*, Lutetiae Parisiorum, 1623; ID.: *La vérité des sciences*, Paris, 1625; ID.: *Traité de l'harmonie universelle*, Paris, 1627; ID.: *Les préludes de l'harmonie universelle*, Paris, 1634; ID.: *Les questions théologiques, physiques, morales et mathématiques*, Paris, 1634; his comprehensive treatises: M. MERSENNE: *Harmonicorum libri ... Harmonicorum instrumentorum IV*, Lutetiae Parisiorum, 1636, and ID.: *Harmonie universelle*, Paris, 1636-1637; and ID.: *Cogitata physico-mathematica*, Parisiis, 1644, and ID.: *Novarum observationum physico-mathematicarum ... tomus III*, Parisiis, 1647. There are also fundamental discussions of acoustics and music with Beeckman, Descartes and other contemporaries in M. MERSENNE: *Correspondance*, editée et annotée par C. DE WAARD, avec la collaboration de R. PINTARD et B. ROCHOT, Paris, 1932-1967, I-X. Cf. H. LUDWIG: *Mersenne und seine Musiklehre*, Berlin, 1935; R. LENOBLE: *Mersenne ou la naissance du mécanisme*, Paris, 1943; see below, chs. 13-15.

[19] G. GALILEI: *Discorsi e dimostrazioni matematiche intorno a due nuove scienze*, Leida, 1638, I (*G. G.*, VIII, 138-150); cf. A. FAVARO: *Amici e corrispondenti di Galileo Galilei*, XXX, *Niccolò Aggiunti*, in *Atti del R. Istituto veneto di scienze, lettere ed arti*, LXXIII, 2 (Venezia, 1914).

[20] G. GALILEI: [*cit. n.* ¹⁹], I, II (*G. G.*, VIII, 113-114, 186-187); cf. L. BELLONI: *Schemi e modelli della macchina vivente nel Seicento*, in *Physis*, V (1963), pp. 259-298; M. D. GRMEK: *La personalité de Galilée et l'influence de son œuvre sur les sciences de la vie*, in CENTRE INTERNATIONAL DE SYNTHÈSE, ed.: *Galilée. Aspects de sa vie et de son œuvre*, Paris, 1968.

[21] I. A. BORELLI: *De motu animalium*, Roma, 1680-1681, pars I-II.

[22] Cf. M. MALPIGHI: *Risposta alla lettera intitolata « De recentiorum medicorum studio dissertatio epistolaris ad amicum »*, in M. MALPIGHI: *Opera posthuma*, Amstelodami, 1698, pp. 289-290.

3. - The nature of the elementary constituents of matter and of heat and light composing the external world conceived as a sheer mechanism.

Galileo developed a corpuscular theory of matter, under the influence of Plato, Democritus and Hero of Alexandria, through the *Discourse concerning bodies placed in water* (1612) [23] and the *Discourses ... concerning two new sciences* (1638) [24]. With Benedetto Castelli he developed a related kinetic   theory of heat and light. Although he had not discussed the nature of light in *Sidereus nuncius* (1610), Galileo had written in this work as if he held it to be something physical travelling from the heavenly bodies to the eye (e.g.: *G. G.*, III, 73). He made this explicit in a letter of May 1611 written to his friend Piero Dini in answer to some doubts expressed by « the leading literary men of Perugia » about the existence of Jupiter's four satellites or « Medicean planets » (*G. G.*, XI, 105, 115). Dealing with the argument that only direct vision could give valid information about the world, he wrote:

« Besides, who would wish to say that the light of the Medicean planets does not arrive on the earth? Are we to make our eyes the measure of the expansion of all lights, so that wherever the images (*specie*) of luminous objects do not make themselves sensible to us, it should be affirmed that light does not arrive from them? Perhaps such stars, that remain hidden from our weak vision, are seen by eagles or lynxes. But let us concede if you like more than the opponents could demand, and suppose that there is nothing in the world except what is seen or understood by us: it does not follow from that, that the light of the stars mentioned fails to arrive on the earth. In fact, since the visible images (*spezie visibili*) are nothing else than shaped light (*luce figurata*), or at least since they do not diffuse (*diffondersi*) without light, where these images arrive there the light also arrives. Now, if the images of four Medicean planets, as they diffused, vanished and were lost before they arrived on the earth, all the crystals Murano has would not be enough to make them visible, because what is nothing cannot be multiplied and enlargement (*dilatazione*) and augmentation presuppose the existence of what has to be enlarged and augmented. So, since the images of the four Medicean planets are seen with the telescope very large and luminous, it cannot be denied that their light diffuses very briskly as far as the earth ».

[23] Cf. *G. G.*, IV, 233-238, 247-248, 263-264, 280-283; K. LASSWITZ: *Galilei's Theorie der Materie*, in *Vierteljahrschrift für wissenschaftliche Philosophie*, XII (1888), pp. 458-476; L. LOWENHEIM: *Der Einfluss Demokrits auf Galilei*, in *Archiv für Geschichte der Philosophie*, VII (1894), pp. 230-268; E. GOLDBECK: *Galileis Atomistik und ihre Quellen*, in *Biblioteca mathematica*, 3 Folge, III (1902), pp. 84-112; W. SCHMIDT: *Hero von Alexandria im 17. Jahrhundert*, in *Abhandlungen zur Geschichte der Mathematik*, VIII (1898), pp. 195-214.

[24] Especially Day I (*G. G.*, VIII, 54-89, 104-105).

Another line of inquiry into the nature of light was reported by La Galla in the treatise *De luce et lumine disputatio* appended to his *De phoenomenis in orbe lunae* (1612). He opened his discussion with an account of some phenomena in which Galileo was to retain his interest to the end of his life: the production of light by various kinds of luminous bodies, raising the question whether there was a common cause. La Galla described how the question was put by Galileo [25]:

« Part of the night had already been spent, when there came together the Most Illustrious Federico Cesi, Marquis of Monte Celio, Patron of Letters in the City, Giovanni Remisani, a man well versed in every kind of learning, distinguished for his eloquence in both Greek and Latin, to whose brilliant mind we owe the new name « telescope », most aptly given to the glass, and also Giovanni Clementi, a most brilliant researcher into natural history, and a rival in our day to the glory of Pliny. We had assembled to meet the Most Excellent Galileo, our purpose being to see Venus display her crescent form through the glass, and other Mercuries revolving round Saturn. But when clouds prevented us from observation of the stars, we spent the meantime discussing various subjects, as often happens with learned men.

« The subject of illumination arose, and in this connection I lamented the weakness of the human intellect, and at the same time its presumption, in that it ventures to investigate all that is not only remotest from our senses, but also positively inaccessible to them, such as the purest and wholly blessed minds and the first principle of all things, the most perfect and highest good. But when it is faced with the thing that is clearest of all and as close and familiar to us as light itself, it is blind, so much so that nowhere else is it plunged in deeper darkness than in the study of this subject. For we are still not agreed in our general classification of it, as to whether it is substance or accident, body or something incorporeal, quality or relation; for such is the weakness of our intellect that it can easily be made to fit all these categories or equally be excluded from them. When I had pronounced this opinion the Most Excellent Galileo expressed his agreement with it and firmly avowed that he would willingly allow himself to be shut up in a dark cell and fed on bread and water, provided that, when he was restored to light in due course, he could perfectly grasp its nature and understand it; a sentiment truly worthy of a philosopher and gentleman. To strengthen this sceptical attitude in ourselves, knowing that we had all alike learnt at school that illumination was an incorporeal quality produced from a luminous body (*corpus lucidum*) and continuously flowing into the transparent (*diaphanum*), Galileo offered to demonstrate the opposite, by separating some light from the illuminated transparent and shut-

---

[25] I. C. LA GALLA: *De phoenomenis in orbe Lunae*, Venetiis, 1612, pp. 57-58; this treatise is not printed in *G. G.* For the attribution of the name « telescopio » to Demisiani (printed here Remisani) see E. ROSEN: *The naming of the telescope*, New York, 1947, pp. 54-61. Bologna stone is a kind of barites discovered about 1604 on Mount Paderno near Bologna by an alchemist called Vincenzio Casciarolo: *G. G.*, XI, 140; VIII, 469-545; XIII, 339.

ting it up so that it appeared to all to be in darkness, without any material being kindled or burnt, as usually happens, but the light alone being taken by itself and as it were dissected from the whole body.

« When this seemed paradoxical to everyone, he promised that he himself would soon demonstrate it. As soon as morning twilight, heralding the sun's rays, lit!the air, he took a little wooden box and showed us the little stones it contained, so that we could see whether they possessed any light. First he showed them by candlelight, then in darkness with all light excluded. When we had all agreed that they contained no light, he held the little wooden box out of the window so that the little stones should be illuminated, not by the sun's rays, which are called primary illumination, but by the still dubious and indistinct twilight or secondary illumination, such as one finds in the shade. After \ a little while he shut the window again and, without letting in any illumination, he showed us the little stones glittering and shining in the utter darkness, just as live coals do, though no heat had been acquired by the stones and no light retained by them. What is still more remarkable, we saw this same light gradually fade, and finally vanish altogether. From which we drew many conflicting inferences; for if light is a quality, and quality is incorporeal, as is obvious, how can it be enclosed and limited by fixed boundaries, for this is the peculiar property of substance? Or if it belongs to quality, it does not belong to quality that is not subject to corporeal conditions, as everyone knows is clearly the case with illumination. Besides, if illumination is a quality emitted (*producta*) from a luminous body into the transparent, so that it is dependent on the luminous body, as it is usually said to be, not only for its genesis but also for its continued existence (for illumination is produced and remains only so long as a luminous body is present in the transparent), then how is it that when the luminous body has been removed, e.g. by shuttering and barring the windows, light or illumination still remains, and shines on for a considerable time without fire and heat? This demonstration certainly struck all of us as remarkable; for although there are many things that in darkness, with all light excluded, so shine that they are not only conspicuous themselves, but also illuminate the ambient air, such as certain rotting woods, the scales, bones and heads of fish, cats' eyes, the underbelly of the glow-worm, and things of that sort, which are beheld with great astonishment; yet these little stones provide occasion for the greatest astonishment of all, since they not only take in illumination, although they are not transparent but opaque, and illumination hitherto used only to enter the transparent, but also they retain it, a property that is attributed neither to the transparent nor the opaque ».

Castelli was bolder than Galileo in pioneering the scientific conception of both heat and light as forms of motion. It was Castelli who had invented the method both used for observing sunspots with a telescope by throwing an image of the sun on a sheet of white paper [26]. By this means they

---

[26] *G. G.*, V, 113, 136; cf. B. DAME: *Galilée et les taches solaires (1610-1613)*, in *Revue d'histoire des sciences*, XIX (1966), pp. 307-370, reprinted CENTRE INTERNATIONAL DE SYNTHÈSE, ed: [*cit. n.* 20], pp. 186-251.

collected the evidence, described in the second and third of Galileo's *Three letters about the sunspots* (1612), that left them in no doubt that the sunspots were changes passing systematically across the sun's actual surface. In May 1612, a few days after Galileo had written his First Letter, Castelli sent him an account of some of his own observations and went on to offer an explanation of sunspots by linking the sun's light with its heat. He attributed both to the rapid motion of particles:

« ... Moved by such a fine occasion to philosophize, I say first, that if it is legitimate to philosophize about the luminous (*lucido*) body of the sun from our own luminous (*luminosi*) bodies, not only is it necessary that these spots are on the body of the sun but I cannot think otherwise. To explain myself better, take the light produced by a piece of white paper set alight by a fire. It is obvious that this luminosity is preceded by a blackness or let us say darkness of the food (*pabulo*) of this light, which, passing little by little through blue and then to red, finally becomes light; and this property (*accidente*) is common to all those bodies that emit (*spandono*) light by themselves. If then light is emitted from the sun, it is not surprising if it makes the transition from black and dark, and that those spots appear. I add (in agreement with my suppositions about light) that a luminous body (*corpo lucido*) being nothing but a body that continuously vibrates (*vibra*) and flings out very rapid corpuscles (*corpuscoli velocissimi*), and the sun being a luminous body and in consequence continuously darting out corpuscles enormously fast, since these bodies cannot begin leaving at the highest speed they will not, while they are moving slowly, certainly take on for me that appearance which I call light. The spots will then necessarily be on the sun, which is what we see » (*G. G.*, XI, 294-295).

Galileo's Third Letter about the Sunspots marks the expression of his natural philosophy in its maturity: the criteria for relevant evidence defining answerable questions and acceptable answers, the use of experimental models, the open frontiers into questions answerable by means of adequate concepts and techniques, and the problem of conceptual frontiers into the apparently unanswerable. He prefaced his discussion of the material nature of the sunspots with an account of what could be known as a basis for physical explanations, and went on to make suggestions resembling Castelli's interesting speculations:

« ... For in our speculating we either try to penetrate the true and intrinsic essence of natural substances, or content ourselves with coming to know some of their properties (*affezioni*). An attempt on the essence I hold to be an undertaking no less impossible and a labour no less vain in the nearest elementary substances than in the most distant and celestial ones. I feel as ignorant of the substance of the earth as of the moon, of the elementary clouds as of the sunspots. I do not see that in understanding these nearby substances we have any other advantage except the abundance of details, but all equally unknown, among which we wander, passing from one to the other with very little or no gain. And if, on asking what is the substance of the clouds, I am told that it is a humid vapour, I shall wish to know next what vapour is. Perhaps I shall be taught that it is water attenuated and resolved into vapour by the power of heat. But, equally doubtful about what water is, on researching into it I shall finally learn that it is a fluid body that runs in rivers and that we continually handle and use. But such information about water is merely closer at hand and dependent on more of the senses; it is no more intimate than the knowledge I had before about clouds. And in the same way I know no more of the true essence of earth or fire than of the moon or the sun; this is the sort of knowledge that is reserved to be learnt by us in the state of blessedness, and not before. But if we wish to stop at the apprehension of some properties (*affezioni*), it does not seem to me that we should despair of being able to reach them in the bodies most distant from us as well as in the nearest ones; rather, some of them perhaps more exactly in the former than in the latter. Who does not understand the periods of the movements of the planets better than those of the waters of different seas? Who does not know that the spherical shape of the lunar body was understood much before that of the earth and much more quickly? And is it not still debated whether this same earth is immobile or rather goes wandering, whereas we are most certain of the movements of not a few stars? Hence I wish to infer that even though it would be useless to try to investigate the substance of the sunspots, nevertheless this does not mean that some of their properties (*affezioni*), such as place, motion, shape, size, opacity, mutability, generation and dissolution, cannot be grasped by us and cannot become the means for being able to philosophize better about other more controversial conditions (*condizioni*) of natural substances. These then finally raising us to the ultimate goal of our labours, that is to the love of the divine Architect (*Artefice*), will keep alive our hope of being able to learn every other truth in Him, the source of light and of truth ».

These properties, he went on, were there for all to see if they made their observations correctly. For « nature, deaf and inexorable to our entreaties, will not alter or change the course of her effects; and those things that we are trying now to investigate and then to persuade others about, have not just occurred once and then vanished, but follow and will follow their own style for a long time, so that they will be seen and observed by many, many people. This should be a great restraint upon us in making us even more circumspect about stating our opinions and about taking care that any feelings, either towards ourselves or towards others, do not make us even slightly turn away from the target of the pure truth ».

He likened sunspots to smoke as well as clouds:

« ... and certainly I do not think that anyone who wanted to imitate them with some of our materials would find a more suitable imitation than to put on a red-hot iron plate some little drops of some kind of bitumen that burns with difficulty: this will impress on the iron a black spot, from which, as from its root cause, will rise a dark smoke, which will become spread out in strange and changing shapes. And even if anyone wanted to hold that probably food and nutriment would have to be continually supplied for the restoration of the immense light that continually diffuses from so great a lamp through the extent of the world, he would have indeed in harmonious agreement not only one but a hundred and all the experiments in which we see all materials on the point of catching fire and changing into light become first black and dark in colour. Thus we see in wood, straw, paper, candles, and in short in all burning things that the flame is planted in and rises from the contiguous parts of these materials, which have first turned black. And I should say further that perhaps, with more accurate observation of the patches mentioned above that are brighter than the rest of the solar disc, it would be possible to discover that these are the very same places where some of the largest spots had dissolved a little earlier. But I do not mean to assert any of these things for certain, nor to oblige myself to maintain it, for I do not like mixing dubious things with what are certain and established » (*G. G.*, V, 187-188, 218-219, 230-231).

In these and their later discussions about heat and light Galileo and Castelli both showed brilliantly constructive physical insight in their transformation of philosophical atomism, and Neoplatonic conceptions of the enormous energy latent in matter, into quantitative mechanistic physics [27]. Galileo in the *Discourses ... concerning two new sciences* later suggested methods of deciding by measurement whether light was a form of motion with a finite speed (*G. G.*, VIII, 87-89). But from his first consideration of the nature of light, through *Il saggiatore* (*G. G.*, VI, 350, 352), down to his last correspondence and controversy with Fortunio Liceti in 1640-1641 he maintained that the evidence could show him only how it behaved, not what it was. In 1640 Liceti sent the aged, blind philosopher his book, *Litheosphorus, sive De lapide Bononiensi* (1640), in which in passing he had cited from La Galla the opinion of « our sublime Galileo, who is said to reckon light to be a body, not an incorporeal quality » [28]. He also sent another work of his published in the same year, *De luminis natura et efficientia libri tres* (1640), in which he mentioned La Galla's account of the experiments Galileo had made with his friends with Bologna stone in their discussion of the nature of light [29]. Galileo wrote on receiving Liceti's second book [30]:

---

[27] See especially the correspondence between Galileo and Giovanni Battista Baliani of 25 and 31 January, 12 March and 8 August 1614 (*G. G.*, XII, 15-16, 19-22, 33-36, 474-478); Galileo's letter of 23 March 1615 to Piero Dini (*G. G.*, V. 297-305); and Castelli's letters to Galileo of 27 June, and 9 and 15 August 1637 (*G. G.*, XVII, 121-123, 150-169). The discussion in these last was inspired by *Il saggiatore*.

[28] FORTUNII LICETI Genuensis *Litheosphorus, sive De lapide Bononiensi, lucem in tenebris conservante liber*, Utini, 1640, p. 175.

[29] FORTUNII LICETI Genuensis *De luminis natura et efficientia libri tres*, Utini, 1640, pp. 16, 21-22, 46.

[30] Galileo to Liceti, 23 June 1640 (*G. G.*, XVIII, 208).

« ... I will have it read to me, hoping soon to be able to understand what, in thinking about it for many, many hundreds of hours, has not come within my capacity; I am speaking of the essence of light, about which I have always been in the dark; and I will consider it my greatest good fortune when, on being made capable of knowing what fire and light is, I will be able to understand how in a small fistfull of cold and black gunpowder there are enclosed twenty casks of fire and many millions of light; besides being also enclosed and kept held in those minute grains, one, so to speak, enormous quantity of tiny little bows which then, in letting fly, bring an astonishing force and speed. Here I would not like to be told that I have not stopped at the truth of fact, for experience shows me that it happens in this way; which, I could say, in all the effects of nature admired by me, assures me of the *an sit* but brings me no gain in the *quomodo* ».

After he had heard what Liceti had published, Galileo wrote again later objecting to his attribution to him of an opinion that he had not written [31]:

« ... I was astonished that because of something mentioned by the philosopher La Galla, you attributed to me the opinion that light is something material and corporeal, when you yourself can read in the same author that I have always held myself so incapable of being able to penetrate what sort of thing light is that I would have offered to stay in prison on bread and water all my life, if I was assured of achieving an understanding of which I so much despair ... ».

He went on to defend himself against the accusation that he was opposed to Aristotelian doctrine, because he was opposed to uses to which it was put. It was in logic that he claimed to be a better Aristotelian than his opponents:

« ... it is against all reason in the world that I am accused of being an opponent of Peripatetic doctrine, when I profess and am sure to observe the Peripatetic, or to put it better Aristotelian teachings more religiously than many others who unworthily pass me off as an opponent of good Peripatetic philosophy. Since to reason and argue well and to deduce the necessary conclusion from the premises is one of the teachings admirably given us by Aristotle in his Dialectics, if, when I see, being deduced from premises, conclusions that have no connection with them and so deviate from the Aristotelian doctrine, I amend and put them straight, I think that I can worthily consider myself a better Peripatetic and that I make a more correct use of this doctrine which others have used incorrectly ... ».

Galileo's final words to Liceti on nature and science repeated once more the famous image of *Il saggiatore* [32]:

---

[31] Galileo to Liceti, 25 August 1640 (*G. G.*, XVIII, pp. 233-234).

[32] Galileo to Liceti, January 1641 (*G. G.*, XVIII, p. 295); cf. *Il saggiatore*, p. 6 (*G. G.*, VI, 232).

« ... if philosophy was what is contained in Aristotle's books, in my opinion you should be the greatest philosopher in the world, you seem to me to have so much at hand and ready all the passages in him. But I really think that the book of philosophy is that which stands perpetually open before our eyes, but because it is written in characters different from those of our alphabet it cannot be read by everybody; and the characters of this book are triangles, squares, circles, spheres, cones, pyramids and other mathematical figures, fittest for this sort of reading ».

4. - The validity of the claim to one true reality discovered by reason.

Galileo's controversies over the Copernican system forced him to define the relationship of the new natural philosophy not only to traditional philosophical learning, but also to revealed belief and to other accepted bases for action. He developed his analysis of this question in the famous series of public letters written during 1613-1615 to Castelli, Piero Dini and Cristina di Lorena, in the *Considerations about the Copernican opinion* (1615), in notes on Bellarmine's letter to Foscarini (1615), and later in the *Letter to Francesco Ingoli* (1624), in the *Dialogue concerning the two principal systems of the world* (1632) and in notes and letters written in the light of the consequences of its publication (1633-1635) [33]. His essential claim was that natural philosophy was able to provide « necessary demonstrations » giving to men knowledge as certain as God's, even though infinitesimal in extent in comparison with His. These truths could not be changed at will like the administrative arrangements of law and commerce, and so could not be rejected because particular interpretations of Scripture seemed to contradict them. God had revealed himself as truly in the mathematical book of nature read by natural science as in the religious and moral book of Scripture, and their different characters and purposes should not be confused. There is a striking contrast between his cautious estimate of his knowledge of light, and his claim throughout the Copernican debate to be able to find « necessary demonstrations » of « the true constitution of the universe. For such a constitution exists, and exists in only one, true, real way, that could not possibly be otherwise » (*G. G.*, V, 330, 102). Here is the language of Aristotle's theory of truly scientific demonstration in the *Posterior analytics* [34]. An examination of this contrast shows the complexity of the elements going into

---

[33] For these writings see the « Scritture in difesa del sistema Copernicano » (*G. G.*, V, 261-370); and *G. G.*, XII, 171-172, 183-185; VI, 509-561; VII, 540-546, 562-568; XV, 24-25; XVI, 215-216, 234-235.

[34] I, 2, 71*b*, 9-72*a*, 24.

Galileo's philosophy. These are illuminating both historically and as an example of scientific thinking.

Paradoxically, Galileo's success as an innovator in scientific strategy was in many ways essentially conservative. In the contemporary debate over the true philosophy, he stood with reformers and conservatives alike in claiming *stare super vias antiquas*. On all his mature work he imposed commitments not only to a conception of the real physical world owing debts to Plato, Democritus and Hero of Alexandria, but also to a conception of scientific demonstration of this based on Aristotle. While he demolished Aristotelian physics, his scientific goal remained the « necessary demonstrations » of the *Posterior analytics* which he saw exemplified by Euclid, Archimedes, and his own science of terrestrial and celestial motion. The Archimedean approach was most successful when he used it to read the book of nature in the mathematical language of the primary properties, as in his treatment of floating bodies, free fall, projectiles and the strength of materials. Through it he created a theoretical real world of mathematical relationships which he was continually fascinated to find realized in the concrete actual world, as in the solutions to mechanical problems found in living structures. This approach also gave him his most fundamental contribution to the cosmological debate, his use of range of confirmation as the criterion of a true theory, which he applied in his first treatment of the arrangement of the elements as a problem of hydrostatics, in his telescopic observations, and in his final dynamical argument for Copernicus from the tides. It was this criterion that was to enable Newton to decide the issue with more adequate dynamics. But by claiming that with it he was giving a « necessary demonstration » in the Aristotelian sense, Galileo claimed more than he needed and ran into two objections already made to Aristotle in the thirteenth century. He was careful to say that he was demonstrating the world as it existed, not God's reasons for creating it so, but he risked the accusation that he claimed to penetrate and find limits to God's inscrutably omnipotent will by human reason. He also exposed himself to the accusation of committing the logical fallacy of affirming the consequent; for he seemed to be asserting that phenomena uniquely determined their causes [35]. His scientific insight in using the criterion of range of confirmation threw open the frontiers of possibilities for both new observations and new theories, but neither he nor his opponents saw that it introduced a different conception of scientific demonstration from Aristotle's. Hence the cross-purposes evident in parts of this debate.

---

[35] Cf. Galileo's *Discorso del flusso e reflusso del mare* (1616) (*G. G.*, V, 371-396); and Antonio Rocco's comments on the *Dialogo* with Galileo's replies (*G. G.*, VII, 628-629, 699-700); A. C. CROMBIE: *The relevance of the Middle Ages to the scientific movement*, in *Perspectives in medieval history*, ed. K. F. DREW and F. S. LEAR, Chicago, 1963, pp. 40-45.

If we examine the whole range of Galileo's scientific activities, and not simply his mechanics, it becomes clear that he pursued throughout a consistent philosophical ideal, but varied his scientific methods and their ancient models according to the problems imposed by the subject matter. He kept in view two clear aims: he insisted on the open frontier into the unknown, and he used his conception of scientific demonstration to distinguish as sharply as possible between what had been and could be established, and what had not and could not, both in general and in any particular case. In the cultural context of his time, he had to put a large amount of effort into establishing the identity of natural philosophy by defining rational criteria for the questions as well as the answers to be admitted, in distinction from literary philosophical erudition, the scholastic exercise of the *disputationis gratia*, uncritical interest in everything from technology to numerology and magic, and mere curiosity. By organizing his combination of ancient models to define « the primary and real properties » of matter in purely quantitative terms that could enter into a mathematical science of nature, and by using range of confirmation as a criterion of truth, he made natural philosophy an open system as the mathematical sciences had been since antiquity. He tried to show by solving specific physical problems that mathematical science created not simply a new and true natural philosophy, but the only available one. But in so defining the field of anwerable questions, he shifted this new philosopy to an area that no Greek would have accepted. In aiming at *episteme, scientia*, true and certain knowledge of the essences of natural things, ancient philosophy had contrasted this with *techne, ars*, the manipulative skills, including mathematics and experiment. Galileo tried to show that the new technical « art » of the « Physico-mathematical Experimental Learning » (to use the Royal Society phrase) [36] yielded the true science of the only nature he believed to exist. The philosophical attempt at *episteme* exemplified most ambitiously by Aristotle became either false or irrelevant, and speculations about possible worlds not aimed at finding the one actual one became a waste of time.

This conception of science had further consequences. Scientific inquiry now became systematically an active manipulation and dissection of nature, rather than simply observation or the search for a consensus between existing opinions. The explicit conception emerged of science as problems to be solved, rather than schemes to be contemplated. In Kant's famous image, the experimental philosopher became with Galileo no longer a pupil accepting everything nature chose to tell him, but a presiding judge who compelled nature to answer the questions that he

[36] C.R.Weld: *A history of the Royal Society*, London, 1848, I, p. 65.

himself devised [37]. The scientific experiment became an active technique for anatomizing phenomena by means of new questions, as well as for reconstructing and explaining them by means of the answers. Natural philosophy was incorporated into the fundamental tone of modern Western civilization, characteristic of its art and its politics as much as its science: its coercive, military approach to nature and mankind, its restless curiosity and striving for progress, in striking contrast with every other civilization. In consequence it became an essential part of natural philosophical inquiry to keep its basic assumptions under constant critical scrutiny. Galileo did not recognize that with the criterion of range of confirmation a new conception of scentific demonstration had been introduced into science, but he led the innovating party towards the explicit recognition of this by Newton and Huygens by emphasizing the transfer of attention from justification of consequences by deduction from accepted principles, to justification of the principles themselves. Further, by actively uncovering the hidden structure of nature, by inventing a language in which nature could speak, and by insisting that nature spoke only in the mathematical language of the primary properties, he introduced the revolutionary principle that, since all natural causes were mechanical, the causes of the behaviour of natural bodies were no different from those of artificial things. In this way he abolished the absolute distinction, accepted from Aristotle, between natural substances generated by nature and artificial things made by man, and at the same time he satisfied Aristotle's condition that in a scientific demonstration the basic principles must all be of the same genus [38]. It followed that, contrary to the Aristotelian view, artificial imitations and models could explain natural processes. If Galileo was a Platonist, he was also an engineer. This conception of the uniformity of all natural causes, since all were mechanistic, gave him in the method of the hypothetical and physical model one of his most powerful ways of putting new questions to nature.

Galileo's extraordinary energy led him to bring into this exacting court of inquiry questions that made him a pioneer over a whole range of contemporary physics and physiology. His insistence on specifying precisely the conditions for valid sensory information gives his physiological psychology a topical as well as an historical interest. But above all he interests us because, by defining both the only kinds of question he held the witness capable of answering and also the available means of checking their dependability, he pioneered accepted norms of scientific thought. « The

---

[37] I. KANT: *Critique of pure reason*, « Preface » to second edition; cf. A. C. CROMBIE: *Augustine to Galileo*, London, 1959, 1979, II, pp. 315-333.

[38] Cf. above *nota* [34]; Descartes was of course to develop philosophical mechanism more systematically than Galileo.

most subtle Galileo, easily the chief of the mathematicians of our time, and the same time a noted philosopher », Liceti described him in yet another book published in 1640, discussing whether the universe was infinite [39]. Galileo's comment illustrates his consistency and his limitations [40]:

« I cannot stop wondering how one single human mind can store all the doctrines scattered in a thousand books by a thousand other rare minds. I have perceived you mentioning me in particular with praise in that place where you discuss at length the magnitude of the universe, whether it should be thought finite or infinite. The reasons given for both sides are very acute, but in my brain neither of them reaches any necessary conclusion, so that I still remain uncertain about which of the two assertions is true; yet one single particular argument of mine inclines me more to the infinite than to the limited, since I do not know how I could imagine it either limited, or unlimited and infinite. And since the infinite *ratione sui* cannot be encompassed by our limited minds, which is not the case with the finite and what is circumscribed by a boundary, I must relate my incomprehension rather to the incomprehensible infinitude than to the finiteness, in which there is no reason for its being incomprehensible. But, as Your Excellency freely affirms, this is one of those questions that happen to be inexplicable by human reasonings, resembling perhaps predestination, free will and other matters, where only the Holy Scriptures and the divine assertions can set us piously at rest ».

n. 8 continued: Galileo's distinction of primary properties from secondary qualities corresponds to that made by the Greek atomists as reported by Galen in *De elementis secundum Hippocratem*, a possible source for Galileo who on 15 November 1590 wrote to his father for Galen's works (*G.G.* x, 44-45).

Further references: A. Carugo and A. C. Crombie, "The Jesuits and Galileo's ideas of science and of nature", *Annali dell' Istituto e Museo di Storia della Scienze di Firenze*, viii.2 (1983) 3-68, and "Galileo and the art of rhetoric", *Nouvelles de la république des lettres* (1988) ii, 7-31, A. C. Crombie, "Alexandre Koyré in Great Britain: Galileo and Mersenne" in *Science: the Renaissance of a History*, ed. P. Redondi (*History and Technology,* iv; London, 1987) 81-92, A. C. Crombie and A. Carugo, "Sorting out the sources", *Times Literary Supplement* (22.xi.1985) 1319-20, (14.ii.1986) 165, (29.viii. 1986) 939, and *Galileo's Arguments and Disputes in Natural Philosophy* (forthcoming); N. Jardine, "Galileo's road to truth and the demonstrative regress", *Studies in History and Philosophy of Science*, vii (1976) 277-318, "The forging of modern realism: Clavius and Kepler against the sceptics", ibid. x (1979) 141-73; W. R. Shea, *Galileo's Intellectual Revolution* (London, 1972); W. L. Wisan, "Galileo's scientific method: a re-examination" in *New Perspectives on Galileo*, ed. R. E. Butts and J. C. Pitt (Dordrecht, 1978) 1-57; see also below ch. 12 p. 354 n. 26 and chs. 13-15.

---

[39] FORTUNI LICETI Genuensis *De quaesitis per epistola a claris viris responsa*, Bononiae, 1640, pp. 270.
[40] Galileo to Liceti, 24 September, 1639 (*G. G.*, XVIII, 106). Liceti had sent him a copy in advance of publication.

12

PHILOSOPHICAL PRESUPPOSITIONS AND
SHIFTING INTERPRETATIONS OF GALILEO

It is entirely appropriate that a discussion of shifting interpretations of Galileo should take as its *terminus a quo* the *très cher maître* of so many of us who took up the history of science professionally immediately after the Second World War: the great Alexandre Koyré. With three or four other rare spirits he was one of those who showed by example the enlightenment that can be gained only by looking beneath the surface of immediate scientific results, by seeking to identify the intellectual and technical conditions that made certain discoveries possible and explanations acceptable to a particular generation or group, others not, and the same not to others. By displaying the science in historical relation to the philosophical assumptions, technical equipment, and social context of its designers and discoverers, they showed how the history of science could illuminate the nature both of European culture and of scientific thinking. This contextual approach establishes the identity of the history of science as a field of study. It shows it clearly to belong in its sources, content and methods of scholarship to history and philosophy, and equally clearly to require some special knowledge of the problems whose records are its primary materials. The history of science might be seen as a history of intellectual behaviour, in the sense both of a history recreating the past and of a comparative natural history of examples, a kind of philosophical anthropology. It is enlightening to compare the different attitudes to nature developed through different periods of European history, and to compare European attitudes with others. Such comparisons involve conceptions both of science and of history, a point which Koyré made fundamental in the evaluation of any interpretation of the history of science.

In his own sophisticated reinterpretation of Galileo's sophisticated thinking, Koyré showed that experimental science was an argument, and that experiments contributed to the argument at logically precise points in its development. In doing this it might be said that he saw Galileo too much through his own Platonic vision: as pointed out by Ludovico Geymonat, and indeed also among others by myself.[1]

---

[1] A. C. Crombie, *Galilée devant les critiques de la posterité* (Les Conferences du Palais de la Découverte, Paris, 1957), cf. on the Galileo Prize, *Physis*, xii (1970) 107; L. Geymonat, *Galileo Galilei* (Milano, 1957; New York, 1965); above chs. 8, 11 below n. 2.

Nevertheless it was from Koyré's *Etudes Galiléennes* (1939) that we all learnt to look at Galileo in a new way: to understand more clearly just how Archimedes was a model for his scientific thinking: that Galileo's view of his procedure in investigating simple but subtle subject-matter like that of motion was first to construct a theoretical world, and then to contrive experiments (real or imaginary) to test whether this was the existing world in which he lived. But we should not forget that in more complex subject-matters, such as those of sunspots, heat, light and floating bodies, experiment had also for Galileo a more directly exploratory role: using then the Aristotelian logical criteria of presence, absence, and agreement in degrees or concomitant variations.[2]

If then the *terminus a quo* of interpretations of Galileo is to be Alexandre Koyré, we might look for likewise sophisticated shifts from that point not in any *terminus ad quem* but in the continuing scholarship relating Galileo and his contemporaries truly to their intellectual and social context: scientific, philosophical, theological, economic, technological, and artistic. And here we might remember those other genial intelligences for whom Galileo was an inspiration: Leonardo Olschki, Edwin Burtt, Giorgio de Santillana, and behind them the masterly scholarship of Rafaello Caverni and Antonio Favaro.

Let me now very briefly indicate a small selection of the characteristics shared by Galileo with his intellectual and cultural context which seem to me to illuminate his intellectual personality and the way he went about his activities, and to illuminate at the same time much other contemporary intellectual behaviour. When we look at Galileo as a man of late Renaissance Italy, we should try to relate the style of his scientific thinking to contemporary styles of thinking in the arts, in philosophy, and in practical affairs. Then through the particular example of Galileo we can offer an analysis of the various elements that make up an intellectual style in the study of nature: conceptions of nature and of science, of scientific inquiry and scientific demonstration and explanation with their diversifications according to subject-matter, of the identity of science within an intellectual culture, and the intellectual commitments and expectations generating attitudes to innovation and change. In exploring these questions we should also keep in view the historical problem of the unique origins of modern science in the society of Western Europe. The example of Galileo gives a central focus to this view in Galileo's style as a Renaissance man of *virtù*. This, in Renaissance

---

[2] See for full documentation of this paper with bibliographies Crombie, *Styles of Scientific Thinking in the European Tradition*, Crombie and A. Carugo, *Galileo's Arguments and Disputes in Natural Philosophy* (both forthcoming); cf. above n.1, below nn.4, 26, 28, 30.

Italian, meant a man with active intellectual power (*virtù*) to command any situation, to control what he did and what he made, whether in mind or matter, in the natural sciences or the constructive arts, in private or political life, as distinct from being at the mercy of events, of the accidents of *fortuna*. The conception of the *virtuoso*, the rational artist aiming at reasoned and examined control alike of his own thoughts and intentions and of his surroundings, seems to me of the essence of the European morality, meaning both habits and ethics, out of which European science was generated and engineered.

The scientific movement generated in Western Europe, above all, a capacity to act with rational intent in the control at once both of argument and calculation, and of a variety of materials and practical activities. It generated, thereby, an effective context for seeing and solving the exemplary technical problems shared by the mathematical sciences with the visual, musical, plastic, and mechanical arts. All exemplified a common mastery of nature by the rational anticipation of effects, whether by means of quantified theory alone, or by modelling a theory with an artifact analytically imitating and extending the natural original. The rational artist and the rational experimenter and observer thus acted alike in conceiving alike an artistic construction and a scientific inquiry first in the mind before executing it with the hands. But, beyond that, there was in the conception of a man of *virtù* a programme for relating man to the world as perceiver and knower and agent in the context of his integral moral and social and cosmological existence. The programme entailed a commitment to reasoned consistency in all things. Let me simply illustrate with some quotations:

Domingo Gundisalvo (late 12th century):

Natural things are those which nature produces by motion visibly operating from potency to actuality.... But artificial things are those made by the art and will of man.... The artist is the natural philosopher who, proceeding rationally from the causes of things to the effects and from effects to causes, searches for principles. By optics... what appears in vision otherwise than it is is distinguished from what appears as it is. For this science assigns the causes by which these things are brought about, and this by necessary demonstrations. ... The science of engines is the science for contriving how one can make all those things agree, of which the measures are expressed and demonstrated in mathematical theory, agree I say in natural bodies .... The sciences of engines therefore teach the ways of contriving and finding out how natural bodies may be fitted together by some artifice according to number, so that the use we are looking for may come from them.[3]

Leon Battista Alberti (1435):

Man is to render praise to God to satisfy him with good works for those gifts of excelling *virtù* that God gave to the soul of man, greatest and preeminent above all

[3] Dominicus Gundissalinus, *De divisione philosophiae*, hrg. L. Baur (*Beiträge zur Geschichte der Philosophie des Mittelalters*, iv.2–3; Münster, 1903) 10, 27, 112, 122.

other earthly animals.[4]

In writing about painting ... we will, to make our discourse clearer, first take from mathematicians those things which seem relevant to the subject. When we have learned these, we will go on, to the best of our ability, to explain the art of painting from the basic principles of nature .... We will now go on to instruct the painter how he can represent with his hand what he has conceived with his mind.[5]

Giorgio Valla (1501):

Nature also follows a path, that is she follows her own order because she carries out everything of that sort with reason as leader. But not with imagination like art, for she does not prepare anything inwardly which she wishes to produce. But the artist reasons when he wants something for himself, fashions and forms it inwardly, and accordingly makes an image for himself of everything that is to be portrayed.[6]

Archytas of Tarentum ... says at the very beginning of his *On Mathematics*: They seem to me to be correct in their estimation and apprehension of mathematical sciences, who consider these to weigh particulars exactly because mathematicians are very well versed in the nature of the whole.[7]

Marsilio Ficino (1469–74):

What is a work of art? The mind of the artist in matter separate from it. What is a work of nature? The mind of nature in matter united with it.[8]

Other living things live either without art or with one single art, to the practice of which they do not apply themselves of their own accord but are drawn to it by a law of fate. Proof of this is that they make no progress with time in the business of constructing things. Men on the other hand are the inventors of countless arts which they pursue of their own will. This is proved by the fact that individuals practise many arts, change, and through long practice become more skilful. And what is remarkable, human arts construct by themselves whatever nature herself constructs, as if we were not slaves of nature but rivals.[9]

Leonardo da Vinci (lived 1452–1519):

Astronomy and the other sciences proceed by means of manual operations, but first they are mental as is painting, which is first in the mind of him who theorizes on it, but painting cannot achieve its perfection without manual operation.[10]

In fact whatever exists in the universe through essence, presence or imagination, the painter has first in the mind and then in the hands.[11]

But first I make some experiment before going any further, because my intention is to cite experience first and then to demonstrate with reason why such an experience is constrained to operate thus in this way; that is the true rule according to which

---

[4] Leon Battista Alberti, *I libri della famiglia*, ed. C. Grayson (*Opere volgari*, i, Bari, 1960) 133; cf. Crombie, 'Science and the arts in the Renaissance: The search for certainty and truth, old and new' *History of Science*, xviii (1980) 233-46.

[5] Alberti, *De pictura*, i.1 and 24, ed. C. Grayson in *On Painting and On Sculpture* (London, 1972) 58.

[6] Giorgius Valla, *De expetendis et fugiendis rebus opus*, i. 3 (Venetiis, 1501).

[7] *Ibid.* vi. 4.

[8] Marsilius Ficinus, *Theologia Platonica*, iv. 1 (*Opera*, Basileae, 1576) 123.

[9] *Ibid.* xiii.3, pp. 295-7.

[10] Leonardo da Vinci, *Treatise on Painting, Codex Urbinas Latinus* 1270, i. 19, transl. A. P. McMahon (Princeton, 1956): a posthumous compilation.

[11] *Ibid.* i. 35.

theorizers about natural effects have to proceed. And although nature starts from the reason and finishes at experience, for us it is necessary to proceed the other way round, that is starting . . . from experience and with that to investigate the reason.[12]

There is no effect in nature without reason; understand the reason and you do not need experiment.[13]

Oh speculator on things, I do not praise you for knowing the things that nature through her order naturally brings about ordinarily by herself; but, I say, rejoice in knowing the end of those things which are designed by your own mind.[14]

Vitruvius on the architect:

His works are born from both construction and reasoning (*De architectura*, i.1.1).
The philological commentary on the earliest Italian translation (1521):
Machinatio . . . may be derived from I cunningly contrive, . . . I deliberate, I think out, . . . stratagem, . . . whence undertaking, thinking, machine and . . . mechanic or mechanical operator.[15]

Machina . . . . Mechanics . . . is commendable whether for its basic imitative resemblance to the divine work of the construction of the world, or for the great and memorable usefulness reached by the human beings enumerated . . . . And that furthermore . . . has been put into practice through a burning desire to produce in sensible works with their own hands that which they have thought out with the mind.[16]

Alessandro Piccolomini (1542):

On the cause on which human happiness depends. Given that the happiness of man consists in acting according to *virtù* in a perfect life, it is reasonable to ask on whom it depends, that is in whose power is this happiness. So it must be noted that according to Aristotle it must derive from one of three causes: divine or human or fortuitous. And if it comes from a human cause, this is either through reasoning or through practice. That it cannot depend on fortune can be seen from the fact that so noble an effect as our own happiness cannot be produced by so vile a cause as fortune, since fortune is not an essential cause but accidental and consequently vile and ignoble. An essential cause surely is what produces the effect according to the intention of that cause, just as an architect produces a house according to his own intention.[17]

Niccolò Tartaglia (1554):

. . . things constructed or manufactured in matter can never be made so precisely as they can be imagined by the mind outside that matter, by which effects may be caused in them quite contrary to reason. And from this and other similar considerations, the

---

[12] Leonardo da Vinci, *Les manuscrits . . . de la Bibliothéque de l'Institut*, Codex E., f. 55ʳ, publiés . . . par . . . C. Ravaisson-Mollien (Paris, 1888).
[13] Leonardo da Vinci, *Il Codico Atlantico nella Biblioteca Ambrosiana di Milano*, . . . transcrizione . . . di G. Piumati, f. 147ᵛ (Milano, 1894–1904).
[14] Leonardo da Vinci, *Les manuscrits . . .* Cod. G., f. 47ʳ, par . . . Ravaisson-Mollien (1890).
[15] Marcus Lucius Vitruvius Pollio, *De architectura libri dece, traducti de latino in vulgare, affigurati, commentati*, i. 3 (Como, 1521) f. 18: begun by Cesare Cesariano and completed by Benedetto Giovio and Bono Mauro; see P. Galluzzi, 'A proposito di un errore dei traduttori di Vitruvio nel '500'', *Annali dell' Istituto e Museo di Storia della Scienza di Firenze*, i.2 (1976) 78-80.
[16] Vitruvius, *ibid.* x. i. f. 162ᵛ.
[17] Alessandro Piccolomini, *De la institutione di tutta la vita de l'homo nato nobile e in un città libera . . .* i. 3 (Venetiis, 1545) f. 16ʳ (first ed. 1542).

mathematician does not accept or consent to demonstrations or proofs made on the strength and authority of the senses in matter, but only on those made by demonstration, and arguments abstracted from all sensible matter.... Similarly, as to those questions that have already been demonstrated with mathematical arguments which are more certain, one should not attempt or believe it possible to certify them better with physical arguments, which are less certain.

Nevertheless

all those things which are known in the mind to be true, and especially by demonstrations abstracted from all matter, should reasonably also be verified in matter by the sense of sight: otherwise mathematics would be wholly useless and of no help or profit to man.[18]

Daniele Barbaro (1556): on Michelangelo:

For the artist works first in the intellect and conceives in the mind, and then signs the external matter with the internal habit.[19]

Art can so far imitate nature, and this comes about because the principle of art which is the human intellect has a great resemblance to the principle that moves nature, which is a divine intelligence; from the resemblance of power and of principles is born the resemblance of operating, which for the present we will call imitation.

But

the intellect of man is imperfect and not equal to the divine intellect, and matter so to speak is deaf, and the hand does not respond to the intention of art;

hence

the architect must think very well and, in order to make more certain of the success of the works, will proceed first with the design and the model, ... and ... he will imitate nature, which does not do anything against its maker. Yet he will not search for impossible things, either as to the matter or as to the form, which neither he nor others can accomplish.... Whence art, observer of nature, wanting also to make something, takes the matter of nature put into existence with sensible and natural form, as is wood, iron, stone, and forms that matter with that idea and with that sign which is reposing in the mind of the artist.[20]

Peter Ramus (1569):

For Archytas and Eudoxus, says Plutarch in his *Marcellus*, transferred mathematical contemplations from the mind, and from things falling within the understanding of thought alone, to examples of sensible and corporal things, enriching geometry with a variety of demonstrations, not only logical but also practical, and they taught that geometry was of the very greatest use in life ... this faculty of geometry is called mechanical and instrumental. But Plato, indignant that they revealed and published the noblest of philosophers to the vulgar and as it were betrayed the secret mysteries of philosophy, deterred both from their undertaking.... How much better and more correctly you judged, when you said that philosophers should be urged from the school and leisure to the government of state, from the contemplation of arts to practising their use.[21]

[18] Niccolò Tartaglia, *Quesiti et inventioni diverse*, vii. 1 (Venetiis, 1546) ff. 78ʳ–9ᵛ.
[19] Daniele Barbaro, *I dieci libri dell'Architettura di M. Vitruvio, tradutti e commentati* ... Proemio (Vinegia, 1556) 9.
[20] *Ibid.* i. 3, p. 26.
[21] Petrus Ramus, *Scholarum mathematicarum libri*, i (Basileae, 1569) 18.

Guidobaldo del Monte (1588):

But if art overcomes nature by imitating her so that those things which are done by art happen contrary to nature, the genius of art will appear by this much more excellent; if indeed in imitating nature it may be said to act contrary to the order of nature (for that will seem perhaps paradoxical, although it is very true). For art with wonderful skill overcomes nature through nature herself, by so arranging things as nature herself would do if she decided that such effects should be produced by herself.[22]

Galileo Galilei (undated):

I have seene all engineers deceiv'd, while they would apply their engines to works of their own nature impossible; in the success of which both they themselves have been deceiv'd, and others also defrauded of the hopes they had conceiv'd upon their promeses ... ; as if, with their engines they could cosen nature, whose inviolable lawe it is, that no resistance can be overcome by force which is not stronger than it. Which belief how false it is, I hope by true and necessary demonstration to make most manifest ... ; and this is according to the necessary constitution of nature .... Nay if it were otherwise, it were not only absurd, but impossible .... And ... all wonder ceases in us of that effect, which goes not a poynt out of the bounds of nature's constitution.[23]

Vincenzo Viviani (1654) on Galileo's decision to live outside the city on his return to Florence in 1610:

There he lived with the more satisfaction because it seemed to him that the city was a kind of prison for speculative minds, and that the freedom of the country was the book of nature, always open to those who enjoyed reading and studying it with the eyes of the intellect. He said that the letters in which it was written were the propositions, figures and conclusions of geometry, by means of which alone was it possible to penetrate any of the infinite mysteries of nature .... He praised indeed all that had been written in philosophy and geometry that was well designed to enlighten and awaken the mind towards similar and higher speculations, but he very aptly used to say that the main doors into the richest treasury of natural philosophy were observations and experiments, which could be opened by the noblest and most inquisitive intellects by means of the keys of the senses .... At all times he took great delight in agriculture, which served him at once as a pastime and as an occasion to philosophize about the way plants feed and grow, the prolific power of seeds, and the other wonderful works of the Divine Architect .... He had a marvellous understanding of the theory of music, and of this he gave a clear example in the First Day of his last Dialogues [i.e. *Discorsi*, 1638]. Besides the delight he took in painting, he enjoyed with exquisite taste works of sculpture and architecture and all the arts subordinate to design.[24]

Living from Michelangelo's death to Newton's birth, Galileo marks the transition between two great European intellectual movements each in its own way dominated by mathematical rationality: the

---

[22] Guidobaldus e Marchio Montis, *In duos Archimidis Aequeponderantium libros paraphrasis scholiis illustrata*, Praefatio (Pesauri, 1588) 2.
[23] Galileo, *Le mecaniche*, ed. naz., direttore A. Favaro (*Le opere*, ii, Firenze, 1968) 155, 189, transl. Robert Payne (1636): transcribed from British Museum MS Harley 6796, ff. 317^r, 329^r-30^r, by A. Carugo: see Crombie and Carugo, op. cit., ch. 2. iii.
[24] Vicenzo Viviani, 'Racconto istorico della vita di Galileo' (1654; *Le opere*, xix) 625, 627.

transition from the world of the rational constructive artist to that of the rational experimental scientist. A product of the integrated intellectual culture of the 16th-century Italian cities, he enjoyed both its interest and its expertise in a rich variety of activities ranging from natural history and the mathematical arts and sciences of music, perspective painting, cartography, architecture, engineering, gunnery, mechanics, and astronomy to philosophy, cosmology, theology and the Italian language as a vehicle of scientific and philosophical expression. When Galileo was negotiating his return to Tuscany in 1610 in the service of the Grand Duke he wrote famously that "as to the title and function of my service, I desire that in addition to the name of mathematician His Highness will add that of philosopher; for I claim to have studied more years in philosophy than months in pure mathematics."[25] It is above all as the author of a philosophical strategy for the sciences of nature, of the design of a scientific style, that Galileo seems to me to illuminate the identity of science within the intellectual culture of early modern Europe.

A pugnacious man like his musical father, Galileo placed himself within what might be called the battle conception of history. He came to see himself battling for two essential elements of an effective strategy for scientific thinking: for principles of explanation applicable to the whole of nature, and for methods of inquiry by which to find accurate and convincing solutions to specific limited problems. One essential criterion for accepting the first was their strict and technical application to the second. These were two aspects of the same search for dependable knowledge. Whether we see Galileo as a Platonist for whom the book of nature was written in mathematical language,. or as a Renaissance artist-engineer who sought to control his materials by taking nature to pieces in a workshop in order to reassemble it from then known principles, he acted also as a humanist scholar debating the best ancient models for true scientific thinking. He could then claim the title of philosopher as an heir to the ancients who transformed their general questions into questions capable of technical scientific answers. This was, and remained long after Galileo, one fruitful approach to the continuing problem of establishing the identity of natural philosophy within the whole varied context of intellectual culture, and with that an agreed conception both of nature and of scientific explanation.

In seeing himself as a pioneer of a new natural philosophy that excluded all others because it uniquely could both define and solve particular and quantitative physical problems and in doing so relate them to a general system of explanation, Galileo was at one with

---

[25] Galileo to Belisario Vinta, 7 May 1610, *Le opere*, x, 353.

conservatives and reformers alike in their paradoxical claim *stare super vias antiquas*. But his ancient guides for selecting the answerable questions defining the true new science came to be less Plato or Democritus than the models for problem-solving set out by Archimedes and the atomic or corpuscular theory of matter offered within a scientific treatise by Hero of Alexandria. His strategy was to establish effective criteria for selecting answerable questions, as well as acceptable answers, to be admitted into an inquiry. The admissible questions came to be, in principle, those answerable by means of mathematical and experimental analysis and an exclusive conception of physical causation. The last criterion came from Aristotle, but Galileo came to make it explicitly mechanistic. True natural science was then distinct from scholastic disputations conducted simply as logical exercises, or building general systems that solved no particular physical problems, or philosophical erudition and theological exegesis like those aiming at concordance in one divine and natural truth, or the uncritical curiosity of natural magic, or the arbitrary transactions of human commerce or law, or constructions for artistic or engineering effect rather than scientific explanation. Galileo's rational experimental science was defined by its integrated search at one and the same time both for reproducible practical results and for corresponding principles of theoretical explanation.

To unravel and date the relative influences on Galileo's scientific style of Plato and Aristotle, and Archimedes and Hero of Alexandria, we must more than ever look below the immediately obvious historical surface of his investigations and disputes and try to grasp the intentions of his arguments. We should distinguish first between the mathematical techniques and conceptions used in exploring the relations within phenomena, for which his essential guide was Archimedes, and the logic of demonstration supposed. The latter was provided by Aristotle's conception of apodeictic demonstration, with its epistemological demand that this should contain a complete explanation in physics through the efficient and material as well as formal causes. By discovering and investigating the date of Galileo's use of textbooks by three Jesuit professors at the Collegio Romano for his essays on Aristotelian natural philosophy misnamed by Favaro *Juvenilia*, and by relating these essays to his other writings, Adriano Carugo and I have established the longevity and depth of the Aristotelian knowledge from which Galileo approached the search for the true cosmology which became the overriding intellectual preoccupation of his life. Work on another unpublished Aristotelian essay, the *Disputationes de praecognitionibus et de demonstratione*, establishes his more fundamentally enduring acceptance of apodeictic search for "necessary demonstrations" of "the true constitution of the universe. For such a constitution exists, and exists in only one, true, real way, that could not possibly be otherwise".[26] From the epistemological demands of such demonstrations came Galileo's consistent search for physical causation, filling the gap left by the Renaissance Platonic acceptance of mathematical harmony and proportion as a sufficient basis for scientific explanation. Before him, his father Vincenzo Galilei had rejected such Platonic conceptions in music and had based his own investigations of musical sensations insistently on searching for physical causes. Galileo in his footsteps based his defence of the telescope as a valid observing instrument on the grounds of there being a valid and stable causal relation between sight and the seen.

Yet in his analysis of the relation of perceiver and knower to the perceived and known Galileo's Platonism also becomes evident. No other inquiries illustrate more clearly both the unity of his intellectual style and the triumphs that led him into matching contradictions. In a contribution to a fashionable debate whether painting or sculpture was the superior, Galileo wrote: "The farther removed the means by which one imitates are from the thing to be imitated, the more worthy of admiration the imitation will be".[27] Hence the representation in painting of a three-dimensional scene on a two-dimensional surface was superior to a merely sculptured relief, just as the representation of emotion by instrumental music was superior to that by song.

---

[26] Galileo, 'Prima Lettera circa le macchie solari' (1612; *Le opere*, v) 102, *Lettera a Madama Cristina di Lorena* (1615; *ibid*) 316, 330; *cf*. Crombie, 'The primary properties and secondary qualities in Galileo Galilei's natural philosophy' in *Saggi su Galileo Galilei* (Firenze, preprint, 1969), 'Sources of Galileo's early natural philosophy' in *Reason, Experiment and Mysticism in the Scientific Revolution*, ed. M. L. Righini Bonelli and W. R. Shea (New York, 1975) 157–75, and above n. 2. Adriano Carugo established during 1968–69 that two of the sources of the *Juvenilia* were Benito Pereira and Francisco de Toledo, and I discovered in June 1971 that a third was Christopher Clavius. William A. Wallace began later to look in the right direction for the first two sources but failed to identify them, writing in 'Galileo and the Thomists', in *St. Thomas Aquinas 1274–1974 Commemorative Studies* (Pontifical Institute of Medieval Studies, Toronto, 1974) 327: "... there is no evidence of direct copying from any of the Thomistic authors mentioned in this study". He did not mention Clavius. In response to a letter of 16 July 1971 with a typed copy of this article I sent him our information on 31 March 1972: "So far as the sources of the *Juvenilia* are concerned, we have shown that three main sources, sometimes copied word for word, are Clavius's commentary on Sacrobosco's *Sphaera*, Pereira's *De communibus omnium rerum naturalium* and Toletus's commentaries on the *Physics* and on *De generatione et corruptione*. Certainly there is no evidence for, and there is negative evidence against, his using Bonamico" (as Favaro had supposed). Later in 1972 after he had visited both myself and Carugo I sent Wallace at his request the relevant sections of our book. A note on p. 330 added subsequently to the published version of his article gives a misleading account of our discoveries, which directed attention to the Collegio Romano; *cf*. also his *Galileo's Early Notebooks: The Physical Questions* (Notre Dame, Indiana, 1977); and references above ch. 11, p. 343.

[27] Galileo to Cardo dà Cigoli, 26 June 1612, *Le opere*, xi, 341, transl. E. Panofsky, *Galileo as a Critic of the Arts* (The Hague, 1954) 36, *cf*. 9.

Likewise, in natural philosophy, Galileo's consistent rating of reason above immediate experience marked a conscious preference for Plato and Democritus, as well as for Archimedes, over Aristotle as a guide to the true nature of things which was to be found in abstract theory. Hence his conclusion that the irreducible minimum existential "conditions" which he found that he must necessarily attribute as he came to "conceive of a piece of matter or of a corporal substance" were not its appearances of colours and tastes and smells and sounds, but the "primary and real properties" of "sizes, shapes, numbers and slow or swift motions".[28] Hence again his judgement on the motion of the Earth: "I can finde no end of my admiration how reason could so much withstand sense in Aristarchus and Copernicus, that, that notwithstanding, this is become the mistresse of their credulitie".[29] This was a triumph. But Galileo's acceptance of mathematics as in some sense nature's true if hidden language led him, when accompanied by his search for apodeictic demonstration, into making an ideal of the impossible. Mathematicians in the 16th century had pointed out the worthlessness of contemporary attempts to put Euclid's geometry into syllogistic form. Galileo's contemporaries likewise rejected his belief that an apodeictic cosmology was even a distant possibility, while he at the same time pursued his ideal by means of the quite different criterion of making the new cosmology ever more probable by its ever increasing range of confirmation.

Finally, in this cosmological debate that was to make Galileo so much an historical symbol, there appeared a further aspect of natural science as an exemplary exercise of *virtù* in all its contexts. An obvious diagnostic characteristic of Western science is that it has been throughout its history as much a moral enterprise as a means of solving physical problems. One form of this has been the view established in different ways by philosophers of many different persuasions since Plato that nature was not just a deductive system, but also a moral order, with accompanying them others insisting like the atomists that, on the contrary, nature was morally neutral. The debate has profoundly affected both the specific intellectual character and the political role of science in Western culture. It has led to tensions repeated formally again and again between doctrines and loyalties derived from radically different sources, tensions often cruel though sometimes fruitful when generated by the insistence of the heirs at once of Aristotle and Moses that the truth must be either one thing or

[28] Galileo, *Il Saggiatore*, q. 48 (1623; *Le Opere*, vi) 347–8, 350; *cf.* Crombie, 'The primary properties . . .' (1969).
[29] Galileo, *Dialago sopra i due massimi sistemi del mondo, Tolemaico e Copernicano*, iii (1632; *Le opere*, vii) 355, transl. Joseph Webbe (c. 1634) in British Museum MS Harley 6320, f. 259ᵛ: see Crombie and Carugo, op. cit., ch. 6. i.

another, universally and exclusively, over the whole range of principle and practice for all that exists.

It may be argued that it was, above all, Galileo who showed how to disembarrass nature of its moral charge, and who through his public controversies and their consequences focussed the moral enterprise of science instead as one of the inalienable freedom of responsible inquiring minds to search for the objective truth. For "Nature, deaf and inexorable to our entreaties, will not alter or change the course of her effects".[30] Nature could not be cheated, and he

being used to study in the book of nature, where things are written in only one way, would not be able to dispute any problem *ad utranque partem* or to maintain any conclusion not first believed or known to be true.[31]

Moreover:

We must not ask nature to accommodate herself to what might seem to us the best disposition and order, but we must adapt our intellect to what she has made, certain that such is the best and not something else.[32]

Theologians (and politicians) should then

consider with all care the difference that there is between opinable and demonstrative doctrines; so that, having clearly in front of their minds with what force necessary inferences bind, they might the better ascertain themselves that it is not in the power of professors of demonstrative sciences to change opinions at their wish, applying themselves now on one side and now on the other; and that there is a great difference between commanding a mathematician or a philosopher and directing a merchant or a lawyer, and that the demonstrated conclusions about the things of nature and of the heavens cannot be changed with the same ease as opinions about what is lawful or not in a contract, rent or exchange.[33]

Hence it was not the scientifically demonstrated conclusions of the new cosmology and their like that threatened humane and responsible intelligence, but rather:

Who doubts that the novelty just introduced, of wanting minds created free by God to become slaves to the will of others, is going to give birth to very great scandals? And that to want other people to deny their own senses and to prefer to them the judgement of others, and to allow people utterly ignorant of a science or an art to become judges

[30] Galileo, 'Terza Lettera delle macchie solare' (1612; *Le opere*, v) 218; *cf.* for these questions Crombie, 'The relevance of the middle ages to the scientific movement' in *Perspectives in Medieval History*, ed. K. F. Drew and F. S. Lear (Chicago, 1963) 35–57, 'Some attitudes to scientific progress: ancient, medieval and early modern', *History of Science*, xiii (1957) 213–30, 'The Western experience of scientific objectivity' in *Proceedings of the Third International Humanistic Symposium* 1975 (Athens, 1977) 428–45: all with further references.
[31] Galileo in 1612 (*Le opere*, iv) 248.
[32] Galileo in 1612 (*ibid.* xi) 344.
[33] Galileo, *Lettera a Madama Cristina di Lorena* (1615; *ibid.* v) 326.

over intelligent men and to have power to turn them round at their will by virtue of the authority granted to them: these are the novelties with power to ruin republics and overthrow states .... Be careful, theologians ...":

for if one doctrine were thus ignorantly condemned, "in the long run, when it has been demonstrated by the senses and by necessity",[34] its opposite might have to be declared heretical instead.

Galileo as a public figure dramatically brought out into the open a subtle shift in the commitments and expectations of disagreement as well as agreement in the intellectual style of early modern Western science. A man of aggressive creative energy who could never be neutral in his own society, contact with him now through the living page of his marvellous baroque Italian, as then in the flesh, may be compared to his own description of the musical interval of the fifth "which, tempering the sweetness by a drop of tartness, seems at the same time to kiss and to bite".[35] In the page, as in the flesh, his account of scientific objectivity is a brisk antidote to the naiver sociological relativism promoted by people evidently ignorant of the distinction between the history of science and the history of ideology. As according to his last disciple and first biographer, Galileo "renovated mathematics and true philosophy in his own country" because he "was endowed by nature with such a marvellous ability to communicate learning",[36] so his arguments communicate the identity of the scientific movement. He communicates this as an intellectual enterprise integrated by its explicit historic criteria for choosing between theories and investigations at different levels of the true, the probable, the possible, the fruitful, the sterile, the impossible and the false. By means of these criteria scientists have exercised a kind of natural selection of theories and investigations which has directed scientific thinking as the history of at once solving problems and embodying them in ever more general explanations.

All this raises fundamental questions of historical interpretation which I have discussed at length in my forthcoming book, *Styles of Scientific Thinking in the European Tradition*.[37] The historiography of

[34] Galileo, notes related to the *Dialago* (*ibid.* vii) 540, 541.
[35] Galileo, *Discorsi e dimostrazioni matematiche intorno a due nuove scienze*, i (1638; *ibid.* viii) 149.
[36] Viviani, 'Racconto ...' (*ibid.* xix) 627–8; *cf.* above nn. 24, 35.
[37] Above n. 2; *cf.* for the concept of scientific styles, and for the historical method of looking for the questions asked or implied by the answers given in any historical situation and for their changes: R. G. Collingwood, *An Autobiography* (London, 1939), *The Idea of Nature* (Oxford, 1945) and *The Idea of History* (Oxford, 1946); also Crombie, *Augustine to Galileo*, introduction (1st. ed. London, 1952, new revised ed. 1979); and the discussion of Galileo's scientific style by Winifred Lovell Wisan, 'Galileo and the emergence of a new scientific style' in *Theory Change, Ancient Axiomatics and Galileo's Methodology*, ed. J. Hintikka, D. Gruender and E. Agazzi, i (Dordrecht, 1981), 311-39.

science is there introduced in the context of intellectual culture, conceptions of nature and of science, technical possibilities, social habits and dispositions especially those favouring or opposing change, and physical and biological ecology. The subject is treated as a kind of comparative intellectual anthropology, the study of human behaviour in situations of habit and opportunity and decision. This provides the historiographical context for the history of styles of scientific thinking as an integral part of cultural identity. Essentially I offer, then, a study of the variety and historical commitments of methods of scientific inquiry and explanation in the situations of intellectual orientation leading to their development. Styles of scientific thinking in Western intellectual history have been dominated and progressively diversified by the interaction of philosophical and practical programmes, embodying antecedent conceptions of nature and of science, with the success or failure of their scientific realization in widening varieties of subject-matter. Scientific experience made explicit the organization of scientific inquiry historically round a series of overlapping types of scientific method and explanation, with characteristic modes of self-correction and criteria of acceptability. These types of science have been differentiated, out of the rational programme initiated by the Greeks, by the demands imposed by diverse subject-matters; the conceptions of nature presupposing what was there to be discovered and so guiding inquiry and supplying the ultimate irreducible explanatory principles; the consequential procedures of research, including the crucial point at which experiment came into a scientific argument; and the theories of scientific demonstration distinguishing kinds of causal and non-causal relations and governing what to accept as having been discovered.

The active promotion and diversification of the scientific methods of late medieval and early modern Europe reflected the general growth of a research mentality in European society, a mentality conditioned and increasingly committed by its circumstances to expect and to look actively for problems to formulate and solve, rather than for an accepted consensus without argument. The varieties of scientific methods so brought into play may be distinguished as the simple postulation established in the mathematical sciences, the experimental exploration and measurement of more complex observable relations, the hypothetical construction of analogical models, the ordering of variety by comparison and taxonomy, the statistical analysis of the regularities of populations and the calculus of probabilities, and the historical derivation of genetic development. The first three of these methods concern essentially the science of individual regularities, and the second three the science of the regularities of populations ordered in space and in time.

ADDENDUM: Further references: see above chs. 8 and 11, p. 343.

Appendix

Reply on receiving the Galileo Prize awarded to the author and Adriano Carugo for their work *Galileo's Natural Philosophy* by the Domus Galileiana, Pisa, to celebrate the fourth centenary of the birth of Galileo and presented at Pisa by Professor Giovanni Polvani, President of the Domus Galileina and Rector of the University of Milan, on 22 December 1969 (*Physis*, xii, 1970, pp. 102-8).

Nearly a century and a half ago Giacomo Leopardi described pessimistically how the same force of intelligence and industry by which scientists and philosophers earn the glory of their achievements, also extinguishes and obscures that glory as the example of each generation is followed by the next. 'Who reads the work of Galileo any more?' he asked. 'But certainly they were marvellous in his time, perhaps none better, none more worthy of a supreme intellect, none so packed with the greatest discoveries and the most splendid concepts possible in those subjects. Yet every average physicist or mathematician of the present day finds himself in either science far superior to Galileo'.[1]

Leopardi was concerned with fame. Since his time the general growth of historical studies, with a sophistication of conceptions of history, and the maturing of the study of the history of science and of the philosophy of science themselves, have led us to look for something more interesting in the historical records of our scientific past.

You have been so generous as to award the Galileo Prize for the study of Galileo's natural philosophy wnich I wrote with the collaboration of my colleague Dr. Carugo. You have been so indulgent as to overlook defects of which I am myself only too conscious. I should like to think that we are really simply the immediate beneficiaries of an act of recognition made to all those historians and philosophers of science and Galileo scholars of many nations whose work during the past century and more has made possible the existence of such a prize, let alone its award.

To name only the dead, before all stand Rafaello Caverni and Antonio

---

1 Leopardi, "Il parini, ovvero della gloria", in *Opere*, a cura di S. Solmi, Milano, 1956, p. 564.

Favaro. I shall be allowed to name also two others, who were an
inspiration to those like myself who took up the history of science
professionally just after the Second World War and who became my
personal friends. I first encountered both while I was still working at
Cambridge: Alexandre Koyré through his Galilean studies published in
Paris on the eve of the War in 1939, and Robert Lenoble through his book
on Mersenne published in the same city in 1943. Contact with these
captivating intelligences was like Galileo's description of the musical
interval of the fifth, something between a kiss and a bite, at once seducing
and awakening. They showed by example the enlightenment to be gained
only by looking beneath the surface of immediate scientific results, by
seeking to identify the intellectual and technical conditions that made
certain discoveries possible and explanations acceptable to a particular
generation or group, others not, and the same not to others. By displaying
the science remembered by later generations in historical relation to the
philosophical assumptions, technical equipment, and social context of its
discoverers, they showed how the history of science could illuminate the
nature both of European culture and of scientific thinking.

This contextual approach establishes the identity of the history of
science as a field of study, an identity for which surprisingly it has
sometimes still to struggle. It shows it clearly to belong in its sources,
content and methods of scholarship to history and philosophy, and
equally clearly to require some special knowledge of the natural sciences
whose records are its primary materials. The history of science might be
seen as a history of intellectual behaviour, in the sense both of a history
recreating the past and of a comparative natural history of examples, a
kind of philosophical anthropology. It is enlightening to compare the
different attitudes to nature developed through different periods of
European history, and to compare European attitudes with others. Such
comparisons involve conceptions of science and of history. For what
enlightenment should we look from Galileo, beside that from Shakespeare
and Christopher Marlowe, and from Michelangelo and Vesalius, in this
heavily subscribed fourth centenary of their births or deaths?

In his view of nature and of science it is easy to see Galileo as a true
product of the world of the Italian cities into which he was born. As an
engineer-philosopher creating a theoretical world of mathematical
relationships realized in the one concrete actual world, his most striking
achievements bear the mark of Archimedes and Plato, then newly re-
edited by the philologists. More surprising at first sight may be the
dominance over his whole natural philosophy, as over that of most of his
contemporaries, of the Aristotelian theory of scientific demonstration. He
appears also as the true successor of the engineer-artists like Alberti,
Brunelleschi, Leonardo da Vinci and Michelangelo who made a rational
conquest of visual space, and of the mathematical theorists from Archytas
and Aristoxenus down to his father Vincenzo Galilei who likewise set out

to show in music the quantitative relationship between perception and rational patterns of time. An engineer of both things and ideas, Galileo made these practical Italian interests in art and technique yield what no Greek philosopher would have thought them capable of yielding, a science of nature.

Galileo has been described as a cultural symbol, transcending history. Rather it seems to me that his reputation illustrates the universal human habit of creating myths to justify attitudes taken to the present and future, myths intimately tied in Western culture to our conception of time and history. As a scientific thinker Galileo has been made by an astonishing variety of philosophical reformers whatever their hearts desired: an experimentalist contemptuous of speculation, a mathematical idealist indifferent to experiment; a positivist in fact hostile to ideas although he may not always have known this himself, an illustration of the role of ideas in scientific discovery; a Platonist, a Kantian, a Machian operationalist. He became also in his own lifetime a symbol of the issue of freedom to exercise personal responsibility implanted in all the cultures receiving the dual inheritance of Greek rational philosophy and Hebrew revelational theology, an issue and a tension reappearing in form, within the minds of individuals as well as externally, in every encounter between doctrines and intellectual loyalties with radically different origins. Shakespeare transcended history in his dramatic mythology of the English kings; Brecht was following a respectable precedent. But our intellectual inheritance is also an essentially critical one, predisposing each generation to take to pieces the history written by its predecessors in their image, before re-writing it in its own; but at the same time, as Galileo might have told us, finding true knowledge, distinguishing what the evidence shows us from what we might incline to impose upon it.

Mr. President, may I conclude with a confession; you are yourself at least the accidental cause of the work which you have so amiably rewarded. When you invited me to contribute to the centennial *Saggi su Galileo Galilei*, I was working on Mersenne's science of music and contemporary physiological theories of hearing and of vision. Into this French herd you sent the Florentine boar, and the result has been twins. In the past year this combined study of Galileo and Mersenne has grown and been divided into two books, which I hope it will be possible to publish together.

In this winter season we may be more conscious than in glorious summer of a discontent with the material inheritance from Galileo's enterprises. But, abrasive as his personality could be, he is a fellow human being who communicates to us in this strange world a hopeful rational simplicity, the simplicity not of innocence but of experience; and the nobility of an eventual acceptance of injustice from which he could not escape and on account of which, as he said, he could never be forgiven because he had committed no crime. I have always thought that one reason for studying history is to extend our range of human contacts,

> As Earth stirs in her winter sleep
> And puts out grass and flowers,
> Despite the snow,
> Despite the falling snow.

In accepting the Galileo Prize on behalf of my collaborator and myself, I should like here also to link it with the memory of all those scholars who have made this field at once critical and creative, with the anticipation of those whom the future will bring, and with the hope that this presnt contact between Oxford and the Domus Galilaeana, and between England and Italy, will grow and flourish.

Presentation of the Galileo Prize: A. C. Crombie, G. Polvani, A. Carugo

13

MATHEMATICS, MUSIC AND MEDICAL SCIENCE*

Two events earlier this summer, perhaps seemingly without relevance either to each other or to my title, when considered together point to common philosophical commitments whose historical origins are the subject of my brief discourse. The death of Helen Keller in June reminds us of the triumph she represents of intelligence over total deprivation of all means of human communication except through touch (¹). The other event was the conference on computer science and communication just held in Edinburgh (²), demonstrating the dramatic growth of this subject. What relevance does music have to either of these examples of medical and mathematical science : to the silent, dark world of the deaf-blind or to the intellectual void within a computer ? The answer is that we learn as children to communicate meaning first through hearing and speech. Parallel to the genetic and structural study of language, states of sensory deprivation of hearing and of vision reduce the study of human communication to its basic psycho-physiological symbolism. We try to imitate this with computer models, with machines. But these contemporary studies of language and communication presuppose a definite conception of both sides of the relationship between the perceiving organism and the world perceived, and of the information communicated, which we need not look far in the literature of science, to say nothing of that of anthropology and genetic psychology, to recognize as the product of very general commitments underlying the sophisticated theory. These are commitments to a view of the subject-matter assumed in advance of detailed research into it. How have they become so much part of Western thinking ?

In 1623, Marin Mersenne opened his scientific discussion of music with the declaration that "nobody can reach perfection in music, nor understand or discuss it, unless he combines the principles of physics and medi-

---

* The research in Italian Libraries was carried out with the support of the Wellcome Trust.

(¹) Obituary, *The Times* (London), 3 June 1968 ; cf. H. KELLER, *The Story of My Life*, 6th ed. (London, 1903).

(²) International Federation for Information Processing, *IFIP Congress 68*, Edinburgh, August 1968.

cine with mathematical reasoning " ([3]). I want to illustrate briefly, with some particular examples, how the invasion of medical science by mathematics in this interesting area of auditory and visual communication reduced the perceiving organism to a mechanism and information to a mathematical symbolism. The mathematical invasion had been a partial and potential programme at least since the protest against the over-simplifications of hypothetical postulates in the Hippocratic treatise *On Ancient Medicine*. It became a complete and actual commitment in the period of Galileo, Kepler, Mersenne and Descartes.

The modern mathematical programme has inherited from the Greek mathematicians two essential elements : the quantification of biological phenomena in an appropriate form, and the demonstration of these quantified phenomena in the "Euclidean" sense of proving that they follow from the principles postulated in order to explain them. Thus the geometrical programme introduced by Euclid's optics into the analysis of visual perception, by postulating linear rays of vision and of light, offered at once a theory explaining the stable relationship between human seeing and the world seen, and at the same time a quantitative method of demonstrating what would be seen under specified conditions of distance, reflection, refraction and so on ([4]). Similarly, in discussing the arithmetical analysis of musical perception, said to have been introduced by the Pythagoreans, Plato's friend Archytas of Tarentum wrote ([5]) :

> Mathematicians seem to me to have an excellent discernment, and it is in no way strange that they should think correctly concerning the nature of particulars. For since they have passed an excellent judgement on the nature of the whole, they were likely to have an excellent view of separate things. They have handed on to us a clear judgement... not least on music... First they have judged that sound is impossible unless there occurs a striking of objects against one another... And so, when things impinge on the perception, those that reach us quickly and powerfully from the source of sound seem high-pitched, while those that reach us slowly and feebly seem low-pitched.

The relating of pitch to speed of motion of some kind, and eventually to frequency of vibration ([6]), again established a stable quantitative rela-

([3]) MERSENNE, *Quaestiones celeberrime in Genesim*, c. iv., vers xxi, q. lvii, art. xvi (Paris, 1623) 1696b. These questions are treated in full in my forthcoming books, *Styles of Scientific Thinking in the European Tradition* and *Mersenne: Science, Music & Language*, and with A. Carugo, *Galileo's Arguments and Disputes in Natural Philosophy*, cf. above ch. 11.

([4]) Cf. A.C. CROMBIE, « The mechanistic hypothesis and the scientific study of vision », *Proceedings of the Royal Microscopical Society*, ii (1967 3-112.

([5]) Quoted by PORPHYRY OF TYRE, *In harmonica Ptolemaei commentarius*, ed. John WALLIS in *Operum mathematicorum volumen tertium* (Oxford, 1699) 236-8; H. DIELS, *Die Fragmente der Vorsokratiker*, 5te Aufl. hrg. von W. Kranz, i, § 47 (Berlin, 1934); K. FREEMAN, *Ancilla to the Pre-Socratic Philosophers* (Oxford, 1948) 78-9. Archytas was probably the main source of the mathematical and physical treatment of sound given by Plato in the *Timaeus* (67 AC, 80 AB); cf. *Timaeus vel de natura* divini Platonis, Marsilio Ficino interprete (Paris, 1536).

([6]) Cf. EUCLID, *Rudimenta musices ciusdem sectio regulae harmonicae...* Ioanne Pena... interprete (Paris, 1557) ff. 7v-8r; M.R. COHEN and I.E. DRABKIN, *Source Book in Greek Science* (New York, 1948) 291; below n. ([11])

tionship between perception and the world perceived. One of the earliest Greek musical discoveries was the identity of the purest consonances with the simplest numerical ratios. The difficulties produced by the somewhat inconsequential demands of the human ear, especially for the Platonic school of mathematical theorists but in fact for all attempts to demonstrate the musical qualities that should be heard with more complicated numerical ratios, are an example of the refusal of complex biological phenomena simply to vanish in the face of theory, however powerful. These difficulties have produced rich developments both in musical scales and composition, and in auditory physiology. But they did not ruin the mathematical programme : they merely complicated it. Thus the severest critic of the Platonic mathematical school, Aristotle's pupil Aristoxenus of Tarentum, wrote of his own, more experimental approach ([7]) : " It is our endeavour that the principles that we assume shall without exception be evident to those who understand music, and that we shall advance to our conclusions by strict demonstration". There is only a short step from demanding strict mathematical demonstrations of biological phenomena to reducing them to a system of mechanisms.

If we count modern science as one product of Western Europe unmatched elsewhere, another is surely the music developed during the same period. But from antiquity music had meant more than simply the ordering of heard sound. It was an intimate part of a world of ideas concerned with the harmony of the cosmos and the ' world soul ', ideal proportions, and occult powers of sounds and words; it was an element in the harmony of the body and the soul, and hence a powerful instrument of education and an efficacious therapy in mental illness. In his standard textbook, *De musica* ([8]), Boethius wrote that " music is involved not only in speculation, but also in morality. For there is nothing so peculiarly human as to be relaxed by sweet melodies, and set on edge by the opposite ". He agreed with Plato that the reason for this was the structural " conformity ", expressed in numerical ratios, between the three kinds of music, *mundana, humana et instrumentalis*, the music of the heavens and the elements, of man, and of sound. Like was induced by like, civilized virtue by moderate and orderly music, lasciviousness by the soft modes, inhuman savagery by the harsh ones. Their music expressed the barbarous habits of the barbarous races and the civilized morality of the civilized ones — though, he wrote, " at the present time these are almost non-existent ". Hence Plato's insistence that children should be taught only healthy music. Boethius illustrated the dangers by the well-known story of the drunken teenager from Taormina excited by " a somewhat Phrygian mode ", who was on his way to burn down the house where his whore was shut up with a rival when Pythagoras, " who happened to be observing the movements of the stars by night, as was his custom ", heard about him. He immediately " ordered the mode to be changed, and so calmed down the spirit of the furious youth to a completely tranquil state of mind ". Another example of the power of music well

([7]) ARISTOXENUS, *Harmonicorum elementorum libri iii*, ii (Venice, 1562) 22 ; H.S. MACRAN, *The Harmonics of Aristoxenus* (Oxford, 1902) 189.

([8]) A.M.T. Severinus BOETHIUS, *De institutione musica libri quinque*, i. 1-2, ed. G. Friedlein (Leipzig, 1867) ; cf. BOETII *De musica* (Venice, 1492).

known to the early philosophers was the acceleration of the heart-beat by its movements. This example of the conformity of music with the body as well as the soul was said to have been reported to Hippocrates by Democritus, when the physician came to cure the philosopher of the alleged insanity for which his fellow citizens had shut him up. Boethius concluded : " From all this it clearly and indubitably appears that music is naturally linked with us in such a way that we could not do without it even if we wished. Therefore our intellectual powers must be applied so that we may also grasp scientifically what has been implanted in us naturally ".

Within this context, part of Greek musical theory, with its stress on simple numerical ratios, remained familiar in medieval education through Boethius, Plato's *Timaeus*, and the study of music with arithmetic in the mathematical *quadrivium*. But between about 1550 and 1650 musical science was transformed by two happenings. The musical theorists were forced by the striking innovations of musical practice, first in polyphony and then in instrumentation, to follow the lead of Aristoxenus in taking the complex responses and demands of the ear into the numerical computation of harmony. At the same time the mathematicians took up the challenge that, as William Wotton was to put it [9] : " Music is a physico-mathematical science, built upon fixed rules, and stated proportions ; which, one would think, might have been as well improved upon the old foundations, as upon new ones, since the grounds of music have always been the same ". The new mathematicians accepted the standing invitation offered by the grounds of music by looking beyond the alleged structural conformity between the human body and soul and the so-called " sounding numbers " [10] of Pythagorean musical theory, and by asking how actually a numerical ratio became a pleasant or unpleasant sensation. Their point of departure was a physical analysis of the relationship between the quantitative ' primary properties ' of sound and the ' secondary qualities ' of sensation these produced through the human ear. In this way the mathematicians began the creation of the modern sciences of physical, psychological and physiological acoustics by making a series of fundamental discoveries.

Boethius [11] had reported the fundamental hypothesis that the pitch of sounds emitted by vibrating strings and other instruments depended on the frequency of impulses transmitted through the air, on the analogy of waves transmitted over the surface of water. The first important advance made in the sixteenth century was Girolamo Fracastoro's physical explanation of resonance published in 1546 [12]. The response of a string to another in unison with it was a popular example of sympathetic magic.

---

[9] William WOTTON, *Reflections upon Ancient and Modern Learning*, 2nd ed. (London, 1697) 329 ; cf. J.M. BARBOUR, *Tuning and Temperament*, 2nd ed. (East Lansing, Mich., 1953), *Die Musik in Geschichte und Gegenwart*, hrg. von F. Blume, 13 Bde. (Kassel und Basel, 1949-68), especially arts. « Harmonie » and « Intervall ».

[10] Cf. Gioseffo ZARLINO, *Le istitutioni harmoniche* (Venice, 1573) 157 (1st ed. 1558).

[11] *De inst. musica*, i. 3, 8-11, 14 ; cf. Gualtherus MIEKLEY, *De Boethii libri primi fontibus* (Jean, 1898). Boethius's main sources were Euclid, Ptolemy, and Nicomachus.

[12] Hieronymus FRACASTORIUS, *De sympathia et antipathia rerum liber unus*, cc. 4 11 (Venice, 1546).

Fracastoro described how one day in a church he noticed some wax images, of which one always moved when a certain bell was rung, while the others stayed still. He pointed this out to some visitors in order to enjoy both their astonishment and his ability to dispel it by explaining that because the moving statue alone happened to be in unison with the bell, it alone responsed to the frequency of the impulses propagated from the bell through the air. These likewise, he said, were the cause of the sympathetic vibrations of a stringed instrument. Another fundamental advance was the mathematical and experimental demonstration that pitch was proportional to frequency and hence that the musical intervals (octave, fifth, fourth, third, etc.) were ratios of frequencies of vibrations, whatever instrument produced them. This was begun about 1563 by Giovanni Battista Benedetti [13], continued between 1589 and 1590 by Galileo's father Vincenzo Galilei [14] and in 1614-1615 by Isaac Beeckman [15], and completed between 1623 and 1634 by Mersenne [16]. Mersenne gave an experimental proof by counting the slow vibrations of very long strings against time measured by pulse beats or a second's pendulum. He then used the laws they had discovered, relating frequency to the length, tension, and specific gravity of strings, to calculate frequencies too rapid to count. The demonstration of these propositions enabled these mathematicians to explain consonance as the physical coincidence in the ear of the impulses produced by the terminations of vibration-cycles, with dissonance increasing as coincidence decreased, and to quantify Fracastoro's explanation of resonance.

We may recognize in Vincenzo Galilei's insistence both on the complexity and on the discoverable regularities of auditory experience something of Galileo's approach to natural science, and certainly a family likeness in the polemical aggressiveness to be made famous by his son. Vincenzo was

[13] Io. Baptista BENEDICTUS, « De intervallis musicis », epist. 2, *Diversarum speculationum mathematicarum et physicarum liber* (Turin, 1585) 283 ; C.V. PALISCA, « Scientific empiricism in musical thought », in *Seventeenth Century Science and the Arts*, ed. H.H. Rhys (Princeton, 1961) 104-9.

[14] Vincentio GALILEI, *Discorso intorno all'opere di messer Gioseffo Zarlino da Chioggia* (Florence, 1589) 103-5 ; « Discorso particolare intorno alla diversità delle forme del diapason » and « Discorso particolare intorno all'unisono », Biblioteca Nazionale Centrale di Firenze, MSS Galileiani 3, ff. 45r - 46r, 54rv, 56r - 57v (c. 1589-90) ; A. PROCISSI, *La collezione Galileiana della Biblioteca Nazionale di Firenze* (Rome, 1959) 4-5 ; PALISCA, *op. cit.* 120-35. Cf. GALILEI's earlier work, *Dialogo della musica antica e della moderna* (Florence, 1581) where he gave an analysis of the fundamental volume of ancient sources : Aristoxeni musici antiquissimi *Harmonicorum elementorum libri iii*. Cl. PTOLEMAEI *Harmonicorum, seu de musica lib. iii.* Aristotelis *De obiecto auditus fragmentum ex Porphyrii commentariis*, omnia nunc primum latine conscripta et edita ab Ant. Gogavino Graviensi (Venice, 1562).

[15] Isaac BEECKMAN, *Journal tenu... de 1604 à 1634*, publié avec une introduction et des notes par C. de Waard, i (La Haye, 1939) ff. 23r - 34r (1614-15).

[16] MERSENNE, *Quaestiones... in Genesim* (1623) 1556-62, 1699, 1710; *La vérité des sciences* (Paris, 1625) 370-1, 567, 614-20; *Traité de l'harmonie universelle* (Paris, 1627) 147-8, 447; *Harmonicorum libri*, lib. i, prop. ii, lib. ii, props. vi-viii, xvii-xxi, xxxiii-xxxv, lib. iv, prop. xxvii (Paris, 1636); *Harmonic universelle* « Traité des instrumens », livre i, props. v, xii, xvi-xix, livre iii, props. vii, xvi-xviii « Traitez de la nature des sons, etc. », livre i, props. i-vii, xiii, livre iii, props. i, v, v [= vi], xiv [= xv], « Traitez de la voix, etc. », livre i, prop. lii, « Traitez des consonances, etc. » livre i, props. vi, x, xii, xvii, xviii, xix, xxii, livre ii, prop. x (Paris, 1636-37); above n.(6), below n.(23).

skilled lutanist, a mathematician, and musical preceptor to the Florentine musical academy of the Camerata. Among the manuscripts inherited by Galileo he left a translation of Aristoxenus into Italian ([17]), and he explicitly followed the example of Aristoxenus in trying to build musical science up from auditory sensation, instead of imposing on it a rigid mathematical scheme in the style of the Platonists. One of his discoveries, described in his last published work and last manuscripts ([18]), was that the traditional ratio 2 : 1, said to have been shown by Pythagoras to produce the octave, did so only with lengths of strings in that ratio : for the tensions of strings the octave ratio was 4 : 1. His ratio for organ pipes was less happy. He poured scorn on the universal harmonies attributed to nature by the Platonists. Even when we knew the mathematical ratios, he pointed out that we could not always determine the quality of our sensations ([19]). This was an observation to be developed by Descartes in distinguishing within the " perfection " or " douceur " of consonances between objective mathematical simplicity and subjective pleasure, between " ce qui les rend plus simple et *accordantes*, et ce qui les rend plus *agréables* à l'oreille " ([20]). It was precisely when Vincenzo was doing this work that Galileo made his retreat from   Pisa   in 1585 and lived mainly in his father's house in Florence, before returning to Pisa as lecturer in mathematics in 1589 ([21]). He reported what were evidently Vincenzo's results in his *Discourses on Two New Sciences* (1638) ([22]), before giving his own proof that the musical intervals were ratios of frequencies and his own physical explanation of resonance, consonance and dissonance.

Before there is any evidence that Galileo had written his account of acoustics in the First Day of the *Discorsi*, Mersenne had written down all the same results and a number of others and had sent some of them to a

([17]) Biblioteca Nazionale Centrale di Firenze, MSS Galileiani 8, ff. 3r - 38v ; Procissi, *op. cit.*, p. 8. Cf. H. Martin, « La " Camerata " du Comte Bardi et la musique florentine du XVIe siècle », *Revue de musicologie*, xiii (1932) 63-74, 152-61, 227-34, xiv (1933) 92-100, 141-51 ; F. Fano, « La Camerata Fiorentina : Vincenzo Galilei (1570 ? - 1591) », *Istituzioni e monumenti dell'arte musicale italiana*, iv (1934) ; D.P. Walker, « Musical humanism in the 16th and early 17th centuries », *The Music Review*, ii (1941) 1-13, 111-21, 220-7, 288-308, iii (1942) 55-71, *Spiritual and Demonic Magic from Ficino to Campanella* (London, 1958), « Kepler's celestial music », *Journal of the Warburg and Courtauld Institutes*, XXX (1967) 228-50 ; C.V. Palisca, *Girolamo Mei (1519-1594) : Letters on Ancient and Modern Music to Vincenzo Galilei and Giovanni Bardi : A study with annotated texts* (American Institute of Musicology, 1960).

([18]) *Discorso...* (1589) 103-5, cf. 92-5, 109, 116-8 ; « Discorso particolare intorno alla diversità delle forme del diapason », MSS Galileiani 3, ff. 45r - 46r ; above n. ([14]). Vincenzo died in 1591.

([19]) V. Galilei, *Dialogo...* (1581), 46-7, 132-3 ; above n. ([14]).

([20]) Descartes à Mersenne, 13. i. 1631, Mersenne, *Correspondance*, ed. C. De Waard, iii (Paris, 1946) 24-5 ; cf. *ibid.* 18. xii. 1629, i. 1630, *ibid.* ii (1937) 338, 371 ; Mersenne, *Harm. univ.*, « Tr. des consonances etc. », i, props. xi, xii, xix, xxi, xxx, xxxii, *Harm. lib.*, iv, props. xvii-xxv.

([21]) Vincenzo Viviani, « Racconto istorico della vita di Galileo », Galileo Galilei, *Opere*, edizione nazionale, direttore A. Favaro, coadiutore I. del Lungo, xix (Florence, 1907) 599-605 ; A. Favaro, « Serie settima di scampoli Galileiani », *Atti e memorie della Reale Accademia di Scienze, Lettere ed Arti in Padova*, n.s. viii (1892) 55.

([22]) Galileo Galilei, *Discorsi e dimostrazioni matematiche intorno a due nuove scienze*, i (Leiden, 1638) ; *Opere*, ed. naz., viii, 138-50, ed. A. Carugo e L. Geymonet (Turin, 1958).

common friend, the musicologist Giovanni Battista Doni, in Rome [23]. One of his outstanding discoveries, related both to vibrating strings and to his concern with measuring time, was the law that the frequency of a pendulum is inversely proportional to the square root of the length. His statement of this was printed by 30 June 1634; Galileo's earliest known statement of it, in the First Day of the *Discorsi*, was written almost certainly in the spring of 1635 [24]. After measuring the frequencies producing different pitches, Mersenne went on to measure the upper and lower audible limits of frequency [25]. With the same technique he showed experimentally that the frequencies of the fundamental note and the harmonics or overtones produced by a vibrating string were in the ratios $1 : 2 : 3 : 4 : 5$ and so on [26]. The explanation, that the string was vibrating simultaneously

[23] Mersenne wrote from Paris on 20.iii.1634 to Nicolas-Claude Fabri de Peiresc in Aix-en-Provence that after more than ten years of work he had finished his « grand œuvre de l'*Harmonie universelle* » of which he sent « le premier cayer » (*Correspondance*, iv, 81-82 ; cf. above n. [16]). The earliest section in which he gave an extensive analysis of the physical quantities determining the notes and intervals produced by vibrating strings, bells and pipes and used this to explain resonance, consonance and dissonance seems to have been the « Traitez des consonances, etc. », livre i, « Des consonances ». This was in print by 2 February 1635 (Mersenne à Doni, *Correspondance*, v, 40-41). Internal references and the *Correspondance*, iv-v, indicate that he was writing at the same time, during 1634, the « Traité des instrumens » (i-iii) and the *Harmonicorum libri* (i-iv). For items sent to Peiresc and Doni cf. also below n.[24], and *Correspondance*, iv, 1, 2, 47, 66, 73-9, 86, 105, 134, 175-7, 181-2, 186-7, 225-7, 233-4, 241, 254-5, 259-60, 267-9, 280-1, 286-7, 345, 368, 379, 384-5, 388, 392-4, 397, v, 33, 35, 136-7 ; cf. iv, 6, 53, 348, 368, v, 2, 35-41. For studies of Mersenne see H. LUDWIG, *Mersenne und seine Musiklehre* (Berlin, 1935) and the outstanding work by R. LENOBLE, *Mersenne ou la naissance du mécanisme* (Paris, 1943). Mersenne's own copy of *Harmonie universelle* with his annotations made between 1637 and 1648 has been published in facsimile by the Centre National de la Recherche Scientifique (Paris, 1965).

[24] Mersenne published this law first in one of his original additions to a work indicating his growing enthusiasm for Galileo : *Les mechaniques de Galilée*, viie Addition (Paris, 1634) 77. The « Privilège du Roy » gives 30 June 1634 as the date on which the printing was completed : cf. MERSENNE, *Correspondance*, iv, 76-7. 207-12, and the new edition of the book by B. Rochot (Paris, 1966). The work was bound with Mersenne's *Les questions théologiques, physiques*, etc. (Paris, 1634) and presumably sent with that to Doni by way of Peiresc in 1634 (Mersenne à Peiresc, 28. vii. 1634, Doni à Mersenne, 8. xi. 1634, *Correspondance*, iv, 267, 384-5 , Appendix iii, pp. 444-55). Elie Diodati sent a copy of *Les mechaniques* from Paris to Galileo on 10 April 1635 (*ibid.* v. 132 ; cf. vi, 242). For Mersenne's use of this pendulum law, and his possible derivation of it from the law of falling bodies, see also *Harm. lib.* ii, props. xxvi - xxix, *Harm. univ.*, « Tr. des instrumens », i. props. xix-xx, « Tr... des sons, etc. », ii, props. xiii-xv, iii, « Du mouvement », props. xx [= xxi], xxii [= xxiii]; above n.[23]. Galileo's correspondence with Fulgenzio Micanzio in Venice between 19. xi. 1634 and 7. iv. 1635 (*Opere*, ed. naz., xvi, 163, 177, 193, 200-1, 203, 208-10, 214, 217-33, 236-7, 239-44, 254) indicates that he had not written the last part of the First Day of the *Discorsi* (where he discussed the pendulum and acoustics) by the latter date. His letter of 9. vi. 1635 to Elie Diodati saying that he had sent a copy to Giovanni Pieroni and subsequent correspondence (*Opere*, xvi, 272-4, 300-4, 359-61) establishes this as the latest date of composition. This copy survives in Biblioteca Nazionale Centrale di Firenze, MS Banco Raro 31 ; cf. G.B.C. de NELLI, *Vita e commercio letterario di Galileo Galilei*, ii (Lausanne, 1793) 616-8 ; GALILEO, *Opere*, viii, 20-22.

[25] MERSENNE, *Harm. univ.*, « Tr. des instrumens », i, prop. xix, iii, prop. xvii, « Tr... des sons... », iii, prop. v [= vi], « Tr. de la voix », i, prop. lii ; *Harm. lib.*, ii, props. xviii, xxxiii.

[26] *Harm. univ.* « Tr. des instrumens », iv, prop. xi [= ix], vi, prop. xlii, vii, prop. xviii « Nouvelles observations ». iv ; *Harmonicorum instrumentorum libri iv* (Paris, 1636) i, prop. xxxiii, iii, prop. xxvii ; cf. *Quaestiones... in Genesim*, col. 1560 ; and the Aristotelian *Problemata*, xix. 8, 23-4, 38-9, 41-2.

as a whole and in these divisions, was sent to Mersenne by Théodore Deschamps on 26 March 1642 ([27]), and was later confirmed experimentally at Oxford by William Noble, Thomas Pigot and John Wallis ([28]). Mersenne also pioneered the experimental measurement of the speed of sound, and showed that speed was independent of pitch and of loudness ([29]). He equated loudness with volume displaced, and related its intensity to the square of the distance from the source ([30]).

It was above all Mersenne who, by his systematic search for a stable and consistent physical basis for the phenomena of auditory sensation, confirmed the mathematical invasion into the medical science of hearing. Between 1625 and 1634, to begin with independently of Galileo and Descartes, he came to the conclusion that animals and plants were nothing but automata ([31]). A limited mechanistic physiology used before this had indicated the general programme. For example Jacob Müller, who became professor of mathematics and medicine at Marburg, in 1617 offered as a public academic exercice a geometrical analysis of muscular action entitled *De natura motus animalis et voluntarii exercitatio singularis, ex principiis physicis, medicis, geometricis et architectonicis deducta* ([32]). The complete theory of the physiological automaton reduced physiology to a branch of the demonstrative science of applied mechanics. For Mersenne the theory came to hand in the first place as a useful weapon in a theological and metaphysical campaign for the uniqueness, responsibility and validity of human reason against two enemies : ' naturalists ' or Neoplatonists such as Telesio, Campanella and Giordano Bruno who linked men with animals and plants as common participants in a world soul; and sceptics who followed Montaigne in using animal intelligence to cast doubt on any superior claims for men. Mersenne distinguished men sharply from animals because God had given men alone reason, conscious discrimination and freedom of choice. But if animals were simply machines, this left him free, as it did Descartes, to use the imitation of natural processes by means of technological artefacts to give experimental philosophy a powerful insight into possible explanations of them.

([27]) Deschamps à Mersenne, 26. iii. 1642, Bibliothèque Nationale, Paris, MS Français nouv. acquis. 6,206, f.196ʳ; cf. MERSENNE, *Corresp.*, iv, 150-1, xi, 81-5; Descartes à Mersenne, 25. ii. 1630, ibid. ii, 397 ; *ibid.*, **22.** vii., 28. xi. 1633, vol. iii, 458-9, 559 ; 15. v. 1634, vol. iv (1955) 143-5 ; Beeckman à Mersenne, 30. v. 1633, *ibid.*, iii, 403-4, 407-8 ; Ismaël Boulliaud à Pierre Gassend, 21. vi. 1633, *ibid.*, iii, 449-51 ; Christophe de Villiers à Mersenne, ix. 1633, *ibid.*, iii, 488.

([28]) John WALLIS, « Letter to the publisher, concerning a new musical discovery ; written from Oxford, March 14, 1676/7, *Philosophical Transactions*, xii (1677) 839-42.

([29]) MERSENNE, *Harm. univ.*, « Tr. ... des sons... », i, props. vii, viii, xiii, xvii, xxi, iii, prop. xxi [= xxii], « De l'utilité de l'harmonie », prop. ix; *Novarum observationum physicomathematicarum... tomus iii*, « Reflectiones physico-mathematicae », c. xx (Paris, 1647).

([30]) *Harm. univ.*, « Tr. ... des sons... », i, props. xii, xv, cf. props. iii, iv cor. xxx, and livre iii, prop. xxi [= xxii] cor. iv; *Harm. lib.* ii, prop. xxxix.

([31]) MERSENNE, *La vérité des sciences* (1625) 16-20; *Les préludes de l'harmonie universelle* (Paris, 1634) 156-9, cf. 118; *Harm. univ.*, « Tr. de la voix », i, prop. li [= lii]; cf. *L'impiété des deistes*, ii (Paris, 1624) 372-8, *Les questions théologiques, physiques, morales, et mathématiques* (Paris, 1634) 229-32. Cf. LENOBLE, *Mersenne* (1943) 74-5, 155-6, 192, 316-25, 501; CROMBIE, references above nn.([3]), ([4]), below n.([39]).

([32]) Giessen. 1617; cf. the later development of this line of analysis by Galileo's pupil Giovanni Alfonso Borelli, *De motu animalium* (Rome, 1680).

Mersenne, like Descartes, used this engineering approach to define the objects of scientific research into the nature of the information mediated by the senses into the living body. In the animal-machine the problem of sensation did not arise, because the light or sound or other external physical motions striking the sense-organs simply stimulated other, internal physical motions of response in accordance with the construction of the machine. This introduced the interesting conception of a purely mechanistic information system. They confined the problem of sensory information to man. Mersenne skirted the philosophical problem of how physical motions of any kind could *cause* something so different in kind as sensations. Instead, he embarked as an experimental physiological psychologist on his impressive programme of exploring the *correlations* between auditory and optical stimuli and the sensations they produced. This work occupied about twenty-five years and had two further products. It led him to envisage a kind of psycho-physiological engineering, through the emotions and dispositions of the soul induced by music, that would surpass in its power of rational control any use of music in medicine or education available to antiquity ([33]). It also led him to make an original analysis of language.

If it was language that chiefly distinguished men from animals, Mersenne said that this was fundamental, for language meant conscious understanding of meaning. The speech and jargon of animals was a kind of communication, but not language, for they mindlessly emitted and responded to messages simply as automata. But what were the basic elements of human language, and was it possible to invent from them a perfect system of communication between all men? He had become interested in language first in his campaign against the Cabalistic belief in the magical and occult powers of words and sounds. The question whether there was a natural human language in which the names of things revealed their natures went back to Herodotus and Plato, had been discussed by Dante, and arose again in the Neoplatonic and Cabalistic speculations of the fifteenth and sixteenth centuries. Mersenne violently rejected the belief that an occult identification gave a name power over the thing named. At first he thought that God might have revealed natural names to Adam in Hebrew, but later he rejected any idea of a natural language and firmly proposed a purely rational theory making words simply arbitrary signs. Because all men in common possessed reason, they had developed languages in which these spoken or written physical signs signified meanings. For the same reason it was possible to translate a common understanding of meaning from one into another of the variety of languages diversified by the different historical experiences, environments, needs, temperaments and customs of the different races. But if no language was naturally prior to any other, Mersenne saw in this analysis of their basic common elements a means of

---

([33]) Cf. MERSENNE, *Quaestiones... in Genesim*, 1619-24; *La vérité des sciences*, pp. 16-17, 32, 69-72; *Les préludes de l'harmonie universelle* (Paris, 1634) 212, 219-22; *Questions harmoniques* (Paris, 1634) 91-9; *Harm. univ.*, Préface générale au lecteur, « Tr... des sons... », i, props. i-ii, « Tr. de la voix ». i. « Tr. des consonances etc. », i, prop. xxxiii; *Harm. lib.* i, prop. ii; LENOBLE, *Mersenne*, pp. 522-31. For his later work on the science of music see *Cogitata physico-mathematica* (Paris, 1644) and *Novarum observationum...* (1647), and on light and vision *Universae mixtaeque mathematicae geometriae synopsis* (Paris, 1644) and *L'optique et la catoptrique* (Paris, 1651).

inventing a perfect universal language that would convey information without error ([34]).

The idea of devising a universal means of communication had arisen in the sixteenth and seventeenth centuries out of comparative studies of ancient and modern languages aiming to find a common language for all nations. Mersenne based his linguistic experiments on a calculus showing the number of possible permutations and combinations of a given number of elements. When in 1629 he tried to interest Descartes in this scheme, he received the famous reply that a language expressing perfectly a perfect knowledge of truth could be achieved only in an earthly paradise ([35]). But this cold water did not quench his optimism. He had argued that natural science could discover only the quantitative externals of things. Hence it should be possible to invent a language of quantities that " could be called natural and universal " ([36]) and would be a perfect means of philosophical communication. He proposed to construct with his combinatory calculus a system of sounds representing the quantitative properties of things, so that the sciences could all be taught with no other language than that of a musical instrument, and two philosophers unable to converse in any other way could communicate with each other perfectly on the strings of two lutes.

All this exemplifies the new vision offered by the mathematical programme and the mechanistic philosophy, when ideas and optimism went far ahead of technical possibilities, but we may recognize in them the origins of familiar contemporary commitments. At the same time our present interests help to sensitize the 'seeing eye' of the historian. The analytical reconstruction of the history of science must inevitably involve also an analysis of science, and so the present and the past illuminate each other by the development of the tradition itself. Contemporary linguistics and interest in very general questions of communication show us Mersenne's

---

([34]) See *Quaestiones... in Genesim*, cols. 23-4, 470-1, 702-4, 1197-1202, 1217, 1383-98, 1692; manuscript continuation, Bibliothèque Nationale, Paris, MS lat. 17, 262, pp. 511, 536 (LENOBLE *Mersenne*, pp. xiii-xiv, 514-7); *L'impiété des deistes*, p. 167; *La vérité des sciences*, pp. 67-76, 544-80; *Traité de l'harmonie universelle*, « Sommaire... » *(item 9); Questions inouyës* (Paris, 1634) 95-101, 120-2; *Harm. univ.*, Préface générale au lecteur, and « Tr. de la voix », Préface, livre i, props. v-xiv, xxxviii; *Harm. lib.*, vii; Mersenne's discussions from 1621 to 1640 with Guillaume Bredeau, Descartes, Jean Beaugrand, Peiresc, Gassendi, Comenius and others in *Correspondence*, 61-3, 102-3, ii, 323-9, 374-5, iii, 254-62, iv, 329, v, 136-40, vi, 4-6, vii, 447-8, x, 264-74; LENOBLE, *Mersenne*, pp. 96-109, 514-21. For conventional theories of language in antiquity cf. the Hippocratic treatise *The Art*, §2, ed. and transl. W.H.S. Jones (Loeb Classical Library, London & Cambridge, Mass., 1923); PLATO, *Cratylus*; DIODORUS OF SICILY, i, 8, ed. and transl. C.H. Oldfather (Loeb etc., 1936); DIOGENES LAERTIUS, *Lives of Eminent Philosophers*, x. 75-6 (Epicurus), ed. and transl. R.D. Hicks (Loeb etc., 1925); LUCRETIUS, *De rerum natura*, v. 1029-80, ed. C. Bailey, 3 vol. (Oxford, 1947).

([35]) Descartes à Mersenne, 20. xi. 1629, MERSENNE, *Correspondance*, ii, 323-9 ; cf· 374-5, iv, 329, 332, v, 134-40, vi, 4, 6.

([36]) *Les questions théologiques*, quest. xxxiv, « Peut-on inventer une nouvelle science des sons, qui se nomme psophologie? », p. 158 (expurgated edition: see LENOBLE, *Mersenne*, pp. xx, 399-401, 518); MERSENNE, *Correspondence*, iv, 74-6, 203-6, 267-71), cf. pp. iii-iv, 2, 11; *Harm. univ.*, «Tr. ... des sons... », i, props. xxiii-xxiv (language played on a lute), « Tr. de la voix », i, props. xii, xlvii - 1 (artificial rational languages), « De l'utilité de l'harmonie », prop. ix (symbolic language, acoustical telegraph); above n.([35]).

problems, and those of Comenius, George Dalgarno, John Wilkins and Leibniz [37], in a new light. Contemporary medical science shows us the power of those commitments to quantification, demonstration, and the hypothetical model brought into physiology by mathematics and all put neatly together in a few words written by Malpighi in 1687. Malpighi described how, in discovering " the mechanisms of our body, which are the basis of medicine ", the investigator " proceeding *a priori* has come to form models *(moduli et typi, modelli)* of them ". He gave as an example Kepler's demonstration of the retinal image by means of a *camera obscura* with a lens, so that " the mathematician produces all the effects that are observed in vision in the state of health and disease in animals, demonstrating *a priori* the necessity of those effects... from knowledge of the mechanism made by man analogous to the eye " [38]. A corresponding model for the ear was offered by a musical instrument. After Thomas Willis, recently Professor of Natural Philosophy at Oxford, had in 1672 identified the cochlea as the sensitive organ of hearing, in the Académie des Sciences the anatomist Joseph Guichard Duverney with the aid of the physicist Edme Mariotte proposed the " conjecture " that it operated by resonance [39]. He suggested that it responded along its spiral selectively to different notes in the same way as the strings of a lute responded to their corresponding fundamentals and harmonics. We can rediscover in these lines of seventeenth-century mathematical medicine, both culminating in Helmholtz, a freshness of intellectual experience made sophisticated by an awareness of the singularity of their methods and of precisely how their conjectures stood in relation to their technical frontiers.

[37] Cf. J.A. COMENIUS, *Via lucis* (1641 ; Amsterdam, 1668) ; George DALGARNO, *Tables of the Universal Character* (Oxford, 1657 ?), *Ars signorum, vulgo character universalis et lingua philosophica* (London, 1661) ; John WILKINS, *An Essay towards a Real Character and a Philosophical Language* (London, 1668) ; and for a systematic historical discussion O.V.C.M. FUNKE, *Zum Weltsprachenproblem in England im 17. Jahrhundert: G. Dalgarno's 'Ars Signorum' (1661) und J. Wilkins' 'Essay Towards a Real Character and a Philosophical Language "* (1668) (*Anglistische Forschungen*, xlix ; Heidelberg, 1929) ; Paolo ROSSI, *Clavis universalis: Arti mnemoniche e logica combinatoria da Lullo a Leibniz* (Milan & Naples, 1960) ; cf. W.C. & M. KNEALE, *The Development of Logic* (Oxford, 1962); below p. 417.

[38] Marcello MALPIGHI, « Responsio ad Epistolam, cui titulus est, De recentiorum medicorum studio dissertatio epistolaris ad amicum » (1664), *Opera posthuma* (Amsterdam, 1698) 276, 289-90 (in Latin and Italian) ; cf. Thomas WILLIS, *De anima brutorum*, i, c. 4 (*Opera Omnia*, Amsterdam, 1682) 22-23 ; CROMBIE, « The mechanistic hypothesis... » (1967), pp. 68-86, above n. [4].

[39] Thomas WILLIS, *De anima brutorum*, i, c. 14 (Oxford, 1672) ; Joseph Guichard DU VERNEY, *Traité de l'organe de l'ouïe* (Paris, 1683) 68, 78-98 ; cf. *Histoire de l'Académie royale des Sciences*, i (Paris, 1733) 395-8 (Année 1684) ; CROMBIE, « The study of the senses in renaissance science », *Proceedings of the Tenth International Congress of the History Science: Ithaca, New York, 1962*, i (Paris 1964) 93-117. William HOLDER, *A Treatise on the Natural Grounds and Principles of Harmony* (London, 1694) cited the analyses of consonance and resonance by Galileo (pp. 9-17, 45-9) and Mersenne (p. 104), and suggested a resonance theory of consonance and dissonance based on Willis's physiology. Cf. H. von HELMHOLTZ, *On the Sensations of Tone as a physiological basis for the theory of music*, 2nd English ed., translated, thoroughly revised and corrected, rendered conformal to the fourth (and last) German ed. of 1877, with numerous additional notes and a new additional appendix..., by A.J. Ellis (London, 1885 ; New York, 1954 ; 1st German ed. 1865), *Treatise on Physiological Optics*, translated from the 3rd German edition [1909], ed. by J.P.C. Southall, 3 vol. (Menasha, Wisc., 1924-25 ; 1st German ed. 1867), both with valuable historical notes ; P.J. KOSTELIJK, *Theories of Hearing. A critical study of theories and experiments on sound-conduction and sound-analysis in the ear* (Leiden, 1950) ; G. von BÉKÉSY, « Current status of theories of hearing », *Science*, cxxiii (1956) 779-83; below p. 377, ch. 14.

For a final legacy of music to medical science we may return again to Mersenne. His study of communication led him to become interested both in musical instruments that could reproduce the human voice by imitating vowel and consonant sounds, and also in the physiology of natural speech. These investigations suggested to him a method of communication for deaf-mutes by teaching them to produce speech by forming the tongue and lips in appropriate positions and to associate these with written words and the things they signified [40]. This problem had been pioneered in Spain, and was taken up by others both in France and in England. One English physician, John Bulwer, in 1644 and 1648, described three methods of communication for the deaf and dumb : by hearing through a stick held in the teeth, by hand signs, and lip reading [41]. Asserting in the rational spirit of Mersenne that " words are nothing else but motion " [42], Bulwer began with an account of the movements of the larynx and mouth in producing speech. This led him to the question : " That the motions of the parts of the mouth in speech are so remarkable, that some have (not without successe) attempted to imitate them by mathematicall motions " [43]. He wrote :

[40] *Harm. univ.*, « Tr. de la voix », i, props. x-xi, li, « Tr. des instrumens », ii, prop. ix; cf. Mersenne à Gassend, 5. i. 1633, Peiresc à Gassend, 4 and 22. ii. 1633, Mersenne à Peiresc. 26. vii and 2 and 13. viii. 1634, *Correspondence*, iii, 354, 358-9, 375, 378, iv, 258-9, 262-3, 280, 289, 294. On instruments for imitating human speech see « Tr. des instrumens », vi, props. xxxi-xxxii, xxxvi, vii, prop. xxx; Pierre Trichet à Mersenne, 9. i. 1631, *Correspondence*, iii, 2-9, de Villiers à Mersenne, xi and 14. xii. 1633, 15. vii, 1635, *ibid.* iii, 538-53. 578-97, v, 293-4, Mersenne à Peiresc, 1 and 15. vii, 17. xi, 1635, and Doni à Mersenne, 30. ix. 1635, *ibid.* v, 269-72, 299-300, 478-82, 410-5.

[41] John BULWER, *Chirologia: or the Naturall Language of the Hand. Composed of the Speaking Motions, and Discoursing Gestures thereof. Whereunto is added Chironomia: or, the Art of Manuall Rhetoricke. Consisting of the Naturall Expressions, digested by Art in the Hand, as the chiesfest Instrument of Eloquence, by Historicall Manifesto's, exemplified out of the Authentique Registers of Common Life, and Civill Conversation. With Types, or Chyrograms* (London, 1644) ; *Philocophus: or, the Deafe and Dumbe Mans Friend, Exhibiting the Philosophicall verity of that subtile Art, which may inable one with an observant Eie, to Heare what any man speaks by the moving of his lips. Upon the Same Ground, with the advantage of an Historicall Exemplification, apparently proving, That a Man borne Deafe and Dumbe, may be taught to Heare the sound of words with his Eie, & thence learne to speake with his Tongue* (London, 1648), *dedication sigs.* A 2-6, pp. 49-54, 71. Sir Kenelm DIGBY (*Two Treatises in the one of which, the Nature of Bodies ; in the other, the Nature of Mans Soule ; is looked into: in way of discovery, of the Immortality of Reasonable Soules*, i, ch. 28, Paris, 1644, p. 257) in arguing that « hearing is nothing else but the due perception of *motion* » (cf. below n. [42]), cited « the ordinary experience of perceiving musike by mediation of a sticke : for how should a deafe man be capable of musike by holding a sticke in his teeth, whose other end lyeth upon the vyall or virginals, were it not that the proportionall shaking of the sticke (working like a dauncing in the mans head) did make a like motion in his braine, without passing through his eare ? and consequently, without being otherwise *sound*, then as bare motion is *sound* » ; cf. HOLDER, *Elements of Speech* (1669) 160 (below n. [49]), DU VERNEY. *Traité de l'organe de l'ouïe*, p. 90, *Histoire de l'Académie royale des Sciences*, i, 397.

[42] *Philocophus*, p. 19 ; cf. pp. 70-1 on the physiology of the ear ; MERSENNE, *Harm. univ.*, « Tr. ... des sons... », i, props i-ii, *Harm. lib.* i, prop. ii.

[43] *Philocophus*, pp. 45-8 ; cf. pp. 110-2 on birds imitating human speech and inanimate noises ; cf. MERSENNE, *Harm. univ.*, Préface générale au lecteur, sig. Aiii ; J. COHEN, *Human Robots in Myth and Science* (London, 1966). On loquacious statues cf. L. THORNDIKE, *A History of Magic and Experimental Science*, ii (New York, 1929) 680, 825, F.A. YATES, *Giordano Bruno and the Hermetic Tradition* (London, 1964) 67, 147-49.

So that if a man (for curiosity or strangenesse sake) would make a puppet or other dead body, to pronounce a word; let him consider on the one part, the motion of the instruments of the voyce; and on the other part the like sounds made in inanimate bodies; and what conformity there is that causeth the similitude of sounds; and by that he may minister light to that effect. But to come neerer to the point. Many of the learned are of opinion, and perswaded in their judgments, that the imitation of the motions of our speech may be effected by insensible creatures, if a dextrous man would employ his time in contriving and making such an instrument to expresse those different sounds; which not having more than seven substantiall differences, besides the vowells (as some who have carefully noted them, doe affirme) it would peradventure be no hard matter to compose such an engine, which because it will be a subtle imitation of the worke of nature, it will be necessary that our artist have this qualification of being more than superficially tinctur'd in anatomy, the better to be acquainted with the muscules, and the nerves inserted into their heads, which are the principles and springs of all those outward motions whereby speech is perform'd and uttered. And I believe the modell must be in fashion of a head, which is the royall part unto which speech is intrusted; for as the tongue and lips articulate, the head resounds. Frier Bacons brazen head, and that statue formed by Albertus Magnus which spake to Thomas Aquine, and which he mistaking for a magical device brake, was certainly nothing else but mathematical inventions framed in imitation of the motions of speech performed by the instruments in and about the mouth.

Bulwer was impressed by the social, civil and legal disabilities of deaf-mutes, who were often considered imbeciles, but he pointed out that most mutes were so because they had been deprived by deafness from birth of any experience of speech and of the normal disciplines of human communication over a growing intelligence ([44]). He quoted from Sir Kenelm Digby the case Digby had met, while he was in Spain in attendance on the Prince of Wales (later King Charles I), of a nobleman who had been " borne deafe, so deafe, that if a gun were shot off close by his eare he could not heare it, and consequently he was dumbe; for not being able to heare the sound of words, he could never imitate, nor understand them ". But the youth's whole manner and appearance, " and especially the exceeding life and spiritfulness of his eyes, ... were pregnant signes of a wel-temper'd mind within ". After " physicians and chyrurgions had long employed their skill, but all in vaine ", he was taught by an apt teacher " to heare the sounds of words with his eyes, and thence learne to speak with his tongue " ([45]). This he learnt so well that, although a little unsteady in controlling the pitch of his own voice, he could recognize that of others and could accurately reproduce the sounds of English and of Welsh spoken by members of the Prince's suite. Bulwer's explanation of this case was strictly rational. He rejected " that supposed infallible sympathy of the nerves of hearing and speech " which " many physicians have confidently affirmed to be the onely cause why a man deafe from his nativity, is consequently dumbe : ... whereas this Lord having got a pair of eare-spectacles before his

([44]) *Philocophus*, pp. 102-9 ; cf. 88-97, 109-38.

([45]) *Ibid.*, pp. 55-61, quoting Sir Kenelm DIGBY, *Two Treatises*, i, ch. 28, pp. 254-6 ; cf. *Philocophus*, pp. 91-2, 155-68. Charles went with Buckingham to Spain in 1623.

eyes, whereby the dependencie that speech had upon the eare was taken away : there remained no signe of a sympatheticall league of silence contracted betweene the tongue and the eare : but the tongue set at liberty, proves free, and being *sui juris*, leaves the unprofitable eare, and by art enters into an auditory league of amity and allyance with the eye, which now officiously becomes *ad succedaneum*, or *quid pro quo*, for eare " [46].

After his encounter with this example of training the eye and mind " in conceiving the visible sound of speech " [47], Bulwer collected together from literature and experience a large number of other cases showing, as he put it, " how the objects of one sense may be known by another ", and how this " community among the senses " provided " other avenewes unto the braine " [48] through which those deprived of their normal sensory equipment could communicate. He cited from Felix Plater one case " of a certaine Abbot, who being made blinde, mute, and deafe by the malignity of the French pox ", could be communicated with only by " drawing letters upon his naked arm " with a finger or a piece of wood. Another case in which touch supplied the deficiency of other senses was that of an ingenious English gentleman " who through some sicknesse becoming deaf, doth notwithstanding feele words, and as if he had an eye in his finger, sees signes in the darke; whose wife discourseth very perfectly with him by a strange way of arthrologie or alphabet contrived on the joynts of his fingers; who taking him by the hand in the night, can so discourse with him very exactly; for, he feeling the joynts which she toucheth for letters, by them collected into words, very readily conceives what shee would suggest unto him " [49].

Bulwer made the interesting point that " if speech were naturall to man, there is no reason but men borne deafe and dumbe (their tongues being commonly free), might come out with it without hearing or teaching ",

[46] *Philocophus*, pp. 113-4.

[47] *Ibid.*, pp. 181-3. Spoken words could be seen at a greater distance and sooner than heard. A friend of mine deaf from childhood tells me that as an undergraduate he used to be able to read with field glasses the conversations of girls in a hostel some distance from the men's hostel where he and some of their sweethearts lived.

[48] *Ibid.*, pp. 64-76, sig. A4.

[49] *Ibid.*, pp. 106-7. For further discussions of this question in England see William HOLDER, *Elements of Speech: an essay of inquiry into the natural production of letters: with an appendix concerning persons deaf and dumb* (London, 1669); John WALLIS, « A Letter of Doctor John Wallis to Robert Boyle Esq., concerning the said Doctors Essay of Teaching a person Dumb and Deaf to speak, and to understand a Language ; together with the success thereof, made apparent to his Majesty, the Royal Society, and the University of Oxford », *Philosophical Transactions*, v (1670) 1087-99 ; HOLDER, *A Supplement to the Philosophical Transactions of July, 1670: With some reflexions on Dr. John Wallis, his letter there inserted* (London, 1678) ; WALLIS, *A Defence of the Royal Society, and the Philosophical Transactions, particularly those of July, 1670, in answer to the cavils of Dr. William Holder* (London, 1678), *Grammatica linguae anglicanae, cui praefigitur, De loquela ; sive de sonorum formatione: tractatus grammatico-physicus, editio sexta. Accessit Epistola ad Thomam Beverley ; de mutis surdisque informandis* (London, 1765 ; 1st ed. Oxford, 1653) ; G. DALGARNO, *Didascalocophus or the Deaf and dumb mans tutor...* (Oxford, 1680) ; cf. Jo. Conrad AMMAN, *Dissertatio de loquela qua non solum vox humana, & loquendi artificium ex originibus suis eruuntur: sed & traduntur media, quibus ii, qui ab incunabulis surdi & muti fuerunt, loquelam adipisci, quique difficulter loquuntur, vitia sua emendare possint* (Amsterdam, 1700); David WRIGHT, *Deafness: A personal account* (London, 1969).

and so " the most unanswerable argument against the naturality of any language is, that they who are naturally deafe, speake not at all " ([50]). Another fundamental question raised by these natural experiments in the extirpation of particular senses was that discussed famously by John Locke ([51]) : what would a man born blind with congenital cateract see after an operation giving him sight ? How do we come to correlate the information received through seeing, touching and hearing into a perception of a single world ? Locke's Oxford contemporary Willis and the mathematical physiologists of the Académie des Sciences ([52]) raised the parallel question of how this humanly perceived world was related to those available to the variety of sensory equipments of the different invertebrate and vertebrate animals. We are still trying to answer these questions. They have a practical application in pre-operative training in cases of restorable deprivation. Above all they enlighten the complexity of that most complex and human of all human phenomena, language itself.

Further references: for music F. de Buzon, " Science de la nature et théorie musicale chez Isaac Beeckman (1588-1637) ", *Revue d'histoire des sciences*, xxxviii (1985) 97-120; H.F. Cohen, *Quantifying Music* (Dordrecht, 1984); P. Costabel, *Démarches* ... (1982) above p. 258; A.C. Crombie, " Alexandre Koyré ... " (1987) above p. 343; S. Dostrovsky, " Early vibration theory ", *Archive for History of Exact Sciences*, xiv (1974/75) 169-218; P.M. Gouk, *The Anatomy of Music* (forthcoming); J.C. Kassler, " The 'science' of music to 1830 ", *Archives internationales d'histoire des sciences*, xxx (1980) 111-36, " Music as a model in early science ", *History of Science*, xx (1982) 103-39; C.V. Palisca, " The science of sound and musical practice " in *Science and the Arts* ... ed. Shirley and Hoeniger (1985) 59-73 above p. 173, *Humanism and Italian Renaissance Musical Thought* (New Haven, 1985); D.P. Walker, " Some aspects of the musical theory of Vincenzo Galilei and Galileo Galilei ", *Proceedings of the Royal Musical Association*, c. (1973-74) 33-47, *Studies in Musical Science in the Late Renaissance* (London, 1978); for the deaf R.E. Bender, *The Conquest of Deafness* (Cleveland, Ohio, 1970); H. Lane, *When the Mind Hears* (New York, 1984), ed. *The Deaf Experience* (Cambridge, Mass., 1984); C.F. Mullett, " 'An Arte to Make the Dumb to Speake, the Deafe to Heare' " *Journal of the History of Medicine*, xxvi (1971) 123-49; see also below chs. 14, and 15 p. 417 for language.

([50]) BULWER, *Philocophus*, pp. 133-5 ; Table, unnumbered sig. b.5. He was arguing against Montaigne.

([51]) *An Essay concerning Humane Understanding*, ii. 9 (London, 1690) ; cf. M. von SENDEN, *Space and Sight : The perception of space and shape in the congenitally blind before nd after operation* (London, 1960) ; CROMBIE, « The mechanistic hypothesis... » (1967) 4-6. For discussions of this question in relation to language cf. Denis DIDEROT, *Lettre sur les aveugles, à l'usage de ceux qui voyent* (London, 1749), *Lettre sur les sourds et muets, à l'usage de ceux qui entendent et qui parlent* (Paris, 1751) ; E. Bonnot de CONDILLAC, *Traité des sensations* (1754) and *Logique* (1780), in *Œuvres complètes*, iii, xxii (Paris, 1798).

([52]) WILLIS, *De anima brutorum*, i, cc. 3-15 ; *Histoire de l'Académie royale des Sciences*, i (1733) 18-19, 36-7 (1667), 117 (1670), 179 (1674), 223-8 (1677), 243-8 (1678), 278-81 (1679), 395-8 (1684) ; cf. MERSENNE, *La vérité des sciences*, pp. 16-20.

14

THE STUDY OF THE SENSES IN RENAISSANCE SCIENCE

It is premature for me to attempt to crystallize my thoughts on this subject at this stage of my investigations *, so this is a brief report intended to raise questions for discussion. The place of the living body in the view of the physical world created by 'Renaissance' science is certainly a subject that we should consider in a symposium on this period, in which an excessive enthusiasm of historians for mathematical physics has sometimes given too short a shrift to the biological and other aspects of scientific activity. In order to relate the study of the living body to the rest of scientific activity, I propose to discuss the history of a biological (and psychological) problem of which, in the terms formulated, a large part arose out of the physics of the period, especially out of the reduction of the physical world to a mechanism and the greater sense of quantitative precision gained in consequence. While this view of the physical world was being created, scientific men put to themselves the question : how does the "animate and sensitive body" receive information about this external world and what is the nature of this information? A study of the investigations by "anatomists, mathematicians and philosophers" into this question gives us a good picture of the analytical methods and philosophical assumptions used in biological research at this time, and of the results imposed and further problems raised by their character and limitations. The field provided physiological problems, such as that of the formation of the retinal image, that could be solved by contemporary physical knowledge. It also provided some striking examples of intellectual behaviour in the face of recognized frontiers of knowledge of more than one kind.

I propose to concentrate on some of the investigations made during the 'Renaissance' into the means by which the sensory mechanisms mediate information about the external world to the living animal. For the purpose of this Symposium, it is assumed that this period includes the 17th century. The general terms in which the problem was investigated are indicated by Galileo's distinction between primary and secondary qualities. It is worth looking, for example, at his account of hearing. He wrote:

> Sounds are made and are heard by us when—without any special "sonorous" or "transonorous" property—a rapid tremor of the air, ruffled into very minute waves, moves certain cartilages of a tympanum within our ear. External means capable of producing this ruffling of the air are very numerous, but for the most part they reduce to the trembling of some body which strikes upon the air and disturbs it; waves are thereby very rapidly propogated, from the frequency of which originates a high pitch and from their rarity a deep sound [1].

The point of the famous conclusion following this passage was of course to eliminate the belief that there were in external bodies any "real qualities" of sound, colour, odour, taste, touch, heat and cold, etc. which could be apprehended immediately through the senses.

* 1962: see above chs. 9, 11, 13 n. 3.

[1]   Galileo, *Il saggiatore* (1623), Question 48.

> I do not believe that for exciting in us tastes, odours, and sounds there are
> required in external bodies anything but sizes, shapes, numbers and slow or
> fast movements; and I think that if ears, tongues and noses were taken away,
> shapes, numbers and motions would remain but not odours or tastes or sounds.
> These, I believe, are nothing but mere names, apart from the living animal...

Galileo's scientific interests led him to study the "sizes, shapes, numbers and slow
or fast movements" exhibited in external bodies, rather than the "ears, tongues and
noses" and the sensations they mediated in the living animal. (He declared that he knew
too little about vision to discuss it.) But here he stated quite clearly, although he did
not invent, the essential programme of contemporary research into sensory physiology. The programme aimed in the first place to discover the mechanisms by means
of which the "sizes, shapes, numbers and slow or fast movements" of external bodies
were translated into sensations whose quality and quantity were correlated with these
quantitative characteristics of external bodies. The first problem, then, was to discover
the mechanisms of the individual special sense organs. But for a general account of how the
"animate and sensitive body" received information about the external world, the further
problem arose of how the sensory mechanism of the body operated as a whole, how
the information received through the different special sense organs was correlated to
give one consistent view of the external world and consistent behaviour in relation to it,
and the extent to which this correlation was 'built into' the body or had to be learned
by experience. Beginning in the first half of the 16th century, research developed along
a number of different lines which broadly speaking also marked stages of inquiry: anatomical, physical and mathematical, and finally psychological, with the relationship
between mind and body presenting a problem to be raised afresh in each scientific
context. It will be convenient to discuss these lines of inquiry in chronological order.

The traditional view generally accepted in the 16th and 17th centuries distinguished
five special senses, in two of which, touch and taste, external bodies acted on the sense
organs directly, whereas in the other three, odour, hearing and vision, they acted through
a medium. The historical sources for the discussions of the sensory mechanisms are the
chapters in anatomical and physiological works dealing with the special senses and with
sensation in general, together with special treatises by investigators who were often
primarily physicists like Kepler and Mersenne as well as biologists like Coiter and Du
Verney. The investigation of the mode of operation of the external world, especially
in the senses where a medium was concerned, was as necessary to the inquiry as the
study of the sense organs themselves, and here the progress in geometrical and later in
physical optics, as well as in the anatomy of the eye, gave the science of vision a considerable lead over that of the other special senses. Vision and the eye had since Galen's
day provided an immediate model for the study of hearing and the ear. I propose to
illustrate the theme of this paper from the history of the inquiry into these two senses.

Consider first the tools of research available. For the study of vision these were
macroscopic anatomy and geometrical optics, and later the philosophical assumption
that the whole physical world, including living bodies, operated as a system of mechanisms, thus defining the problem for research as that of discovering the particular
mechanisms concerned. The recent work of Ronchi as well as the admirable historical
discussions of physiological optics by Helmholtz and other older writers make it unne-
cessary for me to do more than draw attention to some particular characteristics of the
inquiry.

First, although Alhazen and other early investigators had treated the   operation
of the eye as a problem in dioptrics, it was not until the 17th century that the absolute
necessity was recognized of attempting an exclusively mathematical-physical analysis
of the eye as an optical instrument, restricting the problem of vision in the first ins-

tance to those terms. Earlier investigators had complicated this problem for themselves by including other, biological and psychological, aspects, in an attempt to give a comprehensive account of how vision comes about. Kepler made this methodological restriction explicitly when, in *Ad Vitellionem Paralipomena* (1604), he set out to solve one problem first, that of the dioptric mechanism by which the eye throws an inverted image on the retina. "I leave it to natural philosophers", he wrote, "to discuss the way in which this image or picture is put together by the spiritual principles of vision ..." [2]. He was also critical of the lack of technical competence that had led some investigators astray. Thus he wrote of Felix Plater, whose anatomical description of the eye he used : "Compare the true mode of operation of vision as given by me with that given by Plater, and you will see that this famous man is no farther from the truth than is compatible with being a medical man who deliberately does not treat mathematics" [3]. Apart from anatomy, the discovery of the mode of operation of the eye made in this period was almost entirely the work of mathematicians and physicists—Maurolico, Porta, Kepler himself, Scheiner, Descartes, Huygens. Later on Thomas Young and Helmholtz were to retrieve the honour of the medical profession, but it must be admitted that they had a much better knowledge of mathematics and of physics than most of their medical contemporaries. For Kepler and his contemporaries the eye was a piece of optical machinery identical in its mode of operation with the artificial models they made with arrangements of lenses in a camera obscura. To this extent they were able to achieve the 'Cartesian' programme of establishing a complete identity between the artificial and the natural, so that, for example, all biological problems became literally problems in engineering.

The initial restriction of the analysis of vision to a problem in dioptrics, and the solution of that problem, had the immediate effect of allowing further problems to be formulated in such a way that they could be solved. Myopia and hypermetropia and the design of appropriate compensating lenses, accommodation, the formation of a single visual field with two eyes, the relation between direct and indirect vision, and numerous other phenomena were formulated as problems for exact analysis. Even so, it shows the continuing uncertainty of opinion that someone as scientifically competent as Mariotte, the discoverer of the 'blind spot', could still argue that not the retina but the choroid was the sensitive organ. A clear distinction between physiological and psychological problems became possible, and both could be more adequately separated from philosophical problems such as those of the relationship between body and mind. One investigator in this field whose work is insufficiently known is Mersenne. He made experiments from which he concluded that the least angle an object must subtend at the eye in order to become visible is 15″, and he is unusual in this period for giving his actual measurements [4]. He tried to discover experimentally whether single binocular vision is brought about by the axes of the two eyes meeting at the point being looked at, or whether the axes remain parallel and each eye looks at

[2]   Kepler, *Ad Vitellionem Paralipomena* (1604), V, 2; *Gesammelte Werke*, ed. Walter, von Dyck, Max Caspar and Franz Hammer, ii. ed. Franz Hammer (Munich, 1939), 151-2. See my translation, « Kepler : de modo visionis », in *Mélanges Koyré*, ed. I. Bernard Cohen and R. Taton (Paris, 1964), ii, and my   'The mechanistic hypothesis' and the scientific study of vision", *Proc. Roy. Microscopical Soc.*, ii (1967) 3-112: above chs. 9-10 ; V. Ronchi, *Histoire de la lumière* (Paris, 1956). Cf. also E. Boring, *Sensation and Perception in the History of Experimental Psychology* (New-York, 1962); G. S. Brett, *History of Psychology*, ed. and abridged by R. S. Peters (London, 1953); and John Field, H. W. Magoun and Victor E. Hall (editors), *Handbook of Physiology* : Section 1 : Neurophysiology (Washington, D. C., 1959-60), 3 vols.
[3]   Kepler, *op. cit.* V, 4, 187.
[4]   Mersenne, *L'Optique et la catoptrique*, I, Prop. xxx (Paris, 1651), 72.

the point alternately. He came to the conclusion, in agreement with Gassendi, that each eye pays attention to an object alternately and that "le nerf et les muscles de l'un se relaschent, et n'opèrent quasi point, pendant que l'axe de l'autre est bandé pour regarder fixement un objet" [5]. Mersenne made use of this notion of 'attention' to account also for the fact that we actually see only particular objects making up a small part of the visual field focussed upon the retina. He suggested a mechanistic explanation of this psychological phenomenon by supposing that vision was brought about not only by the rays coming from the object to the retina, but also "par les rayons que l'œil jette hors de soi jusques à l'objet" by the mechanical principal that every action produces a reaction — thus reconciling the two ancient conceptions of the visual act [6].

Mersenne, Kepler and most of their contemporaries regarded their methodological restriction of the analysis of vision in the first instance to soluble physical problems as having the effect of excluding what they held to be the most important part of the phenomenon. For example, when Kepler rejected, as optically impossible, Witelo's account of how the "images" or "species" of things seen were carried from the eye through the hollow optic nerve to the seat of the visual faculty of the soul in the brain, he added a note saying: "and yet it is this motion that brings about vision ... and so it is wrong to exclude it from the science of optics simply because, in the present limited state of our science, it cannot be accommodated in optics [7]". And likewise Mersenne wrote:

> Si l'on pouvoit expliquer comme quoy l'âme sent dans le cerveau le mouvement dont l'objet ébranle le nerf qui fait la retine,... nous aurions non seulement le principal point de l'optique, mais ce qui manque de plus excellent à toutes les sciences, qui sont si imparfaites qu'elles ne nous font point concevoir de quelle façon l'âme, ou l'esprit opère... c'est une chose estrange que ce que nous désirons davantage, soit si éloigné de nostre connoissance; et que ce qui nous est le plus intérieur, et ce semble le plus essentiel, nous soit le plus inconnu : ce qui nous doit faire espérer que Dieu nous réserve une autre sorte de veuë où l'entendement trouvera toute sorte de satisfaction [8].

Mersenne was always prepared to confess frankly when he did not know and he urged others to do the same; he said that some philosophers seemed to think that they had established an explanation as true because it had not been proved false, like a murderer whose claim to innocence had not been disproved [9]. But for most of his contemporaries the mechanistic programme of analysis proved too tempting not to be tried out, at least in conjectures, after the facts had been left far behind. Kepler himself speculated in the *Dioptrice* (1611) on the problem he had put aside in the *Paralipomena*, writing:

> To see is to feel the stimulation of the retina, however it is stimulated. The retina is painted with the coloured rays of visible things... But this picture *(pictura)* does not complete the act of vision until the image *(species)* so received by the retina passes through the continuity of the spirits to the brain, and is there delivered to the threshold of the faculty of the soul [10].

[5]   *Ibid.*, Prop. xxvi, 65.
[6]   *Ibid.*, Prop. xxv, 61; cf. référence 26.
[7]   Kepler, *op. cit.* V, 2, 152.
[8]   Mersenne, *L'Optique et la catoptrique*, I, Prop. xxv (Paris, 1651), 62-63.
[9]   *Ibid.*, II, Prop. iv, 88-90. Cf. Newton on this type of argument, in the controversies following the publication of his New Theory about Light and Colours: "the Theory, which I propounded, was evinced by me, not by inferring 'tis thus because not otherwise, that is, not by deducing it only from a confutation of contrary suppositions, but by deriving it from Experiments concluding positively and directly.' (*Philosophical Transactions*, vii, 1672, 5004; reprinted in I. Bernard Cohen, *Isaac Newton's Papers and Letters on Natural Philosophy*, Cambridge, 1958, 93.
[10] Kepler, *Dioptrice*, Prop. lxi; *Ges. Werke*, iv, ed. Max Caspar and Franz Hammer (Munich, 1941), 372.

Perhaps, he continued, the image is transmitted from the eye to the seat of the *sensus communis* in the brain because the optic nerve is filled with visual spirit, and the continuity of the spirit acts in the same way as in the motion of a wave made by a stone thrown into still water which is propagated as far as the surface continues.

Descartes, first in the *Traité de l'homme* and then in *La Dioptrique* (1637) [11], carried this conjecture of visual images impressed on the brain through to the manifestation of their effects in the motor activity of the body (cf. fig. 53). So, by consistently asking the same mechanistic question and allowing no others, by asking only what physical motions followed each preceding motion, beginning with the light impressing an image on the eye and carrying through to the consequential movements of the animal's muscles, he reduced the "animate body" to a system of built-in responses designed to preserve and propagate itself by pursuing the beneficial and avoiding the harmful aspects of the environment acting on it. In human beings, where the system was "sensitive" as well as "animate", Descartes argued that the retinal image was not the object but the means of sensing. The programme there is found in the various proposals made by Descartes, Malebranche and others for correlating different sensations of colour with different modes of motion of particles or waves supposed to constitute light, and perception of shape, size, distance and so on with other physiological clues.

Historically the value of such speculative ideas, extending beyond the contemporary technical and scientific frontiers of testable theory, has been that they may suggest new questions for research; they suggest the form of the answer to be found as the scientific frontiers advance, though there is always the danger that an answer will be found too soon. But in the general history of scientific thinking this danger itself has given to speculative hypotheses another essential if somewhat paradoxical role, as can be seen very clearly, for example, in Newton's intellectual development, especially in relation to Descartes. I eagerly await the publication of R. S. Westfall's researches into this subject, and I am myself particularly grateful to him for drawing my attention to the early notebooks in which Newton devoted many pages to problems of sensory mechanisms, especially in vision. The mechanistic programme in physiology, of which Descartes's *Traité de l'homme* is simply the most extreme example, had the effect of bringing home to physiologists the lesson that the more fruitful the speculative ideas were in suggesting lines of research and explanation, the clearer and stricter must the criteria become for accepting the scientific theories generated. Steno's comments on the *Traité de l'homme* are a good example. He began the *Discours sur l'anatomie du cerveau* :

> Au lieu de vous promettre de contenter vostre curiosité, touchant l'Anatomie du Cerveau, je vous fais icy une confession sincère et publique, que je n'y connois rien [12].

He congratulated Descartes on the beautiful machine he had described to imitate a man; in this he had surpassed all other philosophers. But, he said, Descartes knew well that with existing knowledge it was impossible to describe the true composition of a man. Sylvius had shown that Descartes's machine did not agree with actual dissection and anatomy, and the danger of all systems built on external observations of move-

---

[11] Descartes, *Dioptrique*, IV-VI, *Traité de l'homme*, and *Les passions de l'âme*, Art. 31 ff., in *Œuvres de Descartes*, ed. C. Adam and P. Tannery, vi, xi, (Paris, 1902, 1909). *Traité de l'homme* was published posthumously in Latin (1662) and French (1664). See Norman Kemp Smith, *New Studies in the Phylosophy of Descartes* (London, 1952), 125 ff.; also my "The mechanistic hypothesis ..", référence 2.

[12] *Nicholai Stenonis Opera philosophica*, ed. V. Maar (Copenhagen, 1910), ii, 3.

ments was that the same effect can be explained in different ways. Some people had taken Descartes's machine for an account of the actual body. But:

> Il n'y a que deux voyes, pour parvenir à la connoissance d'une machine : l'une, que le maistre qui l'a composée nous en découvre l'artifice; l'autre de démontrer jusqu'aux moindres ressorts, et les examiner tous séparément, et ensemble... Or le cerveau estant une machine, il ne faut pas que nous espérons d'en trouver d'artifice, par d'autres voyes, que par celles dont on se sert, pour trouver l'artifice des autres machines.

Anatomists and physiologists had been investigating the machinery of the body on the analogy of physical models for over a century in the immediate past before Steno gave this lecture in Paris in 1665; the effect of an explicit statement of the mechanistic programme such as that given by Descartes was not so much to increase this research as to stimulate consciousness of its character. Steno was provoked, as Newton was to be, by the Cartesian use of hypotheses in scientific inquiry, into insisting on a clear recognition of what had been actually established: a recognition in particular instances and not just as a general rule. Theoretical investigators would have greatly assisted others he wrote,

> s'ils eussent fait un récit exact, de ce que les Anatomistes ont écrit du cerveau, ou s'ils eussent étendu, selon les loix de l'Analyse, toutes les manières d'expliquer mécaniquement, les actions animales, ou s'ils se fussent occupez à dresser un catalogue bien exact de toutes les propositions qu'ils y ont trouvées, entre lesquelles il auroit fallu distinguer soigneusement, celles qui sont fondées sur le fait et sur l'expérience, d'avec les autres, qui ne sont que des raisonnemens; mais il n'y a eu personne, jusqu'à cette heure, qui s'y soit pris de la sorte; c'est pourquoy il ne se faut guère arrester, qu'à ceux qui ont travaillé eux mesmes. La première chose qu'on y doit considérer, est l'histoire des parties, dans laquelle il est nécessaire de déterminer, ce qui est vray et certain, pour le pouvoir distinguer d'avec des propositions, qui sont ou fausses, ou incertaines. Ce n'est pas mesme assez de s'en pouvoir éclaircir soy-mesme, il faut que l'évidence de la démonstration oblige tous les autres à en demeurer d'accord; autrement le nombre des controverses augmenteroit, au lieu de diminuer [13].

The history of criteria of cogency and validity in the development of modern science has still to be written, but even a cursory reading shows how consciously the form given to a scientific argument appears in the physiological writings of the time, and how important these are as sources for the history of the logic of scientific inquiry.

The mechanistic programme was at a considerable disadvantage in the investigation of hearing as compared with that of vision because of the primitive state of acoustics. The anatomists who began the investigation in the 16th century had at their disposal only a very elementary, qualitative theory of sound and of hearing inherited from Greek sources, which in no way compared with the well-developed science of geometrical optics. But even so, here again the mechanistic programme, once grasped and reinforced by the successful model presented by the inquiry into the mechanism of vision, offered a clear definition of problems for research. These involved three kinds of investigations: first into the anatomy of the ear and its neural connections with the brain, not only in man and the quadrupeds but also, for comparison, in birds, fish and other types of animals, and in the embryo as well as the adult; secondly, into the physics of sound; and finally, into the problem of relating the results of these investigations in a theory of the auditory mechanism.

Anatomical research, beginning in Italy in the early 16th century not far in advance

---

[13]   *Ibid.*, 16, 19. Cf. G. Canguilhem, "The role of analogics and models in biological discovery", in *Scientific Change*, ed. A. C. Crombie (London and New-York, 1963).

of where Galen had left off, had by the early 17th century clarified and in large part discovered the main macroscopic details of the auditory mechanism (Figs 54-56) [14]. The structures of which anatomical descriptions and illustrations were published in this period include the tympanic membrane or drum, the three ossicles of the middle ear with the tensor tympani and stapedius muscles, the Eustachian tube, and the fenestra rotunda and the fenestra ovalis closed by a membrane attached to the foot of the stapes, and finally the inner ear carved out of the os petrosum beyond these fenestrae and consisting of the vestibule, the three semi-circular canals and the cochlea. The bony spiral of the cochlea was first adequately described by Falloppio, who gave this name to the structure and observed the membranous covering of all the cavities of the labyrinth. The first known drawing of the cochlea was made by Eustachio, who also discovered the membranous lamina spiralis attached to the bony lamina extending into the spiral cavity from the central core (the modiolus) and dividing it longitudinally in two. The first clear description of the membranous lamina was later given by Casserio. Details of the innervation of the ear also began to be clarified at this time, Falloppio observing the passage of the "soft" branch of the auditory nerve into the membranous covering of the cochlea and Eustachio identifying the chorda tympani as a nerve to the tensor tympani muscle. Eventually much fuller descriptions of the innervation of the ear and its associated organs were to be given by Thomas Willis and Du Verney (Figs. 57,58).

According to the theory of hearing which these anatomists inherited from Greek and medieval sources, a sounding body transmitted its motion to the contiguous air which in turn propagated the motion to the ear, where the motion of the external air produced a corresponding motion of the internal air enclosed in the cavities in the bone. As Mondino wrote:

> In order that it may resound, its opening [the external auditory meatus] is long and reaches to the os petrosum, in the cavity of which is implanted the auditory spirit, which is the instrument of hearing. A thin membrane [panniculus; the tympanum] made from the fibres of the auditory nerve covers its opening or cavities [15].

In his commentary on this passage, Berengario da Carpi, who is the author of the first recorded description of the malleus and incus, developed the theory as follows:

> Beyond the membrane *(panniculus)* and within the substance of the aforesaid os petrosum there is in every ear a twisted cavity in which the beating air receives the forms of hearing and offers them to the auditory nerve which is spread out into the membrane; then the sense of hearing comprehends the voice or vocal wave and whatever sound flows to that place... That membrane is called the miringa of the ear, for the miringa or meninga or meninx is nothing except that membrane investing the brain [16].

This view that the drum was an extension of the dura mater originated after Galen and was to be disposed of by Falloppio.

An influential version of the theory in its full form was given by Coiter in the first special monograph to be written on the organ of hearing. He wrote :

[14] Politzer, Adam, *Geschichte der Ohrenheilkunde* (Stuttgart, 1907), i; also a useful guide is J. B. Morgagni, *Epistolae anatomicae duae* (Venice, 1762), especially Epist. I, Art. 92-93. See also references 34-37, below.

[15] Mundinus, *Anatomia*, in Berengario da Carpi, *Commentaria... super anatomia Mundini* (Bologna, 1521), 476.

[16] Berengario, *ibid.*, ff. 476v-477; see C. D. O'Malley and Edwin Clarke, "The discovery of the auditory ossicles", *Bulletin of the History of Medicine*, xxxv (1961) 424-5.

We can discover the mode of action from the definition of the object of hearing, which is sound, and from the mode of communication of the water or air altered by sound with the internal air [17].

The latter he saw as the communication of a representation or "image" of the external world to the sentient thing. He wrote:

> To have a sensation of anything, there must be a mutual action and being affected *(actio et passio)* between the sentient thing and the thing sensed, and for this there must be mutual agreement between the two. Whence it follows that when the external air acts, the internal or implanted air *(aër internus sive implantatus)* is affected, the internal air receiving the alteration of the external air and being moved in the same way from outside. But this does not happen immediately, but through the interposition of the membrane and of certain ossicles wonderfully designed by nature, as follows. The external air affected by the quality of sound meets the myringa membrane, the pulsating myrinx moves the ossicles attached to it, these in turn strike a certain nerve [the chorda tympani] extended across the membrane, and this nerve or cord then rebounds against the membrane. From this the enclosed air receives the alteration and the sounds, but the sound is carried through the twisting and turning windings [the labyrinth and cochlea] of the ears without any disturbance, and reaches the auditory nerve. By means of this passage and agency, the image of the sound *(strepitus imago)* is at last transmitted to the seat of sensation *(principium sentiendi)*.

For Coiter the proper organ \of\ hearing was the "internal air" in the middle ear cavity, which he held was set in motion, as described, by the vibrations of the chorda tympani. In transmitting this motion to the auditory nerve, he thought that the bony labyrinth and cochlea of the inner ear acted like the coils of a musical instrument in strengthing the sound [18].

Discussion of the physiology of hearing by anatomists during this period was concerned principally with the identification of the organ sensitive to sound, and with its mode of operation and that of the other parts of the ear which were held to modulate and transmit the motion of the external air and present the "forms" or "species" or "images" of sound to the sensitive organ for transmission through the auditory nerve to the "common sensory" in the brain. These parts were held to correspond to the coats and humours which protected the sensitive organ of the eye and focussed the visual images on to it. The changes of opinion with progress in anatomical knowledge have been well described by Adam Politzer [14]. The proper organ of sensation was at first held to be the *aer internus* or *aer ingenitus* located in the cavity of the middle ear. This left the function of the ossicles obscure and opinions varied from supposing that they magnified the sound by clattering together when the drum vibrated, to supposing that they controlled the vibrations of the drum, either by modulating their amplitude by changing the tension of the drum by means of the tensor tympani and other muscles (a process which Varolio compared to focussing the eye), or by the attachment of the stapes to the fenestra ovalis acting as a safeguard against excessive movement. Opinions on the function of the labyrinth also varied widely, from Coiter's view supposing that it acted like the coils of a musical instrument in strengthing sound, to the opposite view that it absorbed surplus sound, and prevented echoes. The first person known to me to have located the sensitive *aer* in the labyrinth was the Italian anatomist Guido Guidi (d. 1569), who became Professor of Anatomy in Paris in 1542 and of Philosophy and Medicine

[17] Coiter, Volcher, *De auditus instrumento*, Cap. I, in *Externarum et internarum principalium humani corporis partium tabulae* (Nuremberg, 1573), 89.
[18] *Ibid.*, Cap. xv, 102.

in Pisa in 1548. According to Guidi, "the principal instrument of hearing is the air contained in the inmost cavity where is spread out the nerve of the fifth pair, through which the spirit imbued with the power of hearing is sent from the brain" [19]. He held that the motion of sound in the external air, having set the tympanum and the ossicles in motion, passed into the inner ear through the fenestra ovalis, opened by the motion of the stapes. But, he added, "these are to be understood as conjectures more than as scientific knowledge ».

Guidi's anatomical writings were not published until 1611. Before this date at least one other writer, the French anatomist André du Laurens, had published the view that the cochlea was the location of the proper organ of sensation, and that the motion produced in the drum by the "unda vocalis" in the external air was transferred through the middle ear to the labyrinth and finally to the cochlea, from which the auditory nerve conducted the "sounds" to the "common sensory" [20]. But it was to be over half a century before the proper organ of sensation was firmly located in the cochlea and serious attempts made to envisage its mechanism. Even then argument continued as to whether the motion of the drum was transferred to the labyrinth through the ossicles or through the air in the cavity of the middle ear. Meanwhile Casserio, du Laurens and later most emphatically the German physiologist Günther Christoph Schelhammer (1649-1712) attacked the whole theory of the *aër ingenitus* as the sensitive organ. They argued that the *aër* was a medium and not part of the animate body, and that the proper sensitive organ must be the termination of the auditory nerve analogous (after 1604) to the expansion of the optic nerve into the retina. But it was still believed that the labyrinth was filled with physical air, and this was given an essential mechanical role in all theories of hearing until Domenico Cotugno in 1760 opened a new chapter in the physiological investigation of hearing by replacing the air with the "*humor aqueus labyrinthi*" [21].

While these investigations and speculations were going on, a number of anatomists and physicists became acutely aware of how much the whole physiological inquiry was groping in the dark. "But what need to pursue these things which may in all respects be compared to numerous musical instruments made with great and astonishing care", Vesalius wrote in his letter to Fallopio after a discussion of the ossicles, "since thus far the duties and uses of all of them lie hidden from me; I can understand them no more than the visual and olfactory instruments" [22]. Two essential requirements for the programme of research became recognized. The first was the need to combine anatomy with the quantitative study of the physics of sound. The second was the need to separate the physiological problem of the mechanism of the sense organ from the psychological and philosophical problems arising from sensation and perception, as Kepler had done in the study of vision. The psychology of perception could then become a field of independent empirical inquiry. In the study of hearing neither of these requirements was wholly fulfilled in this period.

The quantitative investigation of the physics of sound in the study of voice and hearing was stressed by Mersenne. "Briefly", he wote, "it should be pointed out that nobody can read perfection in music, nor understand or discuss it, unless he combines

[19] Vidus Vidius, *De anatomia corporis humani libri vii*, VIII, Cap. v (*Ars medicinalis*, Venice, 1611), iii, 322-3.
[20] Laurentius, Andrea, *Historia anatomica humani corporis*, XI, Questiones ix-x (Frankfurt, 1600), 428-9.
[21] Cotugno, Domenico, *De aquaeductibus auris humanae internae anatomica dissertatio* (Naples, 1760).
[22] *Anatomicarum Gabrielis Falloppii observationum examen* (Venice, 1564), 29; see O'Malley and Clarke, *op. cit.*, p. 437.

the principles of physics and medicine with mathematical reasoning" [23]. Following earlier Italian work he made a study of a variety of acoustical phenomena for his *Harmonie universelle*. He distinguished clearly between the motion propagated through the air from particle to particle in producing sound and the actual transport of particles in wind, considered the ratio between the motions of a sounding body and of the air, correlated pitch with the number of "secousses et tremblemens de l'air" [24], studied consonance and dissonance, measured the speed of propagation of sound in air (after Gassendi, who obtained the value 1473 Paris feet per second [25]), compared the study of the reflection of sound with catoptrics, and discussed various illusions of sense in both hearing and vision. Much of the discussion is based on the recognition of formal analogies between sound, light and motion [26]. Mersenne contributed nothing to the physiology of hearing, but his account of the mechanism of perception is worth quoting as an example of this style of approach to a psychological problem; his relations here with Descartes and Hobbes are beyond the scope of our present purposes. He wrote:

L'une des plus grandes difficultez de la Physique consiste à sçavoir comme se font les opérations des sens, et de quelle manière procède l'esprit pour connoistre les objets qui luy sont présentez, et toutes leurs conditions et leurs propriétez dont on s'est figuré un estre représentatif, ou une image et une espèce qui supplée la présence de l'objet, laquelle semble trop grossière pour pouvoir entrer dans le sens, ou dans l'esprit : car puis que la connoissance est une représentation de ce qui est connu, et que la faculté qui connoist doit toucher l'objet auquel elle s'unit, il faut qu'elle le touche et qu'elle s'unisse à luy par le moyen de son image lorsqu'elle ne peut s'unir à sa présence réelle ; et parce que l'image ne peut parfaitement représenter son original si elle ne le contient formellement, ou éminemment, puis qu'il faut avoir ce qu'on représente en la mesme manière qu'on le représente, la faculté qui connoist parfaitement l'une des propriétez de son objet la doit contenir aussi parfaitement comme elle la représente...

Je dis donc premièrement que l'oreille ne connoist pas les sons, et qu'elle ne sert que d'instrument et d'organe pour les faire passer dans l'esprit qui en considère la nature et les propriétez, et conséquemment que les bestes n'ont pas la connoissance desdits sons, mais la seule représentation, sans sçavoir si ce qu'elles appréhendent est un son ou une couleur, ou quelqu'autre chose ; de sorte que l'on peut dire qu'elles n'agissent pas tant comme elles sont agitées, et que les objets font une telle impression sur leurs sens, qu'il leur est nécessaire de la suivre, comme il est nécessaire que les roues d'une horloge suivent le poids ou le ressort qui les tire. Mais l'homme ayant esté touché des sons, il en considère la nature et les propriétez, les distingue d'avec les autres objets, et en forme des connoissances très certaines ; ce qui monstre évidemment qu'il a une faculté et une puissance de connoistre, laquelle dépend nullement des sens.

Or pour revenir à la manière dont l'ouïe aperçoit les sons, je dis en second lieu que l'esprit discerne que ce qui a frappé l'oreille est différent d'avec ce qui frappe l'œil, ou du moins est autrement frappée que luy, et qu'il iuge que ce contact, ou cette impression que l'agent extérieur fait sur l'ouïe luy descouvre d'autres propriétez des corps que l'impression que fait la lumière, ou la couleur

[23] Mersenne, *Quaestiones celeberrime in Genesim*, Cap. IV, Vers, XXI, Quaestio LVII, Art. XVI (Paris, 1623) 1696b; see ch. 13 above.

[24] Mersenne *Harmonie universelle*, « Traitez de la nature des sons », I, Prop. V (Paris, 1636), 12.

[25] Politzer, *Geschichte der Ohrenheilkunde* (Stuttgart, 1907), i, 196. The modern value for the speed of sound in dry air at 0° C. is approximately 331 metres per second, increasing with higher temperatures and decreasing with higher humidities. The value of 1473 Paris feet is approximately 454 metres, which is too high.

[26] Mersenne, *Universæ geometriae, mixtaeque mathematicae synopsis*, Opticae Liber VII, Hypotheses and Prop. III (Paris, 1644), 567-571: this is by Hobbes.

sur l'œil : quoy qu'il soit très difficile de sçavoir comme l'esprit use de l'action, ou plustost de la passion, et de l'émotion de l'oreille, et comme il aperçoit le mouvement et l'émotion du nerf de l'ouïe. Car si l'on considère la manière dont il agit, l'on trouvera qu'il ne peut discerner si le son est extérieur, ou s'il se fait au-dedans de nous mesmes, comme l'on expérimente aux bourdonnemens, et aux bruits que se font au dedans de l'oreille, ou de la teste, qui nous affectent de la mesme manière que s'ils se faisoient au dehors. De là vient que les Anges peuvent tellement émouvoir nos sentimens intérieurs sans qu'ils ayent besoin des objets extérieurs, que nous croyrons que ces objets sont presents...

Mais puis que nous parlons icy de ce qui arrive ordinairement et naturellement, il suffit d'examiner la manière dont l'oreille et l'esprit aperçoivent les sons ; où il faut premièrement remarquer que l'air externe excite l'air interne de l'oreille, et qu'il imprime une émotion dans le nerf de l'ouïe, semblable à celle qu'il a recuë, et que l'esprit qui est tout dans chaque partie du corps, et conséquemment dans ledit nerf, aperçoit aussi tost le mouvement des organes de l'oreille, et iuge par là les qualitez du mouvement du son, et des objets extérieurs qui le produisent : or l'on peut s'imaginer que l'esprit est comme un point indivisible et intellectuel, auquel toutes les impressions des sens aboutissent, comme toutes les lignes du cercle à leur centre, ou comme tous les filets d'une toile de l'araigne qui l'a filée et tissue : car comme l'araigne sent et aperçoit tous les mouvemens et toutes les impressions que reçoivent lesdits filets, de mesme l'esprit de l'homme apperçoit toutes les impressions des muscles, des nerfs, et de leurs fibres, et filamens [27].

The final stage in the macroscopic identification of the proper organ of hearing, and in the hypothetical analysis of its mechanism in the light of the simple macroscopic analogies available at this time, was introduced by Thomas Willis. He introduced his discussion of the problem through a general theory of sensation based on Gassendi's *Syntagma philosophicum* (1658), and resembling in approach that of Mersenne. According to Gassendi, the object of the senses was not itself conveyed to the brain, but was symbolically represented by the motion it created [28]. Willis wrote:

> The object being applied to the sense organ (whether immediately, or through the particles of the air or other intermediate element) impresses its idea or character on the spirits implanted there; and in the same instant, by a continued series of the animal spirits, as it were an irradiation, the type of its impression passes from the sense organ to the head [29].

But, he asked, how was it that the external motions striking the sense organ produced different sensations; how was it, for example, that "the spirits implanted in the eye, do not equally perceive sounds and smells, as they do colours" ? And how were the different kinds of sensation represented distinctly in the same common sensory in the brain ? His answer was that the sense organs were constructed to receive only certain kinds of particles or influences from the external world, so that particles "proportionate to one

[27]   Mersenne, *Harmonie universelle*, « Traitez de la nature des sons », I, Prop. V (Paris, 79-81 ; cf. ch. 15 below.

[28]   Brett, G. S., *The Philosophy of Gassendi* (London, 1908); Paul F. Cranefield, "A seventeenth-century view of mental deficiency and schizophrenia: Thomas Willis on 'stupidity or foolishness'", *Bulletin of the History of Medicine*, xxxv (1961), 291-316.

[29]   Willis, Thomas, *De anima brutorum*, Pars I, Cap. x (London, 1672), 106. The translation, here and below, is corrected from Thomas Willis, *Two Discourses Concerning the Soul of Brutes*, Englished by S. Pordage (London, 1683).

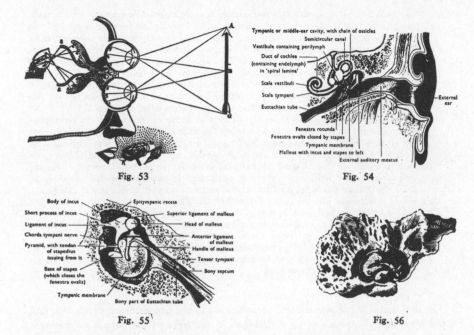

Fig. 53   Fig. 54

Fig. 55   Fig. 56

Fig. 53. From Descartes, *Tractatus de homine* (Amsterdam, 1677), 151 (cf. *Traité de l'homme*, Paris 1664, p. 85). As Descartes wrote in *La Dioptrique*, V: "les images des objets [here A B C] ne se forment pas seulement ainsi au fond de l'œil [at 135], mais elles passent encore au-delà jusques au cerveau [at 246]." Thus is formed "une peinture..., assez semblable aux objets..., en la superficie intérieure du cerveau qui regarde ses concavités. Et de là je pourrais encore la transporter jusques à une certaine petite glande [H; the image of A B C is at *a b c*], qui se trouve au milieu environ de ces concavités, et est proprement le siège du sens commun." In this figure Descartes is illustrating his purely mechanistic, neurological account of how attention is paid to some but not other parts of the sensory field: "pendant que cette glande est retenue ainsi penchée vers quelque côté, cela l'empêche de pouvoir si aisément recevoir les idées des objets qui agissent contre les organes des autres sens : comme ici, par exemple, pendant que tous les esprits que produit la glande H sortent des points *a, b c*, il n'en sort pas assez du point *d* pour y former l'idée de l'objet D, dont je suppose que l'action n'est ni si vive ni si forte que celle d'A B C; d'où vous voyez comment les idées s'empêchent l'une l'autre, et d'où vient qu'on ne peut être fort attentif à plusieurs choses en même temps." (*Traité de l'homme*, p. 86; spelling modernized.) These passages are found in *Œuvres de Descartes*, ed. Adam and Tannery, VI, 128-9 and XI, 185-6, respectively.

Fig. 54. Diagrammatic section of the human ear [a]. The hollow coiled cochlear duct forming the scala media, filled with endolymph, runs inside the "spiral lamina" through its whole length and contains the sensitive organ proper, the organ of Corti; this duct and its organs were discovered only with the improved microscopic techniques introduced in the 19th century. The structures of the inner ear considered in the theories of hearing discussed in this paper are the scala vestibuli ending at the fenestra ovalis closed by the base of the stapes, the scala tympani ending at the fenestra rotunda, the vestibule, and the semicircular canals. This whole system of the scala vestibuli and scala tympani communicating with the vestibule is filled with the perilymph, but before Cotugno (1760) was believed to contain air.

Fig. 55. The tympanic (middle-ear) cavity of the left human ear, seen from the medial side, i.e. looking outwards at the under side of the tympanic membrane with the inner ear removed [b].

Fig. 56. The tympanic (middle-ear) cavity of the calf, seen from the medial side as in fig. 55 with the inner ear removed [c]. A, mastoid bone; B, bony ring forming the true attachment of the tympanic membrane; C, very thin tympanic membrane or "meninx"; D, foot or shank [handle] of malleus; E, oval muscle [tensor tympani]; F, stable incus with two shanks; G, stapes.

[a]   *Cunningham's Textbook of Anatomy*, 9th ed., ed. J. C. Brash. Oxford, 1951, fig. 1002 (modified labelling); reproduced by kind permission of Oxford University Press.
[b]   *Ibid.*, fig. 1015.
[c]   Casserius, *De vocis auditusque organis historia anatomica* (Ferrara, 1600), Tabula IX, fig. XXIII.

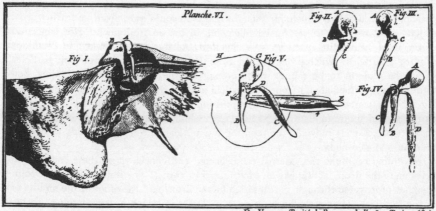

Du Verney, *Traité de l'organe de l'ouïe*, (Paris, 1683).

Fig. 57. Plate VI: the tympanic cavity and its structures in man. Fig. I: the tympanic cavity seen from the outside looking inwards, with the tympanic membrane and outer ear removed. A, malleus; B, incus; c, stapes, seen from the front with its head hidden behind the long shank of the incus; D, os petrosum forming the bottom of the tympanic cavity; E, fenestra ovalis, displayed with the base of the stapes detached from it; F, G, semi-canal in which runs "le muscle interne du marteau" [tensor tympani]; H, I, bony part of the Eustachian tube; i, end of the canal carrying the muscle of the stapes [stapedius]. Fig. V: the malleus with its muscles in situ. A, the head; B, the handle; C, "le muscle externe" [an erroneous interpretation of the anterior ligament of the malleus]; D, its insertion; E, "le muscle interne" [tensor tympani]; F, its insertion below the other muscle. "Cette figure sert à faire entendre de quelle manière les deux muscles du marteau agissent pour faire la tension et le relâchement de la peau du tambour"

sense organ, are incommunicable to the others" [30] These in turn were represented distinctly in the common sensory because "the images of things to be perceived by the senses are not distinctly painted in the common sensory, as on a table; but every impression there shown depends on the motion, as it were by a certain waving of some spirits separate from others", like different wave systems on the surface of water.

Thus the five senses of man and the higher animals were constructed to respond to the five different kinds of particles or influences from the enviroment of which perception was most necessary for survival. On the basis of his comparative neurological studies, one of the most interesting features of *De anima brutorum* [31], Willis thought

[30] Then why does a blow on the eye make us see light? This was seen as an important part of the problem, e.g. by Descartes (*Dioptrique*, VI) and Hobbes (in *Universae geometriae... synopsis*, Opticae Lib. VII, Prop. III, 570). The problem was that which led Johannes Müller to his principle of 'specific nerve energies', writing : « V. Sensation consists in the sensorium receiving through the medium of the nerves, and as the result of the action of an external cause, a knowledge of certain qualities or conditions, not of external bodies, but of the nerves of sense themselves ; and these qualities of the nerves of sense are in all different, the nerve of each sense having its own peculiar quality or energy. ... The nerves of the senses have assuredly a specific irritability for certain influences; for many stimuli, which exert a violent action upon one organ of sense, have little or no effect upon another : for example, light, or vibrations so infinitely rapid as those of light, act only on the nerves of vision, and common sensation; slower vibrations, on the nerves of hearing and common sensation, but not upon those of vision; odorous subtances only upon the olfactory nerves. » (*Éléments of Physiology*, III, v, Preliminary Considerations, trans. W. Baly, London, 1842, ii, 1065; *Handbuch der Physiologie des Menschen*, Coblenz, 1838-40).

[31] Willis, Thomas, *De anima brutorum*, especially I, Cap III (London, 1672): "The Various Kinds of Brutes, together with their respective Souls, and the chief Species of each of them, are rehearsed and described." See also Cap. II, X.

that in lower animals the number of senses might be less than five, in oysters and limpets perhaps reduced only to touch. He thought that God could have given us further senses which would respond to yet further elements in the environmment. His conception of the sense-stimulating particles was chemical. As the eye responded to "luminous or nitrous particles" which produced vision, so the ear responded to "sonorific particles" (which he thought to be saline) which propagated the motion of the sounding body through the intermediate air from one particle to the next "and so the sound, still retaining the character or type of the first impression, is continued to the ear" [32]. These particles enabled him to distinguish sound from wind. He described them as "symbolical particles successively moved", representing the motions of a sounding body as light did those of a visible body.

According to Willis the external ear collected and concentrated these moving particles on to the drum, acting like an ear trumpet or cornet. The impression of the sound was then propagated through the vibration of the drum and the of air in the middle ear to the labyrinth. He concluded from an experiment in which a dog continued to hear for a time after having both drums punctured, that the drum was not absolutely essential to hearing. The function of the ossicles and their muscle and ligament he held to be to control the tension of the drum according to the loudness of the sound, acting in this "as the pupil of the eye is wont, as the matter requires, to be either contracted or dilated". This he held, contrary to earlier views, to be "chiefly involuntary, and that 'tis acted by the instinct of nature". Here he described the phenomenon known as *Paracusis Willisii* in which hearing is facilitated in certain kinds of deafness by a continuous loud noise. "I heard from a credible person", he wrote, "that he once knew a woman, tho' she were deaf, yet so long as a drum was beaten within her chamber, she heard every word perfectly; wherefore her husband kept a drummer on purpose for his servant that by that means he might have converse with his wife".

After discussing the middle ear, Willis goes on to identify the proper organ of hearing, writing:

> But from the aforesaid Den [middle ear cavity], placed behind the Drum, another passage leads towards that part, which is properly the Organ of Hearing; to wit, in the extream side of that Cavern, before-mentioned, there is a door, or certain oval hole, covered with a thin Membrane, commonly called the Window [*the fenestra ovalis*], and beyond that hole, to wit, in the end or sharp process of the stony Bone (*os petrosum*), is the Shell *(cochlea)*, contained: from whence we may think very well, that the impression of the sound brought through its next Chamber from the Drum, is from thence propagated, by an impulse made above the Window, into the Shell.
>
> But the Body of the Shell is an admirable Structure, which being framed in a peculiar recess of the stony Bone, is called by some the Labyrinth, by others the Shell; because its passage or hollowness, after the manner of a Snails shell, is carried about with a turning or spiral Convolution. There are two parts of this, or rather there are two Shells: the former being nigh the chief Oval hole, is less'ned by degrees, from the Spire or more broad Capacity, and ends in a very little one; then from the end of this [33], another Shell, beginning with a very small spire, is inlarged by degrees, in its progress, and its extremity opens with a great aperture [the *fenestra rotunda*], into another Den or Chamber, placed beyond, with an open mouth; this is without any Membrane covering it [34].

[32]   *Ibid.*, I, Cap. xiv.
[33]   Willis and Méry independently discovered the connection (now called the helicotrema) between the two spirals of the cochlea.
[34]   The first of Willis's "Shells" or spirals is now called the scala vestibuli, the second the scala tympani (see fig. 2). He is of course mistaken in supposing that the fenestra rotunda, in which the latter ends, is not closed by a membrane (cf. fig. 8, III).

As to the Shell, the use of it seems to be, that the audible Species being brought thorow such turning and winding Labyrinths, and so receiving an augmentation by reflection, and manifold refraction, it may become more clear and sensible; then further, that every Impression, carried about by this winding and very narrow way, may come more distinct to the Sensory: because by this means, care is taken, that many confused Species together, may not be brought in. After the example and similitude of this Shell, artificial Caverns, and arch'd Meanders, are wont to be framed by Architects, for the increasing of sounds, and for the distinct propagating of them to a wonderful distance. Further, there is another use of the Shell, no less noted, to wit, that the audible Species may be impressed on the Fibres and the ends of the sensible Nerves, inserted in this place, not at once or at large, but by little and little, and as it were in a just proportion and dimension.

We have elsewhere discoursed concerning the Hearing Nerves, which receive the sensible Species, and carry it towards the Common Sensory, and we shewed, that the softer process of either of the seventh pair [35], is destinated to this office; wherefore the end of this Nerve is terminated in the nearest Chamber of the Shell, whence it is manifest, that the sensible Impression, being disposed from the Shell into this Chamber, is conveyed thence towards the Head, by the passage of this Nerve. But moreover (which we took not notice of before) it is observ'd, that this softer auditory process, is cleft into two branches [36]: one whereof is inserted after the manner we have here described, into the aforesaid Chamber; but the other, no less noted branch, is implanted in the Shell itself, about the mid'st of it, or nigh to the meeting of either Labyrinth; so that this branch seems to receive the Depositum of the foremost Shell, and the other aforesaid of the latter Shell.

The extremity of either auditory Nerve, which are implanted about the end of either Shell, ending in slender thrids, seems to cover over the places of Insertions, everywhere with Nervous Fibres spread abroad, as it were into a certain little Membrane [the membranous *lamina spiralis*]; whence it follows, that towards the end of either shell, the proper Sensory of Hearing ought to be placed; for there is the sense, where the Nerve receiving the Idea of Sensation, is implanted; but as the Shell is twofold, and that in like manner there is a double insertion of the forked auditory Nerve, it follows, that in either Ear, there is a twofold Organ of Hearing: but for what use this is so made, does not plainly appear.

That we may give our Conjecture concerning these, perhaps there is need for the audible Species, to be carried toward the common Sensory, that its passage may be the more certain, and that the perception of the sensible thing, may be put out of doubt; but we rather think, that this sensory is made double, that when oftentimes the Idea's of sounds ought to be heard and perceived together, some might pass this way, and others that way, without Confusion. For it is observ'd, that the Hearing, not only as the other Senses, receives many objects together; and by and by whether united or confused, comprehends them, by the same act of the Sense; but moreover, this faculty in the time of Hearing, so distinguishes things, often divers, admitted together at the Ears, that it seems to hear one after another: It ordinarily happen'd, that in a confused multitude of

[35] Willis described the cranial nerves in *Cerebri anatome, cui accessit nervorum descriptio et usus*, Cap. XXII (London, 1664) 156-7; English translation in *Dr. Willis's Practice of Physick* (London, 1684), "Of the Description and Use of the Nerves", p. 117. Here he renumbers the auditory nerve as the seventh, "the ancients" having accounted it the fifth. This seventh nerve, he says, has two branches, a "soft" branch which is the auditory nerve proper (the eighth in modern terminology), and a "hard" branch, which is now called the ninth or glossopharyngeal. Willis in fact says that these two branches "seem to be two distinct nerves."

[36] These two branches of Willis's "soft" branch of the seventh nerve are, in modern terminology, respectively the vestibular and cochlear branches of the eighth (auditory) nerve. A somewhat fuller anatomical description of the branches of the "seventh" nerve, following the terminology used by Willis, is given by Du Verney, *Traité de l'organe de l'ouïe* (Paris, 1683), 44-66.

voices and sounds, that I have myself taken notice to have heard the peculiar voice of a certain Man, and then a little after, I have known that I have heard, at the same time, some other words of another Man, that I did not perceive before; the reason of which is, that this sound being received together with that, reached not at the same instant to the Common Sensory: wherefore, we may believe, that the sensible Species of the former sound, passing thorow only one Shell, is by and by conveyed, by the first branch of the auditory Nerve, sooner to the Sensory; but the other sensible Species, because it could not be carried with it together by the same Nerve, therefore it is carried by a winding about thorow the second Shell, and at length to the second branch of the auditory Nerve, and so coming later to the Common Sensory, is afterwards perceived [37].

The publication of *De anima brutorum* was followed within a few years by a number of different attempts to deal with the essential problem of explaining, by means of an adequate physical hypothesis, how sound produces the appropriate responses in the sensitive organ for transmission along the auditory nerve. I can discuss them only briefly. The main centre of research was the Académie des Sciences. In 1667 Claude Perrault had proposed a programme of research into the structure and functions of the organs composing the bodies of animals; in 1677 he undertook "d'examiner à fond tout ce qui appartient au sens de l'Ouÿe" [38]. The whole programme, carried out by Perrault, Pecquet, Méry. Lamy, Du Verney and other anatomists, is remarkable for its scientific sophistication. The value of the comparative method in physiological inquiry was clearly understood:

> Rien n'est plus advantageux pour l'Anatomie, que la comparaison des Sujets de différentes espèces. Souvent une partie invisible dans une espèce, se rend visible dans une autre; souvent entre deux différentes mécaniques qui doivent être équivalentes, l'une qui est plus marquée, et plus manifestement déterminée à un certain effet, sert à faire comprendre le jeu et l'usage de l'autre, qui est plus enveloppée [39].

Ingenious use in locating certain functions was made of diseases, affecting some parts of the body but not others, as natural experiments in elimination. Arguments from the structures of organs to their functions were made as precise as possible by relating them to known physics. A remarkable consciousness was shown of the form of the argument, beginning with hypotheses leading to experiments which established their probability, and in this a clear grasp was shown of the limits of existing knowledge and the difference between probable conjecture and ascertained fact. There was a growing recognition also of the different kinds of question that can be asked in an inquiry such as that into the sensory mechanisms, of the different 'levels' in the behaviour of an organism which could not be fitted into a single mechanistic scheme, and of the autonomy of psychological questions as a field of empirical inquiry distinct from physiology.

Perrault began his attack on the problem of hearing by attempting a new investigation of the physics of sound, before trying to find out how sound was received by the sensitive organ. He described the results of the whole inquiry in *Du Bruit*, which forms part of his *Essais de physique* [40]. His theory of sound is interesting for the use he made of the concept of air particles as springs, especially in his analysis of speed of propagation, pitch, and consonance and dissonance. His main contributions to the investigation of the mechanism of the ear, for which he used the known functions of the parts of the eye as a guide, were his account of the action of the muscles of the ossicles in controlling the tension of the drum on the analogy of accommodation (though he still thought

[37] Willis, Thomas, *De anima brutorum*, I, Cap. xiv|(London, 1672), 135-6.
[38] *Histoire de l'Académie royale des Sciences*, I (Paris, 1733), 223.
[39] *Ibid.*, p. 117 (1670).
[40] Perrault, Claude, *Essais de physique*, II (Paris, 1680).

that the air and not the ossicles transmitted the motion of sound through the middle ear), and his account of the spiral lamina (in fact the bony lamina) of the cochlea as the sensitive organ, where the auditory nerve fibres spread out as the optic nerve did in the retina. He also identified the short straight "conduit" in birds as corresponding to the cochlea in quadrupeds [41], and denied that the semicircular canals or any other part of the labyrinth except the cochlea contained the sensitive organ. But although he tried to relate the two parts of his inquiry, Perrault did not in fact succeed in offering a theory of hearing precisely based on knowledge of the physics of sound.

The first person to offer a theory of the auditory mechanism based on an exact acoustical law was Joseph Guichard Du Verney. He took up Perrault's programme and acknowledged also the work of Willis, gave a new and detailed systematic description of the anatomy of the ear (figs. 57-8) and its nerves, and wrote that his intention was

> tirer de la mécanique de ces parties quelques conséquences par lesquelles on peut expliquer leur usage et la manière dont nous apercevons les sons et les bruits différents [42].

In this he acknowleged the assistance of the physicist Mariotte. Du Verney's whole theory of the auditory mechanism was based on the physical law of harmonic induction (which Mersenne had studied) as illustraded by the vibrations induced in the strings of a lute when those of a neighbouring lute are plucked. On this he based an account of the control of the tension of the drum by the muscles of the ossicles, writing:

> Je dis donc qu'il faut que la peau du tambour soit différemment disposée, pour recevoir les différens tremblemens de l'air, et qu'en effet il seroit impossible qu'elle pût les transmettre tels qu'ils sont, si elle n'estoit en quelque manière ajustée à leur caractère, et si dans les diverses occasions elle ne s'accommodoit pour ainsi dire, à des tensions propres à représenter les tons différens des corps resonnans. On sçait que quand on met deux luths sur une table, et que l'on pince une corde de l'un de ces luths, si l'on veut qu'une corde de l'autre luth se mette en mouvement, il faut de nécessité qu'elle soit montée à l'unisson avec celle que l'on pince, ou à l'octave ou à quelques autres accords comme la double octave, ou la quinte, ou la quarte, autrement elle fait bien à la vérité quelques tremblemens, mais ils sont très foibles, et jamais ils ne sont sensibles [43].

From the greater strength of the motions transmitted from one lute to another through a solid table than through the air, he argued also that the ossicles (and not the air in the middle ear) played the major role in transmitting the vibrations of the drum to the "air implanté" confined within the labyrinth [44]. In the labyrinth he identified the membranous spiral lamina of the cochlea as the sensitive organ of hearing. Dividing the cochlea longitudinally into two separate spirals connected respectively with the fenestra ovalis and the fenestra rotunda, this membranous lamina had recently been accurately described by Méry. After advancing arguments for its function based on its structure and composition, shape, and neural connections, Du Verney offered a "conjecture" of its mechanism which is best described in his own words:

> Enfin cette lame n'est pas seulement capable de recevoir les tremblemens de l'air, mais sa structure doit faire penser qu'elle peut répondre à tous leurs caractères différens; car estant plus large au commencement de sa première révolution qu'à l'extrémité de la dernière, où elle finit comme en pointe, et ses autres parties

[41] *Ibid.*, pp. 211-2.
[42] Du Verney, *Traité de l'organe de l'ouïe* (Paris, 1683), 68.
[43] *Ibid.*, 78-79. R.S. Stevenson and D. Guthrie, *A History of Oto-Laryngology* (Edinburgh, 1949).
[44] *Ibid.*, I, 42-43.

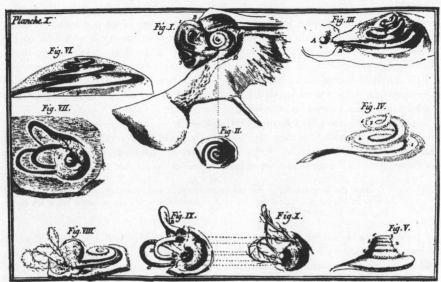

Du Verney, *Traité de l'organe de l'ouïe*, (Paris, 1683),

Fig. 58.\ Plate X: the inner ear and its structures in man. Fig. I: "le limaçon" [cochlea] and the semi-circular canals (1, 2, 3) seen in their natural positions with the middle and external ear removed. A, vestibule; B, fenestra ovalis; C, fenestra rotunda; D, the [bony] spiral lamina, after removing the spiral canal covering it and the membrane attaching it to the surface of the canal (twice natural size). Fig. II: cochlea, showing the spiral canal. Fig. III: vertical section of cochlea, several times enlarged. A, lower part of vestibule; B, fenestra rotunda, closed by a thin membrane. This and Fig. VI show "la rampe supérieure" [scala vestibuli] leading from the fenestra ovalis, and "la rampe inférieure" [scala tympani], leading from the fenestra rotunda. The numbers 1, 2, 3, indicating the two-and-a-half turns of the spiral round its core [modiolus], fall in the scala tympani. Fig. IV: the [bony] spiral lamina (1, 2, 3,), removed from the ear, with its membrane (4, 5, 6) (enlarged). Fig. V: the core with the spiral lamina removed (enlarged). The remaining figures show details of the vestibule with the three semi-circular canals and their blood vessels and nerves.

diminuant proportionnellement de largeur, on peut dire que les parties les plus larges pouvant estre ébranlées sans que les autres le soient, ne sont capables que de frémissemens plus lents qui répondent par conséquent aux tons graves; et qu'au contraire ses parties les plus étroites estant frappées, leurs frémissemens sont plus vistes, et répondent par conséquent aux tons aigus, de mesme que les parties les plus larges d'un ressort d'acier font des frémissemens plus lents, et répondent aux tons graves, et que les plus étroites en font de plus fréquens et de plus vistes, et répondent par conséquent aux tons aigus; de sorte qu'enfin selon les différens ébranlemens de la lame spirale, les esprits du nerf, qui se répand dans sa substance, reçoivent différentes impressions qui représentent dans le cerveau les diverses apparences de tons [45].

With this "conjecture", which Du Verney hoped was "vraisemblable" [46], these early investigations offered for the first time an explanation of hearing similar to Helmholtz's 'resonance theory', which became the basis of more recent explanations. But this similarity must not deceive us into thinking that the state of scientific knowledge in Du Verney's time was capable of allowing anything more than a bright conjectural idea that fell far short of a strictly testable theory. This distinction was well recognized by Du Verney and most of his contemporary investigators. One example of the scientific

[45]   *Ibid.*, II, 96-98.
[46]   *Ibid.*, 68.

uncertainty of opinion is that he himself argued that the vestibule and semi-circular canals were part of the immediate organ of hearing in man and the whole organ in birds and fish which apparently had no cochlea. John Wallis understood only half of Du Verney's theory, while palming it off as his own—getting perhaps as near the truth as is consonant with being a mathematician who knew no anatomy [47]. Immediately after Du Verney's *Traité* appeared, the German physiologist Schelhammer proposed another explanation of the auditory mechanism based on the study of an entirely different branch of acoustics described in Athanatius Kircher's *Phonurgia nova* (1673). Kircher had attempted to give a quantitative explanation of echoes and of the augmentation of sound in wind instruments on the analogy of optical reflection. In his *De auditu* (1684) Schelhammer declared that before he read this work he had been completely lost (in spite of Du Verney, Perrault and Willis), and his explanation of hearing amounted to trying to show how the sound would become concentrated into the cochlea as if the whole ear acted like a complicated echoing tube. Research into hearing was up against a scientific and technical frontier, and even the new form given to Du Verney's theory by Cotugno in 1760 after his discovery that the labyrinth was filled with fluid was a speculative idea that could not be strictly tested by any techniques available. There was no hope of being able to establish any of these explanations firmly inside acceptable scientific doctrine, such as could be done with the dioptrics of the eye, although some of the explanations of hearing could be shown to be unacceptable.

It is an interesting historical phenomenon that by the end of the 17th century both this technical and scientific frontier, and other frontiers to which these inquiries into the sensory mechanism of the body had led, were explicitly recognized. In 1707 the Italian anatomist Valsalva wrote that the progress in the study of hearing would have to await further advances in the physics of sound, such as had taken place in the physics of light [48]. But it was not until the 19th century that real advances in the study of either vision or hearing were made possible, not only by the advances in optics and acoustics but also by the histological studies opened up by the achromatic microscope and the new chemical stains, and by the potentialities of electrophysiology first realized by Johannes Müller's pupils in Berlin, especially Helmholtz.

It was recognized that this scientific and technical frontier could be pushed back by asking further questions of the same kind, as more physical knowledge became available. For example, it could be discovered what happened physically in the nerves behind the retina and the cochlea. But other problems were encountered in following the mechanistic programme that seemed to demand a change in the kind of question. One such problem was that of the co-ordination of the information received through the different senses and of consequent behaviour, a problem that had given rise to the old theory of the "common sensory" that regularly reappears in all the writings on sensory mechanisms. The mechanistic programme had, first, to explain physiologically how the different sense organs produced different sensory information (two of the essential phenomena being that a blow on the eye can produce a sensation of light and that some people hear noises in their ears without an external cause); and secondly, to provide built-in cerebral and neural mechanisms for correlating the sensations received through different sense organs into one consistant view of the world [49] and for producing co-ordinated behaviour. Speculations on these problems led to experimental

[47] Letter to Edward Tyson, May 13, 1701, Oxford MS Bodleian Library Add. D. 105, ff. 127ᵛ and 125ᵛ.
[48] Valsalva, *De aure humana tractatus*, Cap. x (Trier, 1707), 110-11.
[49] Cf. Descartes, *Traité de l'homme* and *Dioptrique*, IV-VI; references 11,|30 and fig. 53.

biological inquiry, especially into the co-ordination of behaviour [50]. But some writers, for example Perrault, questioned whether some of these were problems that properly belonged to the mechanistic programme at all.

The most celebrated essay in showing that physiologists committed to the attempt to provide a completely mechanistic account of sensory perception were asking the wrong question was that made by Berkeley (1709). The effect of Berkeley's arguments was to show that the psychology of perception was a subject for inquiry independant of current physiological theory. This, he said, was incapable of giving an answer—or at any rate the correct answer—to such a question as that put by William Molyneux to John Locke : whether a man born blind and given sight would at once be able to recognize différences in shape by sight, because he had learned to do so by touch [51]. He argued that we learn these things for each sense separately, and also learn by experience to correlate the information received through the different senses. The results of operations for congenital cataract have supported Berkeley's main contentions [52]. For the general history of scientific thinking his is an interesting example of a response made to a frontier of research. He questioned the whole philosophical committment that had created the frontier. As a consequence he assisted the birth of a new field of empirical inquiry.

Since the 17th century the mechanistic programme in physiology has given scientific substance to speculations so-to-speak built into the programme, as, for example the conclusion to which Du Verney was led in his fascinating suggestions for an inquiry into the representation of sensory impressions in the brain: « il est indifférent que les fibres du nerf soient ébranlées du côté de l'oreille ou du côté du cerveau, il en résultera toujours la même sensation » [53]. Yet in 1962 a psychologist can still comment on how the physiological analysis of these physical stimuli looks from his side of the frontier: "Our brains receive information from our sense organs in the form of electrical pulses, but how they use this information to give us knowledge of the world around us is almost entirely mysterious" [54]. Recognition of this frontier has set empirical psychology free to ask its own questions. Perhaps it may be claimed that by their very insistence on a philosophical commitment, the 17th-century investigators of the "animate and sensitive body" brought its limitations out into the light.

Further references: J. Bernhardt, "Hobbes et le mouvement de la lumière", *Revue d'histoire des sciences*, xxx (1977) 3-24, "Le rôle des conceptions d'Isaac Beeckman dans la formation de Thomas Hobbes et dans l'élaboration de son *Short Tract*", ibid., xl (1987) 203-15; R.L. Gregory (1966), (1970) above pp. 271, 258; M.D. Grmek (1985) above p. 258; Y.-C. Zarka, "Visions et désir chez Hobbes" in *Recherches sur le xviie siècle* (CNRS; Paris, 1986) 127-42, "La matière et la représentation: Hobbes lecteur de *La dioptrique* de Descartes" in *Problèmatique et réception du Discours*, ed. H. Méchoulan (Paris, 1988) 81-98; see also chs. 9, 11, 13, 15.

[50]　See the excellent study by Georges Canguilhem, *La formation du concept de réflexe au XVIIe et XVIIIe siècles* (Paris, 1955).

[51]　Berkeley, *A New Theory of Vision*. (1709); Locke, *Essay concerning Human Understanding* (1690), II, Ch. ix. Cf. N. Malebranche, *La recherche de la vérité*, I Paris, 1674); G.W. von Leibniz, *Nouveaux essais sur l'entendement humain* (1704), *Œuvres philosophiques*, ed. R. E. Raspe (Amsterdam & Leipzig, 1765).

[52]　Cf. S. Axelrod, *Effects of Early Blindness : performance of blind and sighted children on tactile and auditory tasks* (American Foundation for the Blind, Research Series No. 7, New York, 1959). See M. von Senden, *Space and Sight. The perception of space and shape in the congenitally blind before and after operation*, trans. Peter Heath (London, 1960; German edition 1932).

[53]　*Op. cit*, 206.

[54]　Gregory, R.L., "How the eyes deceive", *The Listener* (London, 5 July 1962), 15.

MARIN MERSENNE (1588-1648) AND
THE SEVENTEENTH-CENTURY PROBLEM
OF SCIENTIFIC ACCEPTABILITY*

In 1634 the French philosopher Marin Mersenne published in his essay *Les préludes de l'harmonie universelle* a view of the history and present state of the mathematical and natural sciences in Europe. He wrote [1]: « The sciences have sworn among themselves an inviolable partnership; it is almost impossible to separate them, for they would rather suffer than be torn apart; and if anyone persists in doing so, he gets for his trouble only imperfect and confused fragments. Yet they do not arrive all together, but hold each other by the hand so that they follow one another in a natural order which it is dangerous to change, because they refuse to enter in any other way where they are called ». Mersenne's most general contribution to European intellectual life was this vision of the developing community of the sciences. He wrote from experience. Progress, he con-

* This paper was prepared for the course on « The History of Science in Contemporary Culture » held at the Ettore Majorana Centre for Scientific Culture, Erice, Sicily, 15-21 September 1975. It is based on A.C. Crombie, *Marin Mersenne and the Science of Music* (forthcoming).

[1] Mersenne, *Les préludes de l'harmonie universelle*, q. 5 (Paris, 1634) 135-9; cf. for Mersenne's life and thought his *Correspondance*, ed. C. de Waard, R. Pintard, B. Rochot, i- (Paris, 1932-); R. Lenoble, *Marin Mersenne ou la naissance du mécanisme* (Paris, 1943); Crombie, « Mersenne, Marin », in *Dictionary of Scientific Biography*, ix (New York, 1974) 316 sqq.

tinued his argument, could be achieved only by the cultivation of the particular: « Philosophy would long ago have reached a high level if our predecessors and fathers had put this into practice; and we would not waste time on the primary difficulties, which appear now as severe as in the first centuries which noticed them. We would have the experience of assured phenomena, which would serve as principles for a solid reasoning; truth would not be so deeply sunken; nature would have taken off most of her envelopes; one would see the marvels she contains in all her individuals ». These complaints had long been heard, yet, he went on, « most men are glad to find the work done, only a few want to apply themselves to it, and many think that this search is useless or rididulous ». He offered as his own particular reparation of this general fault the pioneering exact science of music which is his chief claim to original fame: a systematic mathematical and experimental investigation of acoustical quantities and of their effects through the physiology of the body on the senses and the emotions and moral dispositions of the soul. Nor did his original investigations into musical science stop there, for they led him to make an original study of the whole subject of the reception of information through the senses and its communication through language and other signs and signals in men and animals.

A conference on the history of science in contemporary culture evidently assumes (as I certainly do) that one good reason for studying history is to understand ourselves. Perhaps at this stage of historical sophistication it hardly needs arguing that for educated understanding of any historical culture yesterday's events may be the least relevant. The categories in which we in the West understand both man and nature now, the intellectual, moral and material satisfactions we demand and the methods by which we get them, are by no means accepted by all mankind and have become ours only through a long process of orientation and reorientation. In order to understand our contemporary culture we need then to see it in the context of both comparative anthropology and of its own intellectual and social history, which might be seen as comparative anthropology extended into the past. Yet if we treat the history of science as a kind of comparative intellectual anthropology, putting ourselves into the minds of the individuals or societies we are studying and trying to understand their questions, satisfactions and discontents, we need to control relativity by objective scientific truth. Science has developed in the characteristically rational Western tradition as an approach to nature effectively competent to solve problems. We may see the origins of our science in the grasp and development by the ancient Greek philosophers, mathematicians and medics of a logic of decision and proof. They introduced decision and proof, a logic of either-or, into speculations both about the general nature of the world and about particular questions. Science has been recognized in our tradition since their time as a cumulative progress of true and effective knowledge. We may see the origins of modern science in the recovery, exegesis and elaboration of the Greek model of rational decision and proof by medieval and early modern Europe. The recovery was made by a new society, with a different view of man and his place in nature and his destiny, a different theology and a different economy, but it was seen first, from the twelfth century, as a continuation of the ancient scientific movement, before its potentialities for elaboration were discovered in application to the many and diverse new problems and subject-matters that have followed. It is objectively illuminating for us then to focus attention on periods of intellectual orientation which have laid down programmes for successful scientific progress[2].

Mersenne's vision of the history of science exemplifies just such a programme, of which much of the essence of our contemporary culture, both explicit and assumed, is a consequence. He belonged, with Galileo, Kepler, Harvey and Descartes, to those gifted generations who, by their selection of problems for private investigation as well as by public controversy, established in the early seventeenth century the identity and accepted norms of thinking and commitment of their new philosophy as a programme of scientific research. Under a combination of intellectual pressures from their whole scientific, philosophical, theological and social ambience, this meant defining rational and workable criteria not simply for accepting the answers proposed, but also for admitting answerable questions. Brushing aside the eclectic possibilities of sixteenth-century Platonism, Hermeticism, magic, atomism, scepticism, the Aristotelian revival and the whole policy of concordance, they made a choice aimed to establish against these possibilities of opinion the identity of natural science as a body of ascertainably true knowledge. They aimed to replace the intellectual habits of eclectic tolerance with the decisiveness needed to solve particular problems. Mersenne made himself responsible for actively promoting the growth of a self-conscious scientific community in Europe, with broad agreement on an acceptable conception of nature, on workable methods of

---

[2] Cf. Crombie, « Some reflections on the history of science and its conception of nature », *Annals of Science,* vi (1948) 54 sqq.; « Introduction » and « A note on history of science as an academic discipline » in *Scientific Change: historical studies in the intellectual, social and technical conditions for scientific discovery and technical invention, from antiquity to the present* (London, 1963); « The relevance of the middle ages to the scientific movement » in *Perspectives in Medieval History,* ed. K. F. Drew and F. S. Lear (Chicago, 1963) 35 sqq.; « Historical commitments of biology », *The British Journal for the History of Science,* iii (1966) 97 sqq.; « Historians and the scientific revolution », *Physis,* xi (1969) 167 sqq.; « Premio Galileo, *ibid.* xii (1970) 106 sqq.; « Some attitudes to scientific progress: ancient, medieval and early modern », *History of Science,* xiii (1975) 213 sqq.;   *Styles of Scientific Thinking in the European Tradition.*

investigating it, and on what could be known about it for certain. He illustrates the complexity of the European intellectual landscape, and the persistent use he made of theological arguments in deciding what was worth knowing, and what could be known, illustrates how misleading it would be for historians to separate the technical science of a period from its ambience of larger intellectual commitments. I shall try to illustrate the relevance of the history of science for contemporary culture by means of the particular example of Mersenne. I shall do so in terms of three questions: (1) the sources motivating an interest in science; (2) the growth of understanding in the scientific community of how to proceed in research: of the variety of methods required by the variety of subject-matters, and of what was acceptable as an adequate result; and (3) what was acceptable as a satisfactory explanation. Mersenne and his contemporaries came to see experimental science as the deliberate product of a union between a theoretical search for reduction to common forms of explanation and a practical demand for accurately reproducible results. Their discussions of the discoverable and the discovered in nature are an illustration of how commitments to general beliefs about nature and about science make certain kinds of question appear cogent and give certain kinds of explanation their power to convince, and exclude others, because they establish, in anticipation of any particular research, the kind of world that is supposed to exist. The comparative historical study of the intellectual and social commitments that may make certain kinds of scientific discovery or practical application intellectually and socially possible in one society, but difficult or impossible in another, has an immediate relevance for the diverse cultures brought into contact with the science of our contemporary world.

Mersenne was educated by the Jesuits at La Flèche before Descartes and then at the Sorbonne, after which he joined the Order of Friars Minor, or Minims. He spent most of his mature life, from 1619 until his death in 1648, at the Minim Convent in Paris near the Place Royale, now the Place des Vosges. This he made a focus for scientific discussions and experiments, and the centre of a European correspondence which helped to bring about a new style of effective scientific communication. He entered upon the European intellectual scene with a defence in his earliest publications of true religion and morality against the dangerous errors of some recent enemies of truth. Central to his argument was his use of the certifiable discoveries of the ancient and modern mathematical sciences, to which he added his first original contributions to optics and acoustics, as a demonstration that truth could be attained, an illustration of divine providence in the order and wonder of the creation, and an example of how reasonably Christians could accept truly demonstrated novelties. He named and attacked one group of the principal enemies of truth in his first two major works, his vast and encyclopaedic commentary *Quaestiones celeberrime in Genesim* (1623), followed by *L'impiété des déistes, athées, et libertins de ce temps* (1624). Among these he identified for attack the Cabalists and believers in magic and the occult, especially Francesco Giorgi, Telesio, Vanini, Patrizi, Bruno, Campanella, and Fludd. In his next work, *La vérité des sciences, contre les sceptiques ou Pyrrhoniens* (1625), he named the other principle enemies of truth. This was a long defence of the possibility of true knowledge against the ancient Greek scepticism of Pyrrho and of the New Academy which had been developed and made popular especially by Montaigne. As before Mersenne found his answer, and hence a rational basis for religion and morality, in natural science.

Theology made Mersenne an apostle of science. When he came to offer, in a series of works published from 1633 to 1637, a programme for natural philosophy and its implementation, he did this in the first place in response on the one hand to magic and the occult and on the other to scepticism, and he did it with a combination of scientific with theological goals. The culmination of this programme was his great *Harmonie universel!* (1636-37), the pioneering study with which he established the modern science of the physics, physiology and psychology of music. After this his interests became more purely scientific, and theology has virtually vanished from the last group of works on the mathematical physical sciences published during his lifetime from 1644 to 1647 and from the posthumously-published work on optics which was also his final essay on the philosophy of science.

The fundamental questions for the early seventeenth-century scientific movement, of what was discoverable in nature and what in any particular inquiry had been discovered, centred round two main issues. The first was the certainty of science, and specifically the validity in physics, in any inquiry for physical causes, of the axiomatic theory of truly scientific apodeictic demonstration embodied in somewhat different forms in Aristotle's logic and Euclid's geometry. The second was the cogency of commitment to a specified natural ontology: for Galileo, Mersenne, Descartes and Gassendi a strictly mechanistic conception of nature, as opposed to other current philosophies with rival claims to expressing the true rationality of nature and its manifest and occult powers. Each issue had consequences not only for the epistemology of science but also for the practice of scientific methods, especially the role given to experiment in a scientific argument. These are illustrated by a comparison of Mersenne with Galileo and Descartes[3].

---

[3] Cf. Crombie, « The primary properties and secondary qualities in Galileo Galilei's natural philosophy » in *Saggi su Galileo Galilei* (Firenze, 1969, preprint); « Sources of Galileo's early natural philosophy » in *Reason, Experiment and Mysticism in the Scientific Revolution*, ed M. L. Righini Bonelli and W. R. Shea (New York, 1975) 157 sqq.; « Some aspects of Descartes' attitude to hypothesis

Galileo's scientific ideal, the postulational method of the Greek geometers, depended for its success in solving problems on the gift which
he shared with Euclid and Archimedes for theoretical intuition into a world
of mathematical simplicity behind complex phenomena. Typical of this
ideal, as he confidently upheld it, were his optimistic view of nature as
an open book to be read in an essentially simple mathematical language,
his habit of giving calculated as distinct from measured numerical values,
and his belief that his method could yield apodeictic demonstration of
causes in nature which uniquely and reciprocally necessitated effects. He
claimed this for his demonstrations of the Copernican hypothesis of the
Earth's motions, as well as for his demonstrations of the motions of projectiles and falling bodies.

Descartes likewise shared this gift for theoretical intuition and took
over the Aristotelian ideal of apodeictic demonstration in natural science
as in mathematics and formal logic. Like Aristotle and the Greek geometers he looked by antecedent analysis primarily for intelligibility in first
principles. These were not open to empirical tests but were taken for granted in the subsequent development of his science: Euclid's axioms, postulates and definitions, Aristotle's matter and form, and Descartes' clear
and simple nature of extension with motion as its mode were in this respect all in the same logical position. He aimed at a completed natural
science, following from the first principles of nature as infallibly as in a
mathematical demonstration. It was true that the realization of this programme in natural scientific knowledge met practical difficulties made by the
complexity of nature. This called for exploration by experiment and by
hypotheses, and the use of experiment to choose between different possible hypotheses. Because of these complications for human knowledge
Descartes recognized that strict demonstration had not been achieved in
many established branches of physics. God alone knew the causes. But
Descartes nevertheless held that human reason could in principle discover
the true causes and from them demonstrate in the full Aristotelian sense
the unique necessarily true explanations of physical phenomena; the validity of human reasoning was guaranteed by the perfection of God who
would not deceive. The completed natural philosophy at which he aimed
would then be the uniquely possible system, built from the foundations,
in which causes explained effects whose existence reciprocally demonstrated these causes.

and experiment » in Académie internationale d'Histoire des Sciences, *Actes du Symposium international des sciences physiques et mathématiques dans la première moitié du XVII siècle, 1958* (Paris,
1960) 192 sqq.; « Descartes, René du Perron » in *Dictionary of Scientific Biography,* iv (1971) 51
sqq.; *Styles* .... ch. 3. iii-v (n. 2 above), citing myself here and elsewhere for ease of reference and
further bibliography. See also for Mersenne's enemies R. H. Popkin, *The History of Scepticism from
Erasmus to Descartes* (Assen, Netherlands, 1964) and F. A. Yates, *Giordano Bruno and the Hermetic
Tradition* (London, 1964).

Mersenne's approch to science differed from both of these in theory and in practice. More profoundly affected by the crisis of scepticism than either Galileo or Descartes, he rejected apodeictic demonstration in natural science on grounds of theology, logic and scientific experience. All these combined to make the whole science of nature a science of intrinsically uncertain possible explanations, and at the same time to give an open view of possible explanations. God's inscrutable omnipotence, which denied us independent rational knowledge of his reasons in defining the essence of things, reduced the order of nature, from man's point of view, simply to an order of contingent fact. The logical fallacy of affirming the consequent established the impossibility of demonstrating in natural things causes uniquely determined by effects. The progress of scientific experience showed that the discovery of contrary instances could never be ruled out. Hence the only knowledge of this contingent created world available to us was that of the quantitative externals of effects, and our only hope of science was to explore these and their connections by means of measurement, experiment and the most probable hypotheses [4]. But this was true knowledge. Mersenne had been encouraged by the successes of recent technology and also by reading Francis Bacon's *Novum organum* soon after it appeared in 1620 [5]. He found in Bacon a programme for real scientific knowledge. The science of nature available to us was able to guide our action [6], even though theology and logic showed it to be less than that claimed by Aristotle, and even though the nature, principles, causes or reasons on which the order of effects depended remained for us an uncertain mystery. In this epistomology Mersenne was nearest among his contemporaries to his friend Gassendi.

Mersenne developed his distinctive philosophy against the enemies of truth he named. Against the sceptics, he argued from the certified discoveries of ancient and modern science that human reason could find true knowledge based on valid information received through the senses. Against believers in a world controlled by unaccountable magical and occult powers, he argued that the actions of nature were limited by accountable rational laws. Against the qualitative verbal physics of the Aristotelian substances and properties he argued that nature was rational, its actions limited by quantitative laws, because it was a mechanism, so that in constructing their machines according to mathematical laws men were imitating the rational works of God. He accepted with enthusiasm the form of rationality expressed in the aphorism coming from Galileo and the sixteenth-century

---

[4] Mersenne, *Les questions théologiques,* Epistre and qq. 2, 4, 22, 24, 46 (1634) 9-11, 18-19, 109-11, 116-7, 229; *Harm. univ.* i, le préface générale, « Tr. de la nature des sons », i, prop. xxxi (Paris, 1636) 73-4, and ii, « Tr. des consonances », Préface (1637); below n. 10.

[5] Mersenne, *La vérité des sciences,* i, ç. 16 (Paris, 1625) 206-13; *Correspondance,* ed. cit. i, 131-2, 169, 379.

[6] Mersenne, *La vérité...,* i, c. 2, p. 14.

Italian mechanicians, that nature cannot be cheated or deprived of its rights, and with equal enthusiasm he accepted the consequential impossibility of the occult marvels entertained by contemporary believers in magic [7]. The distinctive position Mersenne shared with Galileo, Gassendi and Descartes placed them then with the Aristotelians in defending the exclusive and discoverable rationality of nature against the magicians and sceptics, against the Aristotelians in proposing a different conception of the kind of rational nature actually in existence, but against all other contemporary philosophies in closing many currently open questions by insisting upon specified rational criteria for admitting questions as well as answers into natural science.

Mersenne offered his mature natural philosophy then as both a programme and its implementation in response to the fundamental questions raised by his enemies of truth. It involved interlocking conceptions of methods of investigation and demonstration, of explanation, and of existence representing a persistent scientific style. It had two main aspects. First, his experimental science was his reply to the sceptical doubts of the validity both of the human senses and of human reasoning. Hence his scientific investigations of vision and hearing which he held to establish a stable relation between perceiver and perceived, making them receivers of true information, and his insistence that quantitative experiment was the basis of valid rational knowledge of nature. Galileo and Descartes had aimed at certainty in physical science; Mersenne, disbelieving in the possibility of certainty, aimed at precision. This made a considerable difference, and it made him a critic of some aspects of Galileo's performance in his treatment of experimental measurements. Secondly, Mersenne's mechanistic conception of nature was negatively his reply to magic and the occult, and positively an opening he saw into possible explanations of phenomena. Art could not cheat nature, but man, by constructing rational imitations of God's works in nature, could gain some insight into how they operated. Only what man himself could construct, could he be truly said to know [8]. From each of these aspects of his programme, the experimental and the constructional, Mersenne made discoveries and advances in scientific method which indicate an enduring orientation of scientific thinking. These may be illustrated from his science of music and the analysis into which it led him of language and of the general question of the nature and communication of information in men and animals and in machines.

Mersenne opened his scientific discussion of music in 1623 with the declaration that « nobody can reach perfection in music, nor understand

----

[7] Below n. 17.
[8] Below nn. 13-17.

or discuss it, unless he combines the' principles of physics and medicine with mathematical reasoning » [9]. The mathematical programme for relating perceiver to perceived had inherited from the Greek mathematicians — from the Pythagoreans, from Plato's friend Archytas of Tarentum and from Aristotle's pupil Aristoxenus of Tarentum, and from Euclid's two fundamental treatises on optics and on music — not only the geometrical analysis of vision and the arithmetical analysis of music, but also the idea of demonstrating in the Euclidean sense what must be perceived with specified visual and acoustical quantities. The Greek mathematicians made the fundamental instrument of musical analysis the monochord, and they established as a point of departure for all later analysis the fundamental proposition, reported in Boethius' well-known textbook *De musica*, that the pitch of sounds emitted by vibrating strings and other instruments depended on the frequency of impulses transmitted through the air. From the middle of the sixteenth century, musical scientists began to respond to the striking developments in musical practice, for example in polyphony and in the invention of new instruments. Giambattista Benedetti and Galileo's father Vincenzo Galilei in Italy, followed by Isaac Beeckman and Descartes in the Netherlands and then Mersenne himself, undertook a complete revision of Greek acoustics by showing in the first place that pitch was proportional to frequency of vibration, and hence that the traditional musical intervals (octave 2:1, fifth 3:2, fourth 4:3 and so on) were ratios of frequencies of vibrations, whatever instruments produced them. Mersenne's main contribution was to establish experimentally the quantitative relations between the frequencies of vibrating strings and their tension and specific gravity as well as length, and similar relations between the frequencies of wind and percussion instruments.

Beginning with this problem, his work establishes him as a pioneer in the organisation of an experimental inquiry. He deliberately combined the methods of philosophy with those of technology in a systematic quantitative exploration of a whole field, looking at once for a common form of explanation and for accurately reproducible results. He set out to improve the whole conception and practice of what he called « well arranged and well made experiments » [10], the only sure means of unwrapping the envelopes enclosing the complex body of nature. His insistence on the careful specification of experimental procedures, use of controls, repetition

---

[9] Mersenne, *Quaest. in Gen.*, q. 57 (Parisiis, 1623) 1696 b; cf. for what follows Crombie « The mechanistic hypothesis and the scientific study of vision », *Proceedings of the Royal Microscopical Society*, ii (1967) 3 sqq.; « Mathematics, music and medical science », *Actes du XIIe Congrès international d'histoire des sciences, 1968*, i B (Paris, 1971) 295 sqq.; and *Galileo and Mersenne*, ch. 9.

[10] Mersenne, *Harm. univ.* i, « Traitez de la nature des sons et des mouvemens », iii, prop. v, p. 167; cf. Crombie « Mersenne » (1974) n. 29; D. P. Walker, « Some aspects of the musical theory of Vincenzo Galilei and Galileo Galilei, *Proceedings of the Royal Musical Association*, c (1973-74) 33 sqq.

of experiments, publication of the numerical results of actual measurements as well as those calculated from theory, recognition of approximations, and estimation of experimental errors marked a notable step in the experimental method.

To investigate the harmonic phenomena of vibrating strings he used two strings stretched on a frame. One was the control. In the other he kept all the relevant quantities (length, tension, specific gravity) constant except one, and adjusted the variable quantity until it sounded in unison with, and hence vibrated with the same frequency as, the control. To determine the actual frequencies of notes of different pitch, he counted the slow vibrations of very long strings against time measured by pulse beats or a seconds pendulum. Then he used the general laws whose formulation he had completed, relating frequency to the length, tension and specific gravity of strings, to calculate frequencies too rapid to count. This was the first experimental proof that musical intervals were determined by frequencies of vibrations. On it he based a quantitative psycho-physiology of hearing which included the measurement of upper and lower limits of audible frequencies and explanations of consonance, dissonance, and resonance. In exploring further acoustical quantities, he poineered the experimental determination of the speed of sound, first by timing, with the pulse or a seconds pendulum, the difference between the flash or smoke and the report of a gun fired at a given distance. Later he used a method of timing the return of echoes. He trained himself to shout the syllables *Benedicam Dominum* in exactly a second. Then he stood back from a wall to a distance at which the echo began exactly when the voice ceased, giving the continuous syllables *Benedicam Dominum, Benedicam Dominum* [11]. The sound had travelled to the wall and back in a second. The wide variation in values, ranging from about 320 to 450 metres per second on different occasions, led him to point out the need to make measurements with atmospheric conditions as constant as possible. For comparison, the modern value for the speed of sound in dry air at 0° Centigrade is about 330 metres per second, decreasing with humidity and increasing with temperature. He showed that speed was independent of loudness and of pitch. Thus he decided by experiment the ancient question whether pitch depended only on frequency of vibration, as distinct from speed of forward motion. The Stoic theory, that sound was a wave motion propagated through the air in a sphere, led him to equate loudness with the volume displaced. He related the intensity of sound, like that of light, inversely to the square of the distance from its source. He pioneered also the study of harmonics or overtones. A further outstanding discovery was one related

---

[11] Mersenne, ibid., prop. xxii (misprinted xxi) 213 sqq.

both to the vibration of strings and to his concern with measuring time, the law which he published in 1634 that the frequency of a pendulum is inversely proportional to the square-root of its length [12]. This law, attributed to Galileo, became the basis of all clocks.

If Mersenne's experimental science was his answer to scepticism, it might also be argued that he remained a victim of scepticism. Where Galileo and Descartes were clearly decisive if quite often mistaken, Mersenne's empirical caution kept him too often poised in eclectic indecision about the causes of the effects he was measuring. Yet accompanying his reluctance to rule out alternatives and to push forward firmly in order to extract the benefits of one theory as against its rivals, and despite the notoriously idiosyncratic credulity which is perhaps the other face of empiricism, the distinction upon which he insisted between experimentally established regularities and their causes shows a highly critical grasp of scientific acceptability. He accepted that sound, and came to accept that light, were physically motions of some kind, but on the evidence available he refused to commit himself to any definite theory of the media of sound or of light or of the causation of auditory or visual perception. He claimed to demonstrate no more than their effects. Indeed, he wrote: « One is constrained to acknowledge, that man is not capable of knowing the reason for anything other than that which he can make, nor other sciences than those of which he makes the principles himself, as one can demonstrate in considering mathematics » [13]. Elaborating this point with reference to the difficulty of finding true principles in physics, which was concerned with things God had created, he wrote: « We must not be surprised if we cannot find the true reasons and the way they act or are acted upon, because we know the true reasons only for things that we can make with the hand or with the mind; and because, of all the things that God has made, we cannot make a single one, whatever subtlety or effort we bring to it, besides which he could have made them in some other way » [14].

But this definition of what we could know, while ruling out demonstration in the strict sense, gave us an opening into possible explanations of phenomena. We could know fully only what we ourselves constructed, whether in the mind as mathematics or in matter as machines and other

---

[12] Mersenne, *Les méchaniques de Galilée,* VIIe Addition (Paris, 1634) 77; see for the above experiments Crombie, « Mathematics... » (1971) nn, 16, 23-30, « Mersenne » (1974) nn. 42-4, and *Styles* ch. 3. iv (n. 2 above).

[13] Mersenne, *Les questions théologiques,* q. 22 (Paris, 1634) 111; cf. Crombie, *Styles ...* ch. 4. iii.

[14] Mersenne, *Harm. univ.* ii, « Nouvelles observations physiques et mathématiques » p. 8; cf. Descartes, *Principia philosophiae,* iv. 204 (1644); R. Lenoble, « Origines de la pensée scientifique moderne » in M. Daumas (ed.), *Histoire de la science* (Paris, 1957) 369 sqq.; P. Rossi, « Hermeticism, rationality and the scientific revolution », in *Reason, Experiment and Mysticism,* ed. Bonelli and Shea (1975) 247 sqq.; I. Berlin, *Vico and Herder* (London, 1976) 12-27.

products of art. But by imitating God's works in nature by means of these mental or material artifacts we could construct models which, like theories, were experimentally testable by comparison with the natural. In this way Mersenne came to link his experimental science with the second fundamental aspect of his natural philosophy, the conception of nature as a mechanism and the method of the hypothetical model.

The idea not simply that knowledge was construction, that to explain was to be able to reconstruct, but that we could truly know only what we could construct ourselves, introduced into European thinking a profoundly new conception both of science and of nature. Various ingredients contributed to this idea. The ancient and medieval doctrine of art as the imitation of nature had been transformed by the sixteenth century, for example in the thought of Leonardo da Vinci and of Marsilio Ficino as later in that of mechanicians such as Guidobaldo del Monte and Henri Monantheuil, into art as the rival of nature's powers as well as appearances. Human art began like that of the *Deus geometricus et mechanicus* [15] in the mind and issued to completion through the hand. No doubt visions of the potentialities of human manipulation of nature were encouraged by the sceptical doctrine of man as the measure of all things in social philosophy, as the maker of law and ethics, as the maker too of aesthetic taste, and also by the residual influence of magic even after its discredit. Perhaps it was under such influences that ex-Lord Chancellor Bacon took the decisive step, in his discussion of the significance of the arts in intellectual history, of rejecting the absolute distinction between natural and artificial things which had been established in natural philosophy by Aristotle [16]. But art could rival nature's powers only in rearranging or bringing together what God had already created, and God created nature according to fixed laws which art must observe. All philosophers who concerned themselves with this question would have accepted Galileo's distinction between the arbitrary rules of human society and the fixed laws of nature which existed regardless of human opinions and wishes and could not be cheated [17]. Descartes brought the equation of natural with artificial and its potential for explanation through models to a systematic conclusion by reducing natural and artificial alike, equally, completely and exclusively to the laws of matter in motion which were the ultimate laws of nature.

---

[15] Cf. P. Rossi, *I filosofi e le macchine* (Milano, 1962) c. 1 and appendice 1; Crombie, *Galileo Styles* ... chs. 3. ii, 4 (n. 2 above).

[16] Francis Bacon, *De augmentis scientiarum* (1623; *Works,* ed. J. Spedding, R. L. Ellis and D. D. Heath, i, London, 1857) 496-7; cf. Aristotle, *Physics,* ii. 1, 192 b 8 sqq., c. 2, 194a 21 sqq., c. 8, 199a 12 sqq.; Lenoble, Rossi and Crombie, op. cit. above nn. 13-15.

[17] Galileo, *Le opere,* ed. naz. (Firenze, 1968) ii, 155, v, 218, 326; cf. Mersenne, *Les mechaniques de Galilée,* c. 1 (Paris, 1634) 1-2; Descartes, *Princ. phil.* iv. 203; Crombie and A. Carugo, *Galileo's Arguments and Disputes in Natural Philosophy* (forthcoming).

Mersenne developed his general mechanistic theory of nature by an independent route as his reply to magic and the occult. He developed his theory of the animal automaton, which came to guide his whole scientific study of the senses and of language and the communication of information, likewise, and for the same reasons as Descartes and Gassendi, in response to a combined philosophical and theological challenge. They had to consider not only how an animate being could perceive and know a world reduced to matter in motion, but also man's relation to other animals in such a world, and in doing so they had to preserve the Christian doctrine of the spirituality, immortality, and responsibility of each individual person. Mersenne began to consider the nature of animals as distinct from men within his theological campaign for the uniqueness and dignity of the human being and for the validity and stability of human knowledge and of moral and aesthetic judgement. Aristotle had dismissed the suggestion that animals could exercise intelligent choice: only man acted by deliberate art after intelligent inquiry; animals which might appear to do the same were forced to act by natural teleological necessity [18]. Mersenne used this distinction in his campaign against his two named enemies of truth in order to separate men absolutely from all other living creatures [19]. One group had claimed that the alleged sensitivity of plants and intelligence of animals placed them with men as participants in a world soul. This he rejected because it would eliminate individual responsibility. When dealing with the opposing doctrine of the sceptics, who used the alleged sensory acuity and intelligence of animals to throw doubt on any superior claims for human knowledge, he again sharply separated men from animals to make a different point [20]. He argued that all sensory knowledge was so relative that we could not be certain that animals perceived the world in any way as we did. But he insisted that we alone could obtain scientific knowledge of these differences. Eventually he came to deny that animals had any knowledge in any acceptable sense of the word at all. The notion of the animal automaton, to which he and Descartes were led for similar reasons, might then be seen as a mechanized version of Aristotle's natural teleological necessity. Mersenne first published the idea in *Les préludes de l'harmonie universelle* (1634), where he wrote [21]:

... for the animals, which we resemble and which would be our equals if we did not have reason, do not reflect upon the actions or the passions of their external or internal senses, and do not know what is colour, odour or sound, or if there is any

---

[18] Aristotele, *Physics,* ii. 8-9, *De partibus animalium*, i. 1, *Metaphysics*, i. 1, *Nicomachean Ethics*, ii. 1, iii. 3, vi. 3-5.

[19] Mersenne, *Quaest. in Gen.,* q. 35, col. 1262 sqq., *L'impiété des déistes*, ii, cc. 19, 21-2, 24, 26 (Paris, 1624) 360 sqq., 390 sqq., 427 sqq., 470 sqq.

[20] Mersenne, *La vérité des sciences*, i, c. 2, pp. 15 sqq.

[21] *Les préludes,* q. 6, p. 157; cf. Aristotle, *De partibus animalium*, i. 1, 639b 22 sqq.

difference between these objects, to which they are moved rather than moving themselves there. This comes about by the force of the impression that the different objects make on their organs and on their senses, for they cannot discern if it is more appropriate to go and drink or eat or do something else, and they do not eat or drink or do anything else except when the presence of objects or the animal imagination necessitates them and transports them to their objects, without their knowing what they do, whether good or bad; which would happen to us just as to them if we were destitute of reason, for they have no enlightenment except what they must have to take their nourishment and to serve us for the uses to which God has destined them.

So we could say of the animals that they knew nothing of the world impinging upon them, « that they do not so much act as be put into action, and that objects make an impression on their senses such that it is necessary for them to follow it just as it is necessary for the wheels of a clock to follow the weight or the spring that pulls them » [22].

Animals then were purely automatic information systems. If it was language that chiefly distinguished men from animals this was fundamental, for language meant conscious understanding of meaning. The cries and jargon of animals provided a means of communication, but one in which they unconsciously emitted and responded to messages by necessity according to the design suited to the material needs of their species. Mersenne saw the distinction as one fundamentally of intellectual capacity, but matched by physical possibility. This he explored through two parallel investigations, through the comparative anatomy and physiology of voice production in men and a variety of animals, and through the imitation of the vowels, consonants, syllables, and other sounds of the human and animal voice by musical instruments. The artificial model provided a method of analysis and of reproduction of the natural.

Mersenne's conception of human and animal language as both biological and social phenomena, his attempt to base his account of the reception and communication of information in men and animals firmly on a scientific, empirical study of the effects of physical sound and light on the body and the soul, and his rethinking of the physiological coordination of behaviour, led him to ask what were the natural elements common to all human language, and what were the elements common to all forms of communication, whether by human beings, animals or machines. The question whether there was a natural original human language in which the names of things signified their natures, or whether all languages had grown up by fortuitous use in which words acquired meanings by convention, went back to Greek discussions of the origins of man and of civilization. The former

---

[22] *Harm. univ.* ii, « Traitez de la voix » etc., i, prop. lii, p. 79; but they could receive thereby an animal pleasure or pain: *Les préludes,* ibid. 150-1; *Questions harmoniques,* q. i (Paris, 1634) 14-15, 37-38.

view was implied by Herodotus's story of the isolation of children from birth to find out what unprompted words they would first utter [23], and was suggested ambiguously by Plato's account of the alternatives [24]. The conventional theory of language and its origin was described in the Hippocratic treatise, *The Art* [25] and by Diogenes Laertius [26], Lucretius [27] and Diodorus Siculus [28]. The question was considered by Dante [29] and became an issue in the Neo-Platonic and Cabalistic speculations of the fifteenth and sixteenth centuries. Mersenne encountered it first in the Cabalistic belief that an occult identification gave a name power over the thing named. This ancient belief has been very widespread among humanity, and we know that because he forgot it Rumpelstilzchen came to grief.

Mersenne's interest in this aspect of language arose in the first place out of his theological campaign against magic and the occult. From the beginning he violently rejected the Cabalistic belief in the occult power of words and music [30]. He accepted fully the power of music over the emotions and dispositions of the soul. One of his original reasons for taking up the history and science of music had been that he had believed that the Greeks had understood these effects, but he held that they could be understood only through an exact science of sound. He came to envisage a kind psycho-physiological engineering through music and words, surpassing in its potentialities for rational and virtuous control any such use in medicine and education available to the ancients [31]. A first he was undecided whether language had developed by chance or by revelation [32] and he thought that God might have revealed the natural names of things to Adam in Hebrew. But he pointed out that these natural names would have been lost to us through the subsequent growth and differentiation of languages [33]. Soon he hardened his position, rejected the idea of natural names, and firmly proposed a purely rational theory making words simply arbitrary signs by means of which the same meaning could be expressed in different languages [34]. Spoken words were simply physical sounds to

[23] Herodotus, *History*, ii. 1; cf. for bibliography on the language question Crombie, « Some attitudes... » (1975) and *Styles* ... ch. 4. iii (n. 2 above).

[24] Especially *Cratylus*.

[25] Section 2.

[26] *De vitis*, x. 75-6, « Epicurus Herodoto ».

[27] *De rerum natura*, v. 1029 sqq.

[28] i. 8.

[29] *De vulgare eloquentia*, i. 6. 5-7, 9. 5-6, *La divina commedia*, « Paradiso », xxvi. 124 sqq.

[30] Mersenne, *Quaest. in Gen.*, qq. 50-7, col. 1383 sqq., 1549 sqq., 1696 sqq., *L'impiété*, i. 7, pp. 143 sqq.

[31] *Quaest. in Gen.*, Praefatio, and q. 57, col. 1534 sqq., 1619 sqq., *Les préludes*, q. 10, pp. 212 sqq., *Questions harmoniques*, qq. 2, 5, pp. 91 sqq., 252 sqq. esp. 267-8, *Harm. univ.*, Première préface générale and « Tr. de la voix » i.

[32] *Quaest in Gen.*, q. 29, col. 1217-8; q. 28, col. 1197 sqq.

[33] *La vérité*, i, c. 6. pp. 69 sqq.

[34] *Quaest. in Gen.*, continuation in Bibliothèque Nationale, Paris, MS Lat. 17, 262, pp. 511, 536; Lenoble, *Mersenne*, pp. xii-xiv, 515, 517.

which meanings had been attached by use. From this point he elaborated the notable view of the origins, history and empirical science of human language which appeared in *Harmonie universelle*[35]. Because all men in common possessed reason, they had developed languages in which spoken or written words signified meanings, as distinct from the so-called languages of animals. But just as the effects of music varied with race, way of life, period and culture, so different groups of men had come to express their common understanding of meaning in a variety of languages diversified by their different historical experiences, environments, needs, temperaments and customs. Because men shared reason it was possible to translate the expression of a common meaning from any language into any other, but no language was naturally prior to any other. He ingeniously explored the question of identifying the natural elements common to all human language by asking whether it would be possible to use the science of music to invent a language providing natural signification. This led him to the idea of inventing a new universal means of communication between all men.

The need for an effective means of intellectual communication between men of different languages and customs had been recognized for at least three centuries before Mersenne in the theological and geographical context of Christendom. The natural language of mankind might, as it was held, be Hebrew, but its pristine universality had been lost in the consequences of Babel. The universality of Latin stopped at the boundaries of the West. The religious obligation of Christians to communicate the truth revealed to them to the unbelieving Jews and Moslems and the uninstructed pagans forming the bulk of mankind had been pressed in the thirteenth century in Roger Bacon's urgent advocacy of the study of languages[36] and in Raymond Lull's *ars inveniendi veritatem* and its projected use by missionaries trained in schools of Arabic and other oriental tongues[37]. The vision of the unity of truth and of an infallible art such as Lull offered in his combinatory symbolic logic, of a universal method capable of demonstrating the one and certain truth to all who learnt to use it, retained its attraction in the modified context of Europe in the sixteenth and seventeenth centuries. To the infidels and pagans of the Old World had been added those of the New. Christendom had become fragmented by heresy and schism. The idea of finding a common tongue for all nations and peoples was based on new comparative studies of ancient and modern

---

[35] Esp. « Tr. de la voix » i.

[36] *Opus maius,* iii, ed. J. H. Bridges, i (Oxford, 1897) 66 sqq. and iii (London, 1900), *Opus tertium,* c. 27, ed. J. S. Brewer (London, 1859) 100 sqq.

[37] Cf. E. W. Platzeck, *Raimund Lull,* 2 vol. (Roma-Dusseldorf, 1962-64); A. Llinares, *Raymond Lulle* (Paris, 1963); R. D. F. Pring-Mill, « Introductory note » to Raymundus Lullus, *Quattuor libri principiorum* (Wakefield and Paris-La Haye, 1969); also P. Rossi, *Clavis universalis* (Milano-Napoli, 1960); G. Gusdorf, *Les sciences humaines et la pensée occidentale,* iii, 2 (Paris, 1969) 303 sqq.

languages aimed at restoring the religious unity of Europe and at realizing through conversion the ancient ideal of the unity of mankind. The linguistic movement was seen then as essential to the advancement of truth. « For », as Francis Bacon put it in describing the *idola fori*, « it is by discourse that men associate; and words are imposed according to the apprehension of the vulgar. And therefore the ill and unfit choice of words wonderfully obstructs the understanding... For men believe that their reason governs words; but it is also true that words react on the understanding; and this it is that has rendered philosophy and the sciences sophistical and inactive » [38].

Mersenne saw in his own analysis of human knowledge and of its expression through the common elements of human language an opening into the possibility of inventing a perfect system of communication for all men, a new universal language capable of conveying information without error. He began experimenting with the idea of making a new artificial universal language by means of the combinatory calculus showing the number of possible permutations and combinations of a given set of elements with which he had already tried to devise the best tune that could be composed from a given set of notes [39]. Descartes' famous comment, that a language expressing perfectly a perfect knowledge of truth could be achieved only in an earthly paradise, did not quench his enthusiasm [40]. Knowledge of true natures and causes might be reserved for the blessed, but God had disposed of all things by number, measure and weight [41]. Mersenne envisaged a universal language of quantities, and since quantities were the only certain knowledge of things available to us, a language of quantities would be a perfect means of philosophical communication. He proposed a system of sounds and notations constructed with his combinatory calculus so that this language could be expressed in music by persons unable to converse in any common tongue and even by mutes. Two philosophers unable to communicate in any other way could do so perfectly on the strings of two lutes [42]. The extension of historical scholarship, scientific natural history and overseas voyages had made Europeans in the sixteenth and seventeenth centuries increasingly aware of the variety and relativity of cultures and of perceptual worlds which different types of men and animals inhabited. Besides facilitating communication between peoples of different nations, Mersenne became concerned as a matter for both phi-

---

[38] *Novum organum*, ii. 43 and 59; cf. Crombie « Some attitudes... » (1975) nn. 14 sqq.

[39] Mersenne, *La vérité*, iii, c. 10, p. 548; cf. Crombie, « Mathematics... » (1971) 301 sqq.

[40] Descartes to Mersenne, 20. xi. 1629 in Mersenne, *Correspondance*, ed. cit. ii, 323-9.

[41] Mersenne, *Les questions théologiques*, q. 34 (Paris, 1634) 158-65, expurgated edition: see Mersenne, *Correspondance*, ed. cit. iv, 74-6, 156-7, 267-8, 270-1; Lenoble, *Mersenne*, pp. xx, 399-401.

[42] Mersenne, *Harm. univ.* i, « Tr. de la nature des sons » i, props. xxii, xxiv, pp. 39-41, 43; cf. Crombie, « Mathematics, ... » (1971) nn. 34 sqq.

losophy and compassion with the mental world of persons deprived of vision or hearing or another sense and with the problem of communicating with them. His analysis of music and of the human voice made him interested in a method of teaching deaf mutes to speak by forming the tongue and lips in appropriate positions and by associating these with written words and with the things they signified [43]. So music and speech brought about the unity of mankind, and the rational *Harmonie universelle* which God had chosen to exhibit in his creation was shown by research into nature to yield also a moral norm [44].

I have tried to show that when Mersenne was attracted to science as an example of certifiable truth, what he accepted as certifiable depended not only on the logical and experimental validity of an argument, but also on its cogency within his more general beliefs. A persistent characteristic of European culture has been the search for norms of rational thought, applying to every kind of subject-matter and every aspect of life, which appears most obviously in the succession of programmes for intellectual reform such as those of Roger Bacon, Francis Bacon, Descartes and many others before and since. The interaction between the programmes and their realization, and in this between empirical and non-empirical criteria, has provided the dynamics driving natural philosophy to explore ever-widening varieties of questions. At the same time it has sharpened the scientific criteria of evidence, cogency and relevance for accepting both questions and answers, and for agreement and disagreement about particular theories and about the ability of human inquiry to discover general principles of explanation. By placing ourselves at the viewpoint of Mersenne's particular vision of science and nature in the detailed context of his world, we can see how this early seventeenth-century society, making a conscious articulation both with the past and with an expected future, committed its successors to beliefs and methods on a wide front. It would be interesting to make a comparative historical study of the contemporary criteria of evidence and choice used, for example, in science, medicine, law, industry, government, aesthetics and so forth. Mersenne exemplifies the new vision opened by a philosophy of nature and a scientific programme which offered effective intellectual and material power over nature far beyond the immediate technical possibilities, but when this immediate technical limit to ideas was in varying degrees clearly and optimistically grasped. Visions of power and understanding were an ancient part of Western intellectual culture which Mersenne shared with philosophers for whom he had the

---

43 Mersenne, ibid. ii, « Tr. de la voix » i, prop. 1 i, pp. 77-9; Crombie, ibid. nn. 40 sqq.
44 Cf. Mersenne, *Les méchaniques de Galilée,* Épître dédicatoire, pp. 4-6; *Quest. harm.,* qq. 1, 3, 4, pp. 3 sqq., 179 sqq., 235 sqq.

bitterest enmity; but for him and his allies they were acceptable only when made effective by scientific methods tested and developed by a rigorous application. This was their decisive programme. But we must relate any present to any past and any future in their historical contexts. Visions change, historical visions of the past as much as scientific visions of inquiry into nature. History, like any human experience, retains its therapy of surprise.

16

SOME ASPECTS OF DESCARTES' ATTITUDE
TO HYPOTHESIS AND EXPERIMENT

My purpose in this short paper is simple and direct. Historians of mechanics have made us only too well aware of the fact that Descartes' *a priori* reasoning led him to wildly inaccurate conclusions in this field which he was too complacent to check. It seems absurd that he should have left it for Newton to find out whether or not so important a part of his physics as the vortex theory agreed with the facts as expressed by Kepler's laws. His complacency over his laws of motion and of collision, which Huygens and Leibniz had to dismantle, is equally striking. Yet Descartes had a keen interest in the experimental work being done by his contemporaries and was an assiduous experimenter and observer himself, as both his correspondence and his scientific writings amply show. No other great philosopher except perhaps Aristotle spent so much time in experimental observation. He tells us in the *Discours de la Methode* how, during the nine years of combined travel and study after 1619, « I made a variety of observations and acquired a quantity of experience » (¹).

(¹) Descartes, *Oeuvres*, ed. C. Adam and P. Tannery, vi. 29; Paris, 1897-1913, 12 vols. This edition is referred to below as AT. Further published and unpublished letters are included in the new edition of Descartes' *Correspondance*, ed. C. Adam and G. Milhaud, Paris, 1936-56, 6 vols.; further volumes are to follow. The basic biographies of Descartes are Adrien Baillet, *La Vie de Monsieur Descartes*, Paris, 1691; C. Adam, *Vie et oeuvres de Descartes*, AT, xii. Recent studies bearing on the subject of the present paper are: L. J. Beck, *The Method of Descartes*, Oxford, 1952; G. Canguilhem, *La formation du concept de réflexe*, Paris, 1955; R. Dugas, *La mécanique au xvii siècle*, Neuchâtel, 1954; René Descartes, *Discours de la méthode*. Texte et commentaire par E. Gilson, Paris, 1947; A. Gewirtz, « Experience and the non-mathematical in the Cartesian method », *Journal of the History of Ideas*, ii (1941) 183-210; A. Boyce Gibson, *The Philosophy of Descartes*, London, 1931; E. Gilson, *Etudes sur le rôle de la pensée médiévale dans la formation du système cartésien*, Paris, 1930; A. Koyré, *Etudes Galiléen-*

According to his 17th-century biography Adrien Baillet, during this time he dissected and vivisected embryos of birds and cattle and later studied chemistry as well as anatomy. His correspondence describes dissections of dogs, cats, rabbits, codfish and mackerel, and of eyes, livers and hearts obtained from animals slaughtered in an *abattoir* ; experiments on the weight of the air and on the laws of sound – Mersenne's special interest; observations on rainbows and parahelia and other optical phenomena. Many of his scientific writings reflect these activities and show that at least in some fields, especially in optics, physiology and anatomy, his experimental knowledge of the facts was first-hand, genuine and sound. Moreover his correspondence abounds in remarks making the same point as in the sixth part of the *Discours*: « I noticed also with respect to experiments that they become so much the more necessary the more we advance in knowledge » ([2]).

How is it that this expressed attitude to experiment and observation is so different from the indifference that appears in practice in his mechanics? The answer to this question can, I think, be found theoretically in Descartes' conception of completed scientific knowledge in contrast with the process of acquiring such knowledge, and practically in the accidents and circumstances of his own scientific work. There is no space to go far into these subjects. My present purpose is simply to draw attention to the fact that our view of Descartes' attitude to experiment becomes different and more favourable when we look beyond his mechanics and beyond the *Principia* – a premature conception of completed science – to his other work, especially in optics and physiology, where we can observe him in the process of making discoveries.

Descartes had very clear and consistent theoretical conceptions of what constituted scientific knowledge and of how we could acquire it. A word must be said about this explicit and essential framework to his scientific researches. In accordance with the geometrical model which he applied to all reasoning, he held that a completed science consists of demonstrations that begin with premisses that are certain and self-evident and of which the contrary can be seen to be absurd. Descartes' confidence in the applicability of this model to physical science seems to have varied on different occasions. In principle he held that truly scientific knowledge could be claimed, as he wrote

---

nes ii. La loi de la chute des corps. Descartes et Galilée (Actualités scientifiques et industrielles, N. 853) Paris, 1939; G. Leisegang, *Descartes Dioptrik*, Meisenheim am Glan, 1954; G. Milhaud, *Descartes savant*, Paris, 1921; J. A. Passmore, « William Harvey and the philosophy of science », *Australasian Journal of Philosophy*, xxxvi (1958) 85-94; L. Roth, *Descartes, Discourse on Method*, Oxford, 1937; H. Scholz, A. Kratzer and J. E. Hoffmann, *Descartes*, 1951; J. F. Scott, *The Scientific Work fo René Descartes*, London, 1952; Norman Kemp Smith, *New Studies in the Philosophy of Descartes*, London, 1952.

([2]) AT. vi. 63.

to Mersenne in 1640, only when it was possible not simply « to explain how things might be » but « to demonstrate that they could not be otherwise » ([3]). His optimism about the possibility of achieving such demonstrations in practice seems to have depended on which end of the chain of reasoning he was contemplating. When he was considering the results of the analysis that reduced the physical world to the irreducible « simple nature » of extension, with motion as an essential mode of this extension, that is, when he 'was considering the top end of the chain, he seems to have had no doubt that it *would* be possible to show how the composite world we inhabit and observe must follow from these basic, mathematically-conceived constituents. But when he was considering the chain lower down, nearer the complex data the observer and experimenter is faced with, he was far more hesitant. As he wrote to Mersenne in a well-known letter in 1638:

« You ask me whether I think what I have written about refraction is a demonstration. I think it is, at least as far as it is possible, without having proved the principles of physics previously by metaphysics, to give any demonstration on this subject... as far as any other question of mechanics, optics, or astronomy, or any other question which is not purely geometrical or arithmetical, has ever been demonstrated. But to demand that I should give geometrical demonstrations of matters which depend on physics is to demand that I should do the impossible. If you restrict the use of « demonstration » to geometrical proofs only, you will be obliged to say that Archimedes demonstrated nothing in mechanics, nor Vitellio in optics, nor Ptolemy in astronomy, etc., which is not commonly maintained. For, in such matters, one is satisfied that the writers, having presupposed certain things which are not obviously contradictory to experience, have besides argued consistently and without logical fallacy, even if their assumptions are not exactly true » ([4]).

The problem was how to show that all the links, stretching from the general conception of nature as entirely reducible to extension and motion down to the particular data of observation, were really all joined together in a single chain. The paradox of Descartes is that the occasions when he was best as a scientist were those when he was dealing with problems farthest from his ideal, problems where the junction was so difficult that he was forced to leave the top end of the chain alone. His laws of motion were so disastrous just because he thought he had derived empirically exact laws from first principles. In fact he never envisaged the first principles he had discovered by analysis, the conception of matter as extension with motion as its mode, as being open to empirical tests at all. The analysis had ruled out all other possibilities.

([3]) A.T. iii. 39 (11. iii. 1640).
([4]) A.T. ii. 141-2 (17.v. 1638).

It cannot be said too often that Descartes made a contribution to physical science of the first magnitude by re-thinking its basic assumptions and by stating clearly and explicitly the ultimate ideal of all subsequent theoretical physics. This is that the whole of physics should form a single theoretical system in which the last details of observable regularites should be shown to be deducible from a minimum number of fundamental equations, which could be written perhaps on a single page. As everyone knows, Descartes' main failing was his eagerness to rush his fences. The temptation was greatest when he thought he was nearest to this scientific ideal. The paradox of Descartes as a scientist is that his performance improved the more hopeless he saw to be the task of trying to link the problems he was dealing with to the first principles of matter (extension) and motion, from which everything ought to be able to be derived. Standing, as it were, amidst the broken sections of that chain which could not be cast up to heaven, the experimentalist in him came to life. In the Author's Letter prefaced to the French translation of the *Principles* (1647), Descartes said that two and only two conditions determined whether the principles proposed could be accepted as true first principles: « first they should be so clear and evident that the mind of man cannot doubt their truth when it attentively applies itself to consider them » (⁵); and secondly, everything else must be deducible from them. Now we might argue that if we are satisfied in terms of the first condition then there should be no need to make any tests in terms of the second. If the first principles can be seen to be true, then everything else, of which they are the first principles, must follow from them. But Descartes went on to admit: « It is really only God alone who has perfect wisdom, that is to say, who has a complete knowledge of the truth of all things ». What is man to do, without such knowledge of many things? Descartes concluded his Letter by saying that he must experiment. He is thus in the peculiar position of believing that he has discovered the true first principles that form the top end of the chain, while being unable to show how the complexities and enigmas of matter, especially of biology, observable at the bottom end attach to those principles. Hence experiment is necessary in physics, chemistry and biology, but it is an expression of failure, as the sixth book of the *Discourse* shows.

Before considering Descartes' idea of experimental method, I must mention another fundamental characteristic of his conception of scientific knowledge. He held that besides being logically demonstrative this must also be explanatory. In fact in his conception of physics the two went together. The ideal of scientific knowledge in physics would be realised when we were able to describe, as he wrote in the *Principia* (iv. 188), « the universe and the whole visible

---

(⁵) AT. ix. 2. 2-3.

world as if it were a machine, in which there was nothing to consider but the shapes and movements of its parts » ([6]). To such a mechanism it is possible to apply mathematics and calculation, but it is the mechanism – extension and motion – that explains. Descartes' insistence that calculation and description are not sufficient can be seen in his interestingly similar criticisms of Galileo for giving the kinematic law of free fall, and of Harvey for describing the heart's action, without in either case attempting a mechanical explanation. He wrote to Mersenne in 1638 about Galileo: « Without having considered the first causes of Nature, he has only looked for certain particular effects and upon this has built without foundations » ([7]). He himself offered an explanation of both phenomena by trying to show that they followed from the laws of motion and the mechanism of nature which he believed he had discovered.

It was his conception that science must, to be complete, offer explanations in terms of universal mechanism that led Descartes to his masterly grasp of the hypothetical model. In Aristotelian thought a strict distinction was made between natural and artificial things, *naturalia* and *artificialia*. The former were endowed by nature with their natural principles of behaviour and movement. It was beyond man's power to make a natural thing, and artificial imitations could throw no light on the essence of things made by nature. This distinction had become blurred in the partial mechanisation of nature made by some medieval thinkers, and perhaps their influence can be seen in Leonardo da Vinci's insight, that to understand is to construct. Descartes made the identification of the artificial with the natural an instrument of scientific research.

In the *Principia* (iv. 203) he declared that since both natural bodies and the machines made by men operated by means of the same laws of motion, and since these were the ultimate laws of nature and were completely explanatory, he could see no essential difference between natural and artificial bodies. The only difference was that the parts, the basic shapes and motions responsible for the observed behaviour of natural bodies, were too small to be seen, whereas artificial machines were composed of parts large enough to be seen by the men who made them. This being so, Descartes could bring the objectives of the engineer into the game of searching for the nature of things.

Descartes gave his first account of his new physics in terms of the vast hypothetical model of *Le Monde* and *L'Homme*. He transports us to a distant region of space and there constructs before our eyes an imaginary world, built according to the known laws of mechanics, which will imitate everything that we can observe in the actual world. Since we know all its parts and the laws they obey, for we made

---

([6]) AT. viii. 315.
([7]) AT. ii. 380.

them ourselves, we can claim to understand this hypothetical world completely; and since the same events occur in it as in our actual world, we can claim to have shown at least how our world *could* be explained, by analogy with the hypothetical model.

By this move Descartes gave explicit meaning to a wide contemporary practice, for example Harvey's own use of the conception of the heart as force-pump. He exploited this approach in some of his own most successful experimental work. For example, in the *Météores* (viii) he used a model raindrop in the form of a spherical glass flask full of water in order to investigate the properties of the rainbow. It is true that Theodoric of Freiberg had done the same three centuries earlier, but only qualitatively. In *La Dioptrique* (v) Descartes introduced his beautiful investigation of the optics of the eye with a description of a model eye made up out of a *camera obscura*, a lens, and other articles. Then he went on to show how, by means of an experiment already described by Christopher Scheiner, the formation of the image in the eye itself could be investigated. He removed the back of the eye of a freshly dead ox or man and replaced it by a piece of thin white paper or egg-shell. This enabled him to examine experimentally how the eye worked as an optical instrument.

Descartes' innovation was to make the principles of the engineering model the *only* principles operating in nature, thus banishing all mystery and throwing the entire world of matter open to the same form of scientific inquiry. He put himself into the position, allowing a desirable maximum of manoeuvre, of being able to put forward the model of *Le Monde* and *L'Homme* as in the first place an explicitly and unambiguously man-made hypothesis, whose correspondence with actuality was to be investigated.

How was this correspondence to be investigated? In the *Discours* (vi) Descartes wrote: « Reviewing in my mind all the objects that had been presented to my senses, I venture to assert that I have not observed anything that I could not satisfactorily explain by the principles I had discovered. But I must also confess that the power of nature is so vast and extensive, and these principles so simple and general, that I have hardly observed any particular effect that I did not at once recognise to be deducible from them in more ways than one, and my greatest difficulty is usually to discover in which of these ways it depends on them. In such a case, I know no other device than to devise certain experiments such that their result is not the same if it has to be explained in *one* of these ways as it would be if explained in the other » (8). Thus again it is the complexity of nature that forces Descartes back into using hypothetical models and what he called « conjectures », and experiments, in his search for true explanations or « demonstrations » in natural science. Des-

---

(8) AT. vi. 64-5.

cartes used the word   *demonstrer* to cover both the explanation
of the observed facts by the assumed theory and the proof of the
truth of the theory. When challenged with the criticism that this
might involve a circular argument, he wrote in a letter in 1638 contrasting two kinds of hypotheses ([9]). In astronomy various geometrical devices, admittedly false in nature, were used to yield true conclusions only in the sense that they « saved the appearances ». But
physical assumptions were *proposed* as true. He said that he was
persuaded of the truth of the assumption that the material world
consists of particles in motion by the number of effects he could deduce from it, for example such diverse phenomena as the operation
of vision, the properties of salt, the formation of snow, the rainbow,
and so on. He thus made the range of confirmation a criterion of
truth. Some people, he said, might be shocked because he called
the principles from which he demonstrated the facts discussed in
La Dioptrique and *Les Météores* assumptions. But in all natural scientific investigations, he said, the explanation of facts by assumptions
and the proof of assumptions by agreement with facts were intrica-
tely interwoven. He could not resist the temptation to claim that he
could have demonstrated the assumptions made in his optics unambiguously by deducing them from the « primary truths », extension
and motion, had he so chosen. It was by refraining from this dangerous exercise and using assumptions lower down in the hierarchy of
theory, and by relying on experimental criteria, that he produced
his scientific masterpiece, *La Dioptrique*.

Since, as Descartes said, more than one hypothesis could usually
be found to explain the same facts, his procedure was to discover
the differences in their ranges of application and to devise experiments to choose between them on this basis. He gave, as an explicit
example of his conception of this kind of *experimentum crucis*, his
treatment of the problem of the mechanism of the heart in *La Description du Corps Humain* (1648-49). While admitting that Harvey's
theory that the heart is a force-pump might agree with many of the
facts observed, he went on to argue: « that does not exclude the possibility that all the same effects might follow from another cause,
namely from the dilatation of the blood which I have described. But
in order to be able to decide which of these two causes is true, we
must consider other observations which cannot agree with both of
them » ([10]). Descartes of course had proposed the hypothesis that the
heart is a kind of internal combustion engine, from which the blood
is expelled into the arteries by the explosive vaporisation of blood
dropping from the veins into its chambers heated by their natural
fire. Both Harvey and Descartes agreed that the blood left the heart
when it became short, hard and white and entered it when it be-

---

([9]) AT. ii. 197-202 (to Morin 13. vii. 1638).
([10]) AT. xi. 241-2.

came long, soft and red. The crucial difference was that Harvey had said that the heart was contracted in the former condition and expanded in the latter, whereas Descartes claimed the reverse. Harvey's statement agreed with his theory that the blood was forced out of the heart by a muscular contraction, and Descartes' claim agreed with his theory that the blood was forced out by an explosive vaporisation which at the same time expanded the heart. Descartes maintained that observations made by vivisection on a rabbit's heart confirmed his theory, but Harvey was easily able to show, in his *Second Disquisition to Jean Riolan*, that Descartes' observations were mistaken.

Too great a fondness for his own hypotheses was certainly a weakness in Descartes as a scientist. As Gilson said of another example of his work: « La critique si vigilante de Descartes porte beaucoup moins sur les faits que sur leur explication » ([11]). But this weakness sprang from the same source as his greatest strength, his bold imposition of *a priori* theorising upon facts of which he was not content to remain merely a passive observer. But if the power and the failure of his thought both sprang from his application to the world of the mathematician's mode of reasoning, this does not mean that he was indifferent to observed facts, either as a source of information and of scientific problems or as the means of testing theories. Two further examples will illustrate both his strength and his failings.

In his treatment of the problem of falling bodies, soon after his meeting with Beeckman, Descartes appears as a mathematician playing with the world. Beeckman asked for a mathematical description of how a stone falls. Descartes supplied a solution, elegant but mistaken, followed by a further demonstration of how it might fall with different assumptions. One is reminded of Galileo's insistence that he wanted to discover which, among the various mathematical possibilities, is realised in actual fact. Of course Descartes agreed that this was the objective, but he did not really bother to find out whether he had reached it.

It is in *La Dioptrique* that Descartes appears at his best as a physicist and physiologist combining theoretical and experimental inquiry. *La Dioptrique* is significant as one of the « essays in method » without which Descartes said it was impossible to understand his general statements about scientific method. The problem he set out to solve in this work, and in the parallel correspondence with Ferrier, was the construction of a telescope on scientific principles, in place of the instruments so far made simply by trial and error, as in Holland, or with an incomplete knowledge of refraction and the *linea anaclastica* by Galileo and Kepler. The purpose of a telescope, De-

---

([11]) E. Gilson, *Etudes sur le rôle de la pensée médiévale dans la formation du système cartésien*, p. 137.

scartes says, is to increase the power of vision. In order to construct an instrument rationally it is thus necessary for us to have scientific knowledge both of light, by which we see, and of the eye and associated nervous system, which are the natural instruments of sight. The first two *discours* of *La Dioptrique* undertake an analysis of « the nature of light » and a geometrical account of the laws of reflection and refraction. His knowledge of the latter puts Descartes in a position, denied to Galileo and Kepler, to give a scientific account of the working of a telescope and to work out the curvatures of the lenses theoretically. Before taking up this question he devotes the next five *discours* to an analysis of human vision, in both its normal and its pathological states. In this part of the work his anatomical knowledge and skill as an observer are impressively exhibited, for example in his descriptions of the reversal of the image at the back of the eye, of the functioning of the iris, the ciliary muscle, the black pigment preventing internal reflection, and the various forms of co-ordination and accomodation, and of optical illusions. In the eighth and ninth *discours* he gives a synthesis of the two preceding lines of analysis by showing that the cross-section of the surfaces of the lenses used in constructing a telescope should be hyperbolas and ellipses. He did not of course allow for chromatic aberration, a problem not then understood. So that the « artisan » could put the scientific principles discovered into practice, he gives a detailed analysis of these curves, and concludes the whole work in the tenth *discours* with practical advice « on the manner of cutting lenses ». As it turned out Descartes' directions proved difficult to carry out in practice, as the unfortunate Ferrier discovered, but certainly he had shown how in principle to construct a telescope scientifically.

Thus we must not be misled by Descartes' recurringly poor performance, especially in the *Principia*, in checking his theories against the facts, into supposing that he is not perfectly sincere in his castigation, in the *Regulae* (v), « of those philosophers who neglect experiments and expect truth to rise from their own heads like Minerva from Jupiter's » ([12]). He was capable of being a persevering and ingenious experimenter and observer. Neither have we any reason to doubt that, like any other sensible scientist, he intended to put into practice the criteria indicated in his remark to Mersenne in 1638: « there are only two ways to refute what I have written, of which one is to prove by some observations or reasons that the things I have supposed are false; and the other that what I have deduced from those things cannot be so deduced » ([13]). But why did not Descartes apply these criteria more carefully to explanations and statements which his contemporaries soon saw to be obviously false?

Descartes' blind spot arose precisely where it did, I think, because

---

([12]) AT. x. 380.
([13]) AT. ii. 143.

he was always ready, when the opportunity presented itself, to suppose that he had achieved his ideal of completed science when in fact he was far from it. In his work in optics this temptation does not fail to loom over the horizon, but it does not carry off its victim. In *La Dioptrique* he had treated the principles from which the scientific demonstration proceeded as « assumptions », since he does not justify them but simply uses them as sufficient for the limited purpose set by the problem. He explained this practice in the sixth part of the *Discours*, writing:

« If some of the matters of which I have spoken in the beginning of the *Dioptrique* and the *Météores* should, at first sight, shock people because I have called them assumptions, and do not seem to bother about their proof, just have the patience to read these right through and I hope you will be satisfied. For it seems to me that the reasoning is so interwoven that the last are demonstrated by the first, which are their causes, and the first are demonstrated by the last, which are their effects. And let it not be thought that in this I fall into the fallacy which logicians call arguing in a circle, for since experience renders the majority of these effects most certain, the causes from which I deduce them do not so much serve to demonstrate their existence as to explain them; on the other hand, the causes are proved by the effects » [14]. He went on to claim that he considered himself able to deduce his optical principles from the « primary truths » – extension and motion – but had deliberately chosen not to do so. Had he not so chosen the principles used in his optics would have ceased to be mere assumptions. But had a different choice in fact been open to him, had the complex nature of the subject not forced him to start and to remain lower down in the chain of scientific reasoning, with assumptions, hypotheses, models, facts, we may doubt whether his optics would have become the masterpiece of scientific reasoning and experiment that it is. In the *Principia* he thought he could start at the top and derive the whole science of motion from the « primary truths », with disastrous results to his reputation. In *La Dioptrique* and *Les Météores* he was forced by the facts of nature to be better than his ideal.

Further references: Descartes, *Règles* (1977) above p. 258; R.M. Blake, « The role of experience in Descartes's theory of method », *Philosophical Review*, xxxviii (1929) 125-43, 201-18; D.M. Clarke, *Descartes' Philosophy of Science* (Manchester, 1982); P. Costabel (1982) above p. 258; A.C. Crombie (1990) above p. 258 and *Styles* ... chs. 3.v, 4.ii-iii; H.J. Wickes et A.C. Crombie, « A propos de *La dioptrique*: l'expérience dans la philosophie naturelle de Descartes » in *Problématique* ... (1988) 65-79 above p. 398; see also ch. 9.

---

[14] AT. vi. 76.

17

HISTORICAL COMMITMENTS OF BIOLOGY*

"Aussi bien cette solidarité des âges a-t-elle tant de force qu'entre eux les liens d'intel-
ligibilité sont véritablement à double sens. L'incompréhension du présent naît fatalement
de l'ignorance du passé. Mais il n'est peut-être pas moins vain de s'épuiser à comprendre
le passé, si l'on ne sait rien du présent."

(Marc Bloch, *Métier d'historien*)

By an ancient and honourable tradition, which began last year when I
spared you this exercise, the President gives a Presidential Address only
once during his term of office, on retirement. A presidential address in
the summer season is a privileged occasion. Coming at the end of an active
day, it is not the moment for a massive account of research. Rather it is
an occasion when one may indulge with privilege in some directed impres-
sionism, and that is what I propose to do.

I propose to look at the history of biology from the point of view of
the well-known remark by Marc Bloch about the "bonds of intelligibility"
linking past and present in a double sense. The present is incomprehensible without knowledge of the past; but we impoverish our understanding of the past if we are ignorant of the present. No one will be naïve
enough to think that this means reading history backwards, or for that
matter forwards. The fact that historical research is an adventure in self-
discovery does not make it the less objective. I intend to indulge the privilege of the occasion by using some examples with which some of you of
local provenance will be all too familiar. The intelligible links connecting
the past, present and possible future of biology can, I think, be found in
certain commitments persisting and developing through the rich matrix
of beliefs and problems associated with the study of living things. These
throw an interesting light not only on biology as a science but on the
history of scientific thought and on history in general. A clue to the way we
might approach it is given near the beginning of the characteristically
Western scientific enterprise in the comment of Plato's friend, the famous
mathematician Archytas of Tarentum, on the preceding generation of
scientists: "Because they passed excellent judgement on the nature of the
whole world, they were bound to have good judgement on detailed problems." My brief discourse can be regarded as an historical exegesis of
this profound if seemingly paradoxical statement.

Before the general direction of the route to scientific knowledge
had been settled, either in antiquity or in early modern times, two essen-

*Presidential Address given at the Summer Meeting of the British Society for the History of
Science at Oxford on July 1 1966.

tial general questions remained open. It was an open question what kind of world men found themselves inhabiting, and so it was also an open question what kind of means they should use to explore, explain and control it. By deciding on a world about which all applicable propositions must satisfy the condition of non-contradiction, a world of exclusive and discoverable rationality, the Greek philosophers closed for their Western successors all the other routes that before then might have turned out to be the right ones. Anthropology and the comparative history of civilizations have shown that other societies made this commitment and learnt to be scientific systematically only with the Europeanization of the globe. Following this first general decision there are further increasingly particular decisions in the scientific commitment. There may be decisions leading to habits of intellectual and social behaviour that, while not themselves producing any immediate scientific results, may be necessary antecedent conditions for scientific activity. Not all societies make these in the same way: for example ancient society did not, as modern European society did, either use its scientific knowledge technologically on a large scale, or establish through education and communication a philosophical or scientific community with generally agreed aims, methods and criteria of cogency in scientific thought. Within the modern scientific community itself science still proceeds by a series of decisions both about the nature of the world we live in and about means to investigate, explain, control and exploit it. For the student of intellectual behaviour in this field, the doubts, hesitations and unsuccessful theories are as essential a source of data as the successes making up the accepted canon of scientific knowledge.

In this succession of decisions from general to particular we have an invitation to look beneath the surface of particular scientific discoveries for the "bonds of intelligibility" linking past, present and foreseeable future in two ways. There are, first, the historical commitments and conditions that make a given kind of discovery intellectually and socially possible in one period but difficult or impossible in another. The commitments of a period to dominant general beliefs about nature and about science make certain kinds of question appear cogent and give certain kinds of explanation their power to convince, and exclude others, because they establish, in anticipation of any particular research, the kind of world supposed to be there to be discovered. It may be supposed to be a product of divine economy and hence possessing appropriate characteristics of simplicity and harmony, or a system of mechanisms, or a manifestation of probabilities. Such beliefs establish the kind of explanation that will give satisfaction because the supposedly discoverable has been discovered, and they point to what to do in scientific research. Beliefs about nature exercising this influence over the formulation of scientific questions have come in the past from a variety of sources in the social environment, from theology and cosmology as well as analogies with human artefacts which change with the artefacts available. To see how they operate in scientific thinking it is important to make a comparative study which will show how, while cogency may change from one generation to another, each can use its beliefs to add effectively to the sum of valid scientific knowledge. The relevance of historical experience for our imaginations is that it shows us that valid discoveries can be based on beliefs that may seem to us now wholly uncogent.

Secondly, there are the links of logical structure common to different historical situations. Comparative history provides data, beside which a mere study of the present had too restricted a range, for a classification of scientific thinking into logical types differentiated by various related features: by the concept of nature formulating the questions asked, by subject-matter, and by method. It also shows us reasons for the variety of scientific methods. We could dramatize the whole history of scientific thinking from Greek antiquity as a never-ending attempt by mathematics to impose everywhere a simple, homogeneous, postulational, axiomatic system, met by an equally resourceful resistance led by the bio-medical sciences with an excess of experience of the complex, heterogenous enigmas of matter. The simple mathematical programme begun successfully by the Greek geometers was carried to its triumph by classical physics in taking over the whole realm of phenomena that could be analysed into functional relationships with a small number of variables, ideally reduced to two. The discovery that there is such a realm was an insight of genius brought to maturity by the generations from Galileo to Newton. It was essentially the discovery of a realm of simplicity in nature. With some subject-matter, such as mechanics for Galileo, the image of nature might be an open book written in mathematics; scientific research was directed largely towards learning to read the language and soon became a primarily theoretical inquiry carried out in the head. With other subject-matter, such as magnetism and electricity for Galileo's contemporary Gilbert, where theory was still relatively undeveloped, nature was seen as more like a labyrinth or jungle to be explored experimentally with the hands. In whatever subject-matter, the aim of classical physics over its whole range was the discovery and conquest of the realm of mathematical simplicity with few variables, with the suggestion that this was the only realm there is.

The bio-medical resistance had known better since Hippocrates. It was committed to a realm of complexity, and was forced to characterize its problems differently from mathematically simple physics if it was to find answerable questions to put to its subject-matter. It discovered realms of complexity of two kinds, the science of the organized individual and the science of populations, which between them make up biology. The former has used physics and chemistry for its own purposes; the latter in the end has changed the nature of physical science itself.

The biology of the individual can be called, stealing the phrase from Dr. Warren Weaver, the realm of organized complexity. It is distinguished from the realm of simple, universal functions, such as the laws of motion, comprising classical physics because its subject-matter is complex entities each with a specific organization of its simpler components. The biology of the individual is more like engineering than physics, in that each type of living organism is a solution to a specific set of engineering problems—problems of intake and conversion of fuel, locomotion, communication, replication and so on, which it has to solve to survive. This subject-matter has imposed on physiology its characteristic programme: to find out how an organism works by taking it to pieces and trying to put it together again from knowledge of the parts. The programme developed into a search for simpler and more and more general structures and processes from which to reconstruct theoretically not only one complex original but, by means of systematic variations, the whole range of known or possible types of original. This has been carried out by two characteristic methods, both begun by Greek physiologists but made explicit by the genius of their successors in the seventeenth century: the comparative study of the material constituents of living systems, and the modelling of living processes by human artefacts. Since then the history of the biology of the individual has been the discovery by these methods of common structures and processes of increasing generality, from the comparative anatomy and physiology of organs to tissues, cells, protoplasm and so on, to D.N.A. and R.N.A. and the reduction of particular macroscopic physiology to general microscopic chemistry and physics. As everyone knows, this programme is accelerating into the future. How did it start in this explicit modern form and what light do its origins throw on the relation of its commitments to its subject-matter?

We have a clue to both questions in a new "judgement on the nature of the whole world" that can be seen in the history of one **very** important problem in the biology of the individual: the relation of the perceiving organism to the world perceived. How does the living organism receive information about the external world and what is the nature and validity of this information? The best example is the ancient problem of vision, which in Kepler's discovery in 1603/4 of the dioptric mechanism by which the eye produces the retinal image yielded the first major discovery of modern physiology, two decades before Harvey's discovery of the circulation of the blood. Kepler's intellectual moves in making his elementary discovery, with those of Descartes and their immediate successors, illustrate clearly and dramatically how at a given moment a new conception of nature as a whole, which seems to have been impossible before, can give a fresh insight into not just one but a new range of answerable questions.

All the technical knowledge for a solution of the problem of how the

eye operates dioptrically as a receptor of light was available in the geometrical optics and anatomy known to Ptolemy and Galen in second-
century Alexandria. But no Greek saw the problem in this way, let alone
solved it. The barrier seems to have been not technical but conceptual.
The Greeks developed geometrical optics, as part of their profound theoretical commitment to the geometrization of space, as a geometrical theory
of visual perception. Taking the eye as the point of origin of lines of vision,
they developed the science of geometrical perspective as a study of the
visual field seen with direct, reflected and refracted light. They recognized
that the questions of what passed between the eye and the thing seen and
of how it effected sensation were major problems, but they made their
answers serve as immediate explanations of the separate question of visual
perception. All insisted that an eye is a living eye with which we see;
a dead eye was not an eye at all. The most accepted explanation came to
be that vision is effected by images of the object passing into the eye, but
their formulation of the problem did not allow them to see in the eye
itself a subject for optical analysis.

Modern physiological optics began with the brilliant insight of the
medieval Arabic scientist Alhazen that the eye must be treated as an
optical system, and with his attempt to impose on its anatomy a
geometrical-optical model in order to discover how it forms an image. But
Alhazen failed because he again tried to make the dioptric mechanism
give an immediate explanation of visual perception and he was put on the
wrong track by, among other things, the inverted image. Although the eye,
the most complex optical system then known, was assiduously studied by
mathematicians and physiologists following Alhazen, technical advance
still pressed against this inherited conceptual barrier. Kepler finally
succeeded in breaking through it because, as he tells us explicitly, he
came to accept the new judgement that nature, including the human
body, is effectively a system of mechanisms. In the light of this he could
make the strategic decision to separate the physical and physiological problem of the eye's dioptric mechanism from the other, quite distinct questions
of how images effect vision and of what visual perceptions we do in fact
have. He restricted the problem in the first place only to that of discovering
how the eye operates as an optical instrument like any other, in fact as a
dead eye. He solved it by seeing that a well-known model gave the answer:
optically the dead eye was a *camera obscura* with a lens. Having done this
and dismissed the puzzle of the inverted image with a simple rule: for
top read bottom and for right read left, he was in a position to look at
the other questions of vision with a living eye in a new way.

The strategic commitment by Kepler and Descartes and their contemporaries to a mechanistic hypothesis of nature in some form opened
new worlds for discovery in the biology of the individual organism for
two reasons. In the first place, encouraged as Descartes tells us himself

by the various kinds of machines by that time working in Europe and by the evident success of scientific mechanics, the mechanistic hypothesis ruthlessly committed physiology, in advance of making any observations, to asking only one kind of question. This defined the immediate problems to be solved and gave a programme for research in the realm of organized complexity: in a world assumed to be simply a system of mechanisms this was to look for the particular mechanisms concerned in each case—in other words to treat the whole living body as a dead machine. It also made explicit the method foreshadowed in one of Leonardo da Vinci's most pregnant insights: to understand is to construct. The seventeenth-century physiologists became the first masters of the engineering approach to their problems by showing how to use a "relational" model, constructed with formal correspondence to the process modelled but without identity of parts, as a method of antecedent theoretical analysis suggesting new questions to guide experimentation. In this way they used models of the eye, ear, heart, muscles and bones, and other structures, some helpful and others mistaken. Success in the search for mechanisms has depended on the contemporary knowledge by which they have to be characterized, but this search in the seventeenth century both established for physiology its continuing programme of reduction to simpler and more general physico-chemical processes, and gave it a clear view of its technical frontier at any moment.

As might be expected, this ruthless mechanistic commitment to only one kind of question also brought into focus other kinds of question pointing to other frontiers. The Greek formulation of the problem of vision (and indeed of other problems accepting organisms as unanalysed entities) had concealed these. The immediate effect of Kepler's identification and solution of one limited problem of visual machinery was to stimulate strictly physiological analysis of the further mechanisms of the eye in vision, followed by the similar research which has never ceased into hearing and the other senses, and into the nerves as conductors and the brain as co-ordinator of sensory information and of behaviour. But it was soon recognized (although the point gets lost from time to time in physiology) that the discovery simply of mechanisms cannot answer the ancient question of how physical motions of any kind can cause sensations in a living body, as distinct from merely other physical motions as in a dead one. A perceiving organism cannot be reduced logically to a homogeneous set of primitive postulates. Recognizing this, Descartes and Locke drew attention to a new field of empirical inquiry by exchanging the question of how sensations are caused for the different, answerable question of discovering the physical and physiological clues by which the organism makes its distinctions of sensation and perception. It was soon recognized also that the psychology of perception can be studied as another empirical field independently both of current physical theories of these

clues and of the body's apparatus, and of the philosophical, logical problem of causation. So the mechanistic hypothesis itself showed that these
different questions should be liberated from the tyranny of each other
and that in liberty they could create new sciences.

There is a parallel to this in the history of painting. The Italian
quattrocento discovered a new visual world by an explicit use of the Greek
theory of geometrical perspective; but, as Leonardo tells us, the limitation
soon found in a purely geometrical analysis of space itself forced artists
to explore other clues, such as tone and shadow, to represent distance and
scaling. But the creative geniuses who design a programme often see a
need for liberty and variety that becomes lost in the enthusiasm of their
immediate successors. It took a further revolution to open painting to a
free exploration of visual clues by Turner and the French impressionists.
The scientific study of the senses has been liberated in practice from the
largely speculative programme of reduction on the naïve model of physics
partly by experience of the variety of its own subject-matter, and partly
by a more experienced understanding of the physical sciences themselves.

We know now that the passive, camera-like features of the eye
which took such intellectual efforts to discover raise the least interesting
problems of vision. Biochemistry, quantum physics, information theory
and the invention of new physical artefacts have given us a succession
of more likely models of eye and brain: a television camera, a scanning
system with a computer, a system for feeding coded neural information
to the brain which decodes it in the form of visual perceptions. The comparative study of animal sensory systems has shown us a fascinating variety
of solutions to these engineering problems. As the Oxford physiologist
Thomas Willis, as well as the Oxford philosopher John Locke, who also
had a medical training, foresaw in the seventeenth century, these, and
such studies as those of the congenitally blind and of the effects of sensory
deprivation on spacemen and desert hermits, show us the variety of forms
in which our fellow creatures can perceive our common world. Experiments with abnormal perception produced by drugs have shown us that
perception of space is linked with that of time and that both seem to be
correlated with rates of metabolism. We create as it were our own space-
time co-ordinates as a spider creates its web. Time speeds by in childhood
but slows down as our metabolic rate decreases. Drugs stimulating the
metabolic rate make time go faster and space expand so that handwriting
becomes larger; tranquillizers have the opposite effect and make spiders
spin smaller webs. All these physiological studies and many others are leading us to a model showing how the body's machinery decodes its physical
clues and how we may control its operations. But recent work on colour
mixtures has shown us also that too successful a theory of the physical
clues can lose for us phenomena that depend not only on such things as
wave-lengths and intensities but also on what we expect to see. Possibly

the most important result of all from the experimental study of perception has been to show that the living organism, animal as well as human, is not a mere passive recipient of stimuli but actively looks for patterns and meaning in these clues and actively creates from them the meaningful world it perceives.

We create a large part of our own mental ecology, perceptual as well as conceptual, but we can control our belief in it by common, empirical tests. We can model much of this situation with machines and we can construct machines to extend the range of our senses in precision and in detecting new kinds of physical clue. But in the material being modelled we meet the obvious heterogeneity: we do not simply decode information, we know it. In creating the conceptual ecology in which we make our decisions about science and about ourselves as individuals and in society, it would be an arbitrary break in scientific empiricism to exclude from the realm of organized complexity something so obvious as these irreducibly heterogeneous items which are our individual selves.

The second realm of biology, the science of populations, can be distinguished from the first as the realm of unorganized complexity. It is distinguished in logical structure by its method of explaining its subject-matter as a product of statistical mechanisms. To biology it has offered above all a method of explaining the development of ordered complexity by statistical mechanisms operating through time. The history of this approach to the science of living organisms through theories of evolution and genetics is familiar in outline and its present use in biology needs no comment. But if we look briefly at its intellectual origins we will see again how a structural change in far more general beliefs and activities can open a new world of strictly scientific questions. The essence of the change was a new use of time to account for both natural and social order and in consequence a new conception of order itself.

The older view of order inherited from the Greek geometers was essentially spatial. Aristotle thought as a geometer in relating the individual behaviour of the parts to their position in the whole both in living organisms and in the organization of the whole universe. When in the seventeenth century the whole of nature, living and dead, was made into a system of mechanisms, it was still left, for example by Newton, in this essential respect the same: it had been created in a state of stable harmony and so would remain as long as it lasted. The mechanistic philosophers, political as well as natural, saw in the existing order of nature and of the state conditions of stable equilibrium between mechanical forces which had in themselves no power to bring about change. In a famous essay, "On the increase of the habitable earth", Linnaeus applied this belief in the perpetual stability and pre-established harmony, not simply of the laws of nature but of their detailed products, even to the populations of human beings and of the different species of animals and plants found on the earth.

The view of nature and society as in some sense "daughters of time" is as old as Plato and Democritus, and in the seventeenth and eighteenth centuries it was renewed in the study both of human history and of geological strata and their fossils as documents for the history of the earth and of the life on it. The essentially new idea was to apply the mechanistic model to the biology of populations in a new form, making the order of nature and society a succession of states not of pre-established harmony but of statistical equilibrium developing through time. Technically this meant discovering how to quantify a realm of statistical regularities already recognized in antiquity by Egyptian, Assyrian and Hippocratic physicians in their attempts to forecast, at some personal as well as professional risk, the courses of diseases from collections of symptoms frequently but not always associated. The mathematical techniques were first developed in the social sciences. Technically the mathematics of increasingly complex phenomena becomes more difficult if they are treated, as in classical physics, in terms of numerous simultaneous equations, but it becomes easier again if the phenomena are treated as statistical problems of populations. In the sixteenth century the Venetian Republic employed a mathematician to make the actuarial calculations for insuring ships, and by the eighteenth century the techniques were good enough for Voltaire to add to his fortune by speculating in safety on the risks taken by his fellow men. Techniques of scientific demography developed in the same period gave Malthus the basis of his *Essay on Population* (1798), and other techniques made possible Condorcet's analysis of collective political and judicial decisions. But the impulse towards the new model was not simply technical; it was a new conception of nature and society. Descartes had envisaged the construction of machines that could reproduce themselves without outside intervention and saw no difference between these and the natural machines we call alive. In the middle of the eighteenth century the French mathematician and geneticist Maupertius worked out a formal hypothesis showing how increasing diversity, and increasing order in the sense of complexity and degree of adaptation, would be generated in time automatically from unordered inherited variations by the operation of a purely statistical selection through birth, competition and survival. He concluded:

"Cannot we explain in this way how, from only two individuals, the multiplication of the most diverse species could follow? They would owe their first origin only to chance products in which the elementary particles would not keep the order they had in the father and mother animal: each degree of error would make a new species, and from the force of repeated deviations would come the infinite diversity of animals that we see today, which will perhaps go on increasing with the passage of time but to which each century will add only an imperceptible increment" (*Système de la nature*, 1751).

Darwin and Wallace used Malthus's ratio of survival to birth to give factual body to this piece of speculation, but they were able to work with an established commitment to a realm in which it was natural to look for statistical mechanisms as the explanations of economic, social and biological change.

It is no accident that physical science was developing at the same time a statistical conception of the constituents of nature as a whole. In the last decade it has decoded the material link between the two realms of biology. In doing so the spiral of discovery has found that in filling space with repetitive units, geometrical necessity has imposed on the components of viruses and genes the symmetries of the regular solids out of which Plato constructed the five elements and which Kepler found in snowflakes, and the helices studied long ago by Archimedes and Descartes.

I have given you an impressionistic picture of links between some of the past and present commitments of biology. I want to make some suggestions for the future about the relevance of the past and present of biology and the study of biology for human history and the study of history. We are concerned with the decisions, a few large ones and literally millions of smaller ones, that have given our tradition its direction and kept it going through changing circumstances. It might be a useful exercise to look at these in the manner of the eighteenth-century philosophical historians as an aspect of human ecology. Historical and biological research have a large common area of subject-matter and of method. The comparative method pioneered by Aristotle in the study of the organization of states as well as of animal bodies is essential to both. The study of populations is one realm of history as of biology. The search for statistical regularities long practised separately by economists and by ecologists and geneticists, and the use of models and of the comparative method applied to the whole realm of living organisms, together make a common area for research into the past and present of the human race that has only just begun. The bio-medical and the environmental sciences provide essential knowledge of the physical conditions of history, even of political history which is strangely illuminated by such recent work as that on the effects of crowding and isolation on the social behaviour of animals. History with archaeology provides the only material available for the study of human biology in time. The written documents go back over 3,000 years; the parallel anthropological and archaeological evidence extends over a much longer period. Even though this common ground does not include those unique events and irreducible individual decisions that form a large part of the realm of human behaviour, it could have an interesting yield for investment in the immediate future of history and of biology.

More relevant to the historical commitments of biology and of science in general is the mental rather than the physical ecology of human society —especially the mental ecology of innovation and resistance to it within which these decisions are made. History shows us certain constants of intellectual and practical behaviour that can help to explain why ideas and opportunities and certain kinds of tension release creative energy in some circumstances and the reverse in others. Western history has made its mark, as we are told often enough, as a search for control over our physical and mental environment that becomes daily more efficient. The aims of both magic and philosophy have become transposed into science. In some sciences control by highly developed theory has now become so efficient that it may make discoveries more and more difficult, and certainly makes them more and more expensive. This contains a degree of warning for the programming of research, even the most imaginative, because inevitably we plan from past success, which may have paid its main dividends. It also contains a warning both for our understanding of our own history as we watch one belief about nature succeed another, and for our understanding of neighbours with different traditions forced increasingly on our overcrowded globe to endure our enthusiasms. Nature, as Pascal said, remains in herself always unchanged; but nobody knows what she is except whatever it is that falsifies our hypotheses. She also reveals herself, or appears to reveal herself, differently to different ages, societies and individuals. Our contacts with non-Western societies bring not only science, medicine and technology; they bring to them new ways of thinking about themselves, about cosmology, about the value of life, about the meaning of health and disease. Our legitimate pride in the efficiency of our validly established knowledge and our control over life and death can make us insensitive to other kinds of judgement about why life is worth living. This process has parallels in the contacts of confidently sophisticated civilizations with their neighbours in the past. It happened to the West in reverse in the early Middle Ages. So my final suggestion is that we should pay more systematic attention to this aspect of comparative history, for our own benefit as well as that of our neighbours. It is accepted that within the proper field of the history of science we should balance the study of the internal development of different sciences by the study of the scientific activity as a whole in the context of societies and periods: treating history as the study of human behaviour, it would be equally illuminating to compare this evidence with that from societies whose attitudes to nature we should not classify as scientific.

BIBLIOGRAPHY

The subject of this paper has been developed in detail in my forthcoming *Styles* ...; see also my "Contingent expectation and uncertain choice" in *The Rational Arts of Living*, ed.   A.C. Crombie and N.G. Siraisi (*Smith College Studies in History*, vol. 50; Northampton, Mass., 1987).

James Bonner, "The next new biology", *Plant Science Bulletin*, xi (1965), No. 3.

John Cairns, "The bacterial chromosome", *Scientific American*, ccxiv (January 1966).

F. M. Cornford, *Plato's Cosmology. The Timaeus of Plato translated with a running commentary* (London, 1937).

F. H. C. Crick, "The genetic code", *Scientific American*, ccvii (October 1962).

A. C. Crombie, "P. L. M. de Maupertuis, F.R.S. (1698-1759), précurseur du transformisme", *Revue de synthèse*, lxxviii (1957).
—— (editor) *Scientific change. Historical studies in the intellectual, social and technical conditions for scientific discovery and technical invention, from antiquity to the present* (London and New York, 1963).
—— "The study of the senses in renaissance science", *Proceedings of the Tenth International Congress of the History of Science: Ithaca, New York, 1962*, i (Paris, 1964).
—— "Kepler: de modo visionis", in *Mélanges Alexandre Koyré*, ed. I. B. Cohen and R. Taton, ii (Paris, 1964).
—— "Early concepts of the senses and the mind", *Scientific American*, ccx (May 1964).
—— "The mechanistic hypothesis and the scientific study of vision: some optical ideas as a background to the invention of the microscope", *Historical Aspects of Microscopy* (*Proceedings of the Royal Microscopical Society*, ii, 1967.
Charles Darwin and Alfred Russel Wallace, *Evolution by Natural Selection*, with a foreword by Sir Gavin de Beer (Cambridge, 1958).
Descartes, *Traité de l'homme* (1633), *La Dioptrique* (1637), *Principes de la philosophie* (1644).
D. E. C. Eversley and D. V. Glass (editors), *Population in History. Essays in historical demography* (London, 1965).
J. T. Fraser (editor), *The Voices of Time* (New York, 1966).
Kathleen Freeman, *Ancilla to the Pre-Socratic Philosophers*. A complete translation of the fragments in Diels, *Die Fragmente der Vorsokratiker* (Oxford, 1948).
B. Glass, O. Temkin and W. L. Straus, Jr. (editors), *Forerunners of Darwin: 1745-1859* (Baltimore, 1958).
R. L. Gregory, *Eye and Brain* (London, 1966).
Robert Hooke, "Lectures and discourses of earthquakes, and subterraneous eruptions", *Posthumous Works*, ed. R. Waller (London, 1705).
R. W. Horne, "The structure of viruses", *Scientific American*, ccviii (January 1963).
Howard Mumford Jones and I. Bernard Cohen (editors), *Science before Darwin. A nineteenth-century anthology* (London, 1963).
Johannes Kepler, *The Six-cornered Snowflake*, translated by C. Hardie with essays by B. J. Mason and L. L. Whyte (Oxford, 1966).
R. Labat, *Traité akkadien de diagnostics et pronostics médicaux*, transcr. et trad. par R. Labat, 2 tom. (Collection de travaux, Académie international d'histoire des sciences vii, Paris, 1951).
Edwin H. Land, "Experiments in color vision", *Scientific American*, cc (May 1959).
Gustave Lefebvre, *Essai sur la médecine égyptienne de l'époque pharaonique* (Paris, 1956).
Leonardo da Vinci, *Literary Works*, ed. and trans. J. P. and I. A. Richter, 2nd ed., 2 vols. (Oxford, 1939).
—— *The Notebooks*, ed. and trans. E. MacCurdy, 2 vols. (London, 1938).
Linnaeus, "On the increase of the habitable earth", in *Select Dissertations from the Amoenitates Academicae. A supplement to Mr. Stillingfleet's Tracts relating to Natural History*, translated by the Rev. F. J. Brand, 2 vols. (London, 1781). I owe this reference to Dr. R. C. Olby.
P. L. M. de Maupertuis, *Oeuvres*, 2 vols. (Lyon, 1756).
M. W. Nirenberg, "The genetic code. II", *Scientific American*, ccviii (March 1963).
Pascal, *Préface pour le traité du vide* (1647).
Thomas Pennant, *Tour on the Continent 1765*, ed. with notes by G. R. de Beer (London, 1948).
M. von Senden, *Space and Sight. The perception of space and shape in the congenitally blind before and after operation* (London, 1960).
Norman Kemp Smith, *New Studies in the Philosophy of Descartes* (London, 1952).
Benj. Stillingfleet, *Miscellaneous Tracts relating to Natural History, Husbandry, and Physick* (London, 1775).
W. H. Thorpe and O. L. Zangwill (editors), *Current Problems in Animal Behaviour* (Cambridge, 1963).
A. Tenenti, *Naufrages, corsaires et assurances maritimes à Venice, 1592-1609* (Ports, routes, traffics viii, Paris, 1959).
W. Warren Weaver, "Science and complexity", *Rockefeller Annual Report* (New York, 1958).
Robert M. Young, "Scholarship and the history of the behavioural sciences", *History of Science*, ed. A. C. Crombie and M. A. Hoskin, v (1966).

The substance of this address was given at the General Session of the Federation of American Societies for Experimental Biology at its Fiftieth Annual Meeting, at Atlantic City, N.J., on 13 April 1966, and was published in the *Federation Proceedings* (1966).

18

WHAT IS THE HISTORY OF SCIENCE?

The history of thought has been difficult to establish as a legitimate university study in its proper identity, distinct from the peculiar interests alike of unhistorical philosophers and of unphilosophical political historians who dominate history departments, especially in Britain. The history of scientific thought has had to distinguish itself also on a third front from the particular interest of scientists (like that of practising politicians) in the origin of themselves. But it has not been all a matter of existence on unsympathetic or indifferent academic frontiers. Some of the best work on the history of scientific as of other thought has been done not surprisingly by historians of philosophy, and also by historians of literature. Historians of religion and of law have justly located the intellectual centre of their studies in the history of theology and of legal theory. The history of science has been a congenial interest of intellectually sensitive scientists. The history of thought including scientific thought is then a proper part of historical studies as a whole, of which the proper subject is the totality of human experience in all its variety on this spinning globe. With what sort of questions are we concerned in the history of science, in its classical form as the history of scientific thought studied in its context of the history of ideas, of mentalities, of the intellectual and moral commitments, expectations, motivations and achievements of men in societies of many kinds?[1]

1. This paper is based on my forthcoming book, *Styles of Scientific Thinking in the European Tradition* (to be published by Duckworth, London) which contains full documentation and bibliography; cf. also my 'Historical commitments of European science', *Annali dell' Istituto e Museo di Storia della Scienze di Firenze* **vii** (2) (1982), 29–51. The indispensable and only adequately informative single guide to the historiography of science, medicine and technology and its sources is the *Isis Cumulative Bibliography*, ed. M. Whitrow and J. Neu, 5 vols. (London, 1971–80), to which may be added the extensive current bibliographies published in the journal *Isis*, the *Dictionary of Scientific Biography*, ed. C. C. Gillispie, 16 vols. (New York, 1970–80), and the regular reviews of problems and sources in the journal *History of Science*.

Since Greek antiquity the science of nature, *physiologia, scientia* or *philosophia naturalis*, in its whole range from the mathematical to the medical sciences, has been identified as a philosophical approach to nature effectively competent to explore and to solve problems of two related kinds. The first were those presented by particular natural phenomena; the second were those arising in the development of general systems of explanation. An essential criterion for accepting a general system was that it could incorporate the solution of particular problems. In this sense the Greeks might be said to have invented the notion of a problem as distinct from a doctrine. They found the methods of the Babylonians and Egyptians for example in astronomy defective because they lacked *physiologia*: they were techniques without related general explanations.[2] The Greeks then established a scientific tradition with a recognisable identity both in the selection of acceptable questions for scientific inquiry and in the kinds of answer accepted as satisfactory. They introduced the fundamental conception of a scientific system of the world, defined by an exclusively rational causation and entailing a logic of decision and proof. Can we assume that the categories of thought expressed in language have remained sufficiently stable from their time and from their society to ours for meaningful historical investigation of ancient or medieval or other periods of thought to be possible? Can we assume more generally that likewise there is sufficient in common among all mankind for us to be able to understand the intellectual and moral life of any other society or culture historically remote from our own. The whole of historical and anthropological scholarship rests on just that assumption.

But we do not have to look far below the surface of scientific inquiry and its immediate results to see that the whole process has gone on in a context of intellectual and moral commitments, expectations and dispositions that can vary greatly in different societies, periods and groups and also among contemporary individuals. These might entail beliefs about the nature of the world and its knowability; conceptions of scientific method and the organisation of scientific inquiry; expectations of desirable or undesirable ends with consequent motivations; a disposition to master or to accept mastery by events, to change or to resist change and innovation. The nature of the historical inquiry is an invitation to search behind particular scientific results and theories for the antecedent and concomitant intellectual and social and material conditions and commitments that made them possible, and others perhaps impossible, in one historical context, and the reverse in another historical context. Beliefs of varying generality about the nature of the world have affected both the perception of particular problems and the acceptability of different kinds of solution. We can get much enlightenment if we ask, when we read a text, to what questions the author was giving an

---

2. Cf. Adrastus reported by Theon of Smyrna, *Expositio rerum mathematicarum ad legendum Platonem utilium*, recensuit E. Hiller (Leipzig, 1878), pp. 177–8.

answer. Experiment itself may have different meanings and intentions in different contexts. Conceptions of disease as opposed to health have sent medical inquiry and therapeutic practice in diverse directions explicable only within their context, just as acceptance or not of suffering and death whether from disease or by martyrdom or victimisation has depended fundamentally upon beliefs about human nature and the value and end of human life. It required a major philosophical change for mathematical physicists to detach themselves in the seventeenth century from the established Aristotelian conception of cause in order to formulate what became Newton's conception of force, with all its consequences. Belief in providential design made a statistical conception of the economy of nature unacceptable in biology, until Charles Darwin presented his arguments in the wake of the statistical analysis of human economics which provided the persuasive analogy.

Dominant intellectual commitments have made certain kinds of question appear cogent and have given certain kinds of explanation their power to convince, and have excluded others, because they have established, antecedent to any particular research, the kind of world that was supposed to exist and the appropriate methods of inquiry. They established in advance the kind of explanation that would give satisfaction when the supposedly discoverable had been discovered. In this process the cogency of such theoretical worlds might change from generation to generation or from society to society, as each nevertheless added to enduringly valid scientific knowledge. So we are dealing at once with a process of accumulation of objectively certifiable particular knowledge; with the development of general theories which may change; and always with people and their vision. In this way the history of scientific ideas becomes intimately connected, at a highly sophisticated level, with the history of mentalities. The history of ideas and of mentalities is after all the history of people thinking, and when we say that ideas change we mean that people changed their ideas, whether by their own thinking or by exposure to that of others in whatever their circumstances might have been. The history of science can be treated then as a kind of comparative intellectual anthropology, extended into the past. But it would be naive in so treating it to fall into the kind of sociological relativism that fails to distinguish the specific historical identity of science as a problem-solving activity, from a general history of ideas or ideology lacking its specific modes of self-correction and criteria of acceptability. A Hermetic philosopher like Robert Fludd approached the subject of musical or mathematical harmony or of the circulation of the blood with questions different in kind from those of Mersenne and Kepler or of William Harvey, despite certain overlaps in ideology. Galileo's questions about the mathematics of motion were aimed at the solution of problems not held to be fundamental by contemporary scholastic Aristotelians. The perception of the scientifically soluble was of the essence of the intellectual behaviour by which in our comparative historical anthropology we may define the scientific tradition within the context of the more general tradition of Western culture, of which it has always formed a characteristic part.[3] When Galileo insisted that one cannot cheat nature, however much one may cheat ones fellow men, he was defining the identity at once of nature and of natural science.[4] For it was impossible to solve problems in nature whether theoretical or practical by magic or by commercial bargaining or political convenience or chicanery. This was surely a therapeutic experience for mankind, and for historians it points to the most fundamental of truths: the fragility as well as the strength of men and women in the face of problems that are not just intellectual but moral.

We are concerned then in the history of science with a number of different if related questions. The Western scientific movement has been the history of men's relations with nature and mankind as perceiver and knower and agent mediated through particular visions of existence from which the arts and sciences have followed. Historical questions arise at different levels, some given by nature, some made by man. A comprehensive investigation would include historical ecology, the reconstruction of the physical and biological environment and of what men made of it. Essential questions at the level of culture are those of motivation and opportunity, both social and material. At the level of scientific thinking, both in the perception and solution of problems within the technical possibilities available, and in the justification of the enterprise whether intellectual or moral or practical, the history of science has been the history of argument. Scientific argument forms the substance of the scientific movement, a discourse using experiment and observation, instruments and apparatus, but with significance always in relation to the argument. It is illuminating to look at the varieties of scientific argument. We may distinguish six different styles of scientific inquiry and demonstration, diversified by the subject-matters being investigated, by general conceptions of nature, by presuppositions about scientific validity, and by scientific experience of the interaction of programmes with realisations. Three styles or methods were developed in the investigation of individual regularities, three in the investigation of the regularities of populations ordered in space and in time. Each arose within a context in which an assembly of cognate subject-matters was united under a common form of argument. Thus the simple method of postulation exemplified by the Greek mathematical sciences originated within the common Greek search for the rational

3. The alternative catastrophic view denying that there is such a scientific tradition seems to be exemplified by my friend Paolo Rossi, so far as one can judge from his comments upon myself, most recently (though without much discrimination) within a gang of four in the distinguished company of Ernst Cassirer, J. H. Randall and Alexandre Koyré: see his 'Aristotelici e "moderni": le ipotesi e la natura' in *Aristotelismo veneto e scienza moderna*, a cura di L. Olivieri, i (Padova, 1983), 125–9, published in English in *Annali* . . . (as above n. 1), **vii** (1) (1982), 3–7.

4. Galileo, *Le mecaniche*, ed. A. Favaro (*Le opere*, Vol. ii, nuova ristampa, Firenze, 1968), p. 155; cf. his *Lettera a Madama Cristina di Lorena* (1615; *ibid.*, Vol. v), pp. 326–7.

principles alike of the perceptible world and of human reasoning. The exploration by controlled experiment and observation and measurement, required by the scientific search for principles in more complex subject-matters, evolved a form of argument by analysis and synthesis that came to be applied to the most diverse subjects from chemistry and biology to the study of human society and language. Hypothetical modelling, which was developed in a sophisticated form in application to early modern perspective painting and engineering, became likewise an instrument of analysis for the study of society as for physiology and physics. Taxonomy emerged for the logical ordering of almost all subject-matters. The statistical and probabilistic analysis of expectation and choice again took the same forms whether in estimating the outcome of a disease, a legal process, a commercial enterprise, natural selection, or the reasonableness of assent to a scientific theory. The method of historical derivation was applied first to languages and more generally to human cultures, and afterwards to geological history and the the evolution of living organisms. Clearly all this scientific diversity can be understood only within the diversity of thought in the whole historical context.

Almost as important as demonstrations or proofs in the history of the scientific movement have been the arguments aimed at persuasion. The use of such arguments to reinforce or create the power of ideas to convince, especially when the ideas were new and the audience uncertain or unsympathetic, is a somewhat neglected phenomenon in the history of science. Yet it was far from neglected by some of the greatest innovators. Both Galileo and Descartes were masters of the current rhetorical techniques of persuasion. Galileo devoted at least as much energy to trying to establish the identity of natural science within contemporary intellectual culture as to solving particular physical problems. He conducted all his controversies at two levels: one concerned with the physical problem in question; the other concerned with an eloquent advocacy of his conception of natural science as a problem-solving enterprise distinct from the philosophical or theological exegesis of authorities, from a literary excercise, from a commercial or legal negotiation, from magic, and so on. His test of a general explanation was its ability to incorporate the solution of particular problems. Descartes argued likewise at two levels, and this indeed was a general necessity in a period when the nature of the contemporary scientific movement was still to some extent an open question and when its methods and accepted styles of reasoning were still being established. Charles Lyell after legal training practised as a barrister, and like a skilful barrister he set out to present his uniformitarian conception of geology as the only acceptable one and to discredit its hitherto accepted catastrophic rival. Charles Darwin again set out his argument in the *Origin of Species* for evolution by natural selection like a legal brief: marshalling the evidence, demolishing rival explanations, proposing his own solution, raising difficulties against it, meeting them one by one, and finally concluding that his was the only plausible explanation that could account for all the various categories of fact that had to be considered. Persuasion has obviously been aimed at the diffusion of scientific ideas, both at the sophisticated level of the scientific community and also among the general public.

The absorption of scientific ideas into a society and their interactions with accepted beliefs at various levels of education are questions of great interest for the history of science, of ideas and of mentalities alike. For an adequate historical anthropology of science, for a true history of the experience of nature mediated through the specific vision and commitments of a particular society, we need to remind ourselves that many of the categories in which we in the West understand both man and nature now, the intellectual and moral and material satisfactions that we demand and the methods by which we get them, have never been accepted by all mankind and have become ours only through a long process of orientation and reorientation. Moreover scientific visions have always been matched in Western societies by other visions of existence offering quite different satisfactions and explanations with quite different purposes. The dominant element in Western culture remained for long after the seventeenth-century theology. This historical problem is to see how these different interests and categories affected and were affected by the sciences of nature found in the same ambience. We are concerned with the styles and methods at once of opposition, of accommodation and finally perhaps of adoption and use, having much in common in their intellectual and social dimensions whether in response to a new challenge from science or from theology. There are illuminating parallels between the diffusion through a society of scientific and of theological ideas. What must not be forgotten in tracing that diffusion into popular scientific or religious beliefs or practices is the origin of those ideas, usually at the highest and most original and perhaps most difficult level of thinking, within the capacity only of the most highly educated persons. The documentary sources at that level remain an essential part of our historical data.

Much light can be thrown upon the intellectual orientations of European society by its changing apprehensions of its own past and the programmes that have been projected therefrom. We should see the historiography of science, presenting these apprehensions of the history of Western intellectual culture, as an integral part of the scientific movement itself. When philosophers pictured themselves in the twelfth century as dwarfs standing on the shoulders of the giants of Greece and Rome, or like Hugh of St. Victor and Roger Bacon traced the restoration of the divine likeness in fallen man by the restoration of the arts and sciences, or looked in the fifteenth and sixteenth centuries for guidance from a Hermetic wisdom of supposedly Mosaic antiquity, or insisted in the seventeenth century that they were doing something entirely new, they were all making evaluations of the past which entailed programmes for future action. The same applied to the evaluative use of the historical terms dark or middle ages, renaissance, reformation, new philosophy, enlightenment and so on. These may tell us more about the periods in which they were invented than about those to which they refer. The historiography of science developed during the sixteenth to the eighteenth centuries in the same evaluative style as part of a more general historical investigation, initiated especially by Jean Bodin and other contemporary French historians, into the history of civilisation. Their method was to proceed by comparisons among present and past civilisations to a diagnosis of the common causes of their origin, progress, regress or diversification. It became a taxonomy, involving the reconstruction of past human societies, for which their arts and sciences were primary evidence. Francis Bacon and Leibniz again used this method to establish a programme for the historiography of science and technology that would investigate historical causation and provide a guide for present and future action and therapy. The programme assumed that causation was the proper object of the study of human as of natural history, and that it was possible to discover constants of behaviour in human individuals and societies, as it was in natural things. The models were Thucydides and medicine. Thus history had a method by which both to reconstruct the past and to predict the possible future.

This philosophical programme provided an enduring motive for the study of the history of the sciences and arts. Daniel Leclerc in tracing methods and discoveries offered his *Histoire de la médecine, ou l'on void l'origine et le progrès de cet art* as an attempt to '*entrer dans l'esprit de chaque siècle, et de chaque auteur*' (Avertissement; 1696). It was Fontenelle who chiefly promoted what he called in his *Éloge* of Leibniz '*l'histoire de l'esprit humain*' as philosophical history, centred upon the sciences and arts, that would discover the causes of their progress and guide the future. In this style the history of science was developed as a learned discipline especially in France. It is exemplified by d'Alembert's 'Discours préliminaire' (1751) and numerous articles by various authors in the *Encyclopédie*; by Jean–Étienne Montucla's magisterial *Histoire des mathématiques* (1758); by Jean-Sylvain Bailly's beguiling volumes on the history of ancient, modern and oriental astronomy (1775–87); and by the end of the century by a flood of specialised histories of all the main sciences and arts of Europe with some discussion also of those elsewhere. French philosophical historians in the eighteenth century thus integrated the philosophical history of science into the general intellectual culture of Europe and into its historical consciousness both of itself and of its context in the wider world. The history of science became at the same time less programmatically and more factually part of the professional historiographical movement. The historical school at Göttingen above all set out to apply the established methods of classical and biblical philology and diplomatic to produce a general history of human experience, which would display 'the connectedness of the materials of world history',[5]

5. August Ludwig Schlözer, *Weltgeschichte nach ihren Haupt-Theilen im Auszug und Zusammenhang*, Vol. i (Göttingen, 1785), pp. 73–7, cf. p. 120; H. Butterfield, *Man on his Past* (Cambridge, 1955), pp. 6ff.

including in its ample vision the history of governments and religions, of the arts and sciences, and so on. It was a vision and a strategy that came to be distorted, narrowed and clouded during the nineteenth century by the rise to academic dominance of political and constitutional historians who separated what they called history from its context in all other aspects of human experience. In these circumstances the history of science, art, philosophy, religion and of thought in general came to be treated as of merely specialist interest.

The eighteenth-century conception of the history of mankind as essentially the history of intellectual culture, despite the diverse forms given it by Italian, French, Scottish and German thinkers, was no doubt too simple. We may wish to envisage the history of mankind more empirically as the history of the beliefs, memories, habits, dispositions, actions and so forth of men and women in societies and circumstances of many different kinds. But from the virtual exclusion from academically accepted historiography of that most characteristically human experience which is the history of thought, the study of history received a gross impoverishment from which it still suffers. The ordinary type of academic historian reared in political history and saddled with its negative prejudices, which become a vested interest, has acquired little knowledge of the history of thought and its sources belonging to the history of a period, little competence in the analytical disciplines of philosophy, science, economics and so on, and little concern for these deficiencies. Encouraging moves into intellectual and social history too often end for the same reason in presenting simply impressions, a collage of agreeable evocations of atmosphere without analysis and without relation to the hard thought that is the creative force in any intellectual culture. Likewise to restrict the study of the history of science or of any other history to the recent past, on grounds of relevance to our present condition, would grossly impoverish our knowledge of the variety of human expectations and experiences over diverse periods and societies. It would emasculate the comparisons essential to historical enlightenment, and very often the most recent history is the least relevant to our understanding of the problems of the present.

Historiography is a dialogue between an interrogating present and an interrogated past. Separated forever from that living past, the interrogating historian in following his proper art can reconstruct only from what he sees and understands. Clearly he must be competent to understand the sources which define the history of each form of human experience and place it in its context. The context will be wider and may be less technically demanding than the scientific experience of a society, but it would be as absurd for that (or any other) reason to envisage the history of science as the social history of the context without scientific content, as it would be to envisage the history of music without music or the history of visual art without painting and its techniques, or the history of parliament without constitutional law. The requirements of technical competence both scientific and linguistic, and of historical sensitivity and competence of many kinds, apply equally to the classical history of scientific thought and to the programmes recently promoted in the diverse schemata of philosophers; to the vagaries not without some intellectual insights of French structuralists; to the assertive prescriptions derived largely in the Anglo-Saxon world from sociology; to the naively parochial dogmatism of the neo-Puritan, neo-Marxist persuasion, and to presentations of history arising out of any other ideology. The test is not prescription, whatever its pretensions, but performance in true and sensible scholarship. To see the history of science, medicine and technology through the eyes of political interest or popular belief is to classify it contrary to the essential nature of its subject-matter. To see it as a programme calculated for political effect is to classify it outside scholarship altogether.

The questions put to the sources may change with knowledge and viewpoint as one questioning present is succeeded by another. Each may offer fresh insights. We are alerted to the past by experience of the present. Medieval and early modern Europeans set out to recover the sources of ancient thought first because these provided the essential materials for their own treatment of scientific and philosophical problems and because the ancient experience seemed to offer a guide for their own intellectual development. Historical interest then came to focus on those aspects of earlier science that fitted most naturally into the sequence of solutions of problems that generated the accepted body of current scientific knowledge. During the eighteenth and nineteenth centuries progress in the present directed attention to progress in the past and to the conditions that made it possible. New contemporary experiences in our century as earlier have brought into focus hitherto unregarded counterparts in the past. The growing power of probabilistic thinking within contemporary science and logic for example has promoted a fresh look into the intellectual contexts in which it can be seen that concepts of probability have been in substantial use, notably in medicine, law and moral philosophy, from antiquity. The dramatic irrationalism of our time has likewise sensitised us to the irrational in previous societies and individuals, and the study of this has offered historical insights valuable in themselves even if doubtfully relevant to the scientific movement. Again our contemporary experience of the relativity of beliefs and values has emphasised the differences in expectation and behaviour among different societies and cultures, as opposed to an enduring rational similarity of all men. Yet if new insights from our own experience affect the questions we put in a comparative historical anthropology, the basic rationality of our treatment of them remains essentially stable. If each generation in dismantling the history written by its predecessors in their image then rewrites it in its own, we are committed by the whole critical process of scholarship to distinguish evidence from interpretation.

The questions may change also with the intentions of the questioner and with the subject-matter. An historian trying to enter into the mind of his subjects, in order to grasp their problems and expectations in the uncertainty of an unknown future, puts his questions to the sources with a different intention from a philosopher looking in the historical materials for constants of scientific thought or of individual or social behaviour. Such an inquiry can illuminate historical analysis by enabling us to distinguish the historically accidental from the logically essential elements in the succession of scientific systems. An analysis of the history of scientific thought must inevitably involve an analysis not only of how the scientific problems presented themselves at a given time but also of the validity of their solutions in the face of nature. A knowledge of the whole development of the intellectual tradition of natural science, mathematics, logic and philosophy then enables the historian to see the problems and intellectual manoeuvres of Archimedes or Alhazen or Descartes or Darwin in a field of possibilities vastly more extensive than was visible to those thinkers themselves, and to form an appreciation of their achievements and limitations from the wider point of view offered by subsequent knowledge and technique. Provided that their distinctive goals are clearly recognised, historical and logical analysis can each illuminate the other. Some perceptions into the history of scientific thought have been made possible only by more recent mathematical or scientific knowledge. There are fruitful possibilities likewise, for example, in an association between the history of technologies and quantitative analysis of their use and economic effect. Always it is essential to be clear about the differences between these enterprises. What can be achieved is to take consciously into account the fact that the presuppositions, interests and techniques of historians themselves change with the development of these parallel analytical disciplines and so bring about the changing view of the past that is so obvious in the history of historical scholarship.

Again we must distinguish what is common from what is different in the histories of scientific thought and of the practical arts. Theoretical sciences and the practical arts have had close and fruitful relations since antiquity and it would impoverish our historical understanding to envisage the one without the other. Optics and painting, acoustics and music, mechanics and engineering, physiology and medicine for example have shared each with the other in various ways a common social as well as scientific history, common problems, and often a common intellectual style. But even with much in common science and art have different ends. Analytical science as a theoretical inquiry has understanding and explanation as its end. Having taken its subject-matter to pieces and identified its parts, and having understood how they fit together with each other and within a larger theoretical system, it has completed its mission. The objective of medicine by contrast, as of the visual and musical arts and of engineering and practical morality and politics, is not the analysis of the parts but the effect produced in the whole. The effect aimed at by medicine is health, the bodily and mental well-being of the unique individual person. It shares this end rather with religion than with science. Where it differs from religion and belongs with science is in the means. Hence the complexity of relating the intellectual and moral history, and the philosophical anthropology, of medicine and science.

Can historiography be true? Could history be written without a selective vision of events and their relations any more than natural science could proceed without theory? But then is historiography more like a work of literature, an aesthetic or dramatic pattern, than an exercise in the logical control essential to natural science? The art that from antiquity has distinguished history from fiction has been the control of vision by evidence and the distinction by critical scholarship of evidence from interpretation. Shakespeare in his analysis of human character offered generalisations which we recognise at once as true, but our enlightenment from literature comes from applying the analysis of an imaginary world to our experience of the real one. Historiography is an art committed to searching for the real and particular truth. Politicised historiography by contrast is a known form of the art of fiction in the guise of truth, which in a long tradition has aimed not at truth but at effect. Its objective has been not to discover and understand what has happened in fact, but to present an account of events to promote or justify political action. It aims then by the distortion or suppression of evidence or by other rhetorical devices of deception to promote a party line, or perhaps to promote the author himself, by exploiting the trust upon which a true republic of letters must rest. It is a world of half-truth with which true scholarship must live but cannot accept, for

> There is no vice so simple but assumes
> Some mark of virtue on his outward parts:
> . . . in a word,
> The seeming truth which cunning times put on
> To entrap the wisest.

> (*Merchant of Venice* iii.2)

APPENDIX

(a) History and Philosophy at Oxford (1962)

At the Symposium on the History of Science held at Oxford last July a session was devoted to History of Science as an Academic Discipline when there was a discussion of experience in American and Continental as well as British universities. As the discussion will be published in full in the proceedings of the Symposium,* I shall confine myself here to giving a brief account of the arrangements existing at Oxford for postgraduate training and research in the subject and of some of the problems involved.

It will be generally agreed that for any subject to establish itself seriously as an academic discipline two basic requirements need to be satisfied: professional standards need to be established and practical means found for maintaining them by professional training; and primary sources of evidence and critical investigations of problems need to be published in accordance with these standards. The most obvious reason for the recent increase of interest in the history of science and the philosophy of science, and in the history of medicine and the history of technology, is the rapid increase in the recognition of the practical importance as well as the intellectual interest of science itself since the Second World War. But the movement to make history and philosophy of science and related studies part of a liberal education, part of the normal equipment available to an educated person interested in knowing something about these among the other major aspects of the record of human thought and experience, is in danger everywhere of outrunning the supply of scholars of professional standard. To provide for this supply is part of the normal function of a university such as Oxford.

In practice, at least within the British educational system, the only way of providing professional training in this field is through specialisation. No doubt this is in various degrees true of every field, but a discipline requiring some exact knowledge of history, philosophy and science would in practice be impossible to place, without allowing specialisation, in a system such as ours which relies on conventional divisions of subjects with fairly rigid syllabuses. Those ideal beings capable of satisfying scientists, historians and philosophers each at their own professional level, such as are sometimes envisaged by mixed electing committees in the early stages of their discussions, do not and could not

*Scientific Change, ed. A.C. Crombie, London and New York, 1963. The three parts of the appendix which follow mark stages in the introduction of the subject into teaching and research.

exist in modern academic life apart from the unpredictable possibilities of a rare genius. In practice all we can aim to provide for is good professional training within a field of specialisation, as in all other academic disciplines. What this involves in the history and philosophy of science becomes at once apparent by looking at the contents of the subject (or, rather, group of related subjects).

History of science like other historical disciplines is defined by its sources. The immediate problem for both teacher and taught, at every level, is that of mastering the exegesis of these sources. But since history of science (and similarly history of medicine and history of technology) is a subject much wider in scope than science itself, this means mastering both the scientific content of the sources and also the context of thought, available techniques, social conditions, motives and opportunities, and so on. Inevitably in the study of the subject tensions develop between present and past, between the internal history of scientific thought and the external intellectual, technical and social conditions in which it existed, and between the sources and the subject of the student's first degree.

It seems difficult to see how a prospective historian at least of modern science can become really confident of his technical mastery of his materials unless he has had some fairly advanced training (effectively a first degree, or even research experience) in, and experience of the actual *use of* the analytical disciplines of science or mathematics, as distinct from simply studying the historical sources. Moreover, a knowledge of modern science or mathematics (and also of other disciplines such as logic and certain social sciences) enables the historian to see the problems and intellectual manœuvres of an Archimedes, a Nicole Oresme, a Harvey or a Faraday in a field of possibilities vastly more extensive than was visible to these scientists themselves and so to form an appreciation of their achievements and limitations from the wider point of view provided by the subsequent development of knowledge and technique. Yet, if it is necessary, a first degree in, for example, mathematics or physiology is not by itself sufficient equipment for an understanding of the distinctive ideas and techniques of their counterparts in even so recognisably scientific a period as the seventeenth century, and for seeing the problems and the significance of methods and discoveries as these appeared to the people of that period. Until comparatively recently science was very much of a minority interest in societies where it existed at all. To overlook this by concentrating exclusively on scientific content as we would recognise it can only lead to misunderstanding, not only of the relation of science to its external conditions but also of the scientific content itself; indeed one of the main problems in the exegesis of sources which *we* label 'scientific' from earlier periods is to discover what their authors themselves thought they were doing.

In practice, the best previous training to equip historians of science to master the exegesis of their primary sources and the problems of historical investigation depends on the particular sources and periods. It is obvious that more demands are made on scientific equipment by more recent science, and conversely ancient or medieval science, for example, make more demands on philological and usually also on philosophical equipment. Similarly, an historian's training makes him familiar with the handling of sources and with the analysis of social history and institutions in a way science graduates are not, and an economist will be equipped to see the history of technology as something more than simply the history of techniques unrelated to their actual use and its economic or political influence. From whatever first degree the prospective historian of science (or medicine or technology) approaches the subject, he will not usually be equipped to deal with its special problems without postgraduate training in history of science itself. But, by allowing specialisation, different natural routes are opened into the subject, which becomes a natural extension of the subject of the first degree. This, at any rate, is the basis of the arrangements for postgraduate training and research existing at Oxford and will no doubt be that of future policy, and it has certain considerable positive advantages. It fits in with our institutions. It keeps history and philosophy of science in contact with the main body of historical, scientific and philosophical subjects. It encourages the comparative method. And it provides postgraduate students with the valuable experience of working together in the same seminar with people with different but complementary backgrounds.

At Oxford, as at most other British universities, history of science and philosophy of science are usually studied together. This recognises the fact that an analysis of the history of scientific thought must at the same time involve an analysis of science, and conversely that a logical analysis of science would be impoverished by restriction to the present. But it must be recognised also that a philosopher or a scientist may have different reasons from an historian for studying the history of science, according to what they want from it. A scientist or a philosopher may want not so much to understand, for example, the actual processes by, and conditions in which a discovery was made, as to use history to throw light on some scientific concept or theory still in use, or to provide examples of philosophical problems or situations in which he is interested regardless of their history. As long as the differences in their goals are clearly recognised, the historical and the analytical approaches both illuminate and can be indispensable to each other. The method has further fruitful possibilities, for example in a similar association between economic analysis and the history of technology. It has in addition to its other uses the very considerable merit of taking *conscious* account of the fact that the presuppositions, interests and techniques of historians themselves change with the advance of these parallel analytical disciplines and so bring about the *changing* view of the past that is so obvious a feature of the history of historical scholarship.

The main general course of postgraduate training at Oxford is for the Diploma in the History and Philosophy of Science (see appendix). This is arranged as a year's course of instruction open to any graduate of suitable interests and standard. It has been designed to provide both for a general survey of the history of science in which the comparative method can be used, and for detailed study of a choice of special topics. The actual content of study has been made flexible so that graduates can follow the natural route into the subject opened to them by their first degrees, and this is facilitated by basing the teaching for the Diploma on guided reading, classes and tutorials more than on lectures. One useful function of the Diploma is to provide a course of advanced training in this field for candidates going on to work for the D.Phil. or other research degrees. This arrangement also fits in conveniently with the method by which the Department of Scientific and Industrial Research provides grants for postgraduate training. For these reasons the Diploma may perhaps prove a useful model for other universities.

Besides the Diploma, provision is made for the study of both a Chosen Period of Scientific Thought (with options corresponding to those for the Diploma) and the philosophy of science in the course of postgraduate training in philosophy leading to the B.Phil. This places the subject centrally in the principal course of training for graduates intending to take up an academic career in philosophy. In the Honour School of Natural Science there is a Supplementary Subject in the history and philosophy of science open to all candidates, and provision is made for chemists to offer a thesis on a subject in the history of science for Part II. The latter especially is proving a useful ground for recruitment.

These arrangements for building up at Oxford a school of postgraduate training and research in history and philosophy of science are effective as far as they go. At present the number of candidates taking the various courses is over twenty, of whom about half are graduates in science and half in arts. They are brought together for at least one and sometimes two or more seminars each week when a specialised paper is read for discussion. The seminars are attended also by postgraduate students in related fields of history, philosophy and science. By the highest professional standards this experiment must be regarded as being in its early stages and a number of lines of improvement are being considered. It is of particular importance for the professional well-being as well as the breadth of outlook of the subject that it should keep in close touch with related developments in history and other larger academic disciplines. The present arrangement has been especially effective in keeping these contacts with science and with philosophy. It is to be hoped that in the future more historians will overcome their shyness of scientific thought and take up for historical analysis at least the external social and cultural conditions for science. Without an understanding of these, science is scarcely comprehensible as an historical phenomenon, and they are an open field for research.

A candidate for the Oxford Diploma in the History and Philosophy of Science must be, or become, a member of the University and follow a course of instruction of at least three terms. The examination consists of four papers, as follows:

(a) Two papers on General History of Science, studied in relation to the general history of thought and to social history, namely:

    (i) Science in Antiquity.

    (ii) The Origins of Modern Science (to the end of the eighteenth century).

(b) One paper on a Special Period of Scientific Thought. Candidates will be required to study the use of original sources, the history of particular discoveries and theories, the changes in scientific ideas, and the development of scientific methods. Until further notice, candidates may offer *one* of the following:

    *Greek science (especially mathematical and medical).

    Thirteenth- and fourteenth-century science.

    *Seventeenth-century physics and physiology.

    *Nineteenth-century biology.

    Nineteenth-century physics.

    Nineteenth-century chemistry.

(Sources illustrating main themes and problems are specified for each period.)

(c) One paper on Principles of Scientific Thinking with special topics in *either* (i) the physical sciences or (ii) the biological sciences in the nineteenth and twentieth centuries.

* Also options for the Chosen Period of Scientific Thought in the Philosophy B. Phil.

Note: A further option on Early Scientific Instruments was added later to *(b)*. The Diploma has been discontinued.

(b) Quinquennial Application by the Oxford University Committee for the History and Philosophy of Science (1972)

I. *Long-term policy*

The long-term policy of the committee for these subjects is to continue, in close co-operttion with faculty boards (in particular those of Modern History, of Literae Humaniores as responsible for philosophy, and interested science boards) to work towards two main objectives: (*a*) to strengthen the position of Oxford as a centre for research and graduate training, and (*b*) to increase the opportunities for the study of the history and/or philosophy of science as part of undergraduate courses. Policy for the future is related to the position reached so far, and the committee wishes to stress, as in its last quinquennial proposals, four general points made in its replies to the Franks Commission:

1. A large part of the intrinsic intellectual interest of these subjects comes from the fact that they are relevant to a number of different disciplines and thereby help to bring them into contact: for example, the study of the history of science (including medicine and technology) involves also that of science in history; and the philosophy of the sciences deals also with scientific examples of more general philosophical problems.

2. These subjects have suffered severely for these interdisciplinary intellectual virtues, as a minority administrative interest in the competition for funds and posts. Although the committee was set up by the General Board (in its first form in 1956), it has so far received only incidental expenses and no allocation of new posts. Its proposals were adopted by the Modern History Board and included with Priority I in the university's last quinquennial application, but funds for none were in fact granted.

3. Almost unique opportunities for developing these subjects are offered in Oxford, both by the number of its experts in related disciplines and by the richness of its historical collections. The committtee's policy is to make full use of these opportunities and thereby to provide a national and international service. This is in accordance with the recommendation of the British Academy Report drawn up under the Presidency of Sir Maurice Bowra on *Research in the Humanities and the Social Sciences* (Oxford, 1961, paras. 86 and 127, section 7) which is that for the history of science and subjects in **a similar position 'immediate** policy should be directed

towards building up a few strong centres for each study, equipping them adequately with teaching material and research facilities . . .'

4. The range of knowledge and skills involved in the history of science is enormous. Even on a narrow view a subject so embedded in Western history since antiquity requires a range of historical, scientific, philosophical, and linguistic equipment in the whole of which no individual could possibly be an expert. The range required by the philosophy of science is less severe but still formidable if the different sciences are considered. In both cases professional training is required for the expert, and a university intending to treat them seriously must provide posts for enough experts to cover the field.

The committee's policy and its relation to the present position of these subjects is as follows:

(*a*) *Graduate studies*
During the 1960s (after the establishment of the present committee by statute in 1958, following the introduction of the graduate Diploma and papers in the Philosophy B.Phil) graduate students increased to the present number of approximately 40 (approximately half specializing in history of science and half in philosophy of science), making this the largest graduate school in the country. Over the same period 56 graduates have been appointed to university posts (26 in History of Science, 30 in Philosophy of Science) in Britain and overseas. These graduate studies are supported by grants from the Department of Education and Science (which has taken over responsibility for the field from the S.R.C. and M.R.C.), the British Council, the Wellcome Trust, and similar public and private bodies in other countries.

The committee would like to introduce further papers and examinations in keeping with the interdisciplinary character of these subjects which has proved an attraction for graduates. It has in mind the possibility of an independent B.Phil. in History of Science (including medicine and technology), co-ordinated with the B.Phils. in Philosophy, European History, English Studies, Greek and Latin Languages and Literature, Oriental Studies, and others as appropriate. Philosophy of Science is already well provided for in the Philosophy B.Phil. The advantage of this co-ordination is that it equips graduates with a knowledge of these subjects for careers in the historical or philosophical academic professions. The committee does not envisage an increase in the total number of graduate students during the quinquennium.

(*b*) *Undergraduate studies*
The Supplementary Subject in History and Philosophy of Science in the Honour School of Natural Science is offered, as an additional option, only by enthusiasts, whose numbers have, however, now risen to eight. The Special Subject in History of Science in the Honour School of Modern History is offerd by fifteen to twenty candidates, and more may be

expected with the introduction of joint schools of Modern History with Modern Languages and with Economics. Philosophy of Science is included in the new Honour School of Physics and Philosophy; interest in the subject is served in P.P.P., in part, by classes arranged jointly with the Department of Psychology; Philosophy of Mathematics is included in the new Honour School of Mathematics and Philosophy. The committee hopes that (as proposed to the Kneale Committee) these subjects will be given a larger part in combined schools with other arts or science subjects with which they have natural relationships.

The committee draws attention to the fact that these activities are based on two established university teaching posts: one lectureship in History of Science and one in Philosophy of Science. This is extremely inhibiting, even though a considerable role in teaching and supervision is played by several tutorial fellows, by colleagues with non-teaching posts, and by others with an expertise in related fields although not professional historians or philosophers of science.

II. *Proposals*

The committee has already said to the Franks Commission that the principal lack in Oxford is senior posts, in particular a professorship in the History of Science. In fact there have been no new posts in these subjects since 1953 – a contrast with the growth in numbers both of the graduate and undergraduate students here and of the number of teaching posts in other universities. The committee asked for a professorship in its last two quinquennial applications and it now renews its request for a *Professorship in the History of Science* with Priority I. The case for this rests on several grounds. The intrinsic interest and recognized educational value of the subject would be sufficient grounds in themselves, even if there were at present very few students as in some other subjects with chairs. The actual and potential growth of the field in Oxford makes it the more desirable to establish a chair without further delay in order to give recognition to and guarantee the continuity of these devlopments, to consolidate the position of the University as an international centre for research and graduate training, and to encourage the expansion of undergraduate studies. The committee asks for this professorship to start in the first year of the quinquennium, 1972.

In its last two quinquennial applications the committee asked also for a new university lectureship. It requests now the establishment of a new *Lectureship in the History of the Modern Physical Sciences*, with Priority I. This post is required to fill a significant gap in the existing cover of this very large field, and specifically for teaching for the Diploma, the Supplementary Subject, and Part II in Chemistry and Metallurgy, much of which is now done by the Assistant Curator of the Museum of the History of Science in addition to his other duties.

In addition, the committee would welcome any initiative from the Philosophy Sub-Faculty for the establishment of an additional *Lectureship in the Philosophy of Science.*

None of these proposals depends on the provision of additional accommodation.

The committee is sending a copy of this document and of its proposals for library development to the Modern History Board, with the request that the board should take account of them in framing its own proposals.

(c) Beginnings at Oxford (1984)

The monument to efforts to introduce the history of science as an academic discipline at Oxford before World War II is the series of volumes published by R. T. Gunther as *Early Science in Oxford.* These include lectures given by Gunther as first curator of the Museum of the History of Science, an institution which with great courage he effectively created and launched on its way as a cherished part both of the university and of the international scene. Gunther was succeeded in 1940 by Frank Sherwood Taylor, at a time of great difficulty. During the war much of the Old Ashmolean Building was taken over by university and government offices. Sherwood Taylor maintained a reduced display of the collections, acquired important accessions, and with cheerful optimism prepared for the museum's postwar role. One exciting event was the rediscovery of special treasures skillfully concealed by Gunther when war was declared. The museum was officially reopened to the public on a memorable occasion in 1949. In the following year Sherwood Taylor was appointed director of the Science Museum in London, leaving his mark at Oxford not only on the museum but also on the teaching of the history of science.

It was Frank Sherwood Taylor who, by his own lectures and by his efforts to persuade the university to accept the subject within its vision of what should be taught, was directly responsible for the eventual establishment of a teaching post in the history of science. He himself gave regular courses of lectures both on the development of modern science in general and notably on the history of alchemy and early chemistry in particular. To assist with this teaching he arranged for the appointment in 1947 of S. F. Mason, later to become a distinguished chemist, as assistant demonstrator in the museum. At the same time he invited outside historians to give courses of lectures. I remember very well such a course on the history of the idea of evolution, for *pari passu* with my weekly visits Chairman Mao completed his conquest of China. In 1953 the university agreed to establish a senior university post to develop teaching and research in the history of science, which I was invited to fill.

Sherwood Taylor set out his own conception of the history of science as an academic discipline with habitual clarity in the presidential address he gave to the British Society for the History of Science in that same year, published in the society's *Bulletin* (1954, *1*:239–245). His education, first in classics, then (after serving in World War I) in science at Oxford, and finally as a graduate student in the Department of History and Method of Science at University College, London, gave him an ample view. He saw as the sources for the history of science both documents and the instruments and artifacts preserved in museums. A historian of science, he said, had to understand science, but equally he had to understand its context in philosophy and religion. It was not only the medieval natural philosopher whose "interests in the various departments of science and [whose] favourable or unfavourable views of certain theories were much influenced by religious dogmata." In every age theology and natural philosophy have "mutually influenced each other." The historian of science had to know general history, for too often "historian and scientist are at cross-purposes, asking the wrong questions of each other and giving them infertile answers." He had to know languages. If it was very natural to focus on "elucidation of the discoveries and ideas that led up to modern science," that "presents a very incomplete picture." He envisaged rather another approach, which was "to record how scientists went to work in each successive age, how their aspirations changed and how they learned to fulfill those aspirations." This focused less on modern science than on "the way men think and have thought about their work" and about their world. From this approach Albertus Magnus, however wrong his beliefs about the world might seem to us, was "just as interesting as Newton or Darwin: to understand and enter into his point of view is a moving and instructive exercise." Besides, "doubtless we are all wrong *sub specie aeternitatis*. In the shadow of God's knowledge of His universe, to distinguish between the ignorance of Albertus and that of Einstein, is to dispute the precedence of the flea and the louse—which are both equally interesting to the entomologist. That is the sort of history I would wish to be able to write—the fruit of a life of learning to see the world as the men of each former age saw it, and to gain from that seeing the satisfaction that they gained."

The development of the history of science as an academic discipline lay, he insisted, in the hands of the universities. There was "but slender hope of a professional career for a historian of science" until the universities made the subject "a recognized department of studies." How was this to be done? Some had suggested that it was "a subject which could be presented to arts students in order to give them a notion of the place science takes and has taken in the world's affairs. More frequently it is commended as a means of taking off the rawness of the science student who cannot be persuaded to interest himself in the humanities but can be introduced to them through the history of his subject. Again it is commended as a way of introducing the science student to scientific methods" and likewise to help in the teaching of philosophy. Sherwood Taylor concluded firmly that "the study of the history of science for a pedagogic or ancillary purpose is secondary, while its study in and for itself is the primary need." As indeed in every other academic discipline, work in it should be done primarily "with no intention save that the truth should be told."

The problem at Oxford as elsewhere was how to gain the acceptance of the history of science by colleagues in other disciplines and how to relate it to those disciplines. Despite Sherwood Taylor's eloquence and energy, when I came to Oxford in 1954 (having arranged to spend the previous year as a visiting professor in the United States), the subject had not yet been included in any university examinations, and there was no academic committee or board responsible for it. If it were ever to become **part of normal teaching and research**, it was essential to provide for both. The committee with representatives of various arts and sciences, set up first in 1956, became the instrument and center of information through which the subject was introduced into a variety of examinations and initiatives taken in applying for research fellowships, new·teaching posts, and other essential matters. All the examinations for which the subject is now taught at Oxford—in natural science, in history, and in ancient and modern philosophy, and at undergraduate and graduate levels—were introduced between 1957 and 1963.

My aim in organizing teaching, as in the supervision of research, was to make a study of the classical history of scientific thought within the context of the intellectual and moral expectations and commitments and the human experience of the society in which it had its life. The scientific movement has been concerned with man's relations with nature and his fellow beings as perceiver and knower and agent. Above all it seemed to me we should look in its history for people and their vision. The history of ideas, scientific or otherwise, is after all the history of people thinking, and when we say that ideas change we mean that people change their ideas, whether by their own thinking or by exposure to that of others in whatever their circumstances may be. In making this approach I found especial enlightenment in the account given by the Oxford philosopher and archeologist R. G. Collingwood (e.g., in his autobiography) of his historical method. This was to look in the answers given in any historical situation for the questions asked or implied, and for the changes in those often unexpressed questions. The nature of the inquiry into the history of science offers an invitation to look beneath the surface of immediate and particular scientific results and theories for the antecedent and concomitant intellectual and social and material conditions and commitments that made them possible and others perhaps impossible. We may see the subject as a kind of comparative intellectual anthropology. At the same time as we reconstruct events as lived within the mental and social and technical horizons of the persons whose thinking and actions we analyze, we find ourselves dealing in the classical history of science with an approach to nature effectively competent to solve problems and to create coherent systems of explanation. We discover a tradition with a recognizably common logical structure dating from the insights of the Greek mathematicians, physicians, and natural philosophers, and with power to generate a cumulative progress of certifiable objective knowledge. These characteristics of the scientific tradition were recognized by the ancient Greeks themselves, and it is they that have given to that tradition its profound influence upon the whole of Western thought. We recognize an intellectual enterprise integrated by its explicit historic criteria for choosing between theories and investigations at different levels of the true, the probable, the possible, the fruitful, the sterile, the impossible, and the false. We are liberated thereby from the more naive sociological relativism which fails to distinguish the specific history of science from a miscellaneous history of ideas lacking its specific modes of self-correction and criteria of acceptability. These matters were discussed at the symposium I organized at Oxford in 1961, which was published as *Scientific Change* (1963).

My own experience (like that before me of Sherwood Taylor) in establishing the history of science within normal teaching and research at Oxford has a certain sociological interest in itself. For at least a decade after World War II Oxford was still largely an arts university. When I arrived in the early 1950s, about one quarter of both junior and senior members of the university were studying or teaching scientific subjects. Intellectually the dominant subject was philosophy. It was the philosophers who in my case were the most welcoming, and it was on the particular initiative of Gilbert Ryle, John Austin, and William Kneale that an opportunity to study chosen topics in ancient and modern scientific thought was introduced into the graduate course in philosophy. Gwyl Owen and I first taught these topics. Scientists here as elsewhere tended to see the history of science as a study rather of the origins of their own ideas than, as Sherwood Taylor put it, of the scientific thinkers of any period for their own sake and "how their aspirations changed and how they learned to fulfill those aspirations." It was as always the young who accepted with enthusiasm a different conception of the subject, especially after John North joined us and developed the teaching of it.

The Oxford history school remained in this period wholly dedicated to little else beyond the continuous political and constitutional history of England. Colleagues struggled manfully to introduce economic and European history, with some eventual success. The school exemplified in an extreme form the mental and structural obstacles that have prevented the development of an enduring tradition of intellectual history in this country. Despite all this, with the good help of Ernest Jacob and other colleagues, a special subject based on the study of original texts was (after seven years) introduced into the honor school of modern history. I designed the subject with the deliberately chosen title "The Scientific Movement in the Seventeenth Century." By making it firmly European in scope, my aim was to show that the scientific movement, while retaining its own identity, was essentially part of more general intellectual and social movements, and incidentally to show how inappropriate and indeed eccentric an endemic English parochialism must appear in this context. Again it was the young, both the undergraduates who chose it and my colleagues who assisted in teaching it, who confounded the skeptics and made this subject from the start a great success.

One could say that the great merit of our university in its historical and other studies is solidity; matching this too often is an almost structural lack of vision. We in this small field have been perhaps obliged to develop some element of vision in order to survive. Likewise to survive we have needed to develop a solid foundation of scholarship through research and training in research. Some fifty and more graduate students whose work I have myself supervised in the history of science and medicine have been appointed to university posts in various parts of the world.

INDEX